James Hunter is Emeritus Professor
the Highlands and Islands. He has _.. ιne
north of Scotland and about the regio ...ιue diaspora. In the
course of a varied career Hunter has been, among other things,
director of the Scottish Crofters Union, chairman of Highlands and
Islands Enterprise and an award-winning journalist.

'Moving and definitive, this is a hymn to the dispossessed'
Scotland's Books

'Impressively researched and beautifully written . . . brings fresh,
insider sources and voices to the old story. Recommended to all
readers'
Annie Tindley, *History Today*

'Scrupulously researched, lucidly written and beautifully observed'
John Macleod, *Scottish Review of Books*

'This is a book that will be acclaimed and will set a standard . . . the
author should be congratulated on this eye-opening account'
Ray Collier, *Highland News Group*

'May come to be seen not as the most significant book but as the
greatest book written by this Highland historian'
Roger Hutchinson, *West Highland Free Press*

Set Adrift Upon the World

THE SUTHERLAND CLEARANCES

James Hunter

BIRLINN

This edition published in 2016 by

Birlinn Limited
West Newington House
10 Newington Road
Edinburgh
EH9 1QS

www.birlinn.co.uk

First published in 2015

Reprinted 2019

ISBN: 978 1 78027 354 9

British Library Cataloguing-in-Publication Data
A catalogue record for this book is available from the
British Library

Typeset by Hewer Text (UK) Ltd, Edinburgh
Printed and bound by MBM Print SCS Ltd, Glasgow

MIX
Paper from
responsible sources
FSC® C117931

For
Abi, Louisa, Alec and Jamie

'It would be as well for them to be killed as set adrift upon the world'

Soon-to-be evicted residents of the Strath of Kildonan in conversation with one of the sheep farmers who were to take their place

Tuesday 5 January 1813

CONTENTS

LIST OF ILLUSTRATIONS

1. William Clunes by Henry Raeburn.
2. Loch Brora. The green fields across the loch and to the left were part of the pre-clearance township of Carrol.
3. Fields and walls at the Doll, near Brora.
4. Strath of Kildonan, with the village of Helmsdale at its foot.
5. Map of the Strath of Kildonan showing the extent of cultivation around its pre-clearance townships.
6. Suisgill in the Strath of Kildonan.
7. Donald Sage, who grew up in the pre-clearance Strath of Kildonan, called the Helmsdale River 'the finest feature in the landscape'.
8. The Golspie Inn, the focus of the February 1813 'riot'.
9. A roughly inscribed boulder by the shore of Hudson Bay marks the grave of Kildonan protest leader John Sutherland.
10. Churchill Creek, where emigrants from the Strath of Kildonan established their winter camp in the fall of 1813.
11. The Churchill River in winter.
12. York boats on the Hayes River.
13. The author looking out across a frozen Hudson Bay on a December day when the temperature was minus 35 degrees Celsius.
14. Angus McCall, present-day tenant of Culmaily, near Golspie, Patrick Sellar's first farm.

15/16. The foundations of houses destroyed during the clearances are to be seen throughout the Sutherland interior. Members of the Clyne Heritage Society indicate the dimensions of one of the homes.

17/18. The typical dwelling in the pre-clearance straths was a 'long-house', whose walls were a mix of stone and turf on a stone foundation.

19. Looking eastwards across Loch Naver to Achoul, whose tenant, William MacKay, could trace his Strathnaver ancestry through 400 years, was evicted twice during the clearances.

20. Badinloskin, where Margaret MacKay died some days after being carried from a home burned on Patrick Sellar's orders.

21/22. In the course of what organisers of the clearances called 'improvement', hundreds of families were evicted from their long-settled townships in Strathnaver and deposited on three-acre crofts in exposed and previously uncultivated areas like Strathy Point.

23. Much of the Sutherland interior now consists of sporting estates given over mainly to deer-stalking.

24. The Earltown area of Nova Scotia.

25. The Settlers' Monument in the Kildonan area of Winnipeg. An identical sculpture stands in Helmsdale.

26. The Strath of Kildonan's church, deprived of its congregation at the time of the clearances, is today largely disused.

27. The Red River in the heart of Winnipeg.

Map 1: Northern Scotland

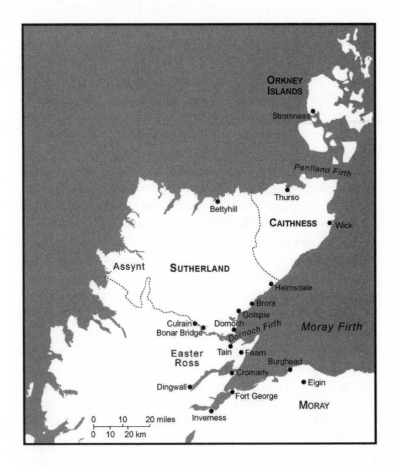

Map 2: Eastern Sutherland

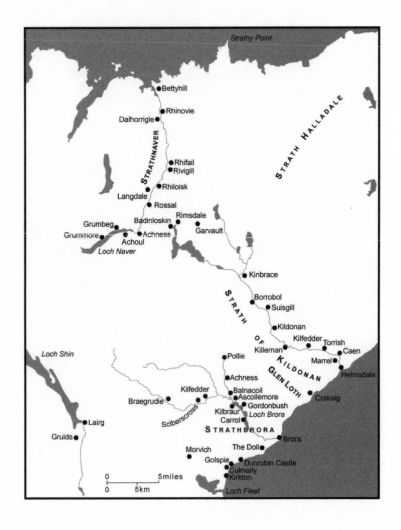

Map 3: North America

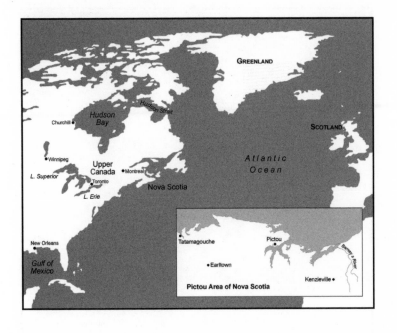

Pictou Area of Nova Scotia

Map 4: Manitoba

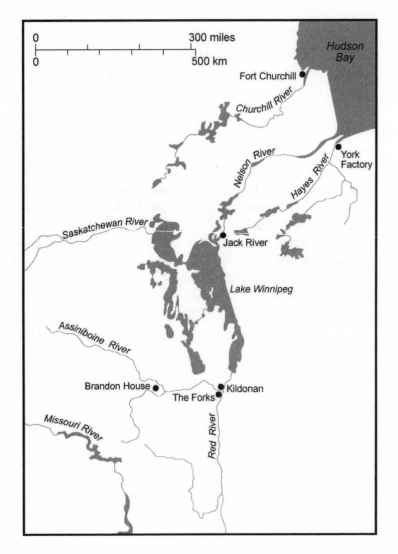

SOME ACTORS IN THE CLEARANCE DRAMA

Auld, William Senior Hudson's Bay Company man with a very low opinion of the Sutherland people the *Earl of Selkirk* recruited for his Red River settlement.

Bannerman, Donald Much-loathed sheriff-officer and constable in charge of the clearance of scores of Sutherland communities.

Brander, James Clerk or secretary to *Patrick Sellar* until 1817. Afterwards Sutherland's procurator fiscal. Supervised many evictions.

Brougham, Henry MP Leading Whig politician. Close friend of *James Loch*. Helped Loch ensure that Sutherland Estate policy was not criticised in parliament.

Cameron, Duncan Senior North West Company man at Red River. Key organiser of efforts to sabotage the settlement there of clearance refugees from Sutherland.

Chisholm, William Tenant at Badinloskin, Strathnaver. The burning of his home by Patrick Sellar in June 1814, and the subsequent death of Chisholm's mother-in-law, Margaret MacKay, led to Sellar being charged with culpable homicide.

Cleugh, John Shepherd. Targeted by 1813 protestors in the Strath of Kildonan. Afterwards sheep-farming tenant of Pollie on the north-western fringes of Strathbrora.

Clunes, William Army officer and member of long-established Sutherland family. The creation of his Torrish sheep farm in the Strath of Kildonan precipitated the Kildonan uprising of 1813.

Colquhoun, Archibald MP Lord advocate who dealt with the repercussions of the opening phase of clearance in Sutherland.

Cranstoun, George Edinburgh lawyer and Sheriff of Sutherland during opening phase of clearance. His independent mindedness led to his falling foul of *James Loch* and the *Staffords*.

Dudgeon, Thomas Easter Ross farmer whose opposition to clearance led to his organising in 1819 a subscription-based mass movement. Seen by *James Loch* and the *Staffords* as a serious threat to their plans for Sutherland.

Edwards, Abel Hudson's Bay Company surgeon who helped care for Kildonan emigrants at their encampment on the Churchill River in the winter of 1813–14.

Gordon, Joseph, of Carrol Sold his Strathbrora estate to the *Staffords* in 1812. Edinburgh-based businessman and lawyer. Opponent of clearance. Acted for several clearance critics. Detested by the *Staffords* and *James Loch*. Helped clearance victims leave for Nova Scotia.

Gordon, Robert, of Langdale Long-established tacksman (tacksmen were traditional tenants of gentry background) at Langdale, Strathnaver. Father-in-law of *David MacKenzie*. Gordon's lands were among those taken over by Patrick Sellar who treated him contemptuously.

Grant, Cuthbert Métis leader who, in alliance with the North West Company, harassed Red River's Kildonan settlers who were seen as a threat to the Métis way of life.

Grant, George MacPherson MP Owed his Sutherland parliamentary seat to the *Staffords*. Very much their poodle. Staunch supporter of clearance.

Gunn, Donald Caithness teenager who, following his recruitment by the Hudson's Bay Company, accompanied emigrants from Kildonan to Hudson Bay. Wrote about this, many years later, in his *History of Manitoba*.

Hall, James Shepherd targeted during 1813 protests in the Strath of Kildonan. Afterwards sheep-farming tenant of Sciberscross, Strathbrora.

Jackson, Andrew Commander of American forces at the Battle of New Orleans where hundreds of Sutherland soldiers, serving with the British army's 93rd Regiment, were killed at a point when, back home, their communities were being destroyed.

Loch, James Commissioner to the Marquis of Stafford and, in effect, chief executive officer of the Stafford business empire. In overall charge of Sutherland Estate developments from 1816. Planned the mass evictions of 1819–20.

McDonald, Archibald Appointed by the *Earl of Selkirk* to help get emigrants from Kildonan to Red River by way of Hudson Bay.

MacDonald, William Recruiting sergeant for the 93rd (Sutherland) Regiment. In 1813 travelled to London on behalf of the Kildonan rebels. Instrumental in involving the *Earl of Selkirk* in Sutherland affairs.

Macdonell, Miles Appointed by the *Earl of Selkirk* as initial governor of the earl's Red River settlement.

MacKay, Angus As a boy of 11, fled from one of Patrick Sellar's evicting parties in Strathnaver. As an old man, testified to *Lord Napier* about his experiences.

MacKay, Angus and Jean Married in Kildonan in 1813. In April of the following year, trekked on snow-shoes from Fort Churchill to York Factory. Settled eventually in Ontario.

MacKay, Donald Strathbrora-born fur trader. Active in the North American interior in the late eighteenth century. Returned to Sutherland and settled at Ascoilemore, Strathbrora. Collaborated with the *Earl of Selkirk*. Leading opponent of clearance.

MacKay, John Successful businessman and railway contractor of Sutherland background. Gave evidence to *Lord Napier* and backed land reform.

MacKay, William, of Achoul Member of long prominent Strathnaver family. Tacksman of Achoul beside Loch Naver. Dispossessed twice in the course of the clearances. In his nineties when evicted for the second time.

MacKenzie, David Minister of Farr, the parish including Strathnaver. Vacillated between endorsement of, and opposition to, clearance.

MacKenzie, William The *Stafford* family's Edinburgh lawyer.

McKid, Robert Sheriff-substitute of Sutherland during opening phase of clearance. Deputy to *George Cranstoun*. With Cranstoun's backing, mounted 1816 prosecution of Patrick Sellar.

MacLeod, Donald Stonemason. Cleared from Strathnaver. Wrote extensively, influentially and bitterly about the clearances. Highly critical of the Sutherland clergy.

Maconochie, Alexander MP Lord advocate in succession to *Archibald Colquhoun*. Helped *James Loch* ease *George Cranstoun* out of Sutherland's sheriffship.

MacPherson, Kate Left her Strath of Kildonan home for Red River in 1813. Nursed typhus sufferers at Sloop's Cove on the Churchill River in the fall of that year. Afterwards settled at Red River.

Munro, John Evicted during Patrick Sellar's 1814 clearances in Strathnaver. Lead organiser of the successful effort to have Patrick Sellar arrested and tried.

Napier, Lord Diplomat and colonial governor. Chairman of 1883 royal commission of enquiry into crofting unrest and crofter grievances.

Rae, William MP Lord advocate in succession to *Alexander Maconochie*. In 1821 persuaded by *James Loch* to send troops to Sutherland to assist with evictions.

Reed, Gabriel Leading Sutherland sheep farmer whose Kilcalmkill farm stretched from Strathbrora to the Strath of Kildonan.

Robertson, Colin Hudson's Bay Company man who succeeded *Miles Macdonell* as governor of the *Earl of Selkirk*'s settlement at Red River.

Ross, Charles Sheriff of Sutherland in succession to *George Cranstoun*. His appointment was subject to the approval of *James Loch* and the *Staffords* whose bidding he did without question.

Ross, Jessie and Gordon Gordon was a Strathbrora schoolmaster. Gordon's protest to the *Marquis of Stafford* about the circumstances surrounding his wife and children's eviction from their Ascoilemore home was treated by the *Staffords* and *James Loch* as a serious threat to them.

Ross, Walter Minister of Clyne, the parish including Strathbrora. Staunch supporter of clearance.

Roy, John Sutherland Estate surveyor.

Sage, Alexander Minister of Kildonan. Generally opposed to clearance.

Sage, Donald Son of *Alexander*. Preacher at Achness, Strathnaver, during later phase of clearance. Author of biography dealing at length with clearance period. Critic of clearance.

Selkirk, Earl of Kirkcudbrightshire estate owner. Impassioned critic of clearance. Hudson's Bay Company shareholder. With HBC backing, helped people quit Kildonan for his Red River settlement – today the city of Winnipeg.

Sellar, Patrick Factor (or manager) of the Sutherland Estate, in association with *William Young*, from 1811 to 1817. Also tenant of several estate farms. His conduct of evictions in Strathnaver in 1814 led, in 1816, to his being tried in the High Court on culpable homicide charges.

Stafford, Marquis and Marchioness of Owners of the Sutherland Estate. Jointly responsible for the Sutherland clearances. She brought her ancestral lands in Sutherland to their partnership. He brought English estates, extensive business interests and immense wealth.

Suther, Francis Principal factor of the Sutherland Estate in succession to *William Young* and *Patrick Sellar*. Lead organiser of the mass evictions of 1819–20.

Sutherland, Alexander Younger brother of *John Sutherland of Sciberscross*. Army officer. Lived in London. Fiercely opposed to clearance. Source of much of the London press's critical coverage of events in clearance-era Sutherland.

Sutherland, Angus MP Descendant of people cleared from the Strath of Kildonan. Influential land reformer. Gave evidence to *Lord Napier*. Successful Land League candidate for Sutherland in the general election of 1886.

Sutherland, John Key leader of the 1813 protests in the Strath of Kildonan. Tradition-bearer and skilled distiller of illicit whisky.

Highly regarded by the *Earl of Selkirk* who helped organise his eventual departure for Red River.

Sutherland, John, of Sciberscross Tacksman at Sciberscross, Strathbrora, where his family lived for several hundred years. At odds with the *Staffords* and strongly opposed to clearance.

Wemyss, William In charge of raising the 93rd (Sutherland) Regiment in 1799 and 1800. Afterwards the regiment's commander. Assisted *William MacDonald* when, in 1813, MacDonald came to London to win support for the Kildonan rebels.

Young, William Factor of the Sutherland Estate, in partnership with *Patrick Sellar*, from 1811 to 1816. Organised the establishment of a number of sheep farms. Dealt, mostly unsuccessfully from a *Stafford* point of view, with the Kildonan and Strathnaver protest movements of the period between 1813 and 1816. Eventually dismissed by *James Loch* and replaced by *Francis Suther*.

INTRODUCTION

What follows is a story. It is the story of how, in the space of seven or eight years in the early nineteenth century, the interior of a large Scottish county was forcibly depopulated. This was accomplished by turning thousands of people out of their homes. Those homes, most of them in long-settled locations, were then destroyed.

Nothing like this – certainly nothing so organised and on such a scale – had taken place in Britain before. Nothing quite like it would take place again. It was an extraordinary episode.

What was done in the course of that episode was planned and carried through by a small group of men and one woman. Most of those men, and the woman too, wrote a great deal about their actions, intentions and feelings. Because the resulting documentation – in the form of letters, memoranda, policy papers and other items of that kind – was produced by, or sent to, individuals who were wealthy, politically significant or both, much of it has been preserved.

There are no equivalent collections of material giving ready insights into the thinking and emotions of the men, women and children ejected from communities that, following their ejection, ceased to exist. This means that the hopes and fears of the dispossessed are harder to access than the aims and ambitions of their dispossessors. Those hopes and fears, however, are by no means irrecoverable. That, at any rate, is one of the beliefs underpinning this book.

1

Another is a conviction that historians, often inclined to deal mainly with the powerful, should also listen out for the voices of humanity at large. The people who emptied homes and made them uninhabitable were more influential than the people whose world was thus turned upside down. But especially if you think (as this book's author does) that it would have been better had settlement after settlement not been eradicated, it is right to give a hearing to folk driven from those places.

And so this telling of the story told here begins with someone who, in the greater scheme of things, was of next to no significance. Her name was Jessie Ross.

I

'INHUMAN TREATMENT'

The destruction of Ascoilemore and one family's experience of clearance

Jessie Ross's life began to be taken apart at about 2 p.m. on Thursday 31 May 1821. That was when as many as ten or a dozen men took possession of the Ross family home in the Sutherland community of Ascoilemore. Those men were there to evict this young mother, her two small daughters, aged five and three, and her two-month-old baby girl. They were also there to empty the house of everything the Rosses owned.[1]

Jessie's baby, whose name was Roberta, had been born less than a year after another baby, a boy who did not live. In just 20 months, then, Jessie Ross had been through two pregnancies, one of which had ended tragically. Unsurprisingly, she was not in good health. This was of no concern to the men invading Jessie's home. Their remit was to make way for the expansion of a nearby sheep farm by ridding Ascoilemore of its inhabitants. There was no possibility, then, of the evicting party, the term its members used of themselves, letting anything or anyone – certainly not Jessie Ross and her children – get in their way.

The man in charge of proceedings, a sheriff-officer called Donald Bannerman, began by ordering out the two Ross girls, Elizabeth and Katherine. Their mother, however, refused to go with them, in the hope, it seems, that her continued presence would lead to the family's belongings being handled with at least a little care. 'She would

3

not leave . . . until the whole furniture was off,' it was afterwards explained. On Jessie Ross also refusing to help move the wooden cradle in which her baby was sleeping, one of the party, William Stevenson by name, picked it up – roughly and angrily it was said – with a view to carrying both cradle and baby outside.

Perhaps, as would be alleged, Stevenson was drunk – he and his colleagues having got through ten bottles of whisky the previous night and another three that morning. Or perhaps he was just clumsy. At all events, Stevenson somehow ran the cradle up against the Ross home's door or doorframe. Two-month-old Roberta, though not tumbled out, was shaken awake and began to cry in alarm. She was still in distress when her cradle was set down in such shelter as an exterior dyke or wall provided from a chill wind out of the north-east.

Although Ascoilemore's other residents had been evicted the day before, there were still people in the vicinity, some of whom now came to the Rosses' assistance. Among them was a woman called Mary Murray. Like Jessie Ross, she was a nursing mother and, doing something that would be thought unacceptable today – but which, judging by the matter-of-fact way it was spoken about, must have been standard practice then – Mary quietened Roberta's cries, a bystander said, by 'giving the child a suck' at her own breast.

The older Ross children were not so easily comforted. Not long after the evicting party got to work, Elizabeth, the five-year-old, was struck in the face by a piece of planking thrown from inside the house, the culprit again being Stevenson. She too began to cry and, though her crying was said to have stopped after 'quarter of an hour', neither Elizabeth nor Katherine, her sister, could have been anything other than traumatised by what was happening to them. Both were reported to have 'looked cold' and to have been 'trembling' or shivering, their misery compounded by the fact that they had, or were incubating, whooping cough.

Nowadays rare, thanks to a vaccine developed in the 1950s, whooping cough was once a common childhood illness. Its symptoms – usually including a fever and the drawn-out cough from which the infection got its name – were always unpleasant, sometimes severe and occasionally fatal. What happened to the three-year-old Katherine Ross some three weeks after the events of 31 May, then, might have happened anyway. But when Katherine died, it is understandable that her father, Gordon Ross, unavoidably elsewhere when his wife and children were evicted, should have insisted that his daughter's death resulted from what he called the 'inhuman treatment' she had experienced the day the Ross family's home was taken from them.[2]

Sutherland, in the north-western corner of the Scottish Highlands, is twenty-first-century Britain's empty quarter. England's average population density is 413 people per square kilometre. Scotland's is 68. But each square kilometre in Sutherland, a county of roughly the same size as Norfolk or Northumberland, contains on average just two people; and since most Sutherland residents live in coastal areas, much of the district's extensive interior is practically uninhabited.

This was not always so. Sutherland's inland straths or valleys, such as Strathnaver, the Strath of Kildonan and Strathbrora, were occupied for a long time, as their plentiful archaeology makes plain, by substantial populations. That changed in the early nineteenth century when, in those three straths, scores of long-established communities, one of them Ascoilemore in the middle part of Strathbrora, were snuffed out in a welter of evictions like the one experienced by Jessie Ross.

Clearances, the term applied in the Highlands to the process of depopulating formerly populated localities, were not confined to Sutherland. The Sutherland clearances, however, were unmatched in scale and ambition. For that reason, they generated, both at the time and subsequently, a great deal of controversy. At the centre of this controversy from the outset were the husband and wife who ordered the obliteration of Sutherland's interior settlements. Although their having done so would forever be held against them in some quarters, this did not affect the couple's standing, during their lifetimes anyway, with people who mattered politically. By these people, the man and woman in question were held in high regard – such high regard that, in due course, they were made Duke and Duchess of Sutherland. But this did not happen until 1833. During the clearances, the future duke and duchess were Marquis and Marchioness of Stafford.

The marquis, whose name was George Granville Leveson-Gower, owed his title – one that, even prior to his becoming a duke, put him near the top of the British aristocracy's pecking order – to his owning substantial estates in Staffordshire. Revenues from those estates and from others elsewhere in England, together with earnings accruing from extensive stakes in coalmines, canals and other enterprises, made Lord Stafford one of early nineteenth-century Britain's wealthiest individuals. Stafford's riches enabled him to become a renowned art collector – his forays into the art market adding lustre to the marquis's several stately homes and to his splendid London residence, Cleveland House. But in spite of his expenditure on paintings of the highest quality, and in spite too of the enormous sums it took to sustain other aspects of his own and his family's opulent lifestyle, Lord Stafford had more than enough cash left over to finance the transformation of the Highland landholdings that came his way as a result of his marrying someone whose aristocratic credentials were as impeccable as his own. This was Elizabeth Gordon, Countess of Sutherland.*

Orphaned when a child, the countess had inherited from her father, the eighteenth Earl of Sutherland, both her title (a countess being the female equivalent of an earl) and the territories her Gordon forebears had amassed in earlier centuries. Those territories, though they included the Assynt district on the county's Atlantic coast,

---

* During the eighteenth century, the Gordon Earls of Sutherland adopted the surname Sutherland. Here, to avoid confusing name changes within the same family, the older name is retained.

consisted mainly of Sutherland's eastern or North Sea coastal plain and the area to its west and north-west, an area that included Strathbrora, the Strath of Kildonan and Strathnaver. Later acquisitions were to make the Sutherland Estate, as the countess's possessions were known, the largest landed property in Victorian Britain. The estate and county of Sutherland would then overlap almost completely. But when events of the Ascoilemore sort were occurring, the Sutherland Estate continued to be centred on the county's eastern half. It is on that area (in particular its interior straths) that this book concentrates.

The clearances that took place there were calculated and considered. But while the thinking behind them was refined over a lengthy period, their key purpose was clear from the first. What Lord and Lady Stafford aimed to bring about was a dramatic expansion of the Sutherland Estate's revenue-producing capacity. The couple's means of doing this involved far-reaching changes in the way their Highland property was organised. First, small-scale agriculturalists of the kind who had long occupied much of the Sutherland Estate's more productive arable land – the bulk of it adjacent to the North Sea – were removed, and the greater part of this land incorporated into large, commercially run farms similar to those already standard on the Marquis of Stafford's English possessions. Second, the interior straths, where people relied more on cattle-rearing than on crop production, were emptied of their inhabitants – whose land was then turned over to sheep farmers. Both the coastal and inland farms thus created were tenanted. But their tenants – a lot of them freshly arrived outsiders – were no simple sons of the soil. Instead they were highly enterprising men of substance, men possessing the stock management and other skills required of any farmer aspiring to operate effectively in the market economy taking shape in conjunction with Britain's industrial revolution. Go-getting and fiercely competitive, the sheep farmers who established themselves in Sutherland during the clearance era were soon cashing in impressively on growing demand for wool – demand generated by the clothing and other needs of emerging manufacturing centres in Lowland Scotland and England. But whether producing wool in the interior or grain and other crops on the eastern coastal fringe, the Sutherland Estate's post-clearance farmers were expected to – and did – generate profits big enough to enable them to pay higher (often much higher) rents than the estate's owners ever got, even in aggregate, from the people the new class of large-scale agriculturalists displaced.

Homes in the communities destroyed in the course of the clearances might be clustered together or more scattered. Either way, they were surrounded by blocks of arable land laid out in long, narrow strips known as rigs. Oats, barley and potatoes (the latter an eighteenth-century introduction to Sutherland) were grown on those rigs, with every farming family in the typical *baile* or township (the Gaelic and English terms applied to such settlements) having the use of agreed numbers of them. Rigs were generally distributed in such a way as to ensure that better and worse tracts of arable were shared out equitably; and especially in inland townships families could also draw on a common resource in the shape of large tracts of hill grazing where cattle could be pastured. During the eighteenth century, more and more of those cattle were sold into southern markets. In Sutherland as elsewhere in the Highlands, that made it possible (because of there being more money in circulation) for estate managers to begin to levy higher rents. But there were limits to this, the pre-clearance landholding structure having originated in a period when high rents were not the priority they afterwards became.

During this period, which lasted for several centuries, the Highlands were often outside the effective jurisdiction of the two countries to which the region successively belonged, those countries being first Scotland and next the British state brought into existence by the Anglo-Scottish union of 1707. In those circumstances, the power and prestige of clan chiefs, the quasi-tribal magnates who held sway in the region, necessarily depended (as had been the case since the Middle Ages) on the number of fighting men their territories could sustain. This was as true of Earls of Sutherland, Elizabeth Gordon's ancestors, as it was of the rest of the Highland nobility. Technically, Sutherland's earls had been granted their earldom by medieval Scotland's monarchy. But they held on to this earldom by conducting themselves, generation after generation, as clan chiefs. This meant that more emphasis was placed on keeping people on the land than on maximising cash returns from it. It also meant that the estate Elizabeth Gordon inherited in 1766, when she was barely one year old, was organised in much the same way at it had been in clanship's heyday.

By 1766, however, that heyday was past. When a number of clan chiefs lined up behind Prince Charles Edward Stuart's 1745 attempt to regain the throne his forebears had lost a lifetime previously, and when the Highland army the prince thus obtained came close to overthrowing Britain's government, London's badly scared politicians – their troops having at last defeated Charles Edward's forces at the Battle of Culloden – promptly set about dismantling clanship. They did so in part by encouraging leading families in the Highlands to turn their backs on much of their heritage, including the Gaelic language all of them had once spoken, and to adopt instead the manners, accents and attitudes of the rest of the British ruling class. The 1785 marriage of Elizabeth Gordon and George Granville Leveson-Gower was bound up with this shift in the relationship between the Highlands and the wider society into which the region was now integrated. Elizabeth, although raised in Edinburgh and London (where she met her future husband) and never more than an occasional visitor to Sutherland, clearly felt – even if only sporadically – that her ancestry imposed on her an obligation to be mindful of people whose family predecessors had been bound to her own forebears by ties of clanship. But Sutherland's population, Elizabeth Gordon came to feel, was not best served by permitting matters in Sutherland to continue as before. Elizabeth's husband who, following the couple's marriage had become (in accordance with then legal practice) the Sutherland Estate's proprietor in her place, backed this view, their shared standpoint helping to explain why Lord Stafford (in a way then unusual) gave his wife a substantial and sometimes decisive say in the policy departures that were to impact calamitously on many Sutherland lives.

The scope for such departures grew in 1803 when Leveson-Gower gained control of his recently deceased father's fortune and, that same year, inherited a further fortune from a childless uncle. Soon the marquis and the marchioness, able now to spend freely, were embarking on the estate management revolution that culminated in the Sutherland clearances.

Although those clearances led to people quitting Sutherland, the Highlands and Scotland, this was not their intended outcome, it being a key component of Lord and Lady Stafford's thinking that dispossessed families could readily be accommodated elsewhere on their property. Hence the efforts made to ensure that people ejected from localities like Ascoilemore headed for the new or growing settlements to which estate managers directed them. Those settlements were of two types. One consisted of villages and small towns on Sutherland's east coast – places like (from north to south) Helmsdale, Brora, Golspie and Dornoch. All such communities gained population at the time of the clearances. So did the further and quite different set of settlements – entirely rural in character – which took shape at the same time. Communities in this category consisted of smallholdings of the kind known in the Highlands as crofts. Such communities, many of them located on land that had not previously been cultivated, were established widely on the inland margins of east coast arable farms as well as on Sutherland's north coast where Strathnaver – exiting the interior from south to north and not, like the Strath of Kildonan and Strathbrora, from west to east – reaches the sea.

Crofting townships were as novel as the sheep farms that gave rise to them. Families settled in these places, instead of having access to rigs of the traditional type, were each allocated a single plot: their croft. Around those crofts there continued to be common grazings.

These, however, were far less generous than had previously been the case. This meant that crofters could keep hardly any cattle. The prospect of their growing worthwhile crops was likewise curtailed both by establishing crofts on poor-quality land and by imposing drastic limits on their size – most crofts laid out in the clearance period being no more than three, four or five acres in extent.

The message was clear. Whatever else Sutherland crofters were to be, they were not to be full-time agriculturalists. But this, the Marquis and Marchioness of Stafford, their advisers and agents said and wrote repeatedly, was a good thing. By concentrating the Sutherland Estate's population in a small proportion of the available acreage, it was claimed, the remainder of the estate could be given over to an up-to-date and highly productive brand of farming. That, it was contended, was exactly what had happened in the rest of the British countryside during preceding centuries, as peasant cultivation everywhere gave way to more advanced modes of husbandry. And just as the dislodged peasantry of rural Staffordshire had helped fuel industrialisation by providing Midland towns and cities with workforces, so the people crowding into Sutherland's crofting townships and coastal villages would find – if only because they had no alternative – new means of making a living. They would find those, this argument ran, in the various businesses the Sutherland Estate's owners and managers were intent on promoting. Among such businesses were fishing, fish-curing, coal mining, brick-making, whisky distilling, brewing, road construction and bridge-building. Incoming farmers, it was pointed out, would require labourers. There would be a need for shopkeepers, shop assistants, domestic servants, bakers, carpenters, coopers, boat-builders, netmakers, stonemasons, tailors and other tradesmen.

From this perspective, then, the Sutherland clearances were simply one aspect of the expansion and diversification of what was, as far as Lord and Lady Stafford were concerned, an under-performing estate economy in manifest need of being dragged into the nineteenth century. What they were about, they maintained, was entirely in tune with the times; it was right, progressive, inevitable; they had history, they believed, on their side. Nor, in their own minds, were the marquis and marchioness motivated wholly, or even largely, by self-interest. Their expenditure on roads, bridges and other infrastructure was likely, they pointed out, to be considerably greater than any short-run return on this investment. Ultimately, of course, the Staffords expected to benefit financially from what they called 'the Sutherland improvements'. But the case for those improvements, as set out by men hired to make them happen, did not dwell on this. That case concentrated rather on the wider consequences of what was going on in Sutherland. Those consequences were said to be wholly positive. A district that had made little contribution to Britain's economic growth would henceforth contribute much more; and among those bound to gain as a result, or so 'improvers' asserted, were people turned out of places like Ascoilemore. Those folk were not so much losing their homes, it was said, as being provided with a fresh start in places where all sorts of opportunities awaited them.

Rhetoric of this sort, a great deal of which was deployed on Lord and Lady Stafford's behalf, is similar to propaganda produced by some of the twentieth century's totalitarian regimes, perhaps because those regimes needed, much like the Staffords, to defend programmes of enforced social and economic change. Such comparisons, to be sure, cannot be pushed too far. When, for instance, Joseph Stalin set about the destruction of peasant farming in the Soviet Union of the 1930s, millions died. Nothing remotely like that occurred in the course of the Sutherland clearances. But the collectivisation of Soviet agriculture and 'the Sutherland improvements' have something in common all the same. The Soviet dictator, like the Marquis and Marchioness of Stafford, thought himself engaged in the modernisation of backward and benighted segments of his country. And while the Staffords would not have countenanced violence of the extreme sort unleashed by Stalin, they nevertheless thought themselves entitled to treat family after family in the way

Jessie Ross and her children were treated in Ascoilemore in 1821. The marquis and marchioness believed themselves so entitled because – and in this their thinking certainly resembles that of total-itarians – they were convinced that the objectives they had in mind for Sutherland and its people were so self-evidently forward-looking as to make it acceptable to secure those objectives by harsh and oppressive means.

Jessie Ross was born in 1793. Her father, George Sutherland, was one of pre-clearance Sutherland's more substantial farmers and was thus of sufficient standing to have ensured that his daughter, unlike many of her Sutherland contemporaries, became fluent in English as well as Gaelic. Jessie's upbringing, then, is likely to have been similar to that of her husband, Gordon, who was born in 1791 and whose father, Hugh Ross, made certain that Gordon got a good schooling. Hugh's being able to provide for his son in this way is a pointer to his having been reasonably well off, his prosperity deriving from his having managed a several-thousand-acre slice of Strathbrora on behalf of its then lairds or proprietors.[3]

Those proprietors belonged to a well-established Sutherland family, the Gordons of Carrol. For centuries, they had been staunch allies – fellow clansfolk in effect – of the other Gordons who became Earls of Sutherland and whose antecedents Carrol's lairds shared. The Gordons of Carrol's readiness to come to the aid of men they regarded as their chiefs is highlighted in a seventeenth-century account of the open warfare that broke out in 1589 between the then Earl of Sutherland and a rival magnate in neighbouring Caithness. When, in response to an armed incursion into his possessions, the earl was in search of someone reliable enough to take charge of the 'thrie [sic] hundred chosen men' he had mobilised with a view to inflicting 'great terror' on Caithness, his choice fell on Alexander Gordon whose descendant, John Gordon of Carrol, would – a couple of hundred years later – make Hugh Ross his factor or estate manager.[4]

Factor Hugh's son Gordon may well have been given his first name by way of honouring the Carrol family. For all this family's long-standing links with Strathbrora, however, John Gordon was its last member to die a laird, the Carrol Estate being bought soon after by the Marquis and Marchioness of Stafford. This was in 1812, by which point Carrol was owned by John's son Joseph. Three years before, the marchioness had assured Joseph, 30 when his father died in 1807, of her 'regard for the old connection subsisting between our families'. She and her husband, Lady Stafford told Joseph, would 'do everything in our power to render your situation in Sutherland agreeable and comfortable'. By 1812, however, this promise had been forgotten, the Staffords now being less interested in their 'old connection' with Carrol than in the fact that Joseph's urgent need for hard cash had presented them with an opportunity to add to their Sutherland acreage.[5]

Joseph Gordon, who began training as a lawyer in Edinburgh in 1804 and who then launched his own legal practice there, was not a poor man. But he was not a rich one either. Unable to afford the Carrol Estate's upkeep and equally unable to service its accumulated debts, Joseph, though reluctant to sell his 'paternal inheritance', felt that 'duty to [his] family' – who might otherwise have found themselves in difficulty – left him with no alternative. 'The thought of getting it pleases me much,' one of the marquis and marchioness's land managers commented on hearing of Carrol's purchase by his employers. Its acquisition, this man added, meant that Stafford control of Strathbrora and adjacent parts of eastern Sutherland was now 'complete'.[6]

Lord and Lady Stafford, however, had got their way at a price – a price that did not begin and end with the £17,000 it cost them to get the Carrol Estate into their possession. What looked to the marquis and the marchioness like a good piece of business, looked very different when viewed from Joseph Gordon's standpoint. This was in part a consequence of bitter disputes as to what exactly Joseph had been offered for Carrol. In conversation with him in Edinburgh,

Joseph said, Lady Stafford had agreed a figure of 16,000 guineas. But the written offer that then reached him was for £16,000 – £800 less. In response to Joseph's protests that he had, in effect, been duped, Lord Stafford eventually gave way. Joseph's account of his dealings with the marchioness, Stafford admitted, was 'correct'. Hence his decision to give Joseph £17,000. This, the marquis added with bad grace, was 'a very large sum for such a property and not a shilling more will be paid . . . for it'.[7]

Despite its being eaten into by debt repayments, the money made from Carrol's sale (around £1 million at today's prices) helped Joseph get properly set up in Edinburgh. His 1812 windfall accounts too for his having become in 1813 an investor in, and a director of, that city's recently launched Commercial Bank. But none of this reconciled Joseph Gordon to his loss of Carrol. Because he lost status when he ceased to be a laird, Joseph (even had he not also been subjected to what he saw as double-dealing) would have been less than human had he not regarded the Carrol Estate's buyers – newly in command of what had been his family's territories – with some resentment. In fact, or so the evidence indicates, Joseph Gordon, from 1812 onwards, loathed the Marquis and Marchioness of Stafford. He certainly went out of his way to cause them a great deal of trouble.[8]

Throughout the clearance period, Joseph Gordon's legal services were made available to some of the most outspoken critics and opponents of evictions; and by 1821, when Ascoilemore was cleared, Joseph – by means (as will be seen) of grants from a fund at his disposal – was assisting dispossessed families, some of Ascoilemore's former residents among them, to emigrate to Nova Scotia. Because eagerness to be off to North America was not at all in accord with Stafford insistence that everyone affected by 'improvement' was benefiting from it, Joseph Gordon's championing of emigration intensified the Stafford camp's already profound mistrust of him. 'Joseph Gordon was always a great enemy of ours,' the marchioness wrote on hearing of his plan to help meet prospective emigrants' costs. Her Edinburgh lawyers were in agreement. Carrol's ex-laird was 'strongly biased against' everything Lord and Lady Stafford were trying to accomplish, one of them commented. Equally forthright condemnation came from James Loch, the Staffords' land management supremo. Hired in 1812 to oversee the marquis's English estates, Loch, though continuing to be based in the south, was in overall charge from 1816 of developments in Sutherland – developments Gordon was intent, or so James Loch believed, on sabotaging. 'Joseph Gordon and all his family are most determined and open enemies to the interests of your Lordship,' Loch informed the Marquis of Stafford.[9]

As James Loch was well aware, Joseph Gordon maintained an extensive network of friends and informants in the Highlands. Among members of this network was Joseph's maternal uncle, Donald MacLeod of Geanies. Like his nephew, MacLeod was a Commercial Bank director. He was also a well-established laird in Ross-shire – Sutherland's neighbouring county to the south – where he had long been that county's sheriff. Joseph Gordon's close links with Donald MacLeod – after whom Joseph named his eldest son – were indicative, as was Joseph's involvement in Edinburgh business circles, of his ready access to individuals of influence. His having such access worried James Loch. So did the extent of Joseph's dealings with some of the many people in Sutherland who thought about opposing, or who actually did oppose, the Marquis and Marchioness of Stafford's plans for them. Loch responded to all such dealings by categorising as a troublemaker anyone known to have participated in them. When, during the month that ended with Ascoilemore's clearance, Joseph Gordon (then in the north) met a number of the township's residents, this accordingly inclined Loch to the view that the people in question were 'a turbulent set'. Among the most turbulent, or so Loch and his management team were soon to conclude, was Gordon Ross, a man prepared, Loch learned in July 1821, to state publicly that his daughter's death was attributable to the way she, her sisters and their mother were treated when turned out of their Ascoilemore home.[10]

*   *   *

Today the Highlands are usually entered from the south by way of the A9 trunk road that links Perth, on the northern edge of the Scottish Lowlands, with Inverness, the Highland capital and the region's only city. The distance between Perth and Inverness is 115 miles. At Inverness, however, anyone travelling from Perth to Strathnaver, say, is barely halfway, while no part of Sutherland is much less than an hour distant. A good deal of that hour is taken up, again on the A9, traversing Easter Ross, the lower-lying, and most intensively farmed, half of Ross-shire. For much of the twentieth century, the A9 got to Sutherland from Easter Ross by following the shores of the Dornoch Firth, the North Sea inlet that is eastern Sutherland's southern boundary. Since the bridging of the firth in 1991, however, the A9 has taken a more direct route that gives speedier access to Dornoch, Sutherland's county town and as such the place housing, at the time of the clearances, both Sutherland's sheriff court and (handily nearby) the county's jail.

From Dornoch, by way of a further stretch of the A9, it takes 20 minutes to reach Golspie, greatly altered in the early nineteenth century by the construction of new buildings including, on the town's northern outskirts, a substantial and still extant inn. Not far beyond the inn is Dunrobin Castle. Much of present-day Dunrobin is Victorian in origin and appearance. But the earlier Dunrobin, though not so ornate, was just as impressive. In 1812, when the clearances were getting under way, 'the ancient seat of the Earls of Sutherland', as the castle was even then described, consisted of 'a well constructed square building' with 'a small court[yard] in the centre'. Some decades previously, Dunrobin had become dilapidated. But the Marquis and Marchioness of Stafford spent heavily on the castle's refurbishment, with a view to its providing them with an acceptable, if always temporary, home when (after journeys that then took days instead of hours) they came north to inspect projects they had initiated.[11]

Many of those projects centred on Brora where a coalmine, for which high hopes were entertained, was meant to underpin a series of other industries. During the nineteenth century's second decade, when those industries were being got up and running, the marchioness was a regular visitor here, the trip from Dunrobin to Brora being reasonably short even when tackled by horse-drawn carriage.

In Brora as in Golspie, the A9 doubles as the town's main street. From this street, at a point just beyond the town centre, a further – narrower – street links the A9 with a single-track road that threads its way westwards or north-westwards into Strathbrora. About five miles up the strath, and occupying its floor for another five miles or more, is Loch Brora which, in the 1790s, the Church of Scotland minister serving this part of Sutherland thought a most attractive 'stretch of water'. The loch was surrounded, the minister went on, by 'lofty mountains at the feet of which are some beautiful villages'. The hills in Loch Brora's vicinity remain as lofty as ever and the loch itself is equally unchanged. But the settlements mentioned by Strathbrora's late eighteenth-century clergyman are nowhere to be seen. They were among the dozens of small communities, collectively containing well over 1,000 people, that disappeared from this single valley in the course of the clearances.[12]

One of these townships was Carrol, the place, about halfway up Loch Brora and on the loch's southern shore, which provided Joseph Gordon's family with their territorial designation. Sheltered from the prevailing westerly wind by a steep hillside, Carrol contained reasonably good arable land. That perhaps is why Joseph's forebears settled here in the Middle Ages. Long before Joseph Gordon sold the Carrol Estate to the Marquis and Marchioness of Stafford, however, his family had transferred their base of operations to another part of the property. Their new home was on Loch Brora's northern shore and near the loch's western end. The spot was called Kilcalmkill. This is an anglicised version of a Gaelic original, *Cill Chaluim Chille*, signifying that the settlement once contained a place of worship dedicated to St Columba, the Irish-born monk believed to have brought Christianity to much of the Highlands. This Kilcalmkill church or chapel was one of seven such foundations

in Strathbrora – another indication that the valley was thickly populated for a lengthy period. But by the end of the eighteenth century
the Kilcalmkill name had been abandoned in favour of a new one,
Gordonbush. Adding 'bush' to a surname in this fashion was one
way that colonists in North America staked a claim to a particular
locality. Whether or not they followed colonial precedent, the
Gordons of Carrol, by renaming Kilcalmkill as they did, were
certainly intent on advertising their connection – one they must have
expected to endure – with the spot where they built a home described
as 'handsome'.[13]

The Marchioness of Stafford, on one of her excursions from
Dunrobin, travelled up Strathbrora towards the end of September
1820. The strath's road, then new, was one piece of Sutherland
Estate infrastructure that had been completed (unlike some others)
on schedule, and Lady Stafford was pleased by it. Writing to her
husband (who had not come north) to tell him about her 'beautiful
drive by the lake', meaning Loch Brora, the marchioness nevertheless confessed to feeling 'rather melancholy' on seeing, 'from the
opposite side of the lake', the 'old town[ship]' of Carrol, cleared
earlier that year and therefore, as Lady Stafford put it, 'empty'.
Today little is left of Carrol homes their occupants were forced to
abandon, and such remnants as survive are not visible from Loch
Brora's northern shore. In the autumn of 1820, however, the settlement's houses – which the last of Carrol's pre-clearance residents
left the previous June – would still have been standing. Already,
admittedly, they would have been roofless. But this, when Lady
Stafford gazed into Carrol from less than half a mile away, may well
have served to accentuate their dreariness and her 'melancholy'. The
marchioness's regrets, to be sure, were for her vanished youth as
much as for Carrol's evicted families. 'You remember we walked
[there]', she commented of Carrol in her letter to Lord Stafford –
evoking a time when both she and her husband, who by 1820 was in
poor health, had been unbothered by age and infirmity. But there is,
all the same, something telling about Elizabeth Leveson-Gower's

reaction to her glimpsing just a little of the destruction resulting
from policies she had helped formulate and carry out. In her letter
touching on it, Carrol's clearance takes on the character of a chance
occurrence in which the Marchioness of Stafford played no part.[14]

Some of Carrol's displaced tenants were allocated freshly laid-
out crofts, lots or allotments (the three terms were used
interchangeably) in a locality, just south of Brora, known as the
Doll. In contrast to Carrol's rigs, which had been cultivated for
generations, those new holdings – their boundaries consisting
initially of nothing other than the scratchy markings made by dragging a plough across open moorland – were located mostly on land
that had never been farmed. This meant that Carrol's newly settled
crofters were expected to contribute to the Sutherland Estate's
'improvement' by somehow getting crops to grow in places where no
crops had ever before been sown or planted. This was not an enticing prospect. Unsurprisingly, then, some of the people meant to
move to the Doll from Carrol, and from other Strathbrora townships cleared in 1819 and 1820, refused to go there, managing instead
to acquire farms in Caithness or to emigrate to North America. But
both Caithness tenancies and Atlantic passages were expensive.
Many Strathbrora families consequently had no option but to take
up crofting in the Doll. There they were told that anyone falling
down on the job of land reclamation – which was supposed to
proceed in tandem with the house construction crofters also had to
undertake – would be evicted for a second time. Reclamation duly
got under way, with results still to be seen all around the Doll in the
shape of boundary walls made from stones and boulders dug and
levered out of each croft's little fields. But this took time, and to
begin with progress was so slow as to suggest that some Doll crofters engaged in deliberate obstructionism. Hence the exasperated
tone of a letter sent to James Loch in February 1820 by Francis
Suther who, as the Staffords' most senior manager in Sutherland,
was responsible for ensuring that matters at the Doll turned out as
intended. 'The Doll allotments are now all fixed,' Suther reported to

Loch. 'I have threatened to turn out [meaning evict] all such as do not begin to improve and get on busily in bringing in the waste [meaning formerly uncultivated] pieces of their lots.' [15]

The Marchioness of Stafford was told nothing of this when, a day or two after her Strathbrora expedition, she was shown around the Doll. She found the settlement a 'pretty' place, the marchioness reported, and was pleased to see its newly installed crofting families 'working at their little harvests'. If, after sighting a newly derelict Carrol, Lady Stafford had felt some momentary qualms as to the long-run wisdom of what she, Lord Stafford and their agents were about, her inspection of the Doll helped set her mind at rest. What the marchioness saw and heard when taken to Gordonbush helped further.[16]

Following the Staffords' purchase of the Carrol Estate in 1812, Gordonbush's earlier name, Kilcalmkill, had been revived. However, it was not now applied to Gordonbush (which retained that name) but to a farm that took shape in 1813 and which stretched from Strathbrora to the Strath of Kildonan, some 15 miles, as the crow flies, further north. This Kilcalmkill farm carried a stock of around 10,000 sheep. Those sheep belonged to the farm's tenant, Gabriel Reed, whom James Loch, not given to flattery, considered 'one of the most intelligent stock farmers' of his day. Underpinning this judgement was Reed's mastery of the complex business of getting large-scale sheep farming under way in Sutherland. Raised in Northumberland, where the Reeds were a well-entrenched family, Gabriel had come to the Highlands in the mid-1790s. Then his centre of operations was the Bighouse Estate on Sutherland's north coast – where Reed installed one of the first of the cheviot flocks (cheviots being a breed originating in the English-Scottish border country) that were to proliferate in Sutherland during the clearance era. Another of the properties which (like Carrol) would eventually fall into Stafford hands, Bighouse, when Gabriel Reed got there, belonged to a Sutherland gentry family, one of whose members became in time Gabriel's wife. But despite his having thus put down roots at Bighouse, not far from Sutherland's boundary with Caithness, Gabriel agreed in 1813 to take on the tenancy of Kilcalmkill, one of the farm's attractions, over and above its cheviot-rearing potential, being the accommodation the Reed family obtained there. Reckoned to be 'a good modern house' of a kind then rare in Sutherland, this accommodation was no common farmhouse but the mansion-like and plantation-surrounded home that had belonged, until 1812, to Joseph Gordon.[17]

'The beauty of it is indescribable,' the Marchioness of Stafford wrote of Gordonbush following her 1820 visit. 'The Reeds', she added, 'are very good sort of people [and] were delighted to see us.' Their home, the marchioness went on, was 'like an English gentleman's place'. While there, she had been delighted to be assured by Gabriel Reed that, thanks to her and the marquis's 'improvements', Sutherland 'would soon be the richest county in England' – England standing, in Lady Stafford's mind, for Britain. Perhaps Gabriel Reed believed this. More probably, however, his purpose was to butter up, and show some gratitude to, the Staffords. Having already profited greatly from the land-use changes the marquis and the marchioness were implementing, Reed in 1820 was looking forward to further gains – because of its having been agreed that an additional piece of Strathbrora would shortly be incorporated into his Kilcalmkill farm. The area in question included one of the few Strathbrora townships to have survived previous clearances. This was Ascoilemore, which, in the autumn of 1820 when the Marchioness of Stafford's Strathbrora expedition took her past the place, was home to Gordon Ross, his two small daughters and his (at this point) three months pregnant wife Jessie.[18]

A mile or so west of Gordonbush is the head of Loch Brora. Further on is a large expanse of flat, potentially cultivable, land intersected by the River Brora – all sweeping curves and deep, dark salmon pools. Here, not far upriver from the loch, the Brora is joined by a smaller but faster flowing watercourse emerging out of the hills to the north. This burn is called in Gaelic *Allt a' Mhuilin*. That means Mill Stream; and though there is no mill in this vicinity today, and has not been for two centuries, Allt a' Mhuilin's name testifies to one having once stood hereabouts. Where there was a mill, moreover, there must have been a settlement. In fact, there were two. One, east of Allt a' Mhuilin, was called Ascoilebeg. The other, beyond the mill burn to the west and a little way up a hillside, was Ascoilemore.

Ascoilemore, before its 1821 clearance, contained several houses. Because nearly 20 decades have passed since those houses ceased to be inhabited, their surviving traces consist of little more than rectangular undulations in the turf. There being no detailed map or plan of Ascoilemore as it was prior to 1821, it is impossible to say which of the township's vestigial ruins marks the spot that was once home to Gordon and Jessie Ross. What can be located, however, is what was said subsequently to be the site of Gordon's place of work. This site is not in Ascoilemore but about half a mile away in Ascoilebeg, and the building that stood there, as can be seen from its remnant footings or foundations, was a substantial one. This goes some way to substantiating its later identification (made well within living memory of the events of 1821) as the school maintained, if not in this precise spot then certainly in this vicinity, by the Society in Scotland for the Propagation of Christian Knowledge (SSPCK). Established in Edinburgh in the early 1700s with a view to civilising Highlanders, then seen widely in the south as barbaric, the SSPCK, by the start of the nineteenth century, had evolved into a charitable body concentrating on the provision of elementary education. The organisation's relationship with the Marquis and Marchioness of Stafford was a chequered one, the marchioness, on one occasion, rejecting as 'totally inadmissible' an SSPCK request that the Sutherland Estate help it financially by not levying rents on its Sutherland schools. But the society, despite those difficulties, remained committed to the county, its Strathbrora school catering, at any given point, for between 40 and 60 pupils.[19]

Gordon Ross may have been one of this school's students and, while still a teenager, may have served as assistant to its then schoolmaster. By 1813, at all events, he had taken that schoolmaster's place. The post carried an annual salary of £15. This is put in perspective by the fact that James Loch's earnings, when Loch was first employed by the Marquis of Stafford, were 70 times greater. But his £15 a year was nevertheless sufficient to enable Gordon to marry Jessie Sutherland and to set up home with her in Ascoilemore. By the standards of their place and time, indeed, the Rosses – until the clearances deprived them of home, income and prospects – enjoyed a good standard of living. Thus the couple employed a maid who helped Jessie manage a home that, unlike most houses in early nineteenth-century Sutherland, ran to two (or at least one and a half) storeys, its ground floor rooms being supplemented by a floored garret or loft. This home appears, in addition, to have been well furnished – no fewer than three cartloads of furniture being taken from it on the day of the family's eviction.[20]

Ascoilemore, when Jessie and Gordon Ross's children were starting to arrive, had four farming tenants: John Baillie, Robert MacKay, Adam MacDonald and Donald MacKay. Those men were jointly in control of the township's hill pasture, its fields or rigs where grain was grown and the drying kiln where this grain was dried prior to its being milled by John MacKay whose mill was on the Ascoilebeg side of Allt a' Mhuilin but whose home was in Ascoilemore. Although other people appear to have lived there, the miller and his family, the Rosses and the township's farming tenants, along with their wives and children, accounted for the largest part of Ascoilemore's population. This population was probably similar to that of Ascoilebeg which had a comparable number of tenants; and since there must have been a lot of to-ing and fro-ing between Ascoilebeg and Ascoilemore, it is likely that all inhabitants of 'the two Ascoiles', as the townships are sometimes called in surviving documentation, were well known to each other. This being so, it makes sense to imagine Gordon Ross, Jessie Ross and their daughters as belonging to a close-knit community numbering (between the two Ascoiles) perhaps 70 or 80 in total. This community, in turn, would have had all sorts of links with those other pre-clearance townships (of which there were several) close enough to have supplied Gordon Ross's school with pupils.[21]

Exactly how Gordon and Jessie Ross were regarded by their neighbours cannot now be established. But it is suggestive, first, that the leading men of Ascoilemore – the two MacKays, MacDonald and Baillie – were well enough disposed towards the Ross family to have put their names in April 1818 to a written record of their having agreed to Gordon being granted 'grass for a cow', this animal's function being to supply Gordon and Jessie (whose second daughter, Katherine, was born the following month) with the milk, butter and other dairy produce needed by a growing family. It is suggestive, second, that 'the schoolmaster', as Gordon Ross is designated in that 1818 document, should also have been provided with what he afterwards called a 'garden' and 'potato land'. It is suggestive, finally, that it was to Gordon Ross that the occupants of Ascoilemore and one or two neighbouring communities turned for assistance when in 1819 they were notified that, although they had escaped that spring's clearance of much of Strathbrora, their townships too had been earmarked for destruction. A number of people duly met more than once with Gordon Ross in his school, where it was decided that, on their and on his own behalf, he should write for help to that Stafford bête noire, Joseph Gordon.[22]

Because Gordon Ross's father was one of the Carrol Estate's key employees, Gordon must have been known personally to Joseph, even though the latter was already a teenager when the future SSPCK teacher was born. As their correspondence cannot be traced, there is no knowing how the two men addressed each other. What can be known, however, is the outcome of their 1819 exchange of letters. There was no prospect, Joseph Gordon told Gordon Ross, of Ascoilemore residents mounting a successful legal challenge to their imminent eviction because, as stated in a subsequent summary of what Joseph had to say, they had 'no ground on which they could resist'.[23]

Since landlords could eject any landholder who did not have a lease, and since the leases Ascoilemore's tenants possessed (leases that spared them eviction in 1819) were due to expire in late 1820, this news cannot have come as much of a surprise to Gordon Ross. Others in Ascoilemore were to make further efforts to hang on there, and, to this end, were reportedly consulting 'a twopenny lawyer' from Tain in Easter Ross just weeks before their eventual dispossession. For his part, however, Gordon Ross now concluded that he had no hope of retaining either his Ascoilemore home or his job. As Strathbrora's last inhabitants were shortly 'to be removed' from the strath, he informed his SSPCK employers, there would soon be 'no occasion' for a school there. But as Gordon well appreciated, this did not mean that Sutherland more generally was ceasing to need schools and schoolmasters. The depopulation of the county's interior valleys had resulted (as mentioned earlier) in newly evicted families flocking into its coastal localities. Among those localities was Helmsdale, 12 miles north of Brora, where the Marquis and Marchioness of Stafford were intent on developing both a harbour and a fishing fleet. A school was required there, and Gordon Ross very much wanted to be appointed its teacher.[24]

Because they controlled all such matters, the Staffords, or more precisely their agents, would have a decisive say in the new school's staffing arrangements. That is why Gordon Ross now tried to curry favour with the marquis and marchioness's Golspie-based factor, Francis Suther. This suited Suther. Being well aware of the efforts Ascoilemore's tenants were making to stave off their eviction, the factor – who thought Ascoilemore folk 'a bad set' – took some satisfaction in having been presented, in the person of a newly obsequious Gordon Ross, with a means of discovering exactly what was going on in the township. This is evident from Francis Suther's correspondence with James Loch. Ascoilemore's tenants were 'determined not to accept' the lots or crofts awaiting them near Brora, Suther told Loch at the start of 1820. At least three of them had consequently 'taken places [meaning farms] in Caithness'. This piece of intelligence, the factor added, came from a man he described as 'my informer Ross' – an informer identified further as 'schoolmaster in Ascoilemore'.[25]

Because there was some prospect at this point of Ascoilemore being cleared in the autumn of 1820, its people were ordered by Francis Suther not to sow or plant crops that spring. As if by way of confirming the factor's opinion of them, most Ascoilemore residents ignored this instruction. One who did not was Gordon Ross. During April and May 1820, the teacher wrote, he 'turned not an inch of . . . [his] potato land', something he is sure to have drawn to Suther's attention when, in May, he made the journey to Rhives, just outside Golspie, where the factor lived and where the Sutherland Estate's administrative headquarters were located. At Rhives, Gordon spoke about his wish to 'be placed at Helmsdale'. Much to his delight, this wish – or so the young man understood Francis Suther to have said – was one the factor was prepared to grant.[26]

But if his dealings with Francis Suther helped Gordon Ross (as he thought) to secure his family's medium-term prospects, those dealings were not without their more immediate downside for the Rosses. Gordon's neighbours, people who had begun by treating the SSPCK teacher as a valuable ally in their developing conflict with the Sutherland Estate, now (or so it was reported) 'withdrew their confidence in him'. However, any consequent unpleasantness (and there is bound to have been some) must have been outweighed, as far as Gordon was concerned, by its having been 'settled', as he put it, that he was to become Helmsdale's schoolmaster.[27]

So matters continued through the rest of 1820 and into the following year – Ascoilemore's clearance having been postponed for some months. Then, in mid-May 1821, no more than a couple of weeks before he, his family and everyone else in Ascoilemore were due to quit the place, Gordon Ross learned, greatly to his distress, that what he had thought to be Francis Suther's promise of a new schoolmastership was no promise at all. Helmsdale's teaching post, it now appeared, was to go not to Ross but to a man whose claim to it was being promoted by George MacPherson Grant, Sutherland's MP and a close friend and ally of the Marquis and Marchioness of Stafford, to whom Grant owed his parliamentary seat. Gordon Ross had no such backer. Immediately, however, he wrote again to Joseph Gordon. The latter, because of his involvement in the professional and commercial life of Edinburgh, is bound to have known some of the Edinburgh-based SSPCK's board of directors – people drawn mostly from the city's business and legal community. It is possible, therefore, that Gordon Ross asked Joseph Gordon to engage in a little lobbying on his behalf, with the aim of persuading the SSPCK to look kindly on their soon-to-be-redundant Strathbrora teacher in connection with any vacancy that might occur elsewhere in the society's network. But if he was to be sure that his employers were made properly aware of his circumstances, Gordon Ross decided, he himself would have to go 'instantly to Edinburgh'. He set out on 24 May. Ascoilemore was to be cleared just six days later.[28]

Before leaving Sutherland for the south, Gordon Ross did everything he could to ensure the safety of his wife and children. He found a place where they could stay temporarily if evicted in his absence, and he attempted to extend by two or three weeks his family's occupancy of their Ascoilemore home. Hence the drawing up of a document signed, according to Gordon, by 'two respectable people' who put their reputations on the line by undertaking to ensure that, as soon as the schoolmaster's trip to Edinburgh was at an end, he, Jessie, their two girls and their baby would remove themselves at once from Ascoilemore. This arrangement, Gordon Ross insisted afterwards, was known to, and agreed by, Francis Suther. If so, Suther's word proved no more reliable in this context than it had done in the case of the promised teaching post in Helmsdale. Gordon learned as much in mid-June when, returning from Edinburgh (where he had failed to get a definite promise of a job) and trudging north through Easter Ross, he chanced to meet a group of people from Strathbrora. Those people were making for the Ross-shire port of Cromarty. There they were to board the Leith-registered *Ossian* and sail for Nova Scotia. The departing emigrants – their voyage financed in part by Joseph Gordon – included at least two families from Ascoilemore. From them Gordon Ross learned that Jessie, Elizabeth, Katherine and Roberta, contrary to his expectations, had already been evicted. This was distressing. More alarming still was the news that Katherine and Elizabeth, as well as their mother, were ill – the girls perhaps dangerously so.[29]

Katherine Ross, then not much more than a month past her third birthday, died some three weeks into June 1821. A week or so later, her father began work on a long letter to the Marquis of Stafford. In this letter, an embittered and angry Gordon Ross outlined how he had been lied to (as he saw it) by Lord Stafford's factor. He then summarised the abuse (as he saw it) his family had experienced.

He had 'always reckoned' Francis Suther 'one of [his] best friends', Gordon Ross wrote. But his efforts to collaborate with the factor had availed him nothing. The job on which he had set his heart had gone to someone else; the arrangement intended to keep his family secure until he got back from Edinburgh had been disregarded. Told of this arrangement on their arrival in Ascoilemore on Wednesday 30 May, the 'evicting party' had held off for just one day. On 31 May – in breach of Suther's assurances, in spite of his wife being in poor health and in spite of his children having been 'taken ill with the [w]hooping cough' – his family, including 'an infant of two months', were ejected from their home, Gordon Ross stated, by men 'who [had] sat up the previous night drinking whisky'. On gaining entry to his house, Gordon continued, one of those men 'began furiously to throw some lumber out of the garret window and knocked down my eldest child'. The same man, the schoolmaster stated, had come close to injuring his baby girl. 'The rest of his conduct,' Gordon Ross went on, 'I shall forbear to mention for decency's sake. Sufficient to say that the mother [and] her three children were exposed to the inclemency of the weather while labouring under the greatest distress of sickness.' The effects of this sickness, Gordon added, had been aggravated by the ill-treatment his wife and daughters had suffered. One of the girls had 'only survived that inhuman treatment twenty-three days'.[30]

He had thought it right to draw those matters to Lord Stafford's attention, Gordon Ross informed the marquis, because he presumed that what had been done to Jessie and her daughters was, as the Strathbrora teacher put it, 'inconsistent with your Lordship's sanction and knowledge'. As for himself, Gordon Ross wrote, he had 'taken advice about the steps' he might take to obtain 'redress'. Acting on this advice, he planned to have his grievances 'laid before a public court'.[31]

The Marquis and Marchioness of Stafford, at this point, were spending some months in Paris. Just over 30 years before, as the French Revolution was beginning, the marquis had gone there when appointed Britain's ambassador to France. His wife, who went with him, greatly enjoyed her time in the French capital, which, being in a ferment politically, was an exciting if sometimes frightening place. But that was then; and the Paris of 1821, its revolution long since snuffed out and its public life quiescent, was not as the Marchioness of Stafford, now in her late fifties, remembered it. 'The life of Paris is less gay than that of London,' she complained; and when, two weeks after its being penned, Gordon Ross's letter reached the Staffords, Lady Stafford's mood could only have darkened further. As both the marchioness and the marquis were quick to recognise, the letter's contents constituted a pressing threat to their position, the Strathbrora schoolmaster's allegations having the potential to embroil them in a reputational crisis of a sort an earlier experience had given them good cause to fear.[32]

Some six years previously, a Sutherland Estate factor had been accused of causing two deaths in the course of evictions he had supervised. The factor in question (of whom more later) was Patrick Sellar, who was duly brought to trial on a charge of culpable homicide – Scotland's equivalent of the English crime of manslaughter. Although Sellar was found not guilty, the action taken against him had generated a great deal of comment – not just in the Highlands but in Edinburgh and London. Much of this comment blurred any distinction there might have been between allegedly brutal evictions and the wider, ostensibly positive, transformations those evictions were meant to bring about. The Staffords, in consequence, found themselves on the receiving end of a great deal of criticism; their Sutherland 'improvements' were set back; there were mutterings – stilled in the Sellar trial's aftermath but by no means forgotten – to the effect that what was going on in Sutherland should perhaps be looked into formally by the United Kingdom's parliament.

Now Gordon Ross's accusations threatened to expose the Marquis and Marchioness of Stafford, together with their senior managers, to renewed attack. There was even a risk, if the Strathbrora schoolmaster's letter was taken at face value, of their being caught up in a trial as damaging to them as Patrick Sellar's had been, for if the Ross family's eviction had indeed been conducted in the way Gordon Ross described, and if injury or death had resulted, then crimes had been committed. Responsibility for those crimes, to be sure, could not be laid directly at Lord Stafford's door. But as had occurred in the Sellar case, there would be plenty of people prepared to implicate the marquis in what had allegedly occurred. Should Gordon Ross succeed in carrying out his threat of getting matters into court, then – irrespective of whether or not the court came down on Ross's side – the Marquis of Stafford, as the Sutherland Estate's proprietor, would be said, and said widely, to be ultimately to blame for a vulnerable woman and her sick children having been cold-heartedly and violently turned out of their home by a set of drunks. Should any such interpretation of events gain acceptance, moreover, it would follow – logically if not legally – that Lord Stafford was also responsible for one of the evicted children having afterwards become so ill that she died.

That was bad enough. Making things worse, from a Stafford perspective, was the source of accusations that, if nothing was done to stop this, might find their way into newspapers which, during the Sellar episode and subsequently, had taken a close interest in what was going on in Sutherland. Gordon Ross, as demonstrated by his letter to Lord Stafford, was no obscure and wholly Gaelic-speaking agriculturalist of the sort constituting the majority of clearance victims. He was fluent in English; he was literate; his background, his profession and connections were such as to help his story gain traction; and he had been in contact with Joseph Gordon who, or so experience suggested, was likely to see in Gordon Ross's litany of complaint an ideal means of once again causing difficulty for the Sutherland Estate and its owners.

Hence the urgency with which Gordon Ross's letter to the Marquis of Stafford was forwarded from Paris to James Loch, then in London. Hence too the tenor of an accompanying note from the marchioness. If there was anything in what the schoolmaster had to say, she instructed Loch, his allegations were not 'to be passed over'. But on enquiry, Lady Stafford was sure, Ross's claims would 'turn out to be gross misrepresentations'. This was to give James Loch a clear steer as to what was expected of him, and, in consequence, to eliminate such slight possibility as there might have been of Loch looking into what had happened at Ascoilemore with anything approximating to an open mind. Writing at once to Francis Suther, Loch ordered the factor to find 'the best means of obliging' Gordon Ross and anyone backing him to 'acknowledge they have told infamous falsehoods'. 'It is out of the question to permit such lies to pass without notice,' Loch went on. Suther, nevertheless, was to 'proceed very cautiously'. In Ross, James Loch warned, 'you have a man who will take advantage of any slip that may be made'.[33]

Francis Suther was Loch's most valued subordinate. So serious was the crisis arising from Gordon Ross's claims, however, that Loch was not prepared to entrust Suther with its resolution. On 28 July 1821, within hours of his getting the first of several Ross-related communications from Paris, James Loch wrote to the Marquis of Stafford to tell him that he personally would shortly be en route for Sutherland. Given the time and effort such a journey required in the early nineteenth century, this was no small undertaking. But not much more than a week later, James Loch had installed himself in Dunrobin Castle. There, in mid-August, he presided over a two-day hearing intended to culminate in Gordon Ross being made to retract his accusations.[34]

In today's Scotland, allegations analogous to those made by Gordon Ross – allegations that might lead to criminal charges – would be investigated by the police. They would report their findings to a procurator fiscal, and the fiscal, in his capacity as public prosecutor, would decide whether or not to bring a suspected offender, or offenders, to trial. But that is not how things worked in Sutherland in 1821, the county's law enforcement mechanisms then being, for most practical purposes, indistinguishable from the Sutherland Estate's administrative machinery. Thus James Loch took it for granted, when writing from London to Francis Suther at the end of July, that Sutherland's procurator fiscal, James Brander, would be party to the planned discrediting of Gordon Ross. Since Brander had himself supervised lots of the evictions on which Ross-instigated court proceedings might throw a harsh light, there was no chance of his not falling in with Loch's wishes. These were clear. If Gordon Ross or anyone else stuck by claims Loch was already describing as 'lies' and 'falsehoods', then Brander was to make all such people aware that he would 'punish them by prosecuting them'.[35]

By involving the procurator fiscal in this way, James Loch may well have succeeded – as he meant to – in confusing the people paraded before him in Dunrobin as to what exactly was going on there. Loch's enquiry had no standing in law. But it cannot have seemed that way to men and women – Loch called them 'witnesses' – who were commanded by James Brander to travel (on foot and for considerable distances in many instances) to Golspie in order to have their answers to Loch's questions recorded in exactly the same manner as if they had been called to testify before a judge.

A key participant in those Dunrobin proceedings was Donald Bannerman, the man 'employed', in James Loch's words, 'to execute the [Ascoilemore] ejections'. On the face of things, Bannerman's 'evidence', as Loch entitled it, carried particular weight because Bannerman, being a constable as well as a sheriff-officer, seemed doubly immune to Sutherland Estate manipulation. The people who gave sheriff-officers and constables their instructions, formally at any rate, were not the Staffords or their representatives but a variety of public office-holders. Those office-holders' duty (supposedly) was to uphold the rule of law; their authority derived (supposedly) from Britain's monarch; they answered (supposedly) to government ministers in Edinburgh and London. In principle, then, Donald Bannerman, in his role as sheriff-officer helped give effect to court orders issued by, or on the authority of, Charles Ross, Sutherland's sheriff. In his other role as constable, Bannerman's line managers, so to speak, were Sutherland's several Justices of the Peace (JPs) – men entrusted by government with the task of appointing and supervising the two dozen or so constables who (as the term *constable* suggests) were the nearest thing early nineteenth-century Sutherland possessed to a police force.[36]

But if in theory Donald Bannerman was a public servant, neither he nor his superiors – whether Sutherland's sheriff or the county's JPs – were any more likely than Procurator Fiscal Brander to cross the Marquis of Stafford, the Marchioness of Stafford or James Loch. On paper, Sheriff Ross might have owed his post to Alexander Maconochie MP, Scotland's lord advocate and the government's main man in Scotland. But Maconochie had assured Loch, prior to Charles Ross's appointment in 1816, that Ross would only become Sheriff of Sutherland if this was 'agreeable to Lord and Lady Stafford' whose 'approval' of any such appointment, Maconochie wrote, he 'thought indispensible'. Nor was Ross himself under any illusion as to what was expected of him. This is clear from a letter the sheriff sent to the Marchioness of Stafford on taking up his position: 'I assure you . . . [of my] most zealous wish to second [meaning assist] by every means in my power your extensive and benevolent projects for the improvement of Sutherland . . . I have only to add that it will be most satisfactory to me at all times to have a communication of what may be your Ladyship's views as to anything to be done in the county.'[37]

Sheriff Ross, then, appreciated precisely where he stood in relation to the Staffords. So did Sutherland's JPs. Prominent among their number were: Francis Suther, the marquis and marchioness's factor; Gabriel Reed, the Gordonbush-based sheep farmer who had gained directly from Ascoilemore's clearance; and Patrick Sellar, no longer a Sutherland Estate employee but a sheep farmer on an even larger scale than Reed. Those men understood what was expected of them by the Staffords. They could be trusted to ensure that Donald Bannerman, one of their longer-serving constables, knew exactly what to say when he appeared before James Loch's Dunrobin tribunal.

Bannerman, moreover, had his own reasons for currying favour with James Loch. In June 1820, when serving removal notices on families at Gruids, a township on a property adjacent to the Sutherland Estate, he had been assaulted by a number of young women who stripped the sheriff-officer naked prior to parading him through a mocking crowd.* Bannerman, who was in his sixties, must have found this humiliating as well as frightening. But despite the attack on him having been precipitated by a clearance the Staffords had no part in, Bannerman, in dealings with the marquis and the marchioness, capitalised shamelessly on what had happened. He informed Lady Stafford that he had been 'brutally used'. He reminded the marchioness of his 'long service' in the cause of clearing areas like Strathbrora. He asked that she and her husband help him stave off 'old age and infirmity' by providing him with some sort of pension.[38]

---

* This episode is dealt with in Chapter 14.

Among testimonials produced by Donald Bannerman in connection with this plea was one from Patrick Sellar who was happy to 'certify' – on the basis of what he had seen in the course of the clearances – that Bannerman 'was almost the only [sheriff-officer in Sutherland] . . . who went straight forward [with] any warrant [of eviction] entrusted to him without fear of the dangers which surrounded him'.[39]

The marchioness, in her response, made known that Donald Bannerman 'should be attended to'. But it would be 'time enough,' she thought, 'to give him [financial] assistance when he stands in need of it'. Whether or not such aid was in the end forthcoming is not known – Bannerman's claim on a Stafford-paid pension having conceivably been jeopardised when, during legal proceedings arising from the Gruids fracas, the doctor who had treated the sheriff-officer said his injuries had amounted to no more than 'a contusion between the shoulders and some scratches upon the body for which he [the doctor] prescribed only one dose of salts'.[40]

That version of events, however, did not become public until a month or more after Bannerman gave James Loch his account of the Ross family's expulsion from Ascoilemore. This account, as well as being coloured by Donald Bannerman's customary loyalty to Sheriff Ross and to JPs like Sellar, Reed and Suther, may have been coloured further, then, by his continuing hopes – at that point anyway – of an eventual cash hand-out from the Marchioness of Stafford.

When he and his evicting party got to Ascoilemore on Wednesday 30 May 1821, Bannerman told Loch's Dunrobin tribunal, it had been his intention to get every one of its homes – except the one where he and his colleagues were to lodge overnight – vacated that day. In the event, however, he left a second home unemptied. This was the one occupied by Jessie Ross, her two daughters and her baby. They were spared eviction, the sheriff-officer explained, because Jessie (in accordance with the document drawn up by her husband before his departure for Edinburgh) 'had given an obligation to remove when she should be asked'. To this extent, Donald Bannerman's take on the Ross family's expulsion from Ascoilemore coincided with Gordon Ross's. But there was little further overlap between the Ross and Bannerman versions of what had occurred.[41]

On the morning of Thursday 31 May, the sheriff-officer said, he had been informed that the Rosses were after all to be evicted immediately because 'Mr [Gabriel] Reed [evidently wanting to have Ascoilemore cleared completely] would not allow [them] to remain'. News of Reed's vetoing of concessions to the Rosses, Bannerman continued, had been brought to him by one of the farmer's shepherds. This was William Stevenson who, during the two days it took to clear the township, was on hand – on his employer's orders – to assist Donald Bannerman and his men.[42]

Also on Thursday morning, Bannerman next stated, he had called on Jessie Ross to tell her that the 'obligation' on which Jessie had been relying had now been countermanded by Reed, and that, in consequence, he wanted her, Elizabeth, Katherine and Roberta to quit their home voluntarily by midday. Following this conversation, Donald Bannerman went on, he and the rest of the evicting party set off for rising ground behind Ascoilemore where they were 'to drive off the cattle' grazing on the township's hill pastures. On his return, at 'about two o' clock in the afternoon', the sheriff-officer said, it was apparent that the Rosses had no intention of leaving of their own volition. At once, therefore, he 'carried [their] ejection into execution'.[43]

This ejection, the sheriff-officer testified, went without a hitch, and he certainly 'saw no violence used'. If this was a slippery formulation which allowed for there having been wrongdoing he had not observed, it was Bannerman's sole concession to that possibility. 'None of [his party] were drunk,' he insisted. The weather, which Gordon Ross had described as 'inclement' in his letter to Lord Stafford, had actually been 'very hot and dry'. Elizabeth and Katherine, far from being ill, hurt and upset, 'were running about' outside. Why, towards the end of the afternoon, he had even 'got a drink of milk' from Jessie Ross who, it was thereby implied, bore neither him nor his colleagues the slightest ill-will.[44]

Four of those colleagues were questioned by James Loch. They were in full agreement with everything that Donald Bannerman had said, and, on hearing this, Loch must surely have thought that, from his perspective, proceedings were going well. There had still to be investigated, however, the conduct of Gabriel Reed's shepherd, William Stevenson, against whom, even in the highly constrained circumstances of James Loch's Dunrobin hearings, there were at least the beginnings of a case to be made.[45]

Stevenson's relationship with the Rosses, it emerged, was not founded on mutual antipathy – rather the reverse. He had been 'very intimate' with Jessie and Gordon Ross. He had been, in other words, their friend. This appears to have attracted attention, perhaps because friendships between Strathbrora people and men like William Stevenson are unlikely to have been common. Many such shepherds, after all, had come north (and Stevenson's non-Highland surname suggests he was in this category) with the sheep farmers who employed them and the sheep they looked after. To begin with anyway, few of those shepherds spoke Gaelic. This precluded much in the way of communication between them and Sutherland's predominantly Gaelic-speaking population – a population which anyway had little time for men thought to be aiding and abetting the farmers and estate managers responsible for uprooting community after community.[46]

But William Stevenson, for all that, was on good terms with Gordon and Jessie Ross. He visited their home, conversing with them there, neighbours recalled, in English, which both Jessie and Gordon, thanks to their upbringing and education, spoke effortlessly. Nor is it hard to guess why this Ross–Stevenson bond might have developed. If (as suggested earlier) the Rosses began to be cold-shouldered by other Ascoilemore families when it became known during 1820 that Gordon was in contact with Francis Suther, this could well have led to the schoolmaster and his wife linking up with another outsider. This, in turn, helps explain both William

Stevenson's conduct on the afternoon of Thursday 31 May 1821 and the ferocity with which Gordon Ross, Stevenson's former but now betrayed friend, reacted to the shepherd's behaviour.

William Stevenson, that afternoon, had to choose between conflicting loyalties: to his employer, Gabriel Reed, on the one side; to Jessie Ross, who had befriended him, on the other. In the end – and to have done otherwise would have been to lose his livelihood – he did his employer's bidding. Hence the shepherd's active participation in the Ross family's eviction. But hence too – or so one might surmise – his opting to dull his guilt (and some guilt there must surely have been) by having recourse to alcohol. That Stevenson had consumed a lot of whisky, that he was in fact drunk, on the day of their eviction: of this the Rosses were in no doubt. Nor, Donald Bannerman's assurances of the evicting party's sobriety notwithstanding, was there any lack of circumstantial evidence to the effect that such was indeed the case.

When, as her eviction got under way, Jessie Ross was asked to take the two-month-old Roberta out of the house, Jessie (as noted earlier) refused point-blank. And when her maid, a girl called Kathleen Fraser, made to pick up the baby's cradle instead, Jessie told her, Kathleen said, 'to let it alone'. 'Stevenson,' Kathleen went on, 'got a little angry at this and took up the cradle and, going out, struck the cradle against the door.' The baby, Kathleen Fraser said, was 'hurt' in the course of this episode, her comment indicating that the cradle came up against the doorway with some force. Given the care people take – almost instinctively – when moving babies, William Stevenson's simultaneously casual and irate handling of Roberta Ross is consistent (to put the matter no higher) with his having been drinking. So is the shepherd's subsequent conduct, notably his throwing a piece of planking into the face of five-year-old Elizabeth Ross and his drenching of Kathleen Fraser with the contents of a tub of urine he came across in the Ross house's garret.[47]

Urine was stored in this way because homespun cloth was customarily soaked in it as a means of fixing the locally produced vegetable dyes applied to all such fabrics. The tub found by Stevenson, then, could well have contained a lot of liquid, all of which, it seems, was poured over Kathleen as she stood below the ladder leading to the Ross home's loft. On Stevenson seeing what he had done, the maid told James Loch, the shepherd 'laughed', as at a joke.[48]

Had Loch been looking to establish misconduct on the part of the Ascoilemore evicting party, then, what he heard from Kathleen Fraser went some way to providing the necessary evidence. But James Loch's purpose was the opposite of this. The person whose wrongdoing Loch was set on proving in the course of the show trial (as good a description as any) he mounted at Dunrobin in mid-August 1821 was not William Stevenson but Gordon Ross. It was essential, therefore, to demonstrate that the shepherd, together with everyone else involved in the Ross family's eviction, had been perfectly sober throughout. With this requirement in view, Loch turned to John MacKay, the man in whose Ascoilemore home Donald Bannerman and his evicting party were accommodated on the night of 30–31 May.

MacKay, the Ascoilemore–Ascoilebeg miller and a leading member of his parish's Church of Scotland congregation, was one of those people whose role in the Sutherland clearances is best described as both critical and obscure: critical because, had estate managers not had the support of individuals like John MacKay, evictions would have been more difficult to carry out; obscure because, while it is clear that such folk got something out of behaving as they did, it is impossible, at this remove, to ascertain what that something was. But if there is no knowing what favours were done for John MacKay in return for the hospitality he extended to the Ascoilemore evicting party, this hospitality was certainly extensive. 'She cooked their victuals for them,' Mary MacKay, the miller's daughter, said of her part in proceedings. 'They had beef and broth for dinner.' Afterwards, Mary continued, she had been sent to fetch whisky – the source, doubtless, being one of the illicit stills that (as recounted later) were then rife in Strathbrora and surrounding areas. 'Ten bottles of whisky were drunk . . . during the first day and night [of the Ascoilemore clearance],' Mary MacKay said. 'Two bottles of whisky were drunk before breakfast [on the second day],' she went on, 'and one immediately after breakfast.' Those bottles, it should be made clear, were probably smaller than their modern counterparts. But the whisky they contained would have been at least half as potent again, perhaps twice as potent, as today's commercial spirit. Since members of Donald Bannerman's party – ten to twelve strong in total – got through more than a bottle apiece on average, it is hard to believe that they were in no way affected. But such was definitely the case, said Mary and John MacKay, who thus put themselves deep in the Sutherland Estate's debt. 'None of the men were drunk,' Mary MacKay insisted. Her father concurred. William Stevenson in particular, he added, 'was not the worse of liquor'.[49]

When John and Mary MacKay's statements were taken in conjunction with those made by Donald Bannerman and his associates, Gordon Ross's contention of drunkenness on the part of the Ascoilemore evicting party was shown, as far as James Loch was concerned, to have no foundation. Gordon's other claims were to be disproved, to Loch's satisfaction, every bit as comprehensively. In part, this was because of the isolated position in which the ex-schoolmaster found himself.

By August, the families from whom Gordon Ross had first heard about the circumstances surrounding Ascoilemore's clearance were in Nova Scotia. Had they been interviewed before they sailed, they might – having by that point no reason to fear repercussions from Sutherland Estate managers – have backed Gordon's account of his family's eviction. But of the many 'witnesses' obliged to appear before James Loch at Dunrobin, none had anything to gain, and all had quite a lot to lose, from endorsing what the estate side had chosen to regard from the outset as evident fabrications. This was most obviously true of people like Donald Bannerman, John MacKay and Mary MacKay who were clearly in the Sutherland Estate camp.

But it was true too of folk whom Gordon Ross might have expected to take his part, Sutherland Estate residents being well aware that their homes and livelihoods could all too readily be lost should they be thought by Loch and his aides to have stepped out of line.

Some people were prepared, despite this, to go at least part way in Gordon Ross's direction. One was Jessie Ross's former maid, Kathleen Fraser. Following her departure from Ascoilemore, Kathleen had got fish-processing work of some sort in Helmsdale. Her job, like every other job in that part of Sutherland, would have been vulnerable to Sutherland Estate pressure. But this did not stop her saying what she said about William Stevenson. Nor were others wholly lacking in the courage needed to take issue with what had been said by Donald Bannerman and his associates. From them James Loch heard that Katherine and Elizabeth Ross were indeed suffering from whooping cough prior to their eviction; that the two girls were seen to be 'cold and trembling' when they found themselves outside their home; that their mother, though 'going about her work' prior to her eviction, was unwell; that Roberta Ross's cradle had indeed been handled roughly by William Stevenson; that the baby's resulting distress was eased only when, as described earlier, Mary Murray (who left shortly afterwards for Nova Scotia) took it on herself to breastfeed and pacify the child; that Elizabeth was indeed struck in the face by a board thrown by Stevenson; that she was hurt and in tears as a result.[50]

But none of this influenced James Loch whose eventual findings gave weight only to what accorded with his own predetermined interpretation of the facts. There was much in this category. When at the Rosses' home, Loch was told, the evicting party 'conducted themselves in a peaceable manner'; they 'used no harshness'; they were 'as careful as they could be of everything'. One man 'did not see any of the [Ross] children hurt or crying'. Another remarked of Elizabeth and Katherine that they 'did not appear very ill' – their whooping cough having developed, this man said, only after their departure from Ascoilemore.[51]

Perhaps this was the way things truly were. Perhaps, as James Loch maintained from the start, Gordon Ross was a fantasist, a liar or worse. Perhaps, as asserted by a number of the 'witnesses' Loch produced to demolish Ross's standing and reputation, the former SSPCK schoolmaster was not, as he had seemed to be, a respectable teacher and family man but a habitual poacher – a lawbreaker (for poaching was a crime) who fished the several Brora River pools below Ascoilemore and who sold (this being thought worse than poaching for domestic consumption) the salmon he caught there. Perhaps, as stated further, Gordon Ross, not confining himself to petty criminality like poaching, was also a troublemaker and agitator who had advised his neighbours to 'oppose' (violently it was implied) their eviction. Perhaps, as also claimed, he had gone so far as to urge Strathbrora people 'to go and set fire to the houses of . . . Gordonbush and Morvich during the night', the homes in question being those occupied by Gabriel Reed and Patrick Sellar. Perhaps the weather which (as mentioned in one of Francis Suther's regular letters to Loch) had brought 'an abundance of snow' to Sutherland as late as 27 May, had turned – just three or four days later and despite the wind still being in the north-east – every bit as 'hot' as Donald Bannerman contended.[52]

But ultimately what was said – whether in support of Gordon Ross or in opposition to him – was neither here nor there. This was because the Ascoilemore schoolmaster, in daring to take on the Sutherland Estate, was assailing the unassailable. The power the Marquis and Marchioness of Stafford exercised in their role as the estate's proprietors, when combined with the wider influence they wielded as a result of their enormous wealth, meant that the Stafford-dominated part of Sutherland had been deprived of anything independent of its owners. Gordon Ross's predicament, it followed, was analogous to that confronting dissenters in the perfectly authoritarian world imagined in George Orwell's *Nineteen Eighty-Four*. As in that world, there remained in Sutherland no autonomous institution to which Gordon Ross could turn. The

Church of Scotland, ostensibly self-administering, was in reality (as will be seen) a Sutherland Estate fiefdom. The county's justice system (as already shown and as will be shown further) was a Sutherland Estate subsidiary. Nor does the parallel with *Nineteen Eighty-Four* end there. In Orwell's fictional dictatorship, where even language has been subverted by the ruling regime, 'war is peace' and 'freedom is slavery'. Similarly, in early nineteenth-century Sutherland – this place the Staffords had made so completely theirs – to depopulate a strath was to 'improve' it and truth, as became apparent in the course of Gordon Ross's Dunrobin ordeal, was whatever James Loch decided truth to be.

Nineteen Eighty-Four ends with its broken rebel, Winston Smith, confessing that everything he had done and thought was wrong. James Loch's enquiry into Gordon Ross's accusations ended in much the same way. First Jessie Ross assented to the proposition, or so James Loch reported, that the contents of her husband's July letter to Lord Stafford had been 'nonsense'. Next Gordon himself, again according to Loch, was left with little alternative but to do likewise. 'After two days examination of witnesses respecting Gordon Ross's complaint to your Lordship,' James Loch informed the Marquis of Stafford on 17 August, 'I have the satisfaction of being enabled to state that the whole of his assertions are false from beginning to end.' It had been proven beyond doubt, Loch continued, 'that the [Ross] children had not the [w]hooping cough when removed [and] . . . that [on the day of their eviction] the greatest care and kindness was shown the family.'[53]

To use that phrase in connection with the events of 31 May 1821 was again to have recourse to proto-Orwellian terminology. For even if James Loch was right to disbelieve everything said and written by Gordon Ross, it remained the case that the Sutherland Estate had removed from her Ascoilemore home a woman whose health was (to put the matter no higher) less than perfect, whose two small daughters were (at the minimum) falling ill, and whose absent husband (because of the Stafford-ordered clearance of Strathbrora) had lost his teaching post. But if it is hard to see where 'care and kindness' had been extended to the Ross family, it is easy to understand the mix of triumph and relief that pervades Loch's 17 August letter to Loch Stafford. Less than three weeks after leaving London for Sutherland, James Loch had closed off any possibility of Gordon Ross doing damage to the marquis and the marchioness's reputation. The former schoolmaster had 'made ample recantation', Loch told Lord Stafford. Ross had also apologised to everyone he had maligned. 'I made him express his sorrow [in particular] to the shepherd [William Stevenson],' Loch wrote.[54]

Inclining now to magnanimity, and having scrutinised Gordon Ross's correspondence (which Ross had been ordered to produce) with Joseph Gordon, James Loch concluded that the schoolmaster had neither incited violence nor engaged in poaching, his taking fish from the River Brora having been sanctioned, it seems, by Francis Suther with whom of course Ross had for a time been on good terms. But when Gordon Ross (aware of the likely impact of his Dunrobin 'recantation' on his future prospects) asked for 'the certificate of indemnification of character' he felt he would need if he were to resume his career, Loch drew the line. 'In demanding the way you do a certificate,' James Loch told Ross, 'you totally forget the nature of the charge which you made to Lord Stafford, [a charge] . . . which has been proved . . . to be untrue in every particular.'[55]

Gordon's consequent lack of an immediate way back into teaching must have further aggravated the Rosses' already desperate plight – the family's homelessness and Gordon's joblessness having had the effect of making them dependent on other people's charity. First to come to their aid were Jean and Alexander MacKay who lived in Ascoilebeg, which, luckily for the Rosses and their fellow refugees from Ascoilemore, escaped clearance a little longer than its neighbouring township. Jean MacKay, it seems, invited Jessie Ross and her children into her home when, on the day of her eviction, Jessie discovered that the emergency accommodation arranged for her before Gordon set off for Edinburgh had been taken by others, the man (another Ascoilebeg resident) with whom the Rosses were to stay having concluded (in the wake of Donald Bannerman's initial, but later countermanded, assurances) that Jessie and her daughters were, for the time being, to be left in place.[56]

Quite how long the Rosses stayed with the MacKays is unclear, but they were definitely there into August. It was at the MacKay home in Ascoilebeg, then, that the three-year-old Katherine Ross died, the child being buried no doubt in the little cemetery still to be seen on the Ascoilemore side of Allt a' Mhuilin. It was in the MacKay home, too, that Jessie Ross, 'through distress, sickness and despair,' as her husband put it, 'lost her milk'. Unable now to feed Roberta, Jessie – probably with Jean MacKay's help – accordingly had to find a wet nurse 'to give the infant suck'.[57]

What happened to Roberta, to Elizabeth, her surviving sister, and to the Ross family more generally during the period that followed is mostly irrecoverable. One or two facts can be established, however. In November 1821, the SSPCK's board of directors, clearly unpersuaded (unlike the Staffords and James Loch) that their former employee had brought his troubles on himself, minuted their decision to forward the sum of £2 (the equivalent of seven weeks' salary) to Gordon Ross, whom they described as 'in distress from the death of a child'. In May 1825, exactly four years after Ascoilemore's clearance, Gordon again features briefly in SSPCK minutes – the organisation's board recording their receipt of a letter 'recommending Gordon Ross . . . to the sympathy and support of the society'. This time Gordon, described as 'now insane' and evidently grappling with mental breakdown, was granted £6. Some part of that sum is likely to have been spent on the Rosses' latest child, a little boy born two years previously. Like his brother, the 1820 baby who died in infancy, this boy was called George. Gordon and Jessie's first son, however, had been christened George Sutherland Ross for Jessie's father. This second boy was named for someone else entirely. He was christened George Granville Leveson Gower Ross. Just as Winston Smith, George

Orwell's fictional rebel, learned in the end to love his country's dictator, so that real-life rebel, Gordon Ross, or so it seems from the name he gave his son, learned if not to love, then certainly to show proper deference to, George Granville Leveson-Gower, Marquis of Stafford.[58]

2

'TRIBES THAT NEVER SAW EUROPEANS BEFORE'

*Ascoilemore fur trader Donald MacKay
and the beginnings of clearance-era
Sutherland's links with Manitoba*

Jessie Ross's resistance to her and her children's eviction – resistance encapsulated in Jessie's refusal to help move her baby from her home – was entirely passive. Donald MacKay, one of Ascoilemore's farming tenants and a man who, in the course of his 68 years, had had to cope often with adversity, gave Donald Bannerman and his evicting party greater trouble.

MacKay had 'removed all the furniture out of [his] house' in advance of his family's eviction on 30 May 1821, Bannerman reported. But some hours later, when the sheriff-officer and his evicting party were busy elsewhere, word reached them that MacKay had resumed possession and 'had put some of [his] furniture into the house again'. On hearing this, Bannerman continued, he had returned to MacKay's home where, with the help of 'some of the party', he 'put [the contents] out and threw down [or demolished] the house'.[1]

Donald MacKay, his wife Mary and their several children were taken in temporarily, like Jessie Ross and her daughters, by an Ascoilebeg householder. The MacKays' rescuer was William Sutherland whose home must have been crammed to bursting point because of his having accommodated not just the MacKays but two further Ascoilemore families. The consequent congestion eased after a fortnight or so, when, with the exception of the MacKays, William Sutherland's guests left for Cromarty, the *Ossian* and Nova Scotia. In the interim, however, the MacKay children, like the Ross girls, had gone down with whooping cough (clearly rife in Ascoilemore just prior to its clearance) and one of them, 'a boy of four years old' according to his father, died.[2]

Though not identified as such in documentation from 1821, the dead child must have been the MacKays' son Hugh, born in 1817. He was buried, no doubt, in the same small graveyard – roughly halfway between 'the two Ascoiles' – as little Katherine Ross. Soon after, Hugh's father (very possibly in emulation of Katherine's father Gordon) wrote to Lord Stafford to inform him of the circumstances surrounding the boy's death and to provide the marquis, as Donald MacKay put it, with some idea of the 'cruelty' being inflicted on Sutherland's population in his, Lord Stafford's, name.[3]

What had happened at Ascoilemore, Donald MacKay raged, was 'so disgraceful to humanity' that he could not 'find language . . . adequate' to describe it. Lord Stafford needed to understand, MacKay continued, that on the day Donald Bannerman and his 'gang' (the term MacKay used of the sheriff-officer's evicting party) were 'demolishing every house [in Ascoilemore] . . . to the very ground', children who were 'sick with the whooping cough' had found themselves without shelter in weather that was 'very cold' because of there having been 'a strong wind from the north-east'. Like Gordon Ross, then, Donald MacKay implied that the Marquis of Stafford was responsible – even if indirectly – for the deaths of Sutherland children. MacKay's language, however, was more forceful than Ross's. The destruction which Bannerman had inflicted on Ascoilemore, MacKay wrote, would be 'visible to the end of time', and he hoped very much that 'those who [were] the authors of such barbarous actions' – the ultimate such authors being the marquis and the marchioness – would one day 'be exposed to the censure of the public'.[4]

Despite the ferocity of its contents, Donald MacKay's letter worried James Loch less than the letter Lord Stafford had received a

few days earlier from Gordon Ross. This was because Loch thought
MacKay an easier man to discredit than the SSPCK schoolmaster.
MacKay, Loch observed, was 'half-crazy', 'a blackguard' and 'a very
great villain' who had for years been embroiled in anti-Stafford plot-
ting of a sort that, according to Loch, had strayed into criminality.
Elaborating on this point, Loch recounted how, on Joseph Gordon
telling Gordon Ross that Ascoilemore's clearance could not be
prevented, Donald MacKay turned elsewhere for legal advice in the
belief – vain as it proved – that he and his neighbours would eventually find some way of retaining their homes. In total, Loch
commented, MacKay and other Ascoilemore tenants 'spent about
£100 [equivalent to several thousand pounds today] in the hope that
they could legally prevent their . . . removing and, finding that
impossible, they urged on their subtenants at Achness to open resistance'. As neither the marquis nor the marchioness needed reminding,
'resistance' to the clearance of Achness, three or four miles from
Ascoilemore, had reached such a pitch in early 1821 that (as
recounted later) evictions there had to be enforced by an army
detachment, the Achness people (whose land was sublet, as Loch
stated, from Donald MacKay and his neighbours) having previously
beaten off the sheriff-officers, constables and Sutherland Estate staff
sent to evict them.[5]

Not content with his having 'incited' violence at Achness, James
Loch went on, Donald MacKay had mailed 'threatening letters' to
the Marchioness of Stafford when, in August and September 1820,
she spent some weeks at Dunrobin. At the time, Loch had advised
Lady Stafford to take no action in response to those letters because
MacKay, or so Loch and Francis Suther understood, had begun
'paying rent for a farm in Caithness' and would thus soon be gone
from Sutherland. Although angered by Donald MacKay having
'openly rebelled in word and deed', as she put it, the marchioness
accepted this advice – with the proviso that, if MacKay persisted,
'we will have him before the sheriff'. On its afterwards becoming
apparent that MacKay had abandoned his planned move to

Caithness and (despite his age) was contemplating a fresh start in Nova Scotia, Loch began to regret that he had dissuaded Lady Stafford from prosecuting MacKay for his role in what the marchioness described as an Ascoilemore-based 'conspiracy' to sabotage Achness's clearance. His 'not having noticed' MacKay's threatening letters, Loch confided to Francis Suther, had simply 'emboldened' their author. But even if it might have served the marchioness better had James Loch turned in 1820 to the ever-pliant Sheriff Ross and got him to jail the Ascoilemore 'madman', as Loch called MacKay, the Stafford position was far from irretrievable, Loch being of the opinion that anything MacKay might say in public about the manner of Ascoilemore's clearance could immediately be countered by evidence of his having engaged in illegality.[6]

But if James Loch was correct to minimise the possibility of Donald MacKay inflicting serious damage on the Staffords, MacKay's July 1821 letter to the marquis – a letter which, unlike Gordon Ross's, was not retracted – shows there were people in clearance-era Sutherland who, though deprived of homes and land, refused to be cowed into subservience. This, in turn, prompts the question of how it came about that Donald MacKay, one such person, considered himself entitled to address the Marquis of Stafford in such unrelentingly caustic terms. James Loch, had he been asked that question, might well have replied that the answer lay (though Loch would have used less sensitive language) in MacKay being unstable psychologically, and in so responding, Loch (as will be seen) might not have been wholly in error. But he would not have been wholly right either. An alternative explanation for MacKay's courageous (and it was courageous) behaviour is to be found in one of his correspondence's most striking features: his signature. All dash and flourishes, it is the signature of a man who had exercised authority.

This was understood by William Young who, as the Sutherland Estate's resident factor between 1811 and 1816, was Francis Suther's predecessor. Reporting on an exploratory trip he made into

Strathbrora in the autumn of the year prior to his appointment, Young told of his finding Donald MacKay living, with his wife and children, 'in a wretched timber hut . . . without a foot of garden ground'. 'Distressed with rheumatism,' Young commented of MacKay for whom the factor felt some sympathy, 'he cannot long hold out in such a habitation and I could wish to see him more comfortable'. Although Donald MacKay was said by the Marchioness of Stafford to have later 'threatened to shoot Young', it may be, then, that the Ascoilemore tenancy which subsequently came MacKay's way was a consequence of his having had the factor's help. The possibility of such help is hinted at in William Young's account of his 1810 encounter with a man who – though Young could not have foreseen this – would afterwards cause the Sutherland Estate much difficulty. 'He pressed me to come in,' Young wrote of Donald MacKay, 'gave me some details of his travels and said he liked to see strangers. On my remarking that his house must be cold in winter, he laughed at my ignorance and said that, although I saw the boards open at present, the rain would make them quite close and prevent the wind from blowing in . . . I had to go [elsewhere] . . . and was obliged to leave poor MacKay in the midst of his travels, after telling him at parting [who] I was, and [that I was] hoping to see him [made] more comfortable in his native land.'[7]

If Donald MacKay truly got to 'the midst of his travels' in the course of just an hour or two's conversation with William Young, he made short work of an intricate life story. As is indicated by his having built in Strathbrora a 'wooden home' approximating to a log cabin, this was a man who had spent more time on various North American frontiers than in Scotland; a man who had been in lots of places which, at the start of the nineteenth century, only a handful of other Europeans had so much as glimpsed; a man who, when he quit Sutherland for the last time in the summer of 1822, would be making his ninth crossing of the Atlantic Ocean.[8]

*   *   *

Donald MacKay was a remarkable individual. Indeed it is an arguable proposition that today's world owes more to MacKay's activities than to the much-trumpeted accomplishments of Loch and the Staffords. Two centuries after the 'improvements' brought about there by James Loch and his employers, Sutherland contains some 13,500 people, about 10,000 fewer, incidentally, than lived there 200 years ago. The population of Manitoba, the Canadian province MacKay's 'travels' helped open up to trade and settlement, is nearly 100 times larger, while a Sutherland town like Brora, of which the Marquis and Marchioness of Stafford expected so much, cannot meaningfully be compared with Manitoban cities like Brandon, its origins traceable to one of Donald MacKay's trading posts, or Winnipeg, which MacKay helped supply with its earliest settlers.

Donald MacKay was born in Strathbrora in 1753. Nothing further is known of him until, in 1779, he enters the historical record as the junior associate of a Montreal fur trader, also of Highland background, called John Ross. The American Revolutionary War was then raging and Montreal, taken from its French founders by the British less than 20 years before, was full of Highlanders. Some were loyalist refugees from independence-seeking colonies to the south; others had served in one of the Highland regiments integral to Britain's ultimately doomed struggle to keep those colonies inside its empire. Since one of his fur trade colleagues was to write of Donald MacKay that 'he had been in the army', it may be that he belonged to the latter group. What is certain is that, within months of Ross hiring him, MacKay, by way of the canoe routes that were the fur trade's equivalent of transcontinental highways, was deep in the North American interior, travelling as far west as the so-called Mandan Villages on the upper reaches of the Missouri River in present-day North Dakota.[9]

The Mandan Villages, permanent settlements in an area where most Native American peoples were nomadic, intrigued their white visitors, not least Meriwether Lewis and William Clark, who headed the Corps of Discovery sent west by US President Thomas Jefferson in 1804. Donald MacKay, who reached the upper Missouri a quarter of a century in advance of Lewis and Clark (key contributors to the USA's territorial expansion) was equally taken by the villages and their inhabitants – something reflected in the several pages devoted to his Mandan experiences in the autobiographical sketch MacKay was to put together when in Nova Scotia.[10]

MacKay's principal field of operations, however, lay further north – on the great rivers, principally the Saskatchewan, the Assiniboine and the Red, that flow into Lake Winnipeg. Here during the 1780s Donald MacKay, whose partnership with John Ross did not last long, traded on his own account, refusing to have anything to do with the consortium then being put together by a number of his compatriots in Montreal. This was the North West Company (NWC), which, for the next 20 or 30 years, would dominate the North American fur trade. Run for much of that period by Simon MacTavish and his nephew William MacGillivray, both of whom came from Stratherrick near Inverness, the company's sphere of operations eventually extended all the way to the Pacific, which one of its leading traders, Alexander MacKenzie, reached in 1793. Aiming always to keep costs low and profits high, MacTavish, MacGillivray, MacKenzie and other 'lords of the lakes and forests' as the Nor'Westers were dubbed by an American observer, were determined monopolists who, if unable to persuade independent traders to join them, were perfectly happy to run such traders out of the interior. Among Nor'Wester targets was Donald MacKay, always his own man, always irascible and already experiencing the periods of 'great trouble and vexation of mind' that were to plague him for much of his life. What MacKay called 'the stratagems and manoeu-vres of the . . . North West Company' were to include his being assaulted and robbed of his trade goods at Grand Portage, a fur trade way station west of Lake Superior. It was in reaction to this and similar episodes that MacKay decided in the end to put his services at the disposal of the one commercial concern with the capacity, potentially at least, to do to the Nor'Westers what they had done to him – that concern being the Hudson's Bay Company (HBC).[11]

Established by royal charter in 1670, this London-based and archetypally imperial corporation was supposedly in sole charge of all the trade conducted in all the territories drained by all the watercourses flowing into Hudson Bay – technically part of the Atlantic Ocean but so vast and so enclosed as to be virtually a sea in its own right. Because Lake Winnipeg's waters drain into the bay by way of the Nelson River, the HBC's domains included, in accordance with its founding charter, the catchments of those other rivers – the Red, the Assiniboine and the Saskatchewan – where Donald MacKay traded in the 1780s. But as MacKay had cause to know, the HBC's claim to those areas, and to richer fur grounds further to the west, had been rendered null and void by the Nor'Westers who, in effect, cut off at source the furs that native peoples had previously been happy to bring to HBC posts – principally York Factory and Fort Churchill – on the shores of Hudson Bay. If this situation was to be altered and the HBC's theoretical control of the fur trade made real, then the previously lethargic corporation, whose Bay-based operatives had shown little inclination to venture inland, was going to have to do what the NWC's ruthlessly enterprising Highlanders had done already – establish a grip on the places where furs originated by adopting native or Aboriginal* technology, in the shape of birchbark canoes, and move ever deeper into the continental interior. This was the approach Donald MacKay began to urge on the HBC, MacKay sailing from Montreal to London in 1788 to make his pitch directly to the company's board.

MacKay's motives were personal. He wanted, he wrote, 'to be revenged on the villains . . . who [had] robbed [him] of his property' at Grand Portage. This was recognised by the Bay Company men with whom he negotiated in London. Equally recognised, however,

---

* The term *Aboriginal*, today standard in Canada, is applied to *First Nation*, *Inuit* and *Métis* peoples. The US equivalent of First Nation is *Native American*.

were Donald MacKay's unrivalled attributes. He knew canoes; he knew the North American interior; he understood its geography more comprehensively than most of the HBC's more established personnel.[12]

Hence Donald MacKay's recruitment by the HBC; and hence the series of expeditions MacKay now launched into the then uncharted wilderness to the west and south-west of Hudson Bay. Despite his coming close to death at times from drowning or starvation, and despite his tendency to seek unnecessary confrontations with his Nor'Wester rivals, Donald MacKay went a long way to providing the HBC with means of reaching from the Bay a series of places that had previously seemed accessible only from Montreal by way of the Great Lakes and Grand Portage. The maps Donald MacKay made in the course of his exploratory travels (the travels William Young was to hear about in Strathbrora nearly 20 years later) would not be superseded in some instances until the development of aerial photography. And when, in 1793, MacKay established a post or trading fort named Brandon House on the Assiniboine, he provided the HBC with the toehold from which the company was eventually to pose an effective challenge to Nor'Wester supremacy in both the Assiniboine and Red River areas.

Donald MacKay's Bay Company bosses – who, when he was in London, presented him with a ceremonial sword – were appreciative of what MacKay did for them. They were less appreciative of the man himself. Displaying tremendous drive and energy at some points, isolating himself at others, and given increasingly to threatening violence to those around him, MacKay became more and more impossible to live with. The Nor'Westers, in the Québécois French that was the lingua franca of the Montreal-based fur trade, had nicknamed him *Le Malin*, the devil. His HBC associates, much as James Loch would do later, called him Mad MacKay. Those same associates, it followed, were not sorry to see Donald MacKay quit Hudson Bay for Scotland in 1799. Nor were they pleased when, with the encouragement of the HBC's London directors, MacKay in 1806 made a brief return to the bay where he overwintered at Fort Churchill. According to the fort's chief trader, William Auld, with whom MacKay quarrelled bitterly, the latter 'when sober, [was] mad, when drunk outrageously so'. There was, then, a certain inevitability about Donald MacKay's 1807 decision to leave Hudson Bay for good. Returning to his native Strathbrora, where he had also spent the years between 1800 and 1806, MacKay – for all that a substantial sum had accumulated in his Bay Company account – chose to live frugally in the 'hut' William Young was to visit in 1810.[13]

In Strathbrora, Donald MacKay's domestic arrangements were complicated. They were also controversial. When with the HBC, MacKay's 'country wife' (the term applied in the fur trade to a man's locally acquired female partner) was Hannah Sutherland, a *Métis* daughter (her mother was Cree) of MacKay's fellow trader and fellow Highlander, James Sutherland. Hannah was to die when she and the couple's two young sons were attacked (for reasons that remain obscure) by a group of Aboriginals. But her boys, William and Donald, survived (despite Donald having been scarred for life) and both were to spend lengthy periods with their father in Ascoilemore. There, not long after his initial homecoming, Donald Senior embarked on a relationship with Mary MacKenzie, more than 30 years his junior and still a teenager when her first child, described by Strathbrora's Church of Scotland minister as Mary and Donald's 'bastard daughter', was born at Ascoilemore in July 1803. Sometime later, however, the couple married prior to having more children, two of whom accompanied their father when in June 1822, taking advantage of subsidised passages Joseph Gordon was then making available, Donald MacKay* sailed from Cromarty for Nova Scotia.[14]

---

* The circumstances surrounding MacKay's emigration are explored in Chapter 14.

Donald MacKay's 1822 departure for North America was not the first of his involvements with transatlantic emigration from Sutherland. That occurred more than ten years before when, at the start of 1812, MacKay was contacted by Thomas Douglas, Earl of Selkirk, then a key figure in the Hudson's Bay Company. Partly with a view to assisting the HBC's continuing efforts to combat Nor'Wester competition and partly in order to provide new opportunities for evicted Highlanders, Selkirk (of whom more later) was setting about the establishment of a settlement colony in the vicinity of Red River's junction with the Assiniboine. Donald MacKay, as Selkirk had discovered, was perhaps the only person then living in the United Kingdom who had not only seen the locality in question but had spent time there. What could MacKay tell him of Red River and its wider setting? the earl enquired. The answer, it became apparent, was a great deal.

'To enter minutely into . . . the nature of this country', Donald MacKay wrote of territories occupied today by Manitoba, Saskatchewan, North Dakota and Minnesota, 'would need a whole volume.' But he would do his best; and in this he was clearly aided (since he supplied Lord Selkirk with sets of latitudes and longitudes) by his having available in Ascoilemore some at least of the charts and journals deriving from his North American explorations. Drawing on these to explain to the earl where Red River lay in relation to the Mississippi–Missouri drainage basin, MacKay could not resist recalling his Missouri exploits of more than 30 years previously. 'I have seen tribes of Indians that never saw any Europeans before,' he boasted, dwelling in particular on periods spent with the 'Big Bellies' (or Mandan) and the 'Snakes' (or Shoshone). Both those peoples, MacKay added, 'treated me with the utmost civility and hospitality'.[15]

But what the Earl of Selkirk really wanted to know, Donald MacKay appreciated, was how prospective colonists – who, in the event, included two contingents from Sutherland – were to get from the Bay Company's York Factory base to Lake Winnipeg and Red

River. 'The distance from York Fort to [Lake] Winnipeg is 350 miles,' MacKay commented. En route, by way of the Hayes and Nelson Rivers, Selkirk's Red River settlers would encounter obstacles in the shape of 'twenty-four carrying places' or portages, where boats or canoes had to be hauled around falls or rapids. There was, then, no disguising the arduousness of a York Factory–Red River journey. But once accomplished, Donald MacKay insisted, that journey – however difficult – would be shown to have been worthwhile.

Besides having easy access to the sturgeon that, according to MacKay, were readily to be taken from Red River itself, people setting up home on the river's banks would be able to draw on lots of other natural resources. 'Red River hath buffaloes, deers of different kinds and, in the fall and spring, geese, swans . . . ducks, heath hens, partridges, rabbits, etc.' As to 'the climate of the country you wish me to describe', Donald MacKay informed Lord Selkirk, it was superior to that of many of North America's already settled districts.

Because he had 'wintered there four years', MacKay wrote of the Red River region, he was well placed to make comparisons between that locality and the St Lawrence Valley where he had spent five years in or around Montreal. Winter weather at Red River, the former fur trader insisted, was 'far milder than in Canada', a term then applied only to the present-day provinces of Quebec and Ontario. By way of demonstrating this to his own satisfaction, MacKay emphasised that the St Lawrence River in the neighbourhood of Montreal, where the river iced over every winter, 'did not break open until April'. The Red River, in contrast, broke 'in March' while the open terrain around it and to the west contained 'better . . . soil' than any to be found in areas fronting the St Lawrence.

In thus portraying Red River as next best thing to the promised land the Israelites found in Canaan, Donald MacKay was engaging in what nineteenth-century Americans called 'boosterism', the business of enticing settlers to some newly opened-up locality by over-egging its attractions. What MacKay had to say of Red River was true – more or less. But there was much he left unsaid, not least the fact that it was going to be hard, verging on impossible, for the HBC and Lord Selkirk to establish at Red River a colony of the sort the latter planned. At the start of the nineteenth century's second decade, after all, the frontier of settlement in British North America (as today's Canada was then called) had not got much further west than the eastern end of the Great Lakes. Since Red River was many hundreds of miles beyond that point, and since the HBC could access Red River only by way of its subarctic and regularly deep-frozen possessions on Hudson Bay, Selkirk's colony (as will be seen) would be for many years one of the most isolated such communities in the world.

Nothing of this is likely to have worried Donald MacKay who, when writing to the Earl of Selkirk from Ascoilemore in February 1812, was anxious to give his full backing to a venture which, if even halfway successful, would create real problems for his old enemies in the NWC, the Nor'Westers being desperate to retain their still powerful grip on the Red River region and Selkirk, in his HBC role, being keen to have that grip loosened. Nor was MacKay any more inclined to sound a note of caution when, in May 1813, the Earl of Selkirk came in person to have dinner with him in the Ascoilemore home that, eight years later, Donald Bannerman and his evicting party were to destroy.

Because Strathbrora at this point was still roadless, Selkirk, when making the journey from Brora to Ascoilemore, was obliged to swap his carriage for a horse. The earl, for all that, is likely to have found the trip worthwhile. As one of those present was afterwards to recall, there were 'a number of persons' waiting for Lord Selkirk 'at Donald MacKay's house'. What was said to them by MacKay and Selkirk was not recorded. But it is probable that, in the course of discussions lasting for two or three hours, the former was every bit as effusive as the latter about the merits of Red River, the Earl of Selkirk's colonisation project now being a means, from Donald MacKay's perspective, of inflicting damage not just on the Nor'Westers but on a new set of foes nearer home.[16]

The Marquis and Marchioness of Stafford's Sutherland 'improvements' had not long been launched in May 1813. But large-scale
clearances were already in an advanced state of preparation, as were
well-organised attempts to stop them. From the outset of the resulting conflict between Sutherland people and the Staffords, MacKay
was clear as to which side he was on. By encouraging eviction-threat-
ened families to reject one of the Sutherland Estate management's
proffered crofts and instead take up Selkirk's offer of a fresh start at
Red River, Donald MacKay, in addition to striking a blow against
the NWC, was helping to subvert 'improvement'.

3

'THERE SHOULD BE BLOOD'

Rebellion in Kildonan

Anyone entering the National Gallery of Scotland, off Edinburgh's
Princes Street, soon encounters a towering portrait – nearly eight
feet high – of a tall, well-set, auburn-haired man wearing the
uniform of one of early nineteenth-century Britain's many military
formations, the 54th (West Norfolk) Regiment of Foot. This
portrait, thought to date from between 1809 and 1811, was painted
by Henry Raeburn, one of Scotland's most renowned artists. But if
the identity of the portrait's painter is clear, its subject has been
something of a puzzle to the National Gallery. The gallery's online
catalogue describes him simply as 'Major William Clunes, died
1829'; and when, in 1997, his portrait was featured in a comprehensive exhibition of Raeburn's work, the exhibition's organisers did
not have much more to say. Observing that 'little is known' of
Clunes,* they added only that he 'is believed to have been a native of
Sutherland' who, having joined the 50th (West Kent) Regiment of
Foot in 1790, was promoted to lieutenant in 1794, to captain in
1797 and to major in 1809 – by which point he had transferred from
the West Kents to the West Norfolks with whom he served until
quitting the army in 1811.[1]

The National Gallery gets wrong the date of William Clunes's
death, which actually occurred in February 1830. Otherwise the

---

* It is likely that the major's surname was pronounced as two syllables, Clu-nes.

gallery's account of him is accurate, if slight. But for all that it might be good if more information were available, no one needs to know who Clunes was in order to appreciate the subtleties of Henry Raeburn's composition – a composition from which the major, his face more brightly lit than its surroundings, looks out self-assuredly at the viewer. Clunes's right hand is on his hip. His left rests on the back of the horse he is about to mount, its head turned away from both Clunes and from his portrait's painter with the result that the animal's tail and hindquarters loom large in the picture's foreground. It is this last feature that led Alison Watt, one of twenty-first-century Scotland's leading artists, to single out the Clunes portrait when asked to pick a particular favourite from among the National Gallery's collection. 'It's almost impossible to choose a favourite', Watt responded, 'but there are several paint-ings I return to again and again. One of those is Raeburn's breathtaking portrait of Major William Clunes . . . Few artists have the skill or chutzpah to design a portrait in which the rippling hindquarters of a horse take up a large proportion of the canvas. It's a dazzling picture.'[2]

What makes this outstanding piece of art all the more significant, in a Sutherland context at any rate, is the insight it offers into the appearance, maybe even the character, of a man whose presence in the Strath of Kildonan on the evening of Tuesday 5 January 1813 – just two or three years after Raeburn painted Clunes's portrait – precipitated the sequence of events that brought the Sutherland clearances to national attention.

Clunes lodged that January night in the home of Alexander Sage, Kildonan's long-serving parish minister. Years later, Donald Sage, the minister's son, was to write an account of his upbringing in that same Kildonan manse. There Sage touches on the major, his family background and his military career. That career, because it commenced just prior to the start of prolonged conflict between Britain and France, resulted in Clunes seeing a lot of action, the major, according to an 1830 obituarist, having 'had the honour of sharing the toils and the fame of our army in the Peninsula [meaning Portugal and Spain], Egypt and [elsewhere]'.[3]

Unsurprisingly, Clunes was wounded more than once and by 1811, or so his father, Gordon Clunes, informed Lady Stafford, was 'in a very bad state'. That, Clunes senior thought, might make it possible – all the more so if the marchioness was prepared to assist – for him to persuade the military authorities to let William return to civilian life. This, Gordon Clunes wrote, had become all the more necessary because his own health was failing and, if William was not permitted to come home, there would be no one to succeed to the tenancy of Crakaig, the Sutherland Estate farm the Clunes family had occupied since the early eighteenth century.[4]

Thus it came about that when Gordon Clunes died in 1812, William – whose case Lady Stafford did indeed take up with the army's high command – was in place to take over at Crakaig. Situated on Sutherland's eastern coastal plain some five miles south of Helmsdale where the Strath of Kildonan opens on to the North Sea, Crakaig contained (as it still does) a substantial tract of arable land. On becoming the farm's tenant, William promptly set about reorganising this land in a manner that attracted the approval of James Loch, who, when visiting Sutherland, was more than once a beneficiary of what Loch called the major's 'gentlemanlike hospitality'. But Loch, despite his being wined and dined from time to time at Crakaig, was never quite sure where William Clunes's ultimate loyalties lay. This was partly because of the complex web of marital connections between the Crakaig family on the one hand and, on the other, the family which, until 1812, owned the Carrol Estate. William's mother was a daughter of one Gordon of Carrol. His sister Anne, whom Donald Sage remembered as a 'dashing young woman', became the wife of another – this being Joseph Gordon whom the Staffords and their senior employees regarded (as already stressed) with unremitting hostility.[5]

Joseph, like James Loch, was an occasional visitor to Crakaig. Exactly how Carrol's ex-laird got on there with William Clunes,

Joseph's cousin as well as his brother-in-law, cannot be known. But it is reasonable to suspect that the two men were sometimes at odds. Joseph Gordon, after all, was an arch-opponent of 'improvement'. William Clunes, in contrast, was among its beneficiaries. By the 1820s, when his rent payments to the marquis and marchioness approached the then enormous sum of £1,000 annually, Clunes, while still tenant of Crakaig, was also in control of much of the Strath of Kildonan, where he kept thousands of sheep on land from which a lot of people had been cleared.[6]

If there was friction between William Clunes and his wife's brother, it is likely to have been aggravated by the beginnings of Clunes's sheep-farming involvements having been bound up with the Staffords' 1812 purchase of Joseph Gordon's Carrol Estate, a necessary prelude (as indicated previously) to the establishment of Gabriel Reed's Kilcalmkill sheep farm. Because that farm stretched from Strathbrora to the Strath of Kildonan, it included Glen Loth, a smaller valley halfway between the two straths. This meant that William Clunes lost access to Glen Loth grazings that had been available to his father and previous Crakaig tenants. His loss, however, was quickly made good by the Sutherland Estate's then newly installed factor, William Young, who took the view that Clunes should get – 'in return' for his surrendered Glen Loth pastures – a sheep farm in the Strath of Kildonan. This farm was to be centred on Torrish, four or five miles up the strath, and its creation, Young calculated, would account for a sizeable proportion of the many evictions that would be required if, in the spring of 1813, William Clunes and Gabriel Reed were to be granted vacant possession of Torrish in the one case and Kilcalmkill in the other.[7]

Although it had been agreed in principle that Clunes should have Torrish in addition to Crakaig, William Young reported to the Marchioness of Stafford, he and the major 'were not at one about [its] value'. With a view to helping fix the farm's rent, Young continued, he had decided that, during the first week of January 1813, Clunes should 'survey' Torrish in conjunction with two men the factor described as 'people of skill'. These were Ralph Reed and James Hall. Both were eventually to become Sutherland Estate tenants in their own right. In 1813, however, Ralph Reed, Gabriel Reed's younger brother, had not yet got a farm of his own, while Hall, who had earlier left Roxburghshire for Caithness, would not move on to the Sutherland Estate until 1818 when (as will be seen) he took over a large part of Strathbrora.[8]

As arranged by William Young, Clunes met with Hall and Reed on the morning of Tuesday 5 January 1813 and, as he put it, 'proceeded up the Strath of Kildonan' in their company. Since, even on horseback, it would have taken the three men a little time to reach their destination and since, in early January, daylight does not last long in the Highlands, the major and his two associates, on getting to Torrish, were able to inspect only 'some part' of the area under review. It was agreed, therefore, that all three should meet again at Torrish the following morning, meantime spending the night in such accommodation as they could find in the vicinity. Leaving his companions to make their own arrangements, Clunes duly rode off to Alexander Sage's manse. This was some four miles distant, the manse being hard by the township of Kildonan which gave the wider strath its name and which owed its own designation (rather like Kilcalmkill) to its supposed connection with one of the Highlands' early medieval saints.[9]

'Major William Clunes', according to a Donald Sage pen-picture that accords with Henry Raeburn's painting, 'was a gigantic, handsome, soldierly-looking man of a truly noble countenance.' The figure that pitched up at the Kildonan manse as dusk was gathering that winter's afternoon in 1813, then, was a striking one. And just as (thanks to Raeburn and Sage) a good deal has been preserved of Clunes's appearance, so it is possible to get a sense of the home where, with night coming on, he hoped to find a bed.[10]

That is because this home (though it no longer houses a minister) is still to be seen in Kildonan. Today one of the locality's oldest residences, it was far from new even in Clunes's time. But the manse

(because all such buildings were intended to accommodate clergymen's visiting colleagues as well as their often large families) was
nevertheless substantial. Its eight rooms made it the largest house in
this part of early nineteenth-century Sutherland and the only one to
have a slated, rather than thatched, roof. As was everywhere standard, the manse also possessed a range of outbuildings more than
sufficient to provide the major, prior to his making his way inside,
with stabling for his horse.[11]

Alexander Sage would prove less than enthusiastic about the
'improvements' that were shortly to depopulate his parish – improvements including the sheep farm Clunes had come up the strath to
look over. Sage would also grow to detest Clunes personally, describing him as a 'vile' man who, though married, had 'debauched' a
series of young women. The first of these – with whom, or so Sage
and his fellow clerics noted, the major eventually 'acknowledged a
criminal connection' – was Janet Matheson who lived near Crakaig
and who, as a result of what appears to have been a brief relationship with Clunes, 'brought forth a child in fornication'. Nothing of
this, however, became public knowledge until 1814; and when, just
five days into the preceding year, the major turned up at Alexander
Sage's door, he appears to have been received warmly enough.
Clunes and his family, after all, were well known to Sage and still
better known to the minister's wife, Jean, who had grown up not far
from Crakaig. Indeed Jean Sage[*] and William Clunes, while not
exactly related, were connected by an intricate kinship chain of a
kind common among the Sutherland gentry class to which both
belonged – Jean's sister, Elizabeth, being an aunt-by-marriage of
William's brother-in-law, Joseph Gordon.[12]

But if, on 5 January 1813, William Clunes expected to enjoy a
restful evening with long-standing acquaintances, he was to be
disappointed. This is clear from evidence collected in the course of

---

* Jean was Alexander's second wife (his first having died) and thus Donald Sage's
stepmother.

enquiries into the turbulent events that were to unfold, over the next 24 hours, both in the vicinity of Alexander Sage's home and elsewhere in the Strath of Kildonan. That evidence includes a statement made by Robert MacKay, a Helmsdale man who happened to call at Kildonan manse just before Clunes's arrival. 'The major', MacKay said, 'had not been long seated when he was informed by Mrs Sage that some people were at the door' and that those people 'wanted to speak with him'.[13]

According to his own subsequent testimony, Clunes, on going out, found four men and a woman waiting for him. Those people asked the major what had brought him to Kildonan. More specifically, they asked who – meaning Ralph Reed and James Hall – he had been with that afternoon and what it was exactly he, Hall and Reed had been doing in and around Torrish. On Clunes supplying at least some of the information thus requested, his interrogators next wanted to know 'whether he had taken a lease' of land or 'grounds' (in the terminology of the time) in Torrish or its neighbourhood – 'to which he [the major] answered that he had not yet taken [these] grounds in tack [or tenancy] but it was likely that he should do so'.[14]

This was not well received by the five-strong deputation clustered around the Kildonan manse's door. Appealing, in vain as it proved, to the major's feelings for his late father, a man warmly regarded locally, Clunes's questioners told the aspiring sheep farmer that his conduct was not what they would have expected of 'his father's son'. Tempers, evidently, were rising. They rose further when one man said angrily 'that if sheep were put upon that ground [meaning land earmarked for inclusion in the planned Torrish sheep farm] there should be blood . . . and that it would be as well for them [the Strath of Kildonan's established occupants] to be killed as set adrift upon the world – to which the [only] woman [present] then added that there should [indeed] be blood and no little of it'.[15]

The origins of the troubles thus initiated – troubles that were to become acute the following day – can be traced to 1810 when

William Young, to whom the Sutherland Estate was then unfamiliar territory, made several forays into the estate's interior. One of those trips (as already noted) resulted in Young's first encounter with Donald MacKay in Strathbrora. Another, made in August 1810, took Young into the Strath of Kildonan.

Today's single-track road through the strath keeps to the left or north bank of the Helmsdale River, reckoned by anglers to be one of the best places in the world to fish for salmon. Young, whose horse would have taken an hour or two to cover the nine miles from the strath's eastern end to Alexander Sage's manse – where he stopped off briefly – followed much the same route. What that route's surroundings looked like can be seen from a large-scale and colourful map commissioned by Britain's military in 1794 when the Highlands were considered a potential target for French raids and incursions. As this map shows, William Young, on riding up a valley he (rightly) thought 'beautiful', would have seen, both on his own side of the River Helmsdale and on the river's opposite bank, township after township. Each of those communities was surrounded, as shown on the 1794 map, by many acres of intensively cultivated land. The crops grown on this land, or so Alexander Sage commented at much the same time as Kildonan was mapped for the military, were sufficient to ensure that the strath's riverside residents, as well as 'supply[ing] themselves with provisions', could export surplus foodstuffs to less favoured localities.[16]

Nor were the minister's parishioners – all of them resident in the Strath of Kildonan or in smaller valleys opening on to it – short of livestock. 'The number of horses in April 1791', Sage wrote, '[was] computed at 812; cows, 2,479; sheep, 5,041; and goats, 570. For these . . . good prices have been got at the markets. Horses of the best kind draw from £4 to £6 sterling; cows from 50 s[hillings] to £4 [and ten shillings].' Since Sage, himself a part-time farmer, appears to have enumerated only breeding cows, it is likely that the Strath of Kildonan, where few such animals are to be seen today, would have contained 4,000 or more cattle when William Young first passed through. And especially if allowance is made for cattle of that time being smaller than their modern counterparts, the prices they obtained – as given by Alexander Sage and converted into present-day cash equivalents – were better than those fetched in Scottish livestock markets at the start of the twenty-first century. Of course, as is true of every agriculturally dependent locality that has ever existed, the Strath of Kildonan experienced bad years as well as good. But the place, it is clear, was more than capable of sustaining a whole set of viable communities, which Alexander Sage's son Donald was afterwards to write about in detail.[17]

'The [Helmsdale] river . . . was . . . the finest feature in the landscape,' Donald Sage recalled of the locality where he spent his boyhood. But he remembered with equal pleasure woodlands William Young would have encountered three or four miles into his August 1810 journey: woodlands of 'black willow, oak, aspen, alder and wild gean [or cherry], the mountain ash or rowan, the black flowering-thorn and the birch tree'. In the vicinity of those woodlands, Young would have rode through the township of Kilfedder, 'a lovely spot,' Sage thought, 'past which a rushing torrent breaks through the copse-wood'. Not far from Kilfedder was Torrish, which William Clunes, James Hall and Ralph Reed were to 'survey' in January 1813 and which, prior to its becoming part of the resulting sheep farm, was a densely peopled settlement where, Donald Sage commented, 'the houses or cottages of the tenantry were built closely together'. Beyond Torrish, Sage went on, were places (and the spellings here are Sage's) like Balbhealach, Dalhalmy and Dibail. This information derives from recollections set down in Donald Sage's old age. But his memory's accuracy is confirmed by the military map of 1794, which shows all the settlements Sage listed and several more besides. On the Helmsdale River's southern bank, for example, the map's compiler, whose name was George Brown, gave precise locations of (from east to west and with Brown's spellings) Manyle, Gruidsarry, Eldrable, Olbsdale, Gilable, Killearnen ('a township of great extent' according to Donald Sage), Tordarroch, Badfleugh and Leist.[18]

In the published version of Donald Sage's memoirs – not made available until 1889 – 20 closely printed pages are given over to an account of these and other settlements as they were at the close of the eighteenth century and the start of the nineteenth. This account concludes: 'I have thus minutely delineated the local features of my native parish for two reasons. First, because with every one of those features is connected a crowd of associations of my early years . . . [Second], because [those same features] are now . . . almost wholly obliterated. The townships . . . which once teemed with happy life are . . . desolate and silent; and the only traces visible of the vanished, happy population are, here and there, a half-buried hearthstone or a moss-grown graveyard.'[19]

Such was the eventual – and still apparent – outcome of William Young's Strath of Kildonan reconnaissance of 1810. At that point, according to Young, there were between 1,200 and 1,500 people living in the Helmsdale River valley and its offshoots.* All or most of them, the factor commented, would one day have to be removed. This followed from its having become 'perfectly clear' to him, Young told the Marquis and Marchioness of Stafford, that the strath was 'adapted for the sheep farming system', sheep farmers, Young stressed, having the capacity to deliver 'much higher' rents than could be looked for from people committed, as was the case in pre-clearance Kildonan, to mixed farming of the sort Young called 'corn and cattle husbandry'.[20]

William Young first arrived in Sutherland in May 1809. Then in his mid-forties, he owned property in both Aberdeenshire and Moray, counties where he launched a variety of business ventures. One of those was centred on the Moray port of Burghead, which Young aimed to expand and revitalise. With this in mind, he came north by sea, in the hope of getting Lord and Lady Stafford to invest in the

---

* According to that year's census, there were 1,574 people in the parish of Kildonan in 1811.

establishment of a regular shipping service between Burghead and
Sutherland. Because road access to Sutherland from the south was
poor in 1809 and would remain so for some time, such a link made
commercial sense. The Staffords duly took a stake in the project and
soon a sizeable sailing craft, 'often full of goods' and carrying 'many
passengers', was leaving every Friday for Burghead from Little Ferry,
located south of Golspie and at the entrance to the narrow channel
linking the saltwater inlet of Loch Fleet with the North Sea.[21]

With him to Sutherland from Moray, William Young brought
some of his business associates. Among them was a 28-year-old man
who, though trained as a lawyer, had been taking a closer and closer
interest in farming. This was Patrick Sellar. Like his companions, he
was familiar with the way that, from anywhere on Moray's coastline, the Sutherland hills – assuming reasonable visibility – are a
constant feature on the north-western horizon. Neither Sellar nor
his companions, however, had previously ventured across the Moray
Firth, the bight-like expanse of North Sea waters separating
Caithness and Sutherland from Moray and points east. But if
Sutherland in 1809 was new to Patrick Sellar, it was also the part of
Scotland where he was to spend much of his life and, by so doing,
make himself wealthy. Hence, perhaps, Sellar's later tendency to
dramatise the impact on him of his first encounter with the Moray
Firth's northern shore: 'We came into Dunrobin Bay . . . a little after
sunrise; and I shall never forget the effect produced on us by the
beauty of the scenery – the mountains, rocks, woods and the castle
reflected on the sea as from a mirror.'[22]

Sellar and Young stayed on in Sutherland for several days, riding
up and down the county's coastal plain. What they saw surprised
and intrigued them. Moray and Aberdeenshire at the start of the
nineteenth century were places where older agricultural systems had
been giving way for some time to farms of the sort still to be seen
there today: farms equipped with substantial, stone-built farm-
houses and the equally substantial barns and other outbuildings
known in Scotland as steadings. In Sutherland in 1809, Young and

Sellar found only one set of such steadings – at Clynelish on Brora's northern outskirts. Everywhere else, farms looked much as they had done for centuries. Neatly walled and carefully drained fields on the southern pattern were nowhere to be seen; neither were the sown grasses and turnips on which Aberdeenshire and Moray farmers increasingly fed their cattle. 'Morayshire [was then] by no means a well-improved county,' Patrick Sellar later remarked of his 1809 inspection of the countryside between Helmsdale and Dornoch. 'But at that time Sutherland seemed a century behind it.'[23]

Paradoxically, however, Sellar and Young scented an enticing opportunity in what seemed to them Sutherland's backwardness. This new found land, as Sutherland was from their standpoint, seemed to the two men to be one they could readily reshape to its – and their – advantage. In much the same gung-ho spirit as was evident among the settlers then transforming Britain's North American, Australian and other colonies, the two Moray men began bombarding the Marquis and Marchioness of Stafford with ideas as to how Sutherland's 'improvement' – something the Staffords were already committed to – could be accelerated, driven through, made real. Up-to-date farms, well-planned villages, harbours, fishing fleets, towns, even factories were envisaged. Detailed proposals as to how all this could be accomplished were drawn up. The originators of those proposals, it was hinted, would themselves be prepared – for appropriate rewards – to make their services available. An impressed, indeed bowled over, marquis and marchioness responded positively. By the summer of 1810, when William Young first explored the Strath of Kildonan, it had accordingly been decided that the Sutherland Estate's previous factor, Cosmo Falconer, was to be dismissed and that, with full effect from May 1811, Young and Patrick Sellar were to take charge of estate administration. One of their priorities, everyone agreed, would be to establish new sheep farms.

As far as the Staffords were concerned, the case for such farms was strong. When, during 1807 and 1808, the Sutherland Estate's then management team had taken the experimental step of creating two tenancies of this new type, it had been shown that any given area of land was likely to be worth at least three times more to the estate if occupied by a sheep farmer instead of by the same area's previous occupants.[24]

The largest of the 1807–08 farms spread across a big expanse of hill country – around 100,000 acres in extent – west of Strathbrora and south of Strathnaver. This farm was tenanted jointly by Adam Atkinson and Anthony Marshall. Like Gabriel Reed, they came from Northumberland and (the sheep-farming fraternity being nothing if not close-knit) their senior employees included Gabriel's brother Ralph, one of the two 'people of skill' who, in January 1813, accompanied William Clunes to Torrish.[25]

It was in Torrish's general vicinity, as it happened, that the second of the 1807–08 farms had taken shape. Named Suisgill, after one of the three settlements it displaced, this farm, as William Young discovered in August 1810, occupied much of the area 'betwixt Kildonan Manse and Kinbrace' in the Strath of Kildonan's upper reaches. However, its tenant, Thomas Houston, unlike Marshall, Atkinson and the Reeds, was no newcomer to Sutherland, Houston having occupied for some time the coastal farm of Lothbeg near William Clunes's Crakaig.[26]

By retaining his Lothbeg tenancy in addition to his Suisgill one, Houston pioneered an arrangement that Clunes was also to adopt and which afterwards became widespread on the Sutherland Estate: sheep farmers, of whom Patrick Sellar was destined to be one of the most successful, usually looking to rent both inland landholdings (laid out in such as way as to include extensive hill grazings) and lower lying farms like Lothbeg. This was sometimes seen as territorial aggrandisement for its own sake. But while such motives may not have been absent, practical considerations loomed larger, notably the benefits to be got from being able to move younger and more vulnerable sheep out of the interior during winter months when those sheep might otherwise have fallen victim to blizzards of the sort that sometimes left higher parts of Sutherland under deep snow for weeks, even months, at a time.

While the Suisgill experience was a pointer to how the wider Strath of Kildonan might be reorganised in the way William Young suggested in 1810, it was well into 1812 before Young was clear as to the precise nature of the 'many valuable improvements' he aimed to bring about in the strath. At the core of the factor's projected changes was the creation of two further sheep farms. These were Kilcalmkill and Torrish; and for all that it had taken Young longer than he would have liked to get to the point now reached, he clearly expected subsequent progress to be faster. At first, this expectation seemed justified. Tenants for the new farms, these being Gabriel Reed and William Clunes, were found readily enough. Nor, looking ahead, did William Young anticipate any difficulty in dealing with the many people who would have to be turned out of Kildonan in advance of Reed's and Clunes's flocks moving in.

Young's blithe assumption that all would be plain sailing may have derived in part from there having been no substantial resistance to the establishment of Thomas Houston's Suisgill farm. This time, however, many more townships were scheduled for clearance: from the south side of the strath in the Kilcalmkill case and from its northern flank in the case of Torrish. It is not surprising, therefore, that some at least of the Strath of Kildonan's about-to-be-ejected residents should have begun to debate what they might do to safeguard their communities from destruction, with the result that, before the end of 1812, Patrick Sellar got 'several dark hints', as he put it, of a 'conspiracy' to thwart the planned evictions. This intelligence, however, was not shared with William Young who, having assured Lord and Lady Stafford that 'improvement' was firmly on track, left Sutherland on Sunday 3 January 1813 to attend to estate business in Edinburgh. Three days later, the Strath of Kildonan was in turmoil.[27]

*   *   *

Before breakfast on the morning of the Wednesday following William Young's Sunday departure for Edinburgh, William Clunes stepped out of Alexander Sage's Kildonan manse in order to see to his horse. He was promptly 'surrounded', he reported subsequently, by as many as 50 men, most of them 'armed with sticks'. One of those men, described as 'spokesman of the party' by Clunes, 'entered into conversation' with him. What this man had to say was much the same as had been said by the people the major had encountered the previous evening. The 'threats' then made to Clunes – threats that blood would be shed if he pressed ahead with his projected sheep farm – were repeated. It was also made clear 'that no inspection of the [disputed] grounds [not just around Torrish but more widely] should be allowed . . . that day'.[28]

Here and there in the Strath of Kildonan that same January morning, life was going on more or less as normal. In the township of Kildonan, not far from the spot where William Clunes was mobbed, two of the township's tenants, John Sutherland and Donald Gunn, both of them among the men who had lobbied Clunes the day before, were busy, as Gunn put it, 'preparing a barn for a wedding'. This wedding took place the next day. The bride was John Sutherland's daughter Jean; the groom a young man by the name of Angus MacKay. When, following their marriage, people gathered in what is likely to have been Jean's father's barn to sing, dance, drink and eat, as was customary in such settings on such occasions, they would be celebrating (as things turned out) the last marriage to take place in the Strath of Kildonan before the strath's families – Angus and Jean (as will be seen) among them – began to be scattered in the way Donald Gunn and his companions feared when telling William Clunes they might as well 'be killed as set adrift upon the world'.[29]

This conviction that nothing could be worse than expulsion from one's home locality helps explain why – though they must have known the odds were very much against their long-term success – so many Strath of Kildonan people took the stand they did on

Wednesday 6 January 1813. Also important, however, was endorsement of their actions by locally influential individuals.

Subsequently it would be claimed that the four men and the woman
(her name was Ann Polson) who sought out William Clunes on the
evening of Tuesday 5 January had been put up to this by George
MacLeod who, like Gordon Ross in Strathbrora, was a schoolmaster
(though his school, unlike Ross's, was one of those run by the Church
of Scotland and not by the SSPCK). MacLeod may or may not have
done as alleged. But what is certain is that the militant stance adopted
by another of the Strath of Kildonan's leading figures, George
MacKay, helped persuade his neighbours to participate in events that
amounted, or so the authorities claimed, to a full-blown riot.[30]

MacKay, an older half-brother of Jean Sutherland's newly
acquired husband, was Kildonan's catechist, meaning that, in close
collaboration with the parish minister, Alexander Sage, he had the
job of subjecting members of the Kildonan congregation to close
and regular questioning of a sort meant to ensure they were
acquainted with the doctrines and teaching of the Church of
Scotland. Recalled by the minister's son Donald as an 'eloquent'
man 'of great natural ability', the catechist was described by John
Gordon, in whose company MacKay spent part of the night of 5–6
January 1813, as 'the wisest person' he knew.[31]

John Gordon was miller in Killernan. George MacKay lived in
Liribol. Both townships were within a mile or two of the Kildonan
manse – Liribol on the north side of the strath and Killernan on the
Helmsdale River's other bank. Although he would have had to ford
the river en route, it would have taken MacKay just a few minutes to
get from his home to John Gordon's mill – one of the places where,
in the run-up to their Wednesday morning confrontation with
William Clunes, a number of people from different Strath of
Kildonan townships met to work out what they might do to forestall
their imminent ejection from their homes.

There was strong – eventually more or less unanimous – feeling
to the effect that, as one participant in the Killernan debate was

reported to have said, 'the men of the Strath of Kildonan ought to rise' and forcibly prevent William Clunes and his associates from completing the survey they had begun on Tuesday 5 January. There was equal feeling that any such action should involve 'both sides of the strath'. While only those townships north of the Helmsdale River were threatened by Clunes's plans, people living on the strath's southern flank, it was agreed, were every bit as much at risk because just as many – indeed more – townships in that quarter would cease to exist if Gabriel Reed's Kilcalmkill farm was permitted to take shape.[32]

Most of the men – from Eldrable, Torrish, Killernan, Liribol, Dalhalmy and other settlements – who argued those matters back and forth in John Gordon's mill while Tuesday turned into Wednesday were among the older and more responsible members of their communities. They were well aware of the risks inherent in what they were proposing. They knew too that, if they stopped William Clunes, Ralph Reed and James Hall going about their business, they would not only be defying their landlord, the Marquis of Stafford, they would also be breaking the law. Perhaps with a view to reassuring themselves that the course they were set on – though illegal – could be considered morally justifiable, they turned to George MacKay, their catechist, for advice. MacKay, it appears, endorsed the proposition that Strath of Kildonan people were entitled to oppose Hall, Reed and Clunes by violent means. The catechist added, however, that he 'would go himself to speak with Major Clunes' whom, he thought, might be dissuaded 'from oppressing poor people'.[33]

The person who acted as 'spokesman' when William Clunes found himself surrounded outside Alexander Sage's manse at first light on Wednesday 6 January, then, was George MacKay, this 'most attractive Christian character', as Donald Sage would one day describe him. But if MacKay hoped that words alone would induce Clunes and his associates to abandon their survey of the area the major intended to rent, the catechist was denied the opportunity to put this to the test. By the time George MacKay met with William Clunes, events in the Strath of Kildonan had acquired their own unstoppable momentum.[34]

On the evening of Tuesday 5 January 1813, when William Clunes went in search of lodgings at the Kildonan manse, his companions, Ralph Reed and James Hall, rode a couple of miles further up the strath to a house occupied by John Turnbull and his family. Turnbull was one of the shepherds hired by Thomas Houston to look after the sheep stock Houston had installed on his Suisgill farm, and Turnbull's home,* built for him by his employer, occupied a spot immediately to the west of the Suisgill Burn's confluence with the River Helmsdale.[35]

Hall and Reed were not John Turnbull's only guests that Tuesday. He had been entertaining a fellow shepherd, John Cleugh, since the preceding Sunday. As Tuesday evening wore on, moreover, the Turnbulls, Reed, Hall and Cleugh were joined by two more shepherds. One was John Cleugh's 18-year-old son, George. The other was James Armstrong, whose place of work was on the Caithness estate belonging to Sir John Sinclair, one of the north of Scotland's most prominent landlords and a man who, like the Marquis and Marchioness of Stafford, very much backed 'improvement' in general and the expansion of sheep farming in particular.[36]

That so many shepherds and sheep farm managers had assembled in the Strath of Kildonan at this point may have owed something to less than a week having passed since New Year's Day, the only holiday granted to working people in early nineteenth-century Scotland. It is more probable, however, that the men who met in John Turnbull's Suisgill home were there because they scented opportunities in the far-reaching changes getting under way on the

---

* This shepherd's cottage was replaced by another such cottage in the 1870s. That building, in turn, has been much renovated and extended in modern times. It is today available for rent by holidaymakers.

Sutherland Estate. Not many years later, after all, no fewer than three of them would be among the estate's leading sheep farmers. That was because John Cleugh, like Hall and Reed, was to make the transition from shepherding or farm management to tenancy, this transition leading, in Cleugh's case, to his leasing (as will be seen) a sheep farm on the upper reaches of the Blackwater not far from Ascoilemore.[37]

Turnbull, the two Cleughs, Armstrong, Reed and Hall had much in common. All of them owed their expertise in sheep management to their having come originally from the England–Scotland border country where large-scale sheep farming had been established during the Middle Ages. All of them were recent arrivals in the north. None of them understood Gaelic, with the exception of George Cleugh who, perhaps because of his being younger than the rest, had picked up a smattering of the language. But linguistic divides can be bridged. What could not be surmounted was the fact that John Turnbull and his friends, rather like settlers on some North American frontier, were at the cutting edge of an increasingly commercialised civilisation's advance into a region where older forms of social organisation remained the norm. Hence the enduring significance of the clash that came to a head in the vicinity of John Turnbull's Suisgill home on Wednesday 6 January 1813. That clash, to be sure, was a lot less violent than analogous conflicts between homesteaders and Native Americans. But the issue at stake in this Sutherland collision was the same as that posed by North America's frontier fighting: which of two incompatible ways of life was to prevail?

The first indication of trouble looming at Suisgill came early on Wednesday morning when a lad called Donald Gunn made his way into John Turnbull's kitchen. Gunn, the son of a Kildonan tenant, also Donald Gunn, was almost certainly acting on his father's instructions. For his part, the father – probably the Donald Gunn then busying himself with wedding preparations and, if so, one of William Clunes's Tuesday evening interrogators – is likely to have had a role in planning what now transpired.

That there had been such planning is clear from subsequent assertions to the effect that various individuals – women as well as men – had gone from house to house in the Strath of Kildonan during the hours of darkness; rousing those homes' occupants; telling folk that 'shepherds were come' to the strath; insisting that the 'shepherds' in question had to be prevented 'from inspecting the grounds' they were intent on looking over. Predictably, some of the men turned out of their beds in this fashion were less willing than others to engage in lawlessness. They were at once informed, or so it was said later, that if they refused to rally round their friends and neighbours, they 'would be dealt with worse' than Major Clunes and his associates.[38]

Donald Gunn junior is unlikely to have needed any such urging. Playing his part to perfection, he told the Turnbulls that he was 'enquiring for a strayed horse' and asked if they had seen it. This seemed innocent enough. In the course of the ensuing conversation, however, Gunn took care to elicit the information that Ralph Reed and James Hall were not yet up and about, but that they soon would be and that it was their intention then to ride back down the strath towards Torrish and their planned rendezvous with the major.[39]

On taking his leave of the Turnbulls, Donald Gunn, according to George Cleugh, recrossed the Suisgill Burn, which he had not long before forded in order to get to the Turnbull home. But instead of returning to Kildonan or searching for his family's ostensibly missing horse, Gunn and 'a parcel of boys' who joined him beside the stream set about 'amusing' themselves, as Cleugh put it, 'at the game of shinney' or shinty* – a sport that had been played by Highlanders, Strath of Kildonan folk included, for centuries.[40]

If, in retrospect, Donald Gunn's conduct was thought suspicious, what happened next was truly alarming. Ralph Reed, having had a bite to eat by way of breakfast, as he said afterwards, had gone 'to

---

* The piece of level ground where this happened has long since been surrounded by a stone wall. But it would still make a reasonable shinty pitch.

put on his greatcoat' preparatory to mounting his horse and, in
James Hall's company, riding back towards Kildonan, Torrish and
– as Reed supposed – the waiting Clunes. But at this juncture, Ralph
Reed went on, 'a woman came running into the house' to say that 'a
number of men' had 'concealed' themselves nearby 'with the view
of attacking' himself and Hall.[41]

This woman was Jean Murray, whose husband Donald operated
a dramshop – then the Strath of Kildonan's nearest equivalent to a
pub – within a short distance of John Turnbull's house but on the
Suisgill Burn's opposite bank. Jean Murray had evidently become
friendly with Mrs Turnbull (whose first name has not been
preserved) but, while anxious to ensure the safety both of her friend
and everyone else in the Turnbull home that morning, she was
equally (and understandably) anxious to conceal her own part in
proceedings. Jean Murray, Ralph Reed recalled, 'requested
Turnbull's wife not to mention' to anyone what she, Jean, had done,
'as she [having betrayed the still hidden conspirators] might be
murdered for it'.[42]

It was now decided that Hall and Reed should at once quit the
Suisgill shepherd's house. Hurriedly mounting their horses – which
John Turnbull was just then feeding at his door – they accordingly
left at speed. Instead of turning down the strath towards Kildonan
and Torrish, however, they turned in the opposite direction, Turnbull
shouting after them, 'For God's sake, gentlemen, make off!'[43]

At this, Donald Gunn was seen to abandon his game of shinty
and run up a nearby hillside in order, it was surmised, to give 'the
watchword to . . . people . . . lying concealed there'. In response, as
many as 50 or 60 men emerged from hiding. Had Ralph Reed and
James Hall made for Kildonan as planned, this substantial force
could readily have 'waylaid' or ambushed them. As it was, all
thought of ambush now abandoned, the previously hidden men,
yelling encouragement to each other in Gaelic, hurtled downhill and
through the Suisgill Burn towards the Turnbull home – some of
them pausing there and others, presumably the younger and fitter

individuals among them, racing past in furious pursuit of the two riders.[44]

Like the equally intimidating group William Clunes found waiting for him that same morning at Alexander Sage's manse, this Suisgill contingent carried 'sticks' or cudgels. And just as their ancestors had done when launching one of the charges characteristic of clan warfare, many of them threw aside their plaids – heavy, blanket-like garments in which they would have wrapped themselves when hiding out that winter's morning. This left these men exposed to the weather. But it also helped them, just as it had helped generations of sword-wielding clansmen, to run as fast as possible.[45]

Although it may seem improbable that their pursuers, being on foot, had any chance of catching up with Hall and Reed, the latter in particular, because his horse was not as sound as it might have been, felt himself seriously at risk of being seized, beaten up and otherwise 'abused'. Nor were his fears without foundation; the fastest of the youths chasing Reed and his companion did not give up until the two mounted men, having passed through Kinbrace at the head of the Strath of Kildonan, reached Achentoul, an isolated settlement on the high plateau beyond the strath's upper end. Here Reed and Hall were eight miles or more from their starting point. They were also approaching the Sutherland Estate's boundary. Beyond that boundary was Strath Halladale, a north–south valley which gave a mightily relieved James Hall and Ralph Reed easy, and mostly downhill, access to the comparative safety of Caithness.[46]

Back at John Turnbull's house, meanwhile, matters were threatening to get out of hand. The men who had halted there while their comrades gave chase to Reed and Hall had soon been joined by others, the new arrivals having hurried on to Suisgill from Kildonan where they had earlier menaced William Clunes. This meant that Turnbull, his wife, their children, James Armstrong and John and George Cleugh were now hemmed in by perhaps 100 people whose blood was up and whose hostility to shepherds and to sheep farming could scarcely have been clearer. Although much of what individuals among the crowd had to say was said in Gaelic and was therefore incomprehensible to the Turnbulls and their guests, the crowd's threatening demeanour became ever more apparent. Among the mob, as it would afterwards be described, were some who counselled caution. But others advocated stern measures. The younger Cleugh, the one man among the encircled shepherds who could follow Gaelic, overheard an especially heated discussion as to what should be done with his father, who had been in Sutherland for some years by this point. Because John Cleugh 'was the first shepherd who came into the country [meaning the Strath of Kildonan area]', it was said, 'his tongue should be cut out of his head or he should be burned alive'.[47]

Those and other equally lurid threats may not have been meant seriously. But there was no mistaking the aggressive intent of those – admittedly few – members of the Suisgill crowd who set about the Cleughs' collie dogs with their sticks. Although they were urged by others to desist, there was a cruel logic to those men's actions. To maim or kill a shepherd's sheepdogs was to deprive him of the tools of his trade, just as to scare shepherds out of Sutherland, which is what many Strath of Kildonan people were trying to do that January morning, would be to leave the county's established and intending sheep farmers, or so those same people hoped, without the means of carrying on farming.[48]

Eventually, with tempers cooling somewhat, one of the crowd's leading moderates, a Liribol tenant by the name of Alexander Fraser, began to impose a kind of order on proceedings. An immediate beneficiary of this development was James Armstrong who, 'being apprehensive of danger', had hidden himself inside John Turnbull's house. Told in English that his life was not at risk and that he would be permitted to go on his way as long as he did not challenge or contradict anything said to him, Armstrong stepped cautiously into the open. There the shepherd was ordered, once more in English, to promise that he would never again show his face in the Strath of Kildonan. He did as he was told. Then, as instructed, James

Armstrong crossed the Suisgill Burn and, doubtless looking repeatedly over his shoulder, began walking quickly in the direction of Kildonan, Torrish, Helmsdale and – though getting there would have taken Armstrong two or three days – his Caithness home.[49]

At Alexander Fraser's insistence, the Turnbulls and Cleughs were also allowed to go in search of places of safety, Fraser directing Mrs Turnbull and her children, in the first instance, to his own house where, he assured the Suisgill shepherd's wife, she would be well looked after. After this, the men surrounding the Turnbull home started to disperse. Their mission, after all, had been accomplished. That is evident from Major William Clunes's reaction to what he learned from James Armstrong whom the major met as the shepherd – 'much frightened and in a state of trepidation' – tramped past Alexander Sage's manse. On hearing from Armstrong something of what had taken place at Suisgill and on discovering, in consequence, that he would be seeing no more of James Hall and Ralph Reed for some time, the major decided that it was 'in vain for him to proceed further in the business' that had brought him to the Strath of Kildonan the day before. Saddling his horse, he rode home to Crakaig.[50]

4

'OPEN AND DETERMINED RESISTANCE'

*The Kildonan rebels consolidate their
gains, take their cause to London and
begin to attract nationwide publicity*

Nothing like the Kildonan uprising had previously occurred on the
Sutherland Estate. This meant that the men then managing estate
affairs had no experience of handling organised opposition. Partly
for that reason, and partly because William Young did not return to
Sutherland from Edinburgh until 21 January, well over a fortnight
passed before steps were taken to deal with the challenge posed to
'improvement' by the dramatic events at Alexander Sage's manse
and at Suisgill. During this period, the 6 January 'rioters', as they
are called in Sutherland Estate correspondence of the time, were free
to build on the victory they had won as a result of their having, in
effect, run Clunes, Hall and Reed out of the Strath of Kildonan.

When, in mid-January, a shepherd by the name of Matthew Short
was bold enough to walk into the strath from the south by way of
Glen Loth, he was accosted, threatened with violence and told that
he and other 'devils who had come into the country' would have
their homes 'set on fire'. Nor was there much sign of the Strath of
Kildonan's prospective sheep farmers responding to belligerence of
this sort by mounting any kind of fightback. William Clunes, for
instance, let it be known that he could do nothing further with
regard to Torrish because he was 'confined to bed by a fit of the
ague', a claim that Patrick Sellar for one regarded as proof of the

major's inherent unreliability. But if Clunes was intent on lying low, so was Gabriel Reed. 'I never saw a man in such terror,' a newly returned Young reported of him. Word had been got to the sheep farmer's then heavily pregnant wife that if her baby turned out to be a boy, the child would be killed to deprive her husband of an heir. This, surely, amounted to no more than posturing on the part of one or two individuals. But perhaps because of what he had heard of the 6 January protests from his badly shaken brother Ralph, Gabriel took all such threats seriously. His wife was sent to her parents' home on the Bighouse Estate, while Gabriel himself took to over-nighting in Dunrobin Castle (the most secure place he could find) and to telling Young he might have to look for another tenant for Kilcalmkill.[1]

On getting back to Sutherland and finding, as he reported, that 'the Kildonan men . . . had risen' and 'would not allow a shepherd to set foot' in the area they now controlled, Young's first instinct had been to open discussions with the rebels. Convinced that Kildonan contained people with whom he could negotiate, the factor 'sent for' those people and met with them in his home at Rhives, where a disenchanted Patrick Sellar, who thought Young should have taken a harder line, watched his colleague 'drawing ale' for men Sellar regarded as criminals. Young, however, was determined to be concil-iatory and to share with his guests his Edinburgh news, which he thought would help him get what he wanted in the Strath of Kildonan.[2]

While in the south, William Young explained, he had finalised the purchase by Lord and Lady Stafford of the Armadale and Strathy Estate on Sutherland's north coast. Previously, the marquis and marchioness had owned comparatively little territory in that quar-ter, their north coast possessions consisting of parcels of land around the estuary of the Naver, Strathnaver's equivalent of Kildonan's Helmsdale River. But now that Armadale and Strathy's previous owner had been persuaded to part with his property in much the same way as Joseph Gordon had been persuaded to sell his Carrol

Estate a year earlier, the Staffords had acquired much of the coastline between the Naver's mouth and Sutherland's border with Caithness. It was there, Young told the Kildonan men he entertained at Rhives, that he intended to settle them, their families and everyone else affected by the proposed Kilcalmkill and Torrish sheep farms. Each of the Strath of Kildonan's evicted tenants, the factor went on, would be allocated a croft consisting of 'about three acres of arable land' in coastal localities where, Young said, 'the climate [was] good [and] the crops certain'. To make it easier for the north coast's future crofters to have their furniture and other belongings taken from their old homes to their new ones, the factor added, he would 'send a vessel' – probably the one usually plying between Sutherland and Burghead – 'to transport' all such goods by sea from Helmsdale.[3]

Among the Strath of Kildonan's residents, William Young acknowledged, there would be people who were too 'old and infirm' to go north. For that reason, as well as to provide for such 'tradesmen and labourers' as might be needed to work on the strath's new sheep farms, he would permit both the elderly and some labouring men to put up homes for themselves on a 150-acre piece of land to be set aside for this purpose in the vicinity of Alexander Sage's manse.[4]

In return for those concessions, Young intimated, he wanted all the Strath of Kildonan's menfolk to meet at the district's parish school on Tuesday 2 February and there put their names to 'a bond for the preservation of the peace'; this bond being intended to prevent any further obstruction or harassment of 'shepherds . . . and all others who are or may be concerned in sheep farming'. To this proposal, it seems, the men with whom the factor spoke at Rhives gave their assent. Despite his scepticism as to the wisdom of awarding anyone from Kildonan any kind of hearing, Patrick Sellar duly informed the Marchioness of Stafford, three or four days in advance of the planned gathering, that it would surely bring about 'a peaceful termination' of the 'mad attempt' that had been made to obstruct 'improvement'.[5]

This optimism proved misplaced. Perhaps the Kildonan tenants who had been 'feasted' as well as plied with beer by William Young had simply told their host what he wanted to hear. Or perhaps Young – who described the individuals in question as 'the most decent' folk he could find in the Strath of Kildonan – had put his trust in a moderate but unrepresentative group who, on going home, found themselves overruled by a more militant majority. On 2 February 1813, at all events, the deputation William Young sent to Kildonan with his carefully drawn-up 'bond' was met by between 100 and 200 men who made clear both that the bond would remain unsigned and that they had no intention of accepting Young's proffered crofts.[6]

In anticipating a radically different outcome, both Young and Patrick Sellar – irrespective of what did or did not take place at Rhives – may well have fallen victim, as they, the Staffords and their allies often did, to their own propaganda. A key contention of this propaganda (as indicated earlier) was the notion that Sutherland's coasts offered the county's inhabitants much better prospects than were available in its inland valleys. Anyone convinced of this – and it became something of an article of faith with Sellar, Young and, a little later, James Loch – was bound to expect people to be willing, even eager, to migrate from the Strath of Kildonan to Strathy and Armadale.

All such expectations foundered on the fact that Kildonan people believed their strath to be a far more appropriate spot in which to grow crops and raise cattle than any north coast locality. Nor were the Kildonan folk alone in this belief. In a book published just as Sellar and Young took over the management of the Sutherland Estate, John Henderson, a Caithness man and an authority on Highland agriculture, endorsed the Kildonan opinion. Because Sutherland's north coast was 'exposed to frequent rains and stormy weather', Henderson observed, its 'crops of corn' were 'so stunted in their growth as to be too short for the sickle'. That of course was why for hundreds, indeed thousands, of years – as the archaeological record demonstrates – people had been much less inclined to set up home on Armadale and Strathy's windswept coastal fringe than in the comparatively sheltered setting of places like Kildonan.[7]

The Strath of Kildonan (to repeat a previous point) was no more immune from occasional crop failures and the hardship they brought with them than was the rest of the early nineteenth-century world – one such failure, in 1807, leading to the loss of hundreds of Kildonan cattle the following spring. But such setbacks (as will be seen) were not nearly so catastrophic as the 'improvement' lobby made out. They were certainly nothing like so damaging as to persuade the strath's agriculturalists that it would be sensible for them to move to three-acre crofts where harvests would be forever meagre and where, as Young conceded, they would be unable to keep more than a couple of breeding cattle apiece, as opposed to the 10, 20, 30 or more that many of them pastured in and around interior townships of the sort Young and Sellar were so anxious to depopulate.[8]

Sutherland's sheriff at this point was George Cranstoun, a leading Edinburgh lawyer. Committed to building up his city-based practice and to keeping in touch with eminent friends like Walter Scott, Cranstoun tended to treat his Highland sheriffship as something of a sinecure, with the result that the administration of justice in Sutherland was, for most practical purposes, in the care of the sheriff's second-in-command or substitute, Robert McKid. McKid would afterwards fall out spectacularly with the Staffords and their estate managers, particularly Patrick Sellar. In 1813, however, Sheriff McKid (substitutes and their principals sharing the same title) was as ready to do William Young's bidding as a later sheriff would be to help with James Loch's persecution of Gordon Ross. In accordance with Young's instructions, therefore, McKid travelled to Kildonan on 2 February in the company of Patrick Sellar and a posse of constables. On encountering the crowd that had gathered outside the Kildonan school in advance of his party's arrival, the sheriff made sure that everyone present understood the terms of Young's bond, one of McKid's subordinates explaining those terms in Gaelic. But this had no effect on people intent on having nothing to do with the factor's plans for them. McKid, in consequence, took his leave. Before he did so, however, he announced that he would be staying overnight in Helmsdale Inn and that anyone willing to reconsider their position could find him there in the morning.[9]

That evening, a number of the Strath of Kildonan's rebel tenants met, as they had done the night prior to the disturbances of 6 January, in the home of John Gordon, Killernan's miller. There they decided to compile, for Robert McKid's benefit, a statement of their aims. This statement took the form of a letter to the sheriff – a letter that began by stressing that its authors were 'loyal' subjects of Britain's king and, as such, 'submitive [*sic*] to all the laws and taxes laid on [them] by government'. What they wanted, the Kildonan men indicated, was a chance to compete on an equal basis for the various 'grounds' the Staffords and their agents were about to let to William Clunes and Gabriel Reed. If granted such an opportunity, or so their letter stated, Kildonan people would match – on a collective basis – rents on offer from Reed, Clunes or any other sheep farmer.[10]

This letter was entrusted to John Bannerman, one of its compilers, who, being resident at Ulbster in the lower part of the strath, was well placed to deliver it, next morning, to Robert McKid. This Bannerman did. To the Ulbster man's fury, however, he found McKid less interested in what the Kildonan tenantry's letter contained than in establishing who had helped write it, the sheriff being convinced, as one of his aides put it, that this 'information . . . might lead to a discovery of . . . illegal proceedings'. John Bannerman, therefore, was placed under guard and 'judicially examined'. On a defiant Bannerman refusing to name names, McKid ordered his arrest and told him that, unless he talked, which he did not, he would be sent under escort to Dornoch Jail.[11]

Word of this development spread quickly up the Strath of Kildonan where yet another meeting was convened at John Gordon's Killernan mill. Some of the people in attendance – and the mill, one of them said, 'was crowded to the door' – were minded to set off south by way of Glen Loth in order to 'intercept . . . and rescue' John Bannerman before Sheriff McKid and his Dornoch-bound party reached Brora. Cooler counsel prevailed, however. Bannerman, it was agreed, had been 'made prisoner contrary to law and justice'. But instead of trying to liberate him by force, his friends and neighbours resolved simply to let the imprisoned Ulbster tenant know that 'money would be collected for him and bail found'. On the necessary £60 (equivalent to an SSPCK teacher's earnings over four years) being quickly raised, Bannerman was released. But such trust as the Kildonan people might have had in McKid or William Young – assumed, rightly or wrongly, to be party to the sheriff's actions – now evaporated. From 3 February forward, neither Young nor Robert McKid was regarded in the Strath of Kildonan with anything other than hostility.[12]

That hostility was reciprocated. William Young, by whom the Kildonan people were increasingly seen as 'a banditti . . . in open rebellion', heartily endorsed Sheriff McKid's decision to follow up the arrest of John Bannerman with the apprehension of as many as possible of the other men involved in a protest movement now more than a month old. At this movement's core, according to Patrick Sellar, were some 50 'desperadoes' or 'daring fellows' of the sort who had told Sellar, when he and McKid met with them in the Strath of Kildonan on Tuesday 2 February that, irrespective of the wishes of the Marquis and Marchioness of Stafford, they were 'entitled to keep possession' of what they defiantly called 'their grounds'. Sellar, as a newcomer to Sutherland, had little chance of identifying people who were mostly strangers to him. But when William Clunes, James Hall, Ralph Reed, the Turnbull family and others who had been on the receiving end of 6 January's 'riotous conduct' were questioned by Robert McKid, some names began to emerge. This enabled

McKid to order the seizure of 15 or more Kildonan residents, warrants for their arrest being entrusted, as was customary, to a sheriff-officer.[13]

The sheriff-officer in question was Donald Bannerman, who eight years later would supervise Ascoilemore's clearance. Bannerman lived near Golspie, but it is by no means improbable that he had some sort of family connection with the Strath of Kildonan where his was a common surname. That, indeed, might be why Bannerman was given the job of serving warrants in the strath, local knowledge being helpful to anyone tasked with finding people not wanting to be found. Conversely of course, a man seen to be harassing and intimidating families he knew, and had perhaps grown up among, would have been regarded with particular loathing, as Donald Bannerman certainly was in much of Sutherland where, well into the twentieth century, his name was recalled (as will be seen) with detestation.

That detestation, to be sure, may have stemmed more from Bannerman's subsequent role in the destruction of hundreds of Sutherland homes than from his activities in February 1813 when, if anything, Kildonan's population got the better of the sheriff-officer and the three colleagues with whom he spent a couple of days in the strath. At the end of their first day, which took them as far west as Suisgill, the four men were taken in for the night by Donald Murray, the dramseller whose wife Jean had warned the Turnbulls and their guests of impending trouble on the morning of 6 January. But the Murrays – whose local unpopularity must have been almost as great as Donald Bannerman's – were the only Strath of Kildonan residents willing to extend a helping hand to the sheriff-officer and his assistants. The men whom he was looking for, Bannerman soon learned, had mostly quit their homes and taken to the hills the moment they heard he had entered the strath. Those who remained were protected by their neighbours who, the sheriff-officer said, 'assembled in crowds around him and his party'. Such was 'the general state of the public mind' in Kildonan, Bannerman went on, that 'if he had proceeded . . . to put . . . warrant[s] into execution . . . he [was] certain that he and his party would have been maltreated if not murdered'. Rather than apprehend anyone, therefore, Donald Bannerman confined himself to making known that the individuals named in his warrants had been ordered to report to Sheriff Robert McKid at Golspie Inn on Wednesday 10 February, when, or so Bannerman appears to have suggested to anyone prepared to listen, the sheriff would do no more than hold an evidence-taking session in connection with his continuing enquiries into the events of early January.[14]

This fooled nobody. Even before he left the Strath of Kildonan, the sheriff-officer acknowledged, he had been accosted by George MacKay, the locality's much-respected catechist, who told him – 'with tears in his eyes' – that practically everyone in the strath was of the opinion that any man who went to Golspie as instructed would be taken into custody in much the same underhand way as John Bannerman had earlier been seized by Robert McKid. If any such arrests were made in Golspie, MacKay warned, there would be trouble such 'as never happened in Sutherland before'.[15]

George MacKay's words proved prophetic. Soon the Kildonan men had resolved to go in force to Golspie on the morning of 10 February with the aim of forestalling further jailings. Not content with this, they decided to beef up their campaign by enlisting allies. In the run-up to 10 February, therefore, envoys were sent both north and south. Those who went north travelled well into Caithness, a county where, the Kildonan emissaries warned, farm rents would be put under upward pressure if or when evicted families from Sutherland came looking for new homes. Although an accurate prediction of what eventually occurred, this was perhaps a less rousing call to action than the one delivered by the strath's southbound representatives whose destination was Strathbrora. There, in township after township, the Kildonan messengers said simply (and correctly) that if Kildonan was depopulated 'to make room for sheep farmers', other localities were bound sooner or later to suffer the same fate. The result was that the Kildonan people, when making for Golspie Inn on the morning of Wednesday 10 February, were reinforced by a substantial contingent from Strathbrora.[16]

Golspie Inn – where Sheriff McKid, Donald Bannerman, several more constables, William Young and Patrick Sellar met early that same morning – was just five years old in 1813. In 1808, the then newly completed inn – owned, like everything else in its vicinity, by Lord and Lady Stafford – was described by the marchioness as 'an excellent house'. Its management, Lady Stafford continued, had been entrusted to James Duncan, formerly a grieve or foreman on the 'home farm' which supplied Dunrobin Castle, less than a mile from the inn, with fresh provisions. Duncan, according to Lady Stafford, was 'an intelligent man [who had] a good-looking wife', such a wife, it seems, being thought an important aid to success in the innkeeping business. But however profitable his Golspie hostelry might have been, James Duncan must have wished himself elsewhere when, on looking out at around midday on 10 February 1813, he saw 'assembled at his door', as he said, 'a vast crowd of people . . . each of them armed with a bludgeon'.[17]

The sheer size of this crowd took James Duncan and his inn's other occupants by surprise. Although men from Strathbrora and Kildonan – men who had left home well before first light – had been entering Golspie for some time, they had succeeded in concealing their numbers by slipping into the village, as one of them put it, in widely separated groups 'of five and six at a time'. For much of the morning, then, McKid, Young and their colleagues appear to have thought that the only people planning to turn up at the inn were the comparatively few folk who had been told by Donald Bannerman, in the course of the latter's otherwise unproductive foray into the Strath of Kildonan, to make themselves available for interview by Sheriff McKid. A less than subtle subterfuge from the outset, this plan – instead of culminating, as McKid had hoped, in several arrests – now looked increasingly likely to end in yet another victory for the Kildonan protest movement. This was confirmed when

Patrick Sellar, a man not lacking in courage, took it upon himself to leave the inn in order to discover the Kildonan and Strathbrora people's intentions. 'Their purpose', Sellar reported, 'was to prevent the arrest of [their] ringleaders . . . [and] they were determined . . . to stand as one man in defence of [what they regarded as] their land and their property. On my endeavouring to point out the folly of a handful of men pretending to fight against [Britain's] laws and . . . constitution . . . they said they were loyal men whose brothers and sons [as was indeed the case] were fighting [Napoleon] Buonaparte* . . . [but] they would allow no sheep to come into the country.'[18]

From the besieged inn's windows, meanwhile, Donald Bannerman had been scanning the people milling about outside and had established, he told Sheriff McKid, that Kildonan men he had ordered to Golspie were among them. On learning this, McKid instructed Bannerman to take 'a party' and 'proceed to apprehend' individuals scheduled for arrest, starting with John Sutherland and Donald Polson. Sutherland (mentioned earlier in connection with his daughter's wedding) was one of the Kildonan uprising's leaders and, like Polson, had been a regular attender at the Killernan meetings where protest tactics were debated and agreed. Both men, on hearing Bannerman order that they be 'take[n] . . . into custody', were inclined initially to step forward and surrender themselves. But seeing this, 'people took hold of [them]', or so it was said later, 'by the skirts of their coats and pulled them [back] into the crowd'. Masterminding this piece of defiance, according to James Duncan who saw what happened, was a young man by the name of Robert Bruce. Bruce, whose home was in one of the communities due to be incorporated into Gabriel Reed's Kilcalmkill farm, grabbed either Polson or Sutherland with his left hand 'while, with his right hand, he brandished his stick above [Donald Bannerman's] head'.[19]

To obstruct, assault or, in legal jargon, 'deforce' a court officer like Bannerman in this way was to commit a crime. Hence Sheriff

---

* Sutherland involvements in the Napoleonic Wars are examined in Chapter 7.

McKid's decision to put formally on record that he had been obliged
to give up his latest attempt to restore order in Sutherland as a result
of Golspie Inn having been 'surrounded by a lawless mob . . . who
have exultingly . . . deforced the officers of the law by preventing
certain individuals from being brought forward for examination'.
He had himself commanded this mob, 'in the king's name', to
disperse, the sheriff went on, and one of his subordinates had translated this edict into Gaelic. But irrespective of the language in which
they were delivered, his orders had been ignored and, fearing for
their safety, he and the people with him had accordingly been obliged
to abandon the inn and retreat – amid, it can be assumed, much
derisive jeering – to Dunrobin Castle.[20]

Secure behind the castle's walls, Robert McKid, William Young
and Patrick Sellar considered their next move. Had they judged it
prudent, Sellar remarked in a subsequent letter to the Marchioness
of Stafford, he and Young could have got together '140 south country men' – themselves, their assistants, sheep farmers and those
farmers' shepherds – with a view to 'speedily' bringing their opponents 'into submission'. 'But . . . by such a measure,' Sellar noted,
'lives would have been endangered and a *judicial investigation*
[would have] followed.' As hinted by Patrick Sellar's underlinings,
indicated here by italics, any such externally directed enquiry (which
Sellar thought would be 'more unpleasant' than the 'riot' of 10
February) was, from his and Young's perspective, to be avoided at all
costs. This was because of the risk of its opening up to public and
political scrutiny the extent of their planned evictions. Much better,
Young and Sellar concluded, to put matters in the hands of Robert
McKid's superior, George Cranstoun, who (in his role as Sutherland's
sheriff-principal) was entitled to ask for backing from the military if,
in his opinion, order could not be restored to his sheriffdom in any
other way. Just such a course of action, Lord and Lady Stafford were
informed, had been suggested to Cranstoun by both McKid and
Young. But they had taken care, Young assured the marchioness, to
let Sheriff Cranstoun know that he should do nothing until he was

clear as to 'Lord Stafford and your Ladyship's pleasure on the subject' – law enforcement being understood by Young, as it was understood by everyone in early nineteenth-century Sutherland, to be less a matter for the state and its appointees than for the Stafford family.[21]

Less than a week after the disturbances of 10 February 1813, events on the Sutherland Estate began to engage the attention of the man who – some years later and by way of completing what William Young and Patrick Sellar had begun – would plan and oversee the almost total depopulation of localities like the Strath of Kildonan and Strathbrora. This man was James Loch. In his early thirties and just six months into his job as the Stafford family's 'commissioner', Loch, whose role approximated to that of chief executive officer (CEO) of a present-day corporation, was already well on the way to becoming what he would remain for more than 40 years – the marquis and marchioness's close confidant as well as their principal man of business. That may be why, despite his formal remit being confined at this stage to Lord Stafford's English properties, Loch did not hesitate to intervene in Sutherland developments, which, he recognised, had the potential to embroil his employer in a crisis of the first magnitude. It was with a view to averting or limiting this crisis that James Loch, in response to the arrival in his London office of the first panicky accounts of what had had transpired in Golspie, wrote at once to George Cranstoun – 'with whom I am acquainted,' Loch noted – to impress on Cranstoun 'in the strongest manner' the 'necessity of his immediately going to Sutherland'.[22]

Cranstoun, a contemporary of Loch's and, like the Stafford commissioner, a product of Edinburgh University, had elected, unlike Loch who moved south on graduating, to remain in the Scottish capital where, by 1813 or shortly after, this up-and-coming lawyer's annual earnings equated to several hundred thousand pounds at present-day values. Described by a colleague as a man of 'decided and confident . . . opinions', Cranstoun did not react positively to James Loch's demand – which is what it amounted to – that, at the busiest time of year in Scotland's courts, he should set aside his caseload and board a coach for the north. Both the sheriff and his clients, the Marchioness of Stafford learned, found compliance with Loch's wishes 'extremely inconvenient'. But George Cranstoun, who had never expected to have to grapple personally with the affairs of what a Scottish politician categorised that same month as a 'distant county', was starting to discover that Sutherland's sheriffship came with strings attached – strings pulled, whenever they felt so inclined, by Lord and Lady Stafford or (which came to the same thing) by James Loch.[23]

Before leaving for the Highlands, Cranstoun made contact with Archibald Colquhoun MP, Scotland's lord advocate and thus the government's principal representative north of the border. Cranstoun, Loch had suggested, should ask Colquhoun for authorisation to call on the army for such assistance as he might find he required when he got to Sutherland. Colquhoun, a man said to be 'most distinguished for his zeal and forwardness' in combating dissent and sedition of all kinds, was happy to oblige. 'In Sutherland', the lord advocate told Lord Sidmouth, whom the prime minister, Lord Liverpool, had made home secretary the year before, 'small farms are . . . converting into sheep farms and the possessors of the small farms are endeavouring by threats of violence to maintain themselves in possession [and] to prevent the new system of sheep farming from being established.' In most circumstances, Colquhoun went on, trouble of this sort could be dealt with by local militia units. These were composed of part-time soldiers and were available for mobilisation in every part of Scotland. No such mobilisation, however, could be contemplated in Sutherland. There, Colquhoun explained, 'most of the local militiamen are either themselves [among] . . . those who are to be dispossessed or entertain the same [anti-sheep-farming] sentiments'. It was for this reason, the lord advocate informed Sidmouth, that General William Wynard, military commander in Scotland, had been instructed to supply Sheriff

Cranstoun, should the need arise, with a battalion of regular troops.[24]

The lord advocate's apprehensions about the intentions of Sutherland militiamen were stoked by Cranstoun in a letter the sheriff mailed to the lord advocate some days after his arrival in the north. In addition to the 300 or more 'able-bodied' males they could call out from their own strath, George Cranstoun reported, the Kildonan protestors were confident of getting support from 'neighbouring parishes' and had accordingly 'give[n] out that they can muster 1,800 men' – 'a great proportion of whom', the sheriff added, were likely to have served in the army or to be militiamen with access to firearms. Cranstoun's fears of an armed insurrection in Sutherland may have been exaggerated, but the sheriff was set on taking no chances. In early March, every militia unit in Sutherland was ordered to turn in its muskets and other weapons. This order, with some reluctance in one or two instances, was obeyed.[25]

Aggressive acts like disarming militiamen had not been on George Cranstoun's agenda when he first reached Sutherland. Knowing, as he acknowledged, that he was seen widely to be 'acting not on behalf of the public but merely [on behalf] of Lady Stafford', Cranstoun declined to take up James Loch's offer of accommodation in Dunrobin Castle, preferring to find his own lodgings. Nor was this his only gesture of independence – an independence which Loch, in time, would find insupportable. William Young and Patrick Sellar, Cranstoun felt, were proceeding far too hastily in the Strath of Kildonan, where they wanted families earmarked for eviction to quit their homes by the end of May. This, George Cranstoun pointed out to William MacKenzie, the marquis and marchioness's Edinburgh lawyer, meant that evicted tenants – most of whose livestock would have to be sold in advance of their moving to Sutherland's north coast – were bound to end up disposing of cattle at a time of year when, with winter just over, these cattle would be in poor condition. The only available buyers, Cranstoun commented to MacKenzie, would be dealers who, 'knowing that [the Kildonan people] must sell would get [their cattle] for nothing'. Even James Loch, not given to backing down, was obliged to acknowledge the justice of this point and to assure Cranstoun that measures would be taken 'to prevent [anyone] losing by their being forced to part with their cattle too speedily'.[26]

Nothing of this went down well with William Young, who felt that both Loch and George Cranstoun were repeating his own mistake of a month earlier by giving too much ground to people Young now thought 'a set of savages'. The factor, in fact, was beginning to wish he had never come to Sutherland. 'All [his] movements', Young was sure, '[were] watched.' He found himself 'situated in this remote quarter', he grumbled, 'without a friend to consult except Mr Sellar'. The one piece of good news Young had to convey to Loch was that Cranstoun had agreed to 'dine' with him at his Rhives home on Saturday 27 February. This, presumably, gave Young a chance to urge the sheriff not to listen to anything said by way of excusing the conduct of the 'Kildonaners' as Young called them. That certainly was the stance the factor took when, next day and no doubt by way of reinforcing arguments advanced the night before, he wrote at length to the sheriff, stressing that no 'oppressive measures' had been taken in the Strath of Kildonan and insisting, as the Staffords and their agents were always to insist, that people expelled from homes in Sutherland's interior would gain, not lose, by being so treated.[27]

'The lands which these people occupy are not adapted for raising grain,' Young wrote of the Strath of Kildonan's inhabitants. Their 'situation' was 'bleak and cold'. The locality was 'only adapted for rearing of sheep' and its occupants would be much better off on the three-acre crofts to be provided for them on Sutherland's north coast where, 'by industry and labour', they would 'earn a decent subsistence' and where, as the factor put it, 'such . . . young men as choose to adventure in fishing may have it in their power to do so'.[28]

William Young's contention that the windswept and harbourless coastline of Armadale and Strathy lent itself to the development of a flourishing fishery was as far-fetched as was the notion that to have a three-acre croft and two cows in that same northerly quarter was a marked improvement on having 10 or 15 times more cattle – to say nothing of a substantial stake in a long-established and well-cultivated township – in the Strath of Kildonan. Had George Cranstoun been minded to repeat Young's offer to the strath's tenants, then, they would have rejected this offer every bit as robustly as when it had first been put to them a month earlier. The sheriff, however, got no such opportunity. When he invited Kildonan people to meet with him in Helmsdale on Tuesday 2 March – thereby 'indulging' lawbreakers in William Young's jaundiced view – only the Reverend Alexander Sage and 'a very few' of the strath's other residents turned up. Word was accordingly conveyed to the men whom Robert McKid had planned to arrest in Golspie on 10 February that, on 9 March, they were to come to Helmsdale where Cranstoun, at what would amount to a specially convened session of Sutherland's sheriff court, planned to subject them to formal questioning.[29]

No such court session took place. At Helmsdale on 9 March, George Cranstoun found himself with nothing to do but read a letter informing him that 'we the people of the parish of Kildonan who was [*sic*] summoned to appear at a court to be held at Helmsdale this day . . . do beg and request as a favour . . . [that Sheriff Cranstoun] defer this court for fifteen days'. This letter, it can be surmised, was the work of the 14-strong 'committee', as its members designated themselves, now co-ordinating the Strath of Kildonan rebellion. The committee – or 'Kildonan Privy Council' as it was dubbed derisively by William Young – consisted of a cross-section of the strath's leading tenants. Among its members were John Sutherland and Donald Polson, the men snatched from Sheriff-Officer Donald Bannerman's clutches at Golspie on 10 February. Polson, Sutherland and their colleagues, it emerged, had taken legal advice – from whom is not clear – and, acting on this advice, they had drawn up and put their names to two 'memorials' or 'petitions'. The first was addressed to the Marquis and Marchioness of Stafford on the slim chance that they might yet be persuaded to call off all planned evictions. The second petition, drafted on the assumption (soon proved correct) that the first would be rejected, contained an appeal for government intervention on the Sutherland Estate tenantry's side.[30]

By Tuesday 9 March, those petitions had reached London, home at that time of year to the Staffords as well as to government ministers. By asking Sheriff Cranstoun to postpone for a fortnight or more the court hearing he had intended to convene in Helmsdale, the Strath of Kildonan committee was looking to gain time. In the course of the ensuing two weeks, or so committee members hoped, news would reach them from the south that their pleas for help had got a hearing.

The Kildonan protestors did not entrust their petitions to the mail. Instead they gave them to a man prepared both to take the petitions personally to London and, on getting there, to negotiate with interested parties on Kildonan people's behalf. This was William MacDonald, whose home was in Brora and who, until his retirement in 1812, had been a recruiting sergeant attached to the army's 93rd Regiment. In 1813, the 93rd (of which more later) was stationed in South Africa. But the regiment had been raised in Sutherland, and it was to Sutherland that its commanders continued to look for recruits of the sort that the 50-year-old MacDonald – who first joined the military in 1779 – had been responsible for finding.[31]

William Young could not make up his mind whether it was best to portray William MacDonald as a politically motivated troublemaker or a wastrel, describing the ex-soldier at different points as an 'infamous vagabond' and 'a perfect incendiary'. But for all the attempts thus made by the Sutherland Estate management to blacken MacDonald's character, members of the Strath of Kildonan's protest co-ordination committee – who provided MacDonald with a travel and expenses fund worth well over £1,000 at present-day values – knew what they were about when they asked the sergeant to act for them. MacDonald might have been vilified and belittled by Young, but he was highly esteemed by his military superiors. One senior officer, Colonel John Halkett, described the sergeant as 'uncommonly assiduous'. This was endorsed by General William Wemyss who had been in charge of the 93rd Regiment when it took shape around 1800 and who, in 1812, was instrumental in securing for MacDonald a service pension of some £33 annually – no small income at a time when an SSPCK schoolteacher like Gordon Ross was expected to get by on less than half that sum. Wemyss, an MP, knew the Marchioness of Stafford – to whom he was related – and was otherwise well connected in London. The general, or so members of the Kildonan 'privy council' must have calculated, could be relied on to put his former recruiting sergeant in touch with people of influence. In so calculating, the Kildonan men were right.[32]

Nor would the Kildonan committee have been unaware of William MacDonald's links with another network whose members were just as likely as General Wemyss to take a pro-Kildonan stance. One of the sergeant's cousins was married to John Sutherland of Sciberscross, whom William Young suspected of having encouraged MacDonald to aid the 'Kildonaner' rebels. While by no means as eminent as William Wemyss, Sutherland, like the general, was an ex-soldier. He was also fiercely critical, as the Kildonan leadership was well aware, of the Staffords and their policies. Equally critical of those policies, and known in the north to be so, was John Sutherland's younger brother, Alexander, who lived in London and who – though this was not yet apparent – would do more than anyone else to ensure that the Sutherland clearances and their organisers acquired the infamy that began to cling to them during 1813 and, to no small extent, would continue to do so for the next 200 years.[33]

Sciberscross, a Strathbrora landholding eventually converted into a sheep farm by James Hall, one of the men chased out of Kildonan at the beginning of January 1813, had been tenanted by successive generations of John and Alexander Sutherland's forebears. While many of the Kildonan tenants whom William MacDonald agreed to represent had equally long-standing links with their locality, there was a key distinction between them and the Sciberscross family. The Kildonan men were working farmers. The Sutherlands of Sciberscross, as indicated by their having a territorial designation attached formally to their surname, belonged to the higher-ranking social group known in Gaelic as *daoine uaisle*, a phrase best, if not quite adequately, translated as 'gentry'. Called tacksmen in English – a tack (as noted previously) being a tenancy – the *daoine uaisle*, who stood just below chiefs in clanship's pecking order, provided Highland clans with their command class. Hence the ease with which men like Alexander and John Sutherland, both of whom reached the rank of captain in infantry regiments, made the transition – following clanship's collapse – from one sort of military service to another. Hence too their aspirations to a status well above that of men who herded cattle, cultivated crops or otherwise worked farms of the Kildonan variety. They were 'comfortable in their accommodations, intelligent, polite in their manners [and] hospitable in their houses', the agricultural commentator John Henderson wrote of tacksmen like the Sutherlands of Sciberscross. They were also accustomed to sustaining their comfortable lifestyles by parcelling out the bulk of their land among hosts of subtenants, the latter, on a typical tack, collectively paying its tacksman a good deal more by way of rent than the tacksman, in turn, paid to his landlord.[34]

From the standpoint of men like William Young and Patrick Sellar, always more interested in boosting estate revenues than in keeping in place what they regarded as a leftover caste of gentlemen warriors, tacksmen were just one more obstacle in the way of commercialised land management. While it was by no means impossible for someone of tacksman background – as shown by William Clunes of Crakaig – to transform himself into the kind of farmer Sellar and Young were anxious to encourage, this was unusual. Most tacksmen, and John Sutherland of Sciberscross was definitely in this category, wanted nothing to do with 'improvement', and so refused point-blank to embrace change of the sort being imposed on the Sutherland Estate. Thus it came about that, in February 1813, John

Sutherland, fearing for his future at Sciberscross and already at daggers drawn with William Young and Patrick Sellar because of steps they had taken to ease him out of another tack he held in the vicinity of Brora, began to give covert aid to the Kildonan rebels. Signing himself 'A Traveller' and mailing his letter (by way of further disguising its authorship) from Tain in Easter Ross, Sutherland wrote to Sheriff Cranstoun whom he urged to listen sympathetically to Kildonan people's grievances. This backfired, the identity of the supposed 'traveller' soon being deduced by the Sutherland Estate management. Of more enduring help to the Kildonan cause was the Sciberscross tacksman's decision, also made in February 1813, to encourage his London-based brother, Alexander, to do what he could to interest the national press in Sutherland people's mounting hostility to the Marquis and Marchioness of Stafford's 'improvement' agenda.[35]

Alexander Sutherland, as it happened, had his own reasons for harbouring a deep dislike of the Staffords and all their works. Some two or three years prior to 1813, Alexander, then in his mid-forties and not long quit of the army, conceived an ambition to come home to Strathbrora where he hoped to lease Gordonbush from its then owner, Joseph Gordon. Joseph, already well embarked on his legal career in Edinburgh, appears to have been open to such an arrangement. But before negotiations could be concluded, the Marquis of Stafford, urged on by the marchioness in Alexander's version of events, stepped in and, by making Joseph Gordon an offer he could not refuse, added Gordonbush (with results described previously) to the Sutherland Estate. 'This she did in sheer malice to me,' Alexander wrote of Lady Stafford's role in these proceedings. That may seem unlikely. But it was a belief Alexander Sutherland never gave up, and it added a highly personal dimension to the attack which, in March 1813, he launched on the marchioness, the marquis and their agents who, as Alexander saw it, had so maltreated and abused the population of the Strath of Kildonan as to have left this population with no alternative but to revolt.[36]

Alexander Sutherland – described by an obituarist as 'a man of considerable intellectual powers and . . . ardent in the interests of . . . the Highlands of Scotland' – lived, during the period following his Gordonbush disappointment, in the fast-growing London borough of Kensington. By Lady Stafford he was nicknamed 'Alex Ink', this being a sneering reference to his relying for part of his income on the ungentlemanly trade of journalism. But his mastery of that trade – Alexander knowing exactly how to conduct an eye-catching press campaign – made him a dangerous adversary. This began to be evident to a duly enraged Marchioness of Stafford on 16 March 1813 when *The Star*, then London's leading evening newspaper, carried an article headlined 'Disturbances in Sutherland'. Attributed simply to 'A Highlander' from that county,* this article described how inhabitants of the 'populous district' of Kildonan, rather than acquiesce in their 'removal . . . from localities very dear to them', had embarked on a campaign of 'open and determined resistance' to their expulsion. This expulsion, it was made clear, had been ordered by Lord and Lady Stafford who, instead of contenting themselves with the immense riches they already possessed, were intent, or so it was implied, on adding to those riches by destroying communities that, quite apart from their other claims on public sympathy, were home to some of the finest troops Britain had ever possessed.[37]

This was a shrewd hit on Alexander Sutherland's part. Readers of *The Star* might not have been gripped by the rights and wrongs of land-use changes in the north of Scotland, but all of them appreciated the contribution Highland regiments had made and were making to the United Kingdom's apparently never-ending war with Napoleonic France, which, as every British patriot was happily aware, had just suffered a massive reverse at the hands of Tsarist Russia. 'I should be glad to know', Alexander Sutherland wrote by way of driving home his point, 'what had been the fate of Russia if

* Sutherland was later to acknowledge his authorship of this and subsequent *Star* articles.

... instead of a populous, brave and loyal peasantry ... she had only [available] to oppose [Napoleon] flocks of sheep.'[38]

By the Stafford camp, Alexander Sutherland was promptly designated 'a wicked libeller' and a 'desperate character' whom William Young wanted taken into custody in the hope that 'letters ... found among his papers' might reveal exactly who, apart from Alexander and his Sciberscross brother, was offering aid and comfort to the Kildonan dissidents. It was 'really quite provoking to see the whole kingdom so much taken up' with the Strath of Kildonan and its doings, Young complained. The marchioness felt similarly. What was needed, she thought, was a counter-attack, one shortly to be launched, at Lady Stafford's instigation, by Sir Humphry Davy, pioneer chemist and one of the foremost scientists of his day.[39]

Davy, though of lowly origins in Cornwall, liked nothing better than to be on good terms with aristocrats, even if, on occasion, they made mock of his provincial upbringing. Thus it came about that when, in the summer of 1812, the then newly married Davy and his bride spent their honeymoon in Scotland, the couple were put up for a week or two at Dunrobin. 'This house is ... delightful, the scenery ... grand and the field sports ... perfect,' Sir Humphry wrote to a friend from Sutherland where, in the space of just a few days, the honeymooning scientist, a keen angler, took no fewer than 30 salmon from the River Brora.[40]

But Dunrobin's delights, Humphry Davy learned in March 1813, were seldom sampled free of charge. Instructed by the Marchioness of Stafford to lobby the editor of *The Star*, a man known to Davy, the scientist had no option but to comply, the paper's editor being pressured, in consequence, to agree that, having already carried two submissions from Alexander Sutherland, he should find space for a letter from 'A Friend to Improvement'. This friend, as the Marchioness of Stafford's correspondence makes clear, was Sir Humphry himself.[41]

Quoting at length from William Young's 28 February letter to George Cranstoun, a copy of which he had been given, Davy set out to rebut Alexander Sutherland's arguments. No 'unprejudiced person', he insisted, could possibly 'censure Lord and Lady Stafford's views with respect to Sutherland'. Their sole aim was 'the permanent benefit of the county and its inhabitants'. Nor was there any question of Sutherland Estate tenants being rendered homeless: 'They are not driven from their country, but may, if it be their choice, be better and more comfortably settled in it . . . They will remain amongst their native mountains, quitting only bleak summits for the warm glen and sheltered plain. They will give up insecurity, as to the means of subsistence, for ample security; and probable distress [meaning hunger] for certain comfort.'[42]

This was a grievous betrayal of his own scientific methods by a man who insisted on accurate observation and who warned repeatedly of the 'dangers of false generalisation'. When in Scotland the previous year, Davy had compiled a geological treatise which concluded that, aside from the area immediately adjacent to the county's east coast, 'the best soils of Sutherland are those in the bottoms of the straths or broad valleys'. Now, at Lady Stafford's behest, he endorsed the emptying of those same 'broad valleys' and the transfer of their population, not to 'warm glens' and 'sheltered plains' of the sort he conjured up for *Star* readers, but to the exposed shores of Armadale and Strathy. The marchioness, however, was pleased by Davy's efforts. Praising the scientist's 'excellent letter', she had 'no doubt things [would] now go on well' with efforts to persuade the public of the justice of what she and her husband were about in the Highlands. In this, the marchioness was mistaken. Days after Humphry Davy got his say in *The Star*, Alexander Sutherland was granted the better part of a broadsheet page on which to develop his analysis of developments in Kildonan.[43]

Reading Alexander Sutherland's words today, it is tempting to assume that his powerful critique of the Staffords and their policies, a critique he elaborated in the years ahead, must have originated in its author's strong sense of solidarity – democratic or even proto-socialist in character – with victims of oppression. This would be wrong. Neither Alexander nor his brother, John of Sciberscross, were in any sense men of the people. Indeed John, when in the end he left the Sutherland Estate, was himself to order evictions – evictions which (as will be seen) were enforced by Donald Bannerman whose activities in Kildonan the Sciberscross tacksman had earlier opposed. The helping hand John Sutherland extended to the Strath of Kildonan's occupants in 1813 is best understood, then, as a product of age-old thinking to the effect that my enemy's enemy (anyone hostile to the Staffords in this instance) is necessarily my friend. Much the same sort of thinking – stemming from his Gordonbush grievances – no doubt played its part in fuelling Alexander Sutherland's anti-Stafford tirades. But those tirades amount, for all that, to rather more than a manifestation of thwarted self-interest. They add up to a comprehensive demolition of 'improvement'.

Alexander, to repeat, was no progressive in the present-day sense. But aggressively expansionist capitalism of the type promoted by the Staffords in Sutherland, it needs recalling in this context, was just as heartily disliked by conservatives as by radicals. Thus early nineteenth-century Britain's most effective scourge of landowning aristocrats like the Staffords was William Cobbett – whose ceaseless castigation of aristocratic conduct was rooted in a profound conviction that the pre-capitalist countryside was in every way preferable to a countryside where cash had become king. Cobbett, towards the end of his life, intended to 'go and inquire . . . into the means used to effect the clearing . . . of the county of Sutherland'. Sadly, he never managed to do this. But if he read Alexander Sutherland's 1813 articles in *The Star*, as he could well have done, William Cobbett would indubitably have agreed with Sutherland's impassioned verdict that there was something far wrong with a world in which 'sheep become the order of the day and Highlanders but objects of secondary consideration'. Like Alexander Sutherland, Cobbett would have wanted those priorities reversed – and the Strath of Kildonan's inhabitants left where they were.[44]

'However plausible on paper', Alexander Sutherland wrote, Lord and Lady Stafford's stated plans for their Highland property were 'in the highest degree illusory'. Some of Kildonan's tenants, he commented, possessed more livestock, especially cattle, than many farmers in England. No one in that position could 'be reasonably expected to feel his condition "improved" by [virtue of his] being transferred to a situation . . . where he is limited to two acres of cornland and grass for two cows'. This was a point which the Marquis of Stafford, his wife, James Loch, William Young and their apologists – whether in 1813 or later – never managed convincingly to refute. Nor were they able to deal satisfactorily with Alexander Sutherland's scornful dismissal of their much-repeated claim that, once installed on Strathy and Armadale crofts, the Strath of Kildonan's former cattle-rearers could instantly be transformed into fishermen.[45]

The locality where this transformation was scheduled to take place, Alexander Sutherland observed, was one where a 'rocky coast' was battered by 'tempestuous seas'. But even if that had not been so, where was the sense in looking to have a fishery manned by people who were – and wanted to remain – agriculturalists? 'If you had a given extent of maritime coast which you thought susceptible of being made a profitable fishing station, in looking around you for the most appropriate crews of boatmen, would it ever enter into your thoughts to fetch those crews from the higher cantons of Switzerland or from the Tyrol? And yet as well might you do so as Mr Young attempt to make fishers of the men of the interior of . . . Kildonan!'[46]

Might material of this sort have been fed to Alexander Sutherland by William MacDonald, who reached London just before Sutherland's *Star* articles began to appear? Sutherland himself denied this – going so far, at one point, as to state he had not met with MacDonald in the capital. That, however, may have been no more than an early instance of a journalist protecting his sources. Sutherland certainly knew MacDonald and, just as certainly, helped

publicise his mission. That was one reason why James Loch, fearing
adverse publicity if he refused to meet with the sergeant, agreed to
do so. But there was an additional such reason. William MacDonald,
as the Kildonan leadership had anticipated, was received hospitably
by General William Wemyss, at whose urging, and in whose London
home, Loch's meeting with MacDonald took place.

This meeting was deplored by William Young who thought that,
if it were not possible to 'apprehend and incarcerate' the sergeant, as
ought to have been done in the factor's opinion, then steps should
certainly have been taken to deprive him of his army pension. Loch
was more realistic. 'MacDonald', he told Young, 'had done nothing
illegal and he therefore could not be touched'. Any attempt to take
away the sergeant's pension, moreover, would at once have been
reported in *The Star* and would have had a bad effect 'upon the
public in London'. Worse, it might well have alienated government
ministers Loch was trying hard to keep on side. William MacDonald,
in short, had to be given his say – which did not imply, James Loch
maintained, any backtracking on his part. 'I saw the ambassador',
James Loch noted condescendingly of his encounter with the
sergeant, 'and desired him to tell [his Kildonan associates] that the
projected arrangements must . . . be carried into full effect.' That
message, Loch hoped, would be reinforced by the imminent deployment in Sutherland of a substantial military detachment.[47]

When, on Tuesday 9 March, the Kildonan men the authorities had
earlier tried to arrest refused for a second time to meet with Sheriff
George Cranstoun in Helmsdale, the sheriff gave the alleged
lawbreakers a last opportunity to come to heel – by letting it be
known that he now expected them to put in an appearance the
following day at Golspie. On nobody from the Strath of Kildonan
turning up that day either, Cranstoun felt himself 'under the disagreeable necessity', as he put it, 'of enforcing the law with the utmost
rigour'. Informing Lord Advocate Colquhoun that 'every conciliatory measure' had been exhausted, the sheriff – acting on the

authority he had obtained before heading north – asked for an army detachment to be sent to Sutherland from Fort George. This was, as it continues to be today, a military base on the Moray Firth's southern shore some 12 miles east of Inverness. Its garrison in 1813 consisted of the 21st Regiment's second battalion.[48]

Although the 21st, which afterwards evolved into the Royal Scots Fusiliers, was one of Scotland's older military formations, its second battalion had been stationed for some years in Ireland – with the result that the unit's rank and file consisted largely of men who were Irish, not Scottish, by birth. Writing nearly 30 years after 1813, Donald MacLeod, a Strathnaver man who became (as will be seen) one of the Stafford family's bitterest critics, made a good deal of this circumstance. Because troops from Sutherland had been deployed against French-backed rebels in Ireland in 1798, MacLeod contended, the 21st Regiment's Irish soldiers welcomed the chance 'to have revenge' on those Sutherland men's home county. In time, that comment would be picked up by novelist Neil Gunn (of whom more later) who saw in this supposed Irish–Highlander clash a typical instance of the British Empire's habit of setting its subject peoples on one another. At various points in the seventeenth and eighteenth centuries, Gunn pointed out, the Gaelic-speaking inhabitants of Ireland and the Highlands had jointly 'threatened the safety of the realm'. 'How wise, therefore, the statecraft that should generate hate between them and send them to destroy each other.'[49]

There is, however, no surviving evidence that Irish troops were despatched to Sutherland with any such purpose. In fact a letter mailed to Alexander Sutherland by an Inverness informant on Monday 15 March, the day that 200 men from the 21st Regiment left Fort George for Golspie in commandeered fishing boats, includes a comment to the opposite effect: 'It was pleasant to hear both officers and men declaring that they would rather . . . meet the French than go against the poor Highlanders.' But if, as it appears, the troops thus shipped across the Moray Firth feared that they might be ordered to fire on Sutherland's civilian population, they need not have worried. The Kildonan people, while willing to do battle with constables and sheriff-officers, had no intention of confronting the 21st Regiment – with the result that, during the week its soldiers were in Sutherland, the only violence they saw resulted from one of them being flogged for having made suggestive remarks to a local woman.[50]

During that same week, as it happened, the Kildonan men whom Sheriff Cranstoun had been trying in vain to interrogate began to present themselves for interview. None, however, were arrested – Cranstoun, to William Young's disgust, soon going so far as to drop all charges arising from either the Kildonan or Golspie disturbances. This conciliatory attitude on the sheriff's part would contribute (as will be seen) to James Loch eventually concluding that George Cranstoun should be levered out of office. In the short run, however, Cranstoun's implicit recognition of the legitimacy of the Kildonan people's aims served mainly to enhance the protest movement's morale. Equally encouraging, from a Kildonan perspective, was news that William MacDonald had succeeded in opening up some prospect of Sutherland people being provided with a future other than the one the Stafford family had in mind for them.

Prior to William MacDonald going south towards the end of February he had been empowered by John Sutherland, Donald Polson and their Kildonan colleagues to approach the British government with a proposal that, if accepted, would result – or so MacDonald was instructed to say – in 700 young men from Sutherland volunteering for military service. This offer was to be made to Frederick, Duke of York, King George III's second son and the British army's commander-in-chief. Since a lot of men from Sutherland were already in the army, and since there was no way that 700 more were available in the Strath of Kildonan alone, this figure could only have been arrived at with the consent of people living in other Sutherland localities such as Strathbrora. That such consent should have been forthcoming is perfectly plausible. There were few

established tenants on the Sutherland Estate who did not feel themselves threatened by 'improvement', and everyone so threatened
would have been delighted if the Duke of York had responded positively to the Kildonan committee's proposition. That was because
this proposition came with strings attached. The promised fighting
men, as emphasised in the documentation taken to London by
William MacDonald, would be put 'at the commander-in-chief's
disposal' only on condition that those men's 'fathers and mothers
and wives and children [could] . . . keep their native home'.[51]

Because Britain's landed interest (consisting of the Marquis of
Stafford and his fellow estate owners) was as dominant politically in
1813 as it was powerful economically, there was next to no chance of
anybody in authority granting any such immunity from eviction to
agricultural tenants – no matter how many soldiers might have been
forthcoming as a result. But if James Loch and the Stafford family
had no fear of William MacDonald getting everything he wanted,
they were nevertheless anxious to minimise the chances of his
extracting concessions of any kind from politicians. Hence the letter
Loch sent on 6 March to James Ingles, a civil servant answering to
Henry Addington, otherwise Lord Sidmouth, the home secretary. At
this point, Loch thought MacDonald would try to make contact,
not with the Duke of York, but with the duke's elder brother, the
future George IV, who had not long before been made Prince Regent
in recognition of the fact that his father had become so ill as to be
incapable of taking decisions. But James Loch's lack of clarity as to
William MacDonald's intentions was neither here nor there. The
Stafford commissioner's primary objective, which he secured, was to
convince government ministers that neither they nor members of the
royal family should have dealings with a man acting on behalf of
people taking part in what the Marchioness of Stafford now called
the 'sort of mutiny' that had broken out in Sutherland.[52]

James Loch's involvement in Sutherland affairs was barely a
month old at this point. But he was already perfecting his favoured
method of dealing with Sutherland dissent – this being to malign

dissenters. In 1821 Loch would brand Ascoilemore's schoolmaster, Gordon Ross, a liar. In 1813 he described the Strath of Kildonan's 'malcontents' in much the same way. Their 'complaints', Loch assured James Ingles, were 'unfounded'. At every point, he wrote, Kildonan's inhabitants had been 'kindly and considerately . . . treated by Lord and Lady Stafford' who, when it 'became necessary to throw a large part of the [Kildonan] district into one farm', had offered affected tenants alternative – and, in Loch's view, superior – landholdings elsewhere. These, however, had been peremptorily rejected by men who had 'openly . . . violated the law and . . . completely defied the power of the local authorities'. There could and should be no concessions to such people – 'or the improvement of . . . [the Sutherland Estate] must forever be abandoned'.[53]

But if it was easy for James Loch to convince James Ingles – and, through him, the home secretary – that William MacDonald should be denied access to royalty and to government, Loch was unable to stop MacDonald winning support from people who, though neither policy-makers nor administrators, were in a position to offer him assistance. Might one of those people have been General William Wemyss, in whose home and in whose company James Loch held his face-to-face meeting with William MacDonald? That surely cannot be ruled out. There is no record of how the 53-year-old Wemyss regarded the patronising, not to say contemptuous, treatment meted out to his veteran sergeant by the 32-year-old and strictly unmilitary James Loch. But it is tempting to suspect that Wemyss may not have been wholly on Loch's side and that he might have had a hand in introducing William MacDonald to the soldier – not far below the general in the army's command structure – who was to ensure that MacDonald did not go back north empty-handed. This was Colonel Archibald Maclaine, a Gaelic-speaking Highlander from Argyll (where his brother owned a substantial estate) and a man with a great deal of military service behind him.

Maclaine's key role in what now unfolded derived from the fact that the instructions given to William MacDonald before he left

Sutherland included a second-best alternative to the Kildonan people's preferred option of being left in place. If the authorities, even in exchange for several hundred troops, were unable or unwilling to prevent the Strath of Kildonan's clearance, then MacDonald was to ask if evicted families – once the promised soldiers were found – might be provided with 'conveyance' to British North America where, as *The Star* reported, they 'had resolved . . . to seek shelter . . . rather than go and starve . . . on the bleak, inhospitable coast pointed out by [Lord and Lady Stafford's] agents as the place of their intended residence'.[54]

James Loch had made it impossible for William MacDonald to put this proposition to ministers. But on its being outlined to Archibald Maclaine, the colonel at once saw its relevance to a venture in which he was then much engaged. This venture was the brainchild of Thomas Douglas, Earl of Selkirk, and arose from the earl's urgent need to grow the population of the colony Selkirk was trying (as he had earlier told veteran fur trader Donald MacKay) to establish at Red River. Since 1811 when (in return for a nominal payment) Selkirk had taken over from the HBC a territory four times the size of Scotland, the earl had not lacked for North American real estate. But peopling this real estate was proving difficult. Just a handful of settlers – from the Hebrides and from Ireland – had been despatched when, in the summer of 1812 and in response to the Royal Navy's seizure of American ships trading with Napoleon's France, the USA declared war on Britain. A US invasion of British territory in present-day Ontario had quickly followed, and, with fighting flaring elsewhere, it looked as if Thomas Douglas's ambitions for Red River would be an early casualty of this new conflict. But nothing if not resourceful, the earl was quick to discern an opportunity where others saw only catastrophe. He decided, as he informed one of his Highland contacts in January 1813, to solve his Red River problem by 'rais[ing] a corps for service in [North] America'. The troops in question, Selkirk believed, could readily be found in the Highlands. But he would embark on their recruitment only if ministers agreed that, once fighting ended, the regiment's soldiers would be settled at Red River and their dependants brought there from Scotland at government expense.[55]

When offered the command of the Earl of Selkirk's projected regiment, Archibald Maclaine – confident that 'the government [would] agree [with] Selkirk's plans' and looking forward, as he put it, to 'trim[ming] the Yankees' jackets in proper style' – had leapt at the opportunity. Now, by way of taking matters forward, Maclaine put William MacDonald directly in touch with Selkirk. A series of meetings followed and to each of the men involved it must have seemed as if the other had been heaven-sent. In William MacDonald, whom he regarded as 'a very active and clever fellow', the Earl of Selkirk saw someone capable of delivering 700 soldiers – the better part of a regiment – who were anxious both to quit the Highlands for North America and to have their families join them there. In Selkirk, the sergeant saw a man of wealth and standing who was keen to recruit troops from Sutherland and who was equally anxious (in consequence of the earl's Red River project) to provide the Strath of Kildonan's population with what seemed, on the face of things, to be a more appealing fresh start than the one on offer from the Sutherland Estate.[56]

At the beginning of April, William MacDonald left London with a commission from Lord Selkirk. This authorised him to compile a list of everyone in the Strath of Kildonan and adjacent districts who might be interested in going to Red River. A fortnight or so later, and just days after MacDonald's return to Sutherland, William Young reported to Lady Stafford on the former recruiting sergeant's new recruitment drive. As it happened, the factor wrote wearily, he too was compiling a list. It contained details of Kildonan residents prepared to take crofts on Sutherland's north coast – and it ran to 'a dozen of names'. On William MacDonald's list, in contrast, were the names of several hundred people. Soon the sergeant's tally would grow to well over a thousand.[57]

5

'DAMNED SAVAGES FROM SCOTLAND'

*Kildonan people leave for Red River and have
to overwinter at Churchill on Hudson Bay*

Five days into April 1814, John Charles, chief trader at Fort
Churchill, a Hudson's Bay Company post close to the bay's western
shore, noted that he had that morning despatched 'an Esquimaux
lad' and an 'Indian' to Churchill Creek 'with a supply of snow-
shoes'. Situated near the spot where the 1,000-mile-long Churchill
River reaches the sea, Fort Churchill was linked to Churchill Creek,
a Churchill River tributary, by a 15-mile trail. At the inland end of
this trail – beyond the boundary between the tundra-like marshes or
muskeg of Hudson Bay's coastal plain and the spruce and tamarack
forests of the subarctic interior – was a little cluster of log cabins.
Thrown up hurriedly the previous fall or autumn, this makeshift
outpost, where John Charles's Aboriginal subordinates unloaded
their snow-shoe-laden sled, was home in April 1814 to between 80
and 90 people from Sutherland.[1]

Those people were ten months into the most gruelling and
protracted journey ever made by emigrants from Europe to North
America. A disease-blighted Atlantic crossing and a bitter Hudson
Bay winter were behind them. But they remained (for reasons
explored shortly) 800 miles short of their intended destination, the
Earl of Selkirk's Red River colony. Hence the Churchill Creek[*]

---

[*] This watercourse has had several names. Originally Churchill Creek, it was known

group's need for the snow-shoes supplied by John Charles. Only with the help of such specialist equipment, or so it was thought by Bay Company men like Charles, would any of Churchill Creek's temporary residents have a reasonable chance of completing their odyssey's next phase – a 150-mile trek to York Factory. This substantial complex was the HBC's North American headquarters. It was also the stepping-off point for anyone venturing into the continental interior by way of the Hayes and Nelson Rivers, which, as explained in Donald MacKay's 1812 letter to Lord Selkirk, constituted the direct route from Hudson Bay to the earl's still-embryonic settlement.

Prior to the advent of air transport, the most straightforward way to get from Fort Churchill to York Factory was by sea. But Hudson Bay in April is frozen coast to coast and, by the HBC's early nineteenth-century operatives, was not reckoned navigable until the third or fourth week of July. From the perspective of emigrants anxious to reach Red River in time to catch the tail end of the crop-sowing season, that ruled out the option of waiting at Churchill until a sea passage to York Factory became feasible. If Red River's aspiring settlers from Sutherland were to obtain any kind of harvest in the fall of 1814, they needed to start voyaging up the Hayes as soon as its ice cover broke in May. This meant that some at least of the Sutherland emigrants needed to quit Churchill Creek for York Factory as soon as winter's grip had slackened sufficiently to make an overland trip possible.

That had long been clear to Archibald McDonald, the man in charge of matters at Churchill Creek. During March, therefore, McDonald selected, from among the younger and fitter of the people for whom he was responsible, the 31 men and 20 women he intended to lead into the snow-blanketed barrens between the Churchill and Hayes Rivers, the latter the more southerly of the two. McDonald,

for a time as Colony Creek because of its 1813–14 association with people bound for Selkirk's colony. Today it is Herriot Creek.

despite (or perhaps because of) his knowing nothing of wilderness travel, expected all to go well. John Charles, aware that nothing akin to McDonald's expedition had been attempted before, was less optimistic. Archibald McDonald's male companions, Fort Churchill's chief trader reckoned, would 'make out with ease', because their frequent winter forays in search of game and firewood, as well as keeping them in training, had accustomed them to the use of snowshoes. Charles worried, however, about the capabilities of what was the first group of European women to have sailed into Hudson Bay. None of the 'females' getting ready to set out for York Factory, Charles pointed out, had walked 'any distance' during the six months they had spent at Churchill Creek. Despite their having been 'directed . . . to be exercised in snowshoes' some days prior to their departure, this did not augur well, Charles thought, for the Sutherland women's capacity to cope with hazards which, the veteran HBC man knew, would test the strongest and ablest of men.[2]

Difficulties – though not always of the sort feared by John Charles – were certainly to arise. But when, just after six o'clock on the morning of Wednesday 6 April, the Sutherland party's long march got under way, it did so in a festive atmosphere. This was encouraged by the stirring sound of the bagpipes played by Robert Gunn who came from the township of Kildonan and who, Archibald McDonald reported, 'took his station in the centre' of the column snaking in 'single files' out of Churchill Creek. At the column's head was an Aboriginal guide (his name featuring nowhere in contemporary records) sent some days earlier from York Factory with a view to ensuring that McDonald and his people took the best way south. The guide, McDonald wrote, was 'followed by the men', all of them hauling sleds piled high with tents, 'bedding' and 'provisions'. This arrangement, Archibald McDonald explained, had the effect – especially in places where 'the snow was soft and deep' – of creating a beaten-down trail that, McDonald hoped, would make it easier for the column's female component to cope with the 'arduous task' of trudging forward, hour after hour, on snow-shoes.[3]

Churchill and the Strath of Kildonan, both of them around 58 degrees north, share the same latitude. But Kildonan Aprils, though they might bring snow and frost on occasion, also bring definite signs of spring, among them, in good years anyway, the early 'bite' of grass so critical, before the strath's clearance, to the well-being of its cattle herds. Nothing like this is true of April on the coasts of Hudson Bay. As in Sutherland, to be sure, the month is characterised by lengthening days and rising temperatures. It followed, then, that Piper Gunn and the other Sutherland people making for York Factory did not encounter intense cold of the kind they had endured at Churchill Creek during December, January and February. But neither did they meet with any real warmth. At times, indeed, Gunn and his companions had to cope with wind chill so severe that some of them, as they recalled long afterwards, were badly affected by frostbite. 'We cannot form an adequate conception of the misery suffered by these people on this trip,' commented Manitoba's earliest historian. 'The females suffered most.'[4]

This was partly because it did not occur to anyone of that era that it might be permissible – even in conditions as extreme as those encountered around Hudson Bay – for women to wear trousers. Instead they wore long, heavy, multilayered skirts and petticoats which made walking in thick snow on snow-shoes all the more demanding, while failing, at the same time, fully to protect tiring legs (even when swathed in woollen 'leggings') from the chilling effect of exposure to the air. Unsurprisingly, then, Archibald McDonald recorded that, with his party just five miles out of Churchill Creek, 'the women began to lose . . . much ground and . . . [had to be] placed in the centre of the men'.[5]

Soon more acute problems were encountered. Much the most prevalent, affecting women and men alike, was snow-blindness – caused by the intense glare of the April sun (now much higher in the sky than during winter) reflecting from apparently limitless expanses of ice and snow. This, like the crippling cramp resulting from prolonged use of snow-shoes, was treated by Archibald

McDonald in accordance with written instructions he had received from a Churchill-based HBC surgeon, Abel Edwards. Having first been dosed with jalops, a herbal 'purgative' or laxative, sufferers from either cramp or snow-blindness were next 'bled', this being the early nineteenth-century medical profession's standard response to almost every ailment. 'A vein ought to be opened', McDonald had been told by Edwards, 'and from ten to sixteen ounces of blood drawn . . . In every case it will be advisable to make rather a large orifice which will allow the necessary quantum of blood to flow in a shorter time . . . Great care should be taken in performing this (easy and safe) operation (as people generally consider it) and [a] vein which does not run contiguous to [an] artery ought to be selected.' Hence the journal entry made by Archibald McDonald at the close of his second day en route to York Factory: 'I bleed Mary Gunn who is very poorly with her eyes.'[6]

Whether Mary, the Kildonan piper's sister, was any less poorly after her bleeding may be doubted. More effective perhaps was McDonald's decision to break camp each morning at around 2 a.m., to get under way by 3 or 4 a.m., when it was barely beginning to get light, and to pause for several hours in the middle part of the day – thus minimising exposure to the sun.

Early starts, however, did nothing to alleviate the impact of cramp – that 'cursed distemper' as it was called by Archibald McDonald. Among its victims was Andrew MacBeath, who came from Borrobol in the Strath of Kildonan's upper reaches and who, at one point, was so 'completely knocked up and disabled' he could barely move. Setting a fire, McDonald 'got boiling a hot decoction . . . with which [MacBeath] was all over smoothly washed after [having had extracted] from his arm from 12 to 14 ounces of blood'. MacBeath, 'with the assistance of his wife', her stamina showing that John Charles had been wrong to doubt female hardihood, was thus enabled 'to keep up with the party' – Archibald McDonald and 'the strongest of the females . . . hauling his [MacBeath's] sled in turn'.[7]

As the trek south continued, disabling cramps and other ailments became more prevalent. Causing Archibald McDonald most concern was Jean MacKay. This was the young woman whose marriage to Angus MacKay, the Kildonan catechist's brother, had been celebrated in Jean's father's barn 15 months before – and who, with her husband, now found herself confronting hazards no one in Kildonan, at the time of Jean and Angus's wedding, could have so much as started to imagine. While there had been repeated 'falls and tumbles' as a result of people losing their footing when 'ascending and descending . . . banks and ridges of hard snow', those had not resulted in serious injury. But on 13 April, a week into a journey that must at times have seemed interminable, Jean MacKay fell so heavily when crossing a stretch of 'bare ice' that she had to be carried into that evening's camp. 'I attended her', Archibald McDonald wrote, 'and found her much inclined to vomit, shivering all over, faintish, abdomen tense, pulse throbbing . . . and somewhat feverish.' Jean, it transpired, was four or five months pregnant. Fearing that she might lose her baby, and in order to give everyone else a chance to recuperate, McDonald decreed that there should be no travel the following day, which, as it happened, 'turned out to snow and blow very fresh'.[8]

Although 'easier in every respect', Jean MacKay, even after a full day's rest, remained unable to walk. Aware that he was now just three or four days short of York Factory, and calculating that the party's progress would be faster if it was shorn of its more incapacitated members, Archibald McDonald ordered John MacKay – 'a very steady man' in McDonald's estimation – to rest up for a further period with his pregnant wife and to take care, in addition, of three exhausted teenagers. The three were Charles McBeath from Borrobol, whose widowed mother had been left at Churchill Creek, and George and Janet Sutherland, Jean's younger brother and sister.[9]

Angus MacKay was supplied by Archibald McDonald with a generous stock of provisions and – on the off-chance that hunting opportunities might arise – with a musket, powder and shot. Nor was MacKay made solely responsible for getting Jean, Charles,

George and Janet to York Factory. Two days before, just prior to
Jean MacKay's fall, the southbound party had met with three men
despatched from York Factory to rendezvous with them. Now one
of those men, another of the HBC's Aboriginal employees, was
instructed by Archibald McDonald to remain with Angus MacKay's
group and, when he judged it safe to proceed, to help the five
Europeans get south.

To have had this help must have been reassuring to MacKay and
his charges. So bad was the weather by this point, however, that even
people who had spent their lives in the vicinity of Hudson Bay could
become disoriented. That is clear from Archibald McDonald's journal entry for Friday 15 April 1814, the day he and the larger party,
refreshed by their 36-hour rest, pushed on. To begin with, the party's
journey lay through 'scrubs of wood'. But by mid-morning, when
McDonald and his companions were crossing a 'a large plain' without shelter of any kind, heavy snow and an 'uncommonly . . . blowy'
wind combined to make movement more and more difficult. 'The
party kept close order', McDonald wrote, 'but could not see above
thirty yards . . . [and] the guide expressed himself much afraid of not
making out the way.' Disaster, in the event, was averted. But at the
height of the blizzard, some at least of the 46 Sutherland people
trudging towards York Factory must surely have wondered – and not
for the first time – if they had been wise, 11 or 12 months earlier, to
sign up as enthusiastically as they had done for the Earl of Selkirk's
colonisation project at Red River.[10]

There was nothing implausible in principle about the regiment-raising venture Lord Selkirk discussed in London during March 1813
with Sergeant William MacDonald. As Selkirk, MacDonald and, for
that matter, the sergeant's Strath of Kildonan associates were well
aware, the United Kingdom was then confronting an acute shortage
of military manpower. Twenty years into almost continuous conflict
with France, Britain (without recourse to French-style conscription)
was simultaneously having to sustain the world's biggest navy, keep

large land forces in action in continental Europe and, in the wake of
the previous summer's declaration of war by the USA, fend off
attacks on its North American territories. Although a US incursion
into those territories had been repulsed in 1812, a more substantial
invasion was feared and, in those circumstances, the Earl of Selkirk's
offer of troops for the North American theatre, where British forces
were desperately scarce, might have been expected to appeal. As was
beginning to be apparent even before William MacDonald left
London for Sutherland, however, official interest in Selkirk's proposals was minimal. This was not because government ministers or
military commanders were congenitally hostile to private initiatives
of the Selkirk type. Nor was it a result of there being something
inherently unacceptable about the notion of the earl's soldiers being
settled eventually at Red River. Earlier conflicts in North America
had been followed by similar settlement schemes, and its Red River
dimension, therefore, would not have constituted an insuperable
obstacle in the way of the Selkirk plan had that plan not been
rendered suspect for reasons rooted in the British ruling order's
long-standing distrust of the plan's originator.

  A key reason for that distrust is traceable to 1792 when the then
Thomas Douglas, in the course of a visit to Paris, received a 'remarkably cool' reception from the future Marquis and Marchioness of
Stafford at a dinner in the British embassy, where George Granville
Leveson-Gower (as mentioned previously) was then in charge and
where there was unconcealed disapproval of the fact that Douglas
had come to France to make the acquaintance of, and show solidarity with, the men directing France's revolution. By 1799, when
Thomas Douglas inherited both his earldom and a Kirkcudbrightshire
estate from his father, his politics, to be sure, were less radical than
they had been. But from the perspective of the Leveson-Gowers and
other members of Britain's landed establishment – an establishment
including many of the country's leading politicians – any credit the
new Earl of Selkirk got from distancing himself from pro-democracy revolutionaries was more than offset by his much publicised

criticisms of the estate management policies favoured by many of his fellow landlords. Those criticisms were levelled in particular at 'improvement' of the Sutherland variety.[11]

Kirkcudbrightshire, where Thomas Douglas grew up, is as far from Sutherland as it is possible to get in Scotland – the young Thomas's interest in the Highlands stemming not from his upbringing but from his having fallen in, when studying law at Edinburgh University, with a fellow student, Walter Scott, whose own enthusiasm for the Scottish north was already well established. The Highlanders with whom Scott identified, however, were long-dead clansfolk of the sort he wrote about in best-selling novels like *Waverley* and *Rob Roy*. Highlanders of his own time, in contrast, held little appeal for Scott, who told Lady Stafford that the Sutherland Estate's recalcitrant tenants would one day 'look back . . . with gratitude to their mistress who pursued their welfare in spite of themselves'. That thought would have seemed nonsensical to Selkirk who, unlike Scott, made great efforts to understand Highlanders as he found them, not as they had been.[12]

Starting in 1792, just after his return from France, the young Thomas Douglas, still in his early twenties, had travelled extensively in the north of Scotland. In the course of his journeys, and with a view to enquiring into the way Highlanders felt about the introduction of sheep farming and the associated beginnings of crofting, Douglas learned Gaelic – something never contemplated (perhaps needless to say) by people like the Marchioness of Stafford, William Young, Patrick Sellar or James Loch. His Gaelic may not have been entirely fluent, but it was certainly sufficient to provide the future earl with what were, by the standards of his time and class, uniquely perceptive insights into the thinking of anti-clearance protestors.

Those insights inform Selkirk's 1805 book, *Observations on the Present State of the Highlands of Scotland*. They inform in particular the book's analysis of the way in which the Highlands of that time were increasingly riven by social conflict – conflict which, in Selkirk's view, was an unavoidable consequence of the

eighteenth-century evolution of clan chiefs into commercial-
ly-minded landowners. Because of its having led to 'the frequent
removal of the ancient possessors of the land', Selkirk wrote, this
development had 'nearly annihilated in the people all that enthusiastic affection for their chiefs, which was formerly prevalent, and [had]
substituted feelings of disgust and irritation . . . [Highlanders]
remember not only the very opposite behaviour of their former
chiefs; they recollect also the services their ancestors performed for
[those chiefs] . . . They reproach their landlord with neglect and
remind him that, but for their fathers, he would now have no estate.
The permanent possession, which they had always retained, of their
paternal farms they consider only as their just right, from the share
they had borne in the general defence, and *can see no difference
between the title of the chief and their own* [italics added].'[13]

Although derided by Young, Sellar, Loch and other estate managers, this belief* – that prolonged occupation of land resulted in a
continuing right to its occupancy – was, as Lord Selkirk recognised,
deeply held by the Sutherland tenants Sellar, Young and their
colleagues were determined to evict. It was for this reason that the
Earl of Selkirk, much to the disgust of the Staffords, refused to
condemn the Strath of Kildonan's 1813 'rioters'. 'According to ideas
handed down to them by their ancestors', Selkirk wrote of the
Kildonan rebels, 'they were only defending their rights and resisting
a ruinous, unjust and tyrannical encroachment on their property.'[14]

Nor did Selkirk hesitate, whether in correspondence or in conversation with the Staffords, to subject their 'improvement' strategy to
criticisms identical to those set out by Alexander Sutherland in *The
Star*. He was 'decidedly of opinion', Selkirk informed Lord Stafford
in April 1813, that 'the more wealthy' of the marquis's Kildonan

---

* The belief in question, enshrined in the Gaelic term *dùchthas*, was integral to clanship and can be traced back for many hundreds of years. The concept was eventually
enshrined in law by means of 1886 legislation that granted crofting families a right to
what amounted to perpetual security of tenure.

tenants would 'spurn' crofts of the sort on offer to them: 'To descend from a farm, stocked with twenty or thirty head of cattle, to a croft of two or three acres and the pasturage of one or two cows is, to a [Highland] peasant, a degradation scarcely less than for a gentleman of two or three thousand pounds per annum to be reduced to so many hundreds.'[15]

So what, in such circumstances, ought to be done? To Selkirk, the answer had long been obvious. If Highland landlords insisted on removing people to make way for sheep, evicted families, instead of being crammed into crofting settlements of the sort planned for the Sutherland Estate, should be helped to emigrate to British North America where they could reconstitute their agricultural operations – and indeed the community life of their original townships – on substantial landholdings of a type that, over there, were readily available. This approach, needless to say, did not commend itself to 'improving' estate owners like the Marquis and Marchioness of Stafford – committed as they were to demonstrating that people moved from one part of an estate to another would ultimately benefit from an enforced change of location. But notwithstanding the abuse that came the Earl of Selkirk's way from fellow aristocrats like the Staffords, his pro-emigration philosophy was one Selkirk adhered to for the greater part of his life; one, indeed, that shaped much of this life; and one that, ten years prior to his being drawn into developments on the Sutherland Estate, Selkirk managed to put successfully into practice on land he had acquired for this purpose on Prince Edward Island (PEI).

In the south-eastern corner of that small colony in the Gulf of St Lawrence in 1803 the Earl of Selkirk installed around 800 people from the West Highland mainland and from adjacent islands, notably Skye. Many of those people had been affected by land-use changes of the kind later implemented in Sutherland, and Selkirk, who accompanied them to PEI, was in no doubt as to his settlers having been well advised to quit Scotland. To begin with, admittedly, chaos reigned. Everywhere he looked, Selkirk wrote, there were 'confused heaps of baggage'; and lacking any alternative, newly arrived families were obliged to 'lodge . . . themselves in temporary wigwams'. But morale, the earl contended, was high. 'They looked to nothing less than a restoration of the happy days of clanship,' he commented of the people he had brought to PEI. That phrase is telling, being indicative of the extent to which Selkirk, as he busied himself with allocating farmland and supervising the beginnings of ground clearance, cast himself in the role of a pre-clearance clan chief. 'I [was] talking my best Gaelic', he commented of the time he spent with his PEI settlers, 'which seemed to have won their hearts.'[16]

This PEI experience, the Earl of Selkirk became convinced, was one he could replicate on a much grander scale at Red River, a place Selkirk first took an interest in when reading, not long after its publication in 1801, Alexander Mackenzie's account of his 1793 crossing of the North American continent. In his book, Mackenzie wrote about Red River and the great plains to its west – plains Mackenzie's *Québécois* voyageurs, in a French term that would be adopted into English, called *les prairies*. Might those prairies be easier to settle than the more easterly and (from a European perspective) more accessible parts of North America where, prior to the nineteenth century, settlement was concentrated but where, because of that region's forest cover, it took a lot of effort to get farming under way? Selkirk, it seems, thought so from as early as 1802; and when, following his 1803 stay in PEI, he travelled to Montreal to find out more about the prairies from Alexander Mackenzie and other Nor'Westers, it became Selkirk's unshakeable conviction that Red River could be transformed into the nucleus of a thriving prairie colony.

Because Selkirk's Red River venture threatened Nor'Wester domination of the North American fur trade, the earl's Montreal hosts were afterwards to maintain that he had tricked them into divulging geographical and other information used to their disadvantage. This was unfair. Selkirk was not duplicitous. But he was aware – or, if not, soon became so – that, irrespective of the NWC's on-the-ground supremacy at Red River and points west, the area in question (as already mentioned) belonged legally to the Montreal men's HBC rivals. Hence the effort Selkirk now put into acquiring, first, a substantial HBC shareholding and, second, the huge slab of territory, centred on Red River, he got the Bay Company to lease to him in 1811. It was this territory, had he succeeded in obtaining official sanction for his projected regiment, that Selkirk intended to populate with hundreds of ex-soldiers and their families once the planned regiment's services were no longer required. But unfortunately for Selkirk, and still more unfortunately for the men, women and youngsters who in April 1814 were to make so desperate a journey from Churchill Creek to York Factory, the peopling of Red River was not to proceed in accordance with the earl's hopes.

When Sergeant William MacDonald came home to Sutherland in mid-April 1813, his mission, as Lord Selkirk understood it, was simply to identify men who might be interested in serving in a Selkirk-recruited military formation, and who might wish thereafter to make homes for themselves, their parents, wives and children at Red River. MacDonald, however, exceeded his authority. According to an increasingly embittered William Young, whose Strath of Kildonan plans the sergeant was helping to wreck, MacDonald 'gave out' that Selkirk, whose regiment-raising scheme was definitively turned down by the authorities in London on 14 April, had in fact secured the British government's wholehearted backing. The sergeant also appears to have indicated, or so circumstantial evidence suggests, that not just men of military age but their dependents also were likely to be shipped within weeks, and at government expense, to North America.[17]

Those confident assertions had the inevitable effect – possibly intended on MacDonald's part – of eliminating any slim chance Young might have had of persuading Kildonan people to abandon their ongoing refusal to take crofts on Sutherland's north coast. But if the sergeant's success in signing up more than 1,000 prospective emigrants proved a Red River homestead to be a more attractive proposition than a Strathy or Armadale croft, the same achievement showed that matters in Sutherland were now spiralling out of Lord Selkirk's control. The large-scale, government-financed emigration he had been trying to bring about was not going to happen. But the people planning to join just such an exodus from the Sutherland Estate did not know this. Some of them were selling their cattle and otherwise preparing for an immediate departure. If his standing and credibility were not to be damaged, and if aspiring emigrants were not to be let down, Selkirk realised during April 1813, he needed to find some way of salvaging something from the wreckage of his earlier scheme. The solution, he decided, lay in getting as many people as possible from Sutherland to Red River that summer.

The one available means of accomplishing this consisted of the HBC ships that set out each June for York Factory from the company's base at Gravesend, not far from London on the lower reaches of the Thames. Prior to crossing the Atlantic, those ships called at the Orcadian port of Stromness, which they reached by means of the North Sea and the Pentland Firth, the narrow strait separating Orkney from Caithness. Passenger accommodation on HBC ships, while limited, was sufficient, Selkirk reckoned, to enable him to get perhaps 70 or 80 young men to York Factory in time for them to make their way inland before the Hayes and Nelson Rivers froze. Once at Red River, Selkirk thought, this advance guard of emigrants would construct homes and otherwise prepare the ground – literally – for the larger party Selkirk hoped to send out in 1814. But given the imminence of the planned clearance of much of the Strath of Kildonan, where were 1814's potential emigrants to be accommodated in the meantime? It was to this issue that the Earl of Selkirk now turned his attention.

In March, when still hopeful of government assistance, Selkirk, had got General Wemyss (William MacDonald's former commanding officer) to take him to Cleveland House, the Stafford family's London mansion, where Lady Stafford was then in residence. There

Selkirk told the marchioness of his plans for what she termed his 'Canada regiment'. Might the families of such Kildonan men as were prepared to join the regiment, Selkirk asked, be left in occupation of their homes until those men's service was at an end? This, Lady Stafford felt, was 'totally inadmissable'. Nor was she any more amenable when, subsequent to the government's rejection of the 'Canada regiment' concept, Selkirk again came to speak with her, this time to float the notion of his renting from the Sutherland Estate 'a few hundred acres' on which intending emigrants could be accommodated until they could be conveyed across the Atlantic. This was an idea to which the marchioness, as she noted, 'could give no encouragement'. Selkirk, it was clear, could expect only obstructionism from the Staffords and their aides. Nothing daunted, however, he left London for Sutherland on Sunday 9 May. Twelve days later, the earl was installed in Golspie Inn.[18]

At the inn, Selkirk was joined by Sergeant William MacDonald and by Archibald MacLellan, a former Kirkcudbrightshire militia officer who was in the earl's employment and who had been sent north, in advance of his boss, to begin selecting the several dozen individuals who, if all went well, would set out for Red River in June. It was at this point that Selkirk (as mentioned previously) rode up Strathbrora to meet with Donald MacKay in the latter's Ascoilemore log cabin. MacKay, Selkirk reported, had for years made the 'beauty' of the Red River country 'a theme of his discourse', and having heard repeatedly of the place from someone who knew it at first hand, people in the eastern part of Sutherland, or so Selkirk thought, 'felt less disinclination' to emigrate to Red River 'than might otherwise have been expected'. Whether or not because of MacKay's influence, the earl was certainly well received in the Strath of Kildonan. 'To such a persecuted people', the son of one Kildonan emigrant remarked a long time later, 'Lord Selkirk came as a rescuing angel' – his welcome made all the more enthusiastic, it can be surmised, by his again deploying, as on Prince Edward Island, his 'best Gaelic'.[19]

Neither William Clunes nor Gabriel Reed, the sheep farmers whose leases of land in the Strath of Kildonan were just then taking effect, gave Lord Selkirk 'the least aid', or so the Marchioness of Stafford was informed by William Young. But the same could not be said of Kildonan's minister, Alexander Sage, from whom Selkirk obtained character sketches of prospective emigrants. Among those selected by Selkirk with Sage's help were several men who had been active in the Kildonan disturbances of some months before. This did not worry Selkirk. What the Staffords were about in Sutherland, he commented, was 'so calculated to excite discontent that there is no reason to be surprised if [such discontent] should occasionally break out into acts of violence'. For this reason, he 'could not consider' their riotous conduct as constituting 'any great imputation of [the] general character' of the 'fine . . . men' he met with in Kildonan. Especially keen to leave for Red River and a most impressive recruit, in Selkirk's opinion, was John Sutherland, someone 'spoken [of]', Selkirk recorded, 'as among the most respectable people in the parish'. Sutherland, in his capacity as a leading member of the Kildonan rebels' organising committee, had played a prominent part (as noted earlier) in what Selkirk called 'the insurrection against the sheep farmers'. But this seems, if anything, to have strengthened Selkirk's faith in his abilities. Because of Sutherland's potential contribution to his Red River colony, the earl commented, he considered him 'a zealous friend [who] ought to be treated with regard'.[20]

Partly because he was so taken by John Sutherland and the several other Kildonan 'insurrectionists' who were equally anxious to quit Scotland, the earl abandoned his earlier idea of a male-only emigration and permitted those men to take their families with them. The resulting emigrant group was thus larger than initially envisaged, numbering well over 90. Most of those people were well enough off to meet upfront the substantial cost (10 guineas a head) of their passages to Hudson Bay; most came from the Strath of Kildonan; and, by this group, their departure for North America in June 1813 must have seemed one among several good outcomes of the strath's

January rebellion. That rebellion, to be sure, had not stopped Gabriel Reed and William Clunes taking occupancy in May of much Strath of Kildonan farmland. But the hundreds of evictions scheduled for that same month had, in effect, been suspended. Nobody was being moved as planned on to crofts at Armadale and Strathy. A good future, or so it seemed, had been secured in North America for as many families as wished to go there. And despite their initial refusal to issue any such guarantee, Lord and Lady Stafford, perhaps fearing further adverse publicity if they evicted intending emigrants, had agreed by July that all such folk were 'to be continued' for the moment in their Strath of Kildonan homes.[21]

In early June John Sutherland and his fellow emigrants left Sutherland, and with such baggage as they could take with them, made their way to Thurso, a small town on Caithness's north coast. There they boarded the *Waterwitch*, the coastal sloop or trading vessel hired by Lord Selkirk to take them across the Pentland Firth to Stromness. Also aboard the *Waterwitch* was a Caithness teenager, Donald Gunn, on his way to Hudson Bay to take up a job with the HBC. Gunn, described by his new employers as 'strong' and 'well made', would in later life become both a prominent resident of Red River and the author of a *History of Manitoba*, a history in which he recounted something of the long voyage that, for him and his fellow passengers, started with the *Waterwitch*'s departure from Thurso's little harbour. 'All things being ready', Gunn wrote, 'the sloop hoisted sail. The [Sutherland people] who had to accommodate themselves on deck . . . raised their bonnets and bade farewell to their beloved friends and relations who had gathered [in Thurso] . . . to give them the last embrace, the last shake of the hand.' By that evening, although laid low by seasickness when crossing the notoriously choppy Pentland Firth, Selkirk's 90-plus recruits were safely ashore in Stromness, where the earl, who had preceded them from Sutherland, was awaiting the arrival of the Bay Company ships which, that year, sailed from Gravesend on 7 June.[22]

The 1813 convoy to Hudson Bay consisted of two HBC vessels, the *Eddystone* and the *Prince of Wales*, together with a naval escort in the shape of HMS *Brazen,* which, single-masted but carrying 28 guns, provided necessary protection at a time when both French and American privateers were active in British and Atlantic waters. As it happened, just such a privateer, flying the US flag, was sighted by the Bay-bound convoy on its second day out of Stromness. The American ship – possibly the privateer reported to have 'committed . . . depredations off the coast of Sutherland' some days previously – was towing a British cargo vessel captured in the North Sea. Its tow, however, was abandoned on the privateer's skipper catching sight of the *Brazen* and (not wishing to engage a heavily armed warship) beating a rapid retreat. But if the HBC convoy was thus kept safe from American attack, it was rapidly to fall victim to an enemy more deadly than any privateer. This enemy was typhus.[23]

Although they had reached Stromness 16 days previously, the *Eddystone*, the *Prince of Wales* and the *Brazen* did not leave there until 28 June. Some part of this hiatus was accounted for by the need to take on stores and drinking water. Much of it, however, was due to persistent 'light airs' that becalmed the three ships for more than a week. Lord Selkirk, who waited in Stromness until the Sutherland emigrants were safely aboard the *Prince of Wales*, the ship on which they were to be accommodated, was 'kept in much anxiety' by this delay. He was right to be worried. Because Stromness's lodging houses were already under pressure as a result of there being a lot of troops in town, the premises where the Sutherland people had been 'billeted' on their arrival were overcrowded and, it can be guessed, none too clean. This made those premises ideal breeding grounds for lice and fleas, the principal means by which typhus-causing bacteria reach human hosts. Unsurprisingly, then, just 'a few days' after the *Prince of Wales* cleared Stromness, one of the ship's passengers – a woman said to have spent several nights in a Stromness home where typhus was later reported – became seriously ill. Soon typhus symptoms – high fever, mental confusion, a dull red rash, persistent coughing, nausea and repeated vomiting – were spreading through the HBC ship's 'between decks' where the Sutherland people were housed in airless and increasingly insanitary conditions that served perfectly to facilitate disease transmission.[24]

One of the first *Prince of Wales* passengers to die was Peter LaSerre, a Jersey-born surgeon who had been hired by the Earl of Selkirk to provide his Red River colony with a resident doctor. Selkirk had put LaSerre in charge of the Sutherland emigrants. With the surgeon's death, responsibility devolved to his second-in-command, Archibald McDonald. Just 23, McDonald, who came from Glencoe in Argyll where his father was one of that locality's tacksmen, had been recommended to Selkirk by one of the earl's Highland contacts at the start of 1812. Selkirk had initially intended to send McDonald to Red River that same year. Impressed by the young man's abilities, however, the earl had taken him instead to London with a view, as Selkirk put it, to providing Archibald with 'an opportunity of acquiring some branches of knowledge that will be useful [to him]'. This 'knowledge' consisted of 'medicine', 'the sciences' and 'mathematics'. But what eventually caused Selkirk to make McDonald responsible, in conjunction with LaSerre, for the 1813 emigrant party was not the training he received in London but his fluency in Gaelic, the only language spoken by most Kildonan people.[25]

His voyage to Hudson Bay was for then 16-year-old Donald Gunn an adventure. Decades later, Gunn remembered clearly his first sighting, near Greenland, of icebergs: 'glittering mountains', he called them. Equally memorable was the HBC convoy's encounter, when in Hudson Strait between the North American mainland and Baffin Island, with what Gunn called 'these extraordinary specimens of humanity, the Esquimaux'. On Sunday 1 August, a 'bright and calm' day in Donald Gunn's recollection, 'numerous fleets' of kayaks put out from the strait's Baffin Island shore to rendezvous with the Bay Company's ships, the kayaks' Inuit occupants exchanging seal oil, ivory and arctic fox pelts for razors, needles and other metal goods. But if Gunn, sailing on the *Eddystone*, had leisure to take in such scenes, that was not true of Archibald McDonald and his charges on the *Prince of Wales*. By 1 August, when a brief note of the convoy's 'trading with the Esquimaux' was entered in his ship's log, John Turner, captain of the *Prince of Wales*, was coping – or trying to – with a first-rate crisis. First passenger after passenger, then seaman after seaman, was recorded in Turner's log as 'ill' or 'very ill'. Within days, some of the same individuals would be mentioned again, this time because of their having 'departed this life'.[26]

Aggravating Captain Turner's difficulties was the HBC convoy's desperately slow progress through Hudson Strait. The *Brazen*, the *Eddystone* and the *Prince of Wales* had first encountered 'isles of ice' and 'straggling ice' on 27 July; and by the beginning of August, though the weather was 'fine', the ships had run into pack ice so dense that, time after time, they were halted completely. On 8 August, when so halted and 'grappled' to a berg, it became apparent – as if things were not problematic enough already – that the *Prince of Wales* was leaking badly as a result of 'a blow she received among the ice'. Soon there were four feet of water in the vessel's hold, while, despite the *Prince of Wales*'s carpenter 'cutting a hole through the ship's side to give more air in the 'tween decks to the sick', typhus was every day more prevalent. With his ship's seaworthiness in doubt and with nearly half his crew either dead or out of action, it is understandable that Captain Turner, on finally getting clear of Hudson Strait and entering the comparatively open waters of Hudson Bay, should have decided on 16 August 'to get into port as soon as possible'. Instead of steering as planned for York Factory, therefore, Turner set a course for the more northerly, and therefore closer, Fort Churchill.[27]

Because the *Eddystone* was bound for neither York Factory nor Churchill but for still remoter outposts towards the foot of the bay, Donald Gunn, scheduled to transfer from the *Eddystone* to the *Prince of Wales* in Hudson Strait, had instead been transferred (in order to keep him out of contact with typhus) to the *Brazen*. Since that ship, it was now decided, should accompany the stricken *Prince of Wales* to Churchill, it was there Gunn first 'beheld,' as he put it, 'the low and uninteresting shores of Hudson's Bay . . . presenting [a] narrow border of yellow sand and a dark blue swamp in the front [and] with [a] dark and dismal looking line of spruce and tamarack in the background. The scenery appeared bleak and desolate beyond the power of description.'[28]

At Churchill the Hudson Bay coastline, generally north–south in orientation, bends markedly towards the west, with the result that the Churchill River, which the Brazen and *Prince of Wales* entered on the evening of Thursday 19 August, flows into the bay from the south. Two northward-tending promontories flank the Churchill estuary. Near the tip of the more westerly of those, the HBC constructed during the eighteenth century an imposing and suppos-edly impregnable strongpoint, Prince of Wales Fort, which, despite its being equipped with a formidable array of artillery mounted on stone-built ramparts, had been captured and destroyed by a French expeditionary force towards the end of the American Revolutionary War. Nosing past the resulting ruins,* now more than 30 years old, the *Prince of Wales* and its escort vessel dropped anchor a couple of miles upstream and just off Sloop's Cove. This little inlet, also on the estuary's western side, owed its name to its use by HBC coastal trad-ing vessels. Their heavy iron mooring rings are still attached today to rocks (where a number of Bay Company men long ago carved their names) just above the cove's shoreline.

Following the destruction of Prince of Wales Fort, HBC opera-tions in the locality had been relocated to Fort Churchill, a complex of mostly wooden buildings some three miles upstream from Sloop's Cove and again on the Churchill River's western bank. But dusk was gathering by the time word of the arrival of the *Prince of*

---

* Prince of Wales Fort was rebuilt by Canadian governments during the 1930s and 1950s and is one of present-day Churchill's visitor attractions.

Wales and the *Brazen* reached there, and though the Fort Churchill
'post journal' records that two men were immediately sent to
Sloop's Cove 'to fire a few guns by way of welcome', it was not until
the following morning, when Captain James Stirling of the *Brazen*
came ashore, that the fort's HBC personnel became aware that both
crew and passengers aboard the *Prince of Wales* were 'in a very
sickly and distressing state with the typhus fever'. At once the fort's
chief trader and his senior colleagues set about providing assistance. Because of the risk of disease spreading to the 40 or so HBC
men based at Churchill, there could be no question of typhus
sufferers being taken into the fort itself. Instead tents were erected
at Sloop's Cove and, in the course of 20 and 21 August, all the sick
were got off the *Prince of Wales* and accommodated – as were those
who had escaped infection – in the resulting encampment.
Vegetables and other 'fresh provisions' were sent from Fort
Churchill. But so, more ominously, were coffins, further deaths
occurring both among *Prince of Wales* seamen and among Kildonan
people who, if all had gone according to plan, would by then have
been setting out from York Factory for Red River.[29]

Survivors of that grim period would for the rest of their lives pay
tribute to Catherine or Kate MacPherson. In her mid-twenties, Kate
had been raised in Gailiable, one of the Strath of Kildonan townships due to be incorporated into Gabriel Reed's Kilcalmkill sheep
farm, and had left there, with her 18-year-old brother John, in the
hope of finding at Red River the secure future no longer to be had in
Sutherland. Kate MacPherson was deeply religious. One of her
granddaughters long afterwards recalled Kate's insistence on devot-
ing time each day to reading from her Bible. It may be, therefore,
that her faith inspired Kate MacPherson to do what she so selflessly
now did: spending hour after hour, day after day, night after night,
whether on the *Prince of Wales* or ashore at Sloop's Cove, helping
ease the sufferings of the many typhus victims.[30]

Despite Kate MacPherson's best efforts, people continued to die,
among them, at Sloop's Cove on Thursday 2 September 1813, John

Sutherland, the man of whom Lord Selkirk had expected so much. Sutherland's, as it happens, is the only grave among the several dug in the Churchill estuary's vicinity at this time to have been marked by a still-surviving headstone. Made from a roughly inscribed boulder, it is to be seen about 100 yards north of the Prince of Wales Fort's north-western corner. That headstone's existence testifies, or so it is legitimate to speculate, to the regard in which John Sutherland was held by his fellow emigrants. Sutherland, to be sure, was no saint. According to Donald Sage, the Kildonan minister's son, he was both a poacher and a 'smuggler', meaning that he was involved in illicit distilling of whisky. But Sutherland, notwithstanding his dabbling in activities reckoned crimes by the authorities, was, as the Earl of Selkirk recognised, a community leader. He was also (and his leadership role may have owed something to this) what present-day anthropologists call a tradition-bearer, someone steeped in his community's largely oral culture.[31]

Predictably, the concept of there being such a culture was rejected by organisers of the Sutherland clearances. Patrick Sellar, for instance, contended that the people he evicted were a 'parcel of beggars' whose 'obstinate adherence' to Gaelic (a 'barbarous jargon' in Sellar's opinion) had, by depriving those same people of 'knowledge and cultivation', condemned them to perpetual backwardness. Although to think like this made it easier for Sellar to rationalise what he was about, the factor's opinions, however confidently asserted, were grounded in nothing more substantial than prejudice. In fact, Highland tradition-bearers like John Sutherland had access, by way of their language, to a rich store of prose and poetry. Some of this had long before been turned into literature, Gaelic, after all, having attained a written form well in advance of English. More of it, however, had been transmitted orally through scores of generations, beneficiaries of such transmission possessing, among other things, an intricate knowledge of the mythical warriors whose heroic exploits constitute the so-called Fenian cycle of Gaelic sagas. Those sagas derive ultimately from Iron Age

Ireland. They reached the Scottish Highlands in the course of migrations that took place within the British Isles and the rest of Western Europe around the time of the Roman Empire's disintegration. Thereafter they survived in the heads of Highland storytellers. One such was John Sutherland, a regular guest, Donald Sage recalled, at Kildonan's manse, where Sutherland's narration of a single Fenian epic could readily occupy the 'three or four hours' it took 'for a log of wood of considerable length' to be reduced to ash in the manse's kitchen fireplace.[32]

What was destroyed by the Marquis and Marchioness of Stafford, by Patrick Sellar, William Young and James Loch, then, was not simply a set of farming townships. Also eradicated was a way of life that had sustained a complex body of belief, ideas and tradition through as many as 2,000 years. If not actually, then emblematically, it was this way of life – the product of a continuity now shattered – that his wife, his children and his friends buried with the body of John Sutherland by the shores of Hudson Bay.

When, in the fall of 1807, Donald MacKay quit Fort Churchill – where he had spent the preceding 12 or so months – and returned to Ascoilemore, the fort's chief trader, hated by MacKay, was William Auld. By 1813, however, Auld had been promoted, and as required by his new role, was dividing his time between Churchill and York Factory. Because he had been awaiting the arrival of the *Prince of Wales* at the latter location, Auld was there when news reached him of the expected ship having put in instead at Fort Churchill. As soon as he could, he headed north, spending two days at sea in an open boat and in weather so bad that he and his crew arrived at Churchill 'drenched in seawater'. What he found on his arrival did not improve Auld's mood. Particularly infuriating, from his perspective, was Captain John Turner's insistence on having nothing further to do with his ship's passengers, whom Turner understandably blamed for having inflicted typhus on his crew.[33]

James Stirling, the *Brazen*'s 22-year-old captain,* would after-wards be complimented on all sides as 'a fine young man' who was due 'great praise' for his having done everything possible 'for the relief of the sick' at Sloop's Cove. Turner's single aim, in contrast, was to return to England as soon as possible. With this objective firmly in view, he not only had the *Prince of Wales* emptied of its passengers, 'cleaned' and 'fumigated'; he also had the ship's cargo – destined for York Factory – put ashore in its entirety. On William Auld discovering this, he instructed Turner to reship his cargo, to reboard 48 settlers who had either escaped typhus or were recovering from it, and then to set sail for York Factory.[34]

If he were able to get at least some of the Sutherland emigrants to York Factory, Auld reasoned, he might be able, even at this late stage, to send them on to Red River; and even if that proved impossible, it would be easier to feed and otherwise look after the emigrant party at the larger and better provisioned York Factory than at Fort Churchill. John Turner, however, was reluctant to fall in with this plan. Nor was William Auld in a position to insist he do so. This was because the two men, or so it was later alleged, had been 'long and deeply engaged in smuggling'. Auld, it seems, had been 'feathering his own nest' by creaming off a proportion of the furs passing through York Factory and, with Turner's conniv-ance, getting those furs conveyed (in the *Prince of Wales*) to London where they were sold privately, Turner and Auld then sharing the proceeds. As Auld's partner in crime, it followed, Captain Turner was well placed to do as he pleased. He duly shil-ly-shallied for several days and, when he finally ran out of excuses for inaction, gave tacit encouragement (or so it can reasonably be suspected) to what amounted to a mutiny by his crew, whose feel-ings about their former passengers were identical to those of their captain and who accordingly refused to have the Sutherland people back aboard.[35]

---

* Later Admiral Sir James Stirling, first governor of Western Australia.

William Auld responded to this challenge by enlisting the help of James Stirling of the *Brazen*. The outcome was that, on the afternoon of Sunday 12 September, Stirling and Auld jointly boarded the *Prince of Wales* off Sloop's Cove. There they 'mustered' the ship's crew who were informed by Captain Stirling that anyone refusing to obey Auld's commands, as conveyed to them by a now chastened Turner, would be pressed into service with the Royal Navy and transferred to the *Brazen*. This was a credible threat. Not only did Stirling have powers to 'impress' seamen in this way, his vessel had been undermanned ever since he had had to put a skeleton crew on the cargo boat recaptured from the American privateer the HBC convoy had encountered off Orkney. Hence the cryptic sentence entered in the *Prince of Wales*'s log on 12 September: 'The men all returned to their duty.'[36]

Over the next few days, then, nearly 50 of Red River's prospective settlers were taken back aboard the *Prince of Wales* – together with their baggage and the ship's previously unloaded cargo. At last, on the afternoon of 15 September, the *Prince of Wales* set sail, only to run aground minutes later on a sandbar at the Churchill River's mouth. Although blamed by Captain Turner on 'the strong set of the tide', there was widespread suspicion ashore that this mishap was a piece of sabotage on Turner's part. That could not be proved, however; and a now intensely frustrated William Auld had no choice but to accede to Turner's demand that, in order to lighten his ship sufficiently to enable its refloating, he be permitted to unload once more his passengers and their belongings. This was done on 16 September amid 'strong gales' and the first heavy snowfall of the now imminent winter. Next day, the *Prince of Wales*'s surgeon, Stainsby by name, wrote formally to Auld to inform him that in his expert opinion (an opinion shared of course by Captain Turner) 'it would not be prudent to take any of the passengers aboard again as in all probability they would [as before] communicate . . . sickness to the ship's company'. Abel Edwards, the HBC surgeon who was to spend the forthcoming winter with the Sutherland people and who reached Churchill from York Factory on 19 September, promptly announced that he agreed with Stainsby; and Auld – aware that there was now no chance of getting anyone to Red River before the coming freeze-up – was thus forced to accept that the entire emigrant party would, as he put it, have to 'winter at Churchill'.[37]

The *Prince of Wales* (rid now of its passengers) eventually quit the Churchill River on 20 September; anchored off York Factory three days later; sailed from there on 6 October; and, having put in briefly at Stromness reached Gravesend on 24 November. With the *Prince of Wales* came Archibald McDonald's dispatches for Lord Selkirk, who, on learning of what had happened to the men, women and youngsters he had seen off five months earlier, was plunged into 'despair at this most unexpected stroke'.[38]

Four thousand miles away at Churchill, William Auld was scarcely less gloomy. Selkirk's intending settlers, he wrote on 16 September, the day after the *Prince of Wales*'s grounding, were in a 'very melancholy and distressed condition'. 'What will become of these miserable people and ourselves', Auld went on, 'the God in Heaven alone can know.' But if unclear as to the eventual fate of the Highlanders who were that same day experiencing their first Hudson Bay snowstorm, the HBC man was certain of those people's congenital incapacity, as he saw it, to help themselves.[39]

William Auld, who joined the HBC in 1790, came originally from Edinburgh. There, as in the rest of Lowland Scotland, Highlanders, despite Walter Scott's romanticisation of their forebears, were habitually regarded with a contempt that, as the eighteenth century turned into the nineteenth, became increasingly racist in tone. By intellectuals and academics like the Edinburgh-born John Pinkerton, writing in the year Auld left Scotland for Hudson Bay, it was axiomatic that Lowlanders, being 'Saxon' or 'Anglo-Saxon', were racially distinct from, and superior to, Highlanders who, like their Gaelic-speaking and similarly categorised cousins in Ireland, were beginning to be labelled 'Celts'. 'In person', Pinkerton observed, 'the Lowlanders are tall and large, with fair complexions, and often with

flaxen, yellow [or] red hair and blue eyes . . . Highlanders are generally diminutive . . . with black curled hair and dark eyes. In mind and
manners the distinction is as marked. The Lowlanders are acute,
industrious, sensible, erect and free; the Highlanders indolent, slav-
ish, strangers to industry.' This was of a piece with Patrick Sellar's
thinking. It was of a piece too with the early nineteenth-century
Scottish press's descriptions of Highlanders as 'lazy', 'filthy', 'ignorant' and 'barbaric'; it was of a piece finally with William Auld's
scorn for the Sutherland people the Earl of Selkirk wished to settle
at Red River.[40]

None of this accorded with early nineteenth-century realities in
North America where (as already noted) the Highlander-dominated
NWC was running rings – commercially and in other ways – around
the more plodding HBC whose senior staff were either Lowland
Scots (like Auld) or English (like most of his colleagues). But
Superintendent Auld was not one to allow such inconvenient truths
to get in the way of entrenched preconceptions. Nor were the various subordinates with whom he exchanged opinions. The
Highlanders huddled in tents at Sloop's Cove, those men thought,
were 'the laziest, dirtiest devils you ever saw'; they were, Auld wrote
by way of summary, 'damned savages from Scotland'. Used to
imposing a quasi-military discipline on a generally pliant (and
English-speaking) workforce recruited mostly in Orkney, HBC men,
it seems, found the Sutherland people's stubbornly independent
outlook as incomprehensible as their language. 'The emigrants',
William Auld complained, 'think [that], because they have paid for
their passage and are not hired servants, they are under no control.'
Informed repeatedly that 'all [Bay Company] orders *must* be
obeyed', the men and women encamped at Sloop's Cove – men and
women who had quit the Strath of Kildonan with a view to gaining
greater control over their lives – simply refused to accept this. Hence
the 'unyielding disposition' and 'refractory spirit' which men like
Auld and his immediate subordinates considered to be the Sutherland
people's most infuriating characteristic.[41]

6

'WHEN AMONG WOLVES, HOWL!'

The struggle to establish a new Kildonan at Red River

On the evening of the first day of their April 1813 trek to York Factory, Archibald McDonald, his 51-strong party and the party's First Nation guide pitched camp on what McDonald called 'the hill opposite Fort Churchill'. Where that hill is exactly is hard to determine in a landscape with little in the way of rising ground. But it is evident that people quitting Churchill Creek for York Factory would, at some point between their winter quarters and the fort, have crossed the frozen Churchill River and, though first following the river's course north, would then have swung sharply away from it. This is because the most serviceable route between Churchill and York Factory leads east and then south on the storm-scoured barrens fringing the Hudson Bay shoreline. That was the route taken by HBC men who carried 'mail packets' between York Factory and Churchill. It was also the route followed in November 1892 by James Tyrrell, an adventurer who, having walked from Churchill to York Factory, published an account of what turned out to be a gruelling journey. That journey, Tyrrell wrote, took him across 'broad plains diversified here and there by stunted, scattered trees, ice-covered ponds, and occasionally the thickly wooded valley of a winding stream'. The Sutherland people of nearly 80 years earlier would have seen much that Tyrrell saw. Like Tyrrell, moreover, they would not have strayed too far from the treeline. Movement in this environment involved a compromise between sticking to open ground where wind-hardened snow makes walking easier and the need, as evening comes on, to have access to the shelter and firewood to be got in forest country.[1]

It is probable, therefore, that Archibald McDonald's 'hill opposite Fort Churchill' is to be found somewhere to the south-east of the present-day Churchill Airport, its 3,000-yard-long runway a legacy of an extensive US military presence that, during the Cold War, turned Churchill (its permanent population today numbering no more than 700) into a substantial community. Take the dirt road that leads south from the airport, and you quickly find tundra giving way to arboreal forest or taiga, the latter consisting of spruce and tamarack trees that, for all their stunted and spindly appearance, might (in consequence of brief growing seasons) be several centuries old. Some of those trees, it follows, could have been glimpsed by the Kildonan people who passed this way 200 years ago. Since then, admittedly, the area immediately to the north and north-west of those people's most likely campsite has been altered radically by the arrival in 1929 of the railway. In the absence of a through road this provides Churchill with an overland link to Winnipeg, a 69-hour train journey away but, for all that, Churchill's nearest urban centre. At the railway's terminus on the Churchill River estuary are tall, rust-streaked silos where, in the weeks prior to each year's freeze-up, Europe-bound ships are loaded with prairie grain. East of those facilities is the little network of streets (a Selkirk Street among them) constituting the modern Churchill. A sizeable North West Company store* serves the local population and a museum (rich in Inuit carved ivory) caters for the tourists who flock each fall to this 'polar bear capital of the world'.

To be in Churchill in December is to have missed the bears, which, by that point, are in search of seals on a frozen Hudson Bay. But to stand on a clear December's morning on the Churchill River's

---

* The present-day NWC dates from 1987 when its founders bought from the HBC that company's stores in the Canadian north.

eastern shore, separated from Sloop's Cove by little more than a mile of ridged and hummocked river ice, is to get some sense, however slight and superficial, of what refugees from the Stafford family's clearances experienced in this vicinity. Because Churchill's latitude is the same as Sutherland's, to come here from Scotland in winter is to find the sun in its familiar, horizon-hugging place. But what is wholly unimaginable by a Scot – until it is encountered – is the impact of a daytime air temperature of minus 35 degrees Celsius. In such conditions, skin exposed to the air chills rapidly. Cold seeps through even half a dozen layers of clothing. Soon there is an irresistible temptation to beat a cowardly retreat to the heated comfort of a nearby vehicle. How on earth, you wonder, did anyone – let alone people recently scourged by typhus – tolerate this, and much worse, for month after month after month? At Churchill Creek during the winter of 1813–14 there was, for sure, no escape to the warmth of a waiting truck or to the still more welcoming interior of one of those present-day Churchill homes where a central heating furnace rumbles steadily for 24 hours every day. At Churchill Creek, two centuries ago, there was nothing to be done but to endure conditions most of us would reckon unendurable.

The emptying of the encampment at Sloop's Cove, where the Sutherland people had by then spent several weeks, began on 21 September 1813 when Archibald McDonald mobilised the encampment's fitter occupants and, taking charge of the reasonably-sized group that resulted, set off upriver by boat. Ideally, McDonald and his charges (many of them still convalescing) would have been housed in the 'four or five . . . frame buildings' constituting Fort Churchill. However, none of this accommodation could be spared; and if they were to exchange their Sloop's Cove tents for something more substantial in the way of protection from the coming winter, the Sutherland emigrants, William Auld ruled, had to be moved 15 or so miles upstream to Churchill Creek. Thereabouts there were fish – walleye, pike, whitefish, trout and the occasional sturgeon – to be had; there was wood to burn and timber to build with; while shelter from snowstorms was provided both by the forest (its trees taller here than nearer Churchill) and by a ridge of higher land a little to the north and west.[2]

Towards the end of September, Abel Edwards, the medical man now in command at Sloop's Cove, organised the transfer of the remaining typhus sufferers – 16 individuals in all – from the cove to what he called 'a small house about three miles above [Fort Churchill]'. While Edwards made arrangements for this building to be 'fitted up as a hospital', McDonald and his people at Churchill Creek were pressing on with house construction. Axes and other necessary tools were sent up from the fort; so was 'one of the [HBC's] old hands' and a more recently arrived Orcadian by the name of William Linklater. Under the HBC men's supervision, tree after tree was felled and soon 'building', as Archibald McDonald reported to Abel Edwards, '[was] going on wonderfully rapid'. By mid-October, when Edwards moved to Churchill Creek with his remaining patients, the place had been equipped with 'a small storehouse', 'four houses . . . for the settlers' and a further such house 'for the officers' – meaning Edwards and McDonald.[3]

According to Angus MacIver, a twentieth-century trapper who set up home near Churchill Creek and established a trap-line there, the 'foundations of several of these dwellings were [still] to be seen in 1930'. Some years later, MacIver wrote, 'spring flooding of the creek [had] covered most, if not all, with mud'. The vanished buildings, the trapper reckoned, were 'about ten by twelve feet'. When occupied, then, they must have been unbearably congested. This helps explain the jaundiced note struck by Donald Gunn when, in his *History of Manitoba*, he set down something of what he had been told about conditions at what Churchill Creek's 1813–14 residents called their 'winter camp'. In the camp's 'shanties', Gunn commented, 'logs had to serve as chairs and mud flooring had to supply the want of beds . . . [H]abitations were of the most simple construction and very ill-adapted to defend their inmates from winter frosts, so often accompanied by heavy gales of wind, while the Fahrenheit thermometer ranged for months from 35 to 50 [degrees] below zero, and many times in the course of the winter fell as low as 55 or even 60 [degrees]* below.'[4]

'The houses in which the settlers reside are numbered [one to four]', Abel Edwards noted in January 1814, 'and each has one of the . . . inhabitants appointed master, whose office it is to see due order and regularity observed, and to report the contrary to the officer in charge.' Among the disciplines thus enforced were rules intended to preserve basic hygiene. Thus the spruce 'brush' or branches spread across floors to serve as beds had to be replaced daily – a chore resented (unsurprisingly) in bitter weather. That same weather, Edwards knew, posed its own risks to health and well-being. Hence the surgeon's stream of injunctions about 'the absolute necessity' of making proper use of the supplies of clothing he had obtained from the HBC's Fort Churchill store. 'Every man and boy on leaving his residence', Edwards ordered, '[is] . . . to have his waistcoat and jacket buttoned closely about his neck and breast, over which he is to wear his toggy or greatcoat. He is likewise to have his handkerchief or stock about his neck, his chin-cloth and mittens . . . and *never* less than two pairs of good socks. A piece of string [is] to be tied round the wrist so as to keep the cuff of the coat close . . . whereby the hand will slip more effectually into the mitten and the wind [will be] prevented from passing up the arm. Every woman [is] to wear *constantly* three petticoats, one of which must be of cloth or thick flannel, also thick leggings, and they are never to go out of doors without . . . hood, mittens and pelisse,† the latter of which may be thrown over the shoulders when going to the river for water.'[5]

---

* Those last two temperatures are equivalent to minus 48 and minus 51 degrees Celsius.

† A *pelisse* was the name given to a fashionable and fur-lined coat of this period. It is improbable that a Hudson Bay pelisse was a high-fashion garment, but it is likely to have been a fur-lined cloak of some kind.

If frostbite was an ever-present danger to people with no previous experience of extreme cold, so was scurvy. A debilitating
and ultimately deadly illness resulting from a diet deficient in
fruit, vegetables and other fresh foodstuffs, scurvy was mostly
kept at bay at Churchill Creek, where only one man showed
symptoms of it. That was due in part to Abel Edwards's insistence on everyone drinking huge quantities of what he called
'decoction of spruce', a herbal tea made from the younger needles found near the tips of a spruce tree's branches. Although so
bitter that it had to be washed down with the help of 'an extra
allowance of molasses', this brew – two pints taken every day –
supplemented the beneficial effects of the frozen cranberries
(gathered before the ground became snow-covered) that were
doled out throughout the winter.[6]

Three more Sutherland people died in the course of the winter –
all of them, it appears, from consumption or tuberculosis. The
ground being frozen hard, the Churchill Creek dead, Angus MacIver
observed, were buried 'Indian fashion'. 'The body was placed on a
layer of logs', MacIver explained, 'and [other] logs were used to
form a small, peaked wood cabin above. So well were the ends of the
logs notched and fitted that no animal could get at the body.' The
resulting 'graves', MacIver wrote, remained visible well over a
century after their construction. They were located, the trapper
added, 'in particularly beautiful locations'.[7]

There were occasions, it seems, when Abel Edwards got overly
close to the people he looked after. This became apparent in
December 1814 when a young and unmarried Kildonan woman
called Betty MacKay – by that point at Red River – was 'delivered of
a female bastard child' whose father, she said, was Edwards. But this
episode notwithstanding, and despite Edwards's often peremptory
manner, the surgeon's supportive stance appears to have been appreciated by the people in his care – all the more so, perhaps, because
his evident concern for their welfare contrasted so markedly with
William Auld's ceaseless hostility.[8]

In September, when Archibald McDonald began rewarding Churchill Creek house-building teams with nightly tots of rum, this was at once forbidden by Auld. Some weeks later – by way of a directive which Donald Gunn afterwards called 'an extraordinary act of despotism' – Auld had the firelock (or firing mechanism) removed from every musket in the Churchill Creek community's possession. Ostensibly, this was to ensure that none of the Sutherland men got lost in the forest as a result of their being tempted into hunting expeditions. But what really lay behind the confiscation of Churchill Creek firelocks, or so it was alleged by men whose guns were thus disabled, was Auld's contention that such game as could be found in the creek's vicinity was HBC property. Prominent among this game were the 'partridges' or ptarmigan which began to appear in the Churchill River area in November and which were to remain there 'in extraordinary numbers' for the rest of the winter. While William Auld had no objection to partridges being eaten at Churchill Creek, he was insistent that a careful record be kept of the numbers of birds thus consumed, and equally insistent that Lord Selkirk (in his role as the Red River settlement's prime mover) should in time be billed for each and every one of them.[9]

Because of Auld's edict, it is known that between 8 November and Christmas Day 1813, exactly 1,350 ptarmigans were consumed by the occupants of Churchill Creek's log cabins. This minimised consumption of HBC-supplied salt beef. It also reduced the need for trips to be made from the creek to the Bay Company store at Fort Churchill. This was a major bonus because each such trip involved, Donald Gunn wrote, 'a return journey of thirty miles on snow-shoes', a journey made all the more demanding by William Auld having told John Charles, the fort's chief trader, to ensure that none of the Churchill Creek party spent more than an hour or two on HBC premises.[10]

As days grew shorter, this ruling became impossible to obey, with the result that, on the evening of 23 November, three 'settlers' (as Red River-bound emigrants are called in HBC documentation) were permitted to overnight at Fort Churchill. There they bedded down in the complex's 'Indian Room' – accommodation set aside for Aboriginals who, though regarded by Auld as less uncivilised than Highlanders, were kept apart from the Bay Company's European personnel. That night the Indian Room caught fire, apparently because such an intense blaze had been stoked up in its stove that the stove's chimney became red-hot and caused boards next to it to ignite. While it is wholly believable that the settler trio in residence – seizing, perhaps, a rare chance to get warm – were responsible, they denied this on the basis that they had set only a 'moderate fire' and on the further grounds that the Indian Room's thickly timbered walls could have been smouldering for some time. While John Charles was inclined to give the settler party the benefit of the doubt, William Auld, still at Fort Churchill at this point, was not. Awakened by his 'consort', as he called his Aboriginal 'country wife' or partner, Auld first took charge of firefighting efforts and next set about attributing blame for what had occurred to 'the imprudence of a party of the settlers who had never been before the fatal night suffered to sleep or even stop at the [fort]'.[11]

Soon after this, as it happened, William Auld left Fort Churchill for York Factory and in his absence the 80-plus people at Churchill Creek were permitted a little more leeway. Christmas was marked with a generous allowance of rum and, as the hours of daylight began gradually to grow, work started on getting everything in 'perfect readiness' for an eventual trek southwards. Between January and March, more than two dozen sleds were constructed. Tents – acquired from Fort Churchill – were put in order; food supplies were accumulated; snowshoes and other gear were got ready. Those settlers unable to walk to York Factory, it was agreed, would remain at Churchill Creek until they could be taken off by sea. The others, with Archibald McDonald in charge, were to quit their winter quarters on 30 March or as soon after that date as proved practicable. In the event, the McDonald-led contingent set off (as described earlier) on Wednesday 6 April.[12]

*   *   *

Twelve days out from Churchill Creek and 'after a great deal of labour', McDonald and his party reached York Factory. Soon they were joined by Jean MacKay, Angus MacKay and the three exhausted (but now recovered) youngsters left in their care. A new 'camp', consisting of five or six large tents and 'a small storehouse', was established on 'the bank of [the] Hayes River about four miles above York Factory'. Oatmeal, rice, dried peas, salt pork, molasses and other provisions were obtained from the HBC; and over the next three or four weeks, as the weather slowly warmed, preparations were made for the upstream voyage scheduled to begin as soon as river conditions permitted.[13]

On the morning of Friday 20 May newly shattered ice on the Hayes River was seen and heard from the Sutherland people's camp to be 'forcing its way down[stream] in a body'. Next day William Cook, York Factory's chief trader, declared the river fit for travel. The HBC 'boatmen' charged with overseeing this last stage of the Sutherland emigrant group's journey were accordingly told to be ready to start for Red River on Monday 23 May.[14]

The voyage up the Hayes and on to Red River was made in two HBC York boats. About 45 feet in length, York boats, constructed by Orcadians in Bay Company employment, were modelled on Orkney fishing boats which, in turn, owed much of their design to the long-ships that had brought Orkney people's Viking ancestors from Norway 1,000 years before. Like longships, York Boats were propelled both by oar and sail, and though much heavier than the birch-bark canoes favoured by the NWC, could be carried around rapids. There were plenty such rapids on the Hayes. There were other obstacles too, most notably the ice that lingered on Swampy Lake, Oxford Lake, Windy Lake and the several other lakes strung out along the river's course. Sometimes it rained and blew 'most tremendously'. Occasionally – still – it snowed. But though intimi-dated initially by 'the rough state of the river', the Sutherland people (none of whom had any previous experience of boat-handling) proved more than capable of coping with adverse weather and with the strenuous task of getting their two craft to the point – towards the Hayes's headwaters – where, by means of a connecting stream called the Echimamish,* it is possible to access the Nelson River's upper reaches.[15]

The Nelson exits the 260-mile-long Lake Winnipeg towards the lake's northern tip. Near here, at Jack River,† the HBC had established a post where, on 11 June, the southbound party – to everyone's delight – met 'with a number of . . . friends and acquaintances'. Those were men in HBC service. Some were Bay Company veterans, among them, very probably, Donald Sutherland, introduced to the fur trade by his Strathbrora uncle, Donald MacKay, in 1795 and based in 1814 in the Lake Winnipeg area. Others were more recent recruits who, like Manitoba's eventual historian Donald Gunn, had left Scotland at the same time as the Kildonan emigrants. Among this latter group, noted Archibald McDonald, was a young man who 'present[ed] to his sister, whom he had the happiness to meet here, a large cake of maple sugar as a positive proof of the goodness of the [Red River] country' where he had spent the preceding winter and spring.[16]

There was dancing that night at Jack River. Next day, a Sunday, in 'rain inclining to sleet', the previous evening's dancers were on Lake Winnipeg. A week or so later, their two York boats reached the lake's southern end, entered Red River and, on Wednesday 22 June, made landfall on the river's left or western bank some two or three miles below 'the Forks' formed by the Red's junction with the Assiniboine.[17]

Today the land adjacent to the Sutherland people's disembarkation point has vanished under the streets, homes, stores and other commercial premises constituting the part of Winnipeg known – appropriately – as Kildonan. In 1814, however, beyond the narrow

---

* The Echimamish is unusual in that it links (with almost no current in either direction) two river systems – those of the Hayes and the Nelson. Although the Nelson, like the Hayes, flows into Hudson Bay not far from York Factory, fur traders preferred the Hayes to the much larger and faster flowing Nelson.

† Afterwards renamed Norway House.

belt of woodland then fringing the river bank, there was nothing but
prairie – griddle-flat, treeless and unbuilt-on – stretching uninter-
ruptedly westwards from the spot where, on the morning following
their arrival, the Red River settlement's newest residents began
planting 42 bushels* of seed potatoes that had been kept in reserve
for them by Miles Macdonell, the man whom the Earl of Selkirk had
placed in day-to-day charge of his Red River venture.[18]

Had matters at Red River unfolded as Selkirk intended, the planting of those potatoes, together with the subsequent allocation of
100-acre landholdings to Sutherland settler families, would have
denoted the commencement of fresh and cheerier chapters in lives
that had been blighted – since the start of Kildonan's troubles in
January 1813 – by one unhappiness after another. But to be a pioneer
settler at Red River, it quickly became apparent, was to be unremittingly beset by difficulties.

Some of those were inherent in the colony's geographical position. Since its beginnings two centuries earlier, European settlement
in North America had expanded gradually outwards from the continent's Atlantic coast. This meant that most frontier settlements
were within fairly easy reach of the more established communities
that together constituted increasingly complex societies of the sort
that, by the early nineteenth century, were taking shape around the
Ottawa and St Lawrence Rivers in Upper Canada (present-day
Ontario). But Upper Canada's farmsteads, villages and small towns
were separated from Red River by a 1,000-mile-wide tract of unsettled territory traversed only – and then just once a year in each
direction – by NWC canoes. Although its consequent isolation from
more populated parts of British North America would in any case
have slowed and checked the Red River colony's development, settler
prospects were rendered still more unfavourable by two further
circumstances. One (already touched on) was the NWC's unyielding
opposition to what Lord Selkirk was trying to accomplish at Red

---

* A bushel of potatoes would have weighed around 50 pounds.

River. The other was the cack-handed way in which Miles Macdonell responded to this opposition.

Like the leading Nor'Westers, many of whom he knew and to some of whom he was related, Macdonell, who first met Selkirk when the earl visited Upper Canada in 1804, was of Highland background. In principle, this should have helped Red River's governor, as Macdonell was designated by Selkirk, to explore ways of defusing – in part at least – NWC hostility to the earl's settlement project. Instead Macdonell acted in ways that had the opposite effect. Possessing little in the way of leadership skills, he gained neither the trust nor the respect of the admittedly hard-to-control and often quarrelsome group of several dozen men – some Scottish, others Irish – who, in the summer of 1812, became the Selkirk colony's first settlers. Neither during that summer, when this initial contingent reached Red River too late in the season to undertake any planting, nor in 1813, when there was less excuse for failing to get worthwhile agriculture under way, was anything of consequence done by either governor or settlers to make the settlement self-sufficient in food. The outcome was a Miles Macdonell 'proclamation' of January 1814. This was intended to secure a reliable supply of foodstuffs by making food exports from the Red River area subject to licences obtainable from Macdonell in his capacity as on-the-ground representative of Lord Selkirk – now, legally at least, the area's proprietor. Instead of putting the Red River colony on a better footing, however, Macdonell's edict endangered its existence.

The exports Miles Macdonell sought to limit consisted principally of pemmican – a concentrated mix of dried buffalo meat, berries and fat. Highly nutritious and easily portable, pemmican fuelled hard-paddling canoe crews in much the same way as more modern transport systems are fuelled by petroleum. The Macdonell proclamation, it followed, further alienated the Nor'Westers – who saw in it an attempt to sabotage their capacity to travel and to trade. Equally antagonised, with still more damaging consequences, was Red River's substantial Métis population. This population consisted of people whose ancestry was traceable to relationships between fur traders and their Québécois canoemen on one side, First Nation women on the other. Then emerging as a distinct ethnic grouping, the Métis depended economically on buffalo hunting, at which they excelled, and on the sale of buffalo-derived products, principally pemmican, to the NWC. Because of its adverse impact on both groups, then, the pemmican proclamation's net effect was to create an anti-settlement alliance between the Nor'Westers and the Métis. That alliance's increasingly explicit objective – one given shape during the five or so months between Macdonell's January proclamation and the mid-June arrival of the Sutherland party – was to bring Lord Selkirk's Red River venture to a close. This, it was agreed, would most effectively be accomplished by the Métis and the NWC pursuing different means to the same end. The company's senior personnel at Red River were to tell settlers that they would find life easier in Upper Canada – while also providing them with a means of getting there. The Métis, for their part, would have the job – should this become necessary – of so harrying the settlement as to make conditions there unbearable. The eventual outcome, if all went to plan, would be to restore Nor'Wester supremacy at Red River. This, in turn, would make it more likely that the NWC would be able to see off the HBC's growing efforts to expand its presence in the many fur-bearing localities Nor'Wester traders had so successfully opened up in Athabasca and the other western territories the Montreal-based NWC could access only through Red River.

Among the Kildonan emigrants who reached Red River in June 1814 was 23-year-old George Bannerman, who, in due course, married and had children. Those children's children, as it happened, would include the mother of John Diefenbaker who, from 1957 to 1963, was prime minister of Canada. Reflecting in his memoirs on the Red River experiences of the 'dispossessed Scottish Highlanders' from whom he descended, Diefenbaker wrote: 'They could not have known that after all they had suffered . . . they would find themselves

caught up in battles waged between two competing fur trade empires
. . . For many this was too much to bear. What they sought was
simply the chance to build anew, not be pawns in a struggle remote
from their understanding or interest.' In thus relaying what his
mother told him of her grandfather's eventual decision to accept the
NWC's offer of transport from Red River to Upper Canada, John
Diefenbaker was (consciously or unconsciously) echoing a verdict
reached, a century earlier, in Donald Gunn's *History of Manitoba*.
So 'wearied and disgusted' were they by the 'trials' they had been
subjected to since leaving Sutherland, Gunn wrote, that it was
scarcely surprising that many of the people in whose company he
had crossed the Pentland Firth in June 1813 should, by the fall of the
following year if not before, have 'heartily wished themselves away
from Red River'.[19]

Despite much of his own life being spent at Red River, where he
settled in 1823 and where he lived for more than 50 years, Donald
Gunn, it should be acknowledged, was a bitter critic of Lord Selkirk,
who, Gunn thought, misled, indeed swindled, the Sutherland families he directed towards his colony. Something of this is reflected in
Gunn's account of his meeting at York Factory, in the summer of
1814, with some of the Sutherland people who had stayed on at
Churchill Creek until it became possible to take them south by sea.
'Their condition', Gunn commented, 'was as miserable and distressing as it could possibly be.' He was particularly affected, Gunn went
on, by the plight of one 'venerable patriarch' and his wife – Donald
and Janet Gunn from Borrobol. Donald, at 65 much the oldest of
the 1813 emigrants, 'had been', Gunn wrote, 'a substantial farmer in
his native land [but] now appeared to be in the most destitute state
imaginable. His habitation consisted of a few poles on which was
stretched, as an apology for a covering, a piece of what had been in
its better day a boat sail, but [was] now so tattered and torn that it
was pervious to every blast of wind that blew and to every drop of
rain that fell.' Prior to quitting Sutherland, Gunn noted, the former
farmer, like other intending emigrants, sold a substantial herd of

cattle. 'Out of the proceeds, he paid [the Earl of Selkirk] . . . ten guineas for the passage of each of his numerous family and [in addition] deposited a considerable sum in the earl's hands to be drawn upon as circumstances might require. But [at York Factory] he could not even get a needle [from the HBC] on the credit of his deposit.' Two of Donald and Janet's children had died at Churchill. The others – months earlier – had left with Archibald McDonald for Red River. 'And here were the aged and broken-hearted parents in their desolation, without shelter and with food barely sufficient to sustain life, deprived of all the property they once possessed, and for what? Exile and misery.'[20]

The settler contingent containing Donald Gunn's 'venerable patriarch' – with whom the future historian shared a name and to whom he may have been related – reached Red River in late August 1814. 'Notwithstanding the troubles they had undergone', Miles Macdonell assured Lord Selkirk in a letter written shortly after this group's arrival, 'they appeared to be in good health and good spirits'. In light of what Gunn observed at York Factory, to say nothing of what had been endured on the *Prince of Wales* and at Churchill, that seems unlikely. The governor, however, was determined to deal only in good news. So was Archibald McDonald. 'They are now all settled in their respective lots', he wrote of Red River's new arrivals, 'and most of their houses [are] in a fair way of building . . . It is with the greatest pleasure I can . . . report to your lordship that they never were happier and more contented in Kildonan than they are here already.'[21]

McDonald's journal entries tell a different story. They record, for example, that Red River's settlers from Sutherland were far from pleased to have had no say in deciding where exactly they should set up home, insisting to McDonald and Macdonell that 'the Earl of Selkirk [had] promised them their choice of lands'. This, McDonald told them, 'could not be heard of', whereupon some at least of the Sutherland menfolk appear to have staged something akin to a sit-down strike by refusing for a day or two to work the farms assigned to them.[22]

Lord Selkirk, needless to say, was given no inkling of this, nor of several other failures to comply with his intentions. Typical of these was the Bay Company's apparent inability to ship to Red River the substantial quantities of emigrant baggage brought ashore from the *Prince of Wales* at Sloop's Cove in August 1813. Containing clothes, bedding and all sorts of other household items, this baggage – as stipulated by Lord Selkirk back in Scotland – had been packed in bales of a size easily accommodated in York boats. Necessarily left behind at Churchill by the group that snow-shoed south in April 1814, scores of these bales were that summer taken by sea to York Factory. But they got no further, and were reported to be 'still lying in [York Factory] stores' in the fall of 1815.[23]

Having their personal belongings with them at Red River might have helped the Kildonan people settle in there. As it was, a lot of them never did. 'We found everything very different to what we had been told should be our condition,' said James MacKay when attempting to explain why his stay at Red River lasted less than a year. 'I was a good deal disappointed,' commented Robert Gunn who had piped the overland party out of Churchill Creek in April 1814 and who was to leave Red River along with MacKay. 'I found nothing like I was told it was going to be,' said Haman Sutherland by way of endorsement.[24]

Others were more specific. 'Farming utensils had been promised,' contended Andrew McBeath and William Gunn. But because heavier implements were unavailable, previously uncultivated prairie had to be tilled without the aid of anything approximating to a plough, while the few light tools on offer could only be acquired for sums equivalent to more than a week's wages in Scotland. 'Hoes were sold at 10 s[hillings],' said McBeath and Gunn, 'axes at 15 s[hillings], thin, small copper kettles at 30 s[hillings].'[25]

The prices charged at Red River for all such manufactured goods were an arguably unavoidable consequence of the place's remoteness. But in insisting on such prices Miles Macdonell was surely in breach of Selkirk's instructions. 'The amount of money to be received from these [Kildonan] people', the earl had informed his governor, 'is a matter of very secondary importance in comparison with their being well satisfied with their treatment'.[26]

Macdonell's reluctance to deal more sympathetically with colonists for whose welfare he was responsible is traceable in part to a snobbish conviction that, as Red River's governor, it was not his business to get alongside the settlement's hoi polloi. Archibald McDonald too appears to have thought himself something of a grandee among people far too inclined, in his view, to get above themselves. The journal McDonald kept daily at Red River during the winter of 1814–15 accordingly degenerates at times into a catalogue of complaints about settlers McDonald considered 'disrespectful' and on whom he imposed petty, and wholly counter-productive, punishments. Thus Robert Gunn, whose eventual quitting of Red River must have owed something to such treatment, was denied tobacco because of his 'bad conduct'. Unsurprisingly, Gunn and other settlers thought McDonald 'harsh and unkind', while he, for his part, found 'the [Sutherland] people so troublesome that', as he commented in February 1815, 'I don't see them but seldom.'[27]

The aloofness thus exhibited by Lord Selkirk's representatives at Red River made it a great deal easier than it might have been for the NWC's key man in the area to woo disgruntled colonists to his side. This was Duncan Cameron. Like Macdonell and McDonald, Cameron had been born into a tacksman family in the Highlands. Like Macdonell he had been taken to New York as a small boy by his parents and, again like Macdonell, he moved north into what remained of British North American territory in the aftermath of the USA's emergence as an independent state. There, however, all similarity between Duncan Cameron and Miles Macdonell ended. For unlike Macdonell – and also unlike Archibald McDonald – Cameron, whom one Red River settler would long afterwards recall as 'a fine old gentleman', possessed no end of people skills. Nor were these his only advantages.[28]

At the Forks, today the bustling heart of downtown Winnipeg and then the strategically significant spot where Assiniboine and Red River canoe routes met, the NWC had constructed in 1809 a sizeable post called Fort Gibraltar. The fort's 18-foot-high palisade surrounded several buildings, much the most imposing being the substantial residence occupied by Duncan Cameron in his capacity as the post's *bourgeois* or boss. Downstream at the altogether more gimcrack Fort Douglas, named for Lord Selkirk and supposedly the administrative headquarters of the Red River country, there was nothing comparable with Cameron's fine home. Still more lacking at Fort Douglas was anything akin to the lavish hospitality in which the Nor'Wester *bourgeois* specialised.

Cameron, Archibald McDonald grumbled, 'began by prevailing upon several heads of [settler] families to visit him at the Forks where he treated them with the greatest attention'. There were 'dinners'; there was dancing; there were 'large allowances of liquors and even of wine'. 'In short', McDonald continued, 'he [Cameron] took every means he could devise to gain [the settlers'] confidence. He had the advantage [because of having been raised in Glenmoriston to the west of Inverness] of being able to talk to them in their native [Gaelic] language, and he very soon began to make them discontented with their situation and prospects. He told them that if they would go down to [Upper] Canada they would receive lands there . . . and that he would find them a passage down in the following spring.'[29]

That last offer was made explicit in January 1815. 'I know all the bad usage you got and the many injustices that were done to every one of you since you left your own country,' Duncan Cameron told the settler community. 'I consider you to be in the very worst of prisons here.' He therefore proposed, Cameron went on, to take 'out of bondage' as many people as wished to be conveyed to Upper Canada – 'a good country,' Cameron told his settler contacts, 'where you may make a decent living for yourselves and your families'.[30]

By way of underlining his capacity to do as promised, Duncan Cameron now took to wearing the military uniform he had

acquired when an officer in the so-called Voyageur Corps established by the colonial authorities in present-day Quebec and
Ontario when, in response to the USA's 1812 declaration of war,
those same authorities were looking to guard against American
incursions into wilderness areas where the NWC's operatives were
more at home than regular troops. To men like the more and more
disenchanted Robert Gunn, the unfailingly genial Duncan
Cameron – presiding over an impressively fortified complex and
dressed in the scarlet tunic of a British army officer – must have
seemed an altogether more impressive, as well as more appealing,
figure than either Archibald McDonald or Miles Macdonell. Hence
the ease with which, in April, several colonists – George Bannerman,
John Diefenbaker's great-grandfather, prominent among them –
were persuaded by Cameron to remove a number of small artillery
pieces from Fort Douglas and to take those upriver to the NWC's
Fort Gibraltar. Everyone involved in this escapade, Robert Gunn
would afterwards tell an Upper Canadian court, was convinced
that 'if the settlers attempted to go away, [the Fort Douglas artillery pieces] would be used to prevent them'. Whether or not
individuals like Gunn truly believed this (and a later enquiry
conducted by a senior colonial official concluded that they did),
the disarming of Fort Douglas had the effect of making the Red
River settlement more vulnerable to the Métis who, during the
spring and early summer of 1815, were to make conditions miserable for those settlers – by now a minority – who continued to
resist Duncan Cameron's blandishments.[31]

It is a pointer to the growing ethnic complexity of early nineteenth-century Manitoba that Métis leadership at this decisive stage
in the Red River settlement's evolution was more and more assumed
by a man who, though born to a Métis woman of mixed Cree and
Québécois descent, had a Highland father. This man was Cuthbert
Grant. His father, also Cuthbert Grant, was a fur trader from
Strathspey, some 30 miles south of Inverness. Hence the extent to
which the Red River troubles of 1815 possess, from a Scottish

perspective, a little of the character of a three-sided Highland civil war transposed to the North American prairies. One set of Highlanders, led by Duncan Cameron and his Nor'Wester associates, was endeavouring to remove from Red River another set of Highlanders, Selkirk's settlers from Sutherland. Equally anxious to be rid of this second Highland grouping was the part-Highland Cuthbert Grant, acting in alliance with Cameron but with his own distinctive agenda deriving from the fact, redolent with irony, that the arrival of Kildonan refugees at Red River posed much the same threat to his Métis community's way of life as was posed to the Sutherland way of life by the beginnings of large-scale sheep farming. Thus it came about that people who, two years before, had set about expelling shepherds and sheep farmers from the Strath of Kildonan now found themselves subjected to similar, though more violent, intimidation.

During the spring and early summer of 1815 settler horses were killed, a bull slaughtered, cattle worried by dogs, homes fired on and, on at least one occasion, settlers taken into temporary captivity. The outcome was exactly as Cuthbert Grant and his associates intended. People already eager to leave for Upper Canada became all the more anxious to be gone; others, though formerly inclined to hang on, concluded that it had become too hazardous to remain. The outcome was the departure from Red River in mid-June of an Upper Canada-bound NWC canoe fleet whose passengers included a majority of the men, women and youngsters who, by way of Churchill and York Factory, had reached Red River from Sutherland just 12 months earlier.[32]

Among the people thus embarking on a further 1,000-mile journey were two babies. One, a 10-month-old girl called Christy or Kirsty Sutherland, was taken east by her mother Margaret (herself just 17) and Margaret's husband William, who, like his wife, came originally from Borrobol. The other was a little boy named John, born at Red River the previous summer and now stowed into a Nor'Wester canoe by his parents, Angus and Jean MacKay. They, it seems certain, would have named their son for the grandfather the boy would never see: Kildonan rebel leader and Sloop's Cove typhus casualty John Sutherland.[33]

The MacKays were eventually to acquire a farm near Port Talbot on the north shore of Lake Erie not far from the present-day Ontarian city of London. Among the several other Kildonan people who settled finally in the same locality was John MacPherson. Twenty when he quit Red River, John was the brother of Kate MacPherson who, on the *Prince of Wales* and at Sloop's Cove, had done so much to care for typhus sufferers. From Port Talbot, where he was joined during the 1820s by two brothers, a further sister and their mother, John would keep in touch, by way of an annual exchange of letters, with Kate. The two, however, were never to see each other again, John spending the rest of his life in Ontario and Kate being unyieldingly determined to cling on at Red River where (but for one or two brief interludes) she would remain until her death in 1867.[34]

On Tuesday 27 June 1815 the settler remnant at Red River – a remnant including Kate MacPherson – took to boats and, by way of Lake Winnipeg, set sail for the safe haven provided by the HBC post at Jack River. Next day their vacated homes were burned by the Métis. This was another reverse for Miles Macdonell who, in what proved to be a vain attempt to placate the Red River settlement's enemies, had two weeks earlier surrendered himself to the Nor'Westers. Their response to this development was to place Macdonell under guard prior to despatching him to Montreal. From a settler perspective, however, Macdonell's consequent removal from the prairie scene had one wholly beneficial consequence. It resulted in the abandoned settlement's demoralised escapees acquiring fresh and more effective leadership in the shape of Colin Robertson. Flamboyant, hard drinking and aggressive, Robertson, who grew up in Perthshire, had some years before forsaken the NWC for the HBC. Much like Donald MacKay at an earlier period, he was firmly convinced that the Bay Company, if it was ever to prevail over the Nor'Westers, needed to adopt the Montreal-based corporation's ruthless methods. This philosophy Robertson summed up in a favourite maxim, 'When you are among wolves, howl!' He was to howl to good effect at Red River where he took charge in July 1815.[35]

In August, Robertson led back to Red River the 30-plus settlers who had fled north at the end of June. In September he supervised both the start of rebuilding and the ingathering of such crops – not least a substantial amount of well-ripened grain – as had survived the earlier Métis onslaught. In October he forced his way into Fort Gibraltar, retook the guns that had been taken from Fort Douglas in April, imprisoned Duncan Cameron and released him only when the shaken Nor'Wester agreed to desist from further harassment of the settlement. 'The crops look well,' Robertson informed Lord Selkirk. 'The wheat and barley are housed; the people are now busy with the hay . . . The settlement . . . [possesses] without exception the most fertile and the easiest cultivated soil I ever saw. It is a perfect paradise.'[36]

Earlier in the year, Duncan Cameron had added to the pressure then being applied to Red River's settlers by telling them that their lives were 'every day in danger' from the region's First Nation peoples who, he warned, would sooner or later kill and scalp the colony's entire population – women and children not excepted. In fact the area's Cree and Saulteaux bands, notably the Saulteaux who taught incoming Highlanders how to hunt buffalo and otherwise survive in prairie country, could scarcely have been more welcoming – mainly, it seems, because they found HBC trading terms more favourable than those on offer from the Nor'Westers. 'The Indians are to a man determined to assist us,' Colin Robertson reported. All that the Earl of Selkirk's settlement now lacked, Robertson felt, was settlers. It came as something of a relief to him, therefore, when in November more than 80 such settlers arrived from Sutherland.[37]

'The situation of the place is still is as you left it,' Kate MacPherson learned at this time from a letter reaching her from a family member still in Gailiable, the Strath of Kildonan township where she had grown up. That was true. Although Gabriel Reed and William Clunes had been for two years in control of much of the strath, and although people had been leaving for Caithness as well as for Red River, there had been, thanks to the impasse resulting from the 1813 protest movement, no widespread evictions. But the clearance of a series of townships continued to be anticipated, and despite what had been learned in 1814 of the difficulties encountered by the previous year's emigrant contingent, there thus remained interest, especially on the part of Kildonan's more substantial farming tenants, in taking up Lord Selkirk's continuing offer of land at Red River – land available to all comers, the earl's agents told inquirers, at five shillings an acre.[38]

Selkirk's principal contact in the Strath of Kildonan at this point was Angus Matheson, an ex-soldier who had met the earl during the latter's Sutherland excursion of May 1813 and who had then so impressed Selkirk that Matheson was now offered 'a free passage to Red River and a free gift of a hundred acres of the best land there'. Matheson was unmarried but was anxious to take with him his widowed mother, a woman of 60, his brother, his brother's wife and the couple's four children, the oldest of whom was ten and the youngest just three months. This was duly arranged, Angus Matheson, by way of rendering Selkirk a return favour, undertaking to have the Strath of Kildonan's new emigrant party, numbering 84 in total, gather at Alexander Sage's church, where the minister read out to them a Gaelic translation of a 'memorandum' the earl had sent north. One object of this exercise was to convey to Sage's hearers Selkirk's assurances that what were referred to as 'the circumstances of [the] last voyage' – the one terminating at Churchill – would not be repeated. Those assurances accepted, it remained only to satisfy intending emigrants' wish that they be accompanied to Red River by a clergyman.[39]

Two years before, Selkirk had attempted to engage just such a clergyman, Alexander Sage's son Donald. Then a newly qualified

Church of Scotland minister, Donald Sage, at that point, had still to
find a parish and was employed as private tutor to the children of
Robert McKid, the Sutherland sheriff-depute called upon to deal
with the Strath of Kildonan's 1813 'rioters'. Although offered a most
attractive annual salary of £50 by Selkirk, the younger Sage declined
in the end to go to Red River, as Selkirk wanted, with the first set of
Kildonan emigrants, on the grounds, it seems, that his Gaelic was
not sufficiently fluent.* Nor was he inclined, it appears, to accompany the Kildonan people who left in 1815. Instead it was agreed
that one of their number, James Sutherland, a man who had served
as one of the Kildonan congregation's elders, would conduct 'divine
service' at Red River where (Alexander Sage having given him some
instruction in such matters) Sutherland was also to oversee 'the
solemnisation of marriages among the settlers'.[40]

As the 1813 party had done, the 1815 emigrants made their way
to Thurso and crossed the Pentland Firth to Stromness. There, in
June, they boarded the *Hadlow*, outward bound for York Factory
and, having been built just a year before, a reassuringly sound vessel.
Aboard an accompanying ship was Robert Semple who, two months
earlier, HBC directors in London had appointed Governor of
Rupert's Land,† the name by which the company's North American
territories were formally known. Once ashore at Hudson Bay,
Semple, a much-travelled businessman then in his late thirties, was
to assume responsibilities formerly exercised by William Auld, who
by now had quit the Bay Company. But if the new governor's duties
were akin to Auld's, his opinions of Highlanders were wholly at
odds with those of his predecessor. Although the young women
among the Kildonan emigrant party did not altogether take his
fancy, being 'more likely,' Semple commented, 'to improve the

---

* Given the nature of Donald Sage's upbringing, it seems unlikely that he had as little
Gaelic as he claimed. Interestingly, Sage makes no reference to this episode in his
memoirs.

† Deriving from Prince Rupert of the Rhine, a cousin of King Charles II and the
HBC's first governor.

strength than the beauty of the breed', he nevertheless thought them, their brothers and their parents 'the mildest people in their manners [he] ever met with'. Red River's latest batch of settlers from Sutherland, HBC headquarters was informed, were 'sober, honest, patient, obedient, willing to oblige and remarkably good natured'.[41]

Among the passengers who had joined the *Hadlow* before the ship sailed for Stromness from Gravesend was John Rogers, a mineralogist hired to make a geological survey of HBC possessions. Being aware of how typhus had overwhelmed the *Prince of Wales*, Rogers made it his business to see that nothing similar occurred on the *Hadlow*. Singling out 'some of the stoutest and most active lads' among the emigrant party, he 'made them scrape the [accommodation] deck quite clean every day and sweep it morning and evening as well', with a view to ensuring that 'no filth could possibly accumulate'. Everyone from Kildonan was encouraged 'to stay on [the upper] deck as much as possible'; 'music and dancing' were organised to 'keep up cheerfulness'; and for some three hours each day John Rogers insisted that emigrant children attended an on-deck school where they began to be made literate in English. 'They certainly made great progress', Rogers commented of these children, 'both in learning the English language as well as [in] learning to read. Their parents were highly delighted.'[42]

Nine weeks and three days out from Stromness, the *Hadlow* dropped anchor off York Factory. 'Perhaps the same number of people under the same circumstances never landed on a foreign shore in higher health or spirits,' John Rogers commented. 'May God grant them every success.'[43]

But at once there was a setback. At York Factory the new arrivals learned for the first time of the springtime turmoil at Red River and the eastward exodus that had followed. This was especially distressing for the several parents in the position which James Sutherland, the Red River settlement's intended preacher, now found himself. Sutherland and his wife Mary had come out on the *Hadlow* with four teenage children, Janet, Catherine, Isabella and James. At Red

River, however, they had expected to meet with two older children, Haman and Barbara, who had left the Strath of Kildonan for Selkirk's colony in 1813. But (as already indicated in Haman's case) both those young people were among the many settlers who, by August, were en route for, or had already arrived in, Upper Canada.[*] On being told this at York Factory, Mary and James Sutherland – with others who got similar news – were understandably 'very much alarmed' and 'cast down'.[44]

James Sutherland's mood, perhaps, was lightened by his being asked to conduct marriage ceremonies that took place at York Factory within days of the *Hadlow* reaching there. These were the product of shipboard romances between three of the Sutherland emigrant group's young women – clearly not so unalluring as Robert Semple made out – and young men who had been destined for HBC service but who were now permitted to become Red River settlers instead. The 'great glee' with which those Hudson Bay weddings were celebrated, Robert Semple felt, went some way to removing initial 'doubts and fears'. Equally helpful in this regard, the governor added, was the 'kind attention' the entire Sutherland group received from HBC men at York Factory. 'Very good tents were pitched for [the disembarking emigrants]; they had the use of the [York Factory] cookhouse with every other convenience the place afforded.' There could have been no greater contrast with the wretched conditions endured at Sloop's Cove two years before.[45]

As a result of the 'contrary winds', 'gales' and 'snowstorms' they ran up against on the Hayes River and on Lake Winnipeg, it was not until early November – by which time both the lake and adjacent watercourses were beginning to freeze over – that this second influx of people from Sutherland won through to Red River. Once there, however, the majority of them would remain; there would be no further departures of the June 1815 sort. Hence its

---

[*] Haman and Barbara were both to settle in the vicinity of Gwillimbury near Toronto.

being possible for this book's author to attend in Winnipeg, on a
snowy winter's afternoon in 2013, an annual general meeting of the
Lord Selkirk Association of Rupert's Land which, in the words of
its website, 'serves as a link to bind together the descendants of the
hardy men and women who first settled on the banks of the Red
River in the early 1800s'. In November 1815, those men, women and
their children numbered just over 100. Today the community they
established has grown into a city of more than 700,000, and
Winnipeggers of Scottish Highland background share what was
once the Red River settlement with people drawn, or so it sometimes seems, from every one of our modern world's cultures and
ethnicities: German, Lebanese, Ukrainian, Polish, Guatemalan,
Filipino, Slovak, Japanese, Chinese, Slovenian, Jewish, Norwegian,
Thai, Russian, Italian, Nigerian, Mexican, Icelandic, Congolese.
The relevant list, in Canadian census data, extends across seven
closely printed pages.[46]

Not least because of his having encouraged people to quit
Scotland for a trouble-plagued Red River, historians from Donald
Gunn forward have often been disapproving of Thomas Douglas,
fifth Earl of Selkirk. As the organisation's name suggests, their views
are not shared by the Lord Selkirk Association of Rupert's Land. At
the association's 2013 general meeting, two members, Cathie
Morgan-Matula and Garnett Lobb, spoke about a trip they had
made to the Strath of Kildonan that summer. There was much interest in seeing, in photograph after photograph, the nowadays scanty
remnants of the Kildonan townships in which so many of Manitoba's
earliest immigrants were born and raised. There was anger at what
was done, on the orders of the Marquis and Marchioness of Stafford,
to those townships. But there was no sense, among this gathering of
Winnipeggers whose ancestry is traceable to people helped by Lord
Selkirk to escape from clearance-era Sutherland, that Selkirk had
done their forebears anything other than a favour.

At the close of each Lord Selkirk Association meeting there takes
place a little ceremony. As the names of early settler families are read

out, descendants of those families stand. And so, in a conference room on the third floor of a soaring office block on Winnipeg's Portage Street, this observer heard, one after another, the surnames of people who returned to Lord Selkirk's colony from Jack River in August 1815 – the surnames too of people who arrived there, in Robert Semple's company, three months later. 'Here the first spectacle that gladdened my eyes', Semple informed Selkirk, 'was twelve or fourteen stacks of corn, a sight perfectly novel in this country.' As the 80-plus Mathesons, Murrays, MacKays, Polsons, Gunns, Sutherlands, Bannermans, MacBeaths and Bruces from the Strath of Kildonan came ashore, Robert Semple went on, 'colours were hoisted . . . guns were fired [and] at night we laughed and drank and danced'.[47]

Houses that had earlier been destroyed had already been rebuilt under Colin Robertson's direction, Semple reported. New homes would follow, he promised, as would a church: 'I shall endeavour by all means to establish the settlers on their respective lots in the spring and in order to inspire confidence shall give it to be understood that I may become a settler myself.'[48]

Robert Semple believed that he and the 1815 emigrants from Kildonan had come to the prairies at what its governor thought 'the end of the difficult part of the history of Red River'. As is evident from even the briefest inspection of today's Winnipeg, the place was certainly destined to prosper. But before it did so, there would be no scarcity of further crises. Of these, much the most lamentable was a settler–Métis clash on 19 June 1816 when Robert Semple and some 20 others died. Inevitably, that Red River encounter involved men from Sutherland. So had an altogether bloodier confrontation, 18 months before, in a quite separate part of North America.[49]

7

'A MOST DESTRUCTIVE AND MURDEROUS FIRE'

The 93rd (Sutherland) Regiment at
the Battle of New Orleans

The *Creole Queen*, a modern replica of a steam-powered paddle-wheeler, takes around 30 minutes to make the downstream voyage to Chalmette from the New Orleans waterfront. During those 30 minutes *Creole Queen* passengers learn a good deal about the great river that is hurrying them south. Here in Louisiana, they are told, the Mississippi is up to three-quarters of a mile wide and 100 or more feet deep; its levees, or artificially raised banks, are the responsibility of the US army's Corps of Engineers; well over half of all America's grain exports (destined for more than 100 countries) are shipped down this single watercourse; some part of the muddy waters flowing past New Orleans will have started out two months before and thousands of miles away in western Canada. Those facts underscore the Mississippi's immense scale. They also serve as pointers to the river's key role in US development. But for the Mississippi's availability as ready-made highway and commercial outlet, the early nineteenth-century opening up of America's Midwest would have been a much more challenging, and economically less productive, process. Hence the significance of what occurred at Chalmette where the *Creole Queen* moors and where its disembarking passengers are met – Chalmette being federal government property – by a US National Park Service ranger.

This, the ranger says, indicating a large and grassy area kept clear of buildings, is the site of one of America's most important battles. Here on Sunday 8 January 1815, the ranger goes on, a hastily put together US army, under the command of Major-General Andrew Jackson, destroyed numerically superior British forces intent on occupying New Orleans and thereby strangling Midwest trade.

During their country's War of Independence, Americans had prevailed more than once over the British. But those successes had depended in part on assistance from France. The Battle of New Orleans, as the Chalmette encounter is known, was different. This was an all-American victory. And it was won, the Park Service ranger tells his *Creole Queen* audience, by an army whose composition shows that the USA, as early as 1815, had begun welding its disparate ethnicities into a single nation. Fighting alongside Jackson's regular troops were members of Louisiana's Creole (and usually French-speaking) planter class, New Orleans 'freemen of colour', a buccaneer detachment from pirate-controlled Barataria Bay in the Mississippi delta, a Native American (principally Choctaw) contingent and – further travelled than any of these – a set of sometimes scruffily clad or 'dirty shirt' frontiersmen and settlers from upriver territories such as Tennessee and Kentucky. By Jackson's British counterparts, most of them of aristocratic background, the American general's polyglot troops were regarded with disdain, even contempt. But the Battle of New Orleans was to overturn all such preconceptions. At the battle's conclusion – and this Chalmette confrontation lasted for barely two hours – British losses were well in excess of 2,000. American losses, as Andrew Jackson would report to President James Madison in Washington, numbered under 20.

Among the British dead were eight men from the Strath of Kildonan. James Fraser, Robert Gunn, Neil MacBeath and Samuel Matheson were killed in action at Chalmette on the morning of 8 January. Alexander MacBeath, Donald MacKay, Adam MacPherson and Duncan Matheson 'died of wounds' either that same day or shortly after.[1]

Those men had served in the British army's 93rd Regiment. All of them, it can safely be guessed, were neighbours, friends or relatives of at least some of the other Kildonan people whose surnames they shared and who, 1,500 miles north of New Orleans, were that same January struggling through their second Manitoban winter. But the Kildonan men who – along with numerous others from Sutherland – were to die beside the Mississippi had left home long before any Kildonan family had cause to think of emigrating to Red River.

The sequence of events that brought Sutherland soldiers to Chalmette had its starting point in Strathnaver, the most westerly, and also most northerly, of the early nineteenth-century Sutherland Estate's interior valleys. There, beside the road that today takes traffic through the strath and a mile or two from this road's junction with a further road leading to Kildonan and Helmsdale, the 93rd Regiment's beginnings are recalled in words inscribed on a metal plaque attached to a stone-built cairn or monument. This monument, its inscription announces, dates from 1914 when it was 'erected by the officers and men of the 2nd Battalion of the Argyll and Sutherland Highlanders', the 93rd's successor unit. The event the monument commemorates – the mustering or assembling of the 93rd Regiment's first set of soldiers – took place, on Sunday 24 August 1800, not far away at Langdale. There, between the road and the River Naver, some two or three hundred yards distant, is a flat and grassy area that can be seen to have the makings of a parade ground. Today this area is occupied by nothing other than a scattering of sheep. That summer Sunday in 1800, however, all must have been stir, noise and bustle hereabouts as 653 young men – a lot of them being seen off by parents and other family members – were lined up, provisioned and otherwise made ready for the start of their march out of Sutherland and into the wider world.

Getting those men together had not been easy. With a view to demonstrating her and her tenantry's patriotism, the Countess of Sutherland (as the future Marchioness of Stafford was known prior to her father-in-law's death in 1803) had committed to raising a regiment for service against France as far back as the opening months of 1799. The regiment, it had been announced, would be commanded by the countess's cousin, General William Wemyss, who had previously been in charge of the Sutherland Fencibles, a 1,000-strong force raised on the Sutherland Estate in 1793 and intended, as all such fencible* corps were intended, for home defence duties. Stationed initially in the Scottish Lowlands, the Sutherland Fencibles (as noted earlier) had been deployed briefly in Ireland during that country's 1798 uprising. Shortly after this the regiment was disbanded, but on the understanding that a large proportion of its officers and men would promptly join the new force Wemyss had undertaken to mobilise on his cousin's behalf. At this point, however, things went seriously awry, few volunteers being forthcoming. The 'delays and difficulties by which . . . recruiting [had] . . . been obstructed', one of the Countess of Sutherland's law agents reported, was due both to 'a relaxation . . . of the ancient spirit of clanship' and to some of the Fencible Regiment's soldiers having picked up 'crude and undigested notions' – meaning pro-democracy ideas – when serving in the south of Scotland and in Ireland.[2]

This was an early indication that Sutherland Estate tenants – as became still more apparent in 1813 and subsequently – could no longer be counted on, as might once have been the case, to fall in line with edicts issuing from Dunrobin Castle. In response, estate managers employed a mix of stick and carrot. Each township, it would afterwards be recalled, was 'required to furnish a rough census of those who were of the age for soldiers . . . If a father had three sons, two were demanded; and if he had two sons, one was demanded.' Conscription of this kind, however, was accompanied by the issuing of written undertakings to the effect that tenants who provided General Wemyss with manpower would be left securely in possession of their landholdings. Those undertakings, when read carefully, turned out to be time-limited. Hence Patrick Sellar's

---

* The term was a contraction of 'defencible'.

reaction when, in February 1813, Kildonan men then resisting eviction produced for Sellar's inspection a number of the documents in question – documents Kildonan parents had understood to mean that, as long as they had sons in the 93rd Regiment, their tenancies would be inviolate. Sellar, as his co-factor William Young reported, found 'the obligations . . . contained [in the papers he was shown] had expired'. Turning to the Kildonan men, Sellar 'told them so'.[3]

Patrick Sellar doubtless thought that the end of the matter. But whatever the legal niceties, many Sutherland parents continued to be convinced, as was said later, that tenants 'who sent their sons into the army' had been told they 'were never to be deprived of their land'. When, as happened in 1813, many such tenants in the Strath of Kildonan were nevertheless threatened with eviction, there was thus much bitter comment from people who, Patrick Sellar's opinions notwithstanding, never ceased to believe that bargains solemnly made had been casually set aside. That is why William Young considered it 'unfortunate' that the promissory documents handed out in the course of the 1799–1800 recruitment drive had ever been distributed. But distributed they definitely were, the papers shown to Patrick Sellar in 1813 having originated, it can be surmised, in exchanges witnessed by Donald Sage, then a boy of ten, when William Wemyss staged an impromptu recruiting fair on what Sage called 'the green' adjacent to his father's Kildonan manse.[4]

This was in May 1800 and General Wemyss, according to Sage, was accompanied by Major Gordon Clunes whose son William would afterwards become one of the Strath of Kildonan's principal sheep farmers. 'The majority [of the prospective soldiers] who assembled', Sage remembered, 'were tall, handsome young fellows who, at the verbal summons of the Countess's ground-officer [or local land manager] . . . presented themselves before General Wemyss that he might have for the asking the pick and choice of them . . . To ingratiate himself with the [young men's fathers]', Donald Sage added, 'General Wemyss . . . sent up to the manse [in advance of his getting there] . . . immense quantities of tobacco-twist and strong, black rapee snuff, together with . . . a large snuff-horn superbly mounted with silver.' The tobacco, it transpired, was unappreciated. 'Smoking', according to Sage, was then 'a luxury . . . utterly unknown to the men of Kildonan' who also, it seems, preferred 'light-coloured' and less potent snuff to the notoriously powerful 'rapee' favoured by Wemyss. But if the general's gifts did not go down as well as they might have done, it was otherwise with Wemyss's 'promise . . . that the [recruits'] fathers should have leases of their farms'. This pledge was warmly received.[5]

That day in Kildonan, or on other days like it, young man after young man stepped forward to be formally enlisted. One of them was William Gunn, then 22 and, at 5 feet 10½ inches, unusually tall by early nineteenth-century standards. Gunn, a military clerk noted, had a 'fresh' complexion, 'brown' eyes, 'brown' hair and was 'round faced'. He signed up for 'unlimited service', the army recorded, and his 'character', according to regimental records, was 'extremely good'.[6]

Did General Wemyss, despite his having handed command of the 93rd to others, remember the undertakings he had given to the father of Kildonan's William Gunn and to the fathers of dozens of men like him when the general's former recruiting sergeant, William MacDonald, came to Wemyss's London home to ask for assistance in obtaining better treatment for Kildonan tenants who, though their sons remained in the 93rd, were about to be dispossessed? And was it a sense of his being under a continuing obligation to the parents of soldiers he had enlisted that caused Wemyss to be so helpful to MacDonald? There can be no definitive answer to those questions. But it is indubitably the case, as William Wemyss would have been well aware, that had pledges of the Kildonan type not been forthcoming, there would have been no *Rèisimeid Chataich*, or Sutherland Regiment, as the 93rd was known to its Gaelic-speaking rank and file. During 1799 the dearth of recruits had been such that Wemyss came close to abandoning his regiment-raising activities on the Sutherland Estate. But by the summer of 1800, thanks in large part to the policy of linking recruitment with immunity (as it was thought) from eviction, the general was able to muster at Langdale a force that became, despite its ranks being so thinned at Chalmette, the nucleus of one of the British army's most formidable formations.*

Entered in the army pay list as the '93rd or Sutherland Regiment of Highlanders', William Wemyss's latest command attracted commendation after commendation from senior officers. Much of that praise stemmed from the conduct of its enlisted men. This was a time when the Duke of Wellington, the British military's most eminent commander and the man who masterminded the ejection of Napoleon's armies from Spain before going on to win the Battle of Waterloo, could describe his soldiers as 'the very scum of the earth', men who, prior to their being dragooned into the forces, eked out precarious livelihoods on the outermost margins of urban society. The troops paraded in front of General Wemyss in Strathnaver in August 1800 were of very different background. They were, it was said, 'the children of respectable farmers'; 'connected by the strong ties of neighbourhood and even of relationship'; 'a sort of family corps'. Thus it transpired that, in an era when military order was customarily maintained by means of frequent floggings, one Sutherland Highlander company went 'nineteen years without having a man punished'. Men of the 93rd, it seems, were 'steady, attentive and . . . regular to a remarkable degree'; 'highly valued'; 'a picture of military discipline and moral rectitude'.[7]

From Inverness in September 1800 *Rèisimeid Chataich* was shipped to the Channel Islands. Two years later the regiment was back briefly in Scotland before being moved to Ireland. From there in 1805 the 93rd was despatched to South Africa where Britain, with a

---

* The 93rd's enduring reputation derives not least from its soldiers having constituted 'The Thin Red Line' against which a Russian cavalry charge foundered during the Battle of Balaclava in 1854.

view to safeguarding trade routes to India and the Far East, aimed to seize Cape Town from the Dutch, then allied with Napoleon.

Take Marine Drive out of today's Cape Town and, keeping Table Bay always to your left, you come after about 15 miles to Bloubergstrand, a Cape Town suburb where the outlook is dominated by Table Mountain, which rears up behind the city centre on the far side of the bay. Due west of Bloubergstrand is Robben Island, separated from Bloubergstrand's sandy beach by a five-mile-wide strait. In this strait, on Friday 4 January 1806, there anchored the British invasion fleet which the 93rd Regiment had joined in Cork some months before.

General Sir David Baird, the officer commanding the 6,500 troops aboard the vessels moored off Bloubergstrand, had intended to disembark his entire force at daybreak on the morning following the fleet's arrival. However, a stiff wind off the South Atlantic raised such a heavy swell that it was not until Sunday 6 January that it became possible to order Baird's soldiers – the 93rd, now about 800 strong, in the vanguard – into the boats that were to carry them ashore. Minutes later, one of those boats, its naval oarsmen struggling to cope with a continuing and 'tremendous' surf, was driven towards rocks still to be seen at the north end of Bloubergstrand beach. The boat 'no sooner touched' those rocks, according to Major John Graham of the 93rd Regiment, 'than she instantly turned bottom up and down went thirty-six of our noble fellows . . . They were so loaded with ammunition [and] accoutrements that they all went down directly; four only were saved of the forty in the boat.'[8]

Opposed by no more than a handful of Dutch 'sharpshooters' at Bloubergstrand, the rest of the Sutherland men landed safely. Two days later, by which point all of Baird's force together with its supplies had been brought ashore, the invading army set off south in what – January being the height of the South African summer – Major Graham called 'intense' heat. 'It is not perhaps in the power of language to describe our sufferings for want of water,' Graham went on. Nor was this the end of his and his men's difficulties. 'It is impossible to give an idea of the badness of the ground over which our line had to advance; very deep sand and completely covered with a sort of brushwood which is something like a gooseberry bush with thorn prickles on it.' Cape Town, then a settlement of some 16,000 people, was now within reach. Between the British and their objective, however, was a Dutch contingent of some 2,000 troops whose artillery was soon subjecting the 93rd to what John Graham called 'heavy fire'. But this, he continued, 'only served to increase the [93rd's] rate of pace . . . At length . . . the order was given to charge and, to be sure, how [the Dutch] did run! . . . Next day we marched towards the town where a flag of truce very soon made its appearance. Several of the outworks were given up immediately, and on the 10th [of January] the whole capitulated.' [9]

Cape Town's defenders, as acknowledged in General David Baird's official account of proceedings, resisted more stubbornly than Major Graham indicated. But British casualties were certainly slight, and Cape Town, which would remain a British possession into the twentieth century, had equally certainly been secured. For the next eight years, the 93rd Regiment was a part of its garrison. This meant that at a time when much of the British army was engaged in the Peninsular War, the name given to Wellington's often bloody campaign against Napoleon's forces in Portugal and Spain, the 93rd's soldiers – each of them pocketing a share of the 'prize money' distributed after Cape Town's capture – saw nothing in the way of action against France. Nor were they to do so after their recall to the United Kingdom in the summer of 1814. Napoleon had by then been defeated and exiled (it was thought permanently) to Elba.* Still to be settled, however, was Britain's continuing war with the USA. This was the conflict the Earl of Selkirk had intended his planned regiment to play some part in. That had not happened. But

---

* From which Napoleon would escape in 1815 as a prelude to organising the campaign that culminated in his final defeat at Waterloo.

when, in September 1814, the 93rd, not long back from Cape Town, was ordered to make ready for a transatlantic voyage, it became apparent that men from Sutherland were, after all, to be drawn into combat in North America.

Fighting on that continent had been sporadic and inconclusive. The USA's principal war aim, the annexation of Canada, had not been and would not be achieved. But Britain, despite its forces having temporarily occupied (and burned much of) Washington, had equally failed to deliver anything approximating to a knock-out blow. Now the British, already attempting to blockade the USA's Atlantic coastline, were looking to obtain control of New Orleans (a city which had been French, Spanish and French again before its acquisition by the USA in 1803) with a view to gaining a chokehold on the Midwest's strategically crucial access to the sea.

By way of Barbados and Jamaica, the 93rd Regiment, which spent nearly as much time afloat as ashore during 1814, was accordingly conveyed in a new invasion fleet (this one 50 vessels strong) to the Gulf of Mexico. There in mid-December the Sutherland Highlanders, along with several other regiments under the overall command of General Sir Edward Pakenham, Wellington's brother-in-law, were put ashore in the vicinity of Lake Borgne, a shallow saltwater lagoon to the east and south-east of New Orleans. But if this 1814 landing was a little bit reminiscent of the lead-up to the 93rd's assault on Cape Town, that was the end of any similarity between the Sutherland men's New Orleans experiences and those that had gone before in South Africa. In the New Orleans case, practically everything that could have gone wrong for the 93rd Regiment, and for the rest of the British expeditionary force, not only did go wrong but did so catastrophically.

By way of a maze of hard-to-navigate bayous and other waterways between Lake Borgne and the Mississippi, Pakenham's force was eventually transported by boat on to one of the few dry-land routes giving access to New Orleans from the south. This route consisted of a strip of territory immediately adjacent to the

Mississippi's left or eastern bank. At Chalmette, where the British were to be repulsed so decisively, that strip was less than a mile wide. Because repeated Mississippi floods had deposited a great deal of silt on the river's banks, the ground here and elsewhere in the vicinity sloped gently downwards from those banks to a broad expanse of cypress swamp. This latter feature, as can be seen by taking a trip to one of present-day Louisiana's surviving examples, consisted of evergreen conifers festooned in Spanish Moss and standing in up to several feet of slow-moving or stagnant water. Terrain of that sort – made all the more uninviting by its being inhabited by alligators, snakes and snapping turtles – was, and is, effectively impenetrable. This meant that, after an initial encounter with the advancing British during the night of 23 December 1814, General Jackson's obvious tactic was immediately to withdraw northwards with a view to creating as strong as possible a defensive line between the Mississippi to his right and the swampland to his left. This Jackson did, choosing to make his stand behind the so-called Rodriguez Canal on the northern boundary of what was then the Chalmet Plantation.

Some seven miles downstream from New Orleans, at that time a rapidly growing town of 25,000 or so people, this was one of dozens of sugarcane plantations occupying the productive and relatively dry soils next to the riverbank. Because it was winter, Chalmet's sugarcane had long since been harvested by the plantation owner's slaves, meaning that, from Jackson's position, his men had a clear field of fire across many hundreds of yards of stubble.

A British probe towards the American frontline – an operation involving the 93rd and several other units – was driven off on 28 December. Another British attack, on New Year's Day, was just as unsuccessful; and for the next week – while Pakenham's troops, their days and nights made miserable by untypically icy and wet weather, regrouped to the south – Andrew Jackson was free to add to the makeshift but highly effective fortifications his men had already thrown up alongside the Rodriguez Canal.

This canal was not, and had never been, any kind of navigation channel. Instead it was an abandoned and mostly dried-up trench created years before in order to direct water downhill from the Mississippi into the swampland to the east, thereby powering a mill which had stood at the canal's lower end. Jackson's soldiers, aided by slaves from nearby plantations, were to spend several days digging out and reflooding the canal, soon six or more feet deep and perhaps 10 to 12 feet wide. The muddy earth thus excavated was meanwhile used – in combination with fence-posts, tree-trunks, cotton bales and other materials of that kind – to construct, on the canal's northern rim, a rampart equipped all along its length with concealed firing positions interspersed, here and there, with emplacements for such artillery pieces as Jackson had managed to acquire.

If this rampart and its defenders were to be overwhelmed, it was clear to Sir Edward Pakenham and his staff, the Rodriguez Canal would first have to be rendered passable by filling stretches of it with what the military called fascines. These usually consisted of pre-prepared bundles of brushwood. At Chalmette, for self-evident reasons, the brushwood was replaced by sugarcane. But the purpose remained as before – to provide attacking troops with safe passage over the canal and to provide, in addition, a solid footing for the ladders that, if they were quickly to scale a parapet with a six or seven feet frontage, the attackers would need to have readily to hand.

Accomplishing first the canal crossing and next the ascent of the American parapet, while all the time exposed to artillery and small-arms fire from well-protected enemies, would have been desperately difficult even if everything had gone exactly as General Pakenham intended. Everything did not.

When, under cover of a low-lying mist on the morning of Sunday 8 January, Pakenham mounted a last, and ultimately disastrous, assault on Jackson's line, his main thrust was intended to break through this line where he and his senior officers judged it weakest: towards the line's merger with the cypress swamp on the British right. However, that thrust soon stalled. This was partly because the attackers, being short of big guns and artillery ammunition, had not managed to silence American cannons which – manned in some cases by pirate gunners from Barataria – cut swathes through the red-coated figures massing in front of them. Still more decisive in determining the battle's outcome, however, was a calamitous failure to bring up the fascines and ladders on which the entire British battle plan depended. The task of rushing this key equipment forward had been entrusted to soldiers of the 44th (East Essex) Regiment. But they had bungled it badly – so badly that the 44th's commander, Colonel Thomas Mullens, would afterwards be court-martialled and dismissed the service. At Chalmette itself, meanwhile, the consequences of those lapses were immediate and, for the 93rd Sutherland Highlanders, tragic.

The 93rd, advancing to the sound of bagpipes, accounted for a substantial part of a detachment – subsidiary to the main attack force – deployed towards the British left and consequently moving forward near the Mississippi's eastern shore. Overall command on this flank had been devolved to one of Pakenham's senior colleagues, General John Keane, who, on seeing the debacle developing to his right, ordered the 93rd to wheel round with a view to reinforcing the faltering British effort in that quarter. This meant that the Sutherland men, instead of approaching Jackson's defences on a comparatively narrow front, found themselves strung out in a long line not far short of the Rodriguez Canal, its waters as impassable to them as to everyone else on account of the necessary fascines still being missing. A diary kept by one of the 93rd's junior officers, Lieutenant Charles Gordon, describes the carnage that now ensued. 'The enemy', Gordon wrote, 'could perceive us plainly.' As a result, he and the men around him were subjected to 'a most destructive and murderous fire . . . of round[shot], grape[shot], musquetry, rifle and buckshot'. Making matters worse was a lack of orders. Keane had been badly wounded. Pakenham had been killed. So had the 93rd's own commanding officer, Lieutenant-Colonel Robert Dale. The 93rd, in consequence, was instructed neither to push on nor to fall back. On the British right, other formations were already in retreat. The 93rd, however, stood – 'like statues' it was said – for minute after minute while, in Lieutenant Gordon's words, 'officers and men . . . were mowed down by ranks'.[10]

From both sides, tributes were afterwards paid to the Sutherland men's refusal to give ground. An American spoke about their 'cool determined bravery and undaunted courage'. A British officer commented that 'nothing could exceed [their] steadiness and gallantry'. But was there perhaps a further factor in the 93rd's apparent unwillingness to become part of what another British officer called the 'confusion' and 'flight' developing all around them? Most of the men that same officer saw quitting the Chalmette battlefield in 'utmost disorder' were veterans of repeated Peninsular engagements. They were unlikely to have survived those engagements – many of them on a far larger scale than the Chalmette clash – had they not sometimes abandoned positions it had become suicidal to hold. Apart from its brief encounter with Cape Town's badly outnumbered defenders, however, the 93rd, prior to its participation in the New Orleans campaign, had no experience of having been under fire. The Sutherland men's motionless acceptance of the devastation inflicted on them at Chalmette might indeed have been the product of unmatched valour. But it may also have owed something to a lack of the sort of initiative that led more hardened soldiers to put their own preservation ahead of any obligation to wait for orders that, with so many commanders out of action, were a very long time coming.[11]

Not until instructed to do so by General John Lambert, on whom overall command devolved following Pakenham's death, were the 93rd's survivors at last to withdraw. By this point, the regiment's killed, wounded and missing numbered somewhere between 500 and 550 – well over half the total strength fielded an hour or two before.[12]

Because Andrew Jackson had no intention of confronting his beaten, but still capable, enemies in the open, the British were able to pull back unmolested. Their immediate destination, two or three miles from Chalmette, was the fine home (its ruins still just visible today) built ten years earlier on the riverside plantation belonging to one of Louisiana's wealthiest sugarcane growers, Pierre Denis de la Ronde. Here the army's surgeons established a field hospital and set about the amputations which, in early nineteenth-century conditions, were the favoured method of treating battlefield wounds that were otherwise liable to become rapidly and fatally gangrenous.

'The scene now presented at [de] la Ronde's', a British artillery officer wrote later, 'was one I shall never forget. Almost every room was crowded with the wounded and the dying . . . I was the unwilling spectator of numerous amputations; on all sides nothing was heard but the piteous cries of my poor countrymen . . . The 93rd Regiment had suffered severely; and I cannot describe the strange feelings created by seeing a basket nearly full of legs severed from these fine fellows.'[13]

Among those treated that day at the de la Ronde plantation was a Sutherland man whose surname has not been preserved but whose first name was John or (in Gaelic) Iain. At Chalmette he had been standing beside his brother when the brother's head was removed entirely by an American cannonball. Now Iain was to lose an arm shattered at the elbow by a bullet. What followed was promptly incorporated into one of those grisly tales military men tell by way of attempting to mitigate the impact of what today is labelled post-traumatic stress.

Iain, it appears, was prone to getting into fights with other soldiers. So no sooner had a surgeon (operating as always in that era without recourse to anaesthetics) sawn through Iain's arm than one of his comrades, stretched out on a neighbouring bench or table, leaned across and (in Gaelic) told Iain that with his right arm now missing he would never again be able to land a blow on anyone. Iain, however, was not having this. Taking hold of his newly sheared-off limb, still within reach of his remaining hand, he swung it towards his tormentor, telling him, or so the story went, that he should think himself honoured to be the last man to feel the weight of what had been a powerful fist.[14]

Back at Chalmette, meanwhile, a two-day truce had been agreed in order to permit the burial of the dead. Something of what this entailed is evident from the subsequent writings of a junior officer, William Gleig, who had earlier been taken to the de la Ronde home to receive treatment for a minor head wound. 'Prompted by curiosity', Gleig commented, 'I mounted my horse [on the first day of the truce] and rode to the front . . . Of all the sights I ever witnessed, that which met me [there] was beyond comparison the most shocking . . . Within the narrow compass of a few hundred yards were gathered together nearly a thousand bodies, all of them arrayed in British uniforms . . . They were thrown by dozens into shallow holes . . . Nor was this all. An American officer stood by, smoking a cigar, apparently counting the slain with a look of savage exultation and repeating, over and over to each individual who approached him, that [the American] loss amounted only to eight men killed and fourteen* wounded.'[15]

Also going about among the dead was another American whose emotions were more mixed than those of his cigar-smoking compatriot, this man's daughter reporting that he had been 'moved to tears' by the killing of so many 'magnificent Highlanders'. 'After the battle', the same woman went on, 'my father took a bible from the body of one of the Highlanders. It had his name . . . and had been given him by his mother.'[16]

In mid-February, just prior to their evacuation by the Royal Navy, the remnants of Britain's New Orleans invasion force learned that the Chalmette slaughter took place more than a fortnight after US and British diplomats, meeting in Europe, had agreed an end to their countries' war. Nothing of this was known, however, in the course of a now demoralised British army's long retreat to the Gulf coast. 'We who only seven weeks [before] had set out in the surest

---

* As indicated earlier, US losses were actually slightly less than stated here.

confidence of glory', wrote William Gleig, 'were brought back dispirited and dejected. Our ranks were woefully thinned . . . our clothing tattered and filthy.'[17]

Every day it rained, Gleig recalled. Some nights, even this far south, there were hard frosts: 'Thus we were alternately wet and frozen.' For the most part, Andrew Jackson's men did not seriously harry their defeated opponents. They did, however, subject British troops to constant psychological pressure. 'To our soldiers', William Gleig wrote, 'every inducement was held out to desert.' Often these blandishments took the form of printed handbills thrown towards sentries in the night. Their Americans pursuers, soldiers found, were 'offering [them] lands' and stressing 'the superiority of a democratical government'. Whether or not in response to propaganda of this sort, there were indeed desertions from the British side. It is unclear if absconders included men from the 93rd Regiment. But it can certainly be argued that a 93rd survivor would have done better to try his luck in the USA than to go home. It would be a long time before there was anything approximating to 'democratical government' in Sutherland. Nor, 15 years on from the Strathnaver muster of 1800, would any soldier returning to that district have any chance of finding there 'lands' of the sort to be had for the asking in America. By 1815, a good deal of Strathnaver was in Patrick Sellar's exclusive occupation. Soon he would be renting the greater part of it.[18]

8

'HE WOULD BE A VERY CRUEL MAN WHO WOULD NOT MOURN FOR THE PEOPLE'

Patrick Sellar establishes himself at Culmaily and begins to clear Strathnaver

Whatever else may be said of him, and he has been castigated and reviled more than any other nineteenth-century Scot, Patrick Sellar was a consummate agriculturalist. Today this is most evident at Culmaily, a Sutherland Estate farm a mile or two south of Golspie. Culmaily is tenanted presently by Angus McCall. While the place bears Angus's imprint – and that of his father who was tenant here before him – Culmaily's layout, Angus says, is still much as planned by Sellar when, on his becoming tenant here more than 200 years ago, he set about reshaping and reorganising a landholding that, before Sellar's arrival, had experienced next to nothing in the way of sudden change.

Patrick Sellar became solely responsible for Culmaily in 1811. Prior to that – other than for a short spell when Sellar and William Young were jointly in charge of it – the farm had been tenanted by one of the Sutherland Estate's long-standing tacksmen. This was Alexander Sutherland who, like many others of his class, had served in the army (though not in the 93rd Regiment in his case) where he had attained the rank of colonel.

Although Sutherland hoped, as he put it, to 'escape unnoticed in the general rage for improvement', pressure on him to quit mounted almost from the moment Young and Sellar took an interest in the

Sutherland Estate. On the Marchioness of Stafford indicating in July 1809 that she would be happy 'to get rid of Sutherland', his connection with Culmaily was brought to an end. Also ended was management of the traditional tacksman type – management leading, as agricultural commentator John Henderson observed in 1812, to much of a typical tacksman's farm being 'let . . . from year to year' to subtenants who, as well as paying rent, were required to provide the tacksman with 'services' in the form of unpaid labour. There were no fewer than 52 such subtenants on Culmaily in 1810, the farm, as a result, being home to more than 250 people.[1]

Most of Culmaily's subtenants appear to have lived on rising ground to the left of the modern A9 (as you approach Golspie from the south) and well above the farm's present-day farmhouse and steadings, themselves on the same side of the road but closer to it. On walking uphill from the present farmhouse to the spot where (given the number of people involved) there must have been a substantial township, you get an extensive view eastwards across the Moray Firth. But other than scattered stones and some traces of foundations there is little sign of the homes that stood here until Patrick Sellar's 1811 takeover.

Following that takeover, the families living in those homes (a 'host of idle beggars' in William Young's opinion) were ejected. The heaped-up rigs on which they had grown their crops were then spread out and flattened, the turf walls and thatched roofs of the former subtenantry's 'levelled' houses, as Lady Stafford noted on one of her trips north, providing useful 'manure' for the fields that took the rigs' place. This was in the summer of 1814, by which point, Sellar was getting Culmaily into 'excellent order' with the help of a workforce that, at times, numbered 30, 40 or more. A few of Sellar's farm labourers may previously have been among Culmaily's subtenants, a small number of local families being retained in cottages on the farm's fringes on condition (as was then customary) that family members turned out en masse at harvest-time when Sellar needed as many as 60 sickle-wielding 'reapers' to bring in ever heavier crops of oats and other cereals. But most of the more highly-skilled men employed at Culmaily (ploughmen and foremen for example) were recruited further afield, Sellar having a strong preference for Moray and other 'south country' workers of the sort he thought about deploying against the Kildonan 'mob' at Golspie in February 1813.[2]

As early as August 1811, when John Henderson paid him a visit, Sellar had equipped Culmaily with 'a handsome dwelling house' and a 'commodious square' of farm buildings. That house and its accompanying steadings were located just below (or on the seaward side) of the A9 and adjacent to Culmaily Burn, the burn's waters powering the 'good mill' and 'threshing machine' described by Henderson. Sellar's mill lade survives. But other than when a dry summer parches a present-day expanse of grass in such a way as to reveal the ground plan of Sellar's 1811 buildings, there is nothing of those buildings to be seen today. That, Angus McCall explains, is because they were demolished in the 1860s or 1870s when they were replaced by a new farmhouse (the one Angus and his wife Evelyn occupy) and more substantial steadings (themselves since modernised extensively) on the top side of the road.[3]

In the absence of Culmaily's first set of steadings, it is on the low-lying land just east and south-east of the A9 – today the most productive part of the farm – that the long-run consequences of Patrick Sellar's endeavours are most apparent. Prior to Sellar's arrival, much of this area was bog. But by 1811, John Henderson reported, it was beginning to be dried out with the help of newly installed drains, some of them, according to Henderson, a remarkable 11 feet below ground. Those drains discharged into the Culmaily Burn's lower reaches, which had themselves been dredged and deepened to form what Henderson called 'a canal'. This linked Sellar's farm with Loch Fleet, the sea inlet where (as already mentioned) William Young had established the northern terminus of his weekly shipping service between Sutherland and Burghead. On the canal, Sellar installed a barge which, at high tide, could be floated out on to Loch Fleet where it was then moored above one of the loch's many sandbars. Those sandbars consist largely of wave-pulverised shells which, being rich in calcium carbonate, were exactly what was needed to neutralise the acidity of the peaty earth in fields reclaimed from marshland. Hence Sellar's use for his barge which, once the outgoing tide had left it beached, could be filled with as much as eight tons of what John Henderson called 'shelly sand'. On the tide coming in again, the now loaded barge was sailed back up to Culmaily where, in Henderson's words, 'the shells [were] conveyed to the [farm's] cattlesheds and there mixed with . . . seaweed and cattle-dung', prior to the resulting combination being delved by hand into increasingly fertile soils that yielded, over five-year cycles, grass, barley, oats, wheat, turnips or potatoes.[4]

Seashells, Angus McCall says, are still turned up regularly when Culmaily's fields are ploughed. Like much else on the farm, they derive from what Patrick Sellar described as 'the numerous little experiments which . . . led him, step by step, to his [eventual] system of management'. At Culmaily this 'system' resulted in the farm's formerly extensive wetlands (together with higher and drier ground where the former subtenantry's rigs had been located) being incorporated into 16 substantial fields or 'enclosures', 'the fences of which', Sellar stressed in a published account of his agricultural activities, '[were] dykes or stone walls' put in place at his, not the Sutherland Estate's, expense.[5]

Some sections of those dykes were removed when the Inverness–Thurso railway sliced through Culmaily in 1868. Others were lost when a part of the farm was taken over by the RAF during the Second World War. But most of them – consisting, Angus McCall points out, of roughly dressed stone from a nearby quarry – still stand. This means that the fields where Angus today produces malting barley and other crops are, in virtually every case, fields that Patrick Sellar first delineated and, in a real sense, created.

Even by present-day standards, Culmaily, with 500 acres of cultivable land and a further 500 acres of hill pasture, is a sizeable farm.

But despite its being emblematic of what 'improvement' could accomplish by way of increased output, Culmaily both in 1811 and after was (as in essence it remains) an arable and cattle-rearing unit of much the same sort as might have come Patrick Sellar's way had he remained in Moray. There was, then, no opportunity here for Patrick Sellar to get into large-scale sheep farming of the sort he was busy introducing, in his factorial capacity, into more inland parts of the Sutherland Estate. This meant that Culmaily was never going to be sufficient outlet for a man increasingly determined to have a personal stake in every aspect of the land-use revolution he was forcing through on behalf of the Marquis and Marchioness of Stafford. What Sellar more and more wanted, it became apparent both to himself and others, was to get into sheep and wool production. His chance to do so came on Wednesday 15 December 1813 when, at Golspie Inn, William Young presided over a 'sett' or auction of lease-expired tenancies.

Among bidders that Wednesday was John Cleugh, one of the shepherds who had been besieged by the Kildonan 'rioters' at Suisgill the previous January. At £75 annually (equivalent to several thousand pounds today), Cleugh's final bid for the tenancy of Pollie, an outlying farm on the north-western fringes of Strathbrora, was £5 a year greater than the next highest offer. This came from John MacDonald, Pollie's established tacksman. By Donald Sage, the Kildonan minister's son, MacDonald was thought 'respectable' and, like other such tacksmen, much given to entertaining 'all comers and goers, from the highest to the lowest, [at] . . . a plentiful and hospitable table'. This positive opinion was not shared by William Young. John MacDonald and his family, Young reported to Lady Stafford, were 'a worthless set'. 'We shall . . . now get clear of them,' he added – his low opinion of the MacDonalds reinforced, no doubt, by suspicion that they were behind what Young called 'an attempt . . . to waylay' John Cleugh as he made his way home from Golspie.[6]

Because of Pollie's isolated situation, five or six miles up the Blackwater, a river that joins the Brora a mile or so upstream from

Ascoilemore, Cleugh's acquisition of its tenancy resulted in comparatively little in the way of enforced depopulation. There would be no
avoiding mass evictions, however, when – as was seen to be imminent in the course of the Golspie Inn proceedings of 15 December
– the sheep-farming frontier advanced into Strathnaver.

As far back as the early seventeenth century, Strathnaver was
described as a well-peopled district 'full of . . . cattle'. It had become
still more thickly settled in the years that followed. 'If you were [to
go] up the strath now', members of a royal commission were told in
1883 by Angus MacKay, whose boyhood had been spent there prior
to Strathnaver's clearance, 'you would see on both sides of it the
places where the town[ship]s were; you would see a mile or half a
mile between every town; there were four or five families in each of
these towns, and bonnie haughs between the towns, and hill pastures
for miles [around] . . . The people [there] had plenty of flocks of
goats, sheep, horses and cattle; and they were living happy.'[7]

Nostalgia for times past might be thought to have coloured this
account. However, early nineteenth-century portrayals of
Strathnaver are almost equally positive about the place. Strathnaver,
according to John Henderson, was 'the most populous' of all
Sutherland's valleys, its 60 or more separate communities (some of
them a lot more substantial than others) containing between them,
or so Henderson calculated, over 2,000 people. Like the Strath of
Kildonan, some 20 or 25 miles to the south-east, pre-clearance
Strathnaver was stock-rearing country, its 338 families (Henderson
was nothing if not precise) owning, in total, around 4,000 breeding
cattle. But cereals were grown here too, as was noted by Benjamin
Meredith, a land surveyor commissioned by the Sutherland Estate in
1810 to compile a report on the 'state of possessions in Strathnaver'.
The strath's climate, Meredith wrote, was 'as salubrious' as that of
coastal localities like Culmaily (where the surveyor was then resident) and its 'crops of grain equally good and early'. Meredith, who
reached Strathnaver by way of what he called 'the black moors and
morasses' on the valley's eastern flank, was much taken by the

long-settled landscapes then to be found on both banks of the River Naver. Strathnaver's 'river, natural woods and arable lands', the surveyor commented, were 'pleasing', 'agreeable' and 'delightful'.[8]

One of Benjamin Meredith's tasks was to assess Strathnaver's sheep-farming potential. This, he informed the Sutherland Estate's proprietors, was by no means unlimited: 'Notwithstanding the great extent of hill and uplands [around Strathnaver] . . . there is . . . but a small portion that can be applied to the raising of sheep, and that wholly confined to the east side of the River Naver.' Although Meredith's findings would eventually be disregarded and virtually the whole of Strathnaver put under sheep, those findings were still influencing estate management thinking when preparations were made for the Golspie Inn gathering at which, in addition to Strathbrora holdings such as Pollie, a number of Strathnaver farms were made available for let. The boundaries of one of those farms, described as 'Rossal and Dalharrold' in the record made of the Golspie sett, were thus in accordance, more or less, with Benjamin Meredith's 1810 recommendations. To the west, the farm was bounded by the River Naver, from (in the north) the Dunviden Burn (which enters the Naver opposite the present-day settlement of Carnachy) to the Mallart River (which joins the Naver just a few hundred yards from the spot where that watercourse exits Loch Naver). From north to south, then, 'Rossal and Dalharrold', or Rhiloisk as it became known, extended for the better part of 15 miles. From west to east, the farm stretched nearly as far, reaching across the Naver–Helmsdale watershed to include, north of Loch Badanloch and Loch Rimsdale, localities closer to the Strath of Kildonan's upper reaches than to Strathnaver. The person who took on Rhiloisk farm, it followed, would become tenant of a substantial slice of the Sutherland Estate. This person, it was decided at Golspie Inn on 15 December 1813, would be Patrick Sellar.[9]

Until that morning, Sellar, by his own account, had not meant to bid for Rhiloisk but for Langdale. That farm – which included the spot where the 93rd Regiment was mustered in 1800 – was on the

River Naver's western bank and, as Culmaily had been, was occupied by a tacksman of the old-style sort. This was Robert Gordon, whose lease had expired and who, that December Wednesday at Golspie, was looking to renew it. Gordon, Patrick Sellar wrote some time later, 'having seen my shepherd traversing the ground [at Langdale] . . . came here [to Culmaily] the day before the sett, took his lodging with me, and imparted his suspicions, as well as his fears, that I should outbid him'. Next morning, Sellar went on, Gordon, having left Culmaily in advance of his (perhaps less than hospitable) host, called at William Young's home at Rhives. There the Langdale tacksman, according to Sellar, 'told some pitiful story' to Young's sister who was then staying at Rhives and who now urged Sellar, when he put in an appearance, 'not [to] think of bidding on [his] guest' of the night before.[10]

Patrick Sellar was not a man to let sentiment get in the way of business. While the lobbying to which he was subject may indeed have caused him, as he wrote, 'to hesitate' about Langdale, what probably proved more decisive was the fact that, at the sett, the Rhiloisk tenancy – dealt with prior to the Langdale one – became subject, as Sellar observed, to fierce competition. The rival bidders, Sellar reported, were 'the people of Rossal', one of several long-inhabited townships inside the farm's borders, and John Paterson, a shepherd employed on the Sandside Estate on Caithness's north coast. Although the day would come when Patrick Sellar's own sheep management skills were unrivalled, that day was not yet. Hence the interest sparked in him by Paterson's evident determination to get hold of Rhiloisk. 'I knew', Sellar commented, 'that the great part of the [Rhiloisk] ground . . . would pay more [under] sheep than people.' He knew too that John Paterson 'was a good judge' of what was, or was not, a sound sheep-farming prospect. As soon as it became clear that Paterson had outbid the Rossal tenants, then, Sellar 'instantly struck in'. Minutes later, to his 'own surprise as well as that of Mr Young', he found himself tenant 'of grounds of which [he] knew little or nothing'.[11]

Although Patrick Sellar (as will be seen) would also acquire Langdale before many years had passed, Robert Gordon was for the moment left in possession. William Young, for his part, had the immediate responsibility of dealing with the implications of the failure of Rhiloisk farm's numerous inhabitants (a substantial group of whom were possibly involved in the bid fronted by the Rossal men) to secure their continued residency in localities where their families, in some instances, had lived for centuries. Since most of the affected individuals knew little or no English, Young (who spoke no Gaelic) had delegated this task to David MacKenzie, a newly ordained Church of Scotland clergyman who was shortly to become minister of Farr. That parish included Strathnaver where MacKenzie was already ministering to communities in the upper part of the strath; and his instructions, MacKenzie recalled, were to tell 'the [Rhiloisk farm] tenants in possession [that] . . . if [their] lands were carried by higher bidders, [then they] . . . were to be provided for in small allotments . . . along the coast'. This of course was exactly the offer made at the start of 1813, and with absolutely no success, to the people Young and Sellar had then been attempting to prise out of the Strath of Kildonan. However, Young – whose complacency, in light of the Kildonan experience, is little short of astonishing – appears not to have anticipated any difficulty on this occasion. 'The Strathnaver men [to be] disposed [of] from the lot [meaning farm] which Mr Sellar got seemed satisfied,' Young informed Lady Stafford. '[They] know that they are all to be provided for . . . There will certainly be no trouble with them.'[12]

William Young's confidence might have been more soundly based had he and John Roy, Benjamin Meredith's replacement as the Sutherland Estate's favoured land surveyor, pushed ahead quickly with the job of pegging out and allocating the crofts – towards the Naver estuary – where evicted families were to be resettled. But bad weather in the autumn, Young lamented, had made it 'quite impossible to get on with fieldwork' of this sort. That was why Sellar, as he commented subsequently, was pressed by Young on the day of the

Golspie sett to 'promise the . . . people [whose lands Sellar had just been granted] . . . that [he] would accommodate as many of them as possible for a year or two until they could make [alternative] arrangements'. This Sellar agreed to do, telling the people in question to meet with him on 15 January when, in his continuing capacity as an estate factor, he would be in the Strath of Kildonan to collect outstanding rents.[13]

The meeting thus arranged duly occurred, being held in the house at Suisgill where John Cleugh, John Turnbull (this Suisgill home's occupier) and other shepherds had been menaced at the start of the Kildonan protest movement. Since the men Patrick Sellar met with in that same house a year later are bound to have known all about the January 1813 'riot' and its aftermath, Sellar's choice of location was perhaps unwise. It could well have served to remind the Suisgill meeting's Strathnaver participants that lots of Kildonan families had for months refused to do as ordered by the Sutherland Estate management team, those same families, either by departing for Red River or by sitting tight, having thereby avoided a move to crofts of the type now on offer in connection with Rhiloisk's planned clearance. Sellar, however, appears to have been as unconcerned as Young about the possibility of renewed dissent. Having 'selected those who should remain' for the time being on his Strathnaver farm, he said afterwards, he 'made a bargain' with them as to the rents they were to pay in their capacity as his temporary subtenants. As for 'the remainder', they were told simply that Sellar and his shepherds were to 'have access at the Whitsunday following' to land which, in the interim, those same people would be obliged to vacate.[14]

During the early part of 1814, when the Kildonan emigrants at Churchill Creek were coping with the full force of a Hudson Bay winter, Patrick Sellar and his shepherds were confronting scarcely less dreadful weather at Rhiloisk. 'The snow [is] better than a yard deep and the frost keener than I ever felt,' Sellar noted. One of his 'guides' to the Sutherland interior, he reported to James Loch, had 'actually lost several of his toes' to frostbite. 'You can scarcely figure the intensity of the [January and February cold] here,' Sellar went on. 'The rivers, lakes and even the [Dornoch] Firth a few miles above Tain were solid [with ice].'[15]

In those circumstances, needless to say, no further progress was made in mapping out crofts in Strathnaver. But if families scheduled to quit Rhiloisk Farm by the Whitsun deadline – meaning 26 May – were no clearer by March or April as to where they were to go, it was soon made starkly apparent that Patrick Sellar very much wished them gone.

During the last week of March, by which point the snow had thawed and a drying wind set in, Patrick Sellar ordered his employees to fire extensive tracts of hill pasture in the vicinity of those townships he was eager to see emptied. Muirburn of this type was and remains a common practice in a sheep-farming context, its purpose being to promote the growth of new grass and heather on land thus stripped of older vegetation. But if, to Sellar, this seemed a perfectly reasonable proceeding, it was thought intimidatory by people still keeping cattle in areas now set suddenly ablaze. That was certainly the common opinion in Rhiloisk, the settlement which (perhaps because it contained the house where Sellar lived when in Strathnaver) gave its name to the wider farm it had become part of. Adjacent to the River Naver and more or less opposite Langdale, Rhiloisk was described by Benjamin Meredith in 1810 as 'a beautiful little place' with 'good land' and with plentiful shelter for its tenantry's cattle in surrounding (and still surviving) woodlands. Now, in the late winter or early spring of 1814, Rhiloisk became one of the first localities in Strathnaver to experience muirburn on a big scale. Because the township's cattle were thus 'deprived of their pasturage', said William Gordon, a Rhiloisk tenant, the animals' condition deteriorated markedly. Nor was the 'burning system', as Gordon called it, in any way confined to more remote spots. 'In many places', he insisted, 'the heath pasturage was burned to within a gunshot [then no more than 100 yards] of the tenants' dwelling houses.' 'It was with difficulty and [only] after a long search that . . . [he] found [his cattle],' one of Gordon's fellow tenants added.[16]

Some way downstream at Rivigill, according to John MacKay, one of that settlement's tenants, he and his neighbours reacted to the burning of their hill grazings by sending 'boys and girls to the hill to try to bring [the cattle] home'. But this proved next to impossible, 'the cattle having been frightened and driven to a distance by the smoke and flames'. Other townships were similarly affected, their inhabitants' consequent anger intensified by Patrick Sellar's assumption that he was entitled to exercise full management rights during March and April over land that would not be formally in his tenancy until the end of May. At Rimsdale, a township on higher land well to the east of the Naver, that point was made in the course of an encounter between a Rimsdale tenant, John Gordon, and Sellar's head shepherd, John Dryden. The shepherd, Gordon reported, told him that he had himself raised exactly this issue with his employer who, by way of reassurance, had replied that 'he [Sellar] would take all the risk and responsibility' both for muirburn and for its consequences.[17]

Back at Golspie, meanwhile, William Young was still awaiting the arrival of John Roy, his land surveyor, whose home was in faraway Aberdeenshire. Eventually, on 20 April, Roy reached Sutherland, only to get word that his wife had fallen ill and that he would at once have to go back south. Told by Young 'to return as soon as he could', Roy at last put in a second appearance at Golspie on 20 May, getting to Strathnaver two or three days later. It was now less than a week before the families Patrick Sellar wanted out of townships like Rimsdale, Rivigill, Rhifail and Rhiloisk were meant to quit their homes. Indeed it would be 4 June – nine days after the removal deadline of 26 May – before, as William Young put it, 'everything was ready' in the various places, further down Strathnaver, where the 150 or so people about to be expelled from Patrick Sellar's farm were at last directed.[18]

There were of course no homes in these localities. When Young said all was in order for their 'reception', he meant only that they had finally been assigned particular crofts – small patches of land on which there were neither houses nor agricultural buildings. Putting these things in place was each newly installed crofter's responsibility, and since they had only just discovered their ultimate destinations, it was assumed by affected families that they would be given at least a few more weeks to make proper preparations for their departure. Nor was this mere wishful thinking on their part. At 'about the end of May', David MacKenzie, the minister whom William Young had asked to help out at the Golspie sett, had been approached by William Gordon – one of the men whose condemnation of Patrick Sellar's muirburn activities has already been quoted – and asked to write to Young on behalf of all the tenants under notice to quit Sellar's farm. What Gordon and others wanted from Young, MacKenzie said later, was 'to know to what places or allotments [they] were to remove themselves . . . as the 26th of May had then passed and an order had come from Mr Sellar to the [still in place] tenants to remove their cattle' from what was now – indisputably – his, Patrick Sellar's, land. David MacKenzie duly did as William Gordon requested. In reply to his letter, the minister said, he got from Young a note stating 'that the tenants might remain in possession until he [Young] could go to the strath [meaning Strathnaver] and make [presumably in collaboration with John Roy] the necessary arrangements for their removal'. By William Gordon and others, Young's letter was interpreted (not unreasonably) to mean that they were under no immediate pressure to take themselves off to crofts that had not, after all, been pointed out to them until several days into June. This, however, was by no means Patrick Sellar's understanding.[19]

Earlier in the year, Sutherland's sheriff court, in response to a request from Sellar in his capacity as a Sutherland Estate factor, had granted removal notices, which were delivered, during February and March, to household after household on Rhiloisk farm. Those notices (fastened to the doors of any tenants not at home) were in the name of the farm's landlord, the Marquis of Stafford. In the standard phraseology of the time, they instructed recipients 'to flit and remove themselves, their husbands, wives, bairns, families, servants, subtenants, cottars, dependants and whole goods and effects' – this flitting and removing to be completed by 26 May 1814. Shortly after that date, which passed (for reasons already touched on) without any sign of movement on the part of Rhiloisk outgoers, Sellar returned to the sheriff court. Without explaining (or so it is reasonable to presume) that no alternative landholdings had at that point been allocated to the people he wanted out, Sellar provided the court with those people's names. Because the individuals thus listed were now technically in breach of the court's earlier orders, Sellar, again in his capacity as factor, was promptly supplied with 'a warrant for their ejectment'. Heading back to Strathnaver, 'with this warrant in my pocket', as he put it, Sellar, on 14 June and without (as far as can be determined) giving much or any advance notice of his intentions, ordered the destruction of homes and other buildings belonging to nearly 30 families who were thus left with no alternative but to vacate localities that have been empty and abandoned ever since.[20]

Patrick Sellar, that June, was under a lot of pressure. Some months previously he had bought a cheviot flock (probably in Roxburghshire which would become his favoured source) and, at substantial cost, had brought this flock north. A few of Sellar's newly acquired sheep had been walked into Strathnaver in March. But at the beginning of June, because of his failure to get vacant possession of any part of his Rhiloisk farm on 26 May, the bulk of Sellar's flock remained quartered at Culmaily where – much of that farm being under crop and the rest given over to cattle – ewe after ewe, as Sellar commented, was 'dying . . . in consequence of the overstock'. 'What did not die', he added, 'were affected by disease which forced me to send a great proportion of them to the knife at one third of their value.'[21]

Nor was there any indication that matters, from Patrick Sellar's standpoint, were likely to improve any time soon. People meant to be gone were still pasturing 'some hundreds of cattle', Sellar wrote, on hill grazings that should long since have been given over to his sheep. Worse, one of his shepherds had been told by the people in question that its new tenant 'never should possess' Rhiloisk farm and that he 'should be a ruined man before they would permit [him] to [have] it'. Combined with the fact that William Young (judging by his letter to David MacKenzie) was in no great haste to have the farm cleared, threats like these must have seemed to Sellar to be tantamount to the beginnings of the sort of stand-off that had developed the year before in the Strath of Kildonan, whose occupants, Sellar had always felt, should never have been permitted (as many of them still were being permitted in June 1814) to remain in place. Hence Patrick Sellar's recourse to force.[22]

It took just two or three days to do everything that had to be done to make sure that a number of townships on Rhiloisk farm were left uninhabitable. During this period, Sellar had at his disposal about two dozen men. Some were sheriff-officers and constables. Others were his own employees. Of the latter, Sellar's shepherds – most of them from the Scottish Borders or from England – were perhaps the most committed to ensuring that family after family was left homeless. Had Patrick Sellar failed to get sheep on to Rhiloisk, after all, his shepherds would have lost their jobs. And those jobs were worth having. A shepherd's wages, as Sellar himself remarked, 'much exceeded' the wages available to ploughmen and other farm workers. Those wages, moreover, were supplemented by profits from the shepherd's 'pack' – the 60 or 70 sheep, from among his employer's flock, he managed on his own account. None of this, to be sure, is likely to have entirely eased the conscience of a man like John Dryden, the Rhiloisk farm head shepherd who had been anxious about his having had to implement Sellar's March muirburning instructions and who must have been still more troubled by what took place in June. But from what is known of one of Dryden's colleagues, Matthew Short, it seems probable that the rights and wrongs of enforced eviction would have concerned him not at all. Short had been employed for a time at Dunrobin Castle's home farm. What led to his eventual dismissal from this post is unknown. But the especially hostile and threatening reception Short got (as mentioned earlier) in the Strath of Kildonan in January 1813 might well have been linked with a reputation which led the Marchioness of Stafford to describe Short, after the shepherd was sacked at Dunrobin, as 'a brute'. Brutes, however, may have been exactly what Patrick Sellar needed in June 1814. Sellar, at all events and to the marchioness's surprise, took on the dismissed Short who thus became a member of the 'evicting party' given the task of putting Sellar's sheriff court 'warrant for ejectment' into effect. The outcome was devastation of a sort not experienced in Sutherland since the ending of inter-clan warfare.[23]

James MacKay, a tenant in Rhiloisk township, had actually moved out with his family before, as it was put by one of MacKay's neighbours, 'Mr Sellar and his party of hatchetmen' arrived. This availed MacKay nothing. His furniture, he explained, had been 'left locked up in his dwelling house' until such time as he was ready to move it. On getting back to Rhiloisk the day after the evicting party had passed through, however, James MacKay found 'that his door had been broken open and smashed to pieces, and the whole of his furniture thrown out, broken and destroyed'. Nor was this all. Both in his home and in his barn and byre or cowshed, the beams and rafters supporting those buildings' roofs had been cut through. The consequent roof collapses not only left home, barn and byre exposed to the weather, they made it impossible for MacKay to make any further use of scarce and valuable timber he had intended to incorporate into his new home.[24]

Had more time been taken, more timber and other materials might have been salvaged. But Patrick Sellar, according at least to people who saw what happened at Rhiloisk, was in a hurry. 'Mr Sellar's usual cry . . . to his party', said Hugh Grant, was 'to make haste [to] throw out . . . furniture and [to] knock down the houses'.[25]

Seeing what was being done to other houses round about, Donald MacKay, described subsequently as 'a feeble old man' in his eighties, clambered up on to his home's roof 'with the aim', he commented, 'of saving the timbers from being cut down and destroyed'. On his shortly after falling from the roof, he was, by his own account, so 'severely hurt' that he had to abandon his house to its fate. Left without anywhere to stay, MacKay sought shelter in woodland of the kind that had so appealed to Benjamin Meredith when he visited Rhiloisk four years before. There MacKay relied for a time on provisions supplied by people living (across the River Naver) on Robert Gordon's Langdale farm. Later he appears to have made his way to a still intact Rhiloisk home that had been appropriated by John Dryden. There this elderly and vulnerable man (the term 'feeble' denoting either physical or mental incapacity) was taken in, at a point (it seems) when the shepherd himself was elsewhere, by Dryden's wife. However, the return of her husband – who would have been all too aware that he could not afford to be found sheltering a Rhiloisk refugee – resulted in Donald MacKay being 'turned out' and, until eventually rescued by relatives, having once more to make what shift he could.[26]

At Rivigill, Rhifail and Rimsdale, events unfolded in much the same way. After 'throwing out' her furniture, said Barbara MacKay, a widow, 'Mr Sellar and party' went on to 'demolish and throw down her dwelling house'. Among her losses, Barbara MacKay continued, was 'a chest with a quantity of [oat]meal in it . . . The chest was broken and the meal scattered about and totally lost.'[27]

At Rhifail, Alexander Manson stood and watched Patrick Sellar's men 'throwing down and demolishing his house'. This was done, Manson explained, 'by cutting the couple trees [key roof supports] all along one side of the house [after] which the roof fell in . . . and the timber was broken and rendered almost useless'. At Rimsdale, in contrast, George Ross's house was left intact. This was because it was wanted, like the similarly unharmed home where Donald MacKay found shelter in Rhiloisk, as accommodation for one of Sellar's shepherds. His home having been taken over in this way, George Ross said, he was unable to strip that home of roofing and other materials that might have helped with the construction of a new house. He was consequently offered cash by way of compensation. But the sum he got, Ross insisted, was equivalent to less than a quarter of his home's true value.[28]

Those comments by George Ross survive – as do remarks made by Alexander Manson, Barbara MacKay, Donald MacKay, Hugh Grant and James MacKay – in documents compiled (for reasons touched on shortly) some 11 months after the occurrences Ross and his neighbours described. But it is to words recorded nearly 70 years later that one must turn in order to get as close as it is now possible to get to the sheer terror (the term is not too strong) engendered among some of the people affected by what Patrick Sellar did in June 1814. Those words were spoken by Angus MacKay, whose description of pre-clearance Strathnaver has already been quoted. MacKay's comments were taken down on Tuesday 24 July 1883 by a civil service clerk in the Free Church at Bettyhill, a post-clearance village that took shape on rising ground immediately to the east of the spot where the River Naver enters the sea. This clerk had travelled by carriage to Bettyhill that Tuesday from Thurso in the company of Francis Napier, the Borders peer and former colonial governor then chairing the six-man commission of inquiry Prime Minister William Gladstone had set up to look into the causes of crofter discontents that, here and there, had erupted into violence. There had been no such violence in Sutherland at this stage. But crofter grievances – many of them dating back to the clearances – were certainly not lacking. Bettyhill's Free Church, as noted by one of the journalists there that day, was consequently 'filled in every part' by local people 'who manifested more than usual interest in the proceedings'. The crowd's attention, it can be taken for granted, would have been captured all the more completely when Donald MacKinnon, one of Napier's colleagues and Professor of Celtic at Edinburgh University, asked Angus MacKay to tell the commission what he remembered of the day when, as a boy of 11, he fled from Patrick Sellar.[29]

MacKay did not say where exactly he spent his childhood. But his answers to MacKinnon's questions show that he grew up in one of the riverside settlements on Rhiloisk farm, perhaps Rhifail or Rivigill. From what MacKay said, moreover, it is clear that the events he described must have taken place on the morning of Monday 13 June 1814. This was the day the Rhiloisk farm clearances began, and it is certain that, had Angus MacKay's parents already seen something of the sort of devastation Patrick Sellar was about to cause in places like Rivigill and Rhifail, they would not have left their children – not just Angus but his younger brothers also – to cope unaided with the hazards they were shortly to face. As it was, Angus's father, mother and older brother – responding to an instruction to get their livestock off Sellar's farm – left very early (and in Sutherland in mid-June it is fully light by 3 a.m.) to drive the family's 'cattle, sheep, a horse, two mares and two foals' to the 'uncultivated piece of ground', as Angus MacKay called it, to which William Young and John Roy (both of whom MacKay mentioned by name) had directed them. Angus and his brothers, meanwhile, were left at home and asleep, their father, as Angus made clear when questioned on the point by Lord Napier, intending to be back in time to get him and his brothers up for breakfast. Well before their father's return, however, the boys were roused by a neighbour shouting that Patrick Sellar and his evicting party had set to work nearby. 'We got such a fright', Angus MacKay said of himself and his brothers, 'that we started out of bed and ran down to the river, because there was a friend of ours living upon the other side, and we wished to go there for protection.' Had he been alone, Angus might readily have forded the River Naver, despite its being, even in dry weather, both deep and fast-flowing. But he had his brothers with him, and the only way Angus could see to get the littlest of them – then just three – safely across was to carry him piggyback fashion. 'The water was that deep', Angus MacKay went on, 'that, when it came up upon his [the three-year-old's] back, he commenced crying and shaking himself upon my back, and I fell, and he gripped round about my neck, and

I could not rise nor move. We were both greeting [sobbing], and took a fright that we would be drowned.' Luckily, however, the two boys were glimpsed by a woman making her way 'up the strath' on the Langdale side. 'She saw us', Angus MacKay said, 'and jumped into the river and swept us out of it.'[30]

He would remember his 'terrible fright', Angus MacKay commented, for the rest of his life. 'You would have pitied them,' he said on being asked about his memories of how people like his parents and their neighbours reacted to being expelled from localities their families had cultivated for generations. 'He would be a very cruel man who would not mourn for the people.'[31]

9

'A COMBINATION AMONG THE BETTER SORT'

The attempt to destroy Patrick Sellar

For all their apparent capriciousness, evictions of the type that took place in Strathnaver in June 1814 were conducted, in principle at any rate, in strict accordance with statute. The legislation in question, cited in every removal notice issued in the course of the Sutherland clearances, was an Act Anent Warning Tenants. This Act, passed by the pre-union Scottish parliament in 1555, regularised the means by which landowners ended tenancies. Central to the 1555 Act – which can thus be seen as an initial step along a road that led centuries later to agricultural occupiers (first crofters, then farmers) gaining security of tenure – was the concept that tenants, as well as their landlords, had rights in land they farmed. Although the 1555 provisions were modified in 1756 when the Court of Session, Scotland's supreme civil court, introduced new procedures in this area, it remained the case that tenants could not be dispossessed, as had once been common, arbitrarily. Hence the requirement, that people be removed from farms (even in circumstances where leases had expired) only at specific points on the calendar, generally Whitsunday. And hence the further stipulation that such removals were lawful only if affected tenants had been given a minimum of 40 days' written notice (in the form of a court-issued order) of their landlord's intentions.

In the case of Patrick Sellar's 1814 evictions from the farm he was then taking over in Strathnaver, those stipulations had been complied with. But what of the further stipulation that outgoing tenants, as noted by an early nineteenth-century authority on those matters, owned – and therefore had a right to harvest – such crops as they might have sown or planted in advance of their removal? 'The principle on which this general rule is understood to be founded', this same authority went on, 'is that a tenant who is entitled to hold his possession during seed-time [some weeks in advance of Whitsun] is also entitled to prepare the ground and to sow it, and [is] consequently entitled to reap the crop which he has sown.' In 1814, as it happened, the Court of Session ruled that such was indeed the case. So where did that leave families ejected from Sellar's Rhiloisk farm in June that year – families who, in law, had an absolute right to harvest crops they had got into the ground well in advance of their ejection?[1]

At the heart of this issue was the fact that Patrick Sellar's evicting party destroyed not just people's homes but also their agricultural buildings, including barns where cereal crops were stored and threshed, peat-fired kilns where the resulting grain was dried and mills where oats in particular were ground into the meal that had long been a Sutherland staple. What took place at Rimsdale – occupying one of the shallow north–south valleys characteristic of the high moorland between Strathnaver and the Strath of Kildonan – was typical, in this regard, of what happened more widely. Some time subsequent to its clearance, the several homes formerly to be found in Rimsdale were replaced by a shepherd's cottage, which today has itself been abandoned. But it is easy to see where the pre-clearance settlement was located; easy to see too that the Rimsdale Burn, flowing past the settlement on its way to Loch Rimsdale, a mile or so distant, would readily have powered a mill. Here in June 1814, said John Gordon, he was told by Sellar's men that 'their orders [were] to throw down [that] mill which orders they were determined to execute'. At Rhifail beside the River Naver, a day or two before, Alexander Manson had 'remonstrated', he said, with Sellar about 'the illegality of his conduct' in depriving the township's tenants – whose barns and other buildings were then being unroofed – of any possibility of their taking in, storing, drying and milling the harvest to which the law entitled them. 'Mr Sellar', Manson commented, 'would hear no word upon the subject, but said he had a right to do what he pleased.' However, Manson, Gordon and a number of others were not prepared to let the matter rest. Over the next several months – indeed over the better part of the next two years – they were to press strongly for something to be done by way of recognising that they had not been treated, or so they contended, in accordance with the law. They began by drawing their grievances to the attention of the Marchioness of Stafford.[2]

On Sunday 3 July 1814, less than three weeks after Patrick Sellar's Strathnaver clearances, Lady Stafford arrived in Sutherland at the start of her regular summer excursion to the Highlands. She had left her overnight lodgings in the Easter Ross village of Alness at six that morning, the marchioness reported to her husband who (as always now) had remained in England. By two that afternoon, Lady Stafford continued, she was safely installed at Dunrobin Castle, 'where they had a very good dinner ready'. En route from the Dornoch Firth crossing point at Meikle Ferry, the marchioness went on, she had noted, when passing Culmaily, that 'Sellar [had] ploughed and smoothed all the rough ground near the road and brought it into order'. Further on, in Golspie, a new mill was 'look[ing] remarkably well'; recently established woodlands were everywhere in 'exquisite' condition; and in the castle gardens there were 'beds of young potatoes and all sorts of greens'.[3]

When at Dunrobin, according to Joseph Mitchell, a civil engineer who was an occasional visitor there, the Marchioness of Stafford 'used every Monday to hold a court on the lawn in front of the castle'. This, Mitchell wrote, was Lady Stafford's way of demonstrating her commitment to conducting estate business 'in accordance with the customs of the chiefs of old'. That such was indeed the marchioness's practice is confirmed by her correspondence from Dunrobin, Lady Stafford's daily letters to the marquis often containing, on Mondays, references to her having been 'very busy' (to quote from one such letter) dealing with 'petitions' she received from estate residents with favours to ask or grievances to express. Among the petitions thus put to the marchioness in July 1814 was one from families Patrick Sellar had, not long before, ejected from their homes.[4]

Those families listed three grounds of complaint. The first arose from Sellar having burned his Rhiloisk farm's hill grazings well in advance of his tenancy commencing. Another had to do with people having been prevented from taking timbers from their old homes to the sites of their new houses. A third stemmed from Sellar's evicting party having 'pulled down . . . houses, barns, kilns and mills contrary', or so Lady Stafford's petitioners maintained, 'to the use and custom of the country which is that [a farm's] removing tenant has [access to] barn, kiln and mill [for] twelve months after removing' – this being essential, the petitioners stressed, if outgoing families such as themselves were to benefit fully from 'the crop left on [vacated] ground'.[5]

This last contention – much the most crucial of the three – turned on what was meant exactly by 'the use and custom of the country'. In some of the comment generated at the time and afterwards by Patrick Sellar's 1814 evictions, the impression is given that the phrase relates to a practice peculiar to Sutherland. This, however, is to misunderstand the force of what was said by the Strathnaver people whose agricultural buildings had been demolished on Sellar's orders. As already indicated, there was not the slightest doubt that, whether in Sutherland or elsewhere in Scotland, tenants removed from farms at Whitsun were entitled in law to harvest such crops as those farms were carrying at the point of removal. Underlying this provision, however, was an assumption (dating from 1555) that, even when a farm's occupier was replaced, agricultural operations on that farm would continue much as before. In such circumstances of course it could never be in anyone's interest, whether landlord or incoming tenant, for 'the whole arable part of [a] farm', as one contemporary text put it, to be left 'waste' (meaning untilled and uncropped) for an entire season, as would have happened were outgoers (still in occupation when fields or rigs needed ploughing and planting) refused harvesting rights. But suppose, as was the case on Sellar's Rhiloisk farm, that a single incoming tenant was taking the place of dozens of previous tenants. Suppose further that this new tenant was implementing a land-use change so drastic that he had absolutely no need to keep arable land in good heart or maintain barns, mills and the like in good order. What then? While such a tenant – Patrick Sellar in this instance – was obliged to permit his farm's former occupants to harvest their grain, was he equally obliged to ensure that they had on-site access to kilns, mills and storehouses? How, in other words, was legislation framed centuries in advance of the Sutherland clearances to be interpreted in this new world where it might be to a landlord's financial benefit to depopulate a whole countryside and – because sheep farming rendered cropping redundant – give up completely on that countryside's cultivation? Those questions (as will be seen) were eventually settled in Scotland's High Court of Justiciary. But when, in the first instance, the Marchioness of Stafford was required to take a view of the matter, she sided less with Patrick Sellar than with his Rhiloisk predecessors.[6]

This was not because the marchioness was reneging either on 'improvement' in general or on the expansion of sheep farming in particular. However, she had two good reasons for offering at least a degree of comfort to Rhiloisk's displaced families. One stemmed from the risk that, if their grievances were simply brushed aside, those grievances might attract further adverse publicity of the sort that had so tarnished the Stafford name in the wake of the 1813 uprising in the Strath of Kildonan. The other was a consequence of the marchioness's long-standing suspicion that Patrick Sellar – from an estate management standpoint – tended to create more problems than he solved.

'Sellar', Lady Stafford had commented as far back as 1811, 'seems to be a clever writer [meaning lawyer] and accountant.' But he lacked 'direction', had 'no sense' and was perhaps overly 'keen about his own interest'. Those early misgivings were reinforced by what the marchioness learned in July 1814 of Patrick Sellar's activities at Rhiloisk. 'The more I see and hear of Sellar', she told her husband, 'the more I am convinced he is not fit to be trusted further than he is at present. He is so exceedingly greedy and harsh with the people. There are very heavy complaints against him from Strathnaver.' Those complaints, Lady Stafford went on, centred on Sellar's refusing any 'indulgence' with regard to 1814's harvest. 'This is to be examined', she concluded, 'and I believe it will be necessary to bring him [Sellar] before [Sheriff] Cranstoun.'[7]

Much the same stance is evident in the emollient tone of the response received by the marchioness's Strathnaver petitioners. Lady Stafford, the petitioners learned, wished to offer evicted tenants a rent rebate equivalent to half the annual rent due to be levied on their new landholdings. 'If any person on the [Sutherland] Estate shall receive any illegal treatment', the same tenants were informed, '[Lady Stafford] will never consider it as hostile to her if they have recourse to legal redress as the most secure way to receive the justice which she always desires they should have.'[8]

One effect of the marchioness's intervention was to ensure that evicted families were no longer debarred – as they had been for a period – from taking away roof and other timbers left behind in the course of the upheavals Patrick Sellar had set in train. But there were no other immediate consequences. Lady Stafford might have given her blessing to some sort of legal action being mounted against Patrick Sellar. But what she had in mind, it seems, was to get either Sutherland's sheriff, George Cranstoun, or failing him, his Caithness counterpart, James Traill, to preside over an arbitration hearing intended to allow both Sellar and the Strathnaver petitioners to give their (doubtless conflicting) accounts of what had occurred in June, after which the presiding sheriff, if he were to find in the complainants' favour, would award appropriate damages against Sellar. Why this approach was not at once adopted is unclear. Perhaps neither

Cranstoun nor Traill, a Caithness landowner, was thought sufficiently neutral by the Strathnaver people. Perhaps, as was suggested
later, 'the [unidentified] lawyer from Ross-shire' whom the
Strathnaver group had engaged was reluctant to tangle with Patrick
Sellar. Perhaps, once the marchioness was again on the road south,
it suited William Young, the Staffords' main man in Sutherland,
simply to let matters slide. Throughout the autumn of 1814 and into
the following winter, at all events, no arbitration mechanism was
put in place. The 'justice' Lady Stafford had promised thus remained
unforthcoming.[9]

Sellar, meanwhile, was trying to counter such adverse effects as
the Strathnaver petition – together with the controversy that gave
rise to it – might have had on his standing with the Staffords. In an
ingratiating letter to the marchioness, penned just days after she had
expressed (though Sellar did not know this) her doubts about him,
he listed his endeavours in the Stafford family's service. Her
Sutherland tenants, he assured Lady Stafford, had 'never' encountered a factor so assiduous 'in exploring . . . fastnesses' whose
inhabitants, he implied, had previously not so much as glimpsed a
Sutherland Estate representative. 'They have seen no vacillation, no
slackening in my duty,' Sellar observed of the people with whom he
dealt on the marchioness's behalf. 'They have no hope [of evading
their obligations] while I am your servant . . . [T]hey know they
cannot cheat me.'[10]

All this was by way of underpinning an early instance of what
was to become a standard Patrick Sellar assertion: that criticism or
condemnation of his conduct originated in his unyielding determination to do his best for his Stafford employers. 'The people of this
country, *high* and *low*', Sellar insisted in his letter to Lady Stafford,
'have an uncommon talent for intrigue.' That statement, in its way,
was prescient. In the summer of 1814, Sellar's suspicions notwithstanding, there was in fact little in the way of an organised conspiracy
– certainly not one involving both ends of Sutherland's social spec-
trum – to do down Sellar. But soon there would emerge, if not a

conspiracy, then certainly a concerted effort to undermine and ulti-mately to destroy all the factor's hopes and ambitions. This campaign, moreover, would indeed have the backing of people drawn from Sutherland society's upper ranks as well as from the county's commonalty, those otherwise distinct groups having been bound together by a shared detestation of Patrick Sellar and everything he stood for.[11]

In the opening sequence of Kathleen Fidler's 1964 novel, *The Desperate Journey*, a book that became both a bestseller and a young people's classic, David and Kirsty Murray, the brother and sister at the centre of Fidler's story, are gathering mussels by Loch Fleet when Patrick Sellar, unseen by the children, approaches on horseback. Dismounting, Sellar makes his way towards Kirsty and David in a manner suggestive of his being the embodiment of forces that are soon to bring about the Murray family's eviction and launch them on the journey of Fidler's title, a journey that ends at Red River. 'His feet made no noise over the wet sandy flats,' Kathleen Fidler wrote of the factor. 'His face became crimson with anger when he saw the creels filled with mussels, and he roared at the chil-dren in a voice of thunder, "What are you young rascals up to?"'[12]

This Loch Fleet encounter, which culminates in Patrick Sellar taking his riding whip to David, is fictional. But to dip into the records of Sutherland's Justice of the Peace Court, where Sellar arraigned a long series of alleged offenders, is to find plenty of evidence to the effect that Kathleen Fidler's portrayal of the factor's behaviour has some basis in fact. On just one occasion in 1814, for example, Sellar had no fewer than 32 people charged with 'repeat-edly carrying off' mussels – in law the property of Lord and Lady Stafford – from the Loch Fleet foreshore. Many more individuals were to be accused of this and numerous other supposed misde-meanours. To be late with a rent payment was to run the risk of a court appearance. To strip trees of their bark – used in tanning leather – was to put oneself equally in danger. Nor was it wise to avoid the tolls levied at bridges built partly or wholly at Sutherland Estate expense. When, at Sellar's instigation, a man by the name of Alexander Campbell was accused in December 1814 of having 'forcibly pass[ed] through the gate of the toll bar' at one such bridge, Campbell responded by saying he had explained to the toll-keeper that, being cashless but being about to sell a sheep, he would pay the toll on his return. This did not impress Sellar. The unpaid toll was a halfpenny. The fine of £1 5s imposed on Campbell was 600 times greater.[13]

None of this did much to enhance Patrick Sellar's local standing. But it was his assaults on what he called the 'nation of poachers and woodstealers' he met with in Sutherland that were to do most to put him at odds with all sorts and classes of people. Those assaults were strictly in accord with Sellar's instructions, as set out in an 1811 'minute of agreement' dealing with his appointment as a Sutherland Estate factor, to 'pay attention . . . to the enforcing of the laws for preserving the plantations and the game'. Sellar, however, had set about that task with unprecedented vigour. This generated a great deal of ill-feeling, indicative of the extent to which 'improvement', as understood and imposed by men like Sellar and William Young, was at odds not just with long-standing tenurial practices but with equally long-standing approaches to the management and use of natural resources.[14]

A thousand years in advance of the beginnings of 'improvement', the 'law tracts' then regulating conduct in Gaelic-speaking communities, whether in Scotland or in Ireland, had stipulated that, irrespective of the formal ownership of such assets, people at large were free to take timber from forests, game from wild country, trout and salmon from streams. Post-medieval developments in the Highlands had ensured that legislation of the type Patrick Sellar applied so enthusiastically – legislation which made naturally occurring trees and wild animals the exclusive property of landowners – was wholly uninfluenced by this earlier thinking. Among Highlanders, however, traces of the older viewpoint survived (and still survive) in deeply entrenched notions of the kind encapsulated in a Gaelic proverb to the effect that every inhabitant of every locality has a right to take a tree from a nearby wood, a deer from a nearby hill, a fish from a nearby river. Hence the enduring Highland belief that, no matter what landlords and courts might say, to kill a stag or take a salmon for one's own consumption is in no way to be equated with theft or other crimes.[15]

Until Patrick Sellar's arrival in the north, Sutherland Estate managers, it seems, had been disinclined to mount any very vigorous challenge to time-honoured reasoning of this kind. That now changed radically. The 'killing of deer or any kind of game', Sellar made clear, was 'prohibited under severe penalities'. Nobody was to 'have in his or her custody . . . at any time . . . any partridges, pheasants, muirfowl, heathfowl, snipes or quails'[*]. Twenty-shilling fines would be imposed on first offenders, higher fines on second offenders, jail sentences on anyone still undeterred.[16]

Perhaps to Sellar's credit, and certainly to the outrage of some of the people thus targeted, those edicts were aimed at 'gentlemen' as well as at humbler folk. As early as December 1810, Sellar was supplying the Marchioness of Stafford with details of prominent tacksmen and other locally eminent individuals 'who by my information', he wrote, 'kill game'. With the marchioness's backing, the individuals in question were informed that, should they persist, 'the most prompt and effectual measures' would be taken against them. Persist, however, some suspected poachers evidently did; and heading up this category, it transpired, was none other than Sutherland's leading law officer, Sheriff-Substitute Robert McKid. He had featured in Sellar's 1810 list of alleged offenders and the factor, or so he reported to Lady Stafford shortly after, duly 'took [McKid] over the coals' by way of warning the sheriff to put away his guns. But McKid – a man quite possibly addicted, as so many poachers

---

[*] Muirfowl are red grouse, heathfowl are black grouse. Quail, though unusual now in Scotland, were once common.

have been, to the risks inherent in illicit sport – had not done as instructed. Hence the new Sellar–McKid clash set in motion on the morning of 10 January 1814 when Walter Nash, a Dunrobin Castle gamekeeper, turned up at Sellar's Culmaily home with what the factor called 'an information against Mr McKid for poaching'. This information, Nash told Sellar, had been conveyed to him by Donald Bannerman, the Golspie-based sheriff-officer and constable who had had a leading role in efforts to combat the previous January's rebellion in Kildonan.[17]

That McKid shot game illegally is undoubted. Equally definite, however, is the fact that he was brought to book by men – Nash, Bannerman and Sellar – who all had their own good reasons for welcoming the opening the sheriff had so rashly made available to them.

In Walter Nash's case, those reasons were bound up with scandal. Just weeks before, as a gossipy William Young observed gleefully, Nash had been found to have been 'carrying on an illicit traffic with his maid', despite, Young added, Nash having 'a wife and three children'. On the maid's resulting pregnancy becoming apparent, and the affair thus becoming public knowledge, the now disgraced girl had been sent 'home to her father'. Walter Nash, unlike his maidservant, had not lost his job. But with scurrilous rumour doubtless swirling around him, the gamekeeper is bound to have been anxious to find means of re-establishing his credentials with his bosses, among whom was Patrick Sellar. This being so, Nash is bound to have been more than usually eager to be seen to be backing Sellar's anti-poaching crusade and must, therefore, have been delighted by his being able to draw Robert McKid's illegal activities to Sellar's attention.[18]

Donald Bannerman is likely to have been equally gratified by his part in what now unfolded, having for some time been at odds with McKid because of the sheriff's refusal to meet his expenses claims. When on duty in or around the then turbulent Strath of Kildonan during February and March 1813, Bannerman had run up

substantial bills relating to food – and more especially whisky –
consumed by himself and three constable colleagues at Helmsdale
Inn. The sheriff-officer had submitted those bills to McKid in the
expectation of their being settled from public funds. This, however,
McKid declined to do on the grounds, first, that 'it [was] not the
practice of the country' to 'feed' waged employees and, second, that
claims arising from the Strath of Kildonan debacle should be
addressed not to him but to the Sutherland Estate. Who, if anyone,
finally covered Donald Bannerman's Helmsdale outlays is unclear.
But because of the sheriff's refusal to do so, the guinea the sheriff-officer pocketed by way of reward for his having informed on McKid
is likely to have made Bannerman feel even better than he might
otherwise have done about his having, in part at least, avenged
himself on the sheriff.[19]

Bannerman, in Sellar's opinion, was 'an excellent police officer'
who had been 'of most effectual service . . . during the [Kildonan]
disturbances'. The sheriff-officer, then, is certain to have been given
a cordial reception when he called at Culmaily on the evening of 10
January to claim his guinea and to divulge what he knew of McKid's
poaching. This had taken place during a period when, as Sellar
explained to Lady Stafford, Sutherland had for 'fourteen days been
bound up in frost and snow' and 'the game [had] come down in
packs from the high [ground]'. 'Nothing could be more mean', the
factor went on, 'than for a gentleman to kill a proprietor's game in
the snow and without being qualified by license or leave of the landlord'. But this was exactly what Robert McKid had done, and he,
Sellar, now had Bannerman's 'affidavit' to prove it.[20]

The exultant tone apparent in these and other comments Patrick
Sellar made about McKid that January cannot be accounted for
solely by the factor's glee at finding another poacher in his clutches.
Although the sheriff and Sellar had, on the face of things, collaborated closely when both were endeavouring to deal with the Kildonan
rebels, tensions between them had been evident even then and had
become more pronounced in the interim. Enraged in the summer of

1813 by the botched job McKid apparently made of a case involving
Sutherland Estate tenants in Assynt, Sellar had persuaded the
marchioness to make it known to George Cranstoun, McKid's principal, that she considered the sheriff-substitute 'in several respects
unfit for his situation'. Cranstoun – again demonstrating the independence of mind that would ultimately lead to Stafford calls for
his, as well as McKid's, dismissal – was not prepared to oblige. 'I
should think it unjust to deprive him [meaning McKid] of his office
and perhaps to ruin him on account of an error of judgement,'
Cranstoun commented.[21]

Robert McKid, as it happened, had come to Sutherland at about
the same time as Patrick Sellar and William Young, giving up a
private legal practice in the Easter Ross town of Tain in exchange for
an annual salary of £90 and, at the same time, taking the tenancy of
a Sutherland Estate farm. This farm, known as Kirkton, shared a
boundary with Sellar's Culmaily, and both Young and Sellar had for
some time been of the opinion, as Young put it, that 'it would
certainly be desirable' to get McKid out of Kirkton with a view to
further enlarging the acreage at Sellar's disposal. McKid's management of Kirkton, Sellar observed, was characterised by 'indolence
and inattention' – deadly sins in the Sellar book. If he were permitted to add Kirkton's fields to Culmaily's, Sellar believed, the cause of
'improvement' was bound to be progressed. That, however, could
only happen if some means were found of making the farm available. The sheriff-substitute's January 1814 embarrassments, Patrick
Sellar is sure to have calculated, were likely to be of help in this
regard, just as they might assist, Sellar is sure to have reckoned also,
ongoing efforts to undermine McKid's standing with George
Cranstoun.[22]

But first the poaching charge had to be made to stick. This took
time. For three weeks, Robert McKid simply denied any wrongdoing on his part, insisting that dead game birds found at Kirkton had
been shot not by himself but by one of his three sons. By one means
or another, however, Walter Nash had eventually provided 'proof',

or so Sellar noted, 'that [the] son [was] innocent and the father guilty'. The outcome, in early February 1814, was that McKid, as Sellar at once informed Lady Stafford, 'struck his colours', confessed his offences and began composing 'a penitential letter' to the marchioness, asking, in effect, for her pardon.[23]

At that point, however, Patrick Sellar lost his nerve. Had he proceeded with a formal prosecution of the sheriff-substitute, and had such a prosecution succeeded, McKid could not have continued in office and, following his dismissal, could readily have been deprived of Kirkton farm. But if such a prosecution were to fail, Sellar warned in a February letter to Lady Stafford, 'he [McKid] would have it in his power . . . to take revenge on us . . . and do us much annoyance'. Since, Sellar went on, 'it were a pity to risk this', it might be better if the marchioness and her husband acceded to McKid's request that his poaching be forgiven. By means of such an 'act of generosity', Sellar argued, the sheriff-substitute could be 'bound to our interest', with the highly beneficial outcome (though Sellar did not make this point explicitly) that sheriff court cases involving Sutherland Estate business would, in those circumstances, be more likely to have pro-estate outcomes.[24]

This was naive. As Sellar suggested, McKid was indeed pardoned. But the result, predictably, was the reverse of what Sellar intended. The sheriff-substitute – already bruised by the 1813 effort to have him dismissed and now humiliated by the discovery of his poaching forays – conceived a deep hatred for the man he regarded, with justice, as his principal persecutor. This became apparent to Sellar when, not long after McKid's pardon had been confirmed, the factor, or so he wrote later, was 'waited upon' by Sutherland's procurator fiscal (and thus the sheriff-substitute's colleague) Hugh Ross. Ross's purpose, originating no doubt in his wish to keep on the right side of the Sutherland Estate and its proprietors, was to tell Sellar that, as the factor commented, 'the sheriff-substitute was lying in wait to do me an injury'. Ross, Sellar went on, had duly 'advised me to be extremely cautious in all my proceedings'. Soon the truth of what Hugh Ross had to say was borne out by developments in Dornoch Sheriff Court where, when Sellar appeared in connection with Sutherland Estate actions having to do with rent arrears and other matters of that kind, he found McKid showing 'every little hostility in his power towards me'. But the sheriff-substitute's capacity to do damage, Sellar assured the Marchioness of Stafford, was limited. 'I have endeavoured to give him [McKid] no room to quibble or trick me,' Sellar wrote. That was in April 1814. Two months later, the Rhiloisk evictions – or, more specifically, what was done in the course of them – would give Robert McKid all the 'room' or opportunity he needed to inflict real harm on Patrick Sellar.[25]

Pressure for something to be done by way of attending to the grievances of people evicted by Patrick Sellar in June 1814 emanated, in the first instance, from those people themselves and, in particular, from two of their number, John Munro and John MacKay. MacKay, before his eviction, had lived in Rivigill. Munro came from Garvault, near the eastern boundary of Sellar's farm and, like Rimsdale, a moorland enclave located, in Garvault's case, north of Loch Badanloch. From Garvault and Rivigill, Munro and MacKay had been relocated, along with their families, to Rhinovie, where they and other refugees from Rhiloisk farm's emptied townships were expected to share that locality's arable and pasture land – on the right bank of the Naver not far from the river's estuary – with its already established residents.

The petition the Marchioness of Stafford received in July 1814 from Rhiloisk's former tenants appears to have been drawn up largely, if not entirely, on John Munro and John MacKay's own initiative. During the winter of 1814–15, however, and still more in the course of the following spring, the two men began to receive backing from beyond the borders of Strathnaver. Some of the allies MacKay and Munro thus acquired may have been motivated by nothing other than a wish to come to the aid of people who had lost land and homes. But as had happened in 1813 when the Kildonan troubles were at their most acute, Strathnaver's discontents were also seized on by people whose antagonism to 'improvement' was rooted in the damage it was doing, or might do, to Sutherland's tacksman class. Prominent members of that class – like Colonel Alexander Sutherland of Culmaily, John MacDonald of Pollie and Robert Gordon of Langdale – had already lost landholdings (as MacDonald and the colonel had done) or come close (as Gordon did in December 1813) to doing so. Others feared, with good reason, that they might be equally vulnerable. Hence their eagerness to capitalise on – even stir up – popular disaffection of a sort that might impede, or perhaps sabotage completely, the Marquis and Marchioness of Stafford's plans for the Sutherland Estate. Hence too the marchioness's growing conviction that she, her husband and their agents were at risk from what, in a letter written in the summer of 1815, Lady Stafford called 'a combination among the better sort'. By 'better sort' the marchioness meant tacksmen. Their purpose, she continued, was 'to effect a demolition of our new system', meaning the land management revolution Sellar and Young had been employed to put in place.[26]

Because backers of combination or 'conspiracy' (a word that features frequently in Sutherland Estate correspondence of the clearance period) were anxious (for obvious reasons) to keep in the background, their identities remain uncertain. But a number can be named. Prominent among this number were John Sutherland of Sciberscross in Strathbrora and his London-based brother Alexander. Both had aligned themselves (as noted earlier) with the Kildonan rebels. Now they offered support to former residents of Patrick Sellar's Rhiloisk farm.

Of the two brothers, Alexander – the 'Sandy Ink' of the marchioness's often angry letters about his journalistic activities – played (as before) an especially crucial role. In so doing, he appears (though details are impossible to pin down) to have had help from others of similar background. Two of London's social networks were important in this connection. One of those was centred on the capital's

Gaelic Chapel. Financed by public subscription*, this church (where services were conducted by a Gaelic-speaking minister) had been completed in 1813, and Alexander Sutherland was, by his own account, a prominent member. Overlapping with the Gaelic Chapel's congregation was a further key network – with which Sutherland was also much involved – consisting of men of tacksman parentage who had gravitated to London, as Sandy Ink himself had done, at the close of careers in the army. This second group was, in turn, a subset of a much larger contingent of former officers (their number augmented by the rapid run-down of the military in the wake of Napoleon's final defeat at Waterloo in June 1815) who found themselves deprived of income, purpose and status in a nation with no further need for their skills. Those men's house journal, as it were, was the *Military Register*. This was a weekly publication concerned, its masthead proclaimed, with 'military affairs and public topics'. Prominent among such topics, from a *Military Register* perspective, were the many grievances of what the periodical's editor called 'the half-pay squad', meaning the legion of ex-lieutenants, ex-captains and others of similar standing who, though recipients of the half-pay that was the early nineteenth-century equivalent of a military pension, often struggled to get by. Men in this situation were eager and sympathetic consumers of stories about the sufferings of veteran soldiers and their families. Patrick Sellar's Strathnaver clearances and their repercussions supplied Alexander Sutherland, one of the *Military Register*'s regular contributors, with an inexhaustible supply of such material.[27]

Starting on 5 April 1815, the *Military Register*'s columns dealt almost weekly with occurrences on the Sutherland Estate where, Alexander Sutherland informed readers, 'a very great number of old tenantry [had] been removed from their strongly cherished localities [in consequence of] the introduction of sheep farms'. Many evicted

---

* One prominent subscriber was the Earl of Selkirk who spent a lot of time in London and who (as mentioned earlier) had learned Gaelic.

tenants, Sutherland stressed, were 'old soldiers' who were being 'reduced to beggary' in the name of 'improvement'. This was bad enough. Making matters worse, however, was 'the conduct of those persons locally charged with carrying the new system into effect'. Their behaviour, Alexander Sutherland alleged, had 'been generally of the harshest and most reprehensible description . . . In truth they act as if they consider North Britons out of the pale of the law.' This was particularly true, Sutherland went on, of one of the Marquis and Marchioness of Stafford's agents or factors who, it was insinuated, had abused his position by ensuring that an especially choice sheep farm had been allocated to none other than himself. 'In taking possession of this farm', Alexander Sutherland wrote of the factor in question, 'he found that the usual custom and law of the land would be too tardy in ridding him of the unfortunate tenants [who had occupied the farm before him]; he therefore . . . applied the *torch* to their habitations . . . In some of [the affected] buildings . . . [were] aged and bedridden persons who narrowly escaped the flames – and some of them, from the affright, precipitancy and circumstances of such a removal, died a few days thereafter in an outhouse, unpitied!!!'[28]

Although he soon would be, Patrick Sellar was not named by the *Military Register* at this stage. But it would have been clear to anyone knowing anything about events on the Sutherland Estate who was meant. It would have been equally clear that the *Military Register* – aggressively committed to 'the legitimate freedom of the press' and to 'maintaining the rights and justice of humanity' – was raising concerns about Sellar's Rhiloisk evictions to a wholly new level. To begin with, the principal issue at stake had been whether or not the factor, by demolishing mills, barns and other buildings, had ridden roughshod over displaced tenants' legal rights to harvest crops sown or planted in advance of their ejection. Now he was accused not just of unroofing homes but of setting them ablaze and, in consequence, causing the deaths of some at least of their occupants. What had previously been a matter to be settled privately or, failing that, in a civil court was now said, in effect, to involve crimes so serious that they could, if proven, result in Patrick Sellar's imprisonment – even, conceivably, his execution.[29]

Just ten days after its publication in London, the 5 April edition of the *Military Register* was shown to Sellar by William Young. The paragraphs dealing with his evictions, Sellar would have seen, were attributed merely to *Miles*, Latin for soldier. But the copy which had come into Young's possession was clearly one that had been put into circulation in the north by John Sutherland of Sciberscross, this being apparent, Sellar reported, from 'some jottings in the margin' which, he saw, were 'in the handwriting' of the Sciberscross tacksman. Given the well-established history of collaboration between John Sutherland and his journalist brother Alexander, Sellar was in no doubt as to the *Military Register* story's authorship. Nor was he under any illusions as to its purpose. Sutherland's tacksman-led 'combination' – this grouping in which Alexander and John Sutherland were principal players – was clearly intent on adding to already-mounting pressure for some sort of official investigation into what exactly had occurred on Patrick Sellar's Strathnaver farm the previous summer.[30]

Hence Sellar's panicky response to what turned out to be the first of many *Military Register* articles by Alexander Sutherland, this response taking the shape of a somewhat incoherent appeal to his employers to stick unswervingly with their 'improvement' mission. Integral to that mission, Sellar recognised, would be many more evictions of the Rhiloisk sort. But there was no need for the Stafford family to apologise for, or feel bad about, this. On the contrary, it needed to be made clear to critics of clearance that there would have been no 'humanity' in 'leaving this race of people [the inhabitants of places like Strathnaver] in barbarous sloth and filth'. Indeed their removal and his own role in that removal, or so Sellar contended in a letter written just hours after his first sight of the *Military Register*'s 5 April issue, could be seen as necessary components of a divinely ordained plan that, in the end, would benefit everyone affected: 'I believe, in my heart, that it is out of the great goodness of Providence that He [God] puts it into the minds of such great people as Lord and Lady Stafford to force us to [do] what is proper for us.'[31]

This letter was mailed to the marquis and marchioness's son and heir who, like his father, was named George Granville Leveson-Gower and who was known formally (as his father had been prior to the death of the younger George's grandfather in 1803) as Earl, or Lord, Gower. Possibly because he was known to be taking a growing interest in the management of the Sutherland Estate, Gower – in his late twenties at this point – had been drawn into the Strathnaver dispute when, in January 1815, he had been sent a petition bearing the names of John Munro, John MacKay and more than 30 other people. This document, John Munro said some weeks later, had been drawn up with a view to making clear to Gower that he and others were angered by their still 'not having received that redress to which they [had] conceived themselves entitled' when, six months before, they first made contact with the earl's mother. Some such redress or recompense was due, the new petition stated, because of the 'cruel usage and oppression' its signatories had suffered at the hands of Patrick Sellar. In one instance, the petition's compilers stated, Sellar had gone so far as to have a home set on fire, 'at the cost of the life' of one that home's occupants.[32]

This was the first the Staffords had heard of the possibility (soon to be made much of by the *Military Register*) that Sellar's conduct in Strathnaver might have been such as to result in criminal charges. A worried Gower, having consulted with his parents, accordingly struck (as Lady Stafford had done the previous July) a conciliatory note. The marquis and marchioness, Gower informed John Munro in early February, were 'desirous' that Munro and his neighbours 'should know that it is always their wish that justice should be impartially administered'. With this end in view, Gower continued, he had written to William Young instructing him to take 'proper steps' to deal with the points made by Munro and his fellow petitioners. Those steps were to culminate, Gower added, in Young 'laying the business' before Sheriff Cranstoun, thereby ensuring, the earl concluded, 'that a full hearing shall be given to all parties'.[33]

In response to Gower's orders, Young drew up a 'submission' which, had Munro, MacKay and their associates put their names to it, would have led to 'all demands, claims, [and] disputes' arising from the June 1814 evictions being aired before Sheriff Cranstoun, prior to the sheriff, as Young commented, 'award[ing] what pecuniary damages he might see due'.[34]

On that offer reaching Strathnaver, however, it was turned down by John MacKay, John Munro and their colleagues. This, or so David MacKenzie – now Farr's parish minister – told William Young, was in part because Munro, MacKay and others had been 'advised' to reject the possibility of an arbitrated settlement and to demand instead that the authorities subject Sellar to a criminal prosecution. One source of that advice, John MacKay confirmed afterwards, was John Sutherland of Sciberscross, who, during March and in the wake of his having made contact with MacKay and Munro, is likely to have supplied his brother with the material that was then published in the *Military Register*.[35]

Perhaps with the Sciberscross tacksman's encouragement, but just as probably on his own initiative, John Munro, towards the end of March, travelled to Golspie to make clear to William Young that a private or semi-private arbitration of the sort advocated by both Lady Stafford and Lord Gower was firmly off Strathnaver people's agenda. He and his neighbours, Munro said, 'now wish[ed] the[ir] case [against Sellar] to be made as public as possible'.[36]

Also in late March, John Munro wrote directly to George Cranstoun, asking, in effect, for advice as to what should happen next. Cranstoun was nothing if not helpful. If Munro and others 'intend[ed] to proceed against Mr Sellar either by nature of a civil or criminal action', the sheriff commented, it would be necessary to have prospective witnesses questioned by himself, as sheriff, or by Robert McKid, as sheriff-substitute. He personally was willing to undertake such questioning, Cranstoun indicated. But because Munro and his associates wanted to press ahead 'immediately', the task would necessarily devolve to McKid. This, Cranstoun explained, was because 'my engagements [in Edinburgh] will not permit me to be in Sutherland until the month of July.' [37]

George Cranstoun, at this point, was also in receipt of correspondence from Patrick Sellar. The charges being levelled against him in Strathnaver, Sellar had insisted in an earlier letter to the Marchioness of Stafford, were nothing but fictions emanating from 'a few tools employed for a purpose'. By 'tools', Sellar meant Strathnaver people like John MacKay and John Munro. By 'purpose', he meant the plot Sellar thought had been hatched with a view to bringing about his downfall. This plot, Sellar now assured Cranstoun, was the work of, among others, Robert McKid. He had been 'basely and artfully traduced' by McKid and his fellow plotters, Sellar complained. This was due in part to his having become 'obnoxious' to McKid in consequence of his role in uncovering the sheriff-substitute's poaching exploits. [38]

The letter containing those comments was sent south from Golspie on 24 March. It is likely – the post from Sutherland to Edinburgh then usually taking under a week – to have been seen by George Cranstoun prior to the sheriff mailing his own 31 March letter to John Munro. But if it was so seen, it was ignored. This may have been due to Sellar's letter reading like a product of runaway paranoia. But it may have owed something also to Cranstoun's (perfectly correct) determination not to be swayed by a man whose prosecution, as indicated by the sheriff's 31 March letter to John Munro, he was more and more inclined to sanction.

Doubtless encouraged by Cranstoun's response to his queries, Munro, for his part, set about exerting further pressure on the authorities. Towards the end of April, he left Rhinovie for Inverness where the High Court – its personnel then making one of their 'circuit journeys' into the north – was in session. In attendance at the court's Inverness sittings was Andrew Clephane, a senior aide or depute to Lord Advocate Archibald Colquhoun. Seeking out Clephane, Munro spoke with him on 2 May and, that same day, handed over to this Edinburgh-based official a sheaf of documents. In the covering letter accompanying those documents, John Munro described them as 'papers which point out many instances of grievous oppression by which [he] and a great many of [his] poor neighbours [had] suffered severely'. He had made the long journey south to Inverness, Munro went on, to 'implore' Clephane 'to see justice done to us'.[39]

Having read John Munro's 'papers' and having had a second meeting with him, Andrew Clephane now made contact with Robert McKid, also in Inverness on High Court business, and gave the sheriff-substitute to understand – as George Cranstoun had done in his exchanges (copied to McKid) with Munro – that formal enquiries into Sellar's behaviour would be in order. On getting back to his Kirkton farm from Inverness, McKid duly wrote to Cranstoun on 8 May both to get final sanction for such enquiries and to ask for guidance as to how they might most effectively be carried out. 'I am extremely sorry that you have so disagreeable a duty to perform and would willingly have relieved you off it,' George Cranstoun told McKid. But he was 'confident', Cranstoun assured his sheriff-substitute, that the 'duty' in question would be handled with McKid's 'usual ability and good sense'.[40]

In his 8 May letter, McKid had asked if he should have Patrick Sellar arrested. Cranstoun, in his reply, did not rule this out. But it would first be necessary, he cautioned, to establish 'if there [was] ground for a criminal proceeding'. McKid should thus go to Strathnaver and there take formal statements from people with first-hand knowledge of Sellar's alleged offences. Such statements, called precognitions, were (and are) commonly recorded in Scotland in advance of possible court actions. While by no means a guarantee that Patrick Sellar was about to be charged, the authorisation of such statement-gathering signalled that John Munro and his backers – both in Strathnaver and beyond – had won a significant victory.

This victory is one that Robert McKid, given his fraught relationship with Sellar, would have been less than human not to have welcomed. Just how warm was his welcome is evident from the speed with which the sheriff-substitute now acted. The letter in which George Cranstoun approved the commencement of investigations in Strathnaver was written in Edinburgh on Saturday 13 May. It is unlikely to have reached Sutherland until, at the earliest, the Thursday of the next week. But on the Monday following that Thursday, McKid was already in Strathnaver and hard at work collecting the first of many pages of testimony amassed in the course of the several days the sheriff-substitute devoted to this task.[41]

On hearing that (despite his best efforts) precognition-taking was under way in Strathnaver, a now thoroughly alarmed Sellar endeavoured – in a way that would today be regarded as unacceptable interference with due process – to bring the authorities round to his view that, by taking his farm's previous occupants out of backwardness and barbarity, he had actually set them on the road to betterment. Hence the long letter Sellar sent, on 24 May 1815, to Archibald Colquhoun.

'Lord and Lady Stafford', Patrick Sellar informed the lord advocate, had been 'pleased *humanely* to order a new arrangement of this country [meaning the Sutherland Estate]'. Basic to that 'arrangement' was the marquis and marchioness's wish to have the Sutherland interior 'possessed by cheviot shepherds [or sheep farmers] and the people brought down to the coast and placed there in lotts [or crofts] under the size of three arable acres'. Such a croft, Sellar maintained, was 'sufficient for the maintenance of an industrious family'. But it was also 'pinched enough' to oblige its occupants – and here Sellar made the 'improvement' lobby's standard link between clearance and marine resource development – to 'turn their attention to the fishing'.[42]

'I presume to say that the proprietors *humanely* ordered this arrangement', Sellar went on by way of further stressing his and the Stafford family's good intentions, 'because it surely was a most benevolent action to put these barbarous hordes into a position where they could better associate together, educate their children and advance in civilisation.'[43]

But for all that it was intended to be helpful to the generality of people on the Sutherland Estate, Patrick Sellar went on, 'improvement' had generated opposition from 'such as had an interest in the former state of things'. This group – and Sellar meant men like Alexander and John Sutherland – had 'induced' the people evicted from Rhiloisk to protest about the manner of their removal. The resulting complaints had been 'publish[ed] anonymously in the public prints'; they had been put to one of Colquhoun's colleagues (here Sellar referred to Andrew Clephane) in Inverness; and they had been much encouraged, if not fomented, by Robert McKid. The latter, or so Sellar asserted, was 'the silent mover' of many of the 'machinations' that had brought matters to the point they had now reached. The sheriff-substitute's enquiries should therefore be halted and he, Sellar, permitted to give his own account of the June 1814 evictions to someone other than McKid – perhaps an equivalent law officer from Inverness-shire, Ross-shire or Caithness.[44]

This was to attempt to resuscitate yet again the Marchioness of Stafford's arbitration proposal of nine months before. But even had Archibald Colquhoun been persuaded by Sellar's 24 May letter to put a stop to Robert McKid's enquiries in Strathnaver, he would have been too late. Before this letter reached Edinburgh, McKid was back in Kirkton with a mass of information as to what had taken place on Sellar's Rhiloisk farm the year before.

Some part of that information consisted of accounts (quoted in the preceding chapter) of the muirburning that occurred well before Patrick Sellar's Rhiloisk lease took effect, together with further accounts (also quoted) of the extent to which homes, barns, kilns and mills had been destroyed. But if evidence of such destruction was potentially damaging to Sellar, it paled into insignificance when set alongside statements dealing with the injuries – and worse – he had allegedly caused.

Patrick Sellar's men, McKid heard, had unroofed one house while it still contained an elderly woman who had been 'bedridden for a score of years' and who, when Sellar's shepherds and their constable colleagues were finished with her home, was left with no shelter other than the portion of roofing immediately above the spot where she lay. A young man, also 'sick in bed', was reported to have been 'forcibly taken out by Mr Sellar and his party' – 'the bed in which he lay [being] broken to pieces' in the process. Barbara MacKay had fallen while trying (in her husband's absence) to remove her home's roof in order to keep its timbers safe from the evicting party's axes. Injured by her fall, Barbara, who was pregnant, had miscarried and lost her baby, but Sellar – who 'would neither listen to argument [n]or to reason' – had rejected pleas that she be allowed to recover before being evicted. In a 'fury', he had ordered 'that she [be] instantly turned out' or have the house 'pulled down about her ears'.[45]

At Rimsdale, said Hugh McBeath, his seriously ill father, Donald, had been 'left . . . cold and comfortless' in a mostly unroofed house. He had asked Sellar if the demolition of the house could be delayed, McBeath continued, but Sellar, 'in a passion', had replied, 'The devil a man of them, sick or well, might be permitted to remain.' His father, Hugh McBeath informed McKid, had died nine days later. And when Hugh's father-in-law, a man by the name of MacKay, had accused Sellar of treating his son-in-law's father in a 'cruel and hard-hearted' manner, the factor, 'seemingly in a rage', had 'pulled out his pocket book', added MacKay's name to a 'proscribed list' and given him to understand that his insolence had put his own tenancy in jeopardy.[46]

Much of this accords with what is known from other sources – not least his own and the Marchioness of Stafford's correspondence – about Patrick Sellar's outlook and character. To him, the people he was dealing with ('aborigines' as he would shortly take to calling them) merited little or no consideration and were accordingly given none. But his farm's original occupants constituted, for all that, an obstacle to Sellar's plans. Had they been allowed to cling on, as many of their Kildonan counterparts had been, to their homes, to their fields and to the hill pastures still swarming with their cattle, Sellar's newly acquired sheep would have continued to die at Culmaily, while his financial position would have deteriorated alarmingly. Hence Sellar's need to demonstrate an unshakeable resolve to make his eviction orders meaningful by rendering homes – indeed entire communities – uninhabitable. 'De'il a one of them shall remain,' he was reported (in a slightly later account of proceedings at Rimsdale) to have told his men who, in some instances anyway, were to claim (as will be seen) that they harboured doubts as to the propriety of leaving the ill and the elderly with next to nothing in the way of shelter. But if, in thus giving no quarter, Patrick Sellar made clear that he, and he alone, was now in charge of his farm, it does not follow that he relished the distress he caused. Sellar, despite the ogre-like reputation he now started to acquire, was no sadist. Nor was he, as shown by his failure to mount a prosecution of McKid, a man of iron will. Hence perhaps the repeated references to Sellar conducting evictions in a 'fury', a 'rage' or a 'passion'. Did he find it necessary, when doing what he had decided he must do, to work himself up into a frenzy? And did this, in turn, lead to his judgement deserting him, as it certainly seems to have done, on the morning of Monday 13 June 1814, at a place called Badinloskin?[47]

That settlement consisted of a house and two or three outbuildings. Located in moorland about a mile west of Loch Rimsdale, Badinloskin's site (where the foundations of its single home are easily found) is best approached today by way of a little-used path leading south from the road linking Syre in Strathnaver with Kinbrace at the upper end of the Strath of Kildonan. As in much of the Sutherland interior, repeated muirburn (of the sort initiated by Patrick Sellar) has combined (or so many ecologists say) with the impact of prolonged overstocking to drain productivity from landscapes that, before they were cleared, carried big herds of cattle. This loss of earlier fertility goes some way to explaining why there are no sheep at or around present-day Badinloskin, something Sellar's shade, if still a visitor here, must find distressing. But on the patch of ground where the family occupying this spot raised their crops, and where the ground was thus manured regularly, the grass remains greener than surrounding vegetation. Hence this spot's attractiveness to the small herd of deer (maybe ten or a dozen beasts and with antlers still in springtime velvet) this book's author disturbed on approaching Badinloskin on a warm morning in June 2014 – exactly 200 years after the settlement's obliteration.

The low ridge between Badinloskin and Loch Rimsdale offers some shelter from the east and south-east. Westward, however, the ground slopes down to a little burn and the view in that direction is extensive – towards the hills behind Dalharrold at the top end of Strathnaver and, beyond that, to higher and more distant peaks. Badinloskin, on the furthest margin of what was potentially cultivable, had not been inhabited for many years in 1814, its occupants enjoying none of the advantages available to people living on longer-inhabited land beside the River Naver. But if it makes sense (and perhaps it does not) to come to any such conclusion on the basis of an hour or two spent here on a fine summer's day, there are likely to have been times when Badinloskin seemed an attractive spot in which to have a home.

This home's location is unmarked by interpretative boards of the sort to be found today in the vicinity of some other places that were cleared. Maybe that is as it should be. But it is surprising all the same. After all, things done here on 13 June 1814 – or, more exactly, the actions Robert McKid took on learning of those things – were to go a long way to ensuring that, in the minds of generation after generation of Scots, early nineteenth-century developments on the Sutherland Estate became synonymous not with 'improvement' but with callousness and brutality.

*   *   *

As Robert McKid was well aware, evidence of supposed wrongdoing on Patrick Sellar's part would carry more weight if it came not just from Sellar's alleged victims but from others. If those others were – in contemporary terminology – 'persons of quality', so much the better. Hence the sheriff-substitute's seeking out of Thomas Gordon.

Gordon was tacksman at Breacachadh. This was a substantial farm perhaps six miles south-east of Badinloskin but, like that homestead, within the catchment area – just about – of the church then serving, as was said in 1815, 'the heights [meaning the upper reaches] of the parishes of Farr and Kildonan'. That church was located at Achness, not far from the northern end of Loch Naver and adjacent to the junction of the Mallart River (flowing out of high country east of the loch) with the River Naver. Here on 12 June 1814 – the Sunday prior to the Monday on which Robert McKid's investigations were more and more to focus – the congregation included Thomas Gordon. Also present was Gordon's fellow tacksman and namesake, Robert Gordon of Langdale, the man who had lodged with Patrick Sellar at Culmaily the night before the Golspie Inn sett at which Sellar had acquired his Rhiloisk tenancy.[48]

At Golspie (as mentioned previously) the future Rhiloisk farm had been described as 'Rossal and Dalharrold'. The second of those townships was barely a mile from Achness. Nearer still were waterfalls over which the Mallart tumbles into the Naver. This meant – since the Mallart was Rhiloisk farm's southern boundary – that Achness and its church were more or less next door to the landholding where, in the early summer of 1814, Patrick Sellar had taken charge. That being so, neither Thomas nor Robert Gordon could have been greatly surprised to see Sellar waiting for them when, on 12 June, they left Achness's church at the end of Sunday service – a service which, being conducted in Gaelic, Sellar would not have wanted to sit through. What followed though was more unexpected, certainly by Thomas, whose dealings with Sellar had hitherto been less extensive than Robert's and who, therefore, had not had much experience of the way Sellar did business.

Thomas and Robert Gordon, it bears repeating, were tacksmen, in Gaelic *daoine uaisle*, people of standing. They constituted what Donald Sage, who knew Thomas Gordon well, called 'a high-souled gentry' whose forebears had occupied positions of leadership in Sutherland for centuries. As Gordons, they were (or believed themselves to be) related; as Gordons, they were (or believed themselves to be) of much the same provenance and ancestry as the Gordon earls from whom the Marchioness of Stafford, originally Countess of Sutherland, had inherited both that title and the estate Patrick Sellar was, as he put it, 'revolutionising'.[49]

Because men like Robert and Thomas Gordon – individuals of the sort Lady Stafford suspected of 'combining' against her – were endangered by the far-reaching changes Sellar was implementing, it was predictable that they, and other tacksmen, should have disliked this incomer who had acquired authority over them. Sellar, for his part, could have mitigated that dislike, or at least prevented it turning into loathing, by treating tacksmen with the respect they considered their due. But this Sellar never did, his manner when dealing with tacksmen often being so offhand as to seem, from a *daoine uaisle* perspective, little short of insulting.

That manner was much in evidence when, on Sunday 12 June 1814 at Achness, Sellar – in the presence of a congregation accustomed to regarding tacksmen as people who gave, not took, orders – treated Thomas and Robert Gordon, both of them much older than him, as his subordinates, messengers and interpreters. First he asked the tacksmen to point out, as worshippers exited the church, someone by the name of William Chisholm. Sellar, being unable to communicate directly with Chisholm whose understanding of English was limited, next told Thomas Gordon (a Gaelic speaker like all Sutherland tacksmen) to tell Chisholm, who had been farming Badinloskin for some years, that he and his family were to quit their home next morning. Gordon was also to make clear to Chisholm, Sellar said, that if his house was not vacated as instructed, then he,

Sellar, would be in Badinloskin by noon on Monday 'to burn or throw it down'.[50]

This was the first indication of the methods Patrick Sellar intended to use to rid his farm of its inhabitants, and Thomas Gordon, by his own account, was shocked. He 'remonstrated with Mr Sellar', Gordon informed Robert McKid, 'and urged him strongly to desist . . . but he was determined'. Chisholm, in consequence, was 'called aside' and Sellar's intentions made clear to him. 'The poor man in answer', or so the Breacachadh tacksman recalled when interviewed by McKid, 'said he would endeavour to obey the order.'[51]

By way of explaining to Thomas Gordon why he wanted William Chisholm put under pressure, Sellar said he had been 'informed [that] Chisholm was a thief'. This information, Sellar afterwards maintained, had first been conveyed to him in January 1814 when he met at Suisgill (as mentioned previously) with his new farm's outgoing tenants. At that meeting, Sellar claimed in his May 1815 letter to the lord advocate, men from the township of Rossal had responded to his request that they curtail their cattle numbers by making any such curtailment conditional on Chisholm's removal. 'They said he had come some years ago', Sellar went on, 'nobody knew from where, [and] had taken up his residence, along with a woman of the country, in a moss [meaning moor] in one of the wildest parts of the parish.'[52]

In fact there was no great mystery about William Chisholm's origins. In his sixties in 1814, he had lived in the Strathnaver area, according to Robert Gordon of Langdale, for some 13 years. Chisholm, Gordon added, was 'a native of Strathglass'. That locality, west of Inverness, had been comprehensively cleared by its landlord between 1800 and 1803. Many of its inhabitants had emigrated to Nova Scotia. But Chisholm, apparently a blacksmith by profession, had evidently preferred to come north. Either then or previously, it seems, he had abandoned his wife and in Sutherland (where, presumably, this wife's continued existence was unknown) had married again. Later, however, the first wife, or so Patrick Sellar said he was told, 'had come to [Badinloskin] . . . with a banditti [and] had threatened [Chisholm] with a gun'. To get rid of this earlier wife (whose name is unknown) and the 'parcel' of despera-does accompanying her, Chisholm had apparently been forced to hand over a proportion of his livestock. In order to make good those losses, Sellar implied, Chisholm had shortly afterwards taken to rustling other people's animals.[53]

In the voluminous paperwork Patrick Sellar generated in the course of attempts to justify what occurred at Badinloskin on 13 June 1814, William Chisholm is called a 'tinker', 'gypsy' or 'caird'. Collectively those terms, which Sellar intended to be derogatory as well as descriptive, imply an itinerant – and, in the case of the Scots word *caird*, a thieving – lifestyle. At Badinloskin, however, Chisholm's existence appears to have been a settled one. Since they had children, including a little girl of 11, he and his Sutherland wife or partner, Henrietta MacKay, had clearly been together for some time. Nor was Chisholm, by early nineteenth-century standards, impoverished. His rent, which there is no word of his being unable to find, was five guineas (£5 5s) a year. That was a substantial sum, being equivalent to more than a third of what an SSPCK teacher like Gordon Ross in Strathbrora then earned annually.[54]

This rent was payable, not to the Sutherland Estate nor to Patrick Sellar, but to the people of Rossal from whom William Chisholm sublet (with the approval, Chisholm said, of Cosmo Falconer who had managed the Sutherland Estate prior to the Young–Sellar takeo-ver) a large tract of land at Badinloskin. Chisholm pastured a cattle herd on this land. On it too he built the home he and Henrietta shared with their children, with Henrietta's sister Janet, and with Janet and Henrietta's mother, Margaret MacKay – an elderly, inca-pacitated and bedridden lady said by Henrietta to be 'aged upwards of ninety years'.[55]

Chisholm, when questioned by Robert McKid, acknowledged that at Achness on Sunday 12 June 1814 Sellar had 'intimated' to him 'that if he was not out of his house with his family and effects upon the following day . . . he [Sellar] would set fire to [it]'. But Chisholm seems to have regarded this threat, passed on to him by Thomas Gordon, as no more than bluster on Sellar's part. He did not believe, he maintained, that Sellar meant what he said. This is borne out by Chisholm not having so much as mentioned what had transpired at Achness to Henrietta who, thus being in ignorance of Sellar's stated intentions, left home on the Monday morning on an errand and was consequently not present at Badinloskin when first Sellar's 'evicting party', then Sellar himself, arrived there.[56]

This was around noon, Sellar and his men having earlier been employed further west where they had demolished homes in townships like the one from which the eleven-year-old Angus MacKay and his brothers fled that same morning across the River Naver. On reaching Badinloskin and finding that his instructions of the day before had not been complied with, Patrick Sellar, Chisholm said, ordered members of the 'evicting party', who had already begun unroofing Chisholm's home and throwing out his furniture, to 'set fire to [the house] in two or three different places'. This was confirmed by others who were present, including one of the evicting party's sheriff-officers who added that, by way of ensuring a fiercer blaze, roof timbers from an adjacent barn were thrown into the burning building. It was also the general consensus (though one disputed by some members of the evicting party) that, when fire was applied to the Chisholm home, Margaret MacKay was still inside. Since the house (judging by its surviving foundations) was a substantial one, and since its interior (probably lit by no more than one or two small windows) would have been dark, it is perfectly plausible that the bedbound Margaret's presence (her bed perhaps in an out-of-the-way corner) may not have been detected by men hurriedly removing pieces of furniture. It is equally plausible that William Chisholm – not expecting the start of his home's unroofing to give way quickly to its being torched – saw no reason to anticipate any immediate harm coming to his mother-in-law. On flames appearing, however, Margaret MacKay at once made her presence known, giving vent to what Chisholm called 'a tremendous and lamentable shriek'. Those words are an English rendition of Chisholm's Gaelic, which may have been more prosaic. But irrespective of what was lost or gained in translation, the overall thrust of William Chisholm's remarks was backed up by Rossal tenants who witnessed the destruction of his home. What Margaret MacKay shouted from inside the burning building, one of them said, was 'Tèine!', Fire![57]

The Rossal men were in Badinloskin that day at Patrick Sellar's request. On 26 May 1814, when Sellar's lease of Rhiloisk farm took effect, they had become his subtenants. This made Chisholm a subtenant of Sellar's subtenants and, since Rossal was not scheduled for immediate clearance, Sellar clearly wanted the township's occupants associated with the eviction of people who were technically their, not his, responsibility. Equally clearly, however, the Rossal men were reluctant to involve themselves in what took place, 'the like of which', one of them commented, 'he had never before seen'. On Sellar urging them to help rescue the screaming woman from the burning house, the same man said, he and his neighbours refused. This, he explained, was from fear that 'the old woman might die [on] their hands', with blame for her death then attaching to them.[58]

In the event, according to a number of the people interviewed by Sheriff McKid, Margaret MacKay was dragged to safety by her daughter Janet and carried to a nearby 'bothy', 'sheep-cot' or outhouse which Sellar's men left intact but which, it was said, 'did not exceed six feet in length'. There Margaret lay until, six days later, she died.[59]

The Chisholm home took time to burn out completely. But flames had certainly died down when, during the afternoon, William Chisholm's wife, Henrietta, got back to Badinloskin, where, she said, she was greeted on her approach by her 11-year-old daughter who, in tears, told her mother 'that Mr Sellar and his party had set fire to, and burned, [their] house'. By way of compensation for the family's losses, Henrietta discovered, her husband had been offered, as he told Robert McKid, 'six shillings', a sum that must have seemed all the more derisory to Henrietta when, on searching through the 'smoking ruins' of her home, she found that £3 in banknotes, hidden for safekeeping in one of the house's walls, had been reduced to ashes.[60]

Enraged by the loss of what would have been to her a considerable sum, Henrietta set out early next day to Thomas Gordon's home at Breacachadh where Patrick Sellar had lodged overnight and where, according to Gordon, he had announced on his arrival that, as promised at Achness, 'he had burned [William Chisholm's] house'. When he and Sellar were breakfasting on the morning of Tuesday 14 June, Thomas Gordon said on being interviewed by McKid, Henrietta MacKay, having just then got to Breacachadh, 'rushed into the room' and, 'crying and roaring in the Gaelic language', demanded recompense for the missing £3. On the Breacachadh tacksman explaining to Sellar in English what had been said, Sellar's reply, as recalled by Thomas Gordon, was to the effect that he accepted no responsibility for the loss of any money at Badinloskin. 'Mr Sellar', Thomas Gordon added, 'did not express the least degree of repentance for his conduct'.[61]

Robert McKid returned to Kirkton from Strathnaver on Saturday 27 May. That same day, Patrick Sellar's clerk, James Brander, delivered to Kirkton a letter Sellar had just written. 'I learn by common report', Sellar informed the sheriff, 'that you have been in Strathnaver expiscating [searching] for evidence against me. I consider it proper to advise you . . . that I am at home [and] that I expect to be informed of what crime it is that you lay to my door.' McKid, who had been warned by George Cranstoun to 'have no extrajudicial communications with Sellar', ignored this letter.[62]

On Monday 29 May, Sellar, having had no reply from McKid, wrote once more to Archibald Colquhoun, copying his letter to George Cranstoun. McKid, Sellar told the lord advocate, had refused to hear his account of events. This was of a piece, Sellar went on, with McKid's 'ill-will' towards him. He had 'little doubt', Sellar added, but that statements made to McKid in Strathnaver would prove to be 'a tissue of misrepresentations'. He was all the more convinced of this, Sellar continued, as a result of his having heard that McKid, 'in examining certain . . . witnesses . . . silenced them as often as they attempted to detail any fact favourable to me'. McKid, Sellar wrote, aimed to 'ruin' him. 'I humbly lay claim', he concluded, 'to your Lordship and Mr Cranstoun's protection from this oppression.'[63]

McKid, meanwhile, spent much of Monday interrogating four of the sheriff-officers or constables Sellar had had with him in Strathnaver in June 1814. They were Kenneth Murray, Alexander MacKenzie, James Fraser and Alexander Sutherland. Although two of them, Sutherland and Fraser, were inclined to stick by Sellar, the others took an opposite tack. So anxious had Sellar been to press ahead with the work of destruction, MacKenzie said, that he 'would not give them [the evicting party] time to eat, drink or take snuff'. Agreeing that he and his colleagues 'threw down . . . dwelling houses, barns and kilns', Kenneth Murray added that the buildings in question had been 'pointed out to them by Mr Sellar' who had also been responsible for the conflagration at Badinloskin. 'They knew well enough they were doing wrong,' Murray continued. But no alternative had been available. Because of their 'dread' of Sellar, Murray claimed, 'they durst not refuse to do anything' he ordered. Alexander MacKenzie concurred. 'He certainly would not have acted as he did but for the express command of Mr Sellar,' MacKenzie said.[64]

Next day, Tuesday 30 May, Robert McKid composed a letter to the Marquis of Stafford. He began by rehearsing the sequence of events that had commenced in July 1814 when Lady Stafford had received from Sutherland Estate tenants in Strathnaver a petition 'complaining', as McKid put it, 'of various acts of injury, cruelty and oppression alleged to have been committed upon their persons and property by Mr Sellar'. Lady Stafford, McKid continued, had been 'graciously pleased' to offer redress. However, this had not been forthcoming (a failure McKid attributed not to the marchioness but to Sellar) and in January the Strathnaver people had accordingly 'approach[ed] Earl Gower' with 'a complaint' similar to that already made to his mother. Subsequent to this, and subsequent to the intervention of Andrew Clephane and George Cranstoun, McKid wrote, 'he had been compelled [meaning commanded] to enter upon an investigation' in Strathnaver where he had interviewed 'about forty' individuals. His inquiries, McKid wrote, had convinced him that, in the course of Patrick Sellar's Rhiloisk evictions, serious offences had been committed.[65]

Those offences, as enumerated by McKid, included: 'wilful fire-raising . . . attended with most aggravated circumstances of *cruelty if not murder*'; 'throwing down and demolishing a mill'; burning 'heath pasture' in advance of the Rhiloisk tenancy having formally changed hands; 'throwing down and demolishing houses whereby . . . lives . . . were endangered if not *actually lost*'; and making it impossible, by destroying barns and other buildings, for evicted tenants to exercise their ownership rights to crops planted or sown before their eviction. Even without the addition of 'innumerable other charges' the sheriff-substitute mentioned but did not specify, this was a formidable list – so formidable, McKid informed Lord Stafford, that 'the laws of the country call upon me to order Mr Sellar to be arrested and incarcerated'.[66]

That same Tuesday, Patrick Sellar, aware that he might shortly be taken into custody, sent James Brander in search of McKid, Brander's task being to establish the terms on which Sellar might be bailed. Like Sellar's earlier attempt to open discussions with the sheriff-substitute, however, this initiative came to nothing, McKid, Sellar alleged, having 'kept purposely out of the way'.[67]

That evening, it was claimed later, McKid – having equipped himself 'with a spyglass' – climbed the hill above Culmaily so 'that he might enjoy the spectacle' he knew was about to unfold. This consisted of 'a sheriff-officer and five assistants' turning up at Patrick Sellar's door and taking him into custody, prior to marching Sellar, now a prisoner, down the road to Dornoch Jail where he arrived in the early hours of Wednesday morning.[68]

Later that day, there were two further developments. The four men Robert McKid had interviewed two days before – Fraser, Sutherland, MacKenzie and Murray – joined Sellar in prison; and Sellar at last got his much-requested face-to-face meeting with the sheriff-substitute. This took the form of an interrogation. During it, Sellar, who must have been both exhausted and shattered emotionally, repeated assertions he had already made in letters to Lady Stafford and to the lord advocate. 'Ignorant people [in Strathnaver]', he said, 'had been stimulated by artful and designing men to complain of oppression.' However, there had been no such oppression. He had instructed his shepherds to burn hill pastures on his farm only after getting permission from the people who, at that point, were still its tenants. The evictions he had ordered took place weeks after his formal entry to the farm and had been undertaken solely because its inhabitants 'repeatedly failed in implementing . . . promises' to quit the place. 'His directions to the officers [conducting those evictions] were that they should lawfully eject [Rhiloisk's former] tenants, and that, after ejecting them, they should remove the roof of every house.' This, Sellar stated, was wholly in accordance with the law. Nor had any injuries or deaths – whether at Badinloskin or anywhere else – resulted from what was done. He had permitted people who were ill, Sellar said, to remain where they were. Yes, he was aware that William Chisholm and his wife claimed that they and their family had been ill-used, 'but he put no dependence on their veracity'. Chisholm was 'a vagrant who had come [to Badinloskin] without authority'. While fire had been employed in the course of his and his family's eviction, this had been confined, Sellar insisted, to the burning of timber removed from the roofs of Chisholm's home and barn.[69]

In the aftermath of his examination, Sellar – his place of confinement evidently well supplied with paper and ink – wrote to Lady Stafford. 'Little did I think when I last had the honour to address your Ladyship,' he began, 'that my next letter should be from Dornoch Prison.' His incarceration he attributed entirely to his 'personal enemy' McKid who, Sellar wrote, had 'inflamed' his (Sellar's) accusers 'with all the art in his power'. He hoped his father, a lawyer by profession, would come north from Moray to take charge at Culmaily, Sellar told the marchioness; and he had instructed his 'man of business' in Edinburgh 'to apply there for redress'. 'I am so overpowered', Sellar ended, 'that I can add no more.'[70]

In Dornoch, the *Military Register* reported, people 'met to cele-brate' Patrick Sellar's downfall with 'the same warm demonstration of joy' they were to mount when, towards the end of June, news came through of Wellington's victory at Waterloo. In the Stafford camp, however, there was consternation. William Young, on the day of Sellar's arrest, announced himself 'more unhinged' than he could 'well express'; and even the usually unflappable James Loch was alarmed. 'You cannot easily conceive the pain and dismay with which I heard . . . of Sellar's story,' Loch informed Young when, on 9 June, word of this latest crisis reached London.[71]

Further reflection did not leave Loch less uneasy. Writing on 10 June to his uncle William Adam, who held high legal office in Scotland, Loch observed: 'You will, I am sure, fully appreciate the delicacy of Lord and Lady Stafford's situation. If they were to communicate [to the authorities in Edinburgh] anything which might be construed in favour of Sellar, it would be said they were using undue influence to protect their factor in acts of oppression and a breach of the law. If they on the other hand let it go abroad, as insinuated by McKid, that they approve of and support the prosecu-tion, there will not be a man in Strathnaver who, from some motive or other, will not swear the worst crime against [Sellar].'[72]

James Loch's anxieties were heightened by his strong suspicion that Sellar had laid himself open to imprisonment by acting 'hastily' and 'unadvisedly' in Strathnaver. Sellar, Loch advised William Adam, was 'extremely unpopular'. While this unpopularity was partly traceable to the many 'disagreeable' things Sellar had had to do in his capacity as a Sutherland Estate factor, it was traceable also, Loch wrote, to the factor's personality and, in particular, to his 'quick, sneering [and] biting way' of expressing himself.[73]

Loch's reservations about Sellar were widely shared. The Marchioness of Stafford, whose misgivings about her factor (as indicated previously) went back a long way, was now more critical than ever. Sellar, the marchioness commented in the aftermath of his arrest, was 'very intemperate and has no command of himself'. He had been 'too precipitate' in Strathnaver, she thought. William MacKenzie, the lawyer who acted for the Sutherland Estate in Edinburgh, was of the same opinion, describing Sellar's 'conduct' in Strathnaver as 'rash'. From the moment of his hearing of Sellar's arrest, however, MacKenzie set about lobbying the lord advocate, Archibald Colquhoun, on the jailed factor's behalf. 'It is in every point of view a matter much to be regretted', MacKenzie remarked of the wider implications of Sellar's plight, 'that the factor on the [Sutherland] Estate should be in such a situation.'[74]

The outcome of MacKenzie's contact with Colquhoun was not reassuring. 'His opinion in point of law', MacKenzie reported of his meeting with the lord advocate, 'is that . . . Sellar is not guilty of wilful fire-raising but is guilty of culpable homicide and criminal oppression.' Colquhoun, MacKenzie went on, was convinced 'that a trial must take place'. Together with other documentation in the case, the precognitions forwarded to Edinburgh by McKid had accordingly been placed in the hands of one of the lord advocate's deputes, Samuel McCormick, who had been instructed to make an assessment of their contents. 'He repeated to me', William MacKenzie noted of a subsequent meeting with McCormick, 'that he considered Mr Sellar's conduct [to be] extremely violent, cruel and oppressive.'[75]

In London, meanwhile, James Loch – firmly of the view that newspaper coverage of the earlier 'Kildonan business' had left 'the public mind of Scotland' suspicious of, or hostile to, Stafford plans for Sutherland – watched with alarm as articles about Sellar's arrest, and about the evictions which had led to it, proliferated in the press.[76]

In the *Military Register*, Alexander Sutherland was predictably exultant. McKid's enquiries – undertaken, Sutherland asserted, as a result of earlier *Military Register* disclosures – had uncovered a 'system of terror'. A man's home had been 'burnt about his family's ears'. Women had been 'seen flying in all directions with their infants in their arms'. Patrick Sellar had responded to people's protests with the comment, 'Dead or alive, you must remove.' In short, the factor and his men – who, Sutherland wrote, considered themselves 'so far north' as to be 'beyond the power of the law' – had behaved like 'a sanguinary invading . . . force giving up a district to pillage'.[77]

This was all the more reprehensible, Alexander Sutherland commented, in the light of the 93rd Regiment's sacrifices at New Orleans – sacrifices which the *Military Register* was then highlighting in a series of articles dealing with the court-martial of the senior officer, Colonel Thomas Mullens, judged responsible (in consequence of his failure to bring up vital fascines and assault ladders) for the Chalmette calamity. 'They did their duty,' the *Military Register* commented of the Sutherland men who had died at Chalmette. 'They fought gallantly . . . [T]hey were unsuccessful. That was the fate of war.' It was a fate, however, that had led to the Stafford family's Highland property now containing 'many a . . . widow and orphan' struggling along in conditions of 'extreme wretchedness'. Because of the sacrifices made by their husbands and fathers, the *Military Register* declared, those same widows and orphans merited 'some humane consideration'. Instead they had 'been turned out of their houses and homes by the torch and by the axe'.[78]

Attempting to minimise this material's impact, James Loch described the *Military Register* as 'an obscure paper'. It was less easy, however, to be dismissive of stories appearing – almost certainly as a result of Alexander Sutherland's efforts – in leading London newspapers like the *Observer* and the *Morning Chronicle*. In their accounts of the events leading up to Patrick Sellar's arrest, both papers went into detail about 'certain charges brought against' Sellar (described as 'under-factor on the Sutherland Estate') by 'tenants in the parish of Farr'. There, the *Morning Chronicle* reported, Sellar had taken 'possession' of 'a large sheep farm' from which everyone had promptly been 'removed'. In the course of those evictions, the newspaper informed its thousands of readers, who included MPs and other people of influence, 'several lives were charged to have been lost' as a result of Sellar's men 'pulling down the houses about the people's heads'. When those alleged crimes had been investigated in the course of what the paper called 'an inquest', the *Chronicle* continued, evicted families had 'proved their case to its fullest extent on the most distinct evidence'.[79]

Late on the evening of Tuesday 6 June, Patrick Sellar, whom William MacKenzie managed to have bailed on a surety of £100, was released from Dornoch Jail, the four men imprisoned with him being freed next day. But with the prospect of a Sellar trial still looming and with adverse press comment continuing, the Marchioness of Stafford, on reaching Dunrobin some weeks later, found little in the north to cheer her. Something of the marchioness's temper is evident in her reaction to being shown a government-financed publication, the *Police Gazette*, in which Sellar's guilt was taken as read. With the backing of James Loch, also in the Highlands that summer, Lady Stafford sent an outraged letter to Lord Sidmouth, the home secretary. The *Police Gazette*, she informed Sidmouth, had stated 'that a charge of murder had been fully proved against a person employed in the management of the Sutherland Estate'. 'While attacks upon the management of [their] property were confined to the common newspapers', the marchioness wrote, she and Lord Stafford had treated those attacks, 'with the contempt they appeared to us to merit. But when I find that such a charge has been published in a paper under the authority of government . . . [it becomes]

incumbent on me to have recourse to your Lordship for your interference and assistance.'[80]

Sidmouth's reply was not as mollifying as it might have been. The
offending article, he explained, had simply been copied into the
Police Gazette from the *Observer*, the *Gazette*'s editor having 'no
grounds for doubting the accuracy' of the *Observer* story – 'as it
appeared to be a regular account of an authorised inquiry'. 'We
must go on in the way we judge best', the Marchioness of Stafford
had earlier written to her husband, 'without minding libels or what
is said.' Sidmouth's failure to offer anything in the way of a *Police
Gazette* retraction doubtless added to her sense – a novel one for the
marchioness – of events slipping beyond Stafford control.[81]

This same sense – of others having somehow managed to impose
their agenda on Sutherland – helps account for the time and effort
the marchioness, James Loch and their aides now put into identifying members of the 'combination' they thought behind Sellar's
jailing. What Patrick Sellar called 'the Strathnaver conspiracy . . .
against his removings' was self-evidently fronted locally by John
Munro and John MacKay, both of whom had all along – and quite
openly – been at the forefront of the protest movement that began
with the July 1814 petition to Lady Stafford. But behind MacKay
and Munro, the Stafford camp was convinced, were other, more
shadowy, figures. Offering a great deal of behind-the-scenes support
and encouragement to Munro and MacKay, it was claimed, were
three other Strathnaver residents. They were John, George and
Malcolm Ross, brothers who, according to Sellar, had been
'concerned' in the anti-clearance 'riots' which had broken out 'many
years ago', as Sellar put it, in Easter Ross. The disturbances in question had occurred in 1792 when a well-organised attempt – foiled
only after military intervention – had been made to expel incoming
sheep farmers and their flocks from Ross-shire. In the wake of that
episode, it seems, the Ross brothers had moved into Sutherland,
settling eventually in the Strath of Kildonan. There, Sellar believed,
Malcolm, George and John Ross had 'incited' the uprising of 1813

before leaving for Strathnaver where they had allied themselves with John MacKay and John Munro, some of the latter's correspondence with the Marchioness of Stafford, Sellar maintained, being in the handwriting of one of the Ross brothers.[82]

Munro, MacKay and the Rosses, it was further said by Sellar, corresponded with Alexander Sutherland in London. He, in turn, was known to have regular dealings not just with his brother, John Sutherland of Sciberscross, but with other members of 'that class of half-pay officers and half-gentlemen who,' James Loch wrote, '[had] long . . . considered the [Sutherland] Estate their own'. This group, from Loch's perspective, was the real source of the Strathnaver troubles, Loch, like Sellar, being firmly of the view that Strathnaver men like John Munro, John MacKay (and, presumably, the three Rosses) were 'merely instruments,' as Loch put it, 'of a few designing tacksmen'. Some of those tacksmen, Loch commented, had close links with the 93rd Regiment. Others had served with different units. But almost all were ex-soldiers and many read the *Military Register*, which, Loch commented, was 'distributed with much industry throughout Sutherlandshire'. In Robert McKid, moreover, this tacksman-led group, had found an eager recruit – John Sutherland of Sciberscross, according to Lady Stafford, being 'always . . . busy with' McKid throughout the summer of 1815.[83]

Either directly or through intermediaries, McKid also appears to have been in communication with John Sutherland's brother, Alexander. The two were said by Alexander to have known each other for more than 20 years. That they were in touch in the immediate aftermath of Patrick Sellar's arrest is confirmed by the fact that, in June 1815, Alexander boasted (incautiously) in the *Military Register* of his being 'in possession of all the documents' (including copies of McKid's Strathnaver precognitions) relevant to the case against Sellar.[84]

But if McKid and the Sutherlands of Sciberscross became prime suspects in the course of the hunt now mounted for anti-Stafford conspirators, they were not the only people thus singled out. A further such plotter, Lady Stafford believed, was Joseph Gordon. Still nursing grievances arising from the Stafford purchase of his Carrol Estate, Gordon was known to have family connections with a number of Sutherland tacksmen and to be a member of what James Loch called the 'large set in Edinburgh, formerly connected with Sutherlandshire, who have ever, with the most determined perseverance, shown their hostility to the Stafford family'.[85]

Like the similar groupings with which Alexander Sutherland was involved in London, this Edinburgh 'set' was composed of people from a Highland gentry background. It followed, in the agitated atmosphere engendered by Sellar's arrest, that to be of such background and to be active on Edinburgh's business and social scene was automatically to have one's actions scrutinised by Patrick Sellar, James Loch and the marchioness. Hence the doubts that began to be expressed at Dunrobin, in the course of the summer of 1815, about the loyalty of a man who, on the face of things, could scarcely have been more supportive of the entire 'improvement' project. This was the Stafford family's Edinburgh-based lawyer, William MacKenzie.

MacKenzie, his brother Colin and their father, Alexander, had between them served the Sutherland Estate for decades. But the MacKenzies, despite their antecedents being in Easter Ross rather than Sutherland, and despite their having been in Edinburgh a lot longer than a man like Joseph Gordon, were in origin a product of much the same social milieu as Gordon or, for that matter, Alexander Sutherland. This milieu was one James Loch, and still more Patrick Sellar, spoke and wrote about with unconcealed contempt. Might his knowing of that contempt have contributed to William MacKenzie's tendency to take an even more negative view of Sellar than the one expressed at times by Loch and the marchioness?

Sellar, MacKenzie thought, was recklessly and dangerously 'quick tempered'. He had met with the then recently released factor at the beginning of July, MacKenzie reported, and had been singularly unimpressed by his account of what had gone on in Strathnaver. 'He answered my disappointment at the plan of burning houses',

MacKenzie wrote scathingly of Sellar, 'by saying [such burning had occurred] by accident and not by intention.'[86]

Sellar, on getting wind of those aspersions, responded – characteristically – by rubbishing MacKenzie in far more intemperate language than MacKenzie had used of him. Her Edinburgh lawyer, Sellar told the marchioness, was 'averse to the present management' of the Sutherland Estate (meaning himself and William Young) and had consequently 'been at pains to lay snares for us'. This, Sellar contended, was because his legal training had enabled him to take on management tasks that would formerly have been carried out by MacKenzie, who, according to Sellar, thus lost 'a considerable thing yearly' by way of income. Robert McKid, Sellar went on, had become Sutherland's sheriff-substitute because William MacKenzie and his family had recommended McKid for the post. That was why MacKenzie, while ostensibly pressurising the Edinburgh authorities on Sellar's behalf, had in fact, or so Sellar claimed, been 'poisoning the mind of the lord advocate' against him in order 'to screen McKid'.[87]

It is suggestive of the beginnings of a persecution complex having taken hold at Dunrobin in the fevered summer of 1815 that the Marchioness of Stafford found this tortuous reasoning persuasive. He 'had better keep clear' of giving MacKenzie any further 'employment' in connection with the Sellar affair, the marchioness instructed Loch.[88]

Irrespective of whether or not William MacKenzie was in any way implicated, Patrick Sellar in particular and 'improvement' more generally were definitely under attack at various points – and not just during 1815 – from elements of what Lady Stafford referred to as Sutherland's 'better sort'. The 'combination' that the marchioness, Loch and Sellar thought the source of all their difficulties can be seen, therefore, to have had a real existence. But does it follow that every manifestation of discontent on the Sutherland Estate should be attributed – as is asserted over and over again in surviving documentation – to this combination's manoeuvrings?

The answer surely is no. Neither John Munro in Strathnaver nor the organisers of Kildonan's 1813 uprising were the passive 'tools' or 'instruments' of Loch and Sellar's imaginings. They were autonomous actors on the Sutherland stage; expressing their own fears and aspirations; waging their own battles with their dispossessors. From an 'improvement' perspective of course, Sutherland's 'aborigines' were not reckoned capable of making their own choices or shaping their own futures. That is why the Sutherland Estate's owners and managers invariably viewed the Sutherland commonalty as other people's puppets. But a moment's reflection on what John Munro accomplished during the year following his eviction from Garvault leaves that sort of reasoning in shreds. Here was a man who organised petitions to the Marchioness of Stafford and to Earl Gower; a man who corresponded with Sheriff Cranstoun; a man who made the long journey from his Rhinovie home to Inverness to negotiate, over a couple of days, with one of Scotland's advocates-depute. Munro indubitably had help from his 'betters'; from John and Alexander Sutherland certainly; maybe from Robert McKid and some others as well. But John Munro, the evidence suggests, used those folk every bit as much as – possibly more than – they used him. And even when the odds against bringing Patrick Sellar to book were huge, as they must have seemed to Munro at the outset of his campaign, neither he nor his Strathnaver colleagues ever abandoned hope. Given that they had lost their homes, their land and so much else, those people's tenacity is remarkable.

That tenacity was much needed in the months following Patrick Sellar's release on bail, months during which, after initial hesitations as to whether or not to back their factor, the Staffords decided that, to some degree at any rate, they had better rally round him. 'I have sent Mr Sellar some herrings today as a sign of goodwill,' the marchioness reported to her husband at the start of her 1815 jaunt to Dunrobin. More substantial support for the factor soon followed, this support being channelled through James Loch, who now found himself urged by Lord and Lady Stafford to involve himself more directly in Sutherland affairs. Although Loch, for his part, was at times still minded (as will be seen) to leave Sellar to fight his own battles, he knew full well that a Sellar trial, from a Stafford perspective, could only be damaging. Over the summer and into the autumn of 1815, therefore, Loch deployed all his formidable lobbying skills in the cause of having such a trial delayed or, better still, avoided.[89]

The marchioness, meanwhile, was regretting such goodwill as she had shown in 1814 to Strathnaver's evicted families. The outcome, she commented to Loch, had been to make them 'think we are favourable to their complaints against Sellar'. On hearing that some of the same families were scheduled to be at Dunrobin on 14 August, one of the Mondays when Lady Stafford was due (in the manner described earlier) to hold court there, she duly resolved to take a harder line, telling her husband that she was determined to make no more concessions. This resolve was maintained in the face of attempts by the Strathnaver contingent to argue that they were entitled to better treatment because of their having provided the army with soldiers of the sort who, earlier that year, had gone into action at Chalmette.[90]

News of the Battle of New Orleans and the slaughter that took place there had reached Britain in early March 1815. Over the next month or two, as details filtered through, it become apparent that no fewer than 13 men from Farr – some of whom are virtually certain to have belonged to Strathnaver – had been consigned to Chalmette's mass graves. This did not move the Staffords. When, on 14 August, the marchioness was shown documents handed to the fathers of Strathnaver recruits by General William Wemyss in 1800 – documents their holders had treated as guarantees of immunity from removal – the marchioness responded much as Patrick Sellar had done when presented with similar material in the Strath of Kildonan in 1813. People whose sons may have been among the Chalmette dead – people who certainly set store by Wemyss's written promises – were informed by Lady Stafford that these promises were 'no longer of any avail'.[91]

John Munro and his associates may not have expected much of the marchioness, whose assurances of the year before had not, after all, been acted on. But they were unsettled by talk that Patrick Sellar might not, in the end, face trial. This was very much the outcome James Loch had been trying to bring about by means of encouraging his more influential Edinburgh contacts – William Adam, his uncle, prominent among them – to do what they could to persuade Archibald Colquhoun, the lord advocate, to back away from his earlier inclination to bring Sellar before the High Court. Rumours to the effect that Colquhoun might indeed be yielding on this point began to circulate in the autumn and resulted in a further letter from John Munro to George Cranstoun. 'Sir,' Munro began, 'Many reports are prevalent here respecting Mr Sellar's trial.' One such report, Munro wrote, had Sellar 'not [being] tried at all'; another had him being pursued for damages 'and not [tried] criminally'. This second option, Munro indicated, was unacceptable. Sellar, he added, 'ought to be in gaol and not at large'.[92]

Soon, however, it was apparent that, notwithstanding John Munro's opposition, the possibility of an arbitrated settlement was once more back on the table. This was confirmed by a December letter from John Campbell, one of Archibald Colquhoun's advisers, to David MacKenzie, now installed formally as Farr's parish minister. The lord advocate, Campbell wrote, wanted MacKenzie to inform people with grievances arising from their treatment by Patrick Sellar that it was thought desirable to have 'the complainants and Mr Sellar' put their respective cases to an arbitrator.[93]

By communicating with Rhiloisk farm's former occupants through their minister, as opposed to writing directly to John Munro, the Edinburgh authorities were perhaps looking to make contact with a hoped-for moderate majority rather than with what they considered a belligerent minority, whose belligerence, those same authorities were told by James Loch, derived from tacksman-organised manipulation. No moderate majority, however, was forthcoming. Although Sellar, now clutching at any straw that came along, responded positively and at once to John Campbell's arbitration offer, the Strathnaver people did the opposite. The strath's dispossessed families, the *Military Register* reported, made clear 'in the firmest manner' that 'no consideration on earth' would 'induce them to swerve' from demanding that Sellar be brought to justice: 'They consider the proposition now made to them as adding fresh insults to their long and crying wrongs.'[94]

If the lord advocate was not going to prosecute Patrick Sellar, the Strathnaver people now concluded, they had better try to do so themselves by engaging the services of what the *Military Register* called 'a proper solicitor' who, in turn, would require the assistance of 'eminent counsel in Edinburgh'. Since expertise of that kind could not be hired cheaply, a meeting was convened in Strathnaver to consider where the necessary cash might come from. The number attending is not known but, according to John Gordon, resettled at Skelpick in the lower part of the strath following his eviction from Rimsdale, 'everybody there paid something'. More, however, was needed; so, either at that same meeting or a little later, it was decided that a delegation should be sent 'into Caithness for the purpose of soliciting subscriptions' to what was, in effect, a fighting fund. This task was taken on by John MacKay, John Munro's close ally, and a second man whose name is not known. Their mission – analogous to the Caithness foray made by Strath of Kildonan rebels in February 1813 – would have a greater chance of success, it was felt, if prospective donors could be shown 'a paper' (signed ideally by someone of status) attesting to Patrick Sellar's alleged iniquities. The requisite document was sought from the Reverend David MacKenzie who provided, if not everything requested, then enough for the fund-raising expedition's purposes. By so doing, MacKenzie exposed himself to an immediate onslaught from a still apprehensive, and therefore more than usually aggressive, Sellar.[95]

The man thus targeted had all along behaved more than a little ambiguously in his dealings with, on the one hand, the people in charge of the Sutherland Estate and, on the other, the families removed from Sellar's Rhiloisk farm. As a son and grandson of tacksmen, David MacKenzie's background made him an obvious candidate for membership of the 'combination' whose hand Sellar and his backers detected in every difficulty they encountered. But if grounds for such thinking were reinforced by the minister's November 1815 marriage to Barbara Gordon, Robert Gordon of Langdale's daughter, there were other circumstances that pointed in the opposite direction. At the Golspie sett in December 1813, for instance, David MacKenzie – clearly trusted by Sutherland Estate managers at that point – had agreed (as mentioned previously) to take on the delicate job of explaining to unsuccessful bidders that, in consequence of their having lost out to others, they would shortly have to exchange their farms for crofts. Some months later, to be sure, MacKenzie (as also noted previously) was happy to write to William Young on behalf of people Sellar was then about to evict. But the minister was equally happy, it seems, to accept Lady Stafford's hospitality at Dunrobin and to tell the marchioness exactly what she wanted to hear about his Strathnaver parishioners. 'He says the people in Strathnaver are excellent people,' commented Lady Stafford in a letter summarising her exchanges with David MacKenzie whom she found 'very good-looking' as well as 'sensible, intelligent and gentlemanlike'. Complaints emanating from evicted families were a result of their having been 'misled', the minister assured the marchioness. There was no reason, MacKenzie said, why such families could not be 'settled comfortably' on new crofts. Lies, the minister went on to hint, had been told in the course of Robert McKid's precognition-gathering. That was why he had found it 'very necessary' to urge his congregation 'to pay due attention to the nature of an oath'. Little wonder, then, that MacKenzie seemed, from the marchioness's perspective, to be 'a great acquisition', 'ready', as he had apparently told his hostess, to help her counter the 'false statements' about 'improvement' that had appeared in the southern press. 'We have drawn out a plan', Lady Stafford informed her husband, 'for

MacKenzie . . . to write to the newspapers to contradict the story of injustice.'[96]

Nothing of this would have come as a surprise to Alexander Sutherland, about whose 'talents for writing and for mischief' Lady Stafford was then complaining. Sutherland, who observed that it did not seem to occur to 'reverend gentlemen' that 'the sheep system' would culminate in their 'preach[ing] to empty pews', had a low opinion of almost all his native county's clergymen. But he reserved particular contempt for David MacKenzie. Not long after he became Farr's minister, or so Alexander Sutherland insisted, MacKenzie had been asked for help by William Chisholm – then dealing with the repercussions of Patrick Sellar's destruction of his Badinloskin home. No such help had been forthcoming. Instead, and in full knowledge of what Sutherland called Sellar's 'pretence' that Chisholm's eviction resulted from the Badinloskin farmer's 'bad moral character', MacKenzie had taken from Chisholm and then burned, or so Sutherland alleged, a 'certificate' Chisholm had earlier obtained from David MacKenzie's predecessor, James Dingwall. This certificate, Alexander Sutherland claimed in an accusatory letter mailed to MacKenzie himself, had testified to William Chisholm being – contrary to what Sellar had put about – a perfectly upstanding person. By destroying the document in question, and by thus aligning himself with people who had turned William Chisholm and his family out of house and home, Alexander Sutherland told the minister, he had behaved in a manner 'at variance with the appropriate conduct of a pastor and a Christian'.[97]

David MacKenzie at once forwarded Alexander Sutherland's letter to William Young. In an accompanying note, the minister, while not denying that he had burned the certificate mentioned by Sutherland, claimed that Chisholm had obtained it improperly. Although the truth of the matter is unlikely ever to be established, MacKenzie, by communicating in this way with William Young, went some way to confirming the validity of Alexander Sutherland's charge that the minister was closer to Sutherland Estate managers than to his parishioners. Shortly afterwards, however, MacKenzie, seemingly incapable of consistency as to whose side to take in the conflict erupting around him, was yet again to change tack, this time by reneging on his promise to correct (as Lady Stafford saw it) press reports about Patrick Sellar's clearance of Rhiloisk.[98]

That promise had been to the effect that MacKenzie would write to *The Star*, the London newspaper which had carried Alexander Sutherland's 1813 articles about the Strath of Kildonan troubles and which, in the summer of 1815, had returned to the attack. James Loch – very much a spin doctor two centuries in advance of that term's invention – had supplied the minister with an appropriate draft. That draft had taken issue with the entire thrust of *Star* coverage of Sellar's 1814 evictions. MacKenzie, however, had stuck to a single and narrow point: that *The Star* (presumably because of confusion in London as to where that summer's emigrant party to Red River set out from) had been in error in reporting that MacKenzie's parishioners (as opposed to those of Alexander Sage) were going to North America in preference to taking crofts of the sort offered by the Staffords. 'As to the circumstances surrounding Mr Sellar', David MacKenzie informed an infuriated Loch, 'since they have a foundation, however exaggerated, it is not my duty to deny them.'[99]

This was a brave gesture on MacKenzie's part. Such courage as the minister possessed, however, deserted him on his receipt, in late December 1815, of a bitingly cold letter from Patrick Sellar. He had been told, Sellar informed MacKenzie, 'that two Strathnaver men [had] been going through Caithness begging money to support a prosecution against me, and that they present[ed] to the public a paper under your hand to certify the truth of their averments'. He very much hoped, Sellar commented, that this report would turn out to be unfounded.[100]

In a grovelling response, MacKenzie at once admitted that what Sellar had heard was 'correct'. On his being approached by John MacKay and John Munro, the minister wrote, he had done as they asked not because he wished Sellar harm but because of his 'simplicity', his 'ignorance' and his susceptibility to 'the arts of some narrators of circumstance'. He now had 'an opportunity of confessing [his] mistake,' MacKenzie continued – a mistake he begged Sellar 'to forgive'. He had learned, the minister added by way of attempting to get back into Sellar's good books, that some of the factor's 'accusers' were 'to apply for certificates of moral conduct' in advance of their being called on to give evidence at any forthcoming trial. He was 'resolved strenuously', the minister assured Sellar, 'to refuse this'.[101]

In the early nineteenth century, it needs mentioning at this point, Church of Scotland clerics were appointed to their parishes not by their congregations, but by those parishes' landlords. This meant that, in the summer of 1815, David MacKenzie had been 'presented' – as the jargon term had it – to his Farr charge by the Marquis of Stafford. It also meant that Patrick Sellar, who took care to remind MacKenzie of this fact in his December letter, was responsible, on behalf of the marquis, for paying the minister's salary or stipend. It may be of course that MacKenzie, in making clear to Sellar that the factor had nothing further to fear from him, cared not at all for his finances and was motivated solely by his stated conviction that nobody evicted from Rhiloisk farm in June 1814 was, in the church's eyes, morally deserving. But either way, Patrick Sellar, from his perspective, had obtained a good result. Farr's parish minister, who could very well have been a danger to him, had been neutralised. This was all the more welcome on its becoming apparent that, following the failure of their December attempt to persuade John Munro, John MacKay and others to accept a last offer of arbitration, the authorities in Edinburgh had decided that there was now no alternative but to bring Patrick Sellar before the High Court.[102]

10

'TO FIND OUT AND PUNISH THE LEADERS OF THE PEOPLE'

The trial of Patrick Sellar and the Sutherland Estate management's revenge on his accusers

All that remains of the building that served as early nineteenth-century Inverness's courthouse is a steeple occupying a corner site at the junction of Bridge Street and Church Street in the city centre. Two plaques have been fixed to this steeple. One, on its Bridge Street face, tells how the courthouse of which the steeple was part – a court-house constructed in 1791 and demolished in Victorian times – took the place of a medieval tolbooth* that once stood on this site. The steeple's second plaque, round the corner in Church Street, announces that it was here, on Tuesday 23 April 1816, that 'the infamous Patrick Sellar' stood trial on charges of 'culpable homicide, fire-raising and cruelty'.

High Court trials were regular occurrences in Inverness. Mostly, however, the individuals prosecuted at those trials were people whose background was such as to ensure that their alleged offences (unless especially heinous) received little or no publicity outside their home localities. It was otherwise with Patrick Sellar. Here was no run-of-the-mill accused. Here was a man establishing himself as a leading agriculturalist; a man employed in a senior

---

* Like most Scottish tolbooths, Inverness's served various functions: as a toll or tax collecting point, a town council meeting place, a courthouse and a jail.

position by one of Britain's wealthiest families; a man who, when carrying out evictions in that family's name, was said to have committed crimes that, if judgment were to go against him, could result in his being sentenced to death. Sellar's trial, then, was nothing if not newsworthy. 'This was a case of great expectation', an Edinburgh newspaper commented, 'and excited much interest in the country.'[1]

Interest was heightened by a belief in the south that a Highland jury might readily take against Sellar. This belief was shared by Sellar's own lawyers, or so the Marchioness of Stafford was informed by George MacPherson Grant of Ballindalloch, the Banffshire laird who (in circumstances touched on later) the Staffords had not long before installed as Sutherland's MP. The Edinburgh advocates engaged by Sellar, Grant wrote, believed 'there [to be] such a strong prejudice [in Inverness] against [their client] that they thought it proper to submit to him . . . whether they would not make a push to get [his] trial removed to Edinburgh'. Sellar rejected that proposal. But Grant, who more than half-expected Sellar to be found guilty, took little heart from the factor's self-assurance. 'I fear his conduct may have been culpably harsh,' the MP commented of Sellar. 'I suspect', he added of what had occurred at Rhiloisk, 'we have not been so fully let into it as we ought to have been.'[2]

What particularly worried not just MacPherson Grant but the Stafford camp more generally was the possibility that Patrick Sellar's defence team, particularly if things went badly for them, might try to shift blame for the Rhiloisk episode from Sellar personally to the Sutherland Estate management apparatus as a whole. This, after all, was a line Sellar himself had adopted (with some justification) as far back as early June 1814 when, in the course of a conversation involving Robert Gordon of Langdale and others, it had been put to him that people could not be expected to quit his Strathnaver farm until they had been told where they were to go. This, Sellar reportedly replied, 'was certainly true, but the fault lay with Mr Young [as indeed it did] and not with him'.[3]

Writing to Lady Stafford from Edinburgh two days prior to Patrick Sellar's trial, William MacKenzie, who had spoken with Sellar's lawyers before they left for the north, expressed 'great anxiety' about the risk of those same lawyers majoring on exactly this point when, as was clearly going to happen, they questioned William Young about the circumstances surrounding Rhiloisk's clearance. 'Young will undergo a very strict examination,' MacKenzie warned. In the course of that examination, he went on, it could readily emerge that the deadline for families to remove themselves from Rhiloisk had come and gone days before Young had so much as started to identify crofts for them. Any such admission, MacKenzie thought, was likely to be seized on as a means of countering a prosecution charge (set out in documentation made available to interested parties some weeks earlier) that Sellar had subjected evicted families to 'oppression'. 'If Sellar's counsel are driven to a defence of the point of oppression', MacKenzie predicted, 'they will say that the oppression was not on Sellar's part.'[4]

This had all along been James Loch's great fear. Sellar, as Loch was only too well aware, had maintained both before and after his arrest that his difficulties stemmed not from his own behaviour but from animosities engendered by the land management policy the Staffords were paying him to implement. Loch, at a point of particular exasperation with Sellar, disputed this. 'I cannot see what connection the system of improvement adopted in Sutherland has . . . with your case,' he told Sellar in October 1815. 'They seem to stand so independent of each other that I think [that] in place of endeavouring to connect them . . . they ought to be kept quite separate.' In his calmer moments, however, James Loch appreciated that neither press nor public were likely to make distinctions of this sort. That was why he insisted, throughout the winter of 1815–16 and into the following spring, on a clearance moratorium in Sutherland.[5]

William Young had planned to turn out of their homes at Whitsun 1816 some of the Strath of Kildonan families who, as a result of the successful protests mounted in the strath in 1813, had been kept in

William Clunes by Henry Raeburn. Two or three years after this portrait was painted, Clunes's inspection of a prospective sheep farm in the Strath of Kildonan precipitated the 1813 protests that brought the Sutherland clearances to national attention. (National Galleries of Scotland)

Loch Brora. The green fields across the loch and to the left were part of the pre-clearance township of Carrol. Ascoilemore was located on the rising ground in the far distance on the right. (Cailean Maclean)

These fields and walls at the Doll, near Brora, were created from previously unculti-vated moorland by families evicted from more productive localities in Strathbrora. (Cailean Maclean)

The lower part of the once densely populated Strath of Kildonan, with the village of Helmsdale at its foot. (© RCAHMS. Licensor www.rcahms.gov.uk)

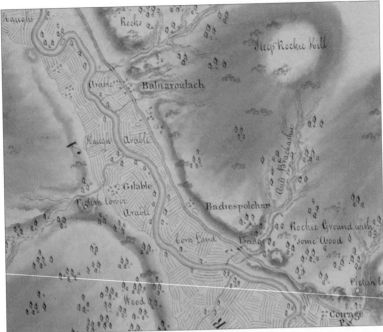

The hatching on this 1794 map of the Strath of Kildonan shows the extent of cultivation around the strath's pre-clearance townships. (National Records of Scotland, RHP11602/3)

Suisgill in the Strath of Kildonan. The house in the middle distance has replaced the home where shepherds were besieged by an angry 'mob' on 6 January 1813. The now walled field was the site of that morning's decoy shinty match. (Cailean Maclean)

Donald Sage, who grew up in the pre-clearance Strath of Kildonan, called the Helmsdale River 'the finest feature in the landscape'. (Cailean Maclean)

Golspie Inn. Focus of the February 1813 'riot' that caused William Young, Patrick Sellar and a posse of sheriff-officers to flee the inn and seek safety in nearby Dunrobin Castle. Military intervention followed. (Cailean Maclean)

A roughly inscribed boulder by the shore of Hudson Bay marks the grave of Kildonan protest leader John Sutherland, who died of typhus at Sloop's Cove on the Churchill River estuary on 2 September 1813. (Jacquie Aitken)

Churchill Creek, where emigrants from the Strath of Kildonan established their winter camp in the fall of 1813. (Rob Bruce-Barron)

The Churchill River in winter, when Hudson Bay and its surroundings remain frozen for several months. (Gary Rea)

York boats on the Hayes River. Kildonan emigrants voyaged up the Hayes in craft like these when making the long journey from York Factory, on Hudson Bay, to Red River. (Hudson's Bay Company Archives)

The author looking out across a frozen Hudson Bay on a December day when the temperature was minus 35 degrees Celsius. In hastily built log cabins, not far from here, families from Kildonan endured these – and much lower – temperatures for several months during the winter of 1813–14. (Evelyn Hunter)

Angus McCall, present-day tenant of Culmaily, near Golspie. This was Patrick Sellar's first farm. Its stone dykes, or walls, date from Sellar's time, as do fields Sellar, an outstanding agriculturalist, laid out, drained and began cropping. (Cailean Maclean)

The foundations of houses destroyed during the clearances are to be seen throughout the Sutherland interior. This home – its dimensions indicated (below) by members of Clyne Heritage Society – stood beside the Skinsdale River, a tributary of the Blackwater, itself a tributary of the Brora, in the heart of what is regarded today as the wildest of 'wild land'. (Nick Lindsay)

The typical dwelling in the pre-clearance straths was a 'longhouse'. Its walls (as shown below) were a mix of stone and turf on a stone foundation. By early nineteenth-century standards, homes of this sort were unusually spacious – with floor areas approaching those of modern three-bedroom bungalows. (Timespan and William Stark)

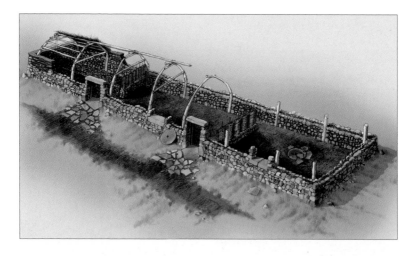

Looking eastwards across Loch Naver from Grumbeg to Achoul. Achoul's tacksman, or tenant, William MacKay, who could trace his Strathnaver ancestry through 400 years, was evicted twice during the clearances – first from Achoul and then (when in his nineties) from Grumbeg. (Cailean Maclean)

Badinloskin, where Margaret MacKay died some days after being carried from a home burned on Patrick Sellar's orders. This elderly lady's death led to Sellar standing trial on a charge of culpable homicide. (Cailean Maclean)

In the course of what organisers of the clearances called 'improvement', hundreds of families were evicted from long-settled townships in Strathnaver (above) and deposited on three-acre crofts in exposed and previously uncultivated areas like Strathy Point (below) where, on this harbour-less coast, they were told to develop a fishing industry. (Cailean Maclean)

Much of the Sutherland interior, where cattle grazed for centuries until replaced (for a time) by sheep, now consists of sporting estates given over mainly to deer-stalking. (Cailean Maclean)

The Earltown area of Nova Scotia where, during and after the clearances, Sutherland families carved farms from virgin forest. (Glen Matheson)

This sculpture, pictured on a snowy winter's day, stands in the Kildonan area of Winnipeg, where it commemorates the clearance victims who were among Manitoba's earliest settlers. An identical sculpture stands in Helmsdale at the entrance to the strath containing the few surviving remnants of the Manitoba immigrants' original homes. (*Winnipeg Free Press*)

The Strath of Kildonan's church, deprived of its congregation at the time of the clearances, is today largely disused. (Cailean Maclean)

The Red River in the heart of Winnipeg. The settlement of New Kildonan, established by clearance refugees in 1814, is today part of a city of more than 700,000. (treisdorfphoto)

place for three years more than Young had originally intended. Loch opposed those evictions. 'If another set of complaints should occur', he commented, 'it will make a most serious impression on the public mind.' Worse still would be renewed unrest. 'If another disturbance takes place', Loch warned Young, 'you may depend upon it becoming a subject for parliamentary enquiry.'[6]

Patrick Sellar's trial began at 10 a.m. in what was reported to have been a 'courtroom crowded to excess'. The trial judge was Lord Pitmilly, thought by one of Patrick Sellar's lawyers, Henry Cockburn, to be a man 'of good sense but moderate ability'. More to the point perhaps was the fact that the judge, when plain David Monypenny, had practised law in Edinburgh in partnership with William MacKenzie and William's brother, Colin. Because the MacKenzies (and maybe at times their partner) handled a great deal of Sutherland Estate business, outside observers were inclined to reckon Pitmilly's presence in Inverness a point in Sellar's favour. But Sellar, believing William MacKenzie less an ally than an adversary, did not expect – though in this he proved wrong – any favours from a man who had been MacKenzie's colleague. What, then, of the jury? Where might its sympathies have been expected to lie? Contrary to external expectations, not with Patrick Sellar's accusers.[7]

The idea that an Inverness jury would automatically be prejudiced against Sellar stemmed from nothing more substantial than a persistent (but anachronistic) Lowland notion that Highlanders, being supposedly given to clannish togetherness, invariably stuck by one another. In fact the 15 men* whose task it was to determine Patrick Sellar's guilt or innocence had more in common with Sellar than with the folk he had allegedly maltreated. Some of the 15, because (like Sellar) they came from Moray, would not have considered themselves in any sense 'Highland'. But they would have been perfectly at ease, for all that, with those other jurymen whose homes

* Prior to the twentieth century, only males served on Scottish juries.

were in Inverness or its immediate hinterland. Since jurors were then
drawn only from society's upper echelons, the Sellar jury consisted
of landowners, substantial farmers, a lawyer and a couple of
'merchants' or businessmen. Some, perhaps a majority, would have
been known to one another. One or two at least (and possibly more)
could well have had dealings either with Sellar personally or with his
lawyer father. All or almost all were men with a financial or professional stake in agricultural and other development of the sort that
had already transformed the Inverness and Moray areas, and was
now being introduced to Sutherland. It followed, then, that when
jury members took their seats that April morning in 1816 and looked
across the Inverness courtroom at Patrick Sellar in the courtroom's
'panel* box', they saw someone whose standing, outlook and
involvements were similar to their own. When, a little later, the court
began to hear (through an interpreter) from the Gaelic-speaking
Strathnaver residents called to testify against Sellar, jurors (few of
whom would have been fluent in Gaelic) are most unlikely to have
felt even the slightest solidarity with people divided from them not
only by language but also by their being products of a social order
that men of the jury's background thought hopelessly outmoded.

Patrick Sellar, in ruling out any attempt to get proceedings
moved to Edinburgh, seems to have had a better grasp than his legal
team of the possibilities inherent in those Highland realities. This
was evident from the manner in which he arranged to be accompanied throughout a trial which was to last (all such trials then having
to be completed in a single session) into the early hours of the day
following its commencement. 'Mr Reed, Kilcalmkill, and Mr Ross,
Clyne, sat with Mr Sellar in the panel box the whole fourteen [in
fact 15] hours,' William Young noted. Subsequent reform would
make it impossible for accused persons to be supported in this way,
and it is easy, in light of Sellar's tactics, to see why. Gabriel Reed (as
indicated previously) was one of the best known and most

---

* *Panel* was, and is, the term applied formally to a defendant in Scots law.

successful sheep farmers in the north. Walter Ross was a Sutherland minister (his parish of Clyne included Strathbrora) and high-profile supporter of 'improvement', not least because of the opportunities it gave him to engage (as will be seen) in farming and related activities. Sellar perhaps derived some comfort from being flanked in this way by friends and allies. This, however, was not the primary purpose of Ross and Reed being there. By so overtly backing Patrick Sellar, Gabriel Reed and Walter Ross were signalling to jurors that their eventual decision, as well as determining Sellar's fate, would amount to a verdict on agrarian change of a type in which not just Sellar, but Reed, Ross and, for that matter, they, the jury, had a substantial stake.[8]

The claim that to condemn Sellar would be to condemn 'improvement' was in accord with the stance taken by the factor himself ever since the first surfacing of allegations of criminal behaviour on his part. It was also a claim which, doubtless at their client's instigation, his advocates were to major on in Inverness, one of them, James Gordon, 'maintaining to the jury that . . . the question at issue involved the future fate and progress of agricultural and even moral improvement in the county of Sutherland'. Were jurors to find Patrick Sellar guilty, Gordon went on, then, though they might think themselves to be upholding 'the laws of this country', they would actually be aiding 'abettors of anarchy and misrule'. Sellar's accusers, according to Gordon, were committed not simply to 'opposing the improvement' of the Sutherland Estate but to subverting, by means of their attacks on Sellar, the rights of 'the noble persons to whom the property belonged'. At a time when the French Revolution was a recent memory and when (as will be touched on later) social unrest was an ever-present threat in many parts of Britain, it was sound strategy thus to present Patrick Sellar as having fallen victim to subverters of established order. As men of property themselves, it was none too subtly being implied, the jury's duty was to stand by property's defenders, of whom Sellar, it was further implied, was clearly one.[9]

None of this, it should be underlined, would have saved Patrick Sellar had the High Court jury been presented with an overwhelmingly convincing case against him. No such case, however, was forthcoming. That at least is the impression conveyed strongly by the only comprehensive account of Sellar's trial, an account which, though compiled and published by one of Sellar's lawyers, deals at some length with what was said by both sides.

At first glance, to be sure, the indictment in which the charges against Sellar were set out was as compendious as John Munro, John MacKay and other victims of Rhiloisk's 1814 clearance could have wished. In the indictment's second sentence, Sellar (addressed directly throughout) was accused of 'culpable homicide . . . oppression and real injury' – an accusation substantiated, or so it appeared, by page after page of detail. Sellar had 'wickedly and maliciously' set fire to hill pastures 'of great extent'. He had engaged in 'violently turning out' of their homes 'pregnant women' and people who were 'aged' or otherwise 'infirm', thus 'cruelly depriving' those people 'of cover or shelter'. This had been accomplished by means of 'setting on fire, burning, pulling down and demolishing . . . dwelling houses, barns, kilns, mills and other buildings'.[10]

Sellar's destruction of Rhiloisk's barns and kilns in advance of their owners being able to harvest their crops was arguably illegal (for reasons explored earlier) in its own right, and was certainly assumed to be so in the indictment presented to the High Court. His destruction of Rhiloisk's homes (though not in itself unlawful) had been conducted, according to the indictment, in a manner that, first, was 'oppressive' and, second, resulted in crimes of great seriousness: 'You . . . Patrick Sellar did . . . culpably kill Donald McBeath, father of Hugh McBeath, then tenant in Rimsdale . . . by unroofing and pulling down, or causing to be unroofed and pulled down, the whole house in Rimsdale . . . where the said Donald McBeath was then lying on his sick bed, saving only a small piece of the roof to the extent of five or six yards, whereby the said Donald McBeath was exposed in a cold and comfortless situation, without cover or

shelter, to the weather; and he, the said Donald McBeath, in consequence of being so exposed, never spoke a word more, but languished
and died about eight days thereafter, and was thereby culpably
killed.' [11]

There was more: 'And further, you . . . Patrick Sellar did . . . set on
fire, burn and demolish, or cause and procure your assistants to set
on fire, burn and demolish, the dwelling-house, barn, kiln, sheepcot
and other buildings then lawfully occupied by William Chisholm in
Badinloskin . . . although you knew that Margaret McKay, a very old
woman of the age of ninety years, less or more, and who had been
bedridden for years, was at the time within the said house . . . [A]nd
the flames having approached the bed whereon the said Margaret
McKay lay, she shrieked aloud in Gaelic, "O Teine", that is to say,
"O the fire", or words to that effect; and was forthwith carried out
by her daughter, Janet McKay, and placed in a small bothy . . . [A]nd
the said Margaret McKay . . . remained insensible from that hour,
and died in about five days thereafter in consequence of the fright
and alarm, and in particular in consequence of her removal, as
aforesaid, from her bed into a cold and uncomfortable place, unfit
for the habitation of any human being; and the said Margaret
McKay was thereby killed by you, the said Patrick Sellar.' [12]

Even at this remove, those words – their impact enhanced by their
having had the potential to set Sellar on a pathway to a gallows –
retain their power. However, the document from which they are
extracted, in consequence of its being so rambling and repetitive as
to verge at times on the incoherent, is cumulatively less than impressive. Although it appears (as indicated earlier) that Archibald
Colquhoun, the lord advocate in whose name Sellar was charged,
was of the view in June 1815 that a Sellar prosecution should
proceed, Colquhoun – in part, no doubt, because of pressure
brought to bear by James Loch and others – had retreated rapidly
from this position. Whether in the early nineteenth century or later,
the precognoscing of witnesses to alleged crimes was normally
succeeded promptly by indictment and trial. But in this instance, the

lord advocate and his colleagues had been party to repeated attempts either to postpone or, better still, avoid bringing Patrick Sellar before the High Court. Those attempts had culminated, during December 1815 and January 1816, in efforts (akin to those made formerly by the Marchioness of Stafford and Earl Gower) to persuade Strathnaver's evicted families to opt for an arbitrated settlement of their complaints. It was only with the foundering of this initiative that the Edinburgh authorities concluded, as William MacKenzie reported, that they 'had no other course to follow' but to bring Sellar to trial. The nature of the indictment they then prepared – a meandering summary of precognitions taken by Robert McKid months before – is suggestive of its being the work of men whose heart was not in the job to which they had at last been obliged to set their hand. The same lack of commitment is evident in the less than resolute way Sellar's prosecution was undertaken in Inverness by Henry Home Drummond, the advocate depute to whom the task had been allocated, who appeared at times to have positively welcomed opportunities to backtrack from the possibility of there having been wrongdoing at Rhiloisk.[13]

Just such an opportunity arose right at the start of the trial when one of Sellar's advocates, Patrick Robertson, took issue, unsurprisingly, with an indictment which, he pointed out, failed repeatedly to deal in 'specific crime[s]' and took refuge instead in 'general charges' of 'destroying a number of houses' or injuring 'a number of tenants'. Drummond at once responded by announcing that he would not press any such charges. This, in turn, provoked an intervention from Pitmilly. While it would be 'improper' for him to comment at that stage on either the prosecution or defence cases, the judge said, he wanted to place on record his opinion of 'the publications' to which Robertson had alluded moments before. By publications, Robertson had made clear, he meant the many articles about Sellar carried by the *Military Register*, articles Robertson described as 'false', 'mischievous' and 'disgraceful'. Pitmilly concurred. The *Military Register*'s coverage of events in Sutherland, he said, 'appear[ed] to be of the most contemptible nature'. This was an early indication that the day might eventually go Patrick Sellar's way. When Home Drummond called his first witness, another such indication followed.[14]

The witness in question was Robert McKid, to whom Sellar's defence immediately objected on grounds of his having 'evinced malice' against Sellar. Drummond having failed to have this objection overruled, the defence was now permitted by Pitmilly – greatly to Sellar's benefit – to explore the extent to which Sutherland's sheriff-substitute, in initiating the factor's prosecution, might have been motivated less by a concern for justice than by his desire to be revenged on a man who had more than once done him harm.[15]

Witnesses, with whom Sellar's lawyers would have had prior contact on this point, were duly called to testify as to prejudice on McKid's part. Hugh Ross, Sutherland's procurator fiscal, recalled his 1814 warning to Sellar – this warning (as noted previously) having been to the effect that McKid had expressed a wish, as Ross now told the High Court, 'to have it in his power to injure Mr Sellar'. William Young, called after Ross, recollected a conversation he had had with McKid on the day following Sellar's arrest, a conversation in the course of which, as Young had reported at the time, the sheriff-substitute remarked that 'Sellar must be hanged or at any rate sent to Botany Bay'*.[16]

From a prosecution standpoint, what Young and Ross had to say was damaging. Hugely more damaging, however, were the contents of the letter, now read to the court, the sheriff-substitute had written to the Marquis of Stafford hours prior to Sellar's imprisonment. In this letter McKid (as already mentioned) had listed Patrick Sellar's supposed offences. That he had thus entered into communication – 'in confidence' as he wrote – with Lord Stafford was bad enough. Worse was the extent to which the supposedly impartial sheriff-substitute, elated by his having (as he thought) brought Sellar to book,

---

* Britain's penal colony in Australia.

expressed himself in ways that (in advance of any trial) both assumed the factor's guilt and (for all McKid's stated 'regret' about what had occurred) took obvious pleasure in so doing. 'A more numerous class of crimes perpetrated by an individual', McKid had written, 'has seldom disgraced any country.'[17]

Because of his reluctance to make it appear as if the marquis and marchioness were throwing their weight behind a possible criminal, James Loch, with Lord Stafford's strong endorsement, had for months been turning down Sellar's requests that McKid's letter be made available to him and his lawyers. The marquis, Loch told the factor, in October 1815 was clear as to 'the impropriety, and therefore impossibility, of furnishing [Sellar] with a copy' of what, Loch pointed out, had been a piece of private correspondence. Continued badgering by Sellar drove Loch to contemplate a leak enquiry (as it would be called today) in order to discover how the factor had come to learn of McKid's letter, while Sellar, for his part, threatened to have Lord Stafford brought north as a trial witness if that should turn out to be the only way of having the letter flushed into the open. The prospect of Stafford thus being put under oath in an Inverness courtroom, it seems, helped force a change of stance on both Loch and his employer. On 8 April, with Sellar's trial only a fortnight away, they consented – albeit grudgingly – to the letter's release. Corresponding subsequently with the marquis, Sellar wrote: 'I beg humbly to thank your Lordship for the communication of Mr McKid's letter.' He was right to do so. By making the letter available, Lord Stafford, as the marquis well knew, did Sellar a great favour.[18]

Following the McKid letter's emergence in the High Court, and in the wake of James Ross and William Young's revelations about their various exchanges with McKid, Home Drummond announced that, in these new circumstances, he would take no evidence from the sheriff-substitute. By thus acknowledging – if only tacitly – some degree of bias on Robert McKid's part, the advocate depute was in effect conceding the possibility that Sellar, as Patrick Robertson had contended when opening for the defence, was a victim of 'conspiracy'. Might Home Drummond have avoided this debacle? Probably not entirely. But he could have taken steps to forestall its occurring at so an early stage in proceedings. His not having done so resulted (because McKid had collected the evidence on which charges against Sellar were based) in the entire prosecution case being launched in circumstances of all too apparent disarray.[19]

Immediately prior to the McKid letter being read aloud in Inverness's congested courtroom, Henry Home Drummond declared himself 'totally ignorant' of it. The advocate depute could not have been unaware, however, of Robert McKid's well-known detestation of Patrick Sellar. Nor could he have been under any illusions as to the likelihood of McKid's loathing of Sellar being drawn, by one means or another, to the High Court's attention. For much of the preceding year, after all, Archibald Colquhoun, Drummond's principal, had been harried by people – not just Sellar himself but James Loch and others – who were firmly (and by no means unjustifiably) of the view that Sutherland's sheriff-substitute, even if not actively engaged in an anti-Sellar conspiracy, certainly had his own axe, or axes, to grind in the Sellar affair. Why, then, did the advocate depute make Robert McKid his first witness? McKid knew nothing at first hand of Sellar's alleged crimes; and even had the sheriff-substitute's letter to Lord Stafford not been in the defence's possession, he was bound to have been cross-examined in ways intended to expose the disputatious, not to say confrontational, nature of his relationship with the man seated in the courtroom's panel box. While there are no grounds – other than the way he went about things in Inverness – for supposing that Home Drummond wanted such an outcome, it is a fact that, had the advocate depute been trying to sabotage his own prosecution, he could scarcely have done better than he did.[20]

Subsequent to the drama surrounding the McKid letter's unheralded appearance, matters took something of an anticlimactic turn. David Ross, McKid's Ross-shire counterpart, was sworn in as interpreter, and 11 Strathnaver people – with whom all exchanges had to be conducted through Ross – were interrogated about the circumstances surrounding their enforced removal from their homes in June 1814. First to appear were William Chisholm and his wife* Henrietta, the burning of whose house at Badinloskin, together with the subsequent death of Henrietta's mother, was central to the prosecution case. Like a number of other prosecution witnesses – notably Hugh McBeath whose father was the other person said to have died as a result of Patrick Sellar's actions – Chisholm appears to have been questioned closely by Sellar's advocates whose preparations, in contrast to Henry Home Drummond's, had been exhaustive. The defence team's 'brief', the Marchioness of Stafford had been told, was 'near 400 pages in length' and, as was plain throughout the Inverness proceedings, its contents ensured that Sellar's lawyers were acquainted with every facet of the case against their client. But there were, for all that, to be no more defence successes on a par with the discrediting of Robert McKid. Some parts of the evidence from Strathnaver – as usually happens in criminal cases of any complexity – were shown to be out of kilter with other parts. But no Strathnaver witness departed in any substantial way from the testimony McKid had collected in May 1815.[21]

This was not for lack of attempts to challenge the veracity of what was said. Thus John MacKay, one of the Rossal men who had witnessed the burning of the Chisholm home at Badinloskin, was made to reveal that, though still resident at Rossal, he had 'been warned out' by Sellar – an admission the defence hoped would detract from the Rossal tenant's standing as a supposedly uninvolved observer of the Chisholm family's eviction. Still more strenuous objections were lodged against a further prosecution witness,

---

* In Inverness, where it appears to have been taken for granted on all sides that Henrietta was indeed William's wife, the earlier allegation that Chisholm had entered into a bigamous marriage did not surface, a fact that creates some doubt as to the story's truth.

another John MacKay. This was the man who, subsequent to his removal from Rivigill to Rhinovie, had become John Munro's close collaborator in the Strathnaver campaign to have Patrick Sellar brought to trial. His efforts in that connection, Sellar's defence team now insisted, demonstrated 'undue and busy interference and agency'. So embroiled had John MacKay been in anti-Sellar activity, in other words, he could have no credibility, or so it was asserted, as a witness to what the factor had or had not done. That accounts for the aggressive way MacKay was questioned about matters such as the time he had spent in Caithness when collecting cash to help with the action Strathnaver people had been intending – in the absence of movement (at that point) in Edinburgh – to raise against Sellar.[22]

This assault did not produce the desired result. 'No agency has been proved,' Lord Pitmilly said of John MacKay. 'I cannot therefore reject this witness as inadmissible. But', the judge added by way of a further broad hint as to where his sympathies lay, 'the jury have heard the objection, and will give what credit to the witness they think he deserves.'[23]

With the exception of David MacKenzie, the minister whom Sellar had successfully intimidated some months previously and who (whether or not in consequence) had little of significance to say, just one more Strathnaver witness was heard after John MacKay. This was Murdo MacKay, whose brief testimony was in accordance with much of what had gone before. 'The barn house and kiln in Ravigill belonging to the witness were thrown down in June 1814,' the court was told. 'There were eight or nine barns and as many houses demolished in Ravigill . . . at [the] desire of Mr Sellar. John MacKay, Hugh MacKay, Charles Gordon, Adam MacKay [and] Donald MacKay as well as the witness sustained loss in their crops in consequence of the want of their barns. By the custom of the country, these barns belong to the outgoing tenant until he thresh out his crop.'[24]

Murdo MacKay should not have been the prosecution's last Strathnaver witness. 'Some other witnesses were called', runs the relevant paragraph in the published record, 'but [were] rejected in respect that they were erroneously described in the list served on the panel.' Since it was reported in Edinburgh that 'the whole tenants complaining [of Sellar's conduct] were cited as witnesses', this explains why John Munro, the most prominent such complainant, was denied an opportunity to testify in Inverness. His not having had that chance accounts, in turn, for the *Military Register*'s claim that 'by far the most material witnesses for the prosecution' were not heard. Since everything known about Munro points to his having been as formidable as he was determined, that was fair comment. By failing to ensure that names, places of residence and other necessary details were got right, Henry Home Drummond had deprived himself of testimony that would have been helpful to his case. This was one more pointer to slipshod preparation on Home Drummond's part. Equally indicative of inadequate groundwork by the advocate depute was the uninformed nature of his cross-examination of William Young, the only senior representative of the Stafford family, other than the accused, to put in an appearance at Inverness.[25]

When Young was obliged to disclose, exactly as William MacKenzie had feared, that his allocation of crofts to Rhiloisk's outgoers had postdated the deadline for their removal, Home Drummond, as far as can be judged, made nothing of this admission. There were no houses on the 'allotments' pointed out to them, Young acknowledged, but, he went on, 'there were barns and byres into which the people might have gone'. By the advocate depute, predictably, there was no probing of its thus being thought acceptable for evicted families to bed down in other people's cowsheds. Continuing silence on Home Drummond's part meant that it was left to Pitmilly to ask Young if it would have been possible for those same families, even after they had been forced from their former homes, to continue to tend – and ultimately to harvest – their crops. 'The new allotments were so near the places from which the tenants were removed', William Young said, 'that they [the Rhiloisk farm outgoers] might easily have carried away their corn.' This was to set aside the extent to which, subsequent to the 1814 clearance, stand-ing crops – left unwatched on abandoned rigs – were eaten and otherwise damaged by Sellar's sheep. It was also to rely on Home Drummond having done next to nothing to inform himself about Strathnaver. Since John Munro's new home at Rhinovie, to cite one instance of the distances involved, was separated from his previous home at Garvault by at least 15 then largely roadless miles, Young – though testifying under oath – was lying when he said that post-clearance homes were 'near' their pre-clearance predecessors. But the advocate depute, no doubt as ignorant of Strathnaver geog-raphy as he was unacquainted with other aspects of his case, let the lie slip by unnoticed.[26]

On Young standing down, the precognition which Robert McKid had taken from Patrick Sellar in Dornoch Jail in May 1815 was read (without comment or addition) into the court record, the advocate depute, at that point, 'declar[ing] the proof for the prosecution concluded'.[27]

By way of commencing their client's defence, Patrick Sellar's advocates, James Gordon, Henry Cockburn and Patrick Robertson, produced three letters testifying, as they put it, to 'Mr Sellar's char-acter'. The letters had been sought from Sir George Abercromby, a leading Banffshire landlord, George Fenton, Moray's sheriff-substi-tute, and James Brodie, one of that county's estate owners. 'I have known him intimately from his infancy,' Brodie wrote of Sellar. 'I always considered him a person of the strictest integrity . . . incapa-ble of being even accessory to any cruel or oppressive action.' Abercromby, for his part, thought Sellar 'incapable of being guilty of the charges brought against him'. Fenton knew Sellar 'to be a man of sympathy, feeling and humanity'.[28]

Two equally prominent individuals were then called to make the same points in person. Thomas Gilzean, Inverness-shire's sher-iff-substitute and someone who dealt regularly with Sellar's father, had 'known the panel from his boyhood' and 'conceive[d] him inca-pable of doing anything cruel or oppressive'. Sir Archibald Dunbar, a further landlord, considered Sellar 'a young man . . . of a good heart' and one 'incapable of doing a cruel or oppressive action'.[29]

In securing endorsements of this kind from men like Dunbar, Gilzean, Fenton, Brodie and Abercromby, Patrick Sellar's lawyers – just as when agreeing to their client being accompanied into the High Court panel box by Gabriel Reed and Walter Ross – were making clear to the jury that Sellar was believed blameless by people of standing. No equivalent character references, needless to say, were available to Sellar's Strathnaver accusers, their minister, David MacKenzie, from whom evicted tenants had hoped to obtain such references, having seen to it that none were forthcoming.

With evening now advancing, it remained only to call witnesses whose evidence was intended by the defence to counter and cancel out what Strathnaver people had had to say about Sellar's conduct at the time of their eviction. Those witnesses, seven in all, were Robert Gunn, John Dryden, Duncan Ross, Andrew Ross, Alexander Sutherland, James Fraser and John Burns. Cumulatively, their testimony suggested that much of what had been said earlier in the day was, to varying degrees, exaggerated or untrue. 'Mr Sellar', Duncan Ross insisted, 'gave strict instructions to hurt nothing belonging to the people . . . [A]fter everything was out of the houses, the [evicting] party, in the gentlest manner, took out the pins [holding roof supports in place] and let the couples fall.' There had been 'no instance of cruelty', Andrew Ross maintained. 'Mr Sellar', according to Alexander Sutherland, 'said [at Rimsdale] . . . that there were sick people in that place and that, therefore, they must not proceed in the ejections'.[30]

There was more to the same effect. None of it appears to have been challenged by Henry Home Drummond. Nor was the advocate depute inclined to replicate the forceful manner in which the credentials of some of his own witnesses had been queried by the defence. This was despite the fact that virtually everybody called by Sellar's defence team was either implicated in the Rhiloisk evictions or had something to lose had they failed to align themselves with Sellar.

Robert Gunn was Patrick Sellar's foxhunter and John Dryden his head shepherd. The two Rosses, Andrew and Duncan, were employed by the Sutherland Estate. James Fraser and Alexander Sutherland were among the sheriff-officers involved in the firing of the Chisholm home at Badinloskin. Only John Burns, a Caithness farmer, was in any way extraneous to what had occurred, and even Burns, since he had presumably come to Strathnaver at Sellar's invitation, was by no means a wholly neutral party.

A committed prosecutor might have made much of such circumstances. Home Drummond, however, was now intent on giving up. In the course of closing comments to the jury, he revealed that, out of all the numerous charges contained in the indictment presented to the jury at the start of Sellar's trial, he proposed to take forward only two. One arose from Sellar's destruction of barns – destruction the advocate depute described as 'irregular', 'illegal' and 'oppressive'. The other concerned what Home Drummond called 'the case of the old woman [whom he does not appear to have dignified with a name] at Badinloskin'. 'He certainly did not think the evidence in this last case was sufficient to establish culpable homicide', the advocate depute assured the court, 'but he argued that the circumstances proved were sufficient to . . . [show that] she had been removed at the risk of her life'.[31]

James Gordon, for the defence, concluded by returning to the manner in which 'certain persons' – acting in accordance with 'a preconcerted plan' – had supposedly 'instigated the people of Strathnaver' to press for Patrick Sellar's prosecution. Pitmilly then summed up.[32]

Of the two charges Home Drummond had retained, the judge disposed quickly of the first. 'There could be no doubt of the practice of the country of retaining . . . barns till the crop should be threshed out,' Pitmilly conceded. 'Neither could it be doubted that Mr Sellar had not left the whole of the barns for the use of the outgoing tenants and, in consequence of this, the tenants suffered damage.' But citing a Court of Session judgment in a civil case, the judge was clear that, though the Rhiloisk outgoers had certainly been entitled in law to harvest the crops they had sown before their departure, Sellar 'was not bound' legally to leave their barns intact and, it followed, was not guilty of any crime in having had those barns destroyed. This meant, Pitmilly continued, that the jury were left with just one alleged offence to consider: the one relating 'to the injury charged to have been done [at Badinloskin] to Margaret MacKay'.[33]

Prosecution witnesses had given one account of events at Badinloskin, defence witnesses another. 'It was the duty of the jury to balance betwixt these two sets of witnesses,' Lord Pitmilly advised. 'If the jury were at all at a loss, they ought to take into view the character of the accused . . . Now here there was, in the first place, real evidence [concerning] . . . the conduct of Mr Sellar in regard to the sick, for this in several instances had been proved [in the course of testimony the jury had heard] to be most humane; and, secondly, there were the letters of Sir George Abercromby, Mr Brodie and Mr Fenton . . . [together with] the testimonies of Mr Gilzean and Sir Archibald Dunbar – all establishing Mr Sellar's humanity of disposition.'

If this is an accurate rendering of Pitmilly's words, he was surely overstepping what were even then the bounds of judicial propriety in asserting that Sellar's conduct had been *proved* humane. In fact it had merely been *said* by defence witnesses (themselves party to the evictions that had given rise to the trial) to be humane. But that, perhaps, is neither here nor there. Pitmilly, when back in Edinburgh, would tell one of William MacKenzie's friends 'how much he [the judge] was satisfied' of Sellar's innocence 'and how evident was the existence of a combination against him'. Hence the steer given from the bench to the High Court's jury. Short of directing the jury to acquit, Lord Pitmilly could not have been clearer as to the verdict he expected. That verdict was duly forthcoming. Fifteen minutes after the jury's retiral, they were back – at around one o'clock in the morning of Wednesday 24 April – to say they had unanimously found Patrick Sellar not guilty.[34]

Pitmilly now 'observed,' as if this needed stating, 'that his opinion concurred with that of the jury'. Scarcely less pleased, it seems, was Henry Home Drummond: 'The advocate depute declared that he thought it fair to the panel . . . to state his conviction that if those witnesses who were rejected on account of errors in their designations had been examined, the result of the trial would have been the same.'[35]

Turning to Patrick Sellar, Pitmilly said: 'Mr Sellar, it is now my duty to dismiss you from the bar; and you have the satisfaction of thinking that you are discharged by the unanimous opinion of the jury and the court. I am sure that, although your feelings must have been agitated, you cannot regret that this trial took place; and I am hopeful it will have due effects on the minds of the country which have been so much, and so improperly, agitated.'[36]

Throughout the preceding day and into the night, or so George MacPherson Grant was told by one of Patrick Sellar's lawyers, 'Sellar bore up very well, but when the verdict of acquittal was pronounced, he burst into tears.' This, MacPherson Grant added, 'had a great effect on the audience', contributing, no doubt, to what Sellar afterwards described as the 'truly gratifying' way in which so many of the people present in the still-crowded courtroom now rushed to congratulate him.[37]

Writing decades later, Donald Sage, whose father had been Kildonan's minister and who was by then a veteran clergyman himself, commented of Patrick Sellar's trial: 'The final issue of it was only what might have been expected when a case came to be determined between the *poor*, as the party offended, and the *rich*, as the lordly and heartless aggressor.' That has been very much the judgement of lots of others down the years. But what mattered in 1816 was not the opinion of posterity but the trial verdict's more immediate implications. For people known to have contributed to having had Sellar brought before the High Court, those implications were severe.[38]

While declaring himself 'quite overpowered with the sympathy and kindness of [his] friends', Patrick Sellar was also intent on being avenged on everyone implicated in what he called 'the late most dangerous conspiracy'. In this he had the backing of the Staffords and their aides. Prior to Sellar's High Court appearance, the marquis, the marchioness, James Loch and other senior figures in the Stafford camp had distanced themselves from their second-in-command (after William Young) in Sutherland. In Sellar's Inverness triumph, however, they saw an opportunity both to reassert their commitment to 'improvement' and to crush all Sutherland opposition to it.[39]

Writing to Sellar on 29 April 1816, the day news of the Inverness verdict reached London, Loch was little short of gushing: 'I cannot let a post leave . . . without congratulating you upon the event of the trial at Inverness, and I am sure you will not think me any less sincere in my congratulations when I say that such a termination was [as] . . . essential for the future progress and prosperity of Sutherland as it was for your future comfort . . . I went to Cleveland House [the Stafford family's London residence] where I found everyone most happy.'[40]

This, from Sellar's perspective, was heartening. The 'permanent improvement of the [Sutherland] Estate', he remarked in response, depended on ensuring that 'the new colony planted here' – by which Sellar meant people like himself – was permitted to 'flourish'. But that would not happen if there were to be any 'repetition' of the 'atrocious attacks' he had had to endure over the preceding two years. Highlanders, Sellar told Loch, were 'crafty . . . and they act in wonderful concert'. In the Highlands, he went on, 'the lower ranks are entirely led by those above them. It occurs to me to be very essential to find out and punish the leaders of the people.' This did not mean, however, that humbler opponents of clearance ought to be spared retribution. They too, Sellar thought, required urgently to be dealt with.[41]

In so thinking, Sellar was at one with George MacPherson Grant, Sutherland's newly returned MP. Grant, whom an English politician called 'a toad of Lady Stafford's', was then intent – as if by way of living up to the Englishman's description – on proving to the marchioness and her husband that he could be relied on to do better by them than his immediate predecessor, James Macdonald. In an earlier indication of his readiness to do Stafford bidding, Grant, who first represented Sutherland in parliament between 1809 and 1812, had uncomplainingly stood aside to make way for Macdonald, one of the marquis's nephews. But on his getting to Westminster the latter had taken up an unexpectedly independent-minded stance on policy matters, and had thus become, as a historian of parliament puts it, 'heavily estranged' from his uncle. Secure in the knowledge that most of early nineteenth-century Sutherland's two or three dozen electors* would fall in automatically with their wishes, the marquis and marchioness duly eased out Macdonald and replaced him, as the same historian observes, with 'the more compliant Grant'. That was in March 1816. Just months later Grant, who had put a lot of effort into modernising tenure arrangements on his own landed properties, embarked on what he described as 'an excursion into the interior of the Sutherland Estate'. The MP's aim was not so much to reacquaint himself with his constituency as to obtain insights into how best to proceed with 'improvement'.[42]

His enquiries in Strathnaver persuaded George Macpherson Grant that, as Rhiloisk farm's evicted families always maintained, William Young had been at fault in 'neglecting to have the allotments intended for dispossessed tenants . . . pointed out to them in proper time'. But Strathnaver's subsequent 'disturbances', Grant reported to James Loch, would not have got off the ground had it not been for the lead given by John Munro, with whom the MP met in the summer of 1816. Munro, Grant believed, was 'the active instigator' (as indeed he was) of Strathnaver people's persistent and ultimately successful efforts to have Patrick Sellar put on trial.

* Prior to the Reform Act of 1832, Scottish county electorates, as a result of voting rights being confined to just a few men of property, were vanishingly tiny.

Munro, Grant continued, had been aided (as indeed he had) by John MacKay. 'Those two men', the MP felt, 'should be removed from the [Sutherland] Estate as an example.'[43]

Loch agreed. In a memo of 19 August 1816, he wrote: 'No delay should take place in communicating to the following persons in Strathnaver, who were connected with the late occurrences, that they are to be turned off at Whitsunday [1817], which ought to be done without fail.' The people Loch named were MacKay and Munro. What happened to them when, three years after their expulsion from Rivigill and Garvault, they and their families were once more evicted – this time from Rhinovie – is not known.[44]

Reporting to James Loch on his Strathnaver encounter with John Munro, George MacPherson Grant noted: 'He [Munro] admits that he was advised by Captain Sutherland in London.' This was Alexander Sutherland who, in the *Military Register*, was still inclined – the April verdict notwithstanding – to insist on Patrick Sellar's guilt. Had it not been for 'the zeal, ingenuity and ability of his counsel', coupled with bias on the part of a judge linked with the Stafford's Edinburgh lawyers, then Sellar, or so the *Register* implied, would have received the punishment that ought to have been his due. As it was, everything that had taken place in connection with the Sutherland 'improvements' since 1813 should be subjected, the paper urged, to parliamentary inquiry.[45]

There was, for the moment anyway, no chance of this. But for as long as Alexander Sutherland's anti-Stafford and anti-Sellar tirades were 'tolerated', William Young warned James Loch, 'the people' (meaning the Staffords' Sutherland tenants) would 'know they [had] him to make a noise' on their behalf. MacPherson Grant concurred. 'I find [Alexander] Sutherland making shameful insinuations as to the impartiality of Sellar's trial', he commented in the course of one of his letters to Loch, 'and really if such publications are permitted there is an end to all [estate] management.'[46]

Sellar's own thirst for vengeance on all the many people he regarded as his persecutors had meanwhile been intensified by his discovering on his getting back to Culmaily from Inverness that 20 recently purchased – and expensive – sheep had had their throats cut in his absence. This 'outrage' by 'pure barbarians', he raged, had to be countered by having its perpetrators found and 'punished with the utmost severity of the law'. As for Alexander Sutherland, whom Sellar regarded as 'the fomentor of all . . . [Sutherland Estate] disturbances if not the very author of them', it was essential 'to give [him] battle' at the earliest opportunity. Hence Patrick Sellar's positive response when, in May 1816, James Loch, with the Marchioness of Stafford's backing, advised him to engage English counsel with a view to suing Sandy Ink, the *Military Register*, or both, for libel.[47]

To Sellar's disappointment, this plan had scarcely been sanctioned when it was abandoned – presumably because, on reflection, Loch and the Staffords realised that it would have done them no good to have the Badinloskin burning, plus other problematic episodes in Strathnaver and the Strath of Kildonan, examined in a London court. But if Alexander Sutherland thus remained beyond the reach of Sellar, Loch, the marquis and the marchioness, it was otherwise with his brother John – seen by the Stafford camp as a key player in the anti-Sellar and anti-clearance activity of the preceding two or three years. The Sciberscross tacksman's lease being due to expire in 1818, it was made clear to him that there was no chance of its being renewed.[48]

Sciberscross, in the upper part of Strathbrora, is some two or three miles beyond Ascoilemore where Jessie Ross (with whom this book began) was probably more taken up in the spring of 1816 with the care of her first child, born in February that year, than with the repercussions of Patrick Sellar's trial. But it is certain, despite this, that Jessie, her husband Gordon and their neighbours would quickly have become aware that John Sutherland had been left with no option but to quit a spot where his forebears, according to John's son William, had 'lived . . . since 1416'. The Ascoilemore Rosses, to be sure, are unlikely to have had much contact with the Sciberscross Sutherlands, who, being *daoine uaisle* or gentry, would have kept themselves apart from the wider population of Strathbrora. But this wider population, for all that, is bound to have been alarmed by news of the planned severing of the Sutherland family's connection with Sciberscross. Irrespective of whether or not William Sutherland was exact in his dating, this connection had lasted for several hundred years. Its termination, as people up and down Strathbrora would at once have recognised, was a clear signal that evictions of the kind Patrick Sellar had implemented in Strathnaver might soon affect them also. If the Sutherlands of Sciberscross, for so long the locality's principal family, could be ordered out of Strathbrora, so – it followed – could everybody else.[49]

Nor was it any easier emotionally for the Sutherlands to leave Sciberscross, where their substantial home was set among what agricultural writer John Henderson called a 'shrubbery of birch, alder and hazel', than it was for other displaced families to quit long-familiar surroundings. That is evident from a letter sent by John Sutherland's wife Mary to the Marchioness of Stafford: 'How can I describe my . . . feelings at the idea of quitting Sutherland for ever! It is so dreary to me that I dread it like annihilation.' Signing herself Mary *Maxwell* Sutherland to make the point that she had been named for the marchioness's mother, also Mary and a daughter of Kirkcudbrightshire laird William Maxwell, Mary Sutherland (a MacDonald by birth) made clear that her husband was perfectly willing to match, or more than match, whatever Sciberscross rent might be available from others: 'If your Ladyship and Lord Stafford would have the goodness and condescension to continue the present possession of Sciberscross [meaning its occupation by her and her family] on terms equal to any other offer, or on any [other] terms agreeable to your Ladyship, God who delights in *mercy* and *forgiveness* would reward [that] generous action.'[50]

Mary Sutherland's plea for 'mercy and forgiveness' on the marchioness's part stemmed from her husband having acknowledged, in one of his own letters to Lady Stafford, that he had indeed played a part – in association with his brother Alexander – in publicising various acts of resistance to 'improvement'. But he had meant only 'to expose' her 'agents', John Sutherland informed the marchioness in the course of a continuing exchange of correspondence, and he resented suggestions that he had been 'engaged in a kind of sedition' or 'had committed a criminal action'.[51]

This in no way weakened Stafford resolve to be rid of the Sciberscross tacksman. Nor did the latter's appeals to history. His father, John Sutherland reminded the marchioness, had come promptly and effectively to the aid of her grandfather, Sutherland's 17th earl, when Dunrobin Castle and the rest of the Sutherland Estate were menaced in the course of the 1745 Jacobite Rebellion, which the earl had opposed. Lady Stafford, John Sutherland continued, 'ought to remember [his] father's services', for which that earlier Sciberscross tacksman had been 'promised Sciberscross . . . all his life free, and to his son after him, by your noble grandfather'.[52]

Neither John nor Mary Sutherland's appeals having made any impression on the marchioness, it was left to their son William to make a last attempt. Like his father, his London-based uncle and lots of others of tacksman background, William had opted for a military career, and by 1816 had attained the rank of captain in the 93rd Regiment. The 93rd, following its Chalmette mauling, had been sent to Ireland to recuperate, and it was from there – from Limerick specifically – that William Sutherland now wrote to Lady Stafford. 'Although my father has unfortunately, and I am sure unintentionally, incurred your Ladyship's displeasure', runs his letter, 'I trust . . . [this] feeling does not extend to his children.' Because it would sadden him to see his family 'entirely removed' from an estate where that same family had 'been so long cherished', William went on, he would be much indebted to the marchioness if she were to consider granting him a lease of Sciberscross 'on equal terms with [those on offer from] any other candidate'.[53]

Like his father's identical proposal – and as had happened when Kildonan people similarly offered to match the rents Gabriel Reed and William Clunes had agreed to pay for their lands – this suggestion was rejected. 'There can be no change in our determination,' the Marchioness of Stafford commented. From May 1818, Sciberscross would be tenanted, it was announced, by James Hall. One of the two men who had had to ride for their lives out of the Strath of Kildonan at the start of January 1813, Hall came originally from Roxburghshire. In his mid-forties when he moved into Strathbrora, James Hall was by trade a shepherd who, prior to his embarking on his Sciberscross venture, had been other people's waged employee. He was of similar background, then, to the Northumberland-born John Cleugh, who had already taken on the tenancy of Pollie, with which Sciberscross shared a boundary. Such men, supremely skilled managers of sheep, were in time to make themselves wealthy. But they had begun life in anything but elevated circumstances. This must have made his departure from Sciberscross all the harder for John Sutherland to bear. He had been displaced, in effect, by a Borders shepherd he is sure to have regarded as having had far, far lowlier origins than himself. To that extent, James Hall's acquisition of Sciberscross – a development redolent of inherited status and privilege giving way to something else entirely – can be seen as a revolutionary moment. The revolution in question, however, brought little or nothing by way of benefit to Strathbrora's population.[54]

'His general intelligence, integrity and kindness of disposition', an obituarist would write of James Hall, 'made him much esteemed and respected by his friends and acquaintances.' Even allowing for the fact that obituaries almost always deal in positives, there is no reason to quarrel with that statement. But Hall – caring and kindly though he may have been – had no option but to comply with the conditions of his lease. Those were to the effect that his Sciberscross farm was to be cleared in advance of his taking occupancy and kept free of people – Hall's shepherds excepted – thereafter.[55]

If being rid of Sciberscross's tacksman pleased the Staffords and their managers, ousting Robert McKid delighted them. McKid's fate had been sealed not so much by Patrick Sellar's Inverness acquittal as by the exposure, in the High Court, of the sheriff-substitute's less than scrupulous handling of Sellar's prosecution. 'McKid', George MacPherson Grant reported to the Marchioness of Stafford in the immediate aftermath of Sellar going free, 'is made as black as possible.' William MacKenzie, the marquis and marchioness's Edinburgh lawyer, was of the same opinion. 'McKid's punishment and dismissal should follow as a consequence [of the trial outcome],' he commented on news of the Inverness verdict reaching the Scottish capital. Lord Pitmilly, MacKenzie informed Lady Stafford some days later, was of the view that McKid had been 'at the bottom' of the entire campaign to bring Sellar to trial. The judge, MacKenzie added, planned to make clear to George Cranstoun, Sutherland's sheriff and McKid's immediate superior, 'what he [Pitmilly] thinks of the conduct of his substitute'.[56]

Not long before Patrick Sellar's trial, McKid had agreed – perhaps because he suspected things might not go his way at the High Court – to give up his tenancy of Kirkton farm. But he appears to have been in no way abashed, in the short run anyway, by his Inverness experiences. McKid, the marchioness learned from William Young some three weeks after the Sellar verdict, was certainly preparing to move out of Kirkton where he had arranged a 'roup' or sale of livestock, farm implements and other items. But the sheriff-substitute, it appears, continued to fulfil all his official functions with an 'assurance' Young found 'astonishing'.[57]

This was a state of affairs Patrick Sellar, for one, was determined to end. In June, with the support of the Staffords and James Loch, Sellar launched a defamation suit against Robert McKid, who was accused, in papers served by Sellar's lawyers, of 'circulating false reports to [Sellar's] prejudice, perverting and abusing his official duty . . . depriving the pursuer [meaning Sellar] of his liberty . . . [and] joining a conspiracy of persons . . . to ruin the pursuer'. McKid, as soon became common knowledge, was being sued for 'exemplary' or punitive damages of £5,000. This sum, equivalent to several hundred thousand pounds today, was one the sheriff-substitute could not possibly have found. But being determined (or so it seemed initially) to fight his corner, McKid engaged the legal services of Joseph Gordon, ex-laird of the Carrol Estate and (as underlined already) a man with no time for the Staffords or for the land management policies they were imposing on Sutherland.[58]

'I shall make a point of having McKid well trounced,' Patrick Sellar told Lady Stafford. So it turned out. Although Joseph Gordon lodged defences on the sheriff-substitute's behalf, McKid at last concluded that he had no option but to throw himself on Sellar's mercy. Gordon duly arranged for the Sellar suit to be dropped on condition that McKid met Sellar's legal expenses of £200 (an amount for which Joseph Gordon stood surety) and made full acknowledgement of his having been at fault in having Sellar charged, arrested and jailed.[59]

The required apology was infused with self-abasement: 'Sir,' McKid wrote, 'Being impressed with the perfect conviction and belief that the statements to your prejudice contained in the precognition which I took in Strathnaver in May 1815 were to such an extent exaggerations as to amount to absolute falsehoods, I am free to admit that, led away by the clamour excited against you, on account of the discharge of the duties of your office as factor for the Marchioness of Stafford . . . I gave a degree of credit to those mis-statements of which I am now thoroughly ashamed and which I most sincerely and deeply regret.'[60]

When bringing George Macpherson Grant up to date with McKid's abject surrender, Sellar observed: 'I found the miserable man involved in such difficulties on all hands, and his family . . . so certainly about to be beggared by my bringing him to heel, that I was well pleased to wash my hands of him.' With his wife and several children – children to whom Donald Sage acted for a time as private tutor – Robert McKid had meanwhile quit Sutherland (as many others did during the clearance era) for Caithness. His resignation from the post of sheriff-substitute was registered formally in the records of Dornoch Sheriff Court, where he had previously presided, on 29 November 1816. At about the same time, McKid was reported to 'be shipping off his furniture [presumably from the Little Ferry pierhead] . . . on board a vessel for Thurso'.* He would play no further part in the public life of Sutherland.[61]

Neither, it transpired, would George Cranstoun. The sheriff had first incurred the Stafford camp's suspicions when, in 1813, he was thought by William Young and Patrick Sellar to have been insufficiently hard on the Kildonan rebels. But it was Cranstoun's conduct during 1815 that made it imperative, from a Stafford perspective, to have him ousted. In the spring of that year, as both Sellar and the Staffords were well aware, Cranstoun had been directly in touch, through John Munro, with the Strathnaver dissidents. Worse, he was suspected (correctly) of having encouraged Robert McKid to push ahead with his investigations into Sellar's Rhiloisk evictions. Hence Lady Stafford's increasingly strident denunciations not just of Sutherland's sheriff-substitute but of the county's sheriff also. 'I am convinced Cranstoun wished to support him [McKid] if he could against us,' the marchioness observed in June 1816. His so doing, she added, stemmed 'from the democratic feeling all those people have in spite of themselves'.[62]

While the notion that George Cranstoun harboured quasi-revolutionary sympathies was – to put it mildly – exaggerated, it was nevertheless the case that his views were at odds with those of a political establishment given to cracking down on dissent of all kinds. This is clear from the extent to which, in the period following Sellar's trial, Cranstoun was prepared to come to the aid of people who found themselves accused of subversion. Prominent among such people was Andrew McKinlay, a radically-inclined Glasgow weaver brought to trial on charges of high treason. For little or

---

* In Thurso McKid set up a legal practice and went into business. Although he got into financial difficulties after three or four years, those proved temporary. First in Caithness and later in Ross-shire, McKid appears to have done reasonably well.

nothing in the way of payment, Cranstoun lent his support to McKinlay's defence team and had the satisfaction of seeing the weaver go free as a result of highly plausible allegations that the advocate depute in charge of the case had offered inducements to (or, more bluntly, bribed) a key Crown witness.[63]

The advocate depute in question was Henry Home Drummond. Although there is no surviving evidence to this effect, it may be that George Cranstoun derived some satisfaction from the consequent discomfiture of the man who had made such a poor fist of Patrick Sellar's prosecution. Cranstoun is also likely – for more personal reasons – to have welcomed the way in which the McKinlay case's collapse redounded greatly to the discredit of the government minister responsible for having brought the weaver and other pro-democracy activists to court. This was Alexander Maconochie, who in July 1816 had succeeded Archibald Colquhoun as lord advocate – a development quickly followed by Maconochie (an especially reactionary member of Lord Liverpool's profoundly illiberal administration) becoming party to a well-organised campaign to have George Cranstoun eased out of his position as Sutherland's sheriff-principal.

This campaign's mastermind was James Loch, who within weeks of the new lord advocate taking office had supplied him with 'a series of papers' summarising the extent of anti-clearance protest in localities like Strathnaver and highlighting, as Loch put it, 'the necessity of some steps being taken' to remedy what Loch called 'the extremely defective execution of the laws' throughout Sutherland. Maconochie could not have been more compliant. 'Acquainted as you are with what is going on in that part of the country,' the lord advocate assured Loch, 'I shall be most happy to receive any communications you will be so obliging as [to] make me upon the [administration] of justice [in] Sutherland and the remedies which you . . . recommend as the most likely to prove effectual for removing the present evils.'[64]

Loch now had his opening. McKid, he explained to Maconochie, could not long survive the exposure of his prejudiced treatment of

Patrick Sellar. But Cranstoun too had to be ousted. What was needed, Loch went on, was a sheriff-principal who, unlike Cranstoun, was prepared to take up permanent or semi-permanent residence in Sutherland – a sheriff, Loch pointed out, being supposedly obliged to spend a minimum of four months a year in his sheriffdom.[65]

Because of safeguards parliament had put in place with a view to guaranteeing judicial independence on a sheriff's part, the lord advocate, in the absence of definitive proof that George Cranstoun had engaged in serious wrongdoing, could not have him sacked. But he could and did put Cranstoun under pressure, with the result that, just three or four weeks after he had first contacted Maconochie, James Loch was able to report to Lady Stafford that the lord advocate or one of his aides had more than once 'told [Cranstoun] that he ought to give up the [Sutherland] sheriffship'. Shortly after, Cranstoun – angered no doubt by his treatment but relieved perhaps to have got clear of his Sutherland embroilments – tendered his resignation.[66]

Loch's correspondence with the lord advocate now moved on to the question of who was to take Cranstoun's place. Sutherland's next sheriff, Loch instructed Maconochie, must be 'of a firm and independent character'. But as so often with Loch, his words are not to be taken at face value. In Sutherland, he had commented in the course of an early letter to the lord advocate, 'a long continuance of old usages and customs' meant that 'improvement' and its attendant need for clearance were 'considered . . . an infringement of the natural and established rights of the inhabitants'. The 'independence' Loch had in mind, then, had less to do with impartiality than with an acceptance that the supposed 'rights' of Sutherland residents – rights, Loch felt, to which Cranstoun was overly attached – should automatically be overridden if they conflicted with what the Stafford family wished to do with their property. Hence Loch's alarm when it began to look as if Maconochie might settle on Cranstoun's replacement in advance of his having had an opportunity to satisfy himself of the new man's suitability.[67]

Matters were proceeding so rapidly in Edinburgh, Loch informed Lady Stafford, that he feared the lord advocate 'might take some steps [in relation to a Sutherland appointment] without any communication with your Ladyship and Lord Stafford. I wrote to him accordingly, stating that this would not do.' Maconochie was reassuring: 'I never intended to recommend anyone to be sheriff [of Sutherland] without Lady Stafford's approval, which I thought indispensable.' He had hoped to meet with the marchioness and the marquis when they were briefly in Edinburgh in the early autumn, the lord advocate continued. That had proved impossible. But he would 'probably be in London before anything is done', and he and Loch would then 'have plenty of time to talk over the subject'.[68]

Maconochie and Loch duly met. They agreed that – subject to the quickly forthcoming consent of the Marquis and Marchioness of Stafford – Sutherland's sheriff-principal should be Charles Ross. A much less prominent lawyer than his predecessor, Sutherland's new sheriff, as would be shown by the way he and his subordinates became party to James Loch's persecution of Strathbrora schoolmaster Gordon Ross, was as amenable to manipulation as Loch and the Staffords could have wished. When, in 1815, tenants evicted from their Strathnaver landholdings by Patrick Sellar looked to George Cranstoun[*] for assistance, they did not look in vain. Future casualties of clearance would receive no such help from Sheriff Ross or from John Law, the lawyer who now moved from Aberdeen to take over Robert McKid's role as Sutherland's sheriff-substitute. Henceforth, as would become painfully evident to Gordon Ross in the summer of 1821, the administration of justice in Sutherland would be subordinate to the requirements of the Staffords and James Loch.

---

[*] His loss of his sheriffdom did not, in the end, impede Cranstoun's advancement. In 1826 he was made a judge.

II

'ABORIGINES OF BRITAIN'

The Sutherland straths; the people who lived there;
how they lived; making a case for their removal

In the summer of 1816, for the second year running, James Loch accompanied the Marchioness of Stafford to Dunrobin. 'Loch', the marchioness had noted the previous August, 'is of infinite use. He is so acute and so sensible . . . and his manners besides are so agreeable to everyone that he is quite a treasure here.' At that point, Loch's role with regard to matters in Sutherland, though more extensive than formerly, remained an advisory one. Twelve months later, as had meanwhile been agreed by Lord and Lady Stafford, Loch was beginning to exercise executive powers over the Sutherland Estate.[1]

Loch, now four years into his position as Stafford family 'commissioner' and aware that his employers were increasingly reliant on him, found his new responsibilities very challenging. 'I left Dunrobin', he wrote at the end of August, 'after having passed as severe a three weeks work as I ever did in my life.' This was in part a consequence of the effort Loch put into ridding Sutherland of Robert McKid and George Cranstoun. More of the commissioner's Dunrobin workload, however, derived from his conviction that management of the Sutherland Estate had hitherto been so slapdash as to make it essential to have administration of the property placed on a properly thought-through basis: 'The thing I wish to do if possible . . . is this, to put the future operation in Sutherland upon some . . . well-digested plan.'[2]

George MacPherson Grant, with whom Loch was in close touch throughout this period, was in full agreement. 'The rapidity with which improvement has been pushed on the Sutherland Estate', the MP remarked to Loch, 'has attracted my astonishment . . . [I]t has frequently appeared to me that too much . . . was aimed at.' With a view to helping Loch obtain the 'authority' the commissioner felt he required, MacPherson Grant put the same point, still more forcefully, to Lady Stafford: 'The want of a general and systematic arrangement has been the great defect hitherto and many things have been decided upon in too great a hurry.'³

The person most responsible for this state of affairs, James Loch felt, was William Young. Many of the difficulties encountered in the Strath of Kildonan in 1813 and in Strathnaver the following year had arisen, Loch was convinced, because Young had 'never given the people [whom he planned to clear] sufficient time to remove'. Young was not without 'merits', Loch conceded, 'but I regret his . . . impatience of delay and [his] eternal fidget to be moving. This prevents him [from] . . . considering his plan beforehand and prevents him too from following it out when begun. It also leads him to a desire to do everything himself in place of trusting to others and [then] confining his attention to a superintendance of their actions.'⁴

Hence James Loch's insistence on a clear-out of the Sutherland Estate's senior managers. Young's employment, as made clear during Loch's August 1816 visit to Dunrobin, was to terminate the following November. Patrick Sellar – though his farm leases were such as to ensure he would remain an estate tenant – was also served with a notice of dismissal. Sellar, however, was permitted – George MacPherson Grant having urged the need for some administrative continuity – to remain in post until May 1817.

While Loch had been gratified by Patrick Sellar's High Court acquittal, he believed that Sellar's abrasive conduct, not just in Strathnaver but more generally, had done Lord and Lady Stafford 'much injury' by 'disposing the minds of [Sutherland] people' against change of every kind. William MacKenzie was of the same opinion. Although he 'could not help regretting that it was necessary he [Sellar] should be in employment for a day after Mr Young's retirement', the Staffords' Edinburgh lawyer told Loch, the decision to have Sellar removed from his factorship was much to be applauded. Sellar was a first-rate farmer, MacKenzie admitted: 'But wherever taste, temper or feeling is required, or even ordinary discretion, he is deficient beyond what I ever met with in any man, so that I don't know one in the whole circle of my acquaintances so ill calculated as him to fill the office of a factor in such a country as Sutherland.'[5]

While MacKenzie, like Loch, had welcomed the Sellar trial's outcome, his suspicions about the factor's judgement – or lack of it – had been reinforced, as had Loch's and MacPherson Grant's, by Sellar's announcement, made within days of his walking free from the High Court, that he intended to bid for the lease of Kirkton, the farm that Robert McKid was then vacating. As was instantly apparent to the factor's colleagues, any such development (coming hot on the heels of the crisis resulting from Sellar's acquisition of Rhiloisk) would have been seen widely as proof that Sellar was more committed to personal aggrandisement than to effective governance of the Sutherland Estate. 'The moment I learned of this,' an infuriated Loch remarked of the Kirkton proposal, 'I remonstrated against it . . . in the strongest manner. In every point of view [a Sellar takeover of McKid's former farm] would have been quite ruinous to the estate and its future management.'[6]

In the event, Patrick Sellar did not obtain Kirkton. But as shown by James Loch's reaction to that possibility, his attempt to do so went a long way to confirming the commissioner in his view that the Young–Sellar duopoly in charge of the Sutherland Estate since 1811 needed urgently to be replaced by a managerial team answering directly to himself. That team began to take shape during Loch's 1816 stay at Dunrobin. From his base in England, Loch from this point forward would determine the overall thrust and content of Sutherland Estate business planning, while, on the ground, his directions would be given effect by three Sutherland-based managers.

Two of these would be located in the Sutherland Estate's more outlying districts; one being in charge of faraway Assynt; the other looking after Strathnaver and the coastal area immediately to its north. Each of those subfactors, Loch ruled, would report to an overseer who, from the Sutherland Estate's Golspie headquarters, would both supervise the work of his Strathnaver and Assynt subordinates and be responsible personally for the more easterly part of the estate, including Strathbrora and the Strath of Kildonan. Of the planned factorial posts, then, the Golspie one was key, and Loch – returning south from Dunrobin in late August 1816 – was clear as to who should fill it. This was Francis Suther, who for the previous two or three years had been principal manager at Trentham, the West Midlands estate regarded as Lord Stafford's premier property.[7]

Suther, according to Loch, was a man of 'good temper and judicious conduct'. At Trentham, Loch wrote, Suther 'had [brought] many very difficult matters to a most satisfactory and profitable issue. He . . . aided me in every plan which I thought it necessary to adopt . . . and, though many of [those plans] were hostile to the feelings of [the local population], he reconciled them to the change, preserved his Lordship's popularity entire, and secured their goodwill to himself'. A skill-set of this sort, Loch considered, was exactly what was required in Golspie if 'improvement' was to be secured. Suther, though appreciative of the trust thus vested in him, was less sanguine. 'I know Trentham and the people I have to deal with [there],' he commented. 'I do not know Sutherland.'[8]

'We all have our faults,' Patrick Sellar observed in the course of a rare moment of self-criticism in the summer of 1816, 'and God knows I am chief of sinners.' That spring, however, he had come home from his Inverness triumph in a mood that was not so much reflective as exultant. Not just he personally, Sellar felt, but his entire philosophy had been vindicated by the High Court verdict of 24 April. Despite his having to deal with a backlog of estate business while also attending to the management of his widely separated farms at Culmaily and Rhiloisk, Sellar – whose energies were unlimited – accordingly found time to set out the principles shaping his approach to land management. The outcome, in the shape of a lengthy 'Note concerning Sutherland', was a complex, but broadly coherent, rationale for the eradication of what remained of Highland clanship and the way of life to which it had given rise. Rooted in its author's belief that he had all along been bringing progress and prosperity to families and communities too backward to achieve those things by themselves, Sellar's 'note' was completed within five weeks of his trial. It remains an intriguing pointer to the factor's conviction that the enforced emptying of the Sutherland interior was just one component of wider processes that, for all the disruption they might cause in the short run, would – or so Sellar supposed – extend the gains arising from Britain's burgeoning economy to less fortunate societies worldwide.[9]

Highlanders, Patrick Sellar wrote, were 'the sad remnant of a people who once covered a great part of Europe and . . . bravely withstood the invading strength of the Roman Empire'. The people Sellar had in mind (and his thinking testifies to the breadth of his reading) were the Celtic populations of localities such as pre-Roman Gaul and pre-Roman Britain, populations that had gradually become confined, or so Sellar contended, to marginal areas like Sutherland. There a Celtic residue had made the grave error, as Sellar saw it, of clinging on to a language that had become hopelessly obsolescent. By failing to abandon Gaelic, Sellar continued, Highlanders had cut themselves off from every sort of modernising influence and sunk to the status of 'savages'. Sutherland's inhabitants, it followed, occupied a position in 'relation to the enlightened nations of Europe . . . [that was] not very different from that betwixt the American colonists and the aborigines of that country. The one', Sellar insisted, 'are the aborigines of Britain shut out from the general stream of knowledge and cultivation flowing in upon the commonwealth of Europe . . . The other are the aborigines of America, equally shut out from this stream.' Wherever it occurred,

Sellar maintained, cultural isolation of this type condemned people to disaster. Both Native Americans and Scottish Highlanders 'live[d] in turf cabins in common with the brutes'; both were 'fast sinking under the baneful effect of ardent spirits'.[10]

That last remark was by way of prelude to an account of what Patrick Sellar regarded as much the most deleterious aspect of the economic order characteristic of Sutherland's inland townships. This was the involvement of many of those townships in illicit whisky distilling. Because the whisky trade was an unlawful one, Sellar observed, it could be carried on only by means of 'lies, chicanery, perjury, cunning . . . [and other] debasing artifices'. A whisky-maker's children, being always 'trained up in deceit', were encouraged to 'exceed their father in turpitude, and the virtue of a Scotch Highlander is [thus] exchanged for the vices of the Irish peasantry.'[11]

That Ireland's Gaelic-speaking countryfolk were sunk still more deeply in depravity than their Highland counterparts was a common-place among people who thought as Sellar did. Equally widespread was apprehension – of a sort apparent in Sellar's May 1816 'note' – that Highlanders, not least those engaged in unlawful whisky production, might be embarking on a course that would culminate in the Highlands becoming as chaotic as parts of rural Ireland already were. This helps explain why, for much of the nineteenth century, protest movements of the Kildonan or Strathnaver variety tended to be seen by the landowning class and its agents as warnings that the Highlands were about to descend into anti-landlord violence of a type common on some Irish estates. It also explains why Patrick Sellar raised the spectre of Ireland immediately prior to advocating a complete clearance of Sutherland's inland valleys. Only by such means, Sellar implied, could Sutherland be protected from pover-ty-fuelled dissent and disorder. Every resident of Strathnaver, the Strath of Kildonan and Strathbrora should therefore 'be brought from the inaccessible interior where [whisky] smuggling is the only possible means of life . . . to the [more] accessible sea coast'. There 'many different fields for . . . industry [lay] open'; there children could be 'bred to honest and useful trades'.[12]

A wholesale emptying of the Sutherland straths would of course have the immediate consequence of making their many square miles of pastureland available to sheep farmers. But this, ostensibly at any rate, was not central to the thinking outlined in Sellar's 'note'. Its closely written pages were instead given over to explaining why, in its author's opinion, the new and expanded coastal communities he envisaged would be more successful than the inland settlements he wanted done away this. His assurance that such would be the case, Sellar wrote, rested on 'two very curious facts'.

'The first fact', he went on, 'is that in no country of which I have yet read or heard of is there in every one person such an accumulation of offices [meaning trades or occupations] as in the Highlands of Scotland. [Here] every man is a quarrier, mason, woodman, carrier . . . carpenter, cooper, turf cutter, thatcher . . . tanner, shoemaker, saddler, shepherd, wool comber, spinner, farmer, cattle dealer, poacher and God knows what, and yet, with all this bountiful provision for every man of them, are they not . . . beggars? The second fact is that nowhere is to be found a peasantry richer, more independent, better lodged, better fed, more virtuous, of higher and nobler spirit, and of more sterling value to society than the people of England; and yet, strange to tell, no man there can get hold of more than one trade or calling, and some only part of one.'[13]

To account for those 'curious paradoxes', as he called them, Sellar turned to the writings of Adam Smith, whose *Wealth of Nations*, first published in 1776, was then beginning to acquire its continuing status as free enterprise capitalism's foundation text. There could have been few farmers in the Scotland of 1816 who had Smith's volumes readily to hand. Patrick Sellar, however, clearly did, his case for the enforced depopulation of the Sutherland straths being underpinned by repeated references to Smith's analysis of what it takes to bring about an economy's expansion.

Basic to Adam Smith's understanding of the growth process was the concept of 'division of labour'. This he famously illustrated with reference to the manufacture of pins. A man making pins entirely on his own account, Smith wrote, 'could scarce perhaps . . . make one pin in a day, and certainly could not make twenty'. But if the various operations involved in pin-making were divided up among 10 or 20 specialists, and if even the most rudimentary machinery became available to them, then daily output would at once soar to the equivalent of several thousand pins per person. For this sort of thing to be feasible, however, population had to be concentrated both to provide a pin-making factory with a workforce and, equally important, to create a market for its output. Hence Adam Smith's dismissal of the possibility of worthwhile economic growth being attained in rural areas, where, by definition, people lived in dispersed settlements and where division of labour could not be achieved by tradesmen forever denied the chance to specialise and collaborate in the way he described.[14]

Smith's 'data', Patrick Sellar maintained, reinforced his own view that the Sutherland Estate's population 'should not be dissipated and scattered in lone and helpless huts and small villages and hamlets over every part of the estate'. Instead people should be forced to live on the estate's North Sea coast between Helmsdale and Brora. 'There is a great danger of planting . . . [removed families] too thin', Sellar warned, 'but none of their being too thick . . . because division of labour can't exist without numbers *thickly* settled.' Once resettlement of this sort had been accomplished, Sellar thought, then 'in place of a Jack-Pudding* mass of confusion' there would be 'correct division of labour'; and 'in place of the poverty . . . of a savage country' there would be 'that state of affluence mentioned by Mr Smith "where a workman of the lowest and poorest order, if he is frugal and industrious, may enjoy a greater

---

* Jack Pudding was a name commonly given to a clown or jokester.

share of the necessaries and conveniences of life than it is possible for any savage to acquire"'.[15]

James Loch was not greatly impressed by Patrick Sellar's 'Note concerning Sutherland'. Sellar's paper, Loch remarked to George MacPherson Grant, contained 'much *very* extraneous matter'. The 'matter' Loch had in mind is likely to have consisted of Sellar's forays into history and economic theory. But issue could also have been taken (if not by Loch then by others) with the factor's analysis of what was going on around him in Sutherland and beyond. Was it truly the case, for instance, that what Sellar called England's 'peasantry' was as wealthy, well housed and well fed as Sellar averred? Given that much of rural England was about to be plunged (as will be seen) into economic crisis and concomitant unrest, perhaps not. Nor can it be assumed that conditions in inland Sutherland – conditions which, to make his prescriptions credible, Sellar *had* to portray in the bleakest available colours – were in fact as grim as the factor described them.[16]

Some families living in Sutherland's interior townships were indubitably poor. But other such families – particularly the families of each township's principal tenants – appear to have been, by the standards of their time, comfortably off. This can be inferred from points made on earlier pages. In 1821, for instance, the four tenants of the then about-to-be-cleared township of Ascoilemore in Strathbrora were jointly able to find about £100 (between six and seven times their SSPCK schoolteacher's annual salary) to meet the cost of legal advice. Tenants in the Strath of Kildonan similarly managed to raise, in the course of just a day or two in February 1813, the £60 needed to bail one of their colleagues, John Bannerman, from Dornoch Jail. A number of the same tenants, a few months later, produced the £50, £60 or more they were required to advance in order to secure family passages to Red River.

Nothing of this is compatible with Patrick Sellar's description of Sutherland as 'a country of sloth and idleness'; a locality sunk perpetually in 'poverty' and 'beggary'. Nor is it difficult to identify the sources of sums of the sort just mentioned. One consisted of remittances from sons serving in the 93rd Highlanders and other regiments – a Plymouth bank, for example, handling 'upwards of £500' in total when, in 1814, some of the 93rd's enlisted men (then in transit from South Africa to Louisiana) were in search of a convenient means of sending money north. Windfalls of that kind, however, were less relied upon than earnings generated nearer home. Thus people who owned 10, 20, 30 or more breeding cows – reportedly a not uncommon state of affairs in the pre-clearance Strath of Kildonan and perhaps in other straths too – would have been able in most years to sell a clutch of younger cattle. In Kildonan and elsewhere, tenants also traded in horses and sheep.* All such livestock sales – especially prior to the price falls that (as touched on shortly) followed the 1815 ending of Franco–British warfare – were a reliable source of hard cash. Equally reliable were earnings deriving from widespread involvement in the business on which Sellar vented so much fury: whisky distilling.[17]

Until well into the eighteenth century, the localised distilling of whisky for domestic consumption had been legal. It was then outlawed by the simple expedient of declaring that whisky could only be produced in stills with capacities well in excess of those in use at community level. This, ironically, can be seen as something of an interference with free markets of the kind preached by Adam Smith and Patrick Sellar in that one set of producers, the owners of large-scale distilleries, was being given a legislatively imposed advantage over another much larger group, people operating stills in farming townships both in Sutherland and other parts of Scotland.

Predictably, attempts to make whisky distilling the preserve of a small number of necessarily monied businessmen were both resented

---

* Those sheep (much less important than cattle in the pre-clearance economy) were native Highland breeds soon to be replaced by the cheviots favoured by farmers like Patrick Sellar and Gabriel Reed.

and ignored, not just by small-scale producers of spirit but by their customers. Thus it came about that even highly respectable (and otherwise law-abiding) rural residents, such as Kildonan minister Alexander Sage, continued to purchase whisky from their long-standing suppliers, Sage going so far as to provide one such supplier with premises. This was John Sutherland, who in September 1813 was to die in the ill-fated emigrant encampment at Sloop's Cove on the Churchill River estuary. 'John', the Kildonan minister's son Donald recalled, 'was . . . a first-rate brewer of malt whisky . . . [and was] often employed . . . in making our annual brewst [sic] . . . We built a cowhouse of stone and turf near the burn [between Kildonan's manse and its church] . . . [This] hovel was also employed for . . . brewing. There often, during the process of our whisky brewst, have I sat with John, watching the process and hearing his tales.' [18]

The fact that Donald Sage described John Sutherland's output as 'malt whisky' goes a long way to accounting for the financial success both of Sutherland and other producers of his type. The distilleries then setting up in Scotland's towns and cities dealt mostly in spirits made rapidly, and in big quantities, from raw, untreated grain of any available sort. The resulting product – 'a most rascally liquor' as Robert Burns called it – was often foul-tasting and, or so people alleged, frequently made its consumers ill. The whisky turned out by men like John Sutherland was, in contrast, produced from barley that had been malted – a time-consuming procedure during which barley was dampened and repeatedly turned over prior to its being dried in much the same sort of kiln as was used to reduce the moisture content of oats in advance of their being ground into meal. When drying, malted barley was exposed to smoke from the peat used to fire kilns. This, in turn, helped give the eventual whisky a flavour thought far superior to that of the spirit emanating from urban distilleries, the overall quality of the Highland product being further enhanced by its producers, unlike their city-based competitors, having ready access to unlimited supplies of clean water. [19]

Far from being a crudely manufactured hooch, then, illicitly made whisky from districts like Sutherland was everywhere thought preferable to its lawfully produced counterpart. Nor was this its only selling point. During the 20-plus years when Britain was engaged in more or less continuous conflict with France, spirits of all sorts were taxed by cash-strapped governments at increasingly punitive levels. Since Highland 'smugglers' (as whisky-makers operating outside the law were known) paid no tax, the contents of the wooden kegs in which they transported their output to market could be sold at prices well below those charged for spirits on which duty had been levied. 'It is . . . not [surprising]', one commentator observed of legally made whisky, '[that] people who can avoid it forbear to purchase at a higher price that which is as nauseous as it is poisonous.'[20]

The authorities made huge efforts to stamp out the illegal trade. For many years, however, this proved not so much difficult as impossible. While acknowledging that 'illicit distillation of spirits prevail[ed] in the country to a considerable extent', Sutherland's JPs were of the view that the practice could not 'effectually be prevented by any coercive measure'. In large part, this was because anti-smuggling laws commanded no widespread support. As with poachers, it followed, the generality of Highlanders were inclined to cheer on any whisky-makers in their midst. Nor was Alexander Sage the only person of comparatively high social standing to have regular dealings with Sutherland smugglers. In 1819, James Duncan, the man in charge of Golspie Inn, was found to have no less than 240 gallons – equal to some 1,500 present-day bottles – of illegally produced whisky in his possession. This was thought bad enough by Sutherland Estate managers. Still more upsetting from their perspective was James Loch's discovery that the whisky handed out freely to guests at Dunrobin Castle had originated in Sutherland's illicit stills.[21]

Given a climate so tolerant of the 'traffic' that exercised Patrick Sellar, the excisemen or 'gaugers' under orders to stamp it out were confronted with an uphill task. Although they had some success in more accessible localities, gaugers found it hard to make undetected approaches to places like the Strath of Kildonan – all the more so because of the care smugglers took to protect themselves. 'The [typical] still', wrote one close observer of the early nineteenth-century Highland scene, 'was generally placed in some secluded spot, in the ravine of a . . . burn or [so] screened by . . . natural woodland . . . that the smoke of the fire [integral to distilling] could scarcely be observed. There were scouts placed around, often three or four savage-looking men, sometimes women or boys.' The resulting scene, this man added, was so 'wild and romantic' as to have constituted 'a fit subject for an artist'.[22]

Smuggling, then, was a communal activity. It also appealed to younger people – in much the same way as drug-dealing can appeal today – because of the opportunities it offered to engage in risk-filled defiance of established order. In this, commented retired Perthshire soldier General David Stewart, whisky smuggling had much in common with the cattle-raiding once so general among Highland clans: 'In smuggling . . . there is a spirit of adventure and hazard which has a charm for the minds of the [Highland] peasantry. An escape or a successful resistance is remembered, and related as a heroic achievement; men encourage each other and a fraternity of feeling is produced among them by a sense of common danger.'[23]

Critics of Sutherland's smugglers, with Patrick Sellar very much leading the charge, strove to create the impression that whisky-makers were worthless incompetents. In fact, whisky-making is a demanding and complex business – the malting and drying of barley being no more than the commencement of a lengthy process requiring a great deal of skill. First the malted and dried barley is ground finely. Next it is added to warm water to produce 'mash'. With the help of lots of stirring, starch-derived sugars, integral to the malted grain, now dissolve gradually into the mix's fluid component. Known as 'wort', this is drained off and, with the addition of yeast, its sugar content is – over a couple of days – enabled to ferment. The weakly alcoholic solution, or 'wash', thus produced then goes into a still. This is a container designed in such a way as to enable the distiller (who must heat the wash-filled still in exactly the right manner) to vaporise, condense and collect the mash's alcohol content. That content, trickling from an outlet at the top of the heated still, is then distilled – more slowly – for a second time. The product of this second distillation consists of the liquor its Sutherland producers and sellers called, in their own language, *uisge beatha*, the water of life.

In present-day distilleries, stills are towering, pear-shaped vessels with capacities of many hundreds of gallons. Those used by Sutherland smugglers were far smaller. In 2013, during an archaeo-logical 'dig' at Caen in the Strath of Kildonan, there were discovered fragments of an early nineteenth-century still. At around two feet high, and with a similar diameter, this Caen still was typical of those used everywhere by smugglers. Like their larger modern counter-parts, all such stills were made from copper. This meant that, in contrast to everything else illicit distillers needed by way of equip-ment, stills such as the one unearthed at Caen could not be manufactured by smugglers themselves. In the northern Highlands they were mostly obtained, it appears, from one or other of Inverness's 'master coppersmiths' – men so unconcerned about their key role in what was a criminal endeavour that they were said to have hung still-shaped signs 'above their shops'.[24]

According to Sergeant William MacDonald, the man who brought the Kildonan rebels' demands to London in 1813, there were then some 300 separate stills in operation in eastern Sutherland, many of them in Strathbrora and the Strath of Kildonan. Because neither of those valleys could grow more than a fraction of the barley needed to meet their smugglers' needs, much of the necessary grain had to be obtained elsewhere. In the case of Strathbrora, most such imports came from nearby coastal farms. But the Kildonan people, being a good bit further north, looked for their supplies, or so Patrick Sellar commented, to Caithness and even Orkney. Some of the resulting whisky went to those same areas. Further quantities doubtless found their way into villages and small towns like Brora, Golspie, Dornoch and their Easter Ross equivalents. But Sutherland whisky was also sent further afield, going south by sea and possibly ending up as far away as Edinburgh.[25]

Despite its being illegal, then, the whisky trade is evidence of Sutherland's inland population having possessed in abundance entrepreneurial and other attributes said by Patrick Sellar – and other advocates of this population's removal – to be wholly lacking among Highlanders. In addition to displaying technical expertise of a high order, Sutherland's whisky-makers demonstrated a decades-long capacity to source raw materials from a distance, to supply faraway markets and to gather in – even from remote customers – the cash due to them. This was a business every bit as multifaceted and demanding as sheep farming, and, it seems, no less profitable.

That is substantiated by archaeological discoveries in and around the remains of the Caen home that yielded up that long-abandoned still. This home was found to have been 'well-constructed'. Its contents included 'high quality glazed ceramics'; and on the 'cobbled and finished' floor uncovered in what were the home's living quarters there would surely have been set out, two centuries ago, furnishings appropriate to a family able to afford dishes and other items manufactured hundreds of miles to the south.[26]

Just before the clearances, Hugh Miller – then a Cromarty schoolboy; later a journalist, author and much else – was an occasional visitor to a Sutherland home akin to the one investigated at Caen. 'The cottage in which we resided', Miller wrote of this home, 'might be regarded as an average specimen . . . It was a low, long building of turf, consisting of four apartments . . . the one stuck on the end of the other and threaded together by a passage that connected the whole.' One of those 'apartments' was, in effect, a byre where 'the master', as Miller called the household's head, housed half a dozen dairy cattle. Next to this cowshed was the

home's principal living area, 'a rude but not uncomfortable apartment with the fire on a large flat stone in the middle of the floor'.
Around this fire, the home's 'inmates' sat 'in a wide circle – the
women invariably ranged on the one side, and the men on the other'.
An adjoining 'apartment' had been 'partitioned into . . . bedrooms'.
Beyond that, at the end of the dwelling furthest from the byre, was
the room where the family entertained and accommodated
'strangers'. This room 'had both windows and a chimney, with
chairs, a table, a chest of drawers, a large box-bed and a small but
well-filled bookcase containing from forty to fifty volumes'.[27]

This was not luxury; and few people today are likely to be
charmed by the thought of a turf-walled home in which smoke from
a chimney-less fire had to find its way out through an aperture in a
thatched roof. But homes of that kind have to be set in the context
of a Scotland characterised at that time and later by some of the
worst housing conditions in Europe. Fifty years after the Sutherland
clearances, as revealed by the national census of 1871, a third of all
Scotland's houses consisted of one apartment (as compared to the
four Miller described) and a further third or more consisted of just
two. Nor was this position to change quickly. In 1913, a century
after the events this book describes, Glasgow alone contained nearly
45,000 one-room tenement flats, which their occupants called 'single
ends'. In those places, dark and sunless because of the cheek-by-jowl
manner in which tenements were built, families – with little in the
way of access to clean water and forced to share with others an
outside, stinking privy – existed in conditions a lot worse than those
described by Hugh Miller.[28]

Pre-clearance Sutherland was, for all that, by no means bereft of
poor housing. Many of the homes occupied by the people Patrick
Sellar evicted from Culmaily were probably in the one-room category – subtenants on coastal farms lacking earning opportunities
(whether from livestock-rearing or whisky-making) of the kind
available in interior communities where significant numbers of
families possessed substantial tenancies of their own. Those inland

settlements, however, were seldom seen by early nineteenth-century visitors to Sutherland – few travellers venturing west of the east coast route that was the modern A9's predecessor. Partly for that reason, and partly because visitors to Sutherland were not anyway very numerous, there was little risk of Sellar and other promoters of clearance running up against contrary testimony – other than from the occasional well-informed journalist like Alexander Sutherland – when they sought to create the impression that localities like Strathnaver or the Strath of Kildonan were a mass of tumble-down hovels whose inhabitants hovered perpetually on the edge of destitution.

The pro-clearance lobby's task was made easier in this respect by the appearance of the homes they were so anxious to destroy. Viewed from outside, Hugh Miller commented of the house he described, that house seemed a 'dingy edifice'. Anyone visiting the present-day Highland Folk Museum at Newtonmore in Badenoch, where a similar home has been re-created, is likely to sympathise with Miller's choice of words. In comparison with modern homes – their neatly perpendicular walls surmounted by equally clean-cut roofs – the Folk Museum building looks decidedly unprepossessing. When a house's walls are low and made largely from turf and when its roof is a mass of well-weathered thatch, then, to modern eyes, that house seems an unrelieved mess. External observers of the early nineteenth-century Highland scene – who were usually comparatively well-off owners of good homes in the south – thought similarly. But as is clear from Miller's writings, and as can be inferred from archaeological findings, the interior of a Sutherland 'longhouse' – the term applied today to homes of the sort excavated at Caen – was by no means as gruesome as is sometimes imagined.[29]

Most Sutherland longhouses are likely to have been less roomy and more ground-hugging than the Highland Folk Museum's reconstructed version. Their basic shape, however, was similar, deriving from a standard method of construction. Key to this method were timbers known as crucks or couples. These were substantial beams, a foot or more in thickness, set firmly into the ground. All such crucks were arranged in pairs – one opposite the other – and together formed a shape somewhere between an inverted V and an inverted U. Successive pairs, planted between five and seven feet apart, provided a house's framework. This meant that its width was restricted, because of the limited distance crucks could span, to between nine and twelve feet. A home's length, however, was in principle unlimited – hence longhouse – and, as is evident from remnant foundations still to be seen throughout Sutherland's straths, houses could be as many as 80, 100 or even more feet long. Even when allowance is made for the fact that a part of this length would be accounted for by a cowshed or byre – usually tacked on to the end of a dwelling in the way Hugh Miller described – this gave a total floor area roughly equivalent to that of a lot of the homes being constructed in present-day Britain.[30]

Crucks were made from timber – mostly birch – sourced from native woodlands of a type then fairly plentiful in localities like Strathbrora, the Strath of Kildonan and Strathnaver. The lighter beams laid lengthwise across crucks to carry the roof might also be birch. Often, however, they consisted of what was called bog, or moss, fir. This was timber deriving from Scots pines that had grown widely in Sutherland during the thousands-of-years long 'climatic optimum' that followed the ending of the Ice Age. The trunks of those pines, so rich in resin as to be impervious to moisture, were here and there preserved in the peat which began to form across much of the Highlands when, around 3000 BC, Britain's weather turned cooler and wetter than it had previously been. Some bog firs were found by accident when peat was dug for fuel. But their presence could also be detected in dry summers when the grasses and other plants immediately above them dried out more quickly than surrounding vegetation. Either way, bog fir was eagerly sought, not least because Scots pine, unlike birch, lends itself to being turned into long, straight planking.

A home's walls were put in place after its cruck framework had been erected. Their base consisted of locally gathered stones or boulders of a sort that can be seen in surviving foundations. Above this was placed course after course of turf, sometimes mixed with further stone, until the wall reached roughly head height. Roofs were multilayered. Above crosswise crucks and lengthwise planking came thinly-cut turfs. These were topped off by straw thatch which, because its waterproofing qualities were lost in the space of a year or two, needed regular renewing.

Crucks and their connecting crossbars had to be kept in place by wooden pegs driven through auger-drilled holes. Otherwise, the building of a longhouse required little in the way of sophisticated tools. That was one of its attractions. Another, apart from its spaciousness, was the fact of its being well insulated – turf walls keeping out cold (or keeping in warmth) much more efficiently than stone or brick. Nor was this the only distinction between longhouses and homes of the sort standard in today's Highlands. Around those homes' right-angled corners and steeply pitched roofs, the wind – in more exposed locations – can whistle and howl for hours on end. No such sound was ever heard from inside a longhouse.

Accurate assessment of housing or other conditions in Sutherland's inland straths was not on James Loch's agenda. What Loch wanted when he assumed overall control of Sutherland Estate management in 1816 was some means of ensuring that neither politicians nor the press were provided with opportunities to accuse the Staffords – whose riches kept them constantly in the public eye – of having maltreated, abused or exploited their Highland tenants. Hence Loch's quest for what the present-day public relations industry calls 'a narra-tive', a pro-clearance storyline that would give at least a degree of credibility to the notion that families were being moved from one part of the Sutherland Estate (its interior) to another (its coasts) not because this would profit the Staffords but because, only by such means, could those same families be rescued from misery and want. Loch's search for such a narrative was made easier by the worldwide impact of a catastrophic event in what was then the Dutch East Indies.

The April 1815 eruption of Mount Tambora on the island of Sumbawa in present-day Indonesia was easily the most significant such eruption of the last thousand or more years. The explosions that blew apart what had been a high peak and turned an estimated 20 cubic miles of rock into ash and lava were heard hundreds of miles away. Sumbawa itself was devastated and many thousands of its inhabitants killed. The sea for miles around was carpeted in floating pumice, and neighbouring islands coated in volcanic debris. These, however, were merely the immediate consequences of an eruption that – for reasons not understood until the later twentieth century – was to bring hardship, hunger and death to people all around the planet.[31]

When Tambora exploded many millions of tons of dust and sulphur dioxide were propelled upwards into the stratosphere. There both dust and gas – the latter transformed gradually into minuscule droplets of sulphuric acid – began to be dispersed across the world. The net effect, as 1815 gave way to 1816, was to produce global cooling on a scale sufficient to cause hugely disruptive changes in weather patterns. For complex reasons, those were more marked in some areas than in others. This, in turn, meant that consequent crop failures – though occurring widely – were concentrated in particular localities. In India the Tambora-related disappearance of 1816's monsoon rains brought famine to Bengal. In Tibet where there were unprecedented July snows, and in China's Yunnan province where August frosts devastated rice crops, low summer temperatures caused similar mass starvation. In the north-eastern United States previously unheard-of meteorological phenomena such as June blizzards and repeated summer frosts came close to wrecking what, in that region at that time, was still a predominantly agricultural economy. In much of southern and western Europe the cold, sunless and often wet weather of 1816 – recalled long after as 'the year without a summer' – impacted equally severely on farming of all kinds.

Such was the scale of crop losses in southern Germany and Switzerland that by the early part of 1817 bread prices there had quadrupled. In those countries, as well as in Italy, France, the Netherlands and elsewhere, governments, local authorities and private charities responded to the threat of famine and to the reality of widespread food riots, beggary and destitution by doling out emergency supplies in order to avert more complete social breakdown.[32]

Nor did the British Isles escape. In Ireland, prolonged rain, harvest failures and an associated typhus epidemic caused much loss of life. In England, crop losses, soaring food costs and consequent disorder – in both countryside and towns – resulted in a Poor Employment Act being rushed through parliament with a view to providing income-creating public works. North of the border, in the Scottish Lowlands, conditions were equally grim. Noting that 'for several months past the foreign journals [had] been almost filled with lamentable accounts of . . . the severe and tempestuous weather' affecting mainland Europe and North America, the Scots Magazine of August 1816 went on to lament the prevalence of thunderstorms, hail, gales and unseasonable cold nearer home. In mid-April, follow-ing heavy and persistent snow, 'the whole country around Edinburgh [had] assumed the aspect of mid-winter'. In mid-May, hills within view of the Scottish capital remained snow-covered. In June, July and August, the 'long continuance of cold [and] rainy weather' resulted in 'a later season than almost ever known'. September, 'which might have been deemed a species of winter', brought no improvement. As in much of the rest of the northern hemisphere, cereal and potato yields were exceptionally low. Food costs, it followed, were high and rising, making the 1816–17 winter, which started with widespread November snowfalls, an especially bleak one for more vulnerable sectors of Scotland's urban population. 'The year 1816 closed bitterly for the poor,' wrote Henry Cockburn, one of the lawyers who had defended Patrick Sellar. 'There probably never were so many people destitute at one time in Edinburgh.'[33]

In Strathbrora, Strathnaver and the Strath of Kildonan, mean-while, 'Eighteen Hundred and Froze to Death', as Americans dubbed

1816, brought difficulties that – though by no means as severe as those affecting places like Ireland, Switzerland or Yunnan – were more acute than anyone in Sutherland could easily recall. People across the north of Scotland, George MacPherson Grant commented in late autumn, confronted 'truly gloomy' prospects, 'for there is still a great proportion of their corn [meaning oats and barley] out [in the open], both cut and uncut, and the potato crop has almost been destroyed by the frost'. Days later, plummeting temperatures had been followed by a mid-November blizzard so intense as to destroy any hope of salvaging grain that remained unharvested. 'The snow is in many places so deep', it was reported, 'that a man can scarcely travel and the corn [still in the fields] is not to be seen.'[34]

Like cattle-rearing pastoralists everywhere, inland Sutherland's pre-clearance farmers were more cushioned from the impact of bad seasons than were occupiers of land given over primarily to arable agriculture. Especially prior to the (mid-nineteenth-century) advent of mechanical reapers and the (much later) appearance of combine harvesters, cereals of all kinds were very vulnerable to prolonged wet weather. Potatoes, while less affected by rain, could readily be lost – as happened widely in 1816 – to summer and early autumn frosts. But cattle, though prone to dying in substantial numbers in long winters when fodder was scarce, could readily come through even the most dreadful summer. Thus it came about that cattle-owning families of the sort who had long accounted for the bulk of the Sutherland interior's population – and who looked to milk, cheese, butter and other dairy products for a good deal of their nutritional requirements – were in principle better equipped than their low-country (and crop-reliant) counterparts to survive 1816's Tambora-induced climatic downturn.

By 1816, however, none of the Sutherland straths were as they had been in the cattle economy's heyday – many of the Strath of Kildonan's leading livestock breeders, to cite just one instance of what had changed, having left for Red River. Both in Kildonan and in neighbouring localities, moreover, extensive hill pastures of the sort on which Highland-style cattle-rearing relied had been lost to sheep farmers like Thomas Houston and William Clunes (in Kildonan), Gabriel Reed (in Kildonan and Strathbrora), John Cleugh (just off Strathbrora), Adam Atkinson and Anthony Marshall (on the southern borders of Strathnaver), and Patrick Sellar (further down Strathnaver). Total cattle numbers, then, were in decline. So were cash returns on beasts put up for sale, livestock prices, high throughout the years of Franco–British conflict, having collapsed (as would happen again after the First World War) when peace was restored and imports once more became available.

Aggravating the effects of pasture losses and price falls was the impact of clearance. In 1816, as would remain the case for another three or four years, removals – thanks to the 1813 uprising in Kildonan and to James Loch's fears of further such resistance – had not been as far-reaching as William Young had planned. A number of townships had nevertheless been emptied on the sheep farms occupied by Atkinson and Marshall, Houston, Cleugh and Sellar. All too often, as both George MacPherson Grant and James Loch observed, this had resulted not (as 'improvement' theory demanded) in movement to the coast but in evicted families, together with their livestock, being 'crowded into' remaining inland settlements, thus putting additional pressure on already shrunken hill grazings as well as on other resources.[35]

The combined effect of all of this – reduced access to pasture-land, increased congestion and plunging prices – was to turn Tambora-related problems that would have anyway occurred into something much more serious. But from James Loch's perspective, if not from that of families running short of food, this was not so much a crisis as an opportunity to manipulate events in ways that helped him bring to fruition the sweeping clearances he began to plan (as will shortly be seen) during the exceptionally cold – and, for many people, hungry – winter of 1816–17.

To help Stafford tenants in Sutherland get through that winter, Loch authorised the purchase, at Sutherland Estate expense, of

substantial supplies of oatmeal. This, he said, was in accordance
with the 'humane and considerate' management philosophy to
which Lord and Lady Stafford were committed. Oatmeal distribu-
tion, however, was undertaken with less charitable aims in view. 'It
[was] an object of some moment', Loch decreed, 'to make the people
[still clinging on in the straths] feel the inconvenience of their present situation.' For this reason, 'a coast side settler' – meaning
someone who had already quit the interior – was 'to be relieved [or
aided] in preference to a hill [or inland] inhabitant'. 'It [was] not
intended [moreover] to bestow any . . . aid gratuitously': 'Let money
be obtained for [meal] in all instances where [this] is possible,' Loch
instructed. Where cash was unforthcoming, he continued, recipients
of assistance were to 'labour' for no money wages on estate construction projects.[36]

But if Loch was committed to obtaining, as it were, a pound of
flesh in return for each pound of meal doled out by Sutherland
Estate employees, he was equally determined to get into circulation
– and have accepted – his interpretation of what it was that had
made such measures necessary. Predictably, this interpretation took
no account of the extent to which the 1816–17 crisis in Sutherland
was a local manifestation of a much wider calamity. Nor did Loch
acknowledge that the land-use changes imposed over the preceding
ten or so years had made it much harder for people living in the
Sutherland Estate's inland valleys to cope with the effects of bad
weather. That was because James Loch was now intent on removing
those people in their entirety, and still more intent on portraying
clearance as a 'necessary' means of 'prevent[ing] the recurrence' of
the 'misery and wretchedness' which, Loch implied, would otherwise be characteristic of the Sutherland interior for all time coming.[37]

In Strathnaver the near-famine of early 1817 resulted in a 'very bad'
outbreak of typhus, which lingered into 1819. Otherwise Sutherland's
1816–17 difficulties proved transient. The 1817 harvest was much
better than its predecessor, while the next year's resulted in what

Sutherland's Church of Scotland clergy, when announcing the dates of thanksgiving services, called 'a very abundant crop . . . safely got in'. This, however, was a harvest unlikely to have brought much gratification to the men, women and children who, that autumn, carried home oats, barley and potatoes from rigs of the sort still being cultivated, at that point, in most parts of Strathbrora, Strathnaver and the Strath of Kildonan. The crops yielded by such rigs in September and October 1818 might have been, as reported, 'most luxurious' and 'uncommonly fine'. But those same crops, as everyone involved in their ingathering well knew, were also the last that would be grown in and around inland communities James Loch had by then earmarked for destruction.[38]

He was appreciative of her wish to press ahead with further 'removals', Loch informed the Marchioness of Stafford in November 1816. But he nevertheless counselled caution. Public opinion 'as well as the feelings of government' – feelings made clear to Loch in the course of his dealings with the lord advocate – were such, the commissioner thought, as to make it essential to get the Sutherland Estate's interior population 'out of the hills gradually'. The more he considered the mechanics of clearance, however, the more Loch became convinced that, though evictions should not be undertaken hastily, neither should they be strung out over a period. It would be a mistake, he wrote, 'to remove a certain portion of the people' in each of several years, not least because sheep-farming tenants, as Loch had come to realise, were more likely to be attracted to farms that had been depopulated in advance of their leases commencing. 'It was determined therefore', Loch commented, 'that the whole of the removals would be completed in the month of May of the years 1819 and 1820 respectively.'[39]

On it becoming apparent that James Loch was now set on having 'the great bulk' of the Sutherland Estate's interior population gone by Whitsun 1819, and on having the remainder moved out a year later, the estate's sheep-farming tenants gave him every possible support. Their motivations varied. Some, most notably Patrick

Sellar, scented expansionary opportunities. Others, such as Gabriel Reed, wanted simply to be assured that they would at last be rid of settlements surviving inside, or adjacent to, the boundaries of farms already in their possession.[40]

When, in the wake of the 1813 protests in the Strath of Kildonan, it had been agreed to suspend evictions scheduled for May that year, the several townships at the Kildonan, or northern, end of Reed's Kilcalmkill farm had not been cleared as promised. This, to Reed, was a source of aggravation. 'I left them [the uncleared townships' occupants] in my farm at the request of your Ladyship's men of business,' Kilcalmkill's tenant complained to the Marchioness of Stafford. 'The first year, I gave to each family the use of their houses with a cow and a calf's keep [meaning access to such pasture as was needed by those animals] for which they paid me 30 [shillings] each, about half its value. The two following years, I let them the place of Borrobol at a rent less . . . than I pay [for that same place] to your Ladyship.' Since Borrobol, in the upper part of the Strath of Kildonan, included substantial hill grazings, Gabriel Reed's subten-ants – as uncleared families on his farm now were – must have managed to hang on to some at least of their cattle for as long as this arrangement lasted. It ended, however, in 1816. That year, Reed remarked of his subtenants, 'I removed them'.[41]

The sheep-farming fraternity's wish to be rid of people Patrick Sellar called 'aborigines' was bound up with a conviction that those same people were contributing to stock losses, which, by 1816, were reckoned to amount to more than 1,500 animals annu-ally. Some of these losses, it was agreed, were attributable to predation by eagles, foxes and other 'vermin'. That is why Sutherland's sheep farmers collectively offered bounties to killers of such predators. One pound (more than many labourers then earned in a month) was paid 'for the head and talons of each full-grown eagle', five shillings 'for the egg of an eagle' and two pounds for 'the face and ears of a bitch fox [or vixen] with young'. The resulting slaughter – intensified by the inclusion of lots of other

birds and mammals in the bounty scheme – was on a scale sufficient to ensure that some species were driven to (or, in the case of
sea eagles and red kites, beyond) the edge of extinction. In just 20
months between August 1819 and March 1821, it was reported, the
overall tally included '112 fully-grown eagles [golden and sea
eagles were not differentiated], 18 young eagles, 211 foxes, 317
wildcats, [pine] martens and polecats, 516 ravens, 281 hawks
[including, presumably, red kites and hen harriers], 1,183 carrion
crows and magpies, and 570 rooks and jackdaws'. This, from a
sheep-farming perspective, was gratifying. Still more pleasing to
men like Gabriel Reed and Patrick Sellar, however, was the prospect of the Sutherland straths being cleared of human beings every
bit as comprehensively as they were being cleared of wildlife.[42]

'The aborigines', Patrick Sellar grumbled in 1817, 'draw . . . a
full rent.' This, he went on, consisted of the 'several hundred
pounds a year' he lost to people who – having intruded on to his
Rhiloisk farm from other, still populated, parts of Strathnaver –
stole his sheep. That Sellar's Rhiloisk flocks had indeed been
depleted was agreed by John MacKay, the ex-military man who
became the Strathnaver district's subfactor in the wake of James
Loch's reorganisation of Sutherland Estate administration.
However, MacKay – whom Donald Sage, no lover of factors, called
'warm-hearted' – told Loch that most Rhiloisk losses resulted, in
fact, from carelessness, even thievery, on the part of Sellar's shepherds. 'I owe it to my own character . . . to state these facts,' MacKay
commented. But Loch, while not questioning the accuracy of what
his subordinate had to say, was in no way swayed by John MacKay's
defence of people MacKay – who himself belonged to a Strathnaver
family – regarded much more positively than Loch ever would.[*] As
long as sheep farms remained 'intermixed with or flanked by' townships of the traditional sort, Loch argued, shepherds would

---

* Perhaps unsurprisingly, given his background and opinions, MacKay soon gave up
his factoring role and emigrated to North America.

continue 'to screen' their 'negligence and knavery' by shifting blame
for stock losses on to the inhabitants of those townships. From this
perspective, then, the shepherding profession's supposed delin-
quencies were simply one more reason for terminating the existence
of virtually all of Sutherland's inland settlements. When shepherds
were thereby deprived of cover for wrongdoing, Loch argued, 'stock
farmer[s]' would at last be able 'to make [them] responsible for the
. . . sheep committed to their charge'.[43]

Hence the soothing tone of Loch's response to Anthony Marshall
when, in December 1817, Marshall contacted Loch about the latter's
plans for Mudale, a settlement on the northern fringes of his and
Adam Atkinson's sheep farm. Mudale, Marshall alleged, was home
to a number of sheep-stealers and the clearances Loch was contemplating, the sheep farmer warned, could 'never be considered
complete' if the township's occupants, as Marshall had heard might
happen, were spared eviction. Marshall's concerns were laid immediately to rest. Mudale's inhabitants, James Loch assured him,
would be gone by Whitsun 1819.[44]

The clearances scheduled for 1819 and 1820 were on an unprecedented scale. When Patrick Sellar began clearing Rhiloisk in June
1814, he evicted 29 families. By the summer of 1818, however, James
Loch was committed, or so he calculated with his usual precision, to
the removal of 704 families in 1819 – with a further 419 to follow in
1820. This meant that, in the course of those two years, something
like 5,500 people* – women, men, children – were to be ordered out
of their homes.[45]

Notices to that effect began to be issued as much as two years
prior to the successive Whitsuns of 1819 and 1820. This lengthy
timescale was meant to help the Sutherland Estate's local management team, headed now by Francis Suther, to avoid mistakes of the

---

* Some of those people were resident in Assynt. However, a large majority of them
lived in eastern Sutherland.

sort Loch thought had been made by William Young. Lady Stafford was of like mind. The difficulties that culminated in Patrick Sellar's trial, she commented in October 1817, had arisen from 'Sellar getting the lease [of Rhiloisk] before all was arranged, which led to his driving [out] the people harshly and prematurely, and [thus] gave an opening to all the trouble which followed'. It was imperative, therefore, that 'sufficient time' be taken to work out exactly how to handle the new – and far more extensive – round of evictions now in prospect. These, Loch replied, were 'wise' words that would be taken fully on board. 'Your Ladyship may rest assured', he continued, 'that nothing shall be done hurriedly or without full consideration . . . I have a very clear and distinct notion of the way in which I think . . . [removals] should be carried into effect.'[46]

Soon Suther and his colleagues were hard at work earmarking areas – on Sutherland's north and east coasts – where evicted families could be installed on newly demarcated crofts. Heads of family, Loch instructed, were to be given the opportunity to select particular crofts from among those on offer – the total might be 30, 40 or more – in the locality to which they had been directed. Individuals who chose crofts 'without delay', Loch further ruled, were to have arrears of rent 'forgiven' and were, in addition, to 'hold their [former] farms, during the last year of their occupation, rent free'. 'The sacrifice is considerable', Loch noted of the estate income thus forgone, 'but it is well worth the object' – this 'object' being to encourage families to start cultivating crofts well in advance of the ending of their previous tenancies. That, in turn, would avoid the risk of anyone laying claim, as had happened in the aftermath of Sellar's Rhiloisk evictions, to crops growing on landholdings they had earlier vacated. Individuals to whom coastal crofts were offered during 1818, say, would have no reason, in the spring of 1819, to sow or plant inland rigs which, that same year, would be incorporated into sheep farms.[47]

When first drawn up in James Loch's London home at 106 Great Russell Street, those procedures seemed straightforward. However, when Francis Suther tried – as he did repeatedly in the spring of 1818 – to put Loch's commands into practice, almost nothing of what Loch intended was achieved. On Tuesday 21 April, Suther informed Loch, he rode from Golspie to Brora to meet people – of whom there were very many – already under orders to quit, by Whitsun the following year, the part of Strathbrora about to be let (as noted earlier) to James Hall. Suther's intention was to give those people the chance to pick out crofts for themselves in various spots on Brora's outskirts. As the factor reported, however, 'not more than half a dozen [men] made their appearance'; all refused to give their names; and none evinced interest in the crofts pointed out to them. Nor did Suther fare any better when, in the course of the following week, he 'went three times' to the several locations around Helmsdale where families from the Strath of Kildonan were supposedly to settle. On the first of his three days in the Helmsdale area, the factor stated in a rueful letter to Loch, 'one man came and took a lot [or croft]'. On the two following days, in the course of which only two men turned up, absolutely nothing by way of croft allocation was accomplished.[48]

Loch afterwards attributed blame for all such reversals to his favoured scapegoats – unidentified agitators and intriguers who, for their own 'selfish purposes', had persuaded families facing eviction that, 'by hold[ing] out to the last', they might force the Marquis and Marchioness of Stafford 'to abandon their arrangements'. In fact, and as had been the case ever since William Young tried and failed to get Kildonan tenants to take north coast crofts in 1813, families threatened with removal could see no good reason – proffered rent abatements and other inducements notwithstanding – to comply willingly with the Sutherland Estate's plans for them. Crofting townships, as compared with interior communities scheduled for destruction, had little in the way of hill grazings. Their component crofts, as laid out by Francis Suther and his subordinates, were invariably small – three, four or five acres at most. Nor were those acres readily cultivable. This was because Loch, as he told Suther, had 'always been against giving good arable land to the settlers', on the basis that relocated families should, wherever possible, be forced into non-agricultural occupations. Hence the tendency to place such families on ground of the kind Suther made available (with consequences described earlier) at the Doll near Brora – ground consisting mostly, in that instance, of stony moorland.[49]

Crofters, besides, were to have no leases. In inland localities it had been common for tenants (especially those rearing stock on a substantial scale) to be granted land for fixed, and reasonably lengthy, periods. However, it was Lady Stafford's wish, or so Loch commented, that 'all the settlers [in crofting townships like the Doll] should . . . [be] tenants at will'. Relocated families, in other words, were to be denied the smallest vestige of security of tenure, which is why Francis Suther was able in 1820 to tell crofters at the Doll that, if they did not press ahead with breaking in the miserably poor land assigned to them, they would be evicted from their new crofts in much the same way as, less than a year previously, they had been turned out of their former possessions in Strathbrora.[50]

On its becoming apparent to James Loch that it was going to be hard to make people do what he wanted, Loch turned for help to Sutherland's Church of Scotland ministers. Those men, as Loch well knew, were mostly eager to oblige the Staffords, with whom they got regular opportunities to meet and socialise, the cordial nature of that socialising being evident from the marchioness's correspondence from Dunrobin. 'I have been passing the pleasantest [evening] I have had since I came [north]', Lady Stafford reported to her husband in August 1815, 'with Mr Sage [of Kildonan] and [George] Gordon [minister of the neighbouring parish of Loth] . . . I am much pleased with . . . Sage [who] has a great wish to see you [again], and to see you drink a glass of whisky . . . which he says you like[d] better than any other spirit . . . [when] in his house at Kildonan. He [Sage] is a very cheerful man and is to write an account of our northern antiquities for me.'[51]

When exactly Alexander Sage and the Marquis of Stafford shared a dram – consisting, presumably, of a gill or two of the illicit whisky the minister bought from John Sutherland – is unclear. Nor is it known if Sage's promised paper on Sutherland's past was delivered. What can be established is that the various other clerics wined and dined at Dunrobin that same summer included Farr's minister, David MacKenzie, by whom Lady Stafford (as noted previously) was much impressed and to whom she had no hesitation in writing when, in May 1816, she felt that MacKenzie's Strathnaver parishioners – certainly those who had given evidence at Patrick Sellar's trial – needed bringing to heel. MacKenzie, who had already been obliged to beg Patrick Sellar's forgiveness for such small aid as he had given the Strathnaver rebels, was now ordered by the marchioness to impress on his congregation 'the necessity of their remaining quiet . . . and conforming with a due spirit of order and submission to the law'. She and Lord Stafford, the marchioness went on, were 'determined on the most decided pursuance of the plans laid down for the benefit of . . . [their] estate . . . Those who are disposed to disturb the public quiet', the marchioness warned, 'will be the first to reap the effects of such ill-judged and useless resistance to measures they cannot defeat.'[52]

Writing to Alexander Sage, the marchioness was equally explicit: 'I request that you should make it known by all possible means that it is our firm determination to persevere in our plans . . . [No] foolish or factious opposition will be of the least avail.' Unavoidable 'ruin', Lady Stafford continued, lay in store for anyone 'who may from weakness and ignorance be led into thinking they can reap any benefit from opposition either to the laws of the country or to the plans . . . we have laid down.'[53]

Sage, MacKenzie and the other clerics to whom Lady Stafford mailed similar instructions appear to have done much as directed. Hence Alexander Sutherland's dismissive treatment of his native county's ministers in the *Military Register*. Hence too the even more impassioned anticlericalism evident in the writings of a man who (though the two are unlikely to have been in contact) was to follow where Alexander Sutherland had led.

This was Donald MacLeod, who was raised in the Strathnaver township of Rossal. Incorporated into Patrick Sellar's Rhiloisk sheep farm in 1814, Rossal was not affected directly by the evictions that led to Sellar's trial. However, the township, along with other remaining settlements on Rhiloisk, was cleared shortly thereafter, at which point MacLeod moved to a coastal township that is today a part of Bettyhill. There, in January 1818, MacLeod, a stonemason to trade, married Jane Gordon who, according to her husband, was to suffer terribly when, in his absence, she and the couple's small children were evicted in retribution, or so MacLeod alleged, for his having failed to 'hold [his] peace' when confronted with the 'oppression and injustice prevailing around [him]'. This episode – which her husband believed to have 'made fatal inroads' on Jane's physical and mental well-being – took place more than ten years after the wholesale clearances of the 1819–20 period. But it accounts both for Donald MacLeod's decision to quit Sutherland and for a good deal of the sheer fury evident in the series of articles the stonemason, who has been described as 'a born journalist', then published in the *Edinburgh Chronicle*, his aim, MacLeod wrote, being to expose the 'thraldom and subjugation' imposed on places like Strathnaver by their 'ruthless and tyrannical' landlords.[54]

Other than the Staffords and their factors, the group who attract most opprobrium in Donald MacLeod's published output are the clergy: 'The oppressors always appealed to them for sanction and justification and were not disappointed. The foulest deeds were glossed over, and all the evil which could not be attributed to the natives themselves, such as severe seasons, famine and consequent disease,* was by those pious gentlemen ascribed to providence, as a punishment for sin. They had always the ear and confidence of the

---

* MacLeod would have seen something at first hand of the post-1817 typhus outbreak in Strathnaver.

proprietors, and I put it to their consciences to say how often, if ever, they exerted their influence in favour of the oppressed.'[55]

Perhaps the extreme example of the sort of clergyman MacLeod had in mind was Walter Ross, one of the two men who, by way of demonstrating their solidarity with Patrick Sellar, had sat alongside the factor throughout his 1816 trial. Minister of Clyne, the parish that included Strathbrora, Ross appears to have devoted next to no time to his parochial duties. He reared and traded in cattle, renting in this connection an extensive tract of land not far from Ascoilemore, the township with which this book began. For a period, Ross served as factor at Balnagown, one of Easter Ross's landed properties, and he was in close contact not just with Sellar but, as their correspondence shows, with Sutherland Estate managers generally. 'His private character', Donald Sage wrote caustically of Walter Ross, 'had no moral weight, for not only was his conversation light, worldly and profane, but it was characterised by exaggeration and absolute untruthfulness.'[56]

Sage's father, Alexander, as it happens, was the one cleric Donald MacLeod exempted from his strictures. As is evident from a surviving letter from Sage senior to his son, Kildonan's minister was certainly critical in private of the clearance – more or less total by 1820 – of his parish. Nor was he afraid to do things, on occasion, of which Sutherland Estate managers disapproved, as when he assisted the Earl of Selkirk to identify prospective emigrants. Actions of that sort help explain why Francis Suther believed Sage to be 'more against the removings' than 'any of' his fellow clerics. But judging by the Marchioness of Stafford's accounts of their dealings, it is improbable that Alexander Sage shared his anti-eviction opinions with her. It is equally improbable that he denounced either clearances or their perpetrators from his Kildonan pulpit; Sage, like most Presbyterian ministers of his time, adhered to a theology that placed stress on it being the duty of Christians to obey, and submit to, all secular authority.[57]

Given the nature of this theology, or so some present-day commentators have contended, it was unreasonable of Donald

MacLeod – and of subsequent authors who took their lead from MacLeod's writings – to have expected Sutherland's ministers to condemn or resist a landed class described by MacLeod as 'desolators of my country and extirpators of my race'. From the Strathnaver stonemason's perspective, however, clerical conduct was rooted less in religious belief than in material advantage. 'Their subserviency to the factors', MacLeod wrote of the ministers he so detested, 'was not for nought. Besides getting their hill pasture enclosed, their tillage lands were extended, new manses and offices . . . built for them . . . and every arrangement made for their advantage. They basked in the sunshine of favour . . . and had the honour of occasional visits, at their manses, from the proprietors themselves.'[58]

Church records from the clearance era do nothing to undermine Donald MacLeod's case: clearances feature in those records only when, as happened in the Strath of Kildonan in 1813, a newly created sheep farm impinged in some way on church property. This episode involved the farm taken over by Major William Clunes, who immediately prior to his being targeted by Kildonan's 'rioters' spent an evening (as recounted earlier) in Alexander Sage's manse. While Sage may or may not have counselled his parishioners to submit quietly to eviction orders issued in connection with the establishment of the farm his guest had come to inspect, it is certain that Sage was in no way minded to accept the loss of land he farmed himself. The land in question, or so Sage argued in a petition he presented to the Presbytery of Dornoch, consisted of hill pastures that from 'time immemorial' had been available to Kildonan ministers. A substantial part of those pastures, it appears, had been leased – whether intentionally or by accident is unclear – to William Clunes. He looked to his co-presbyters, Sage said, 'to defend' him from all such 'incroachments' and, meanwhile, to endorse his decision to take 'the liberty' of 'pasturing . . . his cattle' over 'these [same] grounds'. Taking the view that the Sutherland Estate had subjected Sage to 'great privations which would render his situation most uncomfortable', the presbytery gave Kildonan's minister its full support. Within days, estate managers – in a manner suggestive of what might have happened had the church stood behind congregations as steadfastly as it stood behind ministers – were signalling their willingness to negotiate. Sage, Patrick Sellar reported, had agreed to a deal whereby 60 of Clunes's sheep, though managed at Clunes's expense, would be treated as the minister's own. In addition, such lower ground as remained in Sage's occupation was not only to be protected from future incursion but considerably extended.[59]

It is ironic that Alexander Sage, whom Donald MacLeod held in high regard, should have behaved in 1813 in ways that seem decidedly selfish. It is still more ironic that David MacKenzie, MacLeod's own minister and a man the stonemason despised, should have been the one Sutherland clergyman, so far as is known, to have taken issue with James Loch about the dispossessions planned for 1819 and 1820.

Donald MacLeod's dealings with Farr's minister had been such as to leave the stonemason angry and embittered. When coping with the crisis that left his wife's health so badly impaired, MacLeod had asked David MacKenzie for a 'certificate of moral character', something the stonemason thought would help him counter Sutherland Estate accusations of his having engaged in deliberate trouble-making. MacKenzie, according to MacLeod, at first consented to this request. However, the minister, or so MacLeod alleged, was then subjected to pressure from one of James Loch's under-managers with the result that the desired certificate was, in the end, withheld.

MacLeod's account of MacKenzie's behaviour acquires greater credibility than it might otherwise possess because of its according exactly – though the stonemason appears to have been unaware of this – with the way MacKenzie (someone whose moral courage came and went with remarkable rapidity) had treated requests for identical 'certificates' from people about to give evidence for the prosecution at Patrick Sellar's trial. On that occasion, the minister had caved in to Sellar's bullying of him and refused to sign any such documents. In MacLeod's case, he seems to have yielded in much the same manner to another Sutherland Estate factor. From this factor, MacKenzie informed MacLeod, he had learned that the stonemason had 'told falsehoods of [him]'. That was why the desired certificate would not be forthcoming. 'Donald,' runs MacLeod's rendering of the minister's next remark, 'I would favour you on your father's account, and much more on your father-in-law's account, but after what you have said of me, I cannot.'[60]

Just as the stonemason's father, William MacLeod, had been evicted from Rossal, so his father-in-law, Charles Gordon, a Strathnaver catechist whom Donald Sage regarded as a person of unswerving Christian principle, had been evicted from Rivigill, another of the townships cleared in 1814 by Patrick Sellar. Both men had died prior to Donald MacLeod's encounter with David MacKenzie. But their memory was treasured by MacLeod, and it enraged the stonemason to have MacKenzie compare him so adversely to them: 'I repelled the charge of being a liar, and said, "I do believe that if my father and father-in-law . . . stood at the gate of heaven, seeking admittance, and nothing to prevent them but a false accusation on the part of some . . . factors, you would join in refusing their entrance to all eternity."'[61]

Because of the personal animosity he felt for David MacKenzie, it was inevitable that Donald MacLeod's account of the minister's response to clearances should have been a long way short of flattering. It was 'generally reported' of MacKenzie, MacLeod commented in the course of one of his contributions to the *Edinburgh Chronicle*, that 'there was a letter sent [to the minister's Farr Manse] from the proprietors [meaning the Staffords] . . . requesting to know if removed tenants were well provided for . . . and that the answer was that . . . people were quite comfortable in their new allotments, and that the change was greatly for their benefit'.[62]

This was by no means wide of the mark, in that David MacKenzie, when in Lady Stafford's company at Dunrobin in 1815, had indeed advised her (as noted earlier) that all was well with the families Patrick Sellar had removed from Rhiloisk the year before. That fact, together with MacKenzie's subsequent kowtowing to Sellar, makes it all the more surprising that Farr's minister, in March 1818, should have responded with such marked hostility to a letter in which James Loch both outlined the scale of projected clearance in Strathnaver and sought the minister's help in ensuring compliance with his plans.

'You must be fully aware', Loch informed David MacKenzie, 'that, in contemplating those changes, the welfare of the people has never been lost sight of, as you will know that no proprietors consider more anxiously the happiness of those placed under them than Lord and Lady Stafford do.' MacKenzie, Loch stressed, was 'to point out to [his parishioners] the very favourable terms upon which their removal [was to be] accomplished . . . You will also, at the same time assure them that the measure has been too well considered not to be fully acted upon and too well arranged not to be carried into effect.'[63]

He had complied with these demands, MacKenzie told Loch, by 'showing [the Stafford commissioner's letter] to some, [by] reading it to others, and by satisfying the enquiries of many who only understand the Gaelic language . . . [But] I beg leave to be excused from giving any assurance to the people of the [intended] change being so much for their advantage as you anticipate.' How to account for this unlooked-for (certainly by James Loch) rebelliousness on the Farr minister's part? One part of the explanation surely lies in MacKenzie's father-in-law – rather like Donald MacLeod's – having become a casualty of the tenurial upheavals Loch was forcing through.[64]

This was Robert Gordon of Langdale whose daughter (and only child) Barbara – described by Donald Sage as 'a very shy, pretty, young woman' – had married David MacKenzie in 1815. Barbara's elderly father – whom Sage thought 'a kind old man' – was then, as he had been for many years, tacksman of Langdale, the farm Patrick

Sellar had come close to bidding for in 1813. At Langdale, according to Donald Sage, Gordon lived much as tacksmen of the old style had always lived: 'His house, a rustic cottage, stood on a fairy-like knowe, on the banks of the Naver, and was freely open to all comers of every rank. His farm was parcelled out among a number of subtenants, to whom he granted every indulgence.'[65]

Some of those subtenants (who may have included Donald MacLeod's future father-in-law) were refugees from clearances elsewhere – if not those taking place on Sellar's Rhiloisk farm (separated from Langdale only by the River Naver) then those moved out of the high country east and south of Loch Naver following the 1807 establishment of Adam Atkinson and Anthony Marshall's sheep farm. By providing for such refugees, Robert Gordon, in Donald Sage's estimation, was acting benevolently. Predictably, however, James Loch and Francis Suther took a dimmer view. Gordon, Loch commented, had refused to dispose of his subtenants – as his lease required him to do – and had determinedly 'stuck to . . . old [ways] in lieu of adopting the new'. Suther agreed. 'He has nothing', the factor reported of a visibly impoverished Robert Gordon, 'and his subtenants, who are much in arrear[s] to him, can pay nothing. They are miserably poor.' Patrick Sellar, unsurprisingly, was scathing. Langdale, he informed the Marchioness of Stafford, had 'been filled up . . . with people from all quarters'. Those people – whom Sellar held responsible for many of his stock losses – should be removed forthwith and Langdale, like Rhiloisk, put under sheep. This would most effectively be done, Sellar felt, by himself. Robert Gordon's mounting financial difficulties, and his consequent inability to pay his rent, ought to result, Patrick Sellar thought, in Gordon being obliged to give up Langdale, for which he, Sellar, would be happy to make the sort of offer he had so nearly made when, at the Golspie sett some four years previously, he had bid instead for Rhiloisk.[66]

This represented something of an about-turn on Sellar's part. Not long before, in the autumn of 1816, he had responded to falling wool and livestock prices – and perhaps to that year's dreadful weather – by trying to extricate himself from his Rhiloisk tenancy with a view, he explained, to his concentrating instead on Culmaily. Advised by George MacPherson Grant that it 'would be a very bad precedent . . . to allow anyone to give up his farm from the moment he tires of it,' James Loch turned down this request. Nor were Sellar's attempts to hang on to his factorship beyond May 1817, when he was due to lose it, any more successful. Loch, who regretted that he had retained Sellar's factorial services for as long as he had done, was 'very decidedly against' any such concession and advised Lady Stafford accordingly.[67]

Sellar's 1816 efforts to keep up his income (from his factoring post) and to reduce his outgoings (by relinquishing his Rhiloisk lease) are likely to have originated in pressures stemming both from heavy stock acquisition costs (in connection with Rhiloisk) and the equally heavy expenditure he had incurred as a result of his having hired top-flight Edinburgh lawyers to defend him at the High Court. But by the late summer of 1817, when Sellar began to look covetously in the direction of Langdale, those pressures had eased, not least because of the substantial inheritance that came Sellar's way on his father's death that July.

This upturn in Sellar's fortunes coincided with his becoming engaged to Anne Craig, William Young's niece. His engagement, in Sellar's view, made it essential that prior to his marriage, which took place in 1818, he should acquire a more substantial home than the Culmaily farmhouse in which he had lived since coming to Sutherland. Just such a home was on offer at Morvich. Situated in the lower reaches of Strathfleet, a valley opening on to the sea some three or four miles south of Golspie, Morvich farm – which Patrick Sellar now determined to have – marched (or bordered) with Culmaily. Like Culmaily, Morvich was an essentially arable unit. But unlike Culmaily it possessed a very grand house. Completed in 1812, this house had been intended by the Marquis of Stafford to provide him and the marchioness with an occasional alternative to Dunrobin Castle. However, on its becoming clear that Lord

Stafford's deteriorating health would henceforth prevent him making prolonged trips north, it was decided in 1817 that the Staffords' projected summer home, together with several hundred acres of adjacent farmland, should be made available for lease. 'The house and offices of Morvich', the ensuing advertisement proclaimed, 'are entirely new . . . affording a superior residence for any stock farmer of respectability and capital.' This was true. Its dining room, sitting room, family room, 'writing office', kitchen, pantry, several bedrooms, 'linen room', cellar and 'water-closet' made Morvich House, as the building became known, one of the most up-to-date and prestigious homes in the early nineteenth-century Highlands. And because, as James Loch remarked a little snidely, 'no other man could afford it', Sellar succeeded in renting Morvich relatively cheaply. He was soon to acquire Langdale on an equally favourable basis.[68]

At Langdale, as 1817 turned into 1818, Robert Gordon's position had become untenable. With his rent heavily in arrears and his lease conditions – not least the requirement to rid his farm of subtenants – unfulfilled, Gordon, in return for his debts to the Sutherland Estate being written off, agreed to quit Langdale at Whitsun 1818. On this becoming known, Sellar at once made clear that he was 'most anxious' to have the tenancy of Gordon's former tack – now to be let as a sheep farm – in addition to that of Morvich. Loch, however, was less than enthused by such a prospect. 'I would infinitely [prefer to] have another tenant,' he told Francis Suther. 'I cannot yet say', the commissioner informed Sellar himself in October 1818, 'whether you shall have it [Langdale] or not. [But] I must say my opinion is you *ought not*, as you have enough already.'[69]

As James Loch was well aware, it was not good management practice to permit a single tenant to be as dominant as Sellar now aspired to become. However, Loch, to his evident chagrin, had little alternative but to give Sellar what he wanted. The times were bad agriculturally. Even before the incessant rain, snow and frost of 1816–17, the post-war slump in prices had left hundreds of farms across Scotland without tenants, and rents were everywhere being cut back. Nor had press reports of the unrest generated by the expansion of sheep farming on the Sutherland Estate made it any easier to persuade southern sheep men to take an interest in Langdale or in anywhere else the estate had to offer. Knowing this, Patrick Sellar was convinced – Loch's discouraging noises notwithstanding – that Langdale was destined to be his. 'I am sure', he wrote, 'that Langdale will one day be a part of the farm [of Rhiloisk] . . . because nature meant it so.' So it proved. In December 1818, Loch and Suther concluded that their attempts to get 'a rival to Sellar' had failed. Sellar was to have not just Langdale but the entire western half of Strathnaver from the head of Loch Naver to the River Naver's mouth, a distance, on present-day roads, of about 25 miles. His lease stipulated, moreover, that by the time this huge tract of territory was due to be handed over to him in May 1819, the Sutherland Estate would have ensured that most of it was cleared of its previous occupiers.[70]

'Sellar', George MacPherson Grant commented, 'is universally understood to have an amazing bargain of his new farms.' But if this was a cause of celebration at Morvich House, where Patrick Sellar installed his bride just two weeks prior to his Langdale victory, there must have been corresponding despondency at Farr Manse where Robert Gordon had, by this point, been obliged to move in with his daughter and her husband, David MacKenzie. Not only had the minister witnessed the humiliation and near-bankruptcy of his father-in-law, a man who had for decades been a leading figure in Strathnaver, he had also come close, in consequence of his father-in-law's difficulties, to being ruined himself. At around the time of his marriage to Barbara Gordon, MacKenzie – recklessly but maybe unavoidably – had agreed to stand surety for Barbara's father's rent arrears. On those mounting dangerously, as they soon did, MacKenzie's stipend or salary (payable, as noted previously, by the Sutherland Estate) was stopped on James Loch's instructions, the sums in question, presumably, being set against Robert Gordon's debts in estate accounts. When Gordon's arrears were subsequently cancelled, David MacKenzie's stipend again came through as before. But it is not hard to see why, in those circumstances, the minister should have responded so negatively when Loch asked him to tell Strathnaver's inhabitants that their imminent removal was being undertaken solely with a view to promoting their betterment.[71]

'The mere process of removing . . . people from . . . Strathnaver to the sea coast', MacKenzie maintained, would do nothing to 'ameliorate' their prospects. Nor was it the case, as Loch was inclined to insist, that coastal communities had fared much better in the wake of 1816's harvest failure than their inland counterparts. 'Let me assure you as a positive fact', MacKenzie wrote, 'that the calamities of last year [by which he meant the first part of 1817] were as general, and as severely felt, among inhabitants of the sea coast as . . . [among people living in Strathnaver's] upper parts.'[72]

Many of the north-coast districts where Loch intended to resettle Strathnaver's population, MacKenzie pointed out, were already 'thoroughly inhabited'. It had thus been difficult to find space even for the comparatively small group 'sent down from the heights' when Sellar cleared Rhiloisk. '[H]ow [a] great addition to their number can live comfortably', he could 'not perceive': 'The lands on the coast are not very extensive; neither are they . . . calculated to give good returns; the surface of the ground is extremely rugged and incapable of improvement to any great extent.' It followed that no small croft established on such land could possibly meet the nutritional needs of its occupants: 'From what I have heard of the quantity of land [to be allocated to individual settlers] according to the new arrangements, it will not produce of corn what will support their families for half the year.'

This made it all the more imperative that relocated families were in a position to look to non-agricultural sources of income. Despite contrary claims from advocates of 'improvement', MacKenzie felt, such sources were entirely lacking, and likely to remain so. In the absence of what the minister called 'traffic' (meaning trade) and 'industry', there would, he forecast, be little 'opportunity of earning money by day labour'.

Nor was there much chance of north-coast crofters making a go of the sort of fishery Sutherland Estate managers were urging them to develop: 'The coast is remarkably bald and rocky, the landing places few, and some of them far from being safe.' Families moved to that coast from Strathnaver would, to begin with, be 'totally ignorant of seafaring'. Most of them, moreover, lacked the capital required to 'furnish themselves with boats and fishing implements'. On the north coast, in short, 'a comfortable living' would be every bit as difficult to win from the sea as from the land. 'From this persuasion', Farr's minister told James Loch, 'I cannot attempt to convince the people that the change [about to be imposed on them] will be for their advantage.'

As had happened in 1813, when Alexander Sutherland published similar criticisms of 'improvement' in the columns of *The Star*, neither Loch nor his colleagues made any detailed response to David MacKenzie's critique of their pro-clearance strategy; Loch confined himself to reiterating that he was 'convinced of the necessity of what [he had] advised'. This silence is telling. The statements made by Sutherland in 1813 and by MacKenzie five years later were of a sort that 'improvers', if the case for clearance was as robust as they claimed, should have been able easily to refute. The fact that no convincing refutations were forthcoming is a pointer to Sutherland and MacKenzie having had a better grasp than its backers of where 'improvement' was likely, in the end, to lead. When, 65 years later, an official inquiry was mounted into post-clearance conditions in what had been David MacKenzie's parish, its findings (as will be seen) confirmed the validity of everything the minister had to say in his 1818 letter to James Loch.[73]

12

'THE YEAR OF THE BURNINGS'

The mass evictions of 1819 and their repercussions

On a Sunday at the start of May 1819, just days before James Loch's long-planned clearances were due to begin, Donald Sage conducted a last service in Strathnaver. Sage had moved there four years previously to take up his first ecclesiastical post, as 'missionary' preacher at Achness where, on account of Strathnaver's parish church being in faraway Bettyhill, a subsidiary church had been built to cater for people who would otherwise have found it impossible to get to a place of worship. This Achness church – at which Patrick Sellar had sought out William Chisholm immediately prior to the burning of Chisholm's Badinloskin home – was, according to Sage, 'woefully dilapidated' on his arrival. Nor, despite some subsequent repairs, was it much improved in the course of Sage's tenure. Loch was unwilling to sanction Sutherland Estate expenditure on a building that would, he observed in 1817, 'become unnecessary' when the population it served was moved to the coast. 'The walls were built of stone and clay,' Donald Sage wrote of Achness's church, 'the roof covered with divot [turf] and straw, and the seats were forms set at random . . . on the damp floor.'[1]

Despite those disadvantages, Sage, who completed his ministerial training when still a teenager and then drifted from one teaching or tutoring job to another, was pleased to be in Achness. The house provided for him was as rudimentary as his church. But he furnished it after a fashion with 'a bed and bedding, a carpet and some chairs' he bought when Sheriff Robert McKid – whose children Sage had taught – sold up at Kirkton. Other items were begged or borrowed from his father's Kildonan manse; and in 1816 Sage and his older sister Elizabeth, who took on the role of the newly appointed minister's housekeeper, set up home in a spot that commanded (as is evident from a present-day visit) extensive views of Strathnaver and its northward-flowing river.[2]

Here in 1818 Donald Sage – 'in common with the rest of my people', he commented – took delivery of one of the hundreds of removal notices then being distributed in the Sutherland interior. Sage did not await the arrival of an evicting party. Some months before the date set for his dispossession, he sold the cow that had provided him and Elizabeth with milk, and courtesy of a team of horses belonging to his father, moved his 'few' books and other belongings to Kildonan. This was no desertion of his post, however. Until the spring of 1819 Sage rode regularly into Strathnaver by way of the moorland separating Achness from the Strath of Kildonan's upper reaches. He was thus able (for as long as he retained a congregation) to 'continue the punctual discharge of [his] pastoral duties', the final such duty being the pre-clearance service Donald Sage thought one of 'the bitterest and most overwhelming experiences' of his life.[3]

This service took place not at Achness but further down the strath at Langdale. It was there – Langdale, it seems, having been a long-established meeting place – that the 93rd Regiment had mustered 19 years earlier. As then, lots of people thronged a spot Sage described as 'a beautiful green sward' adjacent to 'the still-flowing waters of the Naver'. But now there was none of the hustle and bustle of that previous occasion. Weighing on everyone present, as Sage's account makes clear, was a bleak realisation that they were about to be deprived forcibly of their homes. Equally distressing was the knowledge that families who had neighboured for as long as they could recall would, on quitting Strathnaver, 'never again . . . behold each other in the land of the living'. Some such families, to be sure, were shortly to find themselves in the same crofting settlements on Sutherland's north coast. But 'many', Strathnaver's subfactor John MacKay reported to Loch, had taken farms in Caithness, while others had chosen, MacKay added, to go 'south'. 'It was indeed the place of parting', Sage wrote, 'and the hour.'[4]

Seated 'right opposite' Donald Sage that morning at Langdale was a man in his nineties – a man Sage knew as 'Old Achoul'. 'As my eye fell upon his venerable countenance,' the minister recalled, 'I was deeply affected, and could scarcely articulate the psalm.' That was not simply because Sage, over the preceding three or four years, had become close to his elderly* parishioner – though he had. In what was being done to Old Achoul in the name of what James Loch considered 'improvement' and Sage labelled a 'system of oppression', the young clergyman saw something emblematic of 'the extinction', as he wrote, 'of the last remnant of the ancient Highland peasantry of the north'.[5]

In some accounts of the Sutherland clearances, and certainly in what was written about the clearances by their organisers, this peasantry – to stick with Donald Sage's term – is presented as an undifferentiated collection of half-starved, moneyless, hopeless and nameless men and women. That is to misunderstand, in all sorts of ways, localities like pre-clearance Strathnaver. For not only did those localities contain (as already stressed) people who were by no means poor, they also possessed a social structure characterised by deeply felt distinctions deriving from a clan-based society that, until its surviving features were given the *coup de grâce* by clearance, had not wholly withered away. Hence the significance of Old Achoul. More than anyone else in Donald Sage's congregation, his standing – a standing his fellow worshippers at Langdale would have been well

---

* In the published version of Sage's account of the Langdale service, Achoul is said to have lived through 'eighty-seven winters'. But this is at odds both with Sage's comment, a few pages earlier, that Achoul had been 18 at the time of the Jacobite Rebellion of 1745–46 and with a newspaper obituary that gives Achoul's age, at the time of his death in 1822, as 99.

aware of – was the product of a time far removed from the one that had conjured up the concept of 'improvement'.

In clanship's heyday, from the fourteenth century to the sixteenth, the dominant families in and around Strathnaver were MacKays. In the seventeenth century and subsequently, those families lost ground – in all senses of that phrase – to the Earls of Sutherland and their Gordon kinsfolk. But despite those reverses, something of the earlier ruling order's status continued to cling to its surviving representatives. Prominent among this group was Old Achoul, otherwise William MacKay. His ancestry – in Gaelic his *sloinneadh* – was traceable, through 400 years, to his clan's founder. The farm on which he lived for the greater part of his life – the farm that provided him with the territorial designation of Achoul – had been occupied by this same clan for just about as long. In 1807, however, that farm, on Loch Naver's south-eastern shore, had been let by the Marquis and Marchioness of Stafford – along with most of the rest of the hill country between Loch Naver and Loch Shin – to Adam Atkinson and Anthony Marshall. When ordered out of Achoul to make way for Marshall and Atkinson's sheep, William MacKay and his wife Janet had moved across Loch Naver to Grumbeg where their daughter and son-in-law were among that township's tenants. But now Grumbeg, along with all the other communities on Loch Naver's western shore and on the west bank of the River Naver from the loch down to the sea, was also to be cleared, this time for Patrick Sellar's benefit. At the Langdale service of April 1819, then, Donald Sage, on finding himself in close proximity to William MacKay, must surely have wondered what could sensibly be said to comfort a man who – for all his great age and for all his deep roots in Strathnaver – was about to lose his home for a second time. It is not surprising that, faced by such a circumstance, Sage was overcome by his emotions.[6]

On getting news of their impending removal, William MacKay, his daughter and son-in-law rejected – like lots more Strathnaver families – all thought of taking one of the diminutive crofts on offer from the Sutherland Estate. Instead they quit Sutherland entirely and rented a farm at Achairn, some six or seven miles on the inland side of the Caithness fishing port of Wick. By early nineteenth-century standards, it was a lengthy journey from Grumbeg to Achairn. This journey, however, was one that Janet MacKay, William of Achoul's wife, was not called on to make, her death having occurred at some point in the run-up to her and her husband's departure from Strathnaver. 'Well Janet', Achoul was heard to say as his wife's coffin was lowered into the ground at the graveyard still to be seen beside the ruins of Donald Sage's Achness church, 'the Countess of Sutherland [as the marchioness was always known to her Highland tenantry] can never flit [move] you any more.'[7]

The countess, however, retained – and in 1819 would exercise – the power to flit thousands of others. Among them were the hundreds who, on what Donald Sage remembered as an 'unusually fine . . . Sabbath morning', gathered around the temporary platform customarily put in place for ministers at occasions like Sage's Langdale service. His 'preparations for the pulpit', Sage wrote, 'always cost [him] much anxiety'. But the prospect of his having to cope with 'this sore scene of parting' brought him 'pain almost beyond endurance': 'I selected a text which had a pointed reference to the peculiarity of our circumstances, but my difficulty was how to restrain my feelings until I should illustrate and enforce the great truths which it involved . . . I preached and the people listened, but every sentence uttered and heard was in opposition to the tide of our natural feelings which, setting in against us, mounted at every step of our progress higher and higher. At last all restraints were compelled to give way. The preacher ceased to speak, the people to listen. All lifted up their voices and wept.'[8]

'People', Donald Sage commented of the ejection process, 'received the legal warning to leave forever the homes of their fathers with a sort of stupor . . . As they began, however, to awaken from the stunning effects of this first intimation, their feelings found vent, and I was much struck with the different ways in which they expressed their sentiments. The truly pious acknowledged the mighty hand of God in the matter. In their prayers and religious conferences not a solitary expression could be heard indicative of anger or vindictiveness, but in the sight of God they humbled themselves, and received the chastisement at His hand.'[9]

While clear as to the wickedness of what was being inflicted on Strathnaver's population, then, Sage was also of the theological persuasion that held it to be one's Christian duty to make no gesture of resistance to clearance. It was this sort of outlook – even when uncontaminated (as in Sage's case) by self-interest – that so maddened the Rossal stonemason Donald MacLeod. The 'anger' and 'vindictiveness' deplored by Sage were, from MacLeod's perspective, perfectly proper responses to the prospect of mass evictions. Nor, despite much clerical emphasis on 'submission', were such feelings ever absent from the pre-clearance scene. That is why James Loch, in a November 1818 circular to Sutherland's ministers, instructed them to tell their parishioners 'once more' that evictions should in no way be opposed and that no one 'should be so inconsiderate as to believe that the intentions with regard to [removals] are not to be carried strictly into effect'.[10]

The locality that both Loch and Francis Suther considered most likely to give trouble was Strathbrora. Some Strathnaver families, Loch commented, had 'settled in their new lots [or crofts] at Strathy', a coastal area to the east of Bettyhill, as early as May 1818. While it is improbable that the people concerned moved north, as Loch insisted, 'with the utmost cheerfulness', it was nevertheless the case that those families – perhaps because of their knowing what happened to the men who pressed most determinedly for Patrick Sellar to be tried – had accepted the inevitability of clearance. It was otherwise in Strathbrora. There it was not until March and April 1819, with the scheduled emptying of much of the strath no more than a month or two away, that Suther was able to report substantial numbers 'coming forward to take lots'. This was not accompanied, however, by any significant movement to the crofts in question – most of them in newly laid-out crofting townships like the Doll. Having met with Suther and put their names down for particular holdings, most Strathbrora men at once rejoined their wives and children in inland townships that were, in consequence, still populated when, on Thursday 6 May 1819, evicting parties set to work.[11]

'I am informed there is an intention to resist the removings in Strathbrora,' Francis Suther noted at the end of April. This was being encouraged, the factor went on, by Colonel Alexander Sutherland, earlier levered out of Culmaily to make way for Patrick Sellar. Following his loss of that farm, Sutherland had retreated, as it were, to Braegrudie, a much less desirable holding at the top end of Strathbrora. The now very elderly Sutherland, in Suther's opinion, was 'getting a little feebleminded' – a 'weakness . . . most apparent', Suther thought, 'in the childish grief' Braegrudie's tacksman showed when meeting with people about to be evicted. But feebleminded or not, Alexander Sutherland, or so the factor considered, remained capable of fomenting unrest. 'The colonel is a decided enemy to the sheep system of farming', Suther wrote, 'and indeed to all improvements that are conducive to strip the interior of the country of its population.' While it was unlikely, in the factor's opinion, that either Alexander Sutherland or anyone else would mount a serious rebellion in Strathbrora, he had resolved, Suther told Loch, to accompany evicting parties into the strath 'in case of force being in any instance necessary'.[12]

Despite Francis Suther's presence, the Strathbrora evictions of May 1819 were formally conducted by Sutherland's procurator fiscal James Brander. Employed at one stage by Patrick Sellar whose clerk or secretary he had been during Sellar's factorship, Brander now combined the role of fiscal with that of a lawyer in private practice. This enabled him to act locally for the Marquis and Marchioness of Stafford while also, in his capacity as a supposedly independent prosecutor, putting alleged lawbreakers (some of them charged at Sutherland Estate instigation) on trial in Dornoch's sheriff court. It was to this court Francis Suther had turned for the eviction warrants Brander had been given the job of enforcing on behalf of Sheriff Charles Ross in whose name, or that of Sheriff-Substitute John Law, those warrants had been issued. Formerly, such enforcement had been left to estate factors. But this had changed on account of James Loch (in a further instance of the extent to which the Sutherland justice system and Sutherland Estate management now overlapped) having instructed Ross (not long after the latter's Loch-engineered appointment) to ensure that his court 'execute [its] own warrants' with a view to avoiding, Loch explained, 'an invidious and improper duty [falling] on . . . [any Sutherland Estate] factor'.[13]

While meaningful to Loch, it is doubtful if distinctions of this sort registered in Strathbrora. There squads of sheriff-officers and constables, technically answerable to Brander, worked alongside men in Sutherland Estate employment. Among the second group was Andrew Ross, a Golspie joiner or carpenter whose task it was to place a value on the timber components of houses earmarked for destruction. Crucks or couples obtained from estate woodlands belonged in law to landlords. But smaller timbers, such as roof planking, doors and doorframes, were considered to be the property of a home's tenant, and had, therefore, to be compensated for. Given the nature of his connection with the Sutherland Estate, Andrew Ross – who did the same job for Patrick Sellar at Rhiloisk in 1814 and who afterwards testified on Sellar's behalf at the latter's trial – is unlikely to have been generous when making the valuations that became the basis of compensation offers to evicted families. Nor were the sums he came up with paid in full. Since clearances were expensive – Brander, for instance, being entitled to a guinea a day and constables to four shillings – and since all such expenses were chargeable to the Sutherland Estate, Francis Suther felt himself entitled to deduct from the cash due to each dispossessed tenant an amount equivalent to the cost of carrying out that same tenant's dispossession. By this means, as the press was shortly to point out, evicted families were left with no alternative but to pay, in effect, for their own eviction.[14]

Treatment of this sort added one more cause of resentment to a situation already replete with such causes. It is unsurprising therefore that, by Saturday 8 May, 'a spirit of determined resistance' was said to be evident in Strathbrora. That afternoon some 'forty persons from the lower part of the strath' – people whose homes had already been dismantled – gathered in the valley's upper reaches. This crowd, according to Suther, was 'resolutely bent on stopping the progress of the [evicting] party had they got . . . that length that evening'. In the event, a potentially explosive confrontation was avoided as a result of James Brander's decision to suspend operations until Sunday – then a generally observed day of rest – had passed. But if that was a point in Brander's favour, it was more than negated by the way he and Suther chose to deal with the non-violent, but highly effective, opposition they encountered from the moment of their starting to demolish the homes they had come to Strathbrora to destroy.[15]

What typically happened, Suther reported, was that families delayed 'tak[ing] their furniture out of their houses . . . [until] aware of the [evicting] party's approach.' Homes thus vacated 'were then demolished to prevent their being taken possession of again', their occupants having 'hung on', as Suther put it, with a view to doing just that. But no matter how comprehensively a house was taken apart, Suther explained, its key components were necessarily left where they fell. This meant that, especially during the hours of darkness, people were able to return to settlements that had theoretically been emptied and there begin the reconstruction of their homes. 'This [Brander] put a stop to', Suther commented, 'by burning the empty houses.' Had those 'strong measures not been taken', the factor went on, it would have been impossible to clear the straths in time to give sheep farmers the vacant possession they had been promised. 'Burning the timber was a step rendered absolutely necessary by the apparent fixed determination of many not to move.'[16]

Such was people's reluctance to quit their homes, Suther wrote, that they were seen on occasion to be 'busy rebuilding' with scraps of timber not 'consumed' when their homes were first set ablaze, a problem that appears to have been solved by a second round of conflagrations. Nor was it the case that cattle, despite evicted families' assurances to the contrary, were got 'off the ground' scheduled for clearance. Instead cattle herds were 'driven out of sight when the evicting party appeared', being retrieved as soon as James Brander, his constables and sheriff-officers had moved on. In the Sciberscross area of Strathbrora, Suther added, by way of underlining why he and Brander considered themselves to have had no option but to act as they did, the 'ground [had been] fairly cleared' in advance of James Hall, the locality's newly installed sheep farmer, taking possession. At Hall's 'own request', however, houses at Sciberscross 'were not burned but levelled'. 'Many are again built, and [Hall] is burning them as he finds clemency in that respect will no longer do.'[17]

In London that May, James Loch was encouraged, to begin with, by the tenor of despatches from the north. Writing from Strathnaver, that district's subfactor, John MacKay, reported that the 'removal of the people' had been 'completed . . . in the quietest manner and with very little trouble'. Initial correspondence from Francis Suther was equally reassuring. Brander and his men had dealt with the Strathbrora 'removings' in under a week, the factor wrote. 'They are [now] gone up the Blackwater [a River Brora tributary] to Kildonan.' Matters there were expected to proceed smoothly. 'The business may be said to be finished.'[18]

Loch 'instantly carried' those letters to the marquis and marchioness to whom he read their contents. It had given Lord and Lady Stafford 'much pleasure', Loch informed one of his Scottish contacts, that 'extensive removals' had been carried out in 'so creditable' a manner. 'To me personally', the Stafford commissioner continued, '[this] is a source of much satisfaction for . . . I hold myself responsible entirely for the measure.'[19]

Then came word as to what had actually occurred. 'I learn with much regret', Loch wrote to Suther, 'that the constables . . . have

burnt the people's houses, a measure I thought would never have
been acceded to after the well founded complaints which this
conduct on the part of Mr Sellar created. I can see no necessity for
such a measure having been resorted to . . . [I]t will give a character
to the proceedings . . . of harshness and severity . . . It has, I understand, created an extensive and, I must confess, well founded
animadversion.' That was most certainly so.[20]

Returning to Strathnaver, days after the valley's clearance, Donald
Sage was appalled by what he saw. 'The spectacle presented', Sage
wrote later, 'was hideous and ghastly. The banks of the lake [mean-
ing Loch Naver] and the river, formerly studded with cottages, now
met the eye as a scene of desolation. On all the houses, the thatched
roofs were gone; but the walls, built of alternate layers of turf and
stone, remained. The flames of the preceding week still slumbered in
the ruins, and sent up into the air spiral columns of smoke; whilst
here a gable and there a long side wall, undermined by the fire, might
be seen tumbling to the ground . . . The sooty rafters of the cottages,
as they were being consumed, filled the air with a heavy and most
offensive odour.'[21]

The Strathnaver evictions, Sage wrote, were the work of 'a strong
body of constables, sheriff-officers and others' who had commenced
'the campaign of burning' at Grummore, a substantial township on
Loch Naver's western shore. This can be confirmed from Sutherland
Estate sources. At Grummore, according to Francis Suther's careful
tallies, 27 families were turned out of their homes. They were
followed by 12 families from Grumbeg, another lochside settlement
a little further north and the place where William and Janet MacKay
had settled when expelled from Achoul. Grumbeg was long-established: present-day archaeological investigations there have
uncovered traces of Bronze Age habitation as well as the site of a
graveyard containing a number of early Christian headstones. Now,
in the space of just a few hours in May 1819, this community – occupying a spot where people had lived for at least 1,000 (and probably
2,000–3,000) years – was snuffed out. 'Their plan of operations',

Donald Sage commented of the men responsible for the destruction of Grumbeg and Grummore, 'was to clear the cottages of their inmates, giving them about half an hour to pack up and carry off their furniture . . . [prior to setting] the cottages on fire.'[22]

Among members of his Achness congregation who thus lost their homes, Sage went on, was a widow, Henrietta or Henny Munro. When younger, as was then common practice, she had followed her soldier husband to war, accompanying his regiment (not the 93rd but some other unit) to Spain where British troops were first deployed against France's occupying forces in 1808. Her husband (whose name is not recorded) having been killed in action or having died from disease, Henrietta had come home to Grumbeg where friends and neighbours had 'built her a small cottage and [given] her a cow'. 'She was a joyous, cheery old creature', Donald Sage recalled of Henny Munro; much given to 'unceasing' talk of 'orders and counter-orders . . . marchings and counter-marchings . . . pitched battles, retreats and advances'. Everyone who 'got acquainted with old Henny Munro', Sage wrote, 'could only desire to do her a good turn were it merely for the warm . . . expressions of gratitude with which it was received.' The men comprising the Strathnaver evicting party of May 1819, however, were not disposed to be kind, whether to this Grumbeg widow or anyone else.[23]

On realising that her home was about to be set on fire, 'Henny', or so Donald Sage was informed, 'plead[ed] for her furniture – the coarsest and most valueless that could well be but still her earthly all. She first asked that, as her neighbours were so occupied with their own furniture, hers might be allowed to remain until they should be free to remove it for her. This request was curtly refused. She then besought [the evicting party] to allow a shepherd, who was present and offered his services for that purpose, to remove the furniture to his own residence on the opposite shore of [Loch Naver], to remain there till she could carry it away. This also was refused, and she was told with an oath that, if she did not take her trumpery off within half an hour, it would be burned. The poor widow [then]

. . . address[ed] herself to the work of dragging her chests, beds, presses [or cupboards] and stools out at the door, and placing them at the gable of her cottage. No sooner was her task accomplished than the torch was applied. The widow's hut, built of very combustible material, speedily ignited, and there rose up rapidly . . . a bright red flame. The wind unfortunately blew in the direction of [Henny's] furniture, and the flame, lighting upon [the widow's belongings] speedily reduced [them] to ashes.'[24]

Would James Brander or Francis Suther have countenanced cruelty of the sort Donald Sage described? Possibly not. But they (being busy in Strathbrora and Kildonan) were not present in Strathnaver; and, not just at Grumbeg but more generally, there appears to have been a tendency, on the part of some individuals involved in enforcing evictions, to set aside everyday decencies and to take a depraved kind of pleasure in imposing gratuitous suffering. Firmly in this latter category, or so Sutherland's population long insisted, was Donald Bannerman, the sheriff-officer and constable who had been much involved in efforts to crush the 1813 uprising in the Strath of Kildonan and who was equally to the fore throughout the 1819 clearances. In Gaelic, Bannerman came to be known as *Domhnall Sgios*, a designation implying that the destruction he caused was (literally) hellish in both scale and intensity. As late as the 1890s, even the 1950s, it would be possible to hear Sutherland people speak with loathing of the manner in which Bannerman and his 'fire brigade' torched house after house after house.[25]

The spring of 1819, as it happened, had brought, in Francis Suther's words, 'a long continuance of cold, dry weather with [an] easterly wind'. Those conditions – common in the Highlands at that time of year – would have had the effect of rendering thatch highly flammable. Equally quick to ignite would have been the 'bog fir' boards holding roofs in place. Bog fir splinters burned so brightly that they were used customarily as candles. Heavier timbers of the same resin-soaked material, on being set ablaze, would thus have generated heat sufficiently intense to cause even turf walls

– especially when dried out, as would have been the case, by sun and wind – to smoulder and smoke in the way Donald Sage reported. Nor would houses have been fired one at a time. At Grummore, the better part of 30 homes, together with all sorts of outbuildings, are likely to have had flames leaping more or less simultaneously from their roofs. The resulting spectacle – redolent of the sort of brute force normally given free rein only in times of war – must have been both terrifying and dispiriting.[26]

Well over 200 families – comprising nearly 1,300 men, women and children – were driven from their Strathnaver homes in May 1819; and what people saw of those evictions would stay with them always. In 1883, a lifetime after the clearances, members of the royal commission then enquiring into crofting conditions took evidence from an Edinburgh resident, John MacKay, a man well into his eighties. MacKay, who left Sutherland when not much more than 20 and whose working life was spent laying cobbled roads and pavements in the Scottish capital, had been brought up in Dalhorrisgle, a small township in the lower part of Strathnaver. 'I mind of my father's house being burned', John MacKay told the 1883 commission's chairman Lord Napier, 'and [the] four [other] houses that were in the place . . . I witnessed the five houses in flames, which really grieved me.'[27]

If accounts of the 1819 clearances had circulated only in the Highlands, James Loch would not have been greatly concerned. What worried him was coverage of the Sutherland evictions in the southern press. There the story was confined initially to the *Military Register*, where Alexander Sutherland, alerted as early as mid-May to 'the burning system being revived', was soon informing readers that 'the whole estate of Sutherland' had become 'a scene of extensive conflagration'. But the *Register* – 'to our agreeable surprise', its editor remarked – quickly found itself just one among many newspapers giving space to what an *Observer* headline called the 'devastation of Sutherland'.[28]

When the Marquis and Marchioness of Stafford set out 'to transform . . . [their] property in the county of Sutherland into one immense sheep farm', the *Observer* reported on 2 August, 'it became necessary to proceed to a kind of expatriation of the inhabitants . . . Many hundreds of dwellings were then committed to the flames'.[29]

This was simply to follow where others, notably *The Scotsman* and *The Times*, had led. June and July stories, copied from one of those papers to the other, told of how 'a posse of men . . . are parading the county of Sutherland and ejecting the poor Highlanders from the homes of their fathers. A valuation is put upon their property; a proportion of the expense is retained, the balance is paid over to the occupier; and his humble dwelling – in which he has gone through the various stages of life and which is endeared to him by a thousand ties and circumstances – is set fire to, and consumed to ashes, before the eyes of himself, his wife and helpless family . . . [Sutherland] is beginning to wear a depopulated and ruinous aspect.'[30]

The Marchioness of Stafford, always sensitive to adverse press coverage of Sutherland Estate affairs, found comment of this kind upsetting. 'We have lately been much attacked in the newspapers,' she lamented in a letter to a friend. 'What is stated is most perfectly unjust.'[31]

James Loch was, if anything, more distressed. 'You have no idea the sensation the story of the burnings [has] made,' Loch informed Francis Suther whom he held responsible for what had occurred. 'The way I feel it personally is that, by one act of improvidence, we have reduced our management to a level with all those that have gone before it . . . [T]he impression is as bad as in Sellar's time, and all the thought, arrangement and management which I have bestowed in the last two years . . . and which I had fondly hoped was to make my administration of Sutherland affairs valued by the public has been thus cast away.'[32]

Neither from Loch nor from the Stafford camp more generally, however, was there any public admission of error or wrongdoing. In a series of letters to senior politicians, Loch condemned press accounts of Sutherland developments as 'the grossest misrepresentations'. Sutherland Estate managers, he wrote, were 'incapable of doing any deliberate act of harshness or unkindness'. The same point was made to journalists and to newspaper proprietors. One of Loch's friends, a man close to *Times* owner John Walter, was asked to 'assure [Walter] on the word of a gentleman' that there was 'not one word of truth' in reports to the effect that the Stafford family's Highland tenants had been maltreated. North of the border, *Scotsman* editor John Ramsay McCulloch was given similar assurances by William MacKenzie, the Staffords' Edinburgh lawyer. McCulloch – whose 'paper [had] behaved most indecently' in James Loch's opinion – was also pressed to reveal the identity of the person or persons providing him and his staff with information about the May clearances and their aftermath. McCulloch, MacKenzie reported, refused to reveal his sources, but he did concede a right of reply to Francis Suther, who duly took the opportunity to describe *Scotsman* coverage of 'the late removals' as 'absolutely false and without foundation'.[33]

In London, meanwhile, Loch managed to have a 'Statement Respecting Improvements in Sutherland' carried by papers like *The Times* and *Morning Chronicle*. This rehearsed the now standard Loch argument that inhabitants of the Sutherland straths were being removed with a view to bettering their conditions – a contention repeated by Suther in a lengthy letter to the *Caledonian Mercury*. An overwhelming majority of evicted families had 'of their own accord quitted their huts and [taken] away their goods' in a wholly 'peaceable manner', Suther informed readers of this Edinburgh newspaper, a much more establishment-oriented publication than the then recently launched *Scotsman*. 'As to the alleged acts of oppression committed by [Sutherland] officers in the execution of their duty,' Suther wrote, 'I distinctly assert such statements to be utterly untrue.' Tales of people 'being burnt out of their huts' were 'unfounded and malicious aspersions'.[34]

But what could not be denied – because it had indubitably occurred – was that, on their being emptied, numerous homes had been set on fire. It was this that ensured that what Gaelic-speakers called *bliadhna na losgaidh*, the year of the burnings, would not readily be forgotten either in Sutherland or much further afield. The impact made by news of what had taken place on the Sutherland Estate in May 1819, Loch forecast, was 'one never to be obliterated'. He was right.[35]

Nor, more immediately, was there to be any silencing of the press. Despite the pressure brought to bear on *Times* proprietor John Walter, the paper's editor, Thomas Barnes, remained unmuzzled. Loch's protestations notwithstanding, Barnes – described by an admiring historian as 'a powerful . . . voice for reform and justice' – continued to publish stories about Sutherland. So did Barnes's *Morning Chronicle* counterpart, John Black, whose paper was then England's best-selling and arguably most influential daily. A Scot brought up by his mother after the death of his Berwickshire farm labourer father, Black was unremittingly hostile to clearances and their perpetrators. Hence this *Morning Chronicle* editorial: 'There is something at which the heart sickens in the idea of turning out the inhabitants of a great division of country to make way for sheep [in order that] a greater profit might be derived by landlords. This approaches almost to a violation of the social union by which the property of the land is allowed to be permanently occupied by certain individuals as most advantageous for the interests of the community. Here the reason for this occupancy ceases to exist, as a turning out of a whole people cannot easily be reconciled with any ideas of general good.'[36]

Doing his best to ensure ongoing press interest in Sutherland throughout the summer of 1819 and into the following winter was a man who became for a time the most formidable – and, from a Stafford perspective, most threatening – critic and opponent of Sutherland Estate policy. This was Thomas Dudgeon who, around

1800, moved from East Lothian in the Scottish Lowlands to Easter
Ross where his elder brother Archibald, whom Thomas came north
to assist, had not long before acquired a farm tenancy at Ardboll.
This locality, some six or seven miles east of Tain, is in the parish of
Tarbat, with whose minister, William Forbes, Thomas was soon
entangled in a protracted, and increasingly bitter, dispute.

This conflict, a pointer to Thomas Dudgeon's lifelong dislike of
authority in all its manifestations, began in June 1803 when Forbes
and his kirk elders were informed that Jean Purves, an unmarried
housemaid employed by Archibald Dudgeon at Ardboll, was 'with
child'. Instructed to report to Forbes's manse in order to account
for her conduct, a heavily pregnant Jean turned up in the company
of her employer's brother who, it emerged, was the father of her
child, born just a day or two later. Egged on it appears by Thomas,
Jean – instead of repenting her sins as expected – called William
Forbes 'a dirty scoundrel', proclaimed herself 'free before God and
man' and, taking Thomas by the arm, strode off unadmonished.
Nor was Jean's lover any more accommodating. Ordered 'to appear
for three Lord's Days before the [Tarbat] congregation to be publicly
rebuked', Thomas Dudgeon, on the first of the three Sundays in
question, told Forbes's parishioners – whose enthralled horror can
readily be imagined – that 'he did not consider [their minister] entitled to give him an admonition'. As for Tarbat's kirk elders, Thomas
Dudgeon added, they were 'a parcel of thieves, liars, backbiters and
hypocrites'.[37]

On his case being referred by William Forbes to the Presbytery of
Tain, Dudgeon was promptly issued with an order 'denying him all
Christian privileges' until he made amends for the 'contempt' in
which he evidently held the church. No such amends being forthcoming, the offending farmer remained at odds with the clerical
establishment until, in 1809, he asked if he might resume his church
membership. Thomas, by this point, had quit Tarbat and was farming on his own account in the nearby parish of Fearn. But before
being allowed to attend church there, it was made clear, he would

have to undergo, back in Tarbat, the three public rebukings he had refused to accept six years before. The outcome was renewed protest on Thomas Dudgeon's part. 'He read a book during all the time of preaching', runs a report of his conduct at the first of the Tarbat services he was told to attend, 'and when he stood up to be rebuked the levity of his behaviour was very offensive.' Although excommunicated all over again, Dudgeon did in the end abase himself sufficiently to enable him to have a succession of sons and daughters baptised in Fearn Parish Church. Their mother, however, was not Jean Purves* – whose pregnancy had led to Dudgeon's original brush with the Revd William Forbes – but Jane MacLeod, whom Thomas appears to have married not long after the eventual restoration of his 'Christian privileges'. Jane, it is probable, was responsible for Dudgeon's reluctant recognition of clerical jurisdiction over him. However, she was also – even if indirectly – the cause of the first of her husband's quarrels with the Sutherland Estate.[38]

When Jane MacLeod married Thomas Dudgeon, Jane's widowed mother was tenant of Morvich, the Sutherland Estate farm Patrick Sellar was to take over in 1818 and which had earlier been earmarked as the site of the Marquis and Marchioness of Stafford's projected summer home. Prior to work on that home starting, it had been necessary to buy out the remaining portion of the Morvich lease held by Jane Dudgeon's mother. From the estate management side, a sum of £300 was offered. That was refused by Morvich's occupant who, as advised in 1810 by her newly acquired son-in-law, asked for double the suggested amount. This figure, according to William Young, then the Sutherland Estate's principal factor, was 'unreasonable'. But despite being obliged finally to settle for rather less than the £600 he wanted, Dudgeon – described at the time by a reluctantly admiring Patrick Sellar as a 'man of considerable skill' – nevertheless succeeded in getting much of what he had demanded. Prior to this point, however, Young had embroiled both Dudgeon

* What happened to Jean Purves and her child is not known.

and his mother-in-law in legal proceedings that, though eventually suspended, left the Fearn farmer with a deep and enduring dislike of Sutherland Estate management methods.[39]

What James Loch called Thomas Dudgeon's 'old grievances about Morvich' may have been one reason for the farmer deciding, towards the end of May 1819, that he should set about helping the Sutherland Estate's evicted tenants 'to concentrate their interests and to act in unison'. But it was not the only such reason. Dudgeon, by his own account, both sympathised and was in contact with some of the urban groupings then pressing more and more aggressively for greater democracy, greater equality, greater social justice. His wish to aid clearance victims was bound up, then, with his politics. It owed something too, or so it can reasonably be guessed, to the devil-may-care disrespect for convention Dudgeon had shown when tangling with the Church of Scotland. Much the same delight in causing trouble was certainly in evidence when, one evening in December 1819, he got fellow members of the ultra-respectable Ross-shire Farmers Club into such an advanced state of 'intoxication' that, staggering to their feet, they toasted, at Thomas Dudgeon's urging, the then highly contentious cause of 'reform'.[40]

This led to Dudgeon's expulsion from the club on the grounds that he was guilty of 'introducing . . . dissension' to its ranks. It is probable, however, that his disbarment had less to do with the stated cause, Dudgeon's proposing of 'political toasts', than with his activities in Sutherland, where, during the preceding six months, he had succeeded in convening a succession of ever larger and, from a Sutherland Estate standpoint, ever more suspect gatherings.[41]

Those took place at Meikle Ferry, which owed its name to its being the northern terminus of the Dornoch Firth sea crossing that then had to be made by anyone looking to access Sutherland from Easter Ross. Attendance at the first such meeting, held on Saturday 12 June, was limited, consisting of what Francis Suther dismissed as 'a rabble of about fifty persons'. Proceedings, however, were clearly more orderly than Suther implied. Because of the 'hard situation' confronting 'tenants . . . removed from their farms on the Estate of Sutherland', it was resolved at this initial gathering, those present considered that it might be necessary for themselves and others 'to abandon their native country and to emigrate to [North] America'. To this end, they agreed to constitute a Sutherland and Trans-Atlantic Friendly Association, to elect Dudgeon as its president and – in order to provide the association with a modicum of funds – to subscribe, in accordance with their means, either sixpence or two shillings and sixpence apiece.[42]

Word of the new association spread quickly. Its next Meikle Ferry meeting, on 17 July, attracted, as Suther was obliged to acknowledge, around 1,000 people. A pre-prepared petition, on being put to the meeting, was signed by no less than 672 heads of family. Sent shortly afterwards to parliament in London, the petition began by making clear that the Trans-Atlantic Association, 'embrac[ing] . . . tenants removed or about to be removed' from the Sutherland Estate, would ideally like to have its members provided with landholdings elsewhere in the United Kingdom. Failing this, the association wanted the British government to grant members 'such pecuniary or other aid as may enable them to emigrate to . . . British [North] America'.[43]

Demands of this sort, not least because of their being publicised in the national press, put pressure on James Loch. Much as had happened in 1813 when Kildonan families had queued up for the Earl of Selkirk's passages to Red River, Sutherland people's apparent eagerness to take themselves overseas was conspicuously at odds with assertion after assertion, from estate management sources, that all was well in the crofting townships where evicted families had been, or were about to be, resettled.

As always, Loch poured scorn on his opponents. Attendance at Thomas Dudgeon's meetings, he wrote, was a consequence of 'the extreme ignorance and credulity' of 'poor people' who had expected Dudgeon to give them financial handouts but who were instead 'induced' to part with sixpences they could ill spare.[44]

In Sutherland assaults of this kind served mainly to enhance the standing of the Trans-Atlantic Association, which by October 1819 was reported to have 'upwards of eleven hundred' members, together with a spreading network of active backers. Prominent among those from the outset were Andrew Thomson and Adam Gibson. Thomson, whose participation helps explain the Trans-Atlantic Association's choice of meeting place, was innkeeper at Meikle Ferry. Gibson taught Latin and other languages at Tain Academy. Described by one of Loch's Ross-shire informants as a man of 'violent dispositions', this Easter Ross teacher, who had come north from Forfar, appears to have shared Dudgeon's pro-reform attitudes. He may also have had some contact with Alexander Sutherland who, despite his living in London, is known to have sent 'three of [his] family', as Sutherland put it, to Tain Academy some two years after the school's opening in 1813. Sutherland, at all events, was quick to give support to the Trans-Atlantic Association, whose founder and president was duly described as 'a man of great ability' in the *Military Register*.[45]

The *Military Register*'s pro-Dudgeon stance – together with the attendance of Alexander Sutherland's brother John, Sciberscross's ousted tacksman, at one Meikle Ferry meeting – caused Loch, Suther and other members of the Stafford camp to suspect that, in Dudgeon and his associates, they were again confronting, albeit in a different guise, the gentry-led 'combination' which, in their estimation, had earlier been behind the campaign to bring Patrick Sellar to trial. This was very much Sellar's own view. And despite its being the case that Dudgeon appears to have acted initially on his own initiative, Sellar, in detecting the hand of what he now called 'the Carrol party' in the latest outbreak of anti-clearance agitation, may have been on to something. It is certainly not difficult to establish connections between Joseph Gordon of Carrol – at loggerheads with the Marquis and Marchioness of Stafford ever since his 1812 sale to them of his Strathbrora estate – and a number of key players in the movement Thomas Dudgeon had so successfully launched in the grounds of Andrew Thomson's inn.[46]

While it may be neither here nor there that both Dudgeon and Joseph Gordon helped finance the school where Adam Gibson was employed, it is noteworthy that Gordon, as well as acting for Patrick Sellar's near-nemesis Robert McKid, acted for Sutherland of Sciberscross. If not through McKid then through the Sciberscross tacksman, it seems likely, Joseph would have been in contact with the latter's brother at the *Military Register*. Of more importance in relation to 1819 developments, however, were Joseph Gordon's links with a new Stafford bête noire, Lachlan Mackintosh, proprietor since 1814 of the *Inverness Journal*, one of the two newspapers (the other being *The Times*) Thomas Dudgeon thought most supportive of the Trans-Atlantic Association. Mackintosh, although by no means in the same league as the Staffords, was a man of considerable wealth, his acquisition of the *Journal*, together with his purchase of a substantial property at Raigmore on the outskirts of Inverness, having been funded from a fortune made in India. There Lachlan, in partnership with his brother Aeneas, had founded Mackintosh and Company, a Calcutta* trading concern in which George Gordon, Joseph's younger brother, was also a partner. This Mackintosh–Gordon entrepreneurial nexus was to be the source (as will be seen) of the cash that eventually enabled Joseph Gordon to bring about assisted emigration of the sort the Trans-Atlantic Association had been set up to promote. But of more immediate benefit to Thomas Dudgeon was the fact that – very possibly through Joseph Gordon's good offices – his association acquired in the *Inverness Journal* an endlessly obliging outlet for material critical of the Sutherland Estate.[47]

A man of distinctly liberal sympathies, Lachlan Mackintosh saw in the *Journal* a means of exposing what he regarded as the excesses of entrenched authority. A favoured target was the little clique of businessmen, lawyers and others who had for ages dominated Inverness Town Council and whose fraudulent electoral practices

---

* Present-day Kolkata.

Mackintosh was to challenge successfully in the courts. The Sutherland Estate, though more distant from Mackintosh's viewpoint than the council faction he wanted driven from office, appears to have been regarded by the *Inverness Journal*'s owner as equally in need of having its powers curtailed. Hence the extent to which Thomas Dudgeon and the Trans-Atlantic Association were able to treat Lachlan Mackintosh's paper as a sort of house magazine. 'I have been told', James Loch commented, 'that the *Inverness Journal* inserts all the statements of the Association gratis, but not to give the appearance of gross partiality, they put them into the form of [paid for] advertisements.'[48]

But if support of this kind helps account for the Trans-Atlantic Association's runaway expansion, it is by no means the sole, or even the major, explanation for the organisation's growth. More critical was the way in which Dudgeon won to his side a group of men with both the capacity and the motivation to recruit others. This group was made up of demobilised soldiers.

During the year or two following the close of a twentieth-century war, the one that ended in 1918, returning servicemen were to stake a claim to land in many parts of the Highlands and Hebrides by seizing and occupying farms illegally. In post-Waterloo circumstances, no similar attack could be mounted on a landowning class then far more dominant politically than it would be a century later. But in 1819, just as in 1919, men recently released from the military took the view, as James Loch acknowledged, that they should have 'land granted to them'. That was how clan chiefs, or so people said, rewarded their fighting men; and on the part of soldiers who had come through ordeals such as the Battle of New Orleans, there was strong feeling that they should be treated similarly. 'The fact is the 93rd [Regiment] consider the Estate of Sutherland as their property,' Loch wrote. 'They are the worst subjects the king has', he remarked of army veterans more generally, 'and by far the worst tenants any estate can be cursed with.' Hence Loch's insistence that former soldiers were not to have crofts: 'Admit none of them as tenants,' he ordered Francis Suther.[49]

Given the consequent refusal of Sutherland Estate managers to extend a helping hand to men the Marchioness of Stafford had once urged into the army, it is unsurprising that individuals in this category were among Thomas Dudgeon's most enthusiastic assistants. With lots of them drawing (then substantial) pensions of between sixpence and two shillings a day, depending on the rank they had reached and the severity of such wounds as they might have sustained, those men gave impetus to Trans-Atlantic Association recruitment drives, travelling across Sutherland at their own expense, it seems, to bring news of proceedings at the association's Meikle Ferry assemblies to localities like Strathnaver that might otherwise have heard little of those gatherings.[50]

While his ex-soldier allies – according to panicky reports reaching Suther – were urging evicted families 'to have blood for blood', Dudgeon himself was concentrating on amassing evidence of Sutherland Estate 'oppression'. At a Meikle Ferry meeting on 27 October, for example, he sought to counter press statements 'from the agents of the Stafford family', as he put it, by collecting affidavits – provided by 'twenty-two respectable men from . . . different districts' – with a view to establishing exactly how May's evicting parties had conducted themselves. By no means every locality affected by clearance was represented on that occasion, Dudgeon conceded. But sworn testimony as to the burning of 271 separate dwellings had nevertheless been amassed. The Trans-Atlantic Association, it was thus demonstrated, had become – in its increasing professionalism as well as in its growing appeal – a force to be reckoned with.[51]

An accordingly alarmed James Loch responded by giving up on his earlier dismissiveness. The Trans-Atlantic Association, he now concluded, had to be neutralised or, better still, destroyed. This, Loch decided, would most effectively be accomplished by portraying the association as a Highland manifestation of the anti-establishment forces Lord Liverpool's administration was looking to tackle by means of the repressive measures which, in the closing months of 1819, ministers were rushing through a parliament given over more and more to fear of revolution. Francis Suther and his colleagues were thus instructed to report to Loch on 'the views of those persons who attend the Meikle Ferry meetings . . . [and] to watch their motions [*sic*] narrowly'. In particular they were 'to trace any connection' between the Trans-Atlantic Association members and what Loch called 'the disturbed districts'.[52]

Especially in Britain's emerging industrial centres, there was at this point no lack of such localities. In depression-hit manufacturing towns throughout the North of England and the Scottish Central Belt, economic discontents and pro-democracy feeling had for some time been jointly fuelling demands for a range of social and political reforms. With no such reforms on offer from Lord Liverpool's government, protest had taken widely to the streets. Resulting confrontations between demonstrators and the authorities had culminated, at St Peter's Field, Manchester, in August 1819, in cavalry charging a thousands-strong crowd, killing a number of people and injuring hundreds more. Dubbed 'Peterloo', by way of ironic comparison with the army's 1815 triumph over Napoleon, this Manchester episode had the effect of convincing more radically inclined reformers that worthwhile change could be brought about only by French-style overthrow of the entire ruling order. Throughout the autumn of 1819, therefore, places like Manchester and Glasgow (the 'disturbed districts' of Loch's correspondence) were convulsed by rumours – some well founded, others not – of imminent insurrection. By ministers and their backers, it followed, social and political dissent of any kind was regarded with the profoundest suspicion. That is what made it good tactics, on James Loch's part, to insist on the 'decidedly radical' nature of the Trans-Atlantic Association.[53]

Thomas Dudgeon had all along been alive to this danger. Although personally supportive of reform, he was at pains to stress that the Trans-Atlantic Association 'disclaim[ed] . . . everything connected with party and politics and only humbly implore[d] the consideration of those able and willing to assist the indigent'. This, however, was disingenuous. Despite its name, the association had never confined itself to helping prospective emigrants find the cash they needed to finance their departure. Past clearances had been denounced. Opposition to further clearances had been mobilised. The whole basis of the Sutherland Estate's 'improvement' strategy – a strategy reliant on the notion that removals were a necessary prelude to general advancement – had been thrown starkly into question. This being the case, Loch had no great difficulty in persuading parliamentarians – few of whom were then inclined to undermine landowning interests – that both Thomas Dudgeon and the organisation he headed ought to be treated as subversive.[54]

One convert to Loch's interpretation of events in Sutherland was William Rae who, in the summer of 1819, had become lord advocate in succession to Alexander Maconochie. In a speech supportive of moves to crush extra-parliamentary opposition to the government, Rae told the House of Commons in December 'that Scotland was in an unpleasant and alarming state which rendered [such] measures . . . absolutely necessary'. The 'march of the radicals onwards to their purpose' was plainest, Rae continued, in Glasgow, Paisley and other urban locations. '[But] even the Highlands . . . had not been exempted from the infection. Taking advantage of the discontent arising from the system . . . of converting farms into sheep-walks, turbulent persons were now endeavouring to excite disaffection in the minds of the brave, gallant and loyal Highlanders, and to promote an unnatural union between them and the miserable radical reformers.'[55]

Gratified by the manner in which the lord advocate had thus 'denounced Dudgeon's proceedings', James Loch turned his attention to two more MPs, William Wilberforce and Henry Brougham. The former, though a Tory and thus a supporter of the Liverpool regime, was the independent-minded and justly famed leader of a succession of campaigns against slavery and the slave trade. He was also known to be deeply concerned about the spread, nearer home, of poverty and destitution. It was in this connection that Thomas Dudgeon had written to him about the plight of Sutherland's evicted families. Wilberforce, according to Dudgeon, had 'taken a kind interest' in the contents of this letter, to which the MP had replied, the Trans-Atlantic Association's president added, 'in the most cheering and friendly terms'. But Wilberforce, his anti-slavery stance notwithstanding, was profoundly conservative by instinct. Lobbied over a Westminster breakfast by Loch and George MacPherson Grant, a man forever anxious to do his bit for his Stafford patrons, Wilberforce – in the course of what Loch called 'a most satisfactory interview' – was easily persuaded to break off all contact with people whom Loch and MacPherson Grant doubtless described as dangerous extremists.[56]

Much the same pitch was made by Loch to Henry Brougham. Then beginning to attract attention as one of the 'coming men' among Whig opponents of Liverpool's Tory ministry, Brougham was a vociferous critic of repression in all its forms. Hence Loch's anxiety when the MP requested a meeting in order to discuss, in Brougham's words, 'your *Northern Rebellion* of which I am in the way of hearing frequent mention'. Brougham's semi-humorous tone reflected the fact that he and Loch had known each other since both had studied law at Edinburgh University. Well aware, however, that he could not rely on their friendship to prevent Brougham from making capital from Highland unrest, Loch promptly set about discrediting everything said or published in the name of the Trans-Atlantic Association. Sutherland 'never was so quiet, so happy or so wealthy'; the association's accounts of the previous May's removals were 'devoid of even [a] vestige of truth'; the organisation was run by 'persons unconnected with and resident out of' Sutherland; 'nine-tenths' of the people who had signed its petition to parliament 'did not understand English'; those people's 'ignorance' made them 'credulous'.[57]

Following a convivial dinner with the Stafford commissioner, Brougham was reassuring. 'My doubts are removed,' he told Loch. 'I hope an opportunity may occur of [my] vindicating your measures either in parliament or elsewhere . . . You know I would not even for your sake do any such thing if I had my doubts, but I really think Lord and Lady Stafford have been ill-treated.'[58]

With Brougham, Wilberforce and Rae on side, Loch felt it safe to assault the Trans-Atlantic Association more directly. He was aided, as 1819 drew to a close, by parliament's adoption of the Seditious Meetings Act – latest of the several pieces of legislation Liverpool's home secretary, Lord Sidmouth, had drafted with a view to curtailing public protest. Nothing if not draconian in scope, the Act laid down that 'no meeting of any description of persons exceeding the number of fifty . . . shall be holden for the purpose of deliberating upon any public grievance or upon . . . [any]thing relating . . . to any matter in church or state'. Penalties for non-compliance with those rulings were severe. In the case of gatherings held with a view to 'considering, proposing or agreeing to any petition, complaint . . . or address', sheriffs and Justices of the Peace were empowered to order participants in such gatherings to disperse – anyone failing to do so being liable to transportation to Botany Bay. In those provisions, Loch realised, were the means of bringing Thomas Dudgeon's activities to a halt.[59]

Dudgeon, as it happened, had made arrangements for a further Trans-Atlantic Association meeting on Tuesday 4 January 1820. Significantly, this was to take place not at Meikle Ferry as before but at Golspie where the Sutherland Estate's headquarters were located and where, seven years before, the Kildonan rebels had forced Francis Suther's predecessors to take refuge in Dunrobin Castle. Perhaps fearing that Dudgeon – though insistent in public on his 'firm attachment' to the law – aimed to stage a repetition of that episode, James Loch decided that, under the terms of the Seditious Meetings Act, the Golspie assembly should be declared illegal.[60]

To begin with, other members of the Stafford camp thought this procedurally difficult because, or so they believed, the Act would not take effect in Scotland until the day following the meeting Loch wanted banned. In correspondence with Loch, however, William MacKenzie, in his capacity as the Stafford family's principal adviser on Scots law, reckoned that it would be legitimate, even in advance of the new legislation coming into force, for Sutherland's sheriff-substitute and JPs to sign 'a notice' that, on Sunday 2 January, would be 'affix[ed] . . . on the doors' of Sutherland's parish churches, this notice to advise non-attendance at Golspie on the ensuing Tuesday. '[I]t will be proper', MacKenzie went on, 'that the magistrates who sign [the] notice should attend [at Golspie] . . . so as to be ready to disperse [any meeting] in case of tumult [or in case of] seditious language being used.'[61]

So it was arranged. On New Year's Day 1820, Robert Nimmo, who had not long before replaced John Law as Sutherland's sheriff-substitute, met with no fewer than 14 JPs – Francis Suther prominent among them – to agree the wording of the 'notice' MacKenzie had suggested. New Year's Day having fallen that year on a Saturday, copies of the resulting document were then rushed to as many Sutherland clergymen as could be reached in under 24 hours. As always, they fell into line. Even Kildonan's Alexander Sage, the minister Suther thought least likely to co-operate, was happy on this occasion to do the factor's bidding. That perhaps owed something to the fact that Jane Sage, one of Alexander's daughters, had married Tarbat's minister, William Forbes, from whom Sage is likely to have heard all about Thomas Dudgeon's earlier clashes with the church. Sage, at all events, shared with Suther the opinion that the Trans-Atlantic Association's president was a 'radical demagogue' who ought to be prevented from getting any kind of hearing.[62]

The notice circulated by Nimmo and his colleagues – its substance conveyed in Gaelic to their congregations by Alexander Sage and other ministers – was more uncompromising than William MacKenzie had advised. Dudgeon and other leading members of the Trans-Atlantic Association, it asserted, were 'men of doubtful principles' whose Golspie meeting was 'illegal'. 'We therefore consider it our duty as magistrates of this county', Sutherland's JPs and sheriff-substitute made known, 'to warn the loyal and peaceable inhabitants of this jurisdiction of the impropriety of their being participatious [*sic*] in such a meeting.'[63]

Nimmo, Suther and their colleagues were aided in their efforts by the weather. Because 'the county [was] so covered in snow', Suther reported to Loch on 2 January, travel was everywhere difficult: 'It has snowed daily for the last ten days. The mails are carried on horseback. All [mail and other] coaches are [stuck] fast in different parts of the road between Inverness and Wick'. In conditions such as those, Suther thought, it was unlikely that big numbers of people, even if inclined to disregard the warnings passed on to them by their ministers, would be able to get to Golspie on 4 January.[64]

The factor was in no mood to take chances, however. Robert Nimmo, who had been summoned to Suther's home at Rhives on Golspie's outskirts on 1 January, stayed with Suther into the next week. At Golspie, on the morning of the day members of the Trans-Atlantic Association were due to gather there, the two men presided over a further 'general meeting' of JPs, one of whom, Patrick Sellar, would have well remembered how, in February 1813, men from Kildonan had both taken over the village and defied all attempts to remove them. With a view to ensuring that, this time, the Sutherland Estate retained control of the situation, Sellar, Suther and their fellow JPs mobilised such constables as could readily reach Golspie and, in addition, swore in another 12 men – most of them estate employees – as temporary additions to this force. Those members of the Trans-Atlantic Association who made it as far as Golspie's cold and snowy main street consequently found themselves monitored closely by more than 20 regular and 'special' constables, all of them under orders 'to perambulate the village' and to report to their superiors when or if 'any assemblage of people [took] place'.[65]

Steps were also taken to warn Thomas Dudgeon, who had left his Mains of Fearn farm on Monday 3 January and spent the following night in Dornoch, that should he press on north to Golspie, he would face arrest. This was plausible. The Seditious Meetings Act made it illegal for a resident of one county (Ross-shire in Dudgeon's case) to attend a meeting (like the one planned for Golspie) in another; and Suther, Nimmo and their colleagues had by now discovered that the Act would, after all, come into force on the morning of 4 January. Understandably, therefore, Dudgeon that same morning quit Sutherland for his home in Fearn. In Golspie meanwhile, those of his followers – at least 100 and possibly more – brave enough to put in an appearance were threatened in much the same way as Dudgeon had already been. In the name of their 'sovereign lord the king', runs the pre-prepared text from which a constable now read aloud, everyone present was 'charge[d] and commande[d] . . . to depart'. What reply, if any, was made to this proclamation by the constable's hearers is not known. What is clear is that, marshalled by two pipers and marching in military formation, they shortly afterwards withdrew from Golspie as instructed.[66]

A delighted James Loch, on being informed of what had transpired, now arranged for Thomas Dudgeon to be subjected to one of the character-blackening onslaughts Loch invariably mounted against the Sutherland Estate's enemies. Loch's chosen vehicle was the *Inverness Courier*. This was a pro-establishment weekly – 'the organ of the oppressors of Sutherlandshire' according to Strathnaver stonemason Donald MacLeod – that had not long before been set up in opposition to Lachlan Mackintosh's *Inverness Journal*. Through a 'person acquainted with the [*Courier*'s] editor', Francis Suther informed a warmly approving Loch, he had 'furnish[ed]' the paper with what the factor called 'some facts' about Dudgeon. The result, towards the end of January, was the publication in the *Courier* of articles in which Thomas Dudgeon was accused of having turned the Trans-Atlantic Association into 'an engine of physical force' which might 'have done infinite mischief' if its adherents – 'inflamed by potations of whisky and the harangues of a radical reformer' – had been permitted free rein in Golspie. Nor were Dudgeon's professions of concern for Sutherland, it was implied, in any way sincere. Dudgeon was 'an East Lothian farmer whose only pretence of connexion with Sutherland [was] . . . residence in the neighbouring county of Ross'. He had set out, deliberately and with malice, 'to estrange the affections' of Sutherland's population from the Marquis of Stafford, 'a princely landlord' and 'a generous and noble-minded man'. He had done so, moreover, from wholly self-interested motives, Dudgeon's 'twopenny association' having been, from the outset, no more than a means of enriching its 'self-elected' president who, the *Courier* insinuated, had 'jobbed' or embezzled association funds.[67]

What Thomas Dudgeon called 'groundless charges' were initially treated by him, he wrote, 'with the contempt they merit[ed]'. Later he gave ground to the extent of publishing a set of Trans-Atlantic Association accounts intended to show that no part of the association's subscription income – amounting to just under £60 – had found its way into his pockets. By that point, however, it was clear to Dudgeon – who eventually emigrated with his family to the USA – that, in the circumstances created by the Seditious Meetings Act and associated legislation, there was no chance of the Trans-Atlantic Association recovering from its Golspie defeat. Not for another 60 years or more would any similar attempt be made to provide Highlanders with a subscription-based organisation capable of standing up to their landlords. Then the Highland Land League – sustained by thousands of members and operating in a less hostile political climate than the one confronting Thomas Dudgeon and his allies – would succeed in winning the legal and other protections that made further clearance impossible. But for the moment, with the Trans-Atlantic Association broken, James Loch, Francis Suther and their Stafford employers were free to proceed with a new round of clearances. This they did.[68]

13

'LAW IS ONE THING AND HUMANITY MAY BE ANOTHER'

Clearances resisted; English consequences of events in Sutherland

The elation experienced by Sutherland Estate managers in the wake of their Golspie victory over Thomas Dudgeon and his Trans-Atlantic Association was short-lived. Although the Seditious Meetings Act now made it possible both to bar Dudgeon from Sutherland and to prohibit further gatherings of the Golspie and Meikle Ferry sort, James Loch, Francis Suther and their colleagues remained anxious about the emergence of organised opposition to the new round of clearances scheduled for May 1820. Prior to the Golspie gathering of 4 January, Dudgeon's 'emissaries' (mostly ex-soldiers) had organised a series of 'kirk door meetings' where 'all the inhabitants of a parish [were] assembled' with the objective, it was reported, 'of considering the [best] way of resisting the [May] arrangements' – arrangements that would involve the removal of a further 200 or more families from the Sutherland interior. It was with a view to countering this activity that Suther, with Loch's strong encouragement, set up an intelligence network consisting of people who, in return for unspecified favours, were prepared to inform on any neighbours planning to defy eviction orders. 'You should keep up some communication in the glens,' Loch instructed the factor. 'Take care', he added, 'you trust the people you confer with.'[1]

Reliable informants were soon in place. 'I have my spies in all the parishes', Suther told Loch in mid-January. Among them (as recounted earlier) was Strathbrora's SSPCK schoolmaster, Gordon Ross. His reports are likely to have been especially valued by Suther. As in 1819, Strathbrora was reckoned the most likely focus of resistance to clearances. Ross, moreover, lived in the same Strathbrora township – Ascoilemore – as the former fur trader, Donald MacKay, whom Suther thought a leading advocate of such resistance.[2]

Francis Suther's worries about the likelihood of serious trouble in places like Strathbrora were intensified, in February and March, by anti-clearance protests at Culrain. This was a Ross-shire locality some 15 miles north-west of Tain and separated from Sutherland only by the narrow, but tidal, waters of the Kyle of Sutherland, a westward extension of the Dornoch Firth. Culrain's owner, Hugh Munro of Novar, customarily resident in London, had not long before taken full charge of properties – most of them further south – he had inherited when a child. On his deciding to let Culrain as a sheep farm and on the successful bidder being guaranteed vacant possession, it had become necessary to eject some 60 tenants, a number of them people who, prior to Hugh Munro reaching adulthood, had been permitted to set up home in Culrain in the wake of their being ordered out of their previous landholdings on the Sutherland Estate.[3]

The necessary removal notices were readily obtained from Tain Sheriff Court. Serving those notices on Culrain householders proved harder. In an echo of earlier exchanges in the Strath of Kildonan, Culrain residents reportedly informed Munro of Novar's agents that 'they would rather die' than move elsewhere; one of those agents, a Tain lawyer named John MacKenzie, noted that, during the opening weeks of 1820, he had 'heard from several quarters that [Culrain's] deluded people were resolved on offering the most determined resistance to the execution of the removings'. The Tain-based sheriff-officers whose job it would be to deliver eviction notices in Culrain had received messages, MacKenzie added, 'threatening to deprive them of their lives' if they so much as approached the community.[4]

On Monday 31 January, one of those sheriff-officers, James Stewart, was instructed 'to serve the different tenants and occupiers' in Culrain 'with citations of removal'. Because Stewart, as he said, '[had] some suspicion that [he] might meet with opposition', he took three men with him for protection. One was Andrew Ross, a constable in Tain; the others were William Munro and Andrew Tallach from the nearby township of Morangie.[5]

Stewart spent Monday night in the inn at Ardgay, about three miles short of Culrain. Tallach, Munro and Ross, however, pressed on to Culrain itself. Although the sheriff-officer was later to swear that 'he had given the most positive instructions to the three men . . . not to let any person know or understand what their objective was', this had predictable results. Munro and Tallach, who bedded down in a Culrain dramshop, may have kept quiet. Ross certainly did not. His sister, who was married to one of Culrain's tenants, lived locally, and the constable, naturally enough, spent the night in her home. On getting there, equally naturally, he was quizzed by his sister and brother-in-law, a man by the name of Urquhart, as to what had brought him and his companions from Tain. 'I suppose', Ross reported his interrogators as saying, 'these are the people [meaning Tallach and Munro] that are come with the summonses for the tenants.' In response, as the constable was afterward to admit, '[he] acknowledged that they were'. Not content with this, Ross also explained – maybe by way of distancing himself from a job he is unlikely to have welcomed – that James Stewart would shortly be arriving to take charge of operations.[6]

Stewart, unaware that word of his mission was now spreading through Culrain, left Ardgay early on Tuesday 1 February, stopping off briefly at Invercarron, one of the communities he passed through, to recruit a further assistant. This was John MacDonald, 'a man', Stewart said, 'who was acquainted [with Culrain] and knew the houses of the different individuals [there]'. Reaching the Culrain dramshop where he expected to find his other three aides, Stewart, to his fury, discovered only Tallach and Munro. Hearing from them that Ross had slept elsewhere, the sheriff-officer sent MacDonald to fetch him. At the Urquhart home, however, MacDonald found no trace of the missing constable. Instead he was told by Ross's brother-in-law to give a message to Stewart. This was to the effect that the sheriff-officer, who 'might go to the devil' for all Urquhart cared, would 'get a broken head' before the day was done. Hurrying back to the dramshop, MacDonald did as instructed. According to James Stewart's subsequent testimony, MacDonald also 'told him [Stewart] he would not follow him any further as he saw the business was attended with danger . . . [because] women were collecting from all quarters'. At this, a now alarmed Stewart asked MacDonald to search further for Constable Ross. 'He positively refused', Stewart said of the Invercarron man, 'and ran away back to his home.'[7]

Leaving Munro and Tallach (who had still been asleep when the sheriff-officer arrived) to struggle into their clothes, James Stewart stepped out of the Culrain dramshop to find himself 'surrounded by a party of furious women to the amount he supposed of 150'. They 'immediately laid hold of him', Stewart said, 'and commanded him to deliver up his papers'. He refused. But 'they rifled his pockets and took every paper he had' – papers amounting, in all, to 57 notices of removal.[8]

From the sheriff-officer's perspective, matters now deteriorated rapidly. While he was kept under close guard by some of his assailants, Tallach and Munro, who had at last appeared, were 'laid hold of . . . and forcibly detained' by others. The women holding him and his colleagues, James Stewart said, 'were armed with sticks or batons'; they had 'handkerchiefs' tied tightly across their faces by way of disguise; and, all the while, 'they made use of the most threatening expressions'. He was convinced, Stewart insisted, that his captors 'would not [have] hesitate[d] to take [the] lives' of their prisoners. They certainly 'spoke of throwing [him] . . . into the [Kyle of Sutherland]'.[9]

William Munro, Stewart said, had at one point 'punched one of the women . . . who fell on her back'. She and her friends responded by urging each other to 'knock the brains out of him'. This was not done, however. Instead Munro was permitted 'to [run] away as fast as he could', while being pelted, as he ran, with stones.[10]

His 'papers', Stewart explained, had meanwhile been carried off by one or two women who told him, as they left, that 'they had as good scholars as he was to read them for them'. The seized documents, the sheriff-officer suspected, had been shown to men 'concealed' nearby. On its being confirmed (whether or not by Culrain's menfolk) that every removal summons had been checked and destroyed, Stewart said, he and Andrew Tallach, 'followed by the whole mob of women', were jostled, pushed and driven out of Culrain 'in a kind of mock triumph'. It was only then, Stewart added, that he at last fell in with the absent Ross. The constable, for his part, was to maintain that he had left his sister's home early that morning and headed for Ardgay with the aim of meeting with James Stewart and warning him of what was likely to happen when the sheriff-officer reached his destination. But he had somehow, according to Ross's own – and not very convincing – account, missed Stewart on the road.[11]

Was it the case, as asserted afterwards, that some of the 'women' involved in the events of 1 February were actually 'men in women's dress'? Almost certainly not. This claim was made only by Alexander Ross, who had seen little of what occurred in Culrain that Tuesday morning, and not by either James Stewart or William Munro, who had seen a great deal. Munro and Stewart, in fact, took care to distance themselves from all such allegations, which perhaps originated in Ross wanting to deflect mocking taunts (of a kind bound to have come his way) about his having fled Culrain rather than risk a confrontation with its womenfolk.[12]

Be that as it may, Culrain's wives and daughters, not its husbands and sons, were clearly at the forefront of the onslaught launched against Munro, Tallach and Stewart. To Francis Suther, the explanation was straightforward. Women played a major part in episodes of the Culrain sort, Suther told James Loch, because it was 'generally believed' in the Highlands 'that a woman could do anything with impunity'. The reason for women's leading role in the destruction of the Culrain removal notices, in other words, was entirely tactical – females being thought less likely than males to face arrest and imprisonment on charges arising from violent clashes with authority. This notion (as will be seen) may have had some foundation in fact. But irrespective of whether or not this was the case, the fact that Culrain's males took little or nothing to do with the attack on James Stewart and his colleagues is not evidence, in itself, of that attack having somehow lacked their backing.[13]

Days or weeks in advance of the Culrain fracas of 1 February, the likelihood of some such confrontation had been widely rumoured in Easter Ross. This is a pointer to the seizure of the Culrain removal orders having been planned – by virtually the entire Culrain community – over a period. So is the well co-ordinated nature of what transpired on the day. Women might have been in the front line. But much of the rest of Culrain's population was clearly involved. '[H]ard by' the spot where he was held captive, James Stewart reportedly 'observed what he conceived to be a large body of men stationed in a wood'. On the Sutherland side of the nearby Kyle, moreover, 'a considerable stir of people' could be seen – those people, it was thought, readying themselves to cross the intervening stretch of water should it have proved necessary to provide Culrain with reinforcements.[14]

On news of his tenantry's actions reaching him in London where (in the manner of the Marquis of Stafford) he was to become a much-praised patron of the arts, Hugh Munro of Novar pronounced himself 'sorry to hear that the Culrain people [had] been behaving in such an *Ultra-Radical* fashion'. Although Culrain's Church of Scotland minister was afterwards to insist that 'no such principles as those of radicalism are known here', this was to detect – as was done widely – the hand of Thomas Dudgeon in what had occurred. 'The rebellion is everywhere imputed to Dudgeon,' Suther informed Loch. An anonymous contributor to the *Inverness Courier* was more specific. Shortly after the dispersal of January's 'radical convention at Golspie', this writer alleged, Dudgeon 'had been busy' at Culrain where, as in Sutherland, he had taken advantage of, and misled, a 'simple and credulous' community. Those remarks, however, have to be set in the context of the stream of anti-Dudgeon material now finding its way into the *Courier*. Tain lawyer John MacKenzie is likely to have been nearer the mark when he commented that the Culrain people had taken the initiative in 'apply[ing] to Mr Dudgeon for his countenance and direction'. This was in accord with what James Stewart heard in Culrain itself. It was in accord too with Thomas Dudgeon's own account of what had occurred. Culrain tenants, Dudgeon acknowledged, had consulted him. He had advised them on how to respond to eviction threats. But he had urged them always – and indeed to have done otherwise would have been foolhardy – to keep within the law.[15]

This the Culrain people had self-evidently not done. On 1 February they had attacked, or deforced, a sheriff-officer. All such deforcements (as indicated previously) were regarded as a serious offence. They were certainly so regarded by Ross-shire's veteran sheriff, Donald MacLeod, an Easter Ross laird who had held the post since 1774 and who, in 1792, had played a leading role in the military-backed suppression of an earlier spate of protests against the advance of sheep farming into the Highlands. This time round, however, MacLeod began by favouring a more conciliatory approach. In correspondence with Munro of Novar's representatives, who wanted the army brought in as soon as feasible, the sheriff underlined his reluctance 'to proceed to the extremity of applying for . . . military [aid] until', as he put it, 'I am satisfied in my own mind that the measures proposed [meaning the clearance of Culrain] cannot be carried into execution by milder means'. MacLeod accordingly sent 'a private message' to men he regarded as Culrain's 'most respectable tenants', individuals whom the sheriff offered to meet in the hope of persuading them to desist from further direct action. This initiative having got nowhere, the sheriff, still intent on avoiding renewed conflict, appears to have asked Thomas Dudgeon to mediate between himself and the Culrain people, something Sutherland Estate managers, who had good cause to be wary of Dudgeon, thought 'very foolish'.[16]

Donald MacLeod, an uncle (as noted previously) of Joseph Gordon, might conceivably have been encouraged to contact Dudgeon by the anti-Stafford nexus to which both the Fearn farmer and Carrol's ex-owner belonged. In the event, however, Dudgeon's mediation efforts – if such they were – suffered much the same fate as the sheriff's own overtures. And when, in mid-February, James Stewart was sent back to Culrain to tell people involved in the earlier disturbances that they were required to present themselves for inter-view at Tain Sheriff Court, he was 'fully worse treated', it was reported, than he had been a fortnight previously. He had again been hustled off the estate, Stewart told Sheriff MacLeod, 'by a mob of women . . . [who] repeatedly declared that they defied all the lawyers and constables in the County of Ross to remove them'. Concluding, in the light of this development, that there was no longer any hope of his engineering a peaceful settlement of the Culrain dispute, MacLeod now applied to the lord advocate, William Rae, 'for some troops to assist the civil power to execute the law'.[17]

No such troops were forthcoming, Rae, according to one of Munro of Novar's agents, taking the line that Ross-shire already possessed enough resources to deal with disturbances the lord advo-cate apparently characterised as 'the howling of a parcel of old women'. If that was the sole reason for Rae's refusal to comply with Donald MacLeod's request for military assistance, then the lord advocate was giving substance to the contention that lawbreaking women always got away with more than lawbreaking men. There are likely, however, to have been additional considerations behind Rae's decision. In the political climate created by the Peterloo killings and their aftermath, the last thing the lord advocate would have wanted was to take responsibility for deploying the army against a new set of demonstrators. Hence Rae's instruction to Donald MacLeod that the sheriff deal himself with the Culrain problem.[18]

The letter containing this directive reached MacLeod on Sunday 27 February. Setting off to Tain from his home at Geanies, some miles to the east, the sheriff promptly set about raising sufficient manpower – as he thought – to do as Rae had ordered. In the absence of the regular troops he had requested, MacLeod turned for help, as the lord advocate had suggested he should, to the Ross-shire militia. But perhaps fearing that its rank and file might be more in sympathy with the Culrain community than with Hugh Munro of Novar, MacLeod mobilised only officers, sergeants and corporals – about 30 men in all. A further six soldiers and an officer – members of a recruiting party that happened to be visiting Tain – were also pressed into service. Tain's four sheriff-officers were joined by ten more sher-iff-officers from Dingwall, Ross-shire's county town. Fifty 'stout young men' were sworn in as special constables; and to the resulting force, already over 100 strong, Donald MacLeod added finally 'about twenty gentlemen'. Drawn from local landowning families, they were described by the sheriff as 'hearty in support of the king's authority' and thus eager to contribute to the crushing of Culrain's rebellion.[19]

Militiamen, soldiers, sheriff-officers and constables – all of them on foot – set off from Tain for Culrain at about five o'clock on the morning of Thursday 2 March. MacLeod and his 'gentlemen' colleagues, who travelled on horseback or by carriage, left about two hours later. Their route lay along the southern shore of the Dornoch Firth, by way of Edderton, to Ardgay. Here the entire party halted for breakfast. At its conclusion, and prior to proceeding any further, MacLeod, by his own account, 'drew up the constables and other unarmed men into four divisions and gave the command of each division to a gentleman on whose discretion and courage [he] had a perfect reliance'. Those four groupings were placed in the vanguard. The militia detachment, each of its members equipped with musket and bayonet, were kept to the rear but ordered 'to be ready to come up when called on'.[20]

Since the Culrain rebels were known to have so-called 'scouts' in Tain, and since those scouts were bound to have kept Culrain people abreast of Donald MacLeod's preparations, the sheriff would not have expected to take the place by surprise. By arriving in such strength, however, he may have hoped to convince the Culrain community of the futility of further resistance. If so, MacLeod was disappointed. On approaching Culrain, the sheriff wrote later, 'we perceived a very considerable mob of women, with some young lads and boys amongst them, coming running . . . towards [us] . . . I immediately came out of my carriage . . . and, having called up the unarmed men, advanced with them . . . The mob took a position behind a stone dike . . . and, with the most horrible screams and yells, assailed us with showers of stones.'

This pitched battle – as it soon became – took place at a spot where a hill burn, flowing out of the high ground to the south, enters the Kyle of Sutherland. Culrain's homes were less than a mile distant. But if Donald MacLeod and his men were to get there, they were first going to have to force a passage through the women confronting them. This proved impossible.

To the sheriff's right, between the road and the Kyle, was a marsh. To his left, on the other hand, the ground rose, immediately behind the burn, in a steep, escarpment-like bank some 50 feet high. From the top of this bank – where it is still possible to find handily-sized stones of the sort the sheriff described – Culrain's defenders could easily rain missiles down on their attackers. The position, then, could scarcely have been better chosen by the women now blocking MacLeod's further progress.

This, from the sheriff's perspective, was bad enough. Still more alarming was the presence, 'a few hundred yards' behind the stone-throwing women and youths, of 'a second line' of people, who might at any point choose to reinforce MacLeod's nearer-hand opponents. This reserve group, according to the sheriff, was 'composed altogether of men . . . many (if not the whole) of them armed with muskets'. Those weapons, MacLeod explained afterwards to the lord advocate, had been obtained 'from a ship wrecked some time [previously] on [Ross-shire's] west coast'. At Culrain, or so the press was to contend, the guns in question were being wielded by 'discharged military' – ex-soldiers who, in the course of Britain's long war with Napoleon, would have had plenty of opportunities to become familiar with the use of firearms.[21]

No doubt aware that to fire on the sheriff and his party would have been to invite all manner of subsequent reprisals, Culrain's ex-soldiers – men who were to show, throughout what followed, much greater discipline than the sheriff's motley force – neither loosed off any shots nor moved from where they stood. Their militia adversaries, in contrast, attempted to force both the burn and its adjacent escarpment at a spot well to the right of most of the 200 or so women facing them. This action – undertaken, Donald MacLeod stressed, 'without any order from me' – was intended to lead to 'the mob' behind the dyke being outflanked. Instead it exposed the militiamen, several of whom were knocked down by well-aimed stones, to renewed attack. This, in turn, led to a number of militiamen – in direct contravention of MacLeod's instructions that they keep their muskets unloaded – firing on the crowd. 'One woman was shot, it is supposed mortally,' Francis Suther wrote three days later when briefing James Loch on those events. 'Another was badly wounded in the mouth and eye by a bayonet.'[22]

Press claims to the same effect were disputed by Donald MacLeod. Only 'two or three shots were fired', he maintained. The militiamen responsible had loaded their muskets, moreover, with buckshot rather than with the heavy and more lethal bullets usually employed. Only 'a young man and a girl' had sustained gunshot wounds. As for such bayonet wounds as had been inflicted, the blame for those belonged entirely to the women who had suffered them: 'They were . . . so infuriated that many of them ran [at] the soldiers [meaning members of the militia] and met with [injuries] inflicted by their own madness'.[23]

Those words were penned more than a week later. On the day itself, the sheriff was preoccupied with survival and escape: 'I was well protected in the retreat by the constables covering me . . . and by that means got into my carriage with little injury . . . [But] many stones were thrown at my coachman . . . and even at my horses; one panel [on the carriage's side] was broken, and the back window drove in . . . On reaching back to the inn at Ardgay [to which MacLeod's entire force now withdrew], we found that [our] casualties amounted to thirteen; five of the militia were much hurt . . . and eight of the constables'.[24]

At Ardgay, in consultation with the now badly rattled 'gentlemen' accompanying him, Donald MacLeod prepared an emergency despatch for the lord advocate. 'I am certain that lives must be lost before these . . . people are removed,' the sheriff informed William Rae. What had taken place that morning at Culrain was nothing less than 'an act of rebellion against the law and the government'. The sternest measures must immediately be taken against everyone involved. '[A] force of 500 regulars with two or three field pieces [meaning artillery] will be necessary to reduce them'.[25]

The 2 March clash at Culrain was of concern to James Loch not least because, much to the Stafford commissioner's irritation, it had the immediate effect of renewing English press interest in clearances and their consequences. Commenting on Munro of Novar's treatment of Culrain's inhabitants, the *Morning Chronicle*, for instance, was scathing: 'There can be no doubt that by the law of this country . . . Mr Munro is entitled, if his tenants have no [legally enforceable] claim to his land, to turn out whatever number of them he pleases . . . But law is one thing and humanity may be another . . . [W]e would ask how the turning out of a number of individuals from their possessions, and it appears to starve, can be possibly reconciled to humanity?' With the next set of evictions in the Sutherland straths less than two months away, this was not the sort of question either Loch or the Staffords wanted posed. Still more unwelcome was the link the *Chronicle* made between Highland dispossessions and what its leader-writer called 'recent occurrences in Staffordshire'. Those occurrences, in the paper's view, showed that a 'penalty for Highland management may be demanded . . . in England'.[26]

This was a reference to the startling outcome in Staffordshire of the general election then going on across the United Kingdom. The favoured candidate for the Staffordshire county constituency, at the contest's commencement, was Earl Gower, the Marquis of Stafford's eldest son. His family had represented Staffordshire continuously in parliament since the early eighteenth century. He himself had been one of the county's MPs since 1815. Towards the end of a noisy and sometimes rowdy campaign, however, Gower – not a man with stomach for a fight – had withdrawn suddenly from the poll and, by so doing, conceded what had been his seat to his challenger, Sir John Boughey.

All sorts of local factors were of course at play in Staffordshire, not least Boughey's much appreciated role in exposing the price-fixing arrangements that had long enabled the Staffords to inflate profits from their coalmines. But the previous May's clearances in Sutherland also played a part. 'Remember when the cries of the houseless orphans resounded from the bleak hills of Brora to the rocky shores of the Orkneys,' one circular advised Staffordshire's electors. While that production's anonymous authors may have been hazy as to the details of Highland geography, their sentiments were clear. So were those of an audience addressed by the earl just days before his abandonment of his parliamentary ambitions. He hoped to have their votes, a *Times* reporter heard Gower tell his listeners. 'You cannot have 'em!' someone yelled, going on, with others, to shout, 'Fire! Scotland!' This, James Loch noted, had become Staffordshire's standard response to Gower's electoral efforts. Wherever the earl appeared, Loch wrote, 'the people cried "Fire!"'. '[A] vast and serious outcry was raised on the subject', Loch told Francis Suther.[27]

Loch was as contemptuous of the generality of Staffordshire's inhabitants as he was of Highlanders. Staffordshire folk, he informed his good friend Henry Brougham, were 'of the most dissolute habits, idle and improvident'. This disdain for people living on the Marquis of Stafford's Midland estates perhaps contributed to Loch's failure to foresee that those same people might take an interest in, and feel some sense of solidarity with, the marquis's Highland tenants. But if he was surprised by the manner in which English voters could be influenced by reports of evictions and burnings in faraway Sutherland, Loch was equally taken aback by the nature of the political response in Scotland to what he called 'the late riot in Ross-shire'.[28]

From Edinburgh it was made brutally apparent to Sheriff Donald MacLeod that William Rae would not be providing either the 500 troops or the three field guns MacLeod had requested. Nor was the lord advocate, a politician as capable as any other of drawing lessons from Gower's fate in Staffordshire, at all agreeable to prosecuting anyone in connection with what had transpired at Culrain. In fact Rae, as Loch was soon to learn, wished nothing more than to have the entire Culrain episode settled as quietly and uncontentiously as possible. 'I learned last night', a horrified Loch wrote to Suther on 1 April, 'that the lord advocate has written to Mr Munro begging of him to let the Culrain people remain'. 'You will admit with me', Loch commented when informing Sutherland's sheriff, Charles Ross, of the same development, 'that it puts every Highland proprietor in a very awkward situation.' After all, if Rae wanted Culrain's clearance put on hold, why should he not take a similar stance with regard to the more extensive removals planned for Sutherland? To delay the final emptying of the Sutherland straths, Loch raged, would be to 'throw away the labour of years'.[29]

Munro of Novar, however, was prepared to consider compromise of a kind that would never have been so much as contemplated on the Sutherland Estate. In this he was helped by the fact that, less than a week after Culrain's women had put Donald MacLeod to flight, several of that locality's 'heads of families', as they described themselves, sent a letter to Munro of Novar's Tain agent. This letter suggested that its signatories and others meet with a sheriff-officer at Ardgay Inn. That meeting took place on Tuesday 14 March. In the course of it, and in the days immediately following, all Culrain's tenants agreed to take delivery of removal notices. This, Sheriff MacLeod claimed, was a consequence of his having urged military intervention, the prospect of such intervention having 'terrif[ied] the [Culrain] people into a sense of the very improper conduct they had hitherto pursued'. Alexander MacBean, Culrain's Church of Scotland minister, begged to differ. MacBean deplored clearances – a 'system of extermination', he called them. Like his clerical colleagues in Sutherland, however, he was unyielding on its being everyone's Christian duty to submit to the will of their landlords. On his having made their obligations clear to them, the minister insisted, Culrain's people had been 'prevailed upon . . . to receive their summonses'.[30]

While minister and sheriff quarrelled openly – in the columns of the Highland and national press – as to who could most convincingly claim credit for restoring peace to Culrain, the township's occupants were negotiating with Munro of Novar's representatives. The outcome was very much the sort of deal the lord advocate had called for. The sheep farmer due to take possession of Culrain in May would do so. But this would be on the basis that – in return, presumably, for an appropriate rent reduction – he would permit Culrain's established occupiers to remain where they were. This arrangement was not one that endured indefinitely. But the Culrain uprising – which resulted (perhaps because of this also being integral to the dispute's settlement) in not one prosecution – was nevertheless a victory of sorts.[31]

Strathbrora's equivalent of Alexander MacBean was Walter Ross, Clyne's parish minister and one of the two men who had sat with Patrick Sellar in the High Court's 'panel box' in 1816. Ross, being in no way critical of clearance, was even more insistent than Culrain's minister on the iniquity of refusing to do a landlord's bidding. Hence the minister's displeasure on learning how his parishioners had treated Francis Suther when, on a Thursday in mid-February, just as the Culrain troubles were at their height, the factor had arranged – as he thought – to meet with a group of Strathbrora tenants at one of the coastal locations where they were to be resettled. '[U]nder a heavy rain,' Suther reported to James Loch, he had waited there for several hours in the hope of being able 'to point out . . . their lots [or crofts]' to the tenants in question. But 'not a soul made their appearance'. He had notified Walter Ross of the missing men's names, Suther went on, and the minister had 'promised to reprimand them all' from his pulpit the following Sunday.[32]

Having the clergy onside with 'improvement' in this manner may have eased Loch's nervousness about the possibility of the Culrain outbreak sparking similar defiance elsewhere. But Loch, as he told Suther in March, remained 'very anxious in every way' about Culrain-type unrest breaking out on the Sutherland Estate. 'I find the Ross-shire gentlemen here [in London]', Loch added of his conversations with Easter Ross landlords then overwintering in the south, 'are . . . saying that the [Culrain] mob was much composed of Sutherland men'. Although 'women' rather than 'men' would have been a more appropriate term, there would certainly have been Sutherland participation in the Culrain protests, if only because the locality (as already noted) had attracted a number of the Sutherland Estate's displaced families. Still more disturbing from Loch's point of view were indications that people still in Sutherland (and perhaps scheduled for eviction in May) had contemplated – or more than contemplated – the possibility of joining Culrain's fight. On 1 February, when he and William Munro were being kicked (more or less literally) out of Culrain, James Stewart had been told that the Culrain rebels 'could command' assistance from 'the people of five parishes in

Sutherland'. A month later, when it was the turn of Sheriff Donald MacLeod and his men to be beaten back from Culrain, the sheriff had seen at least some signs of the truth of that claim. 'There were . . . observed many men running down the hill on the Sutherland side [of the Kyle of Sutherland],' the sheriff reported. This, he continued, was 'with the apparent design of crossing [the Kyle] to assist their neighbours'. That did nothing to ease James Loch's mounting apprehensions about the outcome of May's clearances.[33]

Francis Suther was less concerned. Thanks to Alexander MacBean having taken a hand in the matter, he informed Loch on 19 March, the Culrain people had 'given up all their wild [and] illegal ideas'. This was having a pacifying effect on Sutherland, the factor believed: 'I am certain we shall have no trouble . . . I went through all the places [still to be cleared] in Strathbrora on Thursday last to ascertain what effect the knowledge of the resistance in Ross-shire had made in their minds. It gives me pleasure to say that though the people expressed an anxious wish to remain in their present situations, yet when I explained to them [this] was impossible they readily acknowledged they must submit.'[34]

Ever since Suther had disregarded his orders by permitting the numerous house burnings of the previous spring, however, James Loch had been less convinced than previously that his Sutherland subordinate was wholly reliable. In November 1819, with a view to ensuring that the May 1820 clearances in Sutherland gave no additional 'cause for clamour', as he put it, Loch had supplied Suther with 12 closely written pages of instructions as to how exactly those clearances were to be conducted. Renewed 'burning', Loch made clear, was 'perfectly out of the question'. Now, in the wake both of the Culrain episode and of the Stafford family's humiliation at the hands of an electorate stirred up by endless shouts of 'Fire!', Loch – once more fearful that parliamentarians might start enquiring into Sutherland Estate affairs – stressed again the need to have everything go off quietly in May. '[I]f it does not', Loch told

Suther in March, 'you will cause a flame here [in England] we will have much difficulty in allaying.'

'I must again beg of you', runs a further March letter to Suther from Loch, 'to attend most vigilantly that neither any person acting under your orders, nor under the direction of the [sheep] farmers, permit fire to be used in any way whatever or at any time . . . Pray caution Sellar well about this.'[35]

That last directive stemmed from a number of May's scheduled evictions being Patrick Sellar's responsibility, not the Sutherland Estate's – because they involved people who, at some point in the preceding six or so years, had become Sellar's subtenants. But this circumstance, though important in law, was not sufficient, as Loch appreciated, to shield the Marquis or Marchioness of Stafford from blame in the event of houses going up in flames on one or other of Sellar's farms. As shown by the way the press had dealt with the 1814 burning of William Chisholm's home at Badinloskin, distinctions between this or that type of tenure – Chisholm (as mentioned earlier) having been technically a subtenant of some of Sellar's subtenants – were of no interest to journalists or the public. In newspapers, all evictions on the Sutherland Estate were treated, understandably, as the direct responsibility of its owners. Hence the need to get Patrick Sellar, who had personally taken a hand in some of the preceding year's burnings in Strathnaver, to proceed more circumspectly in 1820.

This Sellar did. So did the evicting parties responsible for ejecting the bulk of the 240 or so families evicted that May. Home after home was unroofed and demolished. But no houses were burned; and nor were there any overt acts of resistance. 'Madam,' Suther reported directly to the Marchioness of Stafford on 27 May, 'The removals are now complete and they have all been effected in the most peaceable and easy manner.' The marchioness and her husband, as is evident from James Loch's account of how his employers received this news, were as relieved as they were delighted. 'I am desired by Lord and Lady Stafford', Loch informed Suther in early June, 'to convey to you their complete and entire satisfaction and approbation at your having accomplished this most delicate but necessary arrangement . . . which the practices of the [Trans-Atlantic] Association and the example of Culrain made still more difficult to manage.'[36]

14

'TO SEEK SHELTER IN SOME MORE
PROPITIOUS QUARTER OF THE WORLD'

*Escaping clearance-era Sutherland; renewed opposition
to removals; army-backed evictions*

Prior to the commencement of large-scale sheep farming on the
Sutherland Estate, anyone making a circuit of Strathbrora,
Strathnaver and the Strath of Kildonan – a journey that, even on
horseback, might take a week – would have passed through, or close
to, somewhere between 150 and 200 distinct (and individually
named) communities. Many were small, consisting of no more than
three or four households. Others were larger. But irrespective of
whether they were home to 20 people or five times that number,
virtually all those settlements (exceptions will be touched on shortly)
had gone by the summer of 1820, their hundreds of landholdings
having been replaced by just eight.

Three men, James Hall, John Cleugh and Gabriel Reed, accounted
for the greater part of Strathbrora, including most of its lower and
more productive areas. Immediately west of Reed, Cleugh and Hall's
farms – Kilcalmkill, Pollie and Sciberscross respectively – was
Anthony Marshall and Adam Atkinson's vast tenancy. In one corner
of Atkinson and Marshall's farm, then, were the higher reaches of
Strathbrora. In another was the part of upper Strathnaver lying to
the east, south-east and south of Loch Naver. Here Marshall and
Atkinson's farm bordered with both of Patrick Sellar's sheep-farming tenancies. The bigger of the two, known as Syre and encompassing

practically the entire western flank of Strathnaver, dated from 1819. Also dating from 1819 was Skelpick, a farm tenanted by John Paterson who, in 1813, had competed unsuccessfully with Sellar for the tenancy of the latter's other Strathnaver landholding, Rhiloisk.

Like Atkinson, Marshall, Reed and Cleugh, Paterson came from Northumberland. Like Cleugh, he was very much a working shepherd made good, having acquired at Skelpick a substantial tenancy situated on the right or east bank of the River Naver and extending from just short of the river's mouth to a point some eight miles upstream. Here Skelpick met with Sellar's Rhiloisk – also on the Naver's right bank and spreading eastwards (as described earlier) into the upper or northernmost section of the Strath of Kildonan. There Rhiloisk shared a march or boundary with Knockfin. Its tenant, Thomas Houston, had previously occupied Suisgill, located (as again described earlier) further down the Strath of Kildonan. One of the Sutherland Estate's first sheep farms, Suisgill was itself now tenanted by William Clunes, against whom so much anger had been directed by Kildonan people in 1813. Also in Clunes's possession, as it had been since its creation precipitated the 1813 protests, was Torrish, the farm immediately east of Suisgill and, like Suisgill, on the Helmsdale's left or northern bank. This meant that, between them, Houston and Clunes controlled many thousands of acres between the Helmsdale River and Sutherland's border with Caithness. In the opposite direction, and thus on the Helmsdale's right or south bank, were riverside localities on the northern rim of Gabriel Reed's Kilcalmkill – much larger than Torrish, Suisgill or Knockfin and extending south, by way of Glen Loth, to this circuit's starting point in Strathbrora.

Everyone dispossessed as a result of the emptying of the Sutherland Estate's interior valleys should, in principle, have been accommodated in one or other of the crofting townships that, by 1820, were to be found on the estate's north and east coasts. In the east, those townships were concentrated around Helmsdale, Brora and

Dornoch; in the north, they occupied virtually the entire coastal strip between Invernaver, on the River Naver estuary, and Strathy, a dozen or so miles to the east. Those places' crofts, however, were no more attractive in 1820 than before to people directed towards them. Hence the efforts evicted families made to remove themselves entirely from the Sutherland Estate.

The 'greater part' of the Strathbrora tenants due to be dispossessed in May 1820, Francis Suther reported during the preceding March, were 'going about Caithness endeavouring to find small farms'. They were not alone. While there was also movement from the Sutherland Estate into Culrain and other Easter Ross localities, Caithness – where landholdings could readily be got by those able to pay for them – was favoured. It was to Caithness (as already seen) that William MacKay of Achoul's family went following their 1819 ejection from Grumbeg, and plenty of others did likewise. Among them were many people evicted from the Strath of Kildonan in 1819 and 1820. From Kildonan those folk headed north into the adjacent Caithness parish of Latheron where they settled thickly in the valleys of the Berriedale and Dunbeath Rivers – localities not at all unlike the one they had left. This, according to Patrick Sellar, was because Kildonan families were 'bred to idleness, illicit distillation and sheep stealing' – activities more readily pursued among the Caithness hills, Sellar reckoned, than in one of the Sutherland Estate's coastal settlements. The fact that so many people had quit the estate in this way, Sellar thought, was no bad thing. Their departure, he informed James Loch, '[has] unloaded you of a great deal of trash of which you are well rid'.[1]

Francis Suther offered a more nuanced analysis of the exodus from Sutherland of what Lady Stafford called 'a very considerable number of middle tenants', by which the marchioness meant the group one or two notches below tacksmen in the pre-clearance hierarchy. 'None have settled in Caithness', Suther explained to Loch, 'who could not get a place to keep at least four milk cows.' What such people wanted, Suther went on, was to remain in full-time farming. That could not be accomplished on a Sutherland Estate croft – the point of such crofts being to force their tenants into the fishing industry and other non-agricultural occupations. This prospect, Suther commented in June 1819, was 'mortally hate[d]' by families of the sort leaving for Caithness. 'Indeed,' he added, 'I have lately found out that the people in the hills [by which he meant residents or former residents of the Strath of Kildonan, Strathbrora and Strathnaver] all consider themselves farmers and look on it as a degradation to be compared to labourers or fishermen.'[2]

Exactly that point had been made over several years by informed critics of the Sutherland 'improvements', such as Alexander Sutherland (notably in his *Star* articles of 1813) and the Earl of Selkirk. This makes it all the more remarkable that no similar thought occurred to Suther, the man with day-to-day responsibility for the mechanics of clearance, until 1819's numerous removals were over. So completely had Suther bought into 'improvement' thinking, it seems, that he simply closed his eyes to the reality of the society he was instrumental in destroying. This society, as the factor had eventually come (even if dimly) to grasp, was not made up entirely – if at all – of the idlers and wasters who populate Patrick Sellar's pro-clearance outpourings. Instead it consisted, in part at any rate, of people who – as well as owning the dairy cows mentioned by Suther – possessed beef cattle herds and other cashable resources on a scale sufficient to enable them to buy their way into Caithness.

Visiting Latheron in the early 1820s, Donald Sage met with 'a goodly number' of those people. Sage's stepmother had died in 1818, and in post-clearance Sutherland, Sage wrote, his father (who would himself die in 1824) now 'lived the life of a hermit' in a district the clearances had stripped of habitation: 'All his family had left [home], and the township [of Kildonan], and indeed the whole parish . . . were depopulated, so that, except [for] his own servants, male and female, the schoolmaster [and one or two others] . . . [my father] had not a human being to converse with for many miles around.' Latheron, in contrast, contained many of the Kildonan minister's former friends and neighbours. Prominent among them, Donald Sage found, was George MacKay. This was the catechist who, on the evening of 5 January 1813, had played a key role in sanctioning the next morning's successful attempt to halt William Clunes's inspection of what subsequently became Torrish farm. 'It would be as well for them to be killed', Kildonan people had told Clunes that same winter's evening, 'as set adrift upon the world.' In the end, however, many Kildonan folk had chosen to leave not just Sutherland but Scotland rather than accede to 'improvement'. Among families broken up in consequence was George MacKay's. Ten years on from 1813, his home was in Latheron. But his brother Angus and Angus's wife Jean, the couple who had married in Kildonan on the day following Clunes's enforced retreat from Torrish, were several thousand miles away, on the Ontario farm they had reached by way of Churchill and Red River.[3]

Although tales of the hazards encountered by emigrants like Jean and Angus MacKay filtered back to Scotland, these by no means eradicated the notion of quitting Sutherland for North America. '*Fhuair sinn bailtean dhuin fhìn*', runs a Gaelic song composed by one of that continent's numerous Highland settlers, "'*S cha bhi uachdrain a chaoidh 'gar lèireadh*': 'We have got farms of our own, and landlords will no more oppress us.' This, from the perspective of Sutherland Estate tenants living constantly with the prospect of losing land and homes, was to conjure up a vision of paradise-like contentment. The Staffords, James Loch and other proponents of 'improvement' might insist that prosperity, as 'improvement' theory demanded, was bound to come the way of people prepared to combine the tenancy of a coastal croft with a non-farming trade. Throughout the clearance era, however, all such claims (as already stressed) were disbelieved. By those who could afford to rent one of its farms, Caithness was preferred to post-clearance Sutherland. By those with the opportunity and the means to get there, North America was reckoned better still.[4]

Some Sutherland people were to join the Kildonan folk who – on being taken from Red River by the North West Company – obtained landholdings in the vicinity of Lake Erie. More, however, made for Nova Scotia. Here families from Sutherland congregated in then thickly wooded country around Pictou, a harbour town on Nova Scotia's north coast. To visit a farm in that locality is, even today, to get a sense of the immense effort it took to create such farms where previously there was virgin forest. It is to get a sense also of the pride taken by pioneer farmers in their achievements. The Pictou area's settlers from Sutherland, remarks present-day Nova Scotian Glen Matheson, were people who 'had never swung an axe' but who found themselves, on their arrival, 'in the midst of hardwood forest' where tree after tree had to be disposed of before crops of any consequence could be grown. Many of Glen's own Sutherland forebears were in this category. Surviving stories of their experiences – stories Glen has spent years collecting – deal in difficulties associated with forest clearance and in hardships suffered during Nova Scotian winters when food was scarce. But a powerful theme of those same stories, Glen Matheson says, consists of what he calls 'the joy of landownership' – the sense that, on reaching Nova Scotia, families whose Sutherland tenancies could so suddenly be taken from them had at last gained independence and security of a kind then unobtainable in Scotland.[5]

Something of what this meant emerges from a petition submitted to Nova Scotia's governor, Sir John Sherbrooke, by an early group of emigrants to Pictou from Sutherland. This group – comprising 17 people in all – consisted of four families. Those families were headed by Robert Baillie, Alexander Sutherland, Hugh MacPherson and Janet Sutherland, a widow accompanied by her son and daughter. None of the four could write, and their petition – in effect an application for a land grant – was drawn up for them, in October 1814, by a Pictou JP, Hugh Denoon.[*] 'Your

---

[*] Denoon had himself been involved, 10 or 12 years earlier, in shipping emigrants from Scotland to Pictou.

memorialists', Denoon commented at the start of a document addressed to Sherbrooke personally, 'emigrated from the county of Sutherland.' They had done so, Denoon went on, in consequence of their having been 'turned out of possessions' that had subsequently been let to 'sheep dealers'. Hence the four families' decision 'to look for an asylum' in Nova Scotia. 'They have [character] certificates from their parish minister', Denoon added of Baillie, MacPherson and the two Sutherlands, none of whom could write but all of whom put their 'marks' to his summary of their case, 'and have nothing to recommend them further but to assure your Excellency that they were faithful subjects at home to his Majesty [King George] and will now so continue.' [6]

Getting to the point of his submission, Denoon noted of Janet Sutherland, Hugh MacPherson, Alexander Sutherland and Robert Baillie 'that as they have followed farming from their infancy they . . . most humbly pray that your Excellency will be pleased to order a location of lands for themselves and families . . . that they may be improving and clearing the woods and brush this winter . . . [in order to plant] a crop the ensuing spring.' This 'prayer' was answered positively. Subject to the standard condition that specified acreages had to be brought into cultivation each year for several years, land grants – requiring little if anything by way of upfront payment – were rapidly forthcoming. Baillie, whose family was 'seven in number', received 350 acres; Alexander Sutherland, with four dependents, got 300 acres; MacPherson, with three, got 250; and Janet Sutherland, with two, was awarded 200. [7]

Baillie and MacPherson are known to have lived in Strathbrora. It is probable that the Sutherlands did so also. If so, the 'sheep dealers' to whom their petition referred were Gabriel Reed and John Cleugh, the former's Kilcalmkill farm dating from 1813 and the latter's Pollie farm from the following year. Establishing Pollie and Kilcalmkill had entailed clearances which, though not so extensive as the blanket removals of 1819 and 1820, were – even to people not directly affected by them – most unsettling. That is why lots of Strathbrora people expressed interest in the Earl of Selkirk's Red River venture at the point, in 1813, when it seemed that Selkirk was about to provide hundreds of passages to North America. Might the Baillie, MacPherson and Sutherland families have hoped to quit Strathbrora for Red River? And might they, when it turned out (because of Selkirk taking limited numbers) they had no chance of being shipped there, have opted instead for Pictou? That question cannot be answered definitively. But it is clear that the choice thus made was a good one. Prior to their departure from the Sutherland Estate, Janet Sutherland, Hugh MacPherson, Alexander Sutherland and Robert Baillie were tenants – highly vulnerable tenants at that – of the Marquis and Marchioness of Stafford. By the close of 1814, less than three months after stepping ashore in Pictou, they had become, between them, the possessors of a 1,100-acre slice of Nova Scotia.[8]

With land came modest affluence. 'The early settlers were strong, industrious and economical,' an early historian of Pictou wrote in the mid-1870s. 'They were poor at first, but with great perseverance they made themselves comfortable homes. There are men . . . who settled . . . in the woods without a guinea in their pockets who [today] have fine houses, large barns, excellent farms and considerable sums at interest.' Success of that sort took time to achieve. But the prospect of eventual betterment had been evident from the first. Hence the manner in which, as across-the-board clearances loomed ever closer, Sutherland people were drawn to Nova Scotia by accounts of the opportunities to be got there.[9]

Since even illiterate settlers could have letters written for them, Robert Baillie and other members of his 1814 party may have been one source of such accounts. Others may have emanated from still-earlier Sutherland emigrants like William MacKenzie, Donald MacIntosh and Angus Sutherland. MacKenzie established himself before 1810 in a locality that evolved into Kenzieville on Barney's River, west of Pictou. Sutherland and MacIntosh, for their part, were principal founders in 1813 of the soon thriving community of Earltown, to the east. By the late 1820s, Earltown and an adjacent locality, Tatamagouche, were home to well over 1,000 settlers. 'Of the[se] . . . settlers', noted that same nineteenth-century historian, 'nearly all came from Sutherlandshire . . . All spoke the Gaelic language and it is still [in 1877] generally used by their descendants.'[10]

In and around both Earltown and Kenzieville, then, there developed what were, in effect, transplanted Sutherland communities. There people expelled from townships destroyed in the course of the clearances could set up home and recommence farming – this time on their own land – in close proximity to relatives, friends and former neighbours. Earltown might be 3,000 miles from Sutherland. Its forests and its climate – Nova Scotia winters being both cold and long-lasting – might make it very different from the Highlands. But by offering its new arrivals the chance to become full-time agriculturalists – in a social setting that was linguistically and culturally familiar – Earltown, together with other Nova Scotia settlements of the same sort, provided homesteaders with lifestyles superior to anything available on three-acre crofts in previously barren parts of Sutherland.

Red River could conceivably have offered Sutherland's dispossessed population an equally desirable alternative to the Sutherland Estate's new crofting townships. But Red River's many troubles – combined with an inaccessibility that was to endure into the 1880s – meant that after 1815 there was for many years little or no movement from Sutherland to Manitoba. Nor was there much interest, once Nova Scotia began to exert its pull, in emigrating to other parts of the world. An obvious place to have gone – not least because of the 93rd Regiment's long stint of garrison duty in Cape Town – was South Africa. However, attempts to channel emigration from Sutherland in that direction were repeatedly to fail.

The first of those attempts was made by John Graham, who helped get the 93rd ashore at Bloubergstrand in January 1806. In South Africa, Graham had quit the 93rd to take command of the locally recruited Cape Regiment, composed of soldiers drawn from the Cape's Khoikhoi people. In 1811 he led his Khoikhoi force and a number of British troops – some men of the 93rd among them – into action against the Xhosa, who held extensive territories around Fish River on the eastern edge of Britain's Cape-centred sphere of influence. In a brutal campaign – calculated, in words used by one of Graham's superiors, 'to impress on the minds of these savages a proper degree of terror and respect' – the Xhosa were defeated. The gains thus made, colonial officials thought, needed to be consolidated by promoting white settlement in a Fish River frontier zone. John Graham agreed. When on leave in Britain in 1813, therefore, he pressed the colonial secretary, Lord Bathurst, to ship to South Africa some of the people then beginning to be threatened with eviction from the Strath of Kildonan and other parts of the Sutherland Estate, a development Graham, who came from the Dundee area, would have heard about from former comrades among the 93rd's officers and men. Neither Bathurst nor other government ministers, however, were any more taken with Graham's scheme than with Lord Selkirk's analogous plan – also circulating in Whitehall in 1813 – to have thousands of Sutherland people relocated to Red River. John Graham's settlement project duly died a rapid death. The next such initiative was no more successful.[11]

This was the brainchild of Adam Gordon, whose father was a long-established tacksman at Griamachary, a modest landholding on the north-eastern borders of Patrick Sellar's Rhiloisk farm. Gordon, who enlisted in the 93rd in 1800, had afterwards followed John Graham into the Cape Regiment. Pensioned off – or put on half-pay – by the army in 1817, he returned to Sutherland. There, in the spring of 1818, by which point removal notices were being distributed in all the Sutherland straths, Adam Gordon declared himself willing to lead a large party of emigrants to South Africa, 'knowing it', he intimated, 'to be one of the finest places in the world'. Probably for the same reason as Red River had appealed five years before – this being that anywhere, whether the North American prairies or the South African veldt, was bound to be an improvement on a Sutherland croft – there appears to have been an initial flurry of interest. But this soon evaporated. In April, Francis Suther reported, Adam Gordon was putting it about that 'more than one half of the inhabitants of [the Strath of] Kildonan [had] expressed their determination to accompany him' to the Cape. By June, however, it was clear that South Africa had in fact been ruled out by prospective emigrants and that Nova Scotia continued to be, on all sides, the popular choice. 'The Kildonan people are determined on going to America',* Suther noted in November 1818, 'and I am rather inclined to think the Strathbrora tenantry . . . intend to embark for [there] also.'[12]

This proved correct. There were many Strathbrora folk among the 20 or 30 families who left Sutherland for Nova Scotia in 1819. In the early summer of 1820 they were followed by another substantial contingent. Among this group were two families from Carrol, the township which, when she glimpsed its emptied and unroofed homes later that same year, would provoke in the Marchioness of Stafford a transient 'melancholy'. Nothing is known of the emotions experienced by the emigrants forced from those same homes by Lady Stafford's employees. All that can be discovered is that there were 19 of them. James Sutherland left Carrol with his wife (whose name was not recorded) and their five children. He was accompanied by William Sutherland, William's wife (again anonymous in the records) and their ten children. By September 1820, when the marchioness looked across Loch Brora at what remained of the houses those people had quit three months earlier, all 19 were in Pictou.[13]

Also sailing on the ship that brought the two Carrol families to Nova Scotia were other families from newly cleared Strathbrora townships. From Scottarie came William Baillie, his wife and four

* 'America', in the early nineteenth century, often signified what is today called North America. The term was applied, in other words, to what became present-day Canada as well as to the USA.

children; from Kilfedder, Catherine Graham, a widow, and her six children; from Kilbraur, Donald Baillie, his (presumably widowed) mother and his two sisters. Like all such emigrants, those people paid heavily (by the standards of that time) for their passage. They sailed on a ship belonging to William Allan, a Leith-based business-man who, for much of this period, was one of the emigration trade's key figures. Allan charged each of his adult passengers £6, with chil-dren under 15 paying £3. This means that William Sutherland from Carrol, some of whose ten children are bound to have been over 15, would have had to find the better part of £60 in order to get his family to Nova Scotia. His ability to do so (to reiterate a point already made) demonstrates that Sutherland's straths, 'improve-ment' rhetoric notwithstanding, were not uniformly sunk in poverty. Strathbrora's schoolmaster, Gordon Ross, whose school was three miles from Carrol and who is sure to have taught a number of the Strathbrora children who left for Pictou in 1820, would have taken four years to earn the amount it cost William Sutherland to secure his family's departure.[14]

Patrick Sellar was pleased to see Sutherland families emigrating en masse. 'There never occurred a better time to get quit of a number of them,' he wrote. 'Highlanders', he added, 'are of all people those who do best in America.' This, Sellar explained, returning to his earlier contention that Sutherland's 'aborigines' and North America's indigenous peoples were equally 'shut out' from civilisa-tion, was because Highlanders, being 'little removed from the first state of society necessarily prevalent in the wilds of that new coun-try', were ideally suited to life in the Nova Scotia backwoods.[15]

James Loch – conscious that widespread eagerness to be off to the other side of the Atlantic was negating claims that betterment awaited everyone taking a Sutherland Estate croft – was not persuaded. That is evident from his exchanges with William Allan who believed he could have filled his ships many times over had all Sutherland's aspiring emigrants been able to find the necessary cash. He had had 'many applications' from every part of the

Sutherland Estate for information about his fares and sailing sched-
ules, Allan told Francis Suther: 'I . . . sent my clerk [north] for the
purpose of encouraging [prospective emigrants], but he found they
had not the money to pay their passage.' Loch, to whom Suther
forwarded Allan's letter, was not amenable to the Leith ship-own-
er's implicit suggestion that poorer people might have their
emigration costs met in part by the Sutherland Estate. 'It is not
Lord Stafford's wish to promote any emigration from the Estate of
Sutherland', Allan was informed, 'as he provides lots [or crofts] for
all he removes from the hills.'[16]

If the Staffords would not subsidise their tenantry's emigration,
some thought, the British government should make good the deficiency. Donald Logan, a Pictou timber shipper, was among those
holding that opinion. He had himself left Sutherland for Nova
Scotia in 1803, Logan informed colonial secretary Lord Bathurst in
November 1818: '[Understanding] that, by reason of various new
arrangements, many of my [Sutherland] friends and acquaintances
were put out of their lands and otherwise rendered uncomfortable, I
returned to my native country and got about one hundred and
twenty of them removed this season to North America. But many
were unable to pay the half of their passage and some not able to
pay . . . anything at all . . . Under these circumstances, several
hundred . . . tenants . . . whose farms the proprietors have considered
more lucrative to lay under sheep, are removed to either waste
ground or . . . [to] allotments so exceedingly unsuitable as to render
it . . . the desire of those unhappy people to seek shelter in some
more propitious quarter of the world.'[17]

Bathurst and his cabinet colleagues, as it happened, were shortly
to sanction the expenditure of £50,000 (equivalent to several million
pounds today) with a view 'to assist[ing] unemployed workmen' to
emigrate to South Africa. But efforts to get Sutherland people to
sign up for the Cape proved as unavailing this time as before, and,
Donald Logan's pleas notwithstanding, there was to be no similar
aid offered, at this stage anyway, to Highlanders looking to reach

North America. From the standpoint of Sutherland's many aspiring emigrants, then, it was fortunate that what Patrick Sellar labelled 'the Carrol party' now stepped in to facilitate their departure.[18]

At his Edinburgh home in the autumn of 1820, Joseph Gordon of Carrol, as the former Strathbrora laird still styled himself, took delivery of a banker's draft for £1,200. This 'munificent sum', as it was described by Lachlan Mackintosh's *Inverness Journal*, had been forwarded to Joseph by his brother George, a partner (as already noted) in Mackintosh & Co. of Calcutta, the business the *Journal's* proprietor had earlier helped to set up. 'My Dear Brother,' began the letter accompanying George's draft, 'The public and private accounts that reached this country about six months ago of the great distress brought upon the poor tenants of . . . Sutherland . . . excited a strong feeling of compassion in many persons here.' He had '[taken] occasion therefore', George Gordon went on, 'to set on foot a subscription' to which his partners – principally Lachlan Mackintosh's brothers – had 'most liberally' contributed. The resulting funds, George informed Joseph, were 'for the behoof of the poor of the county of Sutherland who have suffered from the measures adopted by the Marchioness of Stafford in the conversion of her estate to sheep farms'.[19]

It was George Gordon's intention that the cash resulting from his Calcutta 'subscription' should be distributed by the Edinburgh-based Highland Society, founded in 1784 with the aim of expanding the economy of the Scottish north. Since the society was dominated by landlords and their agents, William MacKenzie, the Staffords' Edinburgh lawyer, was keen to have its members fall in with George Gordon's wishes, George's instructions to his brother making it clear that, should the Highland Society not take charge of the £1,200 from Calcutta, then Joseph (whom MacKenzie loathed) was to be personally responsible for its disbursement. Prior to the society meeting at which the matter was discussed, MacKenzie informed the marchioness, he, Francis Suther and

George MacPherson Grant MP had got together and 'agreed that it would be desirable to keep the subscription money in the hands of the Highland Society rather than permit the management [of it] to be with Joseph Gordon, knowing his sentiments'. This, however, was not accomplished. Although MacKenzie and his allies argued, in effect, that all was well on the Sutherland Estate and that charitable funds were not required there, this was disputed by Joseph Gordon. '[W]hile he candidly admitted that many excellent and benevolent things were done [in Sutherland]', William MacKenzie reported of Gordon, '[he also] said that there was to his knowledge much individual hardship which required to be relieved.' More neutral members of the Highland Society – perhaps eager to steer clear of any Sutherland imbroglio – seem mostly to have kept quiet. But they nevertheless voted to have nothing to do with the cash that had come from India. 'The fund is thus placed at the disposal of Joseph Gordon,' MacKenzie notified Lady Stafford. 'I consider this, with the temper and views he [Gordon] has, very unfortunate . . . Suther says [the Highland Society decision] will do more harm than it is possible to express.'[20]

James Loch, the marquis and the marchioness were of the same opinion. 'I wish we could catch Joseph Gordon writing libels,' Lady Stafford remarked of a man she suspected of having helped foment all the many opposition movements generated by 'improvement', from the Kildonan rebellion of 1813 to Thomas Dudgeon's Trans-Atlantic Association. Gordon, however, was too experienced a lawyer, and too shrewd an operator, to lay himself open to a libel suit. Instead he announced that all funds reaching him from India – funds that were eventually to total a then very substantial £1,700 – would be used to assist emigration. 'This is all very vexatious and troublesome,' Loch commented. Gordon's plans were bound to be seen 'as a sort of attack . . . upon the late arrangements'. Instead of settling down on the crofts assigned to them in 1819 and 1820, evicted families would again begin to think about escaping to North America. It was infuriating, Loch complained to Suther, to have Lord and Lady Stafford 'plagued, and ourselves tormented, by persons . . . having no right to interfere in [Sutherland Estate] affairs'.[21]

Francis Suther and his staff, the Marquis of Stafford instructed, were to 'have nothing to do' with Joseph Gordon 'except privately to have an eye upon him'. In the event, however, the lawyer's intentions were made perfectly clear. The Trans-Atlantic Association may, for all practical purposes, have been suppressed. But Joseph Gordon, who had certainly been in touch (even if indirectly) with Thomas Dudgeon and other association backers, now intended to give effect to the objective encapsulated in the organisation's title. What Lord Stafford called 'the Indian benefaction', it emerged, was to be deployed in such a way as to ease the expense of passages from Sutherland to North America.[22]

In a leaflet circulated in Sutherland in the spring of 1821, Joseph Gordon revealed an improvement on William Allan's transatlantic fares. Adults leaving for Nova Scotia, would pay 'four guineas and a half', 'passengers under fourteen years of age . . . one guinea and a half'. Interest was intense. When, as advertised in his circular and in the *Inverness Journal*, Gordon staged an explanatory event at Golspie Inn on Tuesday 1 May 1821, he 'was met', according to Francis Suther, 'by about 300 people'. Many, significantly enough, were former Sutherland Estate tenants who had moved into Caithness but who now scented an opportunity to get to North America. This Caithness contingent, however, was matched by an equally big group from Strathbrora, where (for reasons touched on shortly) a further, if localised, set of evictions had still to take place.[23]

During the months following his taking charge of the money collected by his brother, Joseph Gordon had begun collaborating closely with William Allan who, within a week or two of the 1 May gathering at Golspie, had signed up enough people to fill the first of the ships he and Joseph Gordon were jointly to dispatch in the next 12 or so months. That vessel, the *Ossian*, sailed for Pictou from the Ross-shire port of Cromarty on 25 June 1821. Two others, the

Harmony and the *Ruby*, left from the same port a year later. The *Ossian* carried just over 100 passengers, the *Ruby* and the *Harmony* a further 250 between them. Courtesy of the funding at Joseph Gordon's disposal, all three ships were well provisioned and their passengers supplied with saws, axes and other tools they would need in Nova Scotia. While those same passengers were certainly glad to be quitting post-clearance Sutherland, their leave-taking – especially for relatives and neighbours left behind – was a time of mixed emotions. On Tuesday 2 July 1822, the day the *Harmony* and the *Ruby* sailed, a 'vast assemblage', or so the *Inverness Journal* reported, 'attended [at Cromarty] to take leave of their friends'. The 'parting scene', the paper continued, 'was of the most affecting nature', such as to leave in tears even those 'spectators unconnected with the [departing] parties'.[24]

Among the 360 or so emigrants thus helped on their way to Nova Scotia were people who had seen something of, or been involved in, the highly charged events surrounding the ejection of Jessie Ross, her two little girls and her baby from their Ascoilemore home. One was Mary Murray, the nursing mother who, on the afternoon of the Ross family's eviction, breastfed and comforted Jessie's baby daughter, Roberta. Another was Alexander MacDonald whose father, Adam MacDonald, was one of Ascoilemore's four principal tenants. Reaching the Earltown district by way of Pictou in 1822, Alexander[*] obtained a land grant on the Tatamagouche River and – as if to underline the extent to which Earltown and surrounding localities were Sutherland communities transposed to Nova Scotia – promptly married someone he had known, and maybe courted, back in Strathbrora. This was Christiana Baillie, one of the two sisters who had accompanied their mother and brother when, in 1820, the Baillie family left for Nova Scotia from Kilbraur, no more than a mile from Ascoilemore but on the River Brora's opposite bank.[25]

---

* Alexander was an ancestor of Glen Matheson – to whom much of this information is owed.

A further arrival in Nova Scotia in 1822 was Donald MacKay, the former fur trader who had been evicted from his Ascoilemore home the day before Jessie Ross and who, like Jessie's husband Gordon, had had the temerity to raise the manner of the township's clearance with the Marquis of Stafford. MacKay (as far as can be established) was not accompanied on to the *Harmony* at Cromarty by his wife Mary, who had perhaps died (though this cannot be established either) some time previously. MacKay took with him, however, two of his and Mary's boys; and in Nova Scotia he was joined by Donald, one of the two sons MacKay had brought back to Strathbrora from York Factory at the end of his Hudson's Bay Company career.

Donald junior's older brother William had returned to Hudson Bay and joined the HBC in 1817. Described in 1832 by the HBC's then governor, George Simpson, as 'a halfbreed of the Cree nation' and 'a steady, well conducted, useful man', William MacKay was to serve the company more loyally than his father, sticking with the HBC for more than half a century, mostly as postmaster (or principal trader) at various HBC trading centres on or to the east of Lake Winnipeg. In 1826, at Norway House, the former Jack River, William married Julie Chalifoux*; and in 1853 – in a development illustrative of the complexity of links between Manitoba and the Highlands – the couple's eldest son, also William, married Elizabeth Grant whose Métis father, Cuthbert Grant, had so effectively harried the Kildonan settlers at Red River.[26]

Some 2,000 miles east of William MacKay's sphere of operations, William's brother Donald had meanwhile settled alongside his father and half-brothers on the upper part of Barney's River. Known to his Nova Scotia neighbours as 'Indian Donald' – because (presumably) of features inherited from his mother – this man, whose childhood experiences included both winter treks across the Hudson Bay

---

* Nothing is known for sure of Julie but she is likely to have been of Métis background.

barrens and stints of cattle-herding on the Strathbrora hills, was said at the end of his life in 1885 to have been 'very industrious, reserved and inoffensive'. If that is an accurate description, Donald MacKay junior's character owed nothing to his father, of whom tall tales were still being told in the Barney's River area more than half a century after the father's death in 1833.[27]

The main originator of such tales was Donald senior himself, a man whose 'trusty rifle', or so it was reported by a Pictou newspaper in 1886, had 'popped' many of the fur trader's numerous enemies. Those same enemies loom large in MacKay's own memoir of his first forays into the then wholly unsettled territories now occupied by Manitoba, Minnesota and North Dakota. This memoir, donated by one of MacKay's descendants to the HBC Archive in Winnipeg, was compiled at the Nova Scotia homestead that MacKay, in exile now forever from Strathbrora, named Gordonbush. At this new Gordonbush,[*] it can be assumed, MacKay wrote at the portable writing desk he had brought with him from Scotland, a desk which, as well as making almost as many Atlantic crossings as its owner, had survived repeated journeyings on the Hayes, Red and Assiniboine Rivers. Those and other travels, MacKay commented, were punctuated by armed confrontations with his fur trade opponents. In the course of one such episode, he recalled, a group of rival traders had queried why they should permit him to be on his way. He replied, Donald MacKay wrote, with those words: 'I only want what is just.' This, to be sure, has all the hallmarks of a gloss put on an ugly, and potentially violent, scene a long time after the event. But it encapsulates, for all that, a truth about this most remarkable man. It certainly captures something of what had motivated Donald MacKay, while still in Sutherland, to wage a final battle with the Staffords and their agents.[28]

*   *   *

---

[*] This name did not survive. The locality where MacKay's Nova Scotia home was situated is today known, more prosaically, as Marsh.

The last mention of Donald MacKay in Sutherland Estate records occurs in a 'List of Small Rents Supposed Irrecoverable at 1st August 1825'. There MacKay is described (inaccurately) as having 'died in America'. He is also stated to have emigrated while still owing the Marquis and Marchioness of Stafford a grand total of sixpence. Lord and Lady Stafford are unlikely to have been perturbed by this loss. They would gladly have surrendered a much larger sum, it seems probable, to be rid of a man the marchioness and James Loch were at one in categorising as a 'villain', a 'rebel' and the principal architect of the 'conspiracy' which, in 1821, resulted in the military being deployed in Sutherland for the first time since soldiers had been sent north in the early months of 1813.[29]

The origins of this new deployment are to be found in the disputed tenurial position of the dozen or so tenants living in Ascoilemore and the adjacent townships of Dalfolly and Ballenleadin, occupying, between them, the mile or so of hillside separating Ascoilemore from Balnacoil where the valley of the Blackwater opens out into Strathbrora. It had originally been intended to evict those tenants, Donald MacKay included, in the spring of 1819. But on hearing of this intention, MacKay and his neighbours had objected on the grounds that William Young, when Sutherland Estate factor, had pledged to keep them in possession until well beyond that date. This, predictably, was disputed by Young's successors and, just as predictably, by Walter Ross, Strathbrora's minister. Ross denied a Donald MacKay claim that the minister, who leased land at Grianan, not far from Ascoilemore, both knew about, and had been party to, an agreement extending Ballenleadin, Dalfolly and Ascoilemore tenancies well into the 1820s.[30]

The fact that Ross came (as usual) to the estate management's aid should have settled matters. But William Young, when contacted by Francis Suther and James Loch, backed up, in part at least, the MacKay version of what had occurred. Some time after he had let Pollie on the Blackwater's upper reaches to John Cleugh, it now emerged, Young had been minded to lease to another shepherd by the name of Potts a further tract of hill pasture also on the Blackwater but some distance downstream. The Ascoilemore people and their neighbours, Young explained to Loch, had made such a 'hideous clamour' about this proposal that he had instead let it to them at an annual rent identical to the one Potts offered, this being 50 guineas. That deal, while not reaching as far into the future as its beneficiaries asserted, did extend, Young confirmed, as far as November 1820. Although limited to landholdings on the Blackwater, and thus not applying to the area where Ascoilemore and adjacent communities were themselves located, this same deal, as Loch and Suther were obliged to accept, constituted a real obstacle to evicting its Dalfolly, Ballenleadin and Ascoilemore beneficiaries. When, in May 1819 and May 1820, most of the rest of Strathbrora was emptied of its inhabitants, the occupants of those three townships were accordingly left in place. They would stay, it was announced, until May 1821.[31]

Heartened by this partial success, the Ascoilemore tenants in particular continued to insist on their entitlement, as they saw it, to remain where they were for several more years. In this connection, they spent heavily (as mentioned earlier) on legal advice – first from Joseph Gordon and then from the so-called 'penny lawyer' (his name was Fraser) they engaged in Tain. On this exercise failing to produce – in the absence of any documentary evidence of William Young's supposed promises – the outcome the Ascoilemore people hoped for, they began (while still seeking legal ways forward) to contemplate other forms of resistance to their removal. In so doing, they are bound to have been encouraged by news from Culrain. Equally encouraging was the way the example set by that Ross-shire community was quickly followed by a second community, this time in Sutherland.

What took place in that community in the summer of 1820 was still recalled a lifetime later in Nova Scotia. Reporting in the 1880s on his conversations with elderly people who – when young – had come to Pictou from Sutherland, a contributor to Nova Scotia's

Eastern Chronicle told how his interviewees had left Scotland when the Staffords (a family those same interviewees clearly detested) 'took it into their heads to convert into . . . stock ranches their estates in Sutherlandshire . . . This', the *Chronicle* account went on, 'made it necessary to drive out the tenantry and, in many cases, burn their cabins to make the work of spoliation doubly sure.' In the run-up to one such episode, *Chronicle* readers learned, 'the landlord's sergeant was . . . delivering the legal notices of ejectment . . . and, the men of the place being absent at the time, a band of Amazons . . . burned the writs and, seizing the officer, suspended him over the bonfire until he was nicely roasted.'[32]

That story came from a man whose mother had been one of the 'Amazons' involved. It contains some errors. The place where the 'sergeant' came to grief was not actually on the Sutherland Estate. Nor were its menfolk – certainly not all of them – elsewhere. What was described, however, was more or less exactly the fate that overtook Sheriff-Officer Donald Bannerman – a 'shocking outrage' James Loch called it – when he attempted to serve removal notices on tenants at Gruids.[33]

Bannerman had confronted the Kildonan rebels in 1813; he had informed on Robert McKid's poaching activities in 1814; and, in 1819 and 1820, he had carried out hundreds of evictions throughout the Sutherland straths. To say he was hated, then, would be grossly to understate the case. Word of what was done to Donald Bannerman or *Domhnall Sgios* at Gruids, it follows, must have been greeted everywhere in Sutherland with glee of the sort that remained evident, well over 60 years later, in the Nova Scotia telling of the tale.

Rather like Culrain, Gruids was an outlying possession of a Ross-shire landlord, in this instance Sir George Munro of Poyntzfield. Also like Culrain, just six or seven miles away, Gruids (where the young Hugh Miller stayed in the 'longhouse' described earlier) was located on the right, or south, bank of the River Shin. Between Culrain and Gruids, however, is the Oykel, the further river that constituted, in the nineteenth century, the boundary between

Sutherland to the Oykel's north and Ross-shire to its south. This meant that, on its being decided that Gruids was to be cleared, the requisite summonses of removal had to be obtained from Sutherland's sheriff court and served by Sutherland sheriff-officers. Thus it came about that, having taken receipt of the relevant 'decreets of removing', Donald Bannerman, accompanied by two colleagues, Alexander Ross and Alexander MacKenzie, arrived at Gruids on the morning of Thursday 15 June 1820.[34]

To get there, the three men had taken the ferry that made regular crossings of the Shin a little way downstream from the present-day village of Lairg. As they approached the Gruids bank, the ferry-man, John Murray, well aware of who his passengers were and why they had made the long journey from Golspie, said sarcastically that they would soon be receiving a warm welcome. Hearing this all three – already more than slightly fearful perhaps of encountering Culrain-style opposition – asked to be returned to the opposite shore. Murray, however, declined to oblige. Left with no alternative but to disembark, Bannerman and his colleagues did so only to see, as Bannerman put it, 'a number of persons, mostly women armed with sticks and cudgels, making towards them'. Soon, said Bannerman, this crowd – about 100 strong – 'violently seized' him. The 'precepts of removing', as the sheriff-officer called the documents he had hidden about his person, were quickly found. Then, while one or two of his assailants went to fetch (presumably from a nearby home) an already burning piece of fuel that could be used to kindle a fire, the rest of the 'mob', young women to the fore, 'stripped him naked . . . threw him down, and bound his hands behind his back'.[35]

A blaze was set alight and the eviction orders thrown on to it. Next Donald Bannerman, who had meanwhile been permitted by older women to get back into his 'britches and stockings', was again grabbed, lifted into the air and suspended over flames fierce enough to scorch him – 'first on the back and then on the belly'. Together with Ross and MacKenzie, who had also been 'laid hold' of,

Bannerman – amid shouted enquiries as to whether he 'had said his prayers that morning' – was next marched back to Murray's ferry-boat. Minutes later, the three captives, escorted by a number of their captors, had been returned to the River Shin's Lairg shore. There Ross managed to escape. Running (as he may have thought) for his life, he found shelter in the home belonging to Lairg's schoolmaster, bolting the house's door behind him as he entered. Soon, however, Ross had been retaken by people John Murray had been busy ferry-ing across the Shin from Gruids, two girls having 'broke[n] in through [a] window' and opened the schoolmaster's locked door from the inside.[36]

Once Ross was back at the point where MacKenzie and Bannerman were being held, both he and MacKenzie appear to have had their freedom restored. Donald Bannerman's ordeal, however, was not yet over. The exhausted sheriff-officer – who, it should be underlined, is described in documentation dealing with his Gruids experiences as 'a widower aged sixty-five years or thereby' – was once more 'felled . . . to the ground'. Only after he had been left to lie there 'for some time' was he at last set on his feet and, with hands still bound and most of his clothes bundled roughly round his neck, left to stumble off in the direction of Golspie.[37]

Two aspects of the Gruids debacle gave the Staffords and James Loch some satisfaction. First, it had not occurred on the Sutherland Estate. Second, the Gruids evictions were being undertaken in the name of Sciberscross's former tacksman, John Sutherland, who, on quitting Strathbrora, had been granted a lease of Gruids by Munro of Poyntzfield. At Gruids, Sutherland may have expected to order matters in the traditional tacksman style by leaving the place in the occupation of subtenants. This was ruled out, however, by the lease Munro had insisted upon. Its terms obliged John Sutherland, as the Poyntzfield laird's lessee, to have Gruids cleared and its population replaced by sheep. Sutherland, who acquired his Gruids tenancy in 1818, had not rushed to fulfil those conditions. But by 1820 he had been compelled to act. Hence the removal orders that resulted in the assault on Donald Bannerman.[38]

The Marchioness of Stafford nurtured a virulent dislike of John Sutherland – a man who had had a hand in so much anti-clearance activity – and was consequently delighted by his Gruids entanglement. She saw the 'finger of justice', the marchioness wrote, in Sutherland 'being the person concerned' in this new clearance. James Loch agreed. Equally to be welcomed, he thought, was the fact that 'Joseph Gordon [was] . . . John Sutherland's agent'. By rendering both men 'guilty of the crime of sheep farming and removing', Loch hoped, developments at Gruids would diminish the authority of two of his most inveterate critics.[39]

For much the same reason, the marchioness derived a malevolent pleasure from reports of Sciberscross's ex-tacksman being 'in a very miserable state, his wife and family constantly quarrelling with him, and he with them'. Soon, however, this pleasure faded. It did so, in part, because of a dawning realisation on the part of Sutherland's sheriff, Charles Ross, that John Sutherland, as Francis Suther informed Loch, may have staged something of a hoax at Gruids. By acting in 'connivance with the measures resorted to by the [Gruids] people', it was suspected, Sutherland aimed to give the appearance of attempting to fulfil his lease conditions while simultaneously ensuring that the attempt was bound to fail.[40]

This, at first sight, may seem nothing more than an extreme instance of the Stafford camp's addiction to conspiracy theory. But Ross (as will be seen) was to become more and more convinced that John Sutherland and his Gruids subtenants were indeed acting in concert – a state of affairs which, though further complicating an already complex situation, did nothing to ease Stafford worries that at Gruids, just as at Culrain, both landlords and the law were being defied with nothing in the way of repercussion. Aggravating those concerns were signs that sympathy with the stand taken at Gruids was widespread on the Sutherland Estate. Nor was such sympathy confined to folk with first-hand experience of eviction. It extended, for example, into the Sutherland county town of Dornoch, as became evident when, in August 1820, efforts were made to draft the 60-strong force of special constables that would be needed, it was felt, if there was to be any chance of getting a second set of removal notices delivered to people who, in June, had consigned the first set to a bonfire.

The decision to recruit this force was made by Francis Suther, Gabriel Reed and others when, in their collective capacity as Sutherland's Justices of the Peace Court, they met on Tuesday 8 August. Over the next week or so, candidates for special constable posts were identified from among tradesmen and businessmen in the Dornoch and Golspie areas. Those candidates – blacksmiths, shop-keepers, an innkeeper, a baker, shoemakers and others – were then ordered to appear at a further court session to be sworn in and briefed as to their duties. This session took place on 19 August in Dornoch's town council chamber, which was housed in the same building as the prison which, five years before, had briefly accommo-dated one of the JP Court's leading members, Patrick Sellar.[41]

'The first ten [men] named and called forward . . . refused to take the oath', Suther reported of the chaos that now ensued, 'and one of them, of the name of Henderson, grossly insulted the court. A warrant was immediately made out for committing him, but the officers [meaning the regular constables on hand] were deforced and the prisoner was rescued on the stair leading from the council room to the jail.' Nobody, it appeared, was willing – not even in return for a special constable's then attractive allowance of four shillings a day – to be seen to be enforcing further clearances.[42]

Neither that Dornoch fracas nor its wider implications would have escaped the notice of Donald MacKay and his associates at Ascoilemore. This Strathbrora township's 'turbulent set' of 'complete Dudgeonites', as Francis Suther called them, were easily the most recalcitrant opponents the factor and Loch had encoun-tered since, in 1816, they had become responsible for the Sutherland Estate's administration. '[U]nder the undue influence of that fellow

MacKay', as Loch put it, the Ascoilemore people had 'from the beginning . . . behaved worse than their neighbours'. They had been regular attenders at the Trans-Atlantic Association's Meikle Ferry assemblies. Preferring 'Dudgeon's sermons' to those of their minister, Suther complained, they had also been prominent among the crowd that – in defiance of clergy-backed warnings of the consequences – had gathered at Golspie for the banned Trans-Atlantic Association meeting of 4 January 1820. People of this stamp, Loch felt, required dealing with harshly.[43]

Individuals like Donald MacKay might think themselves men of substance, James Loch observed. But 'they [were] not so respectable as many who [had] been moved'. They were certainly not to have 'any extraordinary favours' granted to them as a result of their having succeeded in avoiding eviction in 1819 and 1820. On the contrary, they had to be made 'to feel the consequences' of their enthusiastic adherence to Thomas Dudgeon and their attendance at the Trans-Atlantic Association gathering in Golspie. 'I must insist on you intimating to such of them [as were at Golspie]' Loch instructed Suther, 'that they are to be turned off without lots.'[44]

But this, as James Loch recognised in his calmer moments, was no real sanction. Since Donald MacKay and his principal allies – John Baillie and Adam MacDonald in Ascoilemore and Alexander MacKay in Ballenleadin – had 'taken no notice' of earlier offers of coastal crofts, they were not going to be swayed by the absence of further such offers. By 1820, if not before, Donald MacKay – according to intelligence reaching Suther – was anyway 'paying rent for a farm in Caithness'. Others from Ascoilemore and adjacent townships were known to be doing likewise. By the start of 1821, moreover, several of the same 'badly dispositioned' tenants – their Caithness farms notwithstanding – were reported to be showing interest in Joseph Gordon's subsidised passages to Nova Scotia.[45]

Having thus provided themselves with two possible lines of retreat from Strathbrora, Donald MacKay and those around him may well have thought they had nothing to lose from renewed defiance. This became evident as a result of Francis Suther's decision to commence the clearance of the Ascoilemore, Ballenleadin and Dalfolly area by moving, in early 1821, against the three townships' subtenants at Achness. This was a community located, three or four miles up the Blackwater, among the hill pastures that William Young had agreed to lease to the Ascoilemore men and their neighbours. Ten years previously, scarcely anyone had lived at Achness. By 1821, however, the place contained at least eight families, and possibly more. The main explanation for its expansion, according to James Loch, was that it had become 'a nest of smugglers'. From Achness, Loch had learned, it was possible to follow the Blackwater and one of its tributaries, the Skinsdale, to points where – by way of passes at altitudes of no more than seven or eight hundred feet – access could be got, via Borrobol, to the Strath of Kildonan.* From there, other paths led through the hills to the parts of Caithness where Loch (with probable justification) thought many of Kildonan's evicted tenants had re-established their illicit stills. Achness, Loch believed, was 'the connecting point' between Caithness's 'smuggling districts' and those districts' Easter Ross, Inverness and Lowland markets, which were accessed by means of further hill routes leading, or so Loch contended, from Achness, through Gruids, to points south. This connection between the two rebel communities, Loch insisted, was why the one was as determinedly defiant as the other. 'That the preservation of [their] illicit trade is the chief objective of the deluded people [of both Gruids and Achness]', Loch wrote, 'there can be no doubt.'[46]

Achness's inhabitants, James Loch informed William MacKenzie in Edinburgh, were being 'incited by a blackguard by the name of MacKay, a Hudson's Bay man'. Whether or not at MacKay's prompting, it was definitely the case that no one at Achness could be compelled or cajoled into accepting summonses of removal. When,

---

* This was the route followed in 1819 by James Brander and his evicting party when (as mentioned earlier) they moved on from Strathbrora to Kildonan.

not long after New Year, James Brander, who had organised the clearance of much of Strathbrora, went to Achness in the company of several sheriff-officers and constables, the summonses he took with him were at once grabbed and destroyed. When, subsequent to this, a locally recruited Sutherland Estate employee was sent to reason – in Gaelic – with Achness residents, he was instantly sent packing. The settlement's occupants 'would not have heeded' the Archangel Gabriel, Francis Suther remarked of this episode, adding that Strathbrora's minister, Walter Ross, who could be relied on to instruct his congregation to do the Sutherland Estate's bidding, had 'very little influence if any' in Achness, Dalfolly, Ballenleadin or Ascoilemore.[47]

In mid-March a further sheriff-officer agreed to make the long tramp into Achness. 'No sooner [had he] put his foot on the ground', Suther informed Loch, 'than they seized him, stripped him, took every paper he was in possession of and destroyed them before his face.' The Achness stalemate, it was thus made clear, was not going to be broken by any locally available means. The time had come, Loch duly concluded, to persuade William Rae, the lord advocate, to have soldiers sent to Sutherland.[48]

This was Loch's second such endeavour. His first had involved attempts to get 'two companies of infantry' despatched to Gruids in the aftermath of what had been done there to Donald Bannerman. This suggestion, however, had been rebuffed by Rae every bit as firmly as the lord advocate had earlier rejected Sheriff Donald MacLeod's pleas for military intervention in Culrain. Hence the pains Loch took to ensure that this time he got a more positive response.[49]

The starting point of the case made to William Rae was Achness's alleged role in the illicit whisky trade, which Loch knew the government was increasingly eager to put down. All such 'smuggling', Loch argued, was being aided and abetted by ministers' failure to deal decisively with what had been going on in Culrain, Gruids and Achness. Because of that failure, 'a system of resistance to the law

[was] rapidly extending over all the smuggling districts'. This was the government's fault: 'The people [in places like Achness and Gruids] have an idea that . . . government [ministers], if they do not favour their resistance [to eviction], yet wink at it.' It was therefore 'of the greatest consequence' that Rae and his colleagues respond to outbreaks of the Achness, Gruids and Culrain type by showing themselves 'serious in their desire to put an end to them'. Nor should Rae be overly afraid of injury being done to women. Their leading role in what had been going on was entirely 'owing to a silly notion . . . the people have that women are not subject to be punished for riot or assault'. In this connection, cognisance had to be taken of the fact that 'men always collect[ed] the stones' that women and girls threw. There was nothing spontaneous, in other words, about what had taken place at Culrain or Gruids and what was now taking place at Achness. In every instance, attacks on sheriff-officers, constables and others had been the outcome of careful planning. That was why matters were so grave. 'If this [meaning repeated lawbreaking at Achness] is passed over, as well as [what occurred at] Gruids, there is an end to all . . . legal authority.' There was even a possibility, in such circumstances, that 'those who [had] been removed' would 'resume their farms'.[50]

This was all very fine. But the lord advocate, James Loch expected, would respond as always by saying it was the responsibility of the civil authorities – whether in Sutherland or Ross-shire – to enforce court orders. This could be countered, Loch felt, by the contention that such enforcement had become impossible. Not only had Sutherland's JPs been unable to sign up special constables, those constables already in service were not to be relied on. Most of them, Francis Suther told Loch, shared 'the general feeling of [Sutherland] natives' that Achness families had right on their side. This could be seen, Suther went on, 'from the lukewarmness of the majority of those [constables]' who were with James Brander at Achness – but who, despite the rough handling the procurator fiscal received there, had declined to come to his aid.[51]

In late March 1821, James Loch, accompanied by the ever-biddable George MacPherson Grant, met with William Rae in London. At this meeting, all the Stafford commissioner's points appear to have been taken on board. However, the lord advocate, because of the long shadow cast by Peterloo, remained reluctant – even in the face of everything Loch and MacPherson Grant had to say – to run the political risk of injecting soldiers into situations that might result in their killing civilians. Loch had anticipated this. Ever since Peterloo, the Whig opposition in the House of Commons had been harrying the Liverpool administration about its habit, as Whigs saw it, of dealing with protest by resorting over and over again to repression. That was why, before going to see Rae, Loch had ensured that the lord advocate, if he consented to deploy troops in Sutherland, would be spared Whig attack. This had been accomplished with the help of Henry Brougham, a more and more influential presence on the Commons' opposition benches. Brougham, it seems, was amenable to his old friend's suggestion that Sutherland's troubles should not be permitted to become a party matter. As previously agreed with Lady Stafford, Loch now played this card: 'I . . . mentioned to the [lord] advocate Brougham's opinion', Loch told the marchioness, 'and hinted that, through him, we were pretty sure the [parliamentary] opposition would say nothing . . . We saw this had its effect,' Loch went on before adding a little coyly: 'But that is our secret.'[52]

Reassured that he would not be exposed to Whig condemnation in consequence of doing as Loch wanted, William Rae moved fast. On Thursday 5 April, 70 men of the army's 41st Regiment – a Welsh formation – were marched out of Fort George and on to the road north. Pushed along by their commander, a Major Fallon, they made good progress. In just three days they reached Dornoch. Next day they were in Brora. From there, before daybreak on Tuesday 10 April, they set off up Strathbrora in the direction of Ascoilemore and Achness.[53]

James Loch was grateful for 'the vigour' shown by Rae. But there were limits to his gratitude. On learning from William MacKenzie

– liaising on the Sutherland Estate's behalf with the military authorities in Edinburgh – that MacKenzie had instructed Francis Suther to 'see that provisions, particularly bread, be [made] ready for the soldiers', Loch immediately fired off a supplementary order. 'You will keep a distinct account of the amount of provisions furnished for [the 41st Regiment's] use', Suther was instructed, '[so] that you may be repaid by [the] government'. Fallon and his men might be in Sutherland to do, in effect, James Loch's bidding. But, Loch being Loch, there was to be no chance of them getting anything for nothing from the Sutherland Estate.[54]

In Sutherland itself, meanwhile, the Achness-bound military were joined on the morning of their departure from Brora by Sheriff Charles Ross and Francis Suther – Ross heading a substantial contingent of sheriff-officers and constables, Suther in charge of an equally large group of estate employees. In total, then, the force that, just after 8 a.m., passed Donald MacKay's timber-built home – its distinctiveness leading to its featuring in direction-giving correspondence of the time – numbered more than 100. MacKay, who must surely have watched Fallon's dozens of scarlet-coated soldiers swing by, may have found the spectacle (as he was meant to) intimidating. In light of what is known of the former fur trader, however, it is more likely that he derived no little satisfaction from having caused Loch, the Staffords and the British government so much trouble and expense.[55]

Not far beyond Donald MacKay's cabin and just short of Balnacoil, Suther, Ross, Fallon and their men turned right, away from the then recently constructed Strathbrora road and on to a long-established track paralleling the Blackwater's eastern or left bank. A mile or two up this track – as if to make the point that the locality the army was here to depopulate had been inhabited for ages – a broch stood (as it still does) on rising ground above the river. When built, 15 or more centuries before the 41st Regiment's deployment in Sutherland, that castle-like tower is likely to have been garrisoned at times of threat. Neither there nor anywhere else, however, was any opposition offered to the soldiers who, an hour or so into their trek up the Blackwater, marched into Achness.

Because a Latheron man – described by Loch as having 'formerly belonged to that lawless set, the Kildonanites' – had taken part in the January assault on James Brander, there were worries that the Achness people might have received reinforcements from Caithness. But that had not happened. 'On arrival [at Achness]', Suther reported to Loch, 'we found the houses . . . empty [and] not a soul about the place except three old women sitting on a knoll.' Charles Ross had hoped, with the aid of the military, to apprehend men wanted in connection with their participation in one or other of the disturbances that had occurred in Achness since the turn of the year. But word of the troops' approach, Suther noted ruefully, had reached Achness well in advance of their arrival. Having thus 'got a hint to be off', the wanted men, together with almost all the rest of Achness's inhabitants, had disappeared into the hills that, rising steeply beyond the Blackwater, separated the settlement from other pre-clearance communities around and to the north of Sciberscross. Doing battle with the army, it seems, was not on Achness's agenda. Here and there on the approaches to the township, however, there were found 'heaps of stones . . . [that] had been collected', it was surmised, 'to give a warm welcome to the sheriff-officers if they had not been supported by such an overwhelming force'.[56]

The day before, no doubt in response to news of soldiers being en route for Strathbrora, two men from Achness had turned up at Francis Suther's office in Golspie. With them they had brought a letter proposing that, if Achness's residents were left where they were until May, they would then 'remove quietly'. 'I showed this letter to Mr Ross', Suther wrote, 'and he agreed with me that [further delay being thought out of the question] it was absolutely necessary to eject the people and pull down their houses.' This was of questionable legality in that evictions should have been preceded by summonses of the kind that had never been successfully served. But neither Suther nor the sheriff were in the humour to bother with such niceties. Watched by the now resting soldiers, who took no part in these proceedings, Suther's men, as Ross reported to one of William Rae's colleagues in Edinburgh, accordingly set about 'removing . . . furniture and goods' from Achness's homes. They then 'pulled down the roofs' of every house and outbuilding in the township.[57]

There followed one last attempt to give effect to the 'criminal letters' or arrest warrants that had been taken out against a dozen or so Achness men. 'Just as we were coming away', runs Charles Ross's account of this development, 'we descried in different parts of the hills at the distance of nearly a mile, with a river between, two or three small parties of people whom we suspected to be those against whom we had warrants.' At this, Major Fallon 'picked out some of the most active of his men and they . . . gave chase'. On seeing these men run towards the Blackwater, the watchers on the skyline opposite 'started from their hiding places', Suther commented, 'and took up the hillside like mountain deer.' The wanted men, in Suther's words, thus 'got clear off'. They also took some pleasure, it can be guessed, from the fate of one of the 41st's junior officers, a Lieutenant Ash. While 'pursuing one of the flying parties', it appears, Ash, as a result of his taking a header into 'a deep stream', 'came . . . by a severe ducking'.[58]

After Achness, the army's next objective was Gruids. But the direct route to Gruids involved a crossing of the River Shin, and that, it was soon realised, would not be possible. A combination of rain and melting snow had raised the river to a level that made fording it dangerous, and Gruids people had 'carried off all boats'. The problem was solved by Charles Ross commandeering vessels usually stationed at Meikle Ferry and ordering them sailed up the Dornoch Firth and through the Kyle of Sutherland to the point, just below the tidal limit, where the Oykel and Shin meet. There the Meikle Ferry craft were to await the arrival of Fallon and his soldiers who – having reached Ross-shire by way of the then recently constructed crossing that gave the village of Bonar Bridge its name – marched through Ardgay before setting off along the Kyle of Sutherland's southern shore in the direction of the waiting boats. Their route took the troops through Culrain. No removals were scheduled there that spring. But anyone watching the red-coated and musket-carrying infantry tramp by would have understood that – despite earlier failures to bring this about – the army was now liable to be sent against anyone resisting eviction.[59]

Having been ferried across the Oykel just beyond Culrain and having made good speed along the River Shin's western bank, the troops were soon in Gruids. Sheriff Ross had told John Sutherland, Sciberscross's ex-tacksman, to meet him there. But Sutherland, who some days previously had been accused formally by Ross of 'connivance' with his subtenants, was nowhere to be seen. Neither was anyone else. As at Achness, the locality's inhabitants – a number of whom were wanted in connection with the previous year's attack on Donald Bannerman – had taken themselves off before the army's arrival. This meant that no arrests were made. Ejection notices, however, were fixed to every home in Gruids, and the locality's clearance thus hurried along, as a gratified James Loch put it, 'at the point of the bayonet'. Throughout the north of Scotland, Loch considered, it was beginning to be grasped that further resistance to clearance would be dealt with speedily, harshly and effectively.[60]

That lesson, Loch hoped, would shortly be reinforced by the trial of people alleged to have committed criminal offences in the course of the Achness protests. In the event, just three such people – John Matheson, John Sutherland and Ann MacDonald – appeared at the High Court's springtime sitting in Inverness. Sutherland and Matheson were the Achness men who had tried to negotiate with Suther on 9 April and who had instead found themselves sent under armed escort to Dornoch Jail. How or when MacDonald was detained is unclear. But she was probably taken into custody mainly with the aim of making it plain that women

– contrary to popular opinion – were no more immune than men from prosecution. Charged, like Matheson and Sutherland, with 'violently deforcing and obstructing officers of the law', Ann MacDonald went free when, in Inverness, it became apparent that the charges against her and Sutherland could not be sustained by the available evidence. Matheson, however, was sentenced to six months imprisonment.[61]

At Inverness, the several other individuals still being sought in connection with the Achness assault on James Brander were declared 'outlaws and fugitives'. All were said to be 'skulking in the hills' to avoid arrest. But Francis Suther, the Marchioness of Stafford was pleased to learn, anticipated no more trouble from them or their Ascoilemore backers. 'The appearance of the soldiers put an end to all their hopes,' Suther reported of Donald MacKay and his fellow tenants. 'They are completely cowed.'[62]

That seems unlikely. In North America, MacKay's lack of subservience, whether to his HBC superiors or to his many fur trade rivals, had made him disliked and feared in equal measure. Soldiers or no soldiers, that aspect of his character had not changed. Not long after he was, in his own words, 'cast out of [his] wooden house' at the end of May, MacKay would write in the most excoriating terms to the Marquis of Stafford about the 'grief and sorrow' resulting from Ascoilemore's clearance. That was not the action of a man acquiescing tamely in his fate. Nor was MacKay's subsequent departure for Barney's River. A Canadian historian, Marianne McLean, has written persuasively about the 'extraordinarily self-confident' communities established in her country by men and women whose emigration from the Highlands was 'largely triggered by the introduction of sheep farming'. This 'remarkable achievement', McLean comments, was not the work of a beaten-down, disheartened and demoralised people. That is surely the case; just as it is equally the case that the drive and determination so much in evidence among North America's Highland settlers is also discernible in the sheer *élan* with which many of the Stafford family's Sutherland opponents countered policies meant to put them firmly in their place.[63]

There was thus to be no question of people involved in Strathbrora's last stand against clearance now falling in with plans for their 'improvement'. This became apparent towards the end of April when, the earlier bar on offering crofts to families from Achness, Dalfolly, Ballenleadin and Ascoilemore having been rescinded, Francis Suther 'sent an officer among them' with instructions to urge acceptance of coastal 'lots'. That mission, Suther acknowledged, was a failure. Of the 30 or so families who could have done so, only three took up croft tenancies on the Sutherland Estate. Of the others, some went to Caithness. 'But the bulk of them', Suther informed Loch at the beginning of June, 'seem to have a wish to go to America'. Achness's former inhabitants had already been 'promised' help by Joseph Gordon, Suther wrote. Ascoilemore residents, he went on, expected – and were indeed to get – similar assistance. Some sailed that June for Pictou on the *Ossian*. Others – including Donald MacKay who, in the interim, found temporary accommodation in Brora – left the following summer on the *Harmony* or the *Ruby*.[64]

Long before that of course Ascoilemore had ceased to exist. 'Strathbrora is now effectually cleared of all its turbulent people,' Francis Suther reported on 4 June 1821. 'The removings [at Ascoilemore] were completed [last week] . . . and [its] houses demolished . . . [N]o business of this description has yet been done so quietly . . . I went myself with the party in case of opposition, as though I had learned . . . [Ascoilemore's occupants] had given up all intention of resisting, yet knowing their characters I could not altogether trust them.' This mistrust, however, had proved misplaced. All had gone well. The few interior communities that had succeeded, if only for a year or two, in avoiding the fate of all the rest had been dealt with: 'We are now, I think, settled.'[65]

James Loch too was cheerful. 'I am happy to say that the Sutherland removals are entirely completed,' he informed Lord

Stafford – then in Paris. That was in mid-June. Not for another month would it become apparent that one Ascoilemore removal – the one with which this book began – was to cause Loch and his employers more anxiety than any other eviction since Patrick Sellar's destruction of William Chisholm's home at Badinloskin.[66]

15

'INDELIBLE CHARACTERS ON
THE SURFACE OF THE SOIL'

The clearances in retrospect

Winnipeg in the 1880s was a boomtown. Its breakneck expansion was owed to a politician who as a small boy had been brought to British North America by an emigrant father from Sutherland. This politician was John A. Macdonald. A lawyer by profession and a fixer without rival, Macdonald was a driving force in the negotiations that led in 1867 to the former colonies of Nova Scotia, New Brunswick, Quebec and Ontario becoming the self-governing Dominion of Canada. As the new country's prime minister for much of its first quarter-century, Macdonald was determined to turn Canada – extending, to begin with, no further west than the Great Lakes – into a transcontinental union. His first move, made in 1869, was to acquire the territories previously under the jurisdiction of the Hudson's Bay Company; his second, accomplished in 1870, was to turn part of those territories into an additional Canadian province, Manitoba; his third, achieved in 1871, was to persuade residents of faraway British Columbia, on North America's Pacific coast, to join the nation taking shape thousands of miles to the east. To hold the resulting confederation together, Macdonald was clear, it would be necessary to construct a railway around the northern shores of the Great Lakes and on, by way of the prairies and the Rocky Mountains, to a Pacific terminal at Vancouver. Construction of this railway began in 1881. That same year, a dispute about the railway's route was settled in favour of its passing through Winnipeg, a little town in the vicinity of the Assiniboine's junction with Red River, where, nearly three-quarters of a century before, the Earl of Selkirk had installed an emigrant population from the Strath of Kildonan.

Winnipeg in 1871 had perhaps 200 residents. Fifteen years later, it was a thriving city of 20,000, a busy transit point for the thousands of European immigrants who, courtesy of the now completed Canadian Pacific Railway, were transforming Manitoba and the area to its west into one of the world's premier grain-producing regions. Most Manitobans by this point were recent arrivals with little or no awareness of their being, in effect, the fulfilment of Selkirk's belief that the prairies could be settled and farmed. But there was in mid-1880s Winnipeg one man, Charles Napier Bell, secretary to the Winnipeg Board of Trade, who made it his business to commemorate the Selkirk era and to seek out memories of it. 'During this summer', Bell commented in an 1887 publication, 'I have personally interviewed the last survivors of the original [Red River] colony who were old enough on the date of their arrival to remember the events that transpired in connection with the trouble between Lord Selkirk and the Northwest Fur Company. Herewith I give the substance of the information obtained from these old people . . . and, wherever possible, I use their own words.'[1]

Bell's key interviewee, the Board of Trade man wrote, was 'a wonderfully clear-headed and physically active old gentleman' whose recollections filled between four and five densely printed pages. 'My name is Donald Murray,' this man told Bell. 'I was born in Kildonan, Sutherlandshire, in or about the year 1801. I came to this place in 1815 . . . and I have lived here ever since.' Murray went on to speak in detail about Red River's past and, on checking his informant's recollections against such documentation as he could find, Bell judged the 85-year-old's memory 'singularly perfect'. The same is true of Donald Murray's account of his early life. He had indeed been born in 1801 – in October 1801 to be precise – at Suisgill. This was one of the localities incorporated into the Strath of

Kildonan's first sheep farm. That development is likely to have led to the Murray family being moved, when Donald was five or six, to another part of the strath. It may also have resulted in Donald's father, Alexander Murray, being more than usually apprehensive about the likely consequences of the additional sheep farms – Kilcalmkill and Torrish – that began to impact on the Kildonan area in the early part of 1813. Alexander, at all events, ensured that Donald's two older brothers, John and Alexander junior, were among the people who left that year for Red River. The two lads' remit, their younger brother told Charles Bell, was to prepare the way for the rest of the family: Alexander senior, his wife Elizabeth, Donald, a further brother and two sisters, who, in 1815, left Kildonan to join them.[2]

'We had a fine voyage out', Donald Murray said in 1887, 'and no sickness among the people. We left Thurso, as nearly as I can recollect, early in June . . . We arrived at the [Red River] Settlement, I suppose, about the end of October. It was a very cold, snowy fall and we had a hard and stormy journey up from York [Factory].'[3]

At York Factory, Donald Murray recalled, his parents were greeted by the distressing news that their elder sons, as Donald put it in 1887, 'had been sent down to [Upper] Canada by the North West Company'. During their time at Red River, however, the Murray brothers had built two houses. It was in one of these that Donald, his siblings, his mother and father stayed until – in the wake of the settler–Métis clash of June 1816 – they and others fled north to the HBC post at Jack River. There, Donald Murray told Charles Bell, they remained until the summer of 1817 when word came that Lord Selkirk – 'a tall, slender man' in Murray's (entirely accurate) recollection – had himself arrived at Red River at the head of about 100 armed men.[4]

This force had been recruited by Selkirk – who came personally to North America in the fall of 1815 – from among soldiers demobilised at the close of the war that ended with the Battle of New Orleans. With those men's help, Selkirk had at last been able to impose his will on the NWC, whose principal base at Fort William, on the western shore of Lake Superior, the earl seized and occupied. His taking of the law into his own hands in this fashion would embroil Selkirk in complex and stressful legal proceedings that contributed to his early death in 1820. But at Red River in 1817 the earl was nevertheless able to arrange matters to his satisfaction. 'I remember', Donald Murray said of what ensued 'that Lord Selkirk held a great meeting with the colonists . . . At this meeting new arrangements were made with all the settlers as to their lands. Before leaving Scotland the agreement was that we should pay five shillings an acre for our lands, but at this meeting Lord Selkirk gave them to us free of charge.'[5]

Donald Murray would live to see those same acres valued – by the real estate dealers who flooded into 1880s Winnipeg – at hundreds of times the price Selkirk had proposed to charge for them. In the interim, to be sure, the new Kildonan – which Murray served first as a river freighting specialist and afterwards as a magistrate – experienced plenty of setbacks. Crops failed regularly to begin with. The Red River flooded. Winters were skin-searingly cold. Donald Murray, however, never had any regrets about his parents' decision to take him out of Sutherland; and in this he was typical of his community. 'The Scotch', HBC governor George Simpson reported in the course of one of his traverses of the Bay Company's empire, 'consider Red River as much their home as the land of their nativity formerly was. They never will think of leaving the colony.'[6]

That was in 1824, by which point a now peaceful Red River was reaping the benefit of hostilities between the HBC and the Nor'Westers having ended in 1821 when, at the British government's insistence, the two companies amalgamated. Thirty or so years later, Lord Selkirk's colonists from Kildonan were still more securely attached to the farms Selkirk had made over to them. 'These people', one observer commented in the 1850s, 'surpass in comfort those of the same class in most other countries. Rich in food and clothing, all of them have likewise saved more or less money. Abundance on every hand testifies to their industry and economy . . . The evidence of domestic happiness everywhere meets the eye. No want of blankets here on the beds; the children well clothed, and the houses warm and comfortable; the barns teeming with grain, the stables with cattle.' Nothing like that ever would, or could, be written or said about post-clearance Sutherland's crofting townships.[7]

Angus MacKay was Donald Murray's exact contemporary. When Donald was being raised at Suisgill, Angus was growing up in Strathnaver. And just as Murray's experiences were put in print by Charles Bell in 1887, so Angus's life story – a little of it at least – was preserved when, in July 1883 at Bettyhill, he was questioned by Lord Napier and other members of Prime Minister Gladstone's commission of inquiry into crofting conditions. In response to this questioning, Angus MacKay (as recounted earlier) told how he had come close to drowning in the River Naver on the morning in June 1814 when Patrick Sellar's men unroofed his boyhood home. MacKay spoke too of what had happened subsequently to his parents and himself.

Following their 1814 expulsion from Sellar's Rhiloisk farm, Angus said, the MacKay family was sent to Skail. This was on the River Naver's western bank and a little further down the strath. There the MacKays built a new home. It was one they were permitted to occupy for just five years, for in 1819, when Sellar took over the west side of the Naver, the MacKays were again evicted. On this occasion, Angus told Lord Napier and his colleagues, they were allocated a newly demarcated croft on Strathy Point. 'It is just a wild, nasty place,' Angus MacKay said of that rocky, exposed and treeless headland. 'Never a man should be put there at all.'[8]

'Strathy Point is two miles in length on one side', MacKay elaborated, 'and three upon the other. The westerly wind blows upon it; the north-west wind blows upon it; the north wind blows upon it; the north-east wind blows upon it.' Here – where Strathnaver's woods, long-established rigs and plentiful hill grazings at once took on the aura of a paradise now lost – the MacKays were obliged to construct yet another house and to make what shift they could on land so poor it had never before been occupied.[9]

On crofts like those at Strathy Point – and there were hundreds of such crofts on the 'improved' Sutherland Estate – only one crop could be grown in quantity. That crop was potatoes; and when, in the 1840s, potatoes repeatedly fell victim to a devastating blight, food shortages in Sutherland became acute. Before the clearances, James Loch had forecast that crises of this kind would cease as soon as Sutherland's supposedly scarcity-afflicted straths were depopulated. Instead hunger, even starvation, threatened on all sides, disaster being averted only by famine relief measures far in excess of any required prior to 'improvement'.[10]

In such circumstances, there could be no crofting equivalents of the fine homes and well-stocked barns common by the mid-nineteenth century in the several localities – in Nova Scotia and Ontario as well as Manitoba – inhabited by North America's numerous immigrants from Sutherland. In post-clearance crofting settlements, prosperity of that sort was nowhere to be found. Angus MacKay, as the 1883 commission heard, had been obliged to trek regularly into Caithness where, until disabled by a limb-crushing accident, he earned a precarious livelihood in that county's flagstone quarries. Nor were the commission's other Sutherland interviewees any more positive than MacKay about their situation. The only way for someone of Sutherland crofting background to make good, it seemed, was to move elsewhere as soon as possible.

Napier and his team heard from two such individuals. John MacKay had been born in Rogart in 1822, Angus Sutherland near Helmsdale in 1848. MacKay had gone south in the 1840s. There he became involved in railway construction, trained as a civil engineer and, by the 1880s, was managing his own company. Sutherland, for his part, became a pupil-teacher (an older student who helped younger counterparts acquire basic skills) in Helmsdale, went on to take a teacher training course in Edinburgh and, when he appeared before the inquiry commission in 1883, was teaching maths in Glasgow Academy.

Such instances of individual success, it has been suggested, are evidence of 'improvement' having contributed, in the end, to upward mobility of a type that might not otherwise have occurred. That view was not shared by Angus Sutherland or John MacKay. Neither attributed any aspect of their personal advancement to the post-clearance social order from which they had escaped. Both in fact were committed to its destruction. A good deal of MacKay's substantial wealth was invested – by way, for example, of subsidising radical newspapers – in the cause of land reform. Sutherland, by the 1880s, was one of that cause's most eloquent and most effective spokesmen. In this capacity, he collaborated closely with the Irish Land League, which, in 1881, had won security of tenure for its thousands of smallholder members. Both in the Highlands and elsewhere, in speech after speech, article after article, Angus Sutherland insisted that, in order to forestall the possibility of renewed clearances, crofters were entitled to similar safeguards. They were also entitled, he contended, to have restored to them the land from which they, their parents or grandparents had been evicted.[11]

Sutherland's impassioned advocacy of a new deal for crofting communities led to his becoming a key figure in the organisation that, during the 1880s, was to obtain Irish-style security for crofters across the north of Scotland. Known initially as the Highland Land Law Reform Association and later as the Highland Land League, this organisation set out – much as Thomas Dudgeon had tried to do in 1819 – to mobilise crofters with a view to propelling their concerns on to the national stage. In this the Land League was helped by 1884 franchise reforms that gave crofters (male crofters anyway) voting rights and, by so doing, made it feasible for the league to run parliamentary candidates in Highland constituencies. One such candidate was Angus Sutherland, who in 1886 became his native county's MP. Nothing could have been more illustrative of the crofting population's growing assertiveness than the fact that a man

of Angus Sutherland's background now occupied the position filled
for so long by George MacPherson Grant and other Stafford nomi-
nees. Hence the stress laid in an admiring press profile on Angus's
ancestry and, in particular, on the new MP's paternal grandfather
having been 'burnt out of the Strath of Kildonan' prior to his being
'compelled as best he could to build up a new home for himself on a
barren hillside in the vicinity of . . . Helmsdale.'[12]

This same piece of family history was mentioned in the course of
Angus Sutherland's evidence to the 1883 commission. In 1813,
Angus said, his grandfather had not long been married, and had
chosen to stay on in Kildonan when Angus's great-grandparents and
the rest of their family joined what Angus called 'Lord Selkirk's
expedition to Red River'. The great-grandparents* in question were
James and Mary Sutherland – James (as mentioned earlier) having
been the Strath of Kildonan tenant who, prior to his departure for
Red River in 1815, had agreed to serve as the settler community's lay
preacher. As a result of his having seen correspondence that had
long before reached Kildonan from Red River, Angus Sutherland
said, he was well aware of the difficulties his grandfather's parents,
brothers and sisters had encountered initially in Manitoba. But
what he chose to major on, when appearing before Lord Napier,
were the more local consequences of the Strath of Kildonan's
clearance. The 'poverty' and 'present grievances' of crofters in the
coastal townships around Helmsdale, Angus stated in 1883, 'had
their origin' in the period when 'homes were being burned in
Kildonan Strath by those who [then] had the management of the
Sutherland Estate'.[13]

Lord Napier was to hear a great deal of similar testimony – his
Bettyhill hearings, for instance, being enlivened by a declaration to

----

* This book's hardback edition included a footnote asking for information as to who
exactly were Angus Sutherland's emigrant ancestors. The requested information was
forthcoming from Edinburgh resident, Elisabeth Law, whose late mother was a niece
of Angus Sutherland and who shares, in consequence, Angus's descent from the Red
River settlement's first lay preacher.

the effect that the area's crofting difficulties were traceable to hundreds of families having 'been cruelly burnt like wasps' out of Sutherland's straths prior to their being 'forced down to the barren rocks of the seashore'. Privately (as will be seen) Napier had no doubt as to such burnings having taken place. But knowing that their extent (and even their occurrence) would be challenged by beneficiaries of the land-use pattern resulting from mass eviction, Napier took care to stress in his 1884 report that evidence as to the prevalence and impact of clearance was not confined to what had been said to him and his fellow commissioners. While in the Highlands, Napier wrote, he had heard a great deal about 'oppression and suffering' allegedly suffered at the hands of evicting landlords or their agents. 'Many [such] . . . allegations', Napier observed, 'would not bear a searching analysis. Under such a scrutiny they would be found erroneous as to time, to place, to persons, to extent . . . It does not follow, however, that because these narratives are incorrect in detail, they are incorrect in colour or in kind. The history of the economical transformation which a great portion of the Highlands and Islands has during the past century undergone does not repose on loose and legendary tales that pass from mouth to mouth; it rests on the solid basis of contemporary records, and if these were found wanting, it is written in indelible characters on the surface of the soil.'[14]

It was in the hope that Lord Napier would take the chance to see something of these 'indelible characters' that Angus MacKay urged him to inspect the sites of Strathnaver townships like the one Angus had run from on the day of its destruction. 'I am very glad to know that your lordship is to go up the strath,' another of the commission's Bettyhill interviewees, Ewan Robertson, commented on its emerging that Napier was to do as MacKay had advised. Robertson, who had himself explored Strathnaver localities cleared between 1814 and 1819, was right to be gratified. Even today, two centuries after *bliadhna na losgaidh*, it is easy in Strathnaver to find traces of the valley's once plentiful settlements. Well over a century ago, when

Lord Napier inspected what an accompanying *Glasgow Herald* reporter called 'a valley . . . now entirely devoted to sheep farming', those traces must have been a lot more obvious. It is by no means improbable, then, that the hours Napier spent in Strathnaver on Wednesday 25 July 1883 helped frame his contention that the clearance record can be read by anyone who looks around Highland landscapes.[15]

What also became apparent to Lord Napier in Strathnaver was the stark contrast between the quantity and quality of the land occupied by its sheep farmers – the most prominent such farmer in 1883 being one of Patrick Sellar's sons – and the two, three or four acres on which crofters were expected to get by. The 'principal matter of [crofting] dissatisfaction', Napier reported to Gladstone's government, was 'the restriction in the area of [croft] holdings'. This was nowhere more apparent than in Farr, the parish including Strathnaver. Just one of Farr's sheep farmers – Sellar's son and namesake Patrick – occupied land worth two and a half times as much as all the land available to Farr's 293 crofting families. Hence Napier's verdict that Farr exemplified 'the extremes of subdivision and consolidation' resulting from clearance: 'There is a striking absence of intermediate positions; the small farmer and substantial crofter disappear entirely; there is not one single holding which can afford a competent occupation and support to a small tenant [or crofter] labouring his land and living by it; there is a complete extinction of those graduated stations which offer an encouragement to the development of individual intelligence and industry.'[16]

None of late nineteenth-century Farr's crofters, in other words, could aspire to be a full-time agriculturalist of the sort to be found throughout Sutherland's pre-clearance straths. Nor, as predicted by early nineteenth-century opponents of clearance, had it been possible for Farr crofters to capitalise on the marine resources James Loch, Patrick Sellar and the Staffords had insisted would be open to them. Sutherland's north coast, Alexander Sutherland pointed out in his *Star* articles of 1813, lacked harbours and, in their absence, there could be no north coast fishery. Seventy years later, the same point was made over and over again to Lord Napier. The unavoidable consequence, Napier remarked, was that 'the intended fisherman . . . remained an indigent crofter', his plight made all the more unenviable by the fact that crofts, mostly consisting of land that was desperately poor to start with, had been left 'exhausted', as Napier put it, by decade after decade of constant cropping.[17]

In the run-up to the ejection of thousands of Sutherland Estate residents from their homes, Lord Stafford had barred his wife from the Highlands. But in September 1820, the marquis judged it safe for her to venture north again. 'Many, many thanks for letting me come here,' the marchioness wrote to her husband from Dunrobin. He might think her excursions to her ancestral territories nothing other than a giving in to 'childish fancy', Lady Stafford went on. But it brought her 'immense satisfaction', especially since, on this occasion, 'everything [in Sutherland] appear[ed] to be in the most perfect style'. At Dunrobin the castle was 'in a state of neatness and cleanness . . . never [seen] . . . before'; Francis Suther had got the adjacent home farm 'into equal order'; the castle's flowerbeds were filled 'with large fat roses'; its kitchen gardens with strawberries, apples and greengages 'of a richer flavour than [those available] in London'. Further afield, everything hoped for from 'improvement' was in place. The straths were 'entirely cleared'; 'difficulties [were] now really over to all important purposes'; 'the people all quiet'; newly settled crofters 'happy and comfortable on their lots'.[18]

The marchioness was escorted around Sutherland by her son, Earl Gower. Fresh from being greeted everywhere in Staffordshire by shouts of 'Fire!', he must have found it comforting to be among people who, if only from fear of what might follow any hint of discontent, were unfailingly obsequious. 'We went into every house', his mother reported of her and Gower's day-long inspection of crofting townships near Brora, 'and talked to all the people and gave great satisfaction.' There and elsewhere, Lady Stafford added, she had handed out 'prizes to . . . builders of the best cottages'. Similar awards were made to crofters judged to have made most effort to cultivate the 'waste' on which they had been installed. 'I leave . . . with the utmost satisfaction', the marchioness noted at the end of her trip, 'not only in thinking that all is put in so excellent a way . . . but in seeing also that this visit of ours has been a great encouragement . . . to the people who are quite happy in thinking they are attended to.'[19]

James Loch, also in Sutherland at this point, was equally content. Towards the end of 1815, Loch had published a 20-page pamphlet intended to counter the torrent of anti-Stafford comment unleashed by Patrick Sellar's arrest and imprisonment. Now he had seen into print a much expanded – indeed book-length – version. His aim, Loch explained, was to tackle head-on 'malicious' and 'false' claims of the sort the Trans-Atlantic Association and its allies had 'circulated . . . through the medium of the public press'. Stafford policy in Sutherland, Loch maintained, had been – whether in conception or execution – 'humane and considerate'. Statements to the contrary were 'totally and completely false'. Prior to 'improvement', conditions in the Sutherland interior had been 'wretched and deplorable'; 'indolence and sloth' were commonplace; people lived, amid an 'accumulation of filth', in homes 'of the most miserable description'. Now these same people had been provided with coastal crofts they had 'begun to cultivate . . . with much industry' and on which they would 'be enabled to bring up their families in decent comfort'.[20]

'This is the system', Loch wrote of post-clearance Sutherland, 'which a few interested and malignant persons have attempted, for selfish, or pecuniary, or still worse motives to revile . . . [despite its having] brought blessings and happiness . . . of which [the Sutherland Estate's inhabitants] must have forever continued ignorant if it had not been for the steady and praiseworthy perseverance of the owners of this extensive and important property.'[21]

Henry Brougham read James Loch's book 'with the greatest satisfaction and delight'. General David Stewart (of whom more shortly) spoke for critics of 'improvement' in dismissing it as a rehash of arguments Loch had been advancing for several years. Loch, Stewart remarked, was motivated mainly by an 'eager desire to praise Lady Stafford . . . and to run down poor people'. 'I wish to have no feeling in common', the general commented of the Sutherland clearances' principal architect, 'with a person who, for the sake of gain, causes . . . misery to unoffending human beings.'[22]

That Loch was revisiting the standard case for clearance is undoubted. But for all this case's long-standing reliance on one-sided – indeed dishonest – descriptions of life in Sutherland's now emptied straths, Loch was able, by 1820, to point to post-clearance successes. One such success was the transformation of Helmsdale into what a mid-nineteenth-century commentator called a fishing port of 'the first rank'. 'The curing yards at this station', the same commentator went on, 'have long been famed as about the most complete on the [Moray Firth] coast . . . roomy, substantial and having every necessary appendage'. Unlike Sutherland's north coast, then, Helmsdale was provided with a buoyant fishing industry. This, as things turned out, did a lot less than predicted for nearby crofting communities like Marrel, West Helmsdale and Gartymore. Those localities' crofters – many of them evicted from the Strath of Kildonan – lacked the capital required to get into fishing on their own account. At the height of each summer's herring season, it followed, most of the 200 or more boats operating out of Helmsdale were not owned by people from crofting families. But this deficiency notwithstanding, it is easy to understand why the Marchioness of Stafford was so enthused by what she saw of the place when, in the course of her 1820 stay at Dunrobin, she organised – in collaboration with Earl Gower, James Loch, Francis Suther and others – a 'great expedition' to the Strath of Kildonan and to the fast-growing village at its foot.[23]

'I cannot better describe Helmsdale', Lady Stafford informed her husband, 'than by saying we saw about six herring establishments each with their cooperages . . . and so full of people . . . that [the harbour area] looked more like a part of Liverpool than anything else, so handsome are the buildings and so great the bustle . . . Besides these, there are various good houses, shops, [a] post-office, a large inn [with] a room in it calculated for large companies to dine in . . . It is very singular to look out of the windows . . . of this room and to see . . . the curing houses and . . . the port where lay three large vessels from London and Leith to carry off fish and wool . . . the old castle* opposite quite surprised at all those novelties'.[24]

The wool the marchioness mentioned came from Major William Clunes's Kildonan sheep farms. From Helmsdale, Clunes ('dressed,' Lady Stafford observed, 'in a pink and green tartan jacket') escorted the marchioness's party – its members seated in three 'very good' gigs – to Torrish where, Lady Stafford noted, Clunes, had 'built a . . . neat cottage'. The now largely uninhabited Strath of Kildonan, which the marchioness was glimpsing for the first time, seemed to her 'a narrow, wild valley . . . very pretty . . . [its] birchwoods smelling sweet'. Clunes, Lady Stafford added, afterwards invited her and her companions to dine with him at his Crakaig farmhouse where, the marchioness noted approvingly, the major received his guests 'hospitably', providing them with 'a very good dinner in a gentleman-like way [while] a man played on the bagpipes at a distance, so as not to be troublesome.'[25]

Helmsdale's prosperity was not to endure into the twentieth century – the village falling victim, like many comparable communities, to the 1920s' collapse of Scotland's herring industry. But the road on which the Marchioness of Stafford travelled up the Strath of Kildonan to Torrish – a road completed only months before – is still there and still in use. So are the other roads, together with scores of burn-spanning bridges, constructed at much the same time in Strathbrora, Strathnaver and other parts of the Sutherland Estate.

There were Stafford expenditures, then, that continue to yield value. Thousands of vehicles daily cross the Mound, the

---

* Helmsdale Castle, on rising ground south of the harbour, was demolished in the 1970s.

embankment thrown across Loch Fleet between 1814 and 1816 and today an integral part of the A9. At Brora the brewery, brickworks and coalmine on which the Staffords spent heavily are no more. But their Clynelish Distillery, opened in 1819 with a view to utilising barley that might otherwise have found its way to operators of illicit stills, remains in production, turning out what its present-day owners, international drinks combine Diageo, describe as 'a fruity, waxy, slightly smoky single malt'.

Perhaps the most striking survival of the 'improvement' period, however, are the arable farms fringing the modern A9 from Cyderhall (adjacent to the Dornoch Bridge) by way of Culmaily (where Patrick Sellar once farmed) to Crakaig (where, in 1820, William Clunes entertained Lady Stafford). Prior to the commencement of 'improvement', practically all those farms consisted (as they had done for a long time) of rigs occupied, in large part, by subtenants of the sort ejected (as described previously) from Culmaily. This meant that when Cyderhall (to cite one instance) was taken over in 1817 by George Rule, who had moved north from Roxburghshire, the farm was home to a plethora of families whose 'cottages', according to James Loch, 'were dispersed all over it'. 'The small portion of [Cyderhall] that was [then] arable', Loch recalled, 'was interspersed with heaps of stones collected off the land, or with portions of grass which, being pastured, exposed the crop to the continual depredations of . . . cattle.' Three years later, Loch wrote, nothing of this remained: 'The collections of stones have been used either in the construction of dykes . . . or have been employed in the construction of roads. The intermediate portions of grass . . . have been ploughed up, and the farm has . . . begun to assume a regular shape and cultivation. The enclosures [meaning the walled-in fields that took the place of rigs and other open areas] are proceeding . . . and will soon be finished.'[26]

Like their Culmaily counterparts, Cyderhall's cottages were swept away. So were those cottages' occupants who, Loch noted, had 'been settled upon the Dornoch Muirs'. There, in the several crofting settlements that took shape at this time on what had been uncultivated moorland to the west and north-west of Sutherland's county town, Cyderhall's previous occupants joined (or were joined by) people displaced from one or other of the several more Cyderhall-like farms then taking shape on the coastal plain between the Dornoch Firth and Golspie. Unlike the emptying of the Sutherland Estate's inland valleys, however, this aspect of 'improvement' attracted little or nothing by way of critical comment. This may have been due in part to affected families having lacked the financial and other resources that enabled the cattle-rearing and whisky-producing residents of the interior straths to organise all manner of anti-clearance protest. But it is also likely to have owed something to the fact that transformations of the Cyderhall sort were, from a wider Scottish or British perspective, by no means unusual.[27]

As James Loch pointed out in 1820, the open fields that were medieval England's equivalent of Culmaily or Cyderhall's rigs had been subject to 'enclosure' and 'consolidation' from 'as far back' as Tudor times. In Lowland Scotland, identical processes had been under way since the early eighteenth century, spreading north, by the century's close, into Aberdeenshire, Banffshire, Moray and Easter Ross. Had the Sutherland 'improvements' consisted solely of the changes made by men like Cyderhall's George Rule, it follows, no more would have been heard of them than was heard of what thousands of Rule's predecessors and contemporaries had done or were doing in the rest of the country. What brought infamy to Stafford-owned, Loch-managed Sutherland was the total – and fire-accompanied – depopulation of Strathbrora, Strathnaver and the Strath of Kildonan. There had not been, and would not be, any English or Lowland equivalents of that.[28]

The speed, scale, completeness and brutality of the 1819 and 1820 clearances on the Sutherland Estate meant that they attracted lots of press coverage. Over subsequent decades, and for identical reasons, the same clearances were picked over, analysed and almost invariably condemned by a host of commentators. Among the first (as already indicated) was General David Stewart, a Perthshire laird as well as a veteran military man. Stewart's critique of the Stafford and Loch case for clearance was 'founded', he explained, 'on a long intimacy with [Highlanders] both as inhabitants of their native glens and as soldiers'.[29]

David Stewart thought it implausible that troops whose conduct led a senior army commander to call the 93rd Regiment 'an example to all' could have been products of the broken and bankrupt society Loch had supposedly met with in Sutherland. By portraying inhabitants of the Sutherland straths 'as dishonest, irregular in their habits and incapable of managing their farms', Stewart maintained, James Loch had chosen falsely to blacken those people's character in the hope of defending the otherwise indefensible decision to have 'fire . . . applied to [Sutherland homes] to effect their [occupants] more speedy expulsion'. It may well have profited the Staffords, their land managers and their sheep-farming tenants to turn 'whole glens and districts, once the abode of a brave, vigorous and independent race of men, into scenes of desolation'. But nobody should for a moment accept at face value what the organisers of evictions had to say about the communities they destroyed: 'The people [of Sutherland] ought not to be reproached with incapacity or immorality without better evidence than that of their prejudiced and unfeeling calumniators.'[30]

When published in 1822, the book containing those remarks sold 500 copies in London alone in less than a week. Much quoted in the years ahead, David Stewart thus helped keep the Sutherland clearances in the public eye. Plenty of others did likewise. One was Beriah Botfield, a Shropshire-born industrialist and Tory MP who visited Strathbrora when touring the Highlands in the later 1820s. No 'pursuit of prospective advantages', in Botfield's opinion, made it legitimate 'to transgress the laws of humanity', as had been done, he thought, in Sutherland. 'In this secluded valley', Botfield wrote of Strathbrora, 'all was silent and dead; no token of its once peaceful and happy inhabitants remained, save the blackened ruins of their humble dwellings . . . When we reflect that all this desolation has taken place under the abused name of improvement, we must deeply regret that . . . more humane measures were not pursued.'[31]

In a Sutherland context, Botfield was an outsider. Hugh Miller, who (as mentioned earlier) made occasional trips to Gruids from his boyhood home in Cromarty, was not. The adult Miller, however, is unlikely to have had cause to reflect angrily in print on the Sutherland clearances and their consequences had not the Stafford family responded in typically repressive fashion to the 1843 emergence of the Free Church, of which Miller, then a prominent journalist, was an enthusiastic backer.

Disenchantment with the established church – from which the new grouping broke away – was no novelty in Sutherland. But discontents stemming in part from the way the generality of Church of Scotland clerics behaved during the clearances had been fanned in the 1820s and 1830s by lay preachers who operated outside the jurisdiction of the Church of Scotland and posed open challenges to its teachings. Those men attracted followings. By so doing they paved the way for the Sutherland population's practically unanimous adherence to the Free Church, a denomination founded, as its name suggests, on the principle that congregations, not landed proprietors, should appoint ministers. This principle, according to the Free Church, had a theological basis. But it also had secular implications. As was symbolised by the dead dog Free Church supporters suspended over the pulpit in Farr's abandoned parish church, the mass exodus of Sutherland crofters and their families from the Church of Scotland deprived that church of authority. It also deprived estate managers of the means of exercising social control of the sort Sutherland's parish ministers – most of them at any rate – had been all too willing to impose on the Marquis and Marchioness of Stafford's behalf.[32]

By 1843, both the marquis and the marchioness were dead. Ownership of the Sutherland Estate had consequently passed to the former Earl Gower, now (as inheritor of the title his father had been granted in 1833) Duke of Sutherland. 'He scarcely resides there at all,' a leading Free Church minister said of the duke's relationship with his Highland property. 'He can have very little knowledge of [Sutherland] people.' Perhaps not. But the duke was certainly aware of the risks inherent, from a Sutherland Estate perspective, in crofters having ready access to an ecclesiastical institution immune from proprietorial influence. Hence his 1843 rejection of Free Church attempts to buy or lease sites for its churches, manses and schools. In Sutherland, then, Free Church services had to be conducted in the open air. That, in turn, led to Hugh Miller travelling north from Edinburgh, where he now lived, to experience one such act of worship at first hand.[33]

The service Miller witnessed, and went on to write about, was held in a crofting township south of Helmsdale. Prior to its taking place, Miller rode up the Strath of Kildonan. There he saw the 'multitude of scattered patches of green' and the still more numerous ruins – 'well nigh levelled with the soil and . . . still scathed with fire' – that continued to testify to the extent of clearance. 'All is solitude within the valley', Miller wrote of Kildonan, 'except where, at wide intervals, the shieling of a shepherd may be seen; but at its opening, where the hills range to the coast, the cottages for miles together lie clustered as in a hamlet. From the north of Helmsdale to the south of Port Gower, the lower slopes of the hills are covered by a labyrinth of stone fences, minute patches of corn and endless cottages. It would seem as if, for twenty miles, the long withdrawing valley had been swept of its inhabitants, and the accumulated sweepings left at its mouth, just as we see the sweepings of a room sometimes left at the door. And such generally is the present state of Sutherland.'[34]

The congregation he joined, Miller went on, consisted of between 600 and 800 people: 'We have rarely seen a more deeply serious assemblage; never certainly one that bore an air of such deep dejection. The people were wonderfully clean and decent; for it is ill with

Highlanders when they neglect their personal appearance, especially on a Sabbath; but it was all too evident that the heavy hand of poverty rested upon them, and that its evils [in consequence of Sutherland Estate hostility to the Free Church] were now deepened by oppression. It might have been a mere trick of association; but when . . . plaintive Gaelic singing, so melancholy in its tones at all times, arose from the bare hillside, it sounded to our ears like a deep wail of complaint and sorrow.'[35]

Hugh Miller's account of how Sutherland's interior had been 'improved into a desert', drew on David Stewart and on Donald MacLeod, whose press articles about the clearances had appeared just three years before Miller's own. Nor was MacLeod, who became one more of Sutherland's many post-clearance emigrants to North America, himself finished with the topic. In 1857 – by which point he was in Ontario – MacLeod republished his 1840 narrative of what had been done by the Staffords and their agents in places like his native Strathnaver where MacLeod had been among the Rossal men on hand at Badinloskin when, on Patrick Sellar's orders, William Chisholm's home was set alight. To his account of episodes of that sort, Donald MacLeod now added fresh material, its vigour proving that this 'old . . . broken-down stonemason', as MacLeod described himself, had lost none of his facility with words.[36]

MacLeod's revisiting of events of 40 years before had been precipitated, like Hugh Miller's denunciation of the clearances, by the actions of the second Duke of Sutherland, who with the encouragement of his wife, every bit as forceful a personality as her mother-in-law had been, decided in the early 1850s to align herself with the campaign to end slavery in America's southern states. This led to the duke and duchess hosting in London one of the USA's most prominent anti-slavery activists, Harriet Beecher Stowe, who, in gratitude, took it upon herself to castigate MacLeod's 1840 writings, which, Beecher Stowe noted, 'had been industriously circulated in America'. Well briefed by James Loch, still in overall charge of Sutherland Estate matters, Beecher Stowe, in a book entitled *Sunny*

Memories of Foreign Lands, dismissed MacLeod's material as 'ridiculous' and 'absurd'. What had taken place on the Sutherland Estate, she commented, was 'an almost sublime instance of the benevolent employment of superior wealth and power in . . . elevating in a few years a whole community to a point of education and material prosperity which, unassisted, [it] might never have attained.'[37]

MacLeod's rebuttal, *Gloomy Memories in the Highlands of Scotland*, was unforgiving. Slavery was 'damnable' and 'it [was] to be hoped that Americans [would] soon discern its deformity, pollution and iniquity'. But 'the British aristocracy's sympathy with American slaves' was a 'burlesque', a charade. The Duke and Duchess of Sutherland might pose, for self-serving and publicity-seeking reasons, as 'the most liberal sympathisers with foreign victims of oppression and injustice'. Nearer home, however, they were unashamedly benefiting from policies that had turned much of Sutherland into 'a solitary wilderness' and left its inhabitants 'huddled together . . . along the sea-shore' in 'the most impoverished, degraded [and] subjugated . . . condition that human beings could exist in'.[38]

Much the same point was made at much the same time by the London correspondent of the New York *Tribune*, then the most widely read newspaper in the world. It was characteristic of the Duke and Duchess of Sutherland, wrote Karl Marx, to have selected as 'objects' of their 'philanthropy' people 'as far distant from home as possible'. It was equally characteristic of the British press, when reporting the couple's anti-slavery stance, to have failed to notice that 'the history of the wealth of the Sutherland family [was] the history of the ruin . . . of the Scotch-Gaelic population [of their Highland estate]'. In Sutherland 'from 1814 to 1820', Marx went on, 'about 3,000 families were systematically expelled' from their homes. 'All their villages were demolished and burned down, and all their fields converted into pasturage.'[39]

Both in his *Tribune* dispatches and in *Capital*, the book that became the principal source of communism's theoretical underpinnings, Marx portrayed the 'reckless terrorism' of the clearance years as an unavoidable result of capitalism's wider need to have landed properties organised in ways intended to ensure that their owners' financial interests took precedence over all other considerations. In this, as he acknowledged, Marx was following the Swiss economist Jean Charles Léonard de Sismondi, whom Hugh Miller also cited as a powerful critic of developments in Sutherland. Sismondi, in an 'Essay on Landed Property' published in 1834, contended – much as Highlanders themselves contended – that it had been clanship's practice to acknowledge that clansfolk, whether in Sutherland or elsewhere, had rights in the land they occupied. Customary entitlements of that sort, Sismondi argued, ought to be incorporated into law, as had long been the case, he pointed out, in Switzerland and some other parts of continental Europe. Landowners like the Staffords, Sismondi believed, had 'no more right to drive from their homes' the inhabitants of their estates 'than a king to drive out the inhabitants of his kingdom'. If once Britain's landlords came to 'believe that they have no need of the people', he warned, 'the people may in their turn think that they have no need of them.'[40]

Sismondi, Hugh Miller, Donald MacLeod, David Stewart and others were cited by Highland Land League spokesmen like Angus Sutherland. So were later theorists such as Henry George and Alfred Russel Wallace. George's *Progress and Poverty*, published in New York in 1880, was a sustained – and influential – attack on the many iniquities allegedly arising from private property in land. Wallace's *Land Nationalisation*, published in London in 1882, was a call for such property to be brought into public ownership, not least on the grounds that episodes like the Sutherland clearances, which Wallace thought 'a positive crime against humanity', under-lined the cost to society at large of permitting a tiny minority of a country's citizens to do much as they liked with that country's basic resource, its land.[41]

But for all that it was helpful to the Land League to be able to refer to external indictments of Highland landlords, people in Sutherland, or so Farr's Free Church minister Donald MacKenzie said in 1883, needed no such prompting to make them aware of the need for reform. 'We required no one from the outside to come and agitate us,' MacKenzie told Lord Napier at Bettyhill. This, the minister added, was a consequence of demands for security of tenure being fuelled principally by the way in which memories of evictions had been handed down from one generation to the next: 'The accounts of the old men living . . . in the different townships [on Sutherland's north coast]', MacKenzie said of what he had been told about the clearances, 'are more graphic, vivid and harrowing than anything that has been written on the subject.' All such accounts are today beyond recall. But at least a little of their emotional impact, it is safe to guess, is preserved in Gaelic songs and poems dating from a time when dispossession and dispersal were everyday realities.[42]

In his clearance novel, *Consider the Lilies*, written in the 1960s, Iain Crichton Smith, himself a poet as well as an author, imagines a conversation between Patrick Sellar and Donald MacLeod. 'Have you ever read any poetry?' MacLeod asks. 'Poetry?' Sellar is uncomprehending. 'Well, I'll tell you,' MacLeod says. 'There are some poets, we call them bards, who have written songs about you . . . You see, Mr Sellar, you will become a legend . . . Children will sing about you . . . They may even recite poems about you in the schools.'[43]

An especially bitter set of such verses was put together by a song-maker called Donald Baillie, perhaps one of the several Baillies who left Strathbrora for Pictou around 1820. Transmitted from singer to singer in Canada and finally published there in 1890, Baillie's lines date, their content suggests, from the immediate aftermath of Patrick Sellar's 1816 trial, and they are fiercely resentful of Sellar having gone free. ''*S truagh nach robh thu 'm prìosan*,' Baillie's song runs, '*Rè bhliadhnan air uisg' is aran*': 'What a pity that you were not in prison for years, existing on bread and water, with a hard shackle of iron, strong and immovable, about your thigh.'[44]

Baillie takes consolation from his having had a dream in which he sees Sellar burning in hell. So irresistible was this image – an eternity of hellfire suffered by a man who, in life, burned homes – that it became an enduring motif in poetry deriving from, or inspired by, the clearances. In one of Crichton Smith's own poems, while 'stars shine over Sutherland', the factor's 'hot ears' are forever subject to the sound of 'thatch sizzling in tanged smoke'. Sellar fares no less grimly in this Scots version, by twentieth-century poet and folksong revivalist Hamish Henderson, of a Gaelic song made by Ewan Robertson who (as touched on earlier) was one of the men questioned by Lord Napier at Bettyhill:

> Sellar, daith hath ye in his grip;
> Ye needna think he'll let ye slip,
> Justice ye've earned, and, by the Book,
> A warm assize ye winna jouk.
> The fires ye lit tae gut Strathnaver,
> Ye'll feel them noo – and roast forever.[45]

Sellar, by Henderson's time or even Robertson's, had become a historical figure. But that was not so when Donald Baillie's song took shape. His Sellar is a living presence about whom Baillie delights in being offensive. Thus the factor's nose is akin to a porpoise's snout and his lower quarters resemble a donkey's behind. By attributing these and other animal-like features to Sellar, it has been suggested, Baillie was hinting at the factor's iniquity having stemmed from his 'not belong[ing] to the human race'. But even if its deeper meaning is left unexplored, Baillie's description of Sellar – a description tallying, in the case of his prominent nose at any rate, with what is known of his appearance – serves as a reminder that Patrick Sellar was visible in clearance-era Sutherland in a way the Staffords and James Loch were not. Baillie clearly saw Sellar and may have had dealings with him. The same was true of lots of other people on the Sutherland Estate. Loch, the marquis and the marchioness, in contrast, were more rarely glimpsed and still more seldom spoken with. That, in part, is why, in the Sutherland population's collective memory, Patrick Sellar, who died in 1851, came more and more to encapsulate and personify the complex array of influences underpinning 'improvement'.[46]

This, as members of Sellar's family and their descendants were to protest in the later nineteenth century and into the twentieth, was not quite fair. In 1883, in evidence to Lord Napier and in a book published just months later, Thomas Sellar, eldest of Patrick's sons and a man who was himself to die the following year, argued that Sellar senior, when a Sutherland Estate factor, took his orders from Loch who, in turn, was 'acting under Lord and Lady Stafford's instructions'. This, while understandable in light of Thomas Sellar's determination to rescue his family name from 'unmerited obloquy', was erroneous: the Sellar of the clearance era had been anything but the man said by his son to have 'had really no power of initiative'. The underlying point, however, was sound. Ultimate responsibility for the Sutherland clearances, and for everything that happened in the course of them, did not rest with Patrick Sellar. Nor did it rest with William Young, Francis Suther or James Loch. It rested with the Marquis and Marchioness of Stafford.[47]

But Thomas Sellar was not content with allocating, or reallocating, liability for clearances. In the manner of James Loch a lifetime earlier, he set out to show that to have had sheep farmers take the place of the thousands of people removed from the Sutherland interior was, from every point of view, a good thing. This was never a convincing claim. By the 1880s it had been rendered wholly unpersuasive by the financial and other difficulties then confronting inheritors of the sheep-farming structure Loch and Patrick Sellar had been at pains to establish.

Although the price slump that followed Waterloo made for an occasionally rocky start, a great deal of money was made in the

post-clearance straths, not least by Sellar who, in the late 1830s, was
wealthy enough to set himself up on a substantial estate of his own
at Ardtornish in Argyll. The good times, however, were not to
endure. Everywhere they went in 1883 Napier and his colleagues
were dinned with tales of sheep-farming difficulty. In the mid-cen-
tury, it was recalled, soaring wool prices had meant that 'landlords
and sheep farmers alike . . . waxed fat and prosperous'. Now sheep
farmers, as Angus Sutherland took pleasure in informing Napier,
'[were] unable to meet their . . . obligations and going to ruin generally'. This was to exaggerate; but not by very much. Sheep farmers
were certainly struggling. Leases were being thrown in; vacant farms
could not be let; Highland sheep farming, it was beginning to be
apparent, would never again be the wildly successful enterprise* it
had been in the decades following the clearances.[48]

This late nineteenth-century crisis had a number of causes. One
was competition from colonies like Australia and New Zealand
where high quality wool could be produced a lot more cheaply than
in Scotland. But an additional source of trouble lay in the nature of
Highland sheep farming itself. Post-clearance sheep farmers had
benefited hugely from the fertility bequeathed to them by practition-
ers of the mixed farming that had gone on in inland Sutherland for
centuries. Previously cultivated rigs, though no longer put to the
plough, continued to provide what James Loch called 'a sweet and
luxuriant herbage'. Hill pastures, where pre-clearance communities
had grazed their cattle each summer, were similarly productive,
yielding, as a present-day Highland farmer has put it, a 'rich variety
of sweet grasses, herbs and clovers'. But this same farmer, Reay

---

* Such recovery as took place in Highland sheep farming in the twentieth century
depended, for the most part, on government subsidy. It also depended on a switch
from the production of wool (the post-clearance cash crop but one that has yielded
no worthwhile returns in modern times) to the rearing of lambs sold off each autumn
for fattening, or finishing, by low-ground farmers. This trade too has encountered
problems. At the time of writing in 2015 there are fewer sheep in Sutherland than at
any point in 200 years.

Clarke, is unequivocal as to the damage done by practices integral to 'improvement'. Cattle, Clarke points out, consume 'both fine and rough herbage, thus improving the sward'. Sheep, on the other hand, graze selectively with the result that pastures given over to their exclusive use are gradually overrun by coarser and less nutritious types of vegetation. 'In the natural world', Clarke writes, 'all grazing systems have a variety of animals to harvest the herbage. In Sutherland, the mixed summer grazing of former years by cattle with a few sheep, goats and ponies was changed [at the time of the clearances] to an all the year round defoliation by a single species – sheep.' The consequence, as admitted on all sides in the 1880s, was that the stock-carrying capacity of Sutherland's hills was in steep decline while the tracts of old arable around the sites of former townships were increasingly overrun by moss, heather and bracken.[49]

Nothing of this was acknowledged by Thomas Sellar, to whom it seemed as self-evident as it had done to his father that there was no merit in the complex mix of land uses swept away by a sheep monoculture that, like most monocultures, proved – after a first flush – precarious. Instead Thomas sought to defend 'improvement', much as James Loch had done, by disparaging its critics. The charges laid against his father in 1816 were 'a fabric of fiction which had been erected by malice and credulity'. Donald MacLeod's writings were 'sensational'; Hugh Miller's the product of an 'ardent imagination'; Sismondi's and Wallace's little better.[50]

But Thomas Sellar, in finding only virtue in what his father had done and in how he had done it, was spitting in the wind. Both Lord Napier's report and the evidence on which it rested were condemnatory of clearance, and while Napier was by no means supportive of everything the Highland Land League wanted, he was clear as to the pressing need to rescue crofters from the plight they had been left in by management of the Loch variety. Nor were the many journalists and publicists among the Land League's members and sympathisers anything like as circumspect as Napier in their analyses of the population transfers that had contributed so much to creating the problems Napier was trying to solve. What had occurred in Sutherland between 1813 and 1821 began again to be castigated in the press. Alexander MacKenzie, an Inverness-based publisher, produced a best-selling *History of the Highland Clearances* in which the Sutherland experience loomed large. Donald MacLeod's *Gloomy Memories* was reissued and, thanks to its sheer verve, attracted numerous readers.

'I was present at the pulling down and burning of the house of William Chisholm', MacLeod had written of the episode at the centre of Patrick Sellar's trial, 'in which was lying his wife's mother, an old bedridden woman of near a hundred years of age . . . I informed the persons about to set fire to the house of this circumstance, and prevailed on them to wait till Mr Sellar came. On his arrival, I told him of the poor old woman being in a condition unfit for removal. He replied, "Damn her, the old witch, she has lived too long; let her burn." Fire was immediately set to the house, and the blankets in which she was carried were in flames before she could be got out. She was placed in a little shed . . . She died within five days.'[51]

This scene looms large in the literature of modern Scotland, most strikingly in Neil Gunn's *Butcher's Broom*, the finest of several fine novels and plays dealing with the Sutherland clearances. In *Butcher's Broom*, Sellar is Factor Heller – his altered surname hinting perhaps at his being destined for damnation – and presides over evictions identical to those described by Donald MacLeod. Told in Gunn's novel of there being an elderly woman in a house about to be set ablaze, Heller curses 'the old bitch' and calls on his men – 'half-mad with drink and the growing lust of destruction' – to press on. 'Factor Heller', Gunn writes, 'was a wise man. This work had to be done; it would, by God, be done thoroughly . . . Clear them out! Rid the land of such human vermin! . . . House by house they took . . . giving the occupants a brief space in which to haul out their belongings before destroying the dwelling. Pitiful mothers, miserable old men, moaning old women, wailing children, left islanded with their one or two earthly possessions and no home or shelter in the broad world for them. It was a remarkable landscape, acquiring slowly an unearthly, demoniac appearance.'[52]

Neil Gunn grew up in Latheron, the Caithness parish where lots of people from the Strath of Kildonan, some of Gunn's forebears among them, set up home when the strath was emptied. 'They had come from beyond the mountain which rose up behind them', Gunn wrote of those folk, 'from inland valleys and swelling pastures, where they and their people before them had lived from time immemorial. Their landlord had driven them from these valleys and pastures, and burned their houses, and set them here against the sea-shore to live if they could and, if not, to die.'[53]

'I'd always felt the *need* to write of the clearances,' Neil Gunn told a biographer. This requirement was intensified by Gunn's strong sense of Sutherland as a place so scarred by 'improvement' as to make even its landscapes a source of unease. 'In a happy, thriving community', Gunn commented, 'the very land, to our senses, takes on a certain pleasant friendliness . . . On the other hand, in Kildonan there is today a shadow, a chill, of which any sensitive mind would, I am convinced, be vaguely aware, though possessing no knowledge of the clearances. We are affected strangely by any place from which the tide of life has ebbed.'[54]

Something of that same feeling is evident in the recollections of Calum Maclean, a pioneer collector of Gaelic story and tradition. Maclean, who came from the island of Raasay, between Skye and the mainland, first visited Sutherland in the aftermath of the Second World War. Like other visitors, he found the county 'beautiful'. But what 'struck [him] most of all was [its] terrible emptiness', a consequence, Maclean wrote, of Sutherland's population having been 'hounded from the rich inland straths and forced . . . to eke out a precarious livelihood on barren, crowded coasts'. 'There is a strange dignity about them', Calum Maclean wrote of Sutherland's people, 'but deep down in their hearts there is an undercurrent of bitterness and resentment.' Those emotions, Maclean continued, were mostly kept from strangers. They might, however, be shared with other Highlanders who, 'discover that, no matter how it starts, the conversation will sooner or later veer round to the clearances [which] . . . in Sutherlandshire . . . will neither be forgotten nor forgiven'.[55]

When Calum Maclean was in Sutherland – where, two lifetimes after *bliadhna na losgaidh*, he heard Gaelic tales of the cruelties inflicted by *Domhnall Sgios* or Donald Bannerman – Dennis MacLeod was a boy in Marrel, one of the crofting townships near Helmsdale that served as receptacles for families swept, as Hugh Miller's telling image had it, from the Strath of Kildonan. 'Calum Maclean got the clearances – I mean the way the clearances were thought of and spoken about – exactly right,' MacLeod says. 'When crofters got together in Marrel, their talk – once the problems of the day had been sorted out – would often turn to the evictions, to the burnings, to us being confined to Marrel and its none too productive crofts because of our people having been shut out of the strath. Sometimes, I remember, you could detect a feeling of regret – on the part of some folk anyway – that their ancestors hadn't left for Canada when they had had the chance. People were where they were of course. They knew they couldn't turn back the clock and change that. But always, I believe, they felt that they – or, if not them, the folk who'd gone before – had been treated badly, harshly, unjustly. What made this sense of having been wronged much worse, I think, was the lack of any kind of acknowledgement, whether from the British government, the Church of Scotland or anyone else that bad things had happened in Sutherland, that politicians and the church had been party to those things, and that we – I mean people living in places like Marrel – were being left to put up with the consequences.'[56]

In the 1960s, as so many others had done, Dennis MacLeod quit Sutherland. Taking a career path a little reminiscent of the one followed by Rogart-born railway-builder John MacKay in the previous century, Dennis went into mining, first in Zambia, then in

South Africa and finally in Canada. Like John MacKay, Dennis did well. Like MacKay, he set up his own company. Like MacKay, he made money. And like MacKay, Dennis MacLeod wanted, on getting older, to invest a part of his cash in ways that would keep people engaged with the historical significance and continuing implications – global as well as local in MacLeod's opinion – of the depopulation of Sutherland's straths. One outcome was the installation in Helmsdale of a public artwork – pressed for and largely financed by Dennis MacLeod – intended both to commemorate the clearances and to draw attention to the achievements (not least in Canada where MacLeod made his home) of folk the clearances had set adrift.

This artwork, the creation of sculptor and pop artist Gerald Laing, features a family group – an adult couple, their young son and their baby. What he wished this family to depict, Laing wrote, were the feelings of 'loss, disorientation and anxiety' caused by all human displacements – whether 'voluntary or involuntary'. 'I have represented these emotions,' Laing commented, 'in [this] sculpture. The man is tense, wary, anxious but determined. The boy is looking to his father for guidance but, at the same time, is ready for adventure. The woman, holding the newborn child, looks back . . . [up the Strath of Kildonan] at the . . . place she is leaving.'[57]

Because Gerald Laing's sculpture, unveiled at Helmsdale in 2007, was cast in bronze, it could be replicated. Hence the unveiling, the following year, of a twin piece in Winnipeg. There it stands amid traffic in the new Kildonan, just a few feet from the Red River's western bank where, in the summer of 1814 and in the fall of the following year, Sutherland families like the one in Laing's sculpture stepped out of the boats that had brought them from York Factory.

Just as the events that caused those families' departure from the Strath of Kildonan gave rise to one great novel, *Butcher's Broom*, so their arrival in Manitoba is integral to another: Margaret Laurence's *The Diviners*. Central to Laurence's book, published in 1974 and a Canadian classic, is Morag Gunn. Orphaned as a child in the fictional Manitoban town of Manawaka, Morag is raised by Christie Logan. Manawaka's town scavenger and a man inclined to be a drunkard, Christie is a marginalised figure, but he is also a teller of tales; tales featuring Morag's supposed forebear Piper Gunn; tales Christie deploys in ways that have the effect of restoring, building up, enforcing the fragile little Morag's self-esteem.

Piper Gunn – his quasi-magical attributes akin to those possessed by heroes of the Gaelic sagas Donald Sage heard John Sutherland narrate in Kildonan's manse – is not the real-life Piper Gunn who piped the Kildonan emigrants out of their Churchill River encampment at the start of their long trek south. This Piper Gunn, in Christie Logan's or Margaret Laurence's hands, is a towering, almost messianic, figure who, it becomes apparent, is the one person in Sutherland capable of organising its people's escape from the miseries imposed on them by the Marchioness of Stafford, transformed, in Christie's stories, into a villainous 'Bitch-Duchess' whose heart is 'as dark as the feathers of a raven' and who loves 'no creature alive'. 'And her [men] rode through the countryside', Christie says of the Bitch-Duchess, 'setting fire to the crofts and turning out the people from their homes . . . And it was old men and old women with thin shanks and men in their prime and women with the child inside them and a great scattering of small children, like, and all of them was driven away from the lands of their fathers and on to the wild rocks of the shore.'[58]

For a time, Piper Gunn plays laments 'for the people lost, and the people gone, and them with no place for to lay their heads'. Soon, however, he sets his pipes aside and, 'in his voice like the voice of the wind from the north isles', speaks of a ship that is coming and of how all must board this ship 'and go with it into a new world across the waters'. 'But the people were afraid, see,' Christie tells Morag. 'They did not dare. Better to die on the known rocks in the land of their ancestors, so some said. Others said the lands across the seas were bad lands filled with . . . terrors and . . . demons and the beasts of the forests . . . Then Piper Gunn changed his music, and he played the battle music there . . . They say it was like the storm winds . . . like the scree and skirl of all the dead pipers who ever lived, returned then to pipe the clans into battle. Then what happened? What happened then to all them people there homeless on the rocks? They rose and followed! Yes, they rose, then, and they followed, for Piper Gunn's music could put the heart into them and they would have followed him all the way to hell or to heaven with the sound of the pipes in their ears . . . And that was how all of them came to this country, all that bunch, and they ended up at the Red River.'[59]

Towards the close of 1889, from his home in Hereford, John MacKay CE, as that self-made civil engineer always entitled himself, mailed to Lord Napier a copy of *Memorabilia Domestica, Or Parish Life in the North of Scotland*. This was Donald Sage's autobiography, which, 20 years after Sage's death, had been published by his son. MacKay's accompanying letter has not survived. But it is clear from Napier's reply, which has, that John MacKay directed him to what Sage had to say about two issues MacKay had raised when, at Golspie, he appeared before Napier and his royal commission colleagues. One was the extent of the 'burnings' that had occurred in 1819. The other was the maltreatment, as John MacKay saw it, experienced by the 93rd Regiment's New Orleans veterans. One of those, MacKay said at Golspie, was 'an uncle of my father'. Like lots more ex-soldiers, this man had been refused a croft on the Sutherland Estate. But what was worse, in John MacKay's estimation, was the manner in which the estate's owners and managers had reneged, or so MacKay believed, on guarantees that parents of men who joined the 93rd in 1799 and 1800 'were never to be deprived of their land'.[60]

Stafford apologists, as MacKay well knew, were in the habit of querying all such contentions. Had homes really been set on fire? Had men whose sons signed up for military service truly been guaranteed immunity from eviction? On both points, Sage's book offered corroboration of MacKay's position. That was why he sent the book to Napier.

Napier stressed his personal acceptance of what John MacKay had said to him six years before. 'I never had any doubt', he wrote, 'either of the burning of the cottages or the violation of the promises [made to tenants with sons in the 93rd].' House burnings, Napier thought, were a 'natural, almost inevitable, result of the cruel policy of eviction'. As for the Marquis and Marchioness of Stafford's 'faithlessness' in the matter of recruitment, it was to be hoped, Napier commented, that the explanation lay in 'their conscience[s] . . . hav[ing] been perverted by bad counsel and false theories of social management'.[61]

'I have never yet quite understood the real motives of the Duchess-Countess and her husband,' Lord Napier told John MacKay. 'I have always hoped that they were misled by prevalent, though erroneous, views of economical and national policy; that they really believed that they were doing permanent good by [inflicting] transitory suffering; that they were not actually heartless or moved by rapacity. However this may be, I have always thought that there [will] not be a true expiation of the guilt of the great eviction till some representative of the [Stafford] family lead back a band of crofters to repeople, in part at least, the wilderness of Kildonan and Strathnaver.'[62]

Three years prior to this Napier–MacKay exchange, parliament, in response both to Napier's 1884 report and to pressure from the Highland Land League, had granted crofters security of tenure, thus making renewed clearance impossible. Nothing had been done, however, to meet the Land League's further, and equally insistent, demand that people should be restored to places cleared decades earlier. It was with a view to looking into the implications of some such initiative that, in 1892, government ministers established a new royal commission, to report, its remit stated, on whether or not localities that had earlier been emptied of people were 'capable of being cultivated to profit, or otherwise advantageously occupied, by crofters'.[63]

Because of sheep farming's continuing difficulties, much of the land in question had been given over to deerstalking and grouse-shooting, estate managements having found that grouse moors and deer forests were now capable of generating higher revenues than land (other than best-quality arable) in any form of agriculture. This made the remit of the 1892 inquiry, dubbed the Deer Forest Commission by the press, more contentious than it might otherwise have been, Highland landlords being determined to block crofting encroachments on to areas that, despite sheep having gone from them, continued to yield lucrative returns. Predictably, then, the Deer Forest Commission's eventual findings – to the effect that a great deal of formerly settled land could indeed be repopulated – brought nothing in the way of instant action. Towards the nineteenth century's close, however, parliament was persuaded to take tentative steps in the direction of what had come to be called land settlement. A new organisation, the Congested Districts Board (CDB), was made responsible for aiding the inhabitants of hard-pressed and overcrowded townships of the sort Lord Napier had heard so much about when taking evidence on the Sutherland Estate. Much of the CDB's modest budget, it emerged, was earmarked for small-scale infrastructure projects – access roads, piers and jetties being favoured items under this heading. But some funding was available for land settlement initiatives; and, not long after the CDB's formation in 1897, an opportunity for just such an initiative arose in Strathnaver as a result of the Sellar family deciding to sever their last links with Sutherland.

When, in 1898, Patrick Sellar junior died, his son, Patrick senior's grandson, decided not to retain – even at a reduced rent – the Syre farm tenancy his grandfather had taken over in 1819. This development made it possible, a Highland newspaper commented, for the Sutherland Estate 'to do something practical to repair the mischief caused by the management, or rather mismanagement, of a century ago'. But there was to be no prospect of the fourth Duke of Sutherland, the marquis and marchioness's great-grandson, atoning in the way Lord Napier had suggested he might for the Stafford family's role in the clearances. He had no intention, the duke made clear, of renting any part of Strathnaver to crofters. He might consider the transfer of about a third of the farm to the CDB, with the board, rather than the Sutherland Estate, thus becoming responsible for resettlement.* But any such transfer would be on the basis that the CDB pay a full market price for the land on offer. No concession, not even a token one, would be contemplated. Asked privately by a government minister, Lord Balfour, Secretary of State for Scotland in the Conservative government of the time, 'to reconsider the question of price' with a view to facilitating a settlement scheme of obvious symbolic significance, the Duke of Sutherland was adamant. The CDB, if intent on installing crofting families in Strathnaver, must meet his terms. If unable to do so, the board could go hang.[64]

It took the better part of three years for the CDB to finalise its purchase of an area now designated North Syre. But at last, in May 1901, this area – located, the board announced, in a 'beautiful glen' containing a 'considerable' quantity of cultivable land – ceased to be part of the Sutherland Estate. Soon North Syre's former arable had been divided into 29 substantial crofts. Because demand for those crofts was in excess of supply, applicants for them were interviewed by CDB personnel. The successful candidates included Donald John MacKay. Prior to this he had been living at Ardvinglass, one of the townships created at the time of the clearances on rocky, windswept and formerly uninhabited terrain in the vicinity of Strathy Point. There MacKay occupied a croft of around three acres and shared, with several neighbours, a 60-acre common pasture. MacKay's Strathnaver croft, its fields a lot more productive than their Ardvinglass equivalents, was around six times the size of his previous holding. Still more striking was the disparity between Ardvinglass's common grazing and the grazing in which MacKay

---

* 'The present [third] duke', Napier had written of his 'expiation' proposal, 'is now too far gone to do it, [but] his son [the duke with whom the CDB dealt] might still collect some of the grandchildren of the fugitive people, and lead them home.'

now had a stake. The second was nearly 200 times more extensive than the first.[65]

When, in October 1901, the CDB's board members toured North Syre, they were 'greatly pleased,' they reported, 'with the excellent houses which were being erected . . . [on] sites overlooking the River [Naver]'. One of these, still to be seen today, was built by Donald John MacKay. Not far away, on the opposite bank of the Naver, is the site of Rhiloisk, cleared by Patrick Sellar in the wake of his acquiring his first Strathnaver farm. Following the destruction of their homes by one of Sellar's evicting parties, Rhiloisk's inhabitants had been moved (as described earlier) to other parts of Strathnaver. Later, when the strath was emptied completely, they had been moved again, this time to the north coast.[66]

One of the Rhiloisk families treated in this way included a baby girl born in Strathnaver in 1817. When in her early twenties, this girl, Barbara MacKay, married William MacKay, whose parents had been ejected from another of Strathnaver's cleared townships, Rivigill. William and Barbara had several children. The youngest, born in 1859, was Donald John MacKay who, when in his forties, quit Ardvinglass for North Syre. By that point, Donald John's father was dead. But his mother was not, and shortly after he took over his CDB croft she left Ardvinglass, where she and Donald John had shared a home, to join him. This means that when, a year or two into the twentieth century, this elderly woman travelled – probably by horse and cart – from Ardvinglass to Syre, she made a unique journey. Among the thousands of victims of the Sutherland clearances there was only one, Barbara MacKay, who managed at last to come home.[67]

The part of Strathnaver acquired by the CDB in 1901 and still in crofting occupation extends along the River Naver's western bank for several miles. It comprises, however, only a small proportion of the area affected by Strathnaver's clearance. Depopulated localities on the Naver's eastern bank – Rhifail, Rivigill, Rhiloisk and Rossal, for instance – remain uninhabited. So do the strath's upper reaches, including Achoul, Grumbeg, Grummore and other former settlements around Loch Naver.

What is true of the bulk of Strathnaver is true of the Strath of Kildonan and Strathbrora in their entirety. Occasionally there have been attempts to alter this. The one with most prospect of success occurred in the early 1960s when the Highland Panel, an officially appointed group set up to advise government ministers on Highland policy, recommended that land settlement of the sort undertaken more than half a century before at North Syre should be considered in Kildonan. In 1965 this proposal was referred to the then newly established Highlands and Islands Development Board (HIDB), a government agency with responsibilities akin to those the CDB (wound up in 1912) had exercised much earlier. It was expected, said Robert Maclennan, elected Sutherland's MP in 1966, that the board would 'open up to more productive and socially useful purposes' a strath that had become, Maclennan complained, 'the exclusive preserve' of 'sporting estates'. In the event, however, the HIDB ducked this challenge. All concept of renewed land settlement, whether in the Strath of Kildonan or anywhere else, was rejected – the board going so far as to dismiss a request from crofters in Marrel and neighbouring townships that they be provided with some additional grazings in the strath.[68]

Today, therefore, the Strath of Kildonan remains – as far as human presence is concerned – much as it was in the years following its clearance. Strathbrora too is mostly deserted, despite its containing, or so the Deer Forest Commission was assured at September 1893 hearings in Golspie, 'as good land . . . as you can get in any strath in Sutherland'. Prior to its inhabitants being 'cruelly removed . . . to make way for sheep', commission members were told, Strathbrora had contained 'sixty-two townships'. Today those townships – their names read into the record of Deer Forest Commission proceedings – have been abandoned for 200 years. But to walk Strathbrora's single-track and unfrequented road – ideally on a summer's evening when the westering sun picks out the tiniest landscape feature – is to see each long-abandoned settlement's story 'written', as Francis Napier so memorably put it, 'in indelible characters on the surface of the soil'.[69]

Look across Loch Brora from the Strathbrora road near a point where the loch narrows to a couple of hundred yards, and you see, just over the water, the green fields that once surrounded Carrol, which James Sutherland, William Sutherland and their families left for Pictou when, in June 1820, the last of Carrol's houses were unroofed. Continue for a mile or two past Gordonbush, where the Marchioness of Stafford came later that same year to call on Gabriel Reed, and you glimpse, half a mile or so the south, the site of what was once Kilbraur, home, until its clearance, to Donald Baillie, who became another of Strathbrora's Pictou-bound emigrants and who could have been the source (it is tempting to speculate) of the earliest surviving poem about Patrick Sellar and his eventual descent (in the poem at any rate) into the fires of hell.

Nearer hand – within a stone's throw of the road in fact – are the remnants of what is reputed to have been the SSPCK's Strathbrora school. Here (or if not here, nearby) when Gordon Ross was at the start of his teaching career, there must have been no lack of children's laughter, shouting, chatter to be heard. Now, except for the rattle of water in the nearby river, all is silent.

Walking on from this spot by way of the bridge that crosses Allt a' Mhuilinn, you pass close to the graveyard where Katherine Ross, Gordon's daughter, would have been buried when – shortly after this little girl, her mother and her sisters were evicted – she died of whooping cough. Also buried there – though graves of that time seldom have stones or markers of any sort – must be Hugh MacKay, just four years old when, like Katherine Ross, he died in the aftermath of Ascoilemore's May 1821 clearance by *Domhnall Sgios* and his men.

Evidence of Ascoilemore's destruction, the Marquis of Stafford was told by Hugh MacKay's fur trader father Donald, would be 'visible to the end of time'. This evidence has certainly lasted into the twenty-first century. It can be seen, in the shape of one of Sutherland's countless sets of house foundations, by anyone who takes the trouble to go looking.

Just beyond Ascoilemore's now partly wooded site is the hillside where little Hugh's part-Cree half-brothers, William and Donald, came with their father's cattle. From this hillside, you get a wide view of a big part of Strathbrora. Next to no present-day dwellings are in sight. But signs of human impact are everywhere in this landscape: field systems dating from the Middle Ages; a ruined broch; traces of Iron Age, Bronze Age and even earlier habitation. Much of Strathbrora, or so it seems from this vantage point, was occupied – and sometimes densely occupied – for at least 50 centuries. In relation to what went before, then, Strathbrora's present emptiness – this product of 'improvement' – is very, very strange. For that reason, no one should expect it to endure.

One day there will be again, as there was for millennia, a substantial population in Strathbrora. One day there will be homes in places where so many homes were burned down, so many people driven out. When that happens – 10, 50, 100 or more years from now – the clearance of Strathbrora will be seen, in the context of the strath's long history, as an indefensible departure from the way things were and from the way they should have been.

APPENDIX

Jessie and Gordon Ross: their later lives

At some point during the year or two following the eviction of Jessie Ross and her girls from Ascoilemore, Jessie, Gordon and their surviving children moved to Helmsdale where (for reasons that are unclear) the SSPCK schoolmastership Gordon had hoped to obtain had not, after all, materialised. This created an opening for Gordon who, on his eventual recovery, succeeded in opening a school of his own. This school attracted about 100 pupils. But the 'poverty of . . . people' in and around Helmsdale, Gordon Ross commented, was such that many parents could not pay even the minimal fees he requested. It must thus have come as a relief to Gordon – 'now restored', he stressed, 'to soundness of mind and health of body' – when the SSPCK agreed to incorporate his school into its network. This school's founder and sole teacher, one of the society's inspectors reported in 1827, 'seems to be a zealous, active, diligent man . . . He was laid aside by bad health arising from an accumulation of family misfortunes which . . . reduced him to great poverty and involved him in debt from which he has little prospect of being relieved unless the society can do something for him.' Something was duly done: Gordon's newly restored SSPCK salary was back-dated, in effect, for three years.[1]

His having been rehabilitated in this way was doubtless aided both by Gordon Ross's now respectful – not to say submissive – approach to the Staffords and by the death (in 1824) of Francis

Suther whom Gordon, in the aftermath of his daughter's death, had so roundly accused of bad faith. There was to be no repetition of Gordon's 1821 condemnations of Sutherland Estate policy. But neither was his SSPCK position to last: his employers dismissed their Helmsdale schoolmaster in 1834 as a result of his having abandoned the Church of Scotland (with which the SSPCK was closely associated) for an altogether more fervent brand of Christianity. From that point forward, Gordon – one of the lay preachers who laid the groundwork for the Free Church's 1843 success in Sutherland – appears to have combined ecclesiastical activity (and eventual Free Church membership) with continued teaching on his own account. Neither Gordon nor Jessie was to leave Helmsdale. Gordon died there in 1868, Jessie in 1873. The couple's grave in Helmsdale's cemetery is marked by a granite obelisk provided, its inscription states, by Gordon's friends.

ACKNOWLEDGEMENTS

This book owes its existence to Dennis MacLeod and John Macdonald. But for generous donations made by Dennis to the University of the Highlands and Islands (UHI), there would have been no Dornoch-based UHI Centre for History with me as its first director and, to begin with, its sole employee. During my several years in Dornoch, starting in 2005, I had little time for research or writing. But well before I handed over responsibility for the Centre for History to the team who have made it a UHI success story, it had occurred to me that it would be good to produce something about Sutherland. What that something might be became apparent when Rogart crofter and historian John Macdonald (whom I have known since we were both involved in the 1986 launch of the Scottish Crofters Union) helped show UHI's first batch of history students something of what is still to be seen of cleared townships in Strathbrora. That same day, John introduced me to documentation dealing with the Ascoilemore evictions of 1821. Here, I thought, was the starting point for an account of the Sutherland clearances that put dispossessed individuals and families, as far as possible, at its centre. Such an account, I felt, might also serve as a bit of a Centre for History thank-you to Dennis MacLeod who, as mentioned in my concluding chapter, feels strongly about the clearances and their repercussions.

Lots of others have helped along the way. Especially deserving of my thanks is Malcolm Bangor-Jones, who has been exploring

475

Sutherland's history and prehistory for many years and who knows far more about the county's past than I ever will. Malcolm has been generous with information, advice and – on occasion – well-informed criticism. Because our interpretations of what took place in early nineteenth-century Sutherland do not always coincide, Malcolm will not be wholly in agreement with what I have written. But I can assure him that, without his input, the preceding pages would have contained many more errors of both fact and judgement.

I am equally grateful to Marjory Harper of the University of Aberdeen. Marjory, a good friend who (thanks to her being seconded part-time to UHI) also became a Centre for History colleague, carefully read and commented on my chapters as they took shape. Elizabeth Ritchie of the UHI Centre for History and Annie Tindley of the University of Dundee, two of the younger historians of Scotland whom it has been my good fortune to get to know as a result of my UHI involvements, did likewise. So did Eric Richards of Flinders University, Adelaide. Eric, who pioneered academic study of the Sutherland clearances and who continues to take a close interest in the topic, has been generous in his encouragement of this interloper on his patch.

Most fortuitously, a year or so into my researches, I was asked by John Perrin, President of the St Andrew's Society of Winnipeg, to be guest speaker at the society's 2013 dinner. This took Evelyn, my wife, and me to Manitoba with which clearance-era Sutherland had many connections. John and Judith Perrin were the most welcoming of hosts. Ian and Jacquie Ross showed Evelyn and me around the Winnipeg locations where settlers from Sutherland made their homes. Best of all, John Perrin and his St Andrew's Society colleagues made it possible for us to visit Churchill in winter, the time of year when, despite our encountering temperatures of minus 35 degrees Celsius, I wanted to be there in order to get some small sense of what Kildonan people had experienced in that Hudson Bay locality exactly 200 years before.

I am grateful to Calm Air for providing us with free flights from Winnipeg to Churchill. But if getting there mattered, ensuring a productive trip mattered more. Hence the debt I owe to our Churchill expedition's key organiser, Jim Oborne. Jim accompanied us to Churchill, shared with us his knowledge of the Canadian north and put together a Churchill itinerary that delivered everything I hoped for. Helping with this itinerary and providing background information were Cory Young, Doug McGregor, Mike Iwanowsky, Bob Coutts and Scott Stephen. Behind the scenes assistance came from the North West Company (where Jim was for many years a director) and, in particular, from the company's President and CEO, Edward Kennedy. Similar such assistance was provided by Bob Vandewater and Bob Darling. Also integral to our Churchill visit was Alexandra Paul of the *Winnipeg Free Press* whose extensive coverage of my researches in that leading Manitoba paper enabled present-day Manitobans, I hope, to get some sense of their province's long-ago links with Scotland.

At Churchill we were warmly received and shown around by Mayor Mike Spence, Mark Ingebrigston, Gary Rea, Lorraine Brandson, Cam Elliott and Duane Collins. My thanks to all of them for what was, for me, an unforgettable insight into a part of the world I never expected to see.

Back in Winnipeg, again through the St Andrew's Society's good offices, I was invited to meet with members of the splendidly named Lord Selkirk Association of Rupert's Land. In this connection, my particular thanks are due to Phyllis Fraser, Gordon Cameron and, above all, Chloe Clark, the association's genealogist. Like Malcolm Bangor-Jones, Chloe rescued me more than once from bad mistakes.

Many others helped with this book's North American dimension. At Chalmette – in temperatures nearly 70 degrees higher than those I met with in Churchill – Harold Songy of the US National Parks Service dealt patiently with my endless questions about the Battle of New Orleans. Later, Ron Merrill, also of the National Parks Service, commented helpfully on a draft of my account of the battle and the run-up to it.

From Oregon, John C. Jackson, fur trade historian and author of many fine books on Western history, kindly supplied me with a copy of his unpublished account of Donald MacKay – subject only to the less than onerous condition that I downed a dram to that most intriguing man's memory in the vicinity of his Strathbrora home. Marsha MacKay, one of Donald's Nova Scotian descendants, provided all sorts of information I should not otherwise have discovered. Equally generous with the results of his researches into Sutherland settlement in Nova Scotia was Glen Matheson – descended from a number of Strathbrora emigrant families and committed to keeping alive a sense of Nova Scotia's extensive Sutherland heritage.

Marianne McLean, whose *People of Glengarry* is much the most illuminating study of Highland emigration to Ontario, put me in touch with archivists in different parts of Canada. As a result, I was able to consult in the Highland Archive, Inverness, reel after reel of microfilmed documentation sent there by Library and Archives Canada in Ottawa and by the Hudson's Bay Company Archives in Winnipeg.

Fiona MacLeod and her colleagues at the Highland Archive helped me find relevant material in the archive's own collections. Staff at the National Records of Scotland, the National Library of Scotland, the University of Edinburgh archive department and the Staffordshire County Record Office provided much assistance. My travel to these and other sources of information was aided by a generous grant from the Carnegie Trust for the Universities of Scotland.

Among the many Sutherland people who have helped greatly with this project are: Jacquie Aitken of the Timespan Museum and Arts Centre in Helmsdale; Margaret MacDonald, Fiona MacKenzie and Frances Gunn of the Strathnaver Clearance Museum in Bettyhill; Nick Lindsay and Ellen Sutherland of the Clyne Heritage Society; Donald MacLeod of *Am Bratach* and Strathnaver; Angus and Evelyn McCall at Culmaily; Michael Wigan of the Borrobol Estate; and

Rosa Sutherland who, though she lives in Inverness, is very much of Strathnaver ancestry.

Other people on whose expertise – in fields as diverse as whisky-making, ornithology, archaeology, art, family history and sheep farming – I have drawn include Keir Strickland, Reay Clarke, Iain Slinn, Bruce Anderson, Paul Boyle, Lord Selkirk, Alastair Gordon, Bill Machin, Marg Nichols, Norman Newton and Hugh Cheape.

Alison Sandison of the University of Aberdeen's Geography Department provided me with maps, and a whole variety of people helped greatly with my search for illustrations. In this connection, my thanks go in particular to my good friend Cailean Maclean who spent several days photographing a series of widely separated Sutherland clearance locations. Others who took time to supply illustrative material include Gary Rea, Rob Bruce-Barron, Glen Matheson, Jacquie Aitken and William Stark.

Lawrence Osborn expertly copy-edited my typescript. Hugh Andrew, Andrew Simmons, Deborah Warner, Jan Rutherford, Sally Pattle and their colleagues at Birlinn have been great people to work with. I am hugely appreciative of their interest in, and commitment to, this project.

My first book, researched and written more than 40 years ago, was dedicated to Evelyn. It is a measure of time passing that this book is dedicated to our four grandchildren. Since they are aged – at time of publication – from one to eight, they are unlikely to be devouring its contents any time soon. But all of them like to listen to stories. And story-telling is what my kind of history-writing has mostly been about.

One of my great pleasures, during the months following the publication of this book's hardback edition, was to meet, and to be contacted by, lots of people who, 200 years after the Sutherland clearances, remain well aware of their family ties to clearance victims. It was good to learn that, without exception, those people were appreciative of my account of what, to many of them, is still a sensitive and emotive topic. Space precludes my listing every such person. But two people with whom I have met and corresponded deserve special mention. Elisabeth Law, a great-niece of Highland Land League MP Angus Sutherland, solved for me the puzzle of how exactly it came about that Angus descended from one of Red River's settler families. And Donald George MacKay, a direct descendant of George MacKay, the catechist featured in my account of the Kildonan troubles of 1813, enabled me to sort out the relationship between the catechist and Angus MacKay, the young man my book follows (as it were) from Kildonan to Red River and on to Ontario. This new information has been incorporated into this paperback edition. So has a point made to me – politely, I should stress – by lawyer and historian John Macaskill, a friend with his own close links with Sutherland. It will please John to know that I have now got right (as I should have done originally) the date when the Seditious Meetings Act of 1819 came into force.

NOTES

Abbreviations

BCA British Columbia Archives
HA Highland Archive
HBCA Hudson's Bay Company Archives
LAC Library and Archives Canada
NA National Archives (UK)
NLS National Library of Scotland
NRS National Records of Scotland
NSA Nova Scotia Archives
OPR Old Parish Register
SCRO Staffordshire County Record Office
UEA University of Edinburgh Archives

1 'Inhuman treatment'

1. NLS 313/1015: Notes of examination anent the Strathbrora Removings, 13 August 1821; HA Clyne OPR. Subsequent paragraphs in this opening section draw on the same sources.
2. SCRO D593/K/1/3/9: G. Ross to Lord Stafford, 6 July 1821.
3. Scotland's People Website: Death certificates of Gordon and Jessie Ross, 14 October 1868 and 16 October 1873; SCRO D593/K/1/3/9: G. Ross to Lord Gower, 13 August 1821; A. S. Cowper, *Gordon Ross, 1791–1868: SSPCK Schoolmaster and Disciple of Sandy Gair*, Edinburgh, 1981, p. 1. Jessie Ross's father was tacksman of Easter Brora.

4. R. Gordon, *A Genealogical History of the Earldom of Sutherland*, Edinburgh, 1813, p. 198; J. M. Bulloch, *The Gordons of Embo and Other Families of that Name in the County of Sutherland*, Dingwall, 1907, pp. 9–11.

5. NLS 313/3485: Lady Stafford to J. Gordon, 27 May 1809.

6. NLS 313/1577: J. Gordon to W. Young, 6 March 1811; NLS 313/1577: J. Gordon to Lady Stafford, 26 March 1812; NLS 313/1128: W. Young to Lord Gower, 14 March and 11 April 1812.

7. NLS 313/1577: Lord Stafford to A. Gordon, 21 August 1812.

8. J. L. Anderson, *The Story of the Commercial Bank during its Hundred Years: 1810 to 1910*, Edinburgh, 1910, pp. 18, 90.

9. SCRO D593/K/1/3/7: Lady Stafford to Lord Stafford, 27 July 1819; SCRO D593/K/1/3/7: W. MacKenzie to Lady Stafford, 23 July 1819; NLS 313/1153: J. Loch to Lord Stafford, 2 August 1819.

10. SCRO D593/K/1/3/8: F. Suther to J. Loch, 14 February 1820; NLS 313/1153: J. Loch to Lord Stafford, 3 October 1820.

11. J. Henderson, *General View of the Agriculture of the County of Sutherland*, London, 1812, p. 44.

12. W. Ross, 'Parish of Clyne', *Statistical Account of Scotland*, 21 vols, Edinburgh, 1791–99, X, p. 327.

13. Henderson, *County of Sutherland*, pp. 85–86; W. J. Watson, *The History of the Celtic Placenames of Scotland*, Edinburgh, 1926, pp. 273–74.

14. SCRO D6579/9: Lady Stafford to Lord Stafford, 3 October 1820; SCRO D593/K/1/3/8: F. Suther to J. Loch, 17 April, 13 June 1820.

15. SCRO D593/K/1/3/8: F. Suther to J. Loch, 13 February 1820.

16. SCRO D/6579/9: Lady Stafford to Lord Stafford, 3 October 1820.

17. Henderson, *County of Sutherland*, p. 44; J. Loch, *An Account of the Improvements on the Estates of the Marquis of Stafford*, London, 1820, Appendix, p. 33. See also, E. MacKenzie (ed.), *An Historical, Topographical and Descriptive View of the County of Northumberland*, 2 vols, Newcastle, 1825; M. Bangor-Jones, 'Sheep Farming in Sutherland in the Eighteenth Century', *Agricultural History Review*, 50, 2002.

18. SCRO D/6579/9: Lady Stafford to Lord Stafford, 3 October 1820.

19. A. S. Cowper and I. Ross, *The SSPCK and the Parish of Kildonan*, Edinburgh, 1980, p. 2. The evolution of the SSPCK's Strathbrora school can be followed in SSPCK records. See also, Cowper, *Gordon Ross*. The school's reputed site, just above the Strathbrora road about a quarter of a mile short of the Allt a' Mhuilin bridge, is shown on an Ordnance Survey map of 1879, when some at least of Gordon Ross's pupils were still available to tell map-makers where his school was located.

20. NRS GD95/2/13: Minutes of Directors, 1 April 1813.

21. NLS 10853/276: J. Baillie and others to F. Suther, 27 April 1818; NLS 313/1573: Report of P. Sellar on the Sutherland Estate, 1811.

22. NLS 10853/276: J. Baillie and others to F. Suther, 27 April 1818; NLS D593/K/1/3/9: J. Ross to Lord Stafford, 6 July 1821; NLS 313/1015: Notes of Examination anent the Strathbrora Removings, 13 August 1821; NLS 313/1153: J. Loch to Lord Stafford, 19 August 1821.

23. NLS 313/1153: J. Loch to Lord Stafford, 19 August 1821.

24. SCRO D593/K/1/3/9: F. Suther to J. Loch, 18 April 1821; NRS GD95/2/14: Minutes of Directors, 10 February 1820.

25. SCRO D593/K/1/3/8: F. Suther to J. Loch, 14 January 1820.

26. SCRO D593/K/1/3/9: G. Ross to Lord Stafford, 6 July 1821.

27. NLS 313/1153: J. Loch to Lord Stafford, 19 August 1821; SCRO D593/K/1/3/9: G. Ross to Lord Stafford, 6 July 1821.

28. SCRO D593/K/1/3/9: G. Ross to Lord Stafford, 6 July 1821.

29. SCRO D593/K/1/3/9: G. Ross to Lord Stafford, 6 July 1821; SCRO D593/K/1/3/9: Notes of Examination anent the Strathbrora Removings, 13 August 1821; *Inverness Journal*, 29 June 1821.

30. SCRO D593/K/1/3/9: G. Ross to Lord Stafford, 6 July 1821.

31. SCRO D593/K/1/3/9: G. Ross to Lord Stafford, 6 July 1821.

32. NRS GD268/359: Lady Stafford to J. Loch, 24 May 1821.

33. SCRO D593/K/1/3/9: Lady Stafford to J. Loch, 23 July 1821; NLS 313/1141: J. Loch to F. Suther, 28 July 1821; NLS 313/1141: J. Loch to F. Suther, 31 July 1821.

34. NLS 313/1153: J. Loch to Lord Stafford, 28 July 1821.

35. NLS 313/1141: J. Loch to F. Suther, 28 July 1821.

36. NLS 313/1015: Notes of Examination anent the Strathbrora Removings, 13 August 1821; NRS JP32/7/4: List of Constables, August 1820.
37. SCRO D593/K/1/3/4: A. Maconochie to J. Loch, 15 October 1816; SCRO D593/K/1/5/5: J. Loch to Lady Stafford, 27 November 1816; NLS 313/1590: C. Ross to Lady Stafford, 24 December 1816.
38. NLS 313/1141: Petition of Donald Bannerman, 19 March 1821.
39. SCRO D593/K/1/3/8: P. Sellar to J. Loch, 2 September 1820.
40. D593/K/1/3/9: F. Suther to J. Loch, 6 April 1821; *Inverness Journal*, 28 September 1821.
41. NLS 313/1015: Notes of Examination anent the Strathbrora Removings, 13 August 1821.
42. NLS 313/1015: Notes of Examination anent the Strathbrora Removings, 13 August 1821.
43. NLS 313/1015: Notes of Examination anent the Strathbrora Removings, 13 August 1821.
44. NLS 313/1015: Notes of Examination anent the Strathbrora Removings, 13 August 1821.
45. NLS 313/1015: Notes of Examination anent the Strathbrora Removings, 13 August 1821.
46. NLS 313/1015: Notes of Examination anent the Strathbrora Removings, 13 August 1821.
47. NLS 313/1015: Notes of Examination anent the Strathbrora Removings, 13 August 1821.
48. NLS 313/1015: Notes of Examination anent the Strathbrora Removings, 13 August 1821.
49. NLS, SP, 313/1015: Notes of Examination anent the Strathbrora Removings, 13 August 1821; SCRO D593/K/1/3/8: F. Suther to J. Loch, 14 February 1820.
50. NLS 313/1015: Notes of Examination anent the Strathbrora Removings, 13 August 1821.
51. NLS 313/1015: Notes of Examination anent the Strathbrora Removings, 13 August 1821.
52. NLS 313/1015: Notes of Examination anent the Strathbrora Removings, 13 August 1821; SCRO D593/K/1/3/9: F. Suther to J. Loch, 27 May 1821.

53. NLS 313/1147: J. Loch to Lady Stafford, 12 August 1821; NLS 313/1153: J. Loch to Lord Stafford, 17 August 1821.

54. NLS 313/1153: J. Loch to Lord Stafford, 17 August 1821; NLS 313/1153: J. Loch to Lord Stafford, 19 August 1821.

55. SCRO D593/K/1/3/9: G. Ross to J. Loch, 22 August 1821; SCRO D593/K/1/3/9: J. Loch to G. Ross, 24 August 1821.

56. NLS 313/1015: Notes of Examination anent the Strathbrora Removings, 13 August 1821.

57. SCRO D593/K/1/3/9: G. Ross to Lord Gower, 13 August 1821; NLS 313/1015: Notes of Examination anent the Strathbrora Removings, 13 August 1821.

58. NRS GD95/2/14–15: Minutes of Directors, 1 November 1821 and 12 May 1825; HA, OPR Loth, 23 July 1823.

2 'Tribes that never saw Europeans before'

1. NLS 313/1015: Notes of Examination anent the Strathbrora Removings, 13 August 1821.

2. SCRO D593/K/1/3/9: D. MacKay to Lord Stafford, 10 July 1821; NLS 313/1015: Notes of Examination anent the Strathbrora Removings, 13 August 1821.

3. SCRO D593/K/1/3/9: D. MacKay to Lord Stafford, 10 July 1821; HA OPR Clyne.

4. SCRO D593/K/1/3/9: D. MacKay to Lord Stafford, 10 July 1821.

5. SCRO D593/K/1/5/10: J. Loch to W. MacKenzie, 21 March 1821; NLS 313/1153 J. Loch to Lord Stafford, 28 July 1821.

6. SCRO D6579/9: Lady Stafford to Lord Stafford, 3 October 1820; NLS 313/750: Lady Stafford to Lord Stafford, 5 October 1820; SCRO D593/K/1/5/10: J. Loch to W. MacKenzie, 21 March 1821; NLS 313/1015: J. Loch to F. Suther, 22 March 1821; NLS 313/1153 J. Loch to Lord Stafford, 28 July 1821; NLS 313/1153: J. Loch to Lord Stafford, 17 August 1821.

7. R. J. Adam (ed.), *Papers on Sutherland Estate Management*, 2 vols, Edinburgh, 1972, I, p. 37: W. Young to Lady Stafford, 21 October

1810; NLS 313/750: Lady Stafford to Lord Stafford, 5 October 1820.

8.	SCRO D593/K/1/3/9: D. MacKay to Lord Stafford, 10 July 1821.

9.	J. C. Jackson, 'The Voyages of Mad Donald McKay and his Fight for the Fur Trade of the Canadian Northwest' (unpublished biography), p. 23. Jackson's biography (summarised in his entry for Donald MacKay in *Dictionary of Canadian Biography Online*) is the fullest account of MacKay. See also, H. W. Duckworth, 'The Madness of Donald MacKay: An Iron Man of the Fur Trade', *The Beaver*, June–July 1988. MacKay's contribution to the HBC's late eighteenth-century push to the interior features in more general terms in, E. E. Rich, *The History of the Hudson's Bay Company*, 2 vols, London, 1958–59.

10.	HBCA E/233/1: Narrative of Donald MacKay, n.d.

11.	Duckworth, 'Donald MacKay', p. 29. For an overview of the North West Company and its Highland dimension, see, J. Hunter, *A Dance Called America: The Scottish Highlands, the United States and Canada*, Edinburgh, 1994, pp. 49–71.

12.	Jackson, 'Voyages', p. 142.

13.	Jackson, 'Voyages', p. 194.

14.	Donald's family circumstances are touched on in Jackson, 'Voyages'. Further details were supplied to the author by Donald's great-great-great-granddaughter, Marsha MacKay.

15.	MacKay's letter to Selkirk is reproduced in T. Douglas, 'Ossinoboia' [1815], in J. M. Bumsted (ed.), *The Collected Writings of Lord Selkirk, 1810–1820*, Winnipeg, 1987, pp. 22–23.

16.	Anon., *A Narrative of Occurrences in the Indian Countries of North America*, London, 1817, Appendix, p. 21: Affidavit of George Campbell, 19 August 1815.

## 3	*'There should be blood'*

1 .	Duncan Thomson et al., *Raeburn: The Art of Sir Henry Raeburn, 1756–1823*, Edinburgh, 1997, p. 142; National Galleries of Scotland Online	Collection:	http://www.nationalgalleries.org/collection/

simple-search/R/4399/artistName/Sir%20Henry%20Raeburn/recor-
dId/5309. Also, *Army List*, London, 1812, p. 243.

2. National Gallery at 150: http://www.nationalgalleries.org/collection/
   etours/national-gallery-at-150/1; *Inverness Journal*, 12 March 1830.

3. *Inverness Journal*, 12 March 1830.

4. NLS 313/1575: G. Clunes to Lady Stafford, 3 September 1811; NLS
   313/1575: Lady Stafford to Duke of York, n.d.

5. J. Loch, *An Account of the Improvements on the Estates of the
   Marquis of Stafford*, London, 1820, Appendix, p. 34; D. Sage,
   Memorabilia Domestica, Wick, 1899, pp. 151–52; J. M. Bulloch, *The
   Families of Gordon of Invergordon, Newhall and Carrol*, Dingwall,
   1906, p. 110. The Staffords were well aware that William Clunes was
   'much connected' with Joseph Gordon. See, SCRO D593/K/1/3/7: Lady
   Stafford to J. Loch, 17 October 1819.

6. That Joseph Gordon stayed occasionally at Crakaig can be deduced
   from some of his correspondence having emanated from there. See,
   e.g., SCRO D593/K/1/3/6: J. Gordon to J. Loch, 6 April 1818.

7. NLS 313/1580: W. Young to Lady Stafford, 30 December 1812; NLS
   313/1127: P. Sellar to Lord Gower, 21 March 1812.

8. NLS 313/1580: W. Young to Lady Stafford, 30 December 1812; J.
   Henderson, *General View of the Agriculture of the County of
   Caithness*, London, 1815, p. 165; A. MacKay, *Sketches of Sutherland
   Characters*, Edinburgh, 1889, p. 188; A. MacKenzie, *Historical,
   Topographical and Descriptive View of the County of Northumberland*,
   2 vols, Newcastle, 1825, II, p. 247.

9. NRS AD14/13/9: Kildonan Precognitions, (Statement of W. Clunes),
   23 January 1813.

10. Sage, *Memorabilia*, p. 151.

11. Sage, *Memorabilia*, pp. 151–52.

12. CH2/1290/4: Dornoch Presbytery Minutes, 22 November 1814; HA
    D1249/4/2/1: A. Sage to D. Sage, 1 November 1819; Sage, *Memorabilia*,
    pp. 79–81.

13. NRS AD14/13/9: Kildonan Precognitions, (Statement of R. MacKay),
    26 January 1813.

14. NRS, AD14/13/9: Kildonan Precognitions, (Statement of W. Clunes), 23 January 1813.

15. NRS, AD14/13/9: Kildonan Precognitions, (Statement of W. Clunes), 23 January 1813.

16. NRS RHP 11602: Plan of intended road, Kirk of Farr to Helmsdale, 1794; NLS 313/1575: Journal of proceedings to and from Strathnaver, 1810; A. Sage, 'Parish of Kildonan', *Statistical Account of Scotland*, III, p. 445.

17. Sage, 'Parish of Kildonan', p. 449.

18. Sage, *Memorabilia*, pp. 59, 70, 73; NRS RHP 11602: Plan of intended road, Kirk of Farr to Helmsdale, 1794.

19. Sage, *Memorabilia*, p. 75.

20. NLS 313/1575: Journal of proceedings to and from Strathnaver, 1810; R.J. Adam, *Papers on Sutherland Estate Management*, 2 vols, Edinburgh, 1972, I, p. 34: W. Young to Lord Gower, September 1810.

21. J. Henderson, *General View of the Agriculture of the County of Caithness*, London, 1815, p. 145.

22. T. Sellar, *The Sutherland Evictions of 1814*, London, 1883, p. 22: P. Sellar to J. Loch, 1 May 1820

23. Sellar, *Sutherland Evictions*, p. 23: Sellar to Loch, 1 May 1820.

24. S. W. Martins, 'A Century of Farming on the Sutherland Estate, 1790–1890', *Review of Scottish Culture*, X, 1996–97, p. 48.

25. NRS AD14/13/9: Kildonan Precognitions, (Statements of W. Young and R. Reed), 21, 23 January 1813.

26. NLS 313/1575: Journal of proceedings to and from Strathnaver, 1810. A total of 26 tenants were evicted to make way for Houston's Suisgill farm. See, Henderson, *County of Sutherland*, p. 174.

27. SCRO D593/K/1/3/4: P. Sellar to J. Loch, 7 May 1816; NLS 313/1580: W. Young to Lady Stafford, 30 December 1812; NRS AD14/13/9: Kildonan Precognitions, (Statement of W. Young), 23 January 1813.

28. NRS AD14/13/9: Kildonan Precognitions, (Statement of W. Clunes), 23 January 1813.

29. NRS AD14/13/9: Kildonan Precognitions, (Statements of D. Gunn, A. Gunn and D. Polson), 18, 22 March 1813; HA OPR Kildonan.

30. NRS AD14/13/9: Kildonan Precognitions, (Statement of G. MacDonald), 18 March 1813.

31. Sage, *Memorabilia*, p. 95; NRS AD14/13/9: Kildonan Precognitions, (Statement of J. Gordon), 23 March 1813.

32. NRS AD14/13/9: Kildonan Precognitions, (Statements of A. Fraser, G. MacDonald, J. Gordon), 18, 22, 23 March 1813.

33. NRS, AD14/13/9: Kildonan Precognitions, (Statements of G. MacDonald, W. Sutherland), 26 January, 18 March 1813.

34. Sage, *Memorabilia*, p. 95.

35. Adam, *Sutherland Estate*, I, p. 106: Report by Patrick Sellar concerning the state of the interest of landlord and tenant on the Sutherland Estate, March and April 1811.

36. R. Mitchison, *Agricultural Sir John: The Life of Sir John Sinclair of Ulbster*, London, 1962.

37. For Cleugh's obituary, *Inverness Journal*, 3 July 1846.

38. NRS AD14/13/9: Kildonan Precognitions, (Statement of A. Gordon), 21 March 1813.

39. NRS AD14/13/9: Kildonan Precognitions, (Statement of G. Cleugh), 21 January 1813.

40. NRS AD14/13/9: Kildonan Precognitions, (Statement of G. Cleugh), 21 January 1813.

41. NRS AD14/13/9: Kildonan Precognitions, (Statement of R. Reed), 21 January 1813.

42. NRS AD14/13/9: Kildonan Precognitions, (Statement of R. Reed), 21 January 1813.

43. NRS AD14/13/9: Kildonan Precognitions, (Statement of J. Cleugh), 26 January 1813.

44. NRS AD14/13/9: Kildonan Precognitions, (Statement of J. Cleugh), 26 January 1813.

45. NRS AD14/13/9: Kildonan Precognitions, (Statement of G. Cleugh), 21 January 1813.

46. NRS AD14/13/9: Kildonan Precognitions, (Statements of J. Hall and G. Cleugh), 21 January, 13 March 1813.

47. NRS AD14/13/9: Kildonan Precognitions, (Statement of G. Cleugh), 21 January 1813.

48. NRS AD14/13/9: Kildonan Precognitions, (Statement of G. Cleugh), 21 January 1813.

49. NRS AD14/13/9: Kildonan Precognitions, (Statements of J. Armstrong and A. Fraser), 27 January, 22 March 1813.

50. NRS AD14/13/9: Kildonan Precognitions, (Statements of A. Fraser and W. Clunes), 23 January, 22 March 1813.

4 *'Open and determined resistance'*

1. NRS AD14/13/9: Kildonan Precognitions, (Statement of M. Short), 26 January 1813; NLS 313/1128: W. Young to Lady Stafford, 3 February, 1813; NLS 313/1128: W. Young to Lord Gower, 6 February 1813; R. J. Adam, *Papers on Sutherland Estate Management*, 2 vols, Edinburgh, 1972, II, p. 181: P. Sellar to Lady Stafford, 13 February, 1813; SCRO D593/K/1/3/4: P. Sellar to J. Loch, 7 May 1816.

2. NLS 313/1580: W. Young to Lady Stafford, 26 January 1813; NLS 313/1128: W. Young to Lord Gower, 30 January 1813; SCRO D593/K/1/3/4: P. Sellar to J. Loch, 7 May 1816.

3. NLS 313/1578: P. Sellar to Lady Stafford, 11 February, 1813; NRS RH2/4/100: W. Young to the Inhabitants of Kildonan, n.d.; NLS 313/1580: W. Young to Lady Stafford, 3 February 1813; NLS 313/1580: W. Young to Lady Stafford, 8 February 1813.

4. NRS RH2/4/100: W. Young to the Inhabitants of Kildonan, n.d.

5. NRS SC9/7/64: Bond of caution for keeping the peace by tenants of the parish of Kildonan, 2 February, 1813; NLS 313/1578: P. Sellar to Lady Stafford, 11 February, 1813.

6. SCRO D593/K/1/3/4: W. Young to Lady Stafford, 8 February 1813; SCRO D593/K/1/3/4: P. Sellar to J. Loch, 7 May 1816.

7. J. Henderson, *General View of the Agriculture of the County of Sutherland*, London, 1812, pp. 4–5.

8. Henderson, *County of Sutherland*, p. 174.

9. NLS 313/1580 W. Young to Lady Stafford, 3 February 1813; NRS AD14/13/9: Kildonan Precognitions, (Statement of D. Bannerman), 10 February 1813.

10. NRS AD14/13/9: Kildonan Precognitions, ('From the tenants of the Parish of Kildonan to Sheriff McKid', 3 February 1813, as appended to Statement of D. Bannerman), 10 February 1813; NRS AD14/13/9: Kildonan Precognitions, (Statement of J. MacKay), 23 March 1813.

11. NRS, AD14/13/9: Kildonan Precognitions, (Statement of D. Bannerman), 10 February 1813. See also, NRS, AD14/13/9: Kildonan Precognitions, (Documents relating to the disturbances in Kildonan), 3, 5 February 1813; NRS SC9/7/64: Warrant of incarceration of John Bannerman, n.d.

12. NRS AD14/13/9: Kildonan Precognitions, (Statements of J. MacKay, G. MacDonald, A. Gordon, J. Gordon and D. Bannerman), 10 February, 18, 22, 23 March 1813; NRS SC 9/7/64: Petition of John Bannerman, 5 February 1813.

13. NLS 313/1128: W. Young to Lord Gower, 6 February 1813; Adam, *Sutherland Estate*, II, p. 177: P. Sellar to Lord Stafford, 4 February 1813.

14. NRS AD14/13/9: Kildonan Precognitions, (Statements of D. Bannerman and D. Gunn), 10 February, 22 March 1813.

15. NRS AD14/13/9: Kildonan Precognitions, (Statement of D. Bannerman), 10 February 1813.

16. NRS AD14/13/9: Kildonan Precognitions, (Statements of D. Gunn, G. Sutherland, J. MacLeod, G. MacDonald and G. Ferguson), 17, 18, 22, 23 March 1813.

17. Adam, *Sutherland Estate*, II, pp. 80–81: Lady Stafford to Lord Stafford, 27 July 1808; NRS AD14/13/9: Kildonan Precognitions, (Statement of J. Duncan), 11 February 1813.

18. NRS AD14/13/9: Kildonan Precognitions, (Statement of R. Bruce), 13 March 1813; Adam, *Sutherland Estate*, II, p. 180: P. Sellar to Lady Stafford, 13 February 1813.

19. NRS AD14/13/9: Kildonan Precognitions, (Documents relating to proceedings at Golspie and statements of D. Polson, J. Sutherland and J. Duncan), 10–21 February, 13, 22 March 1813.

20. NRS AD14/13/9: Kildonan Precognitions, (Documents relating to proceedings at Golspie), 10–21 February 1813.

21. NRS AD14/13/9: Kildonan Precognitions, (Documents relating to proceedings at Golspie), 10–21 February 1813; NLS, SP 313/1580: W. Young to Lady Stafford, 11 February 1813; Adam, *Sutherland Estate*, II, p. 181: P. Sellar to Lady Stafford, 13 February 1813.

22. SCRO D593/K/1/5/2: J. Loch to W. Young, 15 February 1813.

23. H. Cockburn, *Life of Lord Jeffrey*, 2 Vols., Edinburgh, 1852, I, p. 211; NLS 313/1579: W. MacKenzie to Lady Stafford, 15 February 1813; NRS RH2/4/100: A. Colquhoun to Lord Sidmouth, 19 February 1813. For Cranstoun's earnings, NLS 313/1588: W. MacKenzie to Lady Stafford, 28 November 1816.

24. M. Fry, *The Dundas Despotism*, Edinburgh, 1992, p. 294; NRS RH2/4/100: A. Colquhoun to Lord Sidmouth, 19 February 1813.

25. NRS AD14/13/9: G. Cranstoun to A. Colquhoun, n.d.; NLS 313/1580: W. Young to Lady Stafford, 12 and 13 March 1813.

26. NLS 313/1579: W. MacKenzie to Lady Stafford, 15 February 1813; SCRO D593/K/1/5/2: J. Loch to G. Cranstoun, 18 February 1813.

27. SCRO D593/K/1/3/1: W. Young to J. Loch, 7 and 21 February 1813; NRS RH2/4/100: W. Young to J. Cranstoun, 28 February 1813.

28. NRS RH2/4/100: W. Young to J. Cranstoun, 28 February 1813.

29. Adam, *Sutherland Estate*, II, p. 186: W. Young to Lady Stafford, 14 March 1813.

30. NRS AD14/13/9: Kildonan Precognitions, 1813 (Documents relating to developments at Helmsdale, 9 March 1813); SCRO D593/K/1/3/1: W. Young to J. Loch, 20 March 1813; LAC MG19-E1 14058–59: J. Armour to W. MacDonald, 27 February 1813; NLS 313/1581: Lord Selkirk to W. Munro, 27 March 1813.

31. NA WO121/119: Discharge documents of William MacDonald, March–April, 1812.

32. Adam, *Sutherland Estate*, II, p185: W. Young to Lady Stafford, 4 March 1813; NLS 313/1580: W. Young to J. Loch, 13 March 1813; NA WO121/119: Discharge documents of William MacDonald, March–April, 1812.

33. NLS 313/1580: W. Young to Lady Stafford, 12 March 1813. See also, M. Sutherland, *A Fighting Clan: Sutherland Officers, 1250–1850*, London, 1996, pp. 180–81.

34. Henderson, *County of Sutherland*, p. 50.

35. NLS 313/1580: W. Young to Lady Stafford, 12 and 20 March, 1813; NLS 313/1126: J. Sutherland to Lady Stafford, 12 August 1813; NLS 313/1578: P. Sellar to J. Sutherland, 10 August 1813.

36. NLS 313/991: A. Sutherland to W. Ross, 20 July 1815. This was a letter sent by Alexander to one of his correspondents in Sutherland. Like many such letters, it found its way into the hands of Stafford family employees. Also, Sutherland, *Fighting Clan*, pp. 147–48.

37. *Gentleman's Magazine*, September 1834; NLS 313/749: Lady Stafford to Lord Stafford, 13 August 1815; *The Star*, 16 March 1813.

38. *The Star*, 16 March 1813.

39. NLS 313/1578: W. Young to Lady Stafford, 13 March 1813; NLS 313/1578: P. Sellar to Lady Stafford, 14 March 1813; SCRO D593/K/1/5/2: J. Loch to W. Young, 3 April 1813; Adam, *Sutherland Estate*, II, p. 193: W. Young to Lady Stafford, 15 April 1813.

40. J. A. Paris, *The Life of Sir Humphry Davy*, London, 1831, p. 222: H. Davy to J. G. Children, 21 August 1812; R. Holmes, *The Age of Wonder: How the Romantic Generation Discovered the Beauty and Terror of Science*, London, 2009, pp. 235–304.

41. NRS GD268/216/13: Lady Stafford to J. Loch, 25 March 1813; NRS GD268/216/18: Lady Stafford to J. Loch, n.d. 1813.

42. *The Star*, 24 March 1813.

43. Holmes, *Age of Wonder*, p. 272; NLS 314/16: H. Davy, Sketches of the geology of the east coast of Sutherland, 1812; NRS GD268/216/13: Lady Stafford to J. Loch, 25 March 1813.

44. W. Cobbett, *Tour in Scotland*, London, 1833, p. 155.

45. *The Star*, 5 April 1813.

46. *The Star*, 5 April 1813.

47. NLS 313/1580: W. Young to J. Loch, 13 March 1813; Adam, *Sutherland Estate*, II, p. 188: J. Loch to W. Young, 16 March 1813; SCRO D593/K/1/5/2: J. Loch to W. Young.

48. Adam, *Sutherland Estate*, II, p. 187: G. Cranstoun to J. Loch, 12 March 1813.

49. D. MacLeod, *Gloomy Memories of the Highlands of Scotland*,

Glasgow, 1892, p. 7; N. M. Gunn, *Butcher's Broom*, London, 1977, pp. 308–09.

50. *The Star*, 22 March 1813; NLS 313/1580: W. Young to Lady Stafford, 20 March 1813.

51. LAC MG19-E1 14058–59: J. Armour to W. MacDonald, 27 February 1813.

52. A. Allardyce (ed.), *Letters to and from Charles Kirkpatrick Sharpe*, 2 vols, Edinburgh, 1888, II, pp. 76–77: Lady Stafford to C. K. Sharpe, 22 March 1813; Lady Stafford to C. K. Sharpe, 22 March 1813; SCRO D593/K/1/3/2: J. Loch to J. Ingles, 6 March 1813.

53. SCRO D593/K/1/3/2: J. Loch to J. Ingles, 6 March 1813.

54. *The Star*, 22 March 1813. Also, SCRO, SC, D593/K/1/3/2: J. Loch to G. Cranstoun, 6 March 1813.

55. UEA La.II.202: Selkirk to A. MacDonald, 23 January 1813. LAC MG19-E1 14101–02: A. MacDonald to Selkirk, 9 February 1813. For wider background to Selkirk's proposed regiment, see, J. Bumsted, *Lord Selkirk: A Life*, East Lansing, 2009, pp. 200–33.

56. LAC MG19-E1 14056–57: List of officers submitted to Lord Selkirk, 13 February 1813; UEA La.II.202: Selkirk to A. MacDonald, 30 April 2013; Sel P 703–12: Selkirk to M. Macdonell, 30 June 1813.

57. NLS 313/1580: W. Young to Lady Stafford, 15 April 1813; LAC MG19-E1 14043–44: H. Torrens to Selkirk, 14 April 1813; UEA La.II.202: Selkirk to A. MacDonald, 8 May 1813.

5 'Damned Savages from Scotland'

1. HBCA B42/a/140: Fort Churchill Post Journal, 5 April 1814.

2. HBCA B42/b/69: Fort Churchill Correspondence Book, 5 April 1814.

3. LAC MG19-E1 1107–16: A. McDonald to Selkirk, 22 May 1814; BCA A/B/20/C47E: Journal of Abel Edwards, 1 April 1814.

4. D. Gunn, *A History of Manitoba from the Earliest Settlements to 1835*, Ottawa, 1880, p. 103.

5. LAC MG19-E1 18178–242: Journal of Archibald McDonald, 6 April 1814.

6. BCA A/B/20/C47E: Copy of Instructions to Mr McDonald, 25 March 1814; LAC MG19-E1 18178–242: Journal of Archibald McDonald, 7 April 1814.

7. LAC MG19-E1 1107–16: A. McDonald to Selkirk, 22 May 1814.

8. LAC MG19-E1 18178–242: Journal of Archibald McDonald, 13–14 April 1814; BCA A/B/20/C47E: A. McDonald to A. Edwards, 21 April 1814.

9. LAC MG19-E1 18178–242: Journal of Archibald McDonald, 14 April 1814.

10. LAC MG19-E1 18178–242: Journal of Archibald McDonald, 15 April 1814.

11. J. M. Bumsted, *Lord Selkirk: A Life*, East Lansing, 2009, p. 45.

12. W. Fraser, *The Sutherland Book*, 3 vols, Edinburgh, 1892, II, p. 320: W. Scott to Lady Stafford, 19 November 1811.

13. T. Douglas (Earl of Selkirk), *Observations on the Present State of the Highlands of Scotland*, London, 1805, pp. 119–20.

14. J. P. Pritchett, *The Red River Valley: A Regional Study*, New Haven, 1942, p. 120: Selkirk to M. Macdonell, 12 June 1813. Pritchett drew on Selkirk family papers that were subsequently destroyed by fire.

15. NLS 313/1581: Selkirk to Lord Stafford, 22 April 1813.

16. Selkirk, *Observations*, pp. 198, 200; P. C. T. White (ed.), *Lord Selkirk's Diary, 1803–04: A Journal of his Travels*, Toronto, 1958, p. 17.

17. NLS 313/1580: W. Young to Lady Stafford, 15 April 2013.

18. NRS GD268/216/18: Lady Stafford to J. Loch, n.d.; NLS 313/1581: Notes by Lady Stafford, 18 March, 13 April 1813; SP 313/1581; NLS 313/1581: Selkirk to Lord Stafford, 22 April 1813; NLS 313/1581: W. Young to Lady Stafford, 21, 23 May 1813.

19. LAC MG19-E1 650–54: Selkirk to M. Macdonnell, 12 June 1813; R. G. MacBeth, *The Selkirk Settlers in Real Life*, Toronto, 1897, p. 18.

20. NLS 313/1581: Selkirk to W. Munro, 27 March 1813; UEA La.II.202: Selkirk to A. MacDonald, 12 June 1813; LAC MG19-E1 655–57: Selkirk to M. Macdonnell, 12 June 1813.

21. A. Allardyce (ed.), *Letters to and from Charles Kirkpatrick Sharpe*, 2 vols, Edinburgh, 1888, II, p. 85: Lord Gower to C. Kirkpatrick Sharpe, 12 July 1813.

22. HBCA Biographical Sheets: Donald Gunn; Gunn, *Manitoba*, p. 91; HBCA C.1/778: *Prince of Wales* log, 7–12 June 1813.

23. NLS 313/1129: W. MacKenzie to Lady Sutherland, 13 July 1813; Gunn, *Manitoba*, p. 94.

24. HBCA C.1/778: *Prince of Wales* log, 21–28 June 1813; Gunn, *Manitoba*, pp. 91–92; A. McDonald, *Reply to the Letter Lately Addressed to the Earl of Selkirk by the Rev. John Strachan*, Montreal, 1816, p. 21.

25. UEA La.II.202: Selkirk to A. MacDonald, 9 July, 4 August 1812. Archibald McDonald's background is explored in J. Hunter, *Glencoe and the Indians*, Edinburgh, 1996, pp. 44–71.

26. Gunn, *Manitoba*, pp. 94–95; HBCA C.1/778: *Prince of Wales* log, 30 July–6 August 1813.

27. HBCA C.1/778: *Prince of Wales* log, 27 July–19 August 1813.

28. Gunn, *Manitoba*, p. 96.

29. HBCA B42/a/140: Fort Churchill Post Journal, 18–19 August 1813; HBCA C.1/778: *Prince of Wales* log, 22–25 August 1813; HBCA B42/a/140: Fort Churchill Post Journal, 20–30 August 1813.

30. Memories of Kate MacPherson are preserved in W. J. Healy, *Women of Red River*, Winnipeg, 1923, pp. 53–55.

31. D. Sage, *Memorabilia Domestica*, Wick, 1899, pp. 130–31.

32. Sage, *Memorabilia*, pp. 130–31; NLS 313/991: P. Sellar, Note concerning Sutherland, 24 May 1816.

33. LAC MG19-E1 875–78: W. Auld to W. Hillier, 25 September 1813.

34. HBCA C.1/778: *Prince of Wales* log, 23–24 August 1813; LAC MG19-E1 822–24: M. Macdonell to Selkirk, 7 September 1813; HBCA B42/1/140: Fort Churchill Post Journal, 9 September 1813; LAC MG19-E1 875–78: W. Auld to W. Hillier, 25 September 1813; LAC MG19-E1 886–97: O. Keveny to M. Macdonell, 26 September 1813.

35. LAC MG19-E1 1572–75: R. Semple to Selkirk, 22 June 1815; LAC MG19-E1 1831–39: P. Fidler to R. Semple, 27 December 1815.

36. HBCA C.1/778: *Prince of Wales* log, 12 September 1813.

37. HBCA C.1/778: *Prince of Wales* log, 15–17 September 1813; HBCA B42/a/140: Fort Churchill Post Journal, 17 September 1813; UEA

La.II.202: Selkirk to A. MacDonald, 16 November 1813; BCA A/B/20/
C47E: Journal of Abel Edwards, 19–20 September 1813.

38. HBCA C.1/778: *Prince of Wales* log, 20 September-24 November 1813;
UEA La.II.202: Selkirk to A. MacDonald, 16 November 1813.

39. LAC MG19-E1 843–64: W. Auld to A. Wedderburn, 16 September
1813.

40. K. Fenyó, *Contempt, Sympathy and Romance: Lowland Perceptions of
the Highlands and the Clearances during the Famine Years, 1845–1855,*
East Linton, 2000, pp. 30, 51, 62–63.

41. LAC MG19-E1 843–64: W. Auld to A. Wedderburn, 16 September 1813;
LAC MG19-E1 875–78: W. Auld to W. Hillier, 25 September 1813; LAC
MG19-E1 836–42: R. Noss to W. Auld, 26 September 1813; BCA A/B/20/
C47E: Journal of Abel Edwards, 27 September, 12 October 1813.

6 'When among wolves, howl!'

1. LAC MG19-E1 18178–242: Journal of Archibald McDonald, 6 April
1814; L. E. Brandson, *Churchill Hudson Bay: A Guide to Natural and
Cultural Heritage,* Churchill, 2012, pp. 86–87; J. W. Tyrrell, *Across the
Sub-Arctics of Canada,* Toronto, 1897, p. 223.

2. HBCA B42/a/140: Fort Churchill Post Journal, 21 September 1813;
BCA A/B/20/C47E: Journal of Abel Edwards, 21–23 September 1813;
Tyrrell, *Across the Sub-Arctics,* p. 210.

3. BCA A/B/20/C47E: A. Edwards to M. Macdonell, 12 January 1814;
BCA A/B/20/C47E: A. McDonald to A. Edwards, 28 September 1813;
BCA A/B/20/C47E: Journal of Abel Edwards, 17 October 1813; LAC
MG19-E1 836–42: R. Noss to W. Auld, 26 September 1813; LAC
MG19-E1 1091–1107: A. McDonald to Selkirk, 22 May 1814.

4. A. and B. MacIver, *Churchill on Hudson Bay,* Churchill, 2006, p. 149;
D. Gunn, *A History of Manitoba from the Earliest Settlements to
1835,* Ottawa, 1880, p. 100.

5. BCA A/B/20/C47E: A. Edwards to M. Macdonell, 12 January 1814;
BCA A/B/20/C47E: Circular to the Emigrants at Churchill Creek, 12
February 1814.

6. BCA A/B/20/C47E: A. Edwards to W. Auld, 14 December 1813.

7. MacIver, *Churchill*, p. 150.

8. LAC MG19-E1 13384: Examination of Betty MacKay, December 1814.

9. LAC MG19-E1 1091–1107: A. McDonald to Selkirk, 22 May 1814; Gunn, *Manitoba*, pp. 101–02; J. P. Pritchett, *The Red River Valley*, New Haven, 1942, p. 125; BCA A/B/20/C47E: A. Edwards to M. Macdonell, 12 January 1814.

10. HBCA B42/a/140: Fort Churchill Post Journal, 25 December 1813; BCA A/B/20/C47E: A. Edwards to Macdonell, 12 January 1814; Gunn, *Manitoba*, p. 100.

11. HBCA B42/a/140: Fort Churchill Post Journal, 24 November 1813; BCA A/B/20/C47E: A. Edwards to W. Auld, 21 December 1813; LAC MG19-E1 1262–66: W. Auld to M. Macdonell, 13 March 1814; LAC MG19-E1 1091–1107: A. McDonald to Selkirk, 22 May 1814.

12. BCA A/B/20/C47E: Journal of Abel Edwards, 25 December 1813; BCA A/B/20/C47E: A. Edwards to M. Macdonell, 12 January 1814; BCA A/B/20/C47E: W. Auld to A. Edwards, 7 February 1814; BCA A/B/20/C47E: A. Edwards to J. Charles, 30 March 1814;

13. LAC MG19-E1 18178–242: Journal of Archibald McDonald, 18–20 April 1814.

14. LAC MG19-E1 18178–242: Journal of Archibald McDonald, 20–21 May 1814.

15. LAC MG19-E1 18178–242: Journal of Archibald McDonald, 23 May, 5 June 1814.

16. LAC MG19-E1 18178–242: Journal of Archibald McDonald, 11 June 1814. See also, HBCA: Biographical Sheets.

17. LAC MG19-E1 18178–242: Journal of Archibald McDonald, 12, 20 22 June 1814.

18. LAC MG19-E1 1170–75: A. McDonald to Selkirk, 24 July 1814.

19. J. Diefenbaker, *One Canada: Memoirs*, Toronto, 1973, pp. 4–5; Gunn, *Manitoba*, 115.

20. Gunn, *Manitoba*, pp. 105–06.

21. LAC MG19-E1 1215–26: M. Macdonell to Selkirk, 9 September 1814; LAC MG19-E1 1170–75: A. McDonald to Selkirk, 24 July 1814.

22. LAC MG19-E1 18178–242: Journal of Archibald McDonald, 29–30 June 1814.

23. LAC MG19-E1 1654: R. Semple to C. Robertson, 5 September 1815; J. Strachan, *A Letter to Lord Selkirk on his Settlement at the Red River*, London, 1816, pp. 64–65.

24. A. Amos, *Report of Trials in the Courts of Canada relative to the Destruction of the Earl of Selkirk's Settlement on the Red River*, London, 1820, pp. 366, 378, 382–83.

25. Strachan, *Letter to Lord Selkirk*, pp. 64–66.

26. LAC MG19-E1 650–54: Selkirk to M. Macdonell, 12 June 1813.

27. LAC MG19-E1 18243–18370: Journal of Archibald McDonald, 2 February, 4 March 1815; Strachan, *Letter to Lord Selkirk*, p. 65.

28. C. N. Bell, *The Selkirk Settlement and the Settlers*, Winnipeg, 1887, p. 12.

29. A. McDonald, *Narrative Respecting the Destruction of the Earl of Selkirk's Settlement on Red River*, London, 1816, p. 6.

30. LAC MG19-E1 1740–43: D. Cameron to H. MacEachen, 10 January 1815.

31. Amos, *Report of Trials*, p. 366. See also, W. Coltman, *Statement and Report Relative to the Disturbances in the Indian Territories of British North America*, London, 1818, pp. 167–68.

32. Coltman, *Statement and Report*, pp. 169–72; LAC MG19-E1 18243–18370: Journal of Archibald McDonald, 14 June 1815.

33. LAC MG19-E1 1542–46: List of families and servants carried off from Red River Settlement by the North West Company, 18 June 1815; LAC MG19-E1 18178–18242: Journal of Archibald McDonald, 11, 23 August 1814.

34. LAC MG19-E1 1542–46: List of families and servants carried off from Red River Settlement by the North West Company, 18 June 1815; W. J. Healy, *Women of Red River*, Winnipeg, 1923, p. 63. See also, L. Tegelberg, 'Catherine Sutherland of Point Douglas: Woman of Heart and Head', *Mantitoba Pageant*, Autumn 1975.

35. P. C. Newman, *Caesars of the Wilderness: The Story of the Hudson's Bay Company*, New York, 1988, p. 109.

36. LAC MG19-E1 20250–52: C. Robertson to Selkirk, 5 October 1815.

37. LAC MG19-E1 1744–45: D. Cameron to H. MacEachen and D. Livingston, 10 March 1815; LAC MG19-E1 1547–56: J. Pritchard to Selkirk, 20 June 1815; LAC MG19-E1 20250–52: C. Robertson to Selkirk, 5 October 1815.

38. Timespan Letters to Sutherland Family: W. MacPherson to J. and C. MacPherson, 7 July 1815.

39. LAC MG19-E1 22036–37: Selkirk to A. Matheson, 7 March 1815; LAC MG19-E1 20140–42: A. Matheson to Selkirk, 27 March 1815; LAC MG19-E1 1658–61: List of passengers landed at York Factory, 26 August 1815; UEA La.II.202: Selkirk to A. MacDonald, 26 February 1814.

40. LAC MG19-E1 20140–42: A. Matheson to Selkirk, 27 March 1815; LAC MG19-E1 1528: W. Sutherland and others to J. McDonald, 9 May 1815; LAC MG19-E1 20057: Selkirk to M. Macdonell, 19 May 1815; A. Ross, *The Red River Settlement: Its Rise, Progress and Present State*, London, 1856, pp. 30–31; D. Sage, *Memorabilia Domestica*, Wick, 1899, p. 96.

41. LAC MG19-E1 18545–49: Report from R. Semple, 17 June 1815; Sel P 1661–66: Statement re voyage out, 7 September 1815.

42. LAC MG19-E1 1661–66: Statement re voyage out, 7 September 1815.

43. LAC MG19-E1 1661–66: Statement re voyage out, 7 September 1815.

44. LAC MG19-E1 20227–29: A. Macdonell to Selkirk, 5 September 1815; Sel P 1661–80: R. Semple to Selkirk, 5 September 1815; Sel P 1658–61: List of passengers landed at York Factory, 26 August 1815.

45. LAC MG19-E1 20227–29: A. Macdonell to Selkirk, 5 September 1815; Sel P 1661–80: R. Semple to Selkirk, 5 September 1815.

46. LAC MG19-E1 2718–34: R. Semple to Selkirk, 20 December 1815.

47. LAC MG19-E1 2718–34: R. Semple to Selkirk, 20 December 1815.

48. LAC MG19-E1 2718–34: R. Semple to Selkirk, 20 December 1815.

49. LAC MG19-E1 2718–34: R. Semple to Selkirk, 20 December 1815.

7 'A most destructive and murderous fire'

1. R. H. Burgoyne, *Historical Records of the 93rd Sutherland Highlanders*, London, 1883, pp. 45–51.

2. R. J. Adam, *Papers on Sutherland Estate Management*, 2 vols, Edinburgh, 1972, II, pp. 4–7: C. Mackenzie to Lady Sutherland, 14, 23 September, 1 October 1799.

3. *Report of Commissioners of Inquiry into the Condition of the Crofters and Cottars in the Highlands and Islands of Scotland*, Evidence, p. 2509; NLS 313/1580: W. Young to Lady Stafford, 3 February 1813.

4. *Crofters and Cottars*, Evidence, p. 2510; SCRO D593/K/1/3/3: W. Young to J. Loch, 8 December 1815. Also, Adam, *Sutherland Estate*, I, Introduction, xxvi–xxviii.

5. D. Sage, *Memorabilia Domestica*, Wick, 1899, p. 101. Also, P. Groves, *History of the 93rd Sutherland Highlanders*, Edinburgh, 1895, pp. 3–4.

6. NRS RH2/8/99: Sutherland Highlanders Descriptive Roll Book, 1799–1831.

7. P. Henry, *Notes of Conversations with the Duke of Wellington*, New York, 1888, p. 18; D. Stewart, *Sketches of the Character, Manners and Present State of the Highlands of Scotland*, 2 vols, Edinburgh, 1822, II, p. 280; A. E. J. Cavendish, *An Rèisimeid Chataich: The 93rd Sutherland Highlanders*, London, 1928, pp. 13, 15, 20, 26; H. Miller, *Sutherland as it Was and Is*, Edinburgh, 1843, p. 42.

8. Cavendish, *Rèisimeid Chataich*, p. 30.

9. Cavendish, *Rèisimeid Chataich*, pp. 28–32.

10. Cavendish, *Rèisimeid Chataich*, p. 44.

11. Cavendish, *Rèisimeid Chataich*, p. 47.

12. There are various estimates of the 93rd's New Orleans casualties. One of the more detailed contemporary accounts puts the total at 536. See, W. James, *A Full and Correct Account of the Military Occurrences in the Late War between Great Britain and the United States of America*, 2 vols, London, 1818, II, p. 555.

13. B. E. Hill, *Recollections of an Artillery Officer*, 2 vols, London, 1836, II, 14–15.

14. A. MacKay, *Sketches of Sutherland Characters*, Edinburgh, 1889, p. 161.

15. G. R. Gleig, *The Campaigns of the British Army at Washington and New Orleans*, London, 1827, p. 182.

16. Cavendish, *Rèisimeid Chataich*, p. 47.

17. Gleig, *Campaigns*, p. 191.

18. Gleig, *Campaigns*, p. 186.

8 'He would be a very cruel man who would not mourn for the people'

1. NLS 313/1127: A. Sutherland to Lord Gower, 14 August 1809; R. J. Adam, *Papers on Sutherland Estate Management*, 2 vols, Edinburgh, 1972, II, p. 92: Lady Stafford to Lord Gower, 13 July 1809; NLS 313/990: Census of the inhabitants of Culmaily, April 1810; J. Henderson, *General View of the Agriculture of the County of Sutherland*, London, 1812, p. 121.

2. Adam, *Sutherland Estate*, II, p. 226: Lady Stafford to Lord Stafford, 18 July 1814; P. Sellar, 'Farm Reports: County of Sutherland: Strathnaver, Morvich and Culmaily Farms', in J. F. Burke (ed.), *British Husbandry Exhibiting the Farm Practice in Various Parts of the United Kingdom*, London, 1834, p. 69.

3. Henderson, *County of Sutherland*, pp. 150–51.

4. Henderson, *County of Sutherland*, pp. 150–51; Sellar, 'Farm Reports', p. 68.

5. Sellar, 'Farm Reports', p. 68.

6. Adam, *Sutherland Estate*, I, pp. 144–45: Lands on the Estate of Sutherland set at Golspie Inn, 15 December 1813; Adam, *Sutherland Estate*, II, pp. 204–05: W. Young to Lady Stafford, 19 December 1813; D. Sage, *Memorabilia Domestica*, Wick, 1899, p. 154.

7. R. Gordon, *A Genealogical History of the Earldom of Sutherland*, Edinburgh, 1813, p. 11; *Crofters and Cottars*, Evidence, p. 1616.

8. Henderson, *County of Sutherland*, pp. 24–26; Adam, *Sutherland Estate*, I, pp. 16–17: Report on the present state of possessions in Strathnaver, 1810.

9. Adam, *Sutherland Estate*, I, pp. 23–24: Report on the present state of possessions in Strathnaver, 1810.

10. Adam, *Sutherland Estate*, II, p. 238: P. Sellar to Lady Stafford, 18 February 1815.

11. Adam, *Sutherland Estate*, II, p. 238: P. Sellar to Lady Stafford, 18 February 1815.

12. NRS CS232/S/23/2: Strathnaver Precognitions, (Statement of D. MacKenzie), 22 May 1815; NLS 313/1581: W. Young to Lady Stafford, 3, 19 December 1813.

13. SCRO D593/K/1/3/1: W. Young to J. Loch, 22 October 1813; Adam, *Sutherland Estate*, II, p. 239: P. Sellar to Lady Stafford, 18 February 1815.

14. Adam, *Sutherland Estate*, II, p. 239: P. Sellar to Lady. Stafford, 18 February 1815; P. Robertson, *Report of the Trial of Patrick Sellar*, Edinburgh, 1816, pp. 42–43.

15. NLS 313/1578: P. Sellar to Lady Stafford, 27 January 1814; SCRO D593/K/1/3/2: P. Sellar to J. Loch, 3 March 1814.

16. Adam, *Sutherland Estate*, I, p. 22: Report on the present state of possessions in Strathnaver, 1810; NRS CS232/S/23/2: Strathnaver Precognitions, (Statement of W. Gordon and J. MacKay), 22 May 1815; NRS CS232/S/23/2: Strathnaver Precognitions, (Statement of P. Sellar), 31 May 1815.

17. NRS CS232/S/23/2: Strathnaver Precognitions, (Statements of J. MacKay and J. Gordon) 23 May 1815.

18. Robertson, *Trial*, p. 39.

19. NRS CS232/S/23/2: Strathnaver Precognitions, (Statement of D. MacKenzie), 22 May 1815.

20. SCRO D593/K/1/3/3: P. Sellar to J. Loch. 28 June 1815; NRS SC9/7/63: Summons of removing [against] tenants in the parishes of Lairg, Dornoch, Rogart, Golspie, Clyne and Kildonan, 26 February 1813. The Sutherland Sheriff Court eviction notice quoted here was issued a year prior to the one Sellar obtained in 1814. However, the wording of all such notices was standard.

21. SCRO D593/K/1/3/3: P. Sellar to J. Loch 28 June 1815; NRS

CS232/S/23/2: Strathnaver Precognitions, (Statement of J. MacKay), 25 May 1815.

22. SCRO D593/K/1/3/3: P. Sellar to J. Loch 28 June 1815.

23. Robertson, *Trial*, p.27; Sellar, 'Farm Reports', p. 77; NLS 313/749: Lady Stafford to J. Loch, 12 August 1815.

24. NRS CS232/S/23/2: Strathnaver Precognitions, (Statements of J. MacKay and H. Grant), 22 May 1815.

25. NRS CS232/S/23/2: Strathnaver Precognitions, (Statement of H. Grant), 22 May 1815.

26. Robertson, *Trial*, p. 7; NRS CS232/S/23/2: Strathnaver Precognitions, (Statement of D. MacKay), 22 May 1815.

27. NRS CS232/S/23/2: Strathnaver Precognitions, (Statement of B. MacKay), 22 May 1815.

28. NRS CS232/S/23/2: Strathnaver Precognitions, (Statements of A. Manson and G. Ross), 23 May 1815.

29. *Aberdeen Journal*, 25 July 1883.

30. *Crofters and Cottars*, Evidence, pp. 1617–18.

31. *Crofters and Cottars*, Evidence, pp. 1616–17.

9   'A combination among the better sort'

1. R. Bell, *A Treatise on Leases*, Edinburgh, 1820, pp. 473–77.

2. NRS CS232/S/23/2: Strathnaver Precognitions, (Statements of J. Gordon and A. Manson), 23 May 1815.

3. NLS SP 313/748: Lady Stafford to Lord Stafford, 3 July 1814.

4. J. Mitchell, *Reminiscences of My Life in the Highlands*, 2 vols, London, 1883, II, p. 95; NLS 313/750: Lady Stafford to Lord Stafford, 24 September 1820.

5. NLS 313/991: Heads of the complaints against Mr Sellar, July 1814.

6. Bell, *Treatise on Leases*, p. 474. See also, W. Ross, *A Discourse Upon the Removing of Tenants*, Edinburgh, 1782.

7. NLS 313/754: Lady Stafford to Lord Gower, 20 July 1811; NLS 313/748: Lady Stafford to Lord Stafford, 20 July 1814.

8. NRS CS232/S/23/2: Lady Stafford's answer to a petition presented by tenants removed from Mr Sellar's farm, 22 July 1814.

9. NLS 313/991: G. M. Grant, Observations on an excursion into the interior of the Sutherland Estate, 1816; NRS CS232/S/23/2: Strathnaver Precognitions, 23 May 1815 (Statement of G. Ross); *Military Register*, 8 May 1816. For Traill, see, J. T. Calder, *Sketch of the Civil and Traditional History of Caithness*, Glasgow, 1861, pp. 214–18.

10. NLS 313/1578: P. Sellar to Lady Stafford, 27 July 1814.

11. NLS 313/1578: P. Sellar to Lady Stafford, 27 July 1814.

12. K. Fidler, *The Desperate Journey*, Edinburgh, 2002, pp. 7–9.

13. NRS JP32/5/21: Petition against mussel depredators, 1814; NRS JP32/5/21: Petition of P. Sellar against A. Campbell, 1814; NRS JP32/5/22: Claim of P. Sellar against sundry tenants, 2 April 1815; NLS 313/991: Report concerning the natural woods on the Sutherland Estate, 1815.

14. SCRO D593/K/1/3/3: P. Sellar to J. Loch, 16 October 1815; R. J. Adam, *Papers on Sutherland Estate Management*, 2 vols, Edinburgh, 1972, I, p. 42: Minute of agreement with W. Young and P. Sellar, 1811.

15. See J. Hunter, *On the Other Side of Sorrow: Nature and People in the Scottish Highlands*, Edinburgh, 1995, pp. 62–66. Also J. Hunter, *The Making of the Crofting Community*, Edinburgh, 1976, pp. 156–60.

16. NRS JP32/5/21: Complaint against poachers, 1814.

17. Adam, *Sutherland Estate*, II, pp. 133–34: P. Sellar to Lady Stafford, 11 December 1810; Adam, *Sutherland Estate*, II, p. 206: P. Sellar to Lady Stafford, 10 January 1814; NLS 313/1578: P. Sellar to Lady Stafford, 10 January 1814.

18. SCRO D593/K/1/3/1: W. Young to J. Loch, 5 December 1813.

19. NRS JP32/71: Accounts and notes, 16 November 1814.

20. NLS 313/1578: P. Sellar to Lady Stafford, 10 January 1814; Adam, *Sutherland Estate*, II, p. 206: P. Sellar to Lady Stafford, 10 January 1814.

21. NLS 313/1129: G. Cranstoun to W. MacKenzie, 17 September 1813.

22. NLS 313/1127: P. Sellar to Lord Gower, 19 March 1811; NLS 313/1581: W. Young to Lady Stafford, 17 October 1813.

23. NLS 313/1578: P. Sellar to Lady Stafford, 31 January 1814; Adam, *Sutherland Estate*, II, p. 207: P. Sellar to Lady Stafford, 2 February 1814.

24. Adam, *Sutherland Estate*, II, pp. 207–08: P. Sellar to Lady Stafford, 2 February 1814.

25. T. Sellar, *The Sutherland Evictions of 1814*, London, 1883: P. Sellar, Statement in answer to certain misrepresentations, December 1825; NLS 313/1578: P. Sellar to Lady Stafford, 7 April 1814. Also, Robertson, *Trial*, p. 25.

26. NLS 313/749: Lady Stafford to Lord Stafford, 13 August 1815.

27. NLS 313/1016: A. Sutherland to J. Bethune, 30 June 1815; *Military Register*, 7 February 1816; G. C. Cameron, *The Scots Kirk in London*, Oxford, 1979, pp. 104–06. Also E. Richards, 'The *Military Register* and the Pursuit of Patrick Sellar', *Scottish Economic and Social History*, 16, 1996.

28. *Military Register*, 5 April 1815.

29. *Military Register*, 28 June 1815.

30. NLS 313/1127: P. Sellar to Lord Gower, 15 April 1815.

31. NLS 313/1127: P. Sellar to Lord Gower, 15 April 1815.

32. NRS CS232/S/23/2: Strathnaver Precognitions, (Statement of J. Munro), 24 May 1815; NRS CS232/S/23/2: Petition sent to Earl Gower by the tenants of Mr Sellar's farm, 1815.

33. NRS CS232/S/23/2: Lord Gower to J. Munro, 8 February 1815.

34. NLS 313/1128: W. Young to Lord Gower, 16 February 1815; SCRO D593/K/1/3/3: W. Young to J. Loch, 15 June 1815.

35. SCRO D593/K/1/3/3: W. Young to J. Loch, 15 June 1815; NLS 313/991: G. M. Grant, Observations on an excursion into the interior of the Sutherland Estate, 1816.

36. NLS 313/1586: Grant (Young's clerk) to W. Young, 27 March 1815.

37. NRS CS232/S/23/2: G. Cranstoun to J. Munro, 31 March 1815.

38. NLS 313/1586: P. Sellar to Lady Stafford, 15 February 1815; NLS 313/991: P. Sellar to G. Cranstoun, 24 March 1815.

39. NRS CS232/S/23/2: J. Munro to A. Clephane, 2 May 1815.

40. NRS CS232/S/23/2: R. McKid to G. Cranstoun, 8 May 1815; NRS CS232/S/23/2: G. Cranstoun to R. McKid, 13 May 1815.

41. NRS CS232/S/23/2: G. Cranstoun to R. McKid, 13 May 1815.

42. NLS 313/991: P. Sellar to A. Colquhoun, 24 May 1815.

43. NLS 313/991: P. Sellar to A. Colquhoun, 24 May 1815.

44. NLS 313/991: P. Sellar to A. Colquhoun, 24 May 1815.

45. NRS CS232/S/23/2: Strathnaver Precognitions, (Statements of J. Munro, J. Campbell, M. MacKay, W. MacKay and J. MacKay), 22–24 May 1815.

46. NRS CS232/S/23/2: Strathnaver Precognitions, (Statements of H. MacBeath and G. Ross), 23 May 1815.

47. Robertson, *Trial*, p. 33.

48. NRS CS232/S/23/2: Strathnaver Precognitions, (Statement of D. MacKenzie), 22 May 1815.

49. D. Sage, *Memorabilia Domestica*, Wick, 1899, p. 155; NLS 313/1586: P. Sellar to Lady Stafford, 15 July 1815.

50. NRS CS232/S/23/2: Strathnaver Precognitions, (Statement of T. Gordon), 25 May 1815.

51. NRS CS232/S/23/2: Strathnaver Precognitions, (Statement of T. Gordon), 25 May 1815.

52. NRS CS232/S/23/2: Strathnaver Precognitions, (Statement of T. Gordon), 25 May 1815; NLS 313/991: P. Sellar to A. Colquhoun, 24 May 1815.

53. SCRO D593/K/1/3/3: R. Gordon to W. Munro, 12 February 1816; Adam, *Sutherland Estate*, II, p. 238: P. Sellar to Lady Stafford, 18 February 1815.

54. NRS CS232/S/23/2: Strathnaver Precognitions, (Statement of W. Chisholm), 25 May 1815.

55. NRS CS232/S/23/2: Strathnaver Precognitions, (Statements of W. Chisholm and H. MacKay), 25 May 1815.

56. NRS CS232/S/23/2: Strathnaver Precognitions, (Statements of W. Chisholm and H. MacKay), 23 May 1815.

57. NRS CS232/S/23/2: Strathnaver Precognitions, (Statements of W. Chisholm, D. MacKay, W. MacLeod, J. MacKay and K. Murray), 23, 29 May 1815.

58. NRS CS232/S/23/2: Strathnaver Precognitions, (Statement of D. MacKay), 23 May 1815.

59. NRS CS232/S/23/2: Strathnaver Precognitions, (Statements of W. Chisholm, H. MacKay and D. MacKay), 23 May 1815.

60. NRS CS232/S/23/2: Strathnaver Precognitions, (Statements of W. Chisholm, H. MacKay and D. MacKay), 23 May 1815.

61. NRS CS232/S/23/2: Strathnaver Precognitions, (Statement of T. Gordon), 25 May 1815.

62. NRS CS232/S/23/2: P. Sellar to R. McKid, 27 May 1815; NRS CS232/S/23/2: G. Cranstoun to R. McKid, 13 May 1815.

63. NRS CS232/S/23/2: P. Sellar to A. Colquhoun, 29 May 1815.

64. NRS CS232/S/23/2: Strathnaver Precognitions, (Statements of K. Murray, A. MacKenzie, J. Fraser and A. Sutherland), 29 May 1815.

65. Robertson, *Trial*, pp. 21–24: R. McKid to Lord Stafford, 30 May 1815.

66. Robertson, *Trial*, pp. 21–24: R. McKid to Lord Stafford, 30 May 1815.

67. NRS CS232/S/23/2: Summons of wrongous imprisonment, 27 June 1816.

68. NRS CS232/S/23/2: Summons of wrongous imprisonment, 27 June 1816; HA BD/1/14/1–3: Dornoch Jail Book, 31 May 1815.

69. HA BD/1/14/1–3: Dornoch Jail Book, 31 May–2 June 1815; NRS CS232/S/23/2: Strathnaver Precognitions, (Statement of P. Sellar), 31 May 1815.

70. Adam, *Sutherland Estate*, II, pp. 241–42: P. Sellar to Lady Stafford, 31 May 1815.

71. NLS 313/1584: W. Young to Lady Stafford, 31 May 1815; SCRO D593/K/1/5/4: J. Loch to W. Young, 9 June 1815.

72. SCRO D593/K/1/5/4: J. Loch to W. Adam, 10 June 1815.

73. SCRO D593/K/1/5/4: J. Loch to W. Adam, 10 June 1815.

74. NLS 313/749: Lady Stafford to Lord Stafford, 4, 15 August 1815; NLS 313/1579: W. MacKenzie to Lady Stafford, 5 June 1815; NLS 313/1579: W. MacKenzie to Lady Stafford, 3 June 1815.

75. NLS 313/1579: W. MacKenzie to Lady Stafford, 9 June 1815.

76. SCRO D593/K/1/5/4: J. Loch to P. Sellar, 25 June 1815.

77. *Military Register*, 14, 21 June 1815.

78. *Military Register*, 9 August 1815.

79. SCRO D593/K/1/5/5: J. Loch to W. Adam, 21 May 1816; *Observer*, 18 June 1815; *Morning Chronicle*, 19 June 1815.

80. NLS 313/1579: W. MacKenzie to Lady Stafford, 5 June 1815; HA BD/1/14/1–3: Dornoch Jail Book, 6, 7 June 1815; SCRO D593/P/18/2: Lady Stafford to Lord Sidmouth, 24 August 1815.

81. SCRO D593/P/18/2/2: Lord Sidmouth to Lady Stafford, 11 September 1815; NLS 313/749: Lady Stafford to Lord Stafford, 17 August 1815.

82. NLS 313/1588: P. Sellar to Lady Stafford, 8 April 1816; SCRO D593/K/1/3/5: P. Sellar to J. Loch, 18 March 1817.

83. NLS 313/1133: J. Loch to Lord Stafford, 14 August 1815; SCRO D593/K/1/5/5: J. Loch to W. Adam, 21 May 1816.

84. NRS CS232/S/23/2: Summons of wrongous imprisonment, 27 June 1816; *Military Register*, 14 June 1815, 8 May 1816.

85. NLS 313/749: Lady Stafford to Lord Stafford, 5, 10, 13 August 1815; NLS 313/1015: J. Loch to F. Suther, 21 January 1820.

86. NLS 313/1579: W. MacKenzie to Lord Stafford, 12 July 1815; NLS 313/1579: W. MacKenzie to Lady Stafford, 25 July 1815.

87. NLS 313/1586: P. Sellar to Lady Stafford, 3 July 1815.

88. SCRO D593/K/1/3/3: Lady Stafford to J. Loch, 21 July 1815.

89. NLS 313/749: Lady Stafford to Lord Stafford, 9 August 1815.

90. SCRO D593/K/1/3/3: Lady Stafford to J. Loch, 25 July 1815.

91. R. H. Burgoyne, *Historical Records of the 93rd Sutherland Highlanders*, London, 1883, pp. 45–51; NLS 313/749: Lady Stafford to Lord Stafford, 14, 18 August 1815; Adam, *Sutherland Estate*, II, pp. 162–63: Lady Stafford's answer to the petition of the Strathnaver people, 16 August 1815.

92. Extracts from Munro's letter to Cranstoun were published in the *Military Register* of 29 November 1815.

93. Extracts from Campbell's letter to MacKenzie were published in the *Military Register* of 28 February. Campbell wrote to Sellar in similar terms on the same day, 25 December 1815.

94. NLS 313/1588: J. A. Campbell to P. Sellar, 25 December 1815; NLS 313/1588: P. Sellar to D. MacKenzie, 16 January 1816.

95. *Military Register*, 28 February 1816; Robertson, *Trial*, pp. 35–36; NLS 313/1588: P. Sellar, 24 December 1815.

96. NLS 313/749: Lady Stafford to Lord Stafford, 14, 21 August 1815.

97. NLS D593/K/1/3/3: Lady Stafford to J. Loch, 25 July 1815; NLS 313/1016: A. Sutherland to D. MacKenzie, 16 June 1815; NLS 313/991: A. Sutherland to W. Ross, 20 July 1815.

98. NLS 313/1016: A. Sutherland to D. MacKenzie, 16 June 1815 (together with attached note).

99. SCRO D593/K/1/3/3: D. MacKenzie to J. Loch, 25 August 1815.

100. NLS 313/1588: P. Sellar to D. MacKenzie, 24 December 1815.

101. NLS 313/1588: D. MacKenzie to P. Sellar, 12 January 1816.

102. For a more sympathetic interpretation of David MacKenzie's behaviour, D. Paton, '"Brought to a Wilderness": The Rev David MacKenzie of Farr and the Sutherland Clearances', *Northern Scotland*, 13, 1993. Paton does not seem to have been aware of MacKenzie's January 1816 letter to Sellar.

10   'To find out and punish the leaders of the people'

1. *Caledonian Mercury*, 2 May 1816.

2. SCRO D593/K/1/3/4: G. McP. Grant to J. Loch, 6 April 1816; NLS 313/1587: G. McP. Grant to Lady Stafford, 27 April 1816.

3. NRS CS232/S/23/2: Strathnaver Precognitions, (Statement of D. MacKenzie), 22 May 1815.

4. SCRO D593/K/1/3/4: W. MacKenzie to Lady Stafford, 21 April 1816.

5. SCRO D593/K/1/5/4: J. Loch to P. Sellar, 3 October 1815.

6. SCRO D593/K/1/5/4: J. Loch to W. Young, 29 November 1815; R. J. Adam, *Papers on Sutherland Estate Management*, 2 vols, Edinburgh, 1972, II, p. 270: J. Loch to W. Young, 18 December 1815.

7. P. Robertson, *Report of the Trial of Patrick Sellar*, Edinburgh, 1816, p. 67; H. Cockburn, *Memorials of His Time*, Edinburgh, 1856, p. 299.

8. NLS 313/1589: W. Young to Lady Stafford, 24 April 1816.

9. Robertson, *Trial*, pp. 64–65.

10. Robertson, *Trial*, pp. 5–13.

11. Robertson, *Trial*, p. 9.

12. Robertson, *Trial*, p. 10.

13. NLS 313/1588: W. MacKenzie to Lady Stafford, 22 March 1816.

14. Robertson, *Trial*, pp. 15–17.

15. Robertson, *Trial*, p. 19.

16. Robertson, *Trial*, pp. 25–26; Adam, *Sutherland Estate*, II, p. 243: W. Young to Lady Stafford, 7 June 1815.

17. Robertson, *Trial*, pp. 21–24.

18. SCRO D593/K/1/3/3: P. Sellar to J. Loch 14 September 1815; SCRO D593/K/1/5/4: J. Loch to P. Sellar, 26 October 1815; SCSCRO D593/K/1/5/5: J. Loch to G. MacP Grant, 3 February 1816; SCRO D593/K/1/5/5: J. Loch to P. Sellar, 8 April 1816; NLS 313/1588: P. Sellar to Lord Stafford, 24 April 1816.

19. Robertson, *Trial*, pp. 15–16, 26.

20. Robertson, *Trial*, p. 20.

21. SCRO D593/K/1/3/4: W. MacKenzie to Lady Stafford, 21 April 1816.

22. Robertson, *Trial*, pp. 31, 36–37.

23. Robertson, *Trial*, pp. 36–37.

24. Robertson, *Trial*, pp. 37–38.

25. *Scots Magazine*, May 1816, p. 393; *Military Register*, 3 July 1816; Robertson, *Trial*, p. 38.

26. Robertson, *Trial*, pp. 38–40.

27. Robertson, *Trial*, pp. 41–53.

28. Robertson, *Trial*, pp. 54–57.

29. Robertson, *Trial*, pp. 57–58.

30. Robertson, *Trial*, pp. 59–62.

31. Robertson, *Trial*, p. 64.

32. Robertson, *Trial*, pp. 64–65.

33. Robertson, *Trial*, pp. 65–66.

34. NLS 313/1588: W. MacKenzie to Lady Stafford, 4 May 1816; Robertson, *Trial*, p. 66.

35. Robertson, *Trial*, p. 67.

36. Robertson, *Trial*, p. 67.

37. NLS 313/1587: G. MacP. Grant to Lady Stafford, 27 April 1816; SP 313/1588: P. Sellar to Lady Stafford, 24 April 1816.

38. D. Sage, *Memorabilia Domestica*, Wick, 1899, p. 198.

39. SCRO D593/K/1/3/4: P. Sellar to J. Loch, 7 May 1816.

40. SCRO D593/K/1/5/5: J. Loch to P. Sellar, 29 April 1816.

41. SCRO D593/K/1/3/4: P. Sellar to J. Loch, 7 May 1816; SCRO D593/K/1/3/4: P. Sellar to J. Loch, 23 May 1816.

42. D. R. Fisher, 'Sutherland, 1790–1820', 'George Macpherson Grant, 1790–1820', 'George Macpherson Grant, 1820–32', in *The History of Parliament*: http://www.historyofparliamentonline.org/.

43. NLS 313/991: G. M. Grant, Observations on an excursion into the interior of the Sutherland Estate, 1816.

44. NLS 313/1580: J. Loch, Memorandum, 19 August 1816.

45. NLS 313/991: G. M. Grant, Observations on an excursion into the interior of the Sutherland Estate, 1816; *Military Register*, 22 May, 3 July, 10 July 1816.

46. SCRO D593/K/1/3/4: W. Young to J. Loch, 15 May 1816; SCRO D593/K/1/3/4: G. M. Grant to J. Loch, 16 May 1816.

47. SCRO D593/K/1/5/5: P. Sellar to W. Young, 7 May 1816; SCRO D593/K/1/5/5: J. Loch to W. Adam, 21 May 1816; SCRO D593/K/1/5/5: J. Loch to P. Sellar, 25 May 1816; SCRO D593/K/1/5/5: J. Loch to P. Sellar, 12 June 1816; SCRO D593/K/1/3/4: P. Sellar to Lady Stafford, 2 June 1816.

48. NLS 313/1591: Note of farms out of lease at Whitsunday 1818.

49. SCRO D593/K/1/3/5: W. Sutherland to Lady Stafford, 8 March 1817.

50. NLS 313/1591: M. Sutherland to Lady Stafford, 4 September 1817.

51. SCRO D593/K/1/3/5: J. Sutherland to Lady Stafford, 24 April 1817; SCRO D593/K/1/3/5: J. Sutherland to Lady Stafford, 17 October 1817.

52. SCRO D593/K/1/3/5: J. Sutherland to Lady Stafford, 24 April 1817; NLS 313/1591: J. Sutherland to Lord and Lady Stafford, 4 September 1817.

53. SCRO D593/K/1/3/5: W. Sutherland to Lady Stafford, 8 March 1817.

54. NLS 313/1591: Lady Stafford to J. Sutherland, 27 September 1817.

55. *Inverness Courier*, 24 September 1834.

56. NLS 313/1587: G. M. Grant to Lady Stafford, 27 April 1816; NLS 313/1588: W. MacKenzie to Lady Stafford, 26 April 1816; NLS 313/1588: W. MacKenzie to Lady Stafford, 4 May 1816.
57. NLS 313/1589: W. Young to Lady Stafford, 12 May 1816.
58. NRS CS232/S/23/2: Summons of wrongous imprisonment, oppression and damages, Sellar against McKid, 27 June 1816.
59. NLS 313/1015: P. Sellar to Lady Stafford, 1 May 1816; NRS CS232/S/23/2: Defences for Robert McKid, 4 February 1817.
60. NRS CS232/S/23/2: R. McKid to P. Sellar, 22 September 1816.
61. SCRO D593/K/1/3/5: P. Sellar to J. Loch, 23 September 1817; NRS SC9/1/3: Dornoch Sheriff Court, Minutes, 29 November 1816; NLS 313/1587: G. Dempster to Lady Stafford, 3 December 1816. For a summary of McKid's subsequent career, see E. Richards, *Patrick Sellar and the Highland Clearances*, Edinburgh, 1999, pp. 211–12.
62. NLS 313/755: Lady Stafford to Lord Gower, 27 June 1816.
63. For details of the McKinlay trial, see G. W. T. Omond, *The Lord Advocates of Scotland*, 2 vols, Edinburgh, 1883, II, pp. 244–46; Cockburn, *Memorials*, pp. 329–37; P. B. Ellis and S. Mac a' Ghobhainn, *The Scottish Insurrection of 1820*, London, 1989, pp. 110–11; B. P. Lenman, *Integration and Enlightenment: Scotland, 1747–1832*, Edinburgh, 1981, p. 152.
64. SCRO D593/K/1/5/5: J. Loch to A. Maconochie, 25 August 1816; SCRO D593/K/1/3/4: A. Maconochie to J. Loch, 31 August 1816.
65. SCRO D593/K/1/5/5: J. Loch to A. Maconochie, 12 September 1816.
66. NLS 313/1587: J. Loch to Lady Stafford, 20 September 1816.
67. SCRO D593/K/1/5/5: J. Loch to A. Maconochie, 12 September 1816.
68. SCRO D593/K/1/5/5: J. Loch to Lady Stafford, 27 November 1816; SCRO D593/K/1/3/4: A. Maconochie to J. Loch, 15 October 1816.

11 'Aborigines of Britain'

1. NLS 313/749: Lady Stafford to Lord Stafford, 14 August 1815.
2. SCRO D593/K/1/5/5: J. Loch to F. Suther, 30 August 1816; SCRO D593/K/1/5/5: J. Loch to G. M. Grant, 31 May 1816.

3. SCRO D593/K/1/3/4: G. M. Grant to J. Loch, 10 June 1816; NLS 313/1587: G. M. Grant to Lady Stafford, 28 August 1816.

4. SCRO D593/K/1/5/4: J. Loch to W. Young, 29 November 1815; NLS D593/K/1/5/5: J. Loch to G. M. Grant, 31 May 1816.

5. SCRO D593/K/1/3/4: W. MacKenzie to J. Loch, 19 October 1816; SCRO D593/K/1/5/5: J. Loch to W. MacKenzie, 23 October 1816.

6. SCRO D593/K/1/5/5: J. Loch to G. M. Grant, 31 May 1816.

7. R. J. Adam, *Papers on Sutherland Estate Management*, 2 vols, Edinburgh, 1972, I, pp. 191–95: J. Loch, Memorandum respecting the management of the Estate of Sutherland, 18 August 1816.

8. J. Loch, *An Account of the Improvements on the Estates of the Marquis of Stafford*, London, 1820, p. 66; SCRO D593/K/1/3/4: F. Suther to J. Loch, 6 September 1816; SCRO D593/K/1/5/6: J. Loch to P. Sellar, 13 May 1817.

9. SCRO D593/K/1/3/4: P. Sellar to J. Loch, 5 July 1816.

10. NLS 313/991: P. Sellar, Note concerning Sutherland, 24, 31 May 1816.

11. NLS 313/991: P. Sellar, Note concerning Sutherland, 24, 31 May 1816.

12. NLS 313/991: P. Sellar, Note concerning Sutherland, 24, 31 May 1816.

13. NLS 313/991: P. Sellar, Note concerning Sutherland, 24, 31 May 1816.

14. A. Smith, *An Inquiry into the Nature and Causes of the Wealth of Nations*, 2 vols, Hartford, 1811, I, p. 4.

15. NLS 313/991: P. Sellar, Note concerning Sutherland, 24, 31 May 1816. Sellar is here quoting from Volume I, Chapter I of the *Wealth of Nations*.

16. SCRO D593/K/1/5/5: J. Loch to G. M. Grant, 8 June 1816.

17. NLS 313/991: P. Sellar, Note concerning Sutherland, 24, 31 May 1816; D. Stewart, *Sketches of the Character, Manners and Present State of the Highlands of Scotland*, 2 vols, Edinburgh, 1822, II, pp. 289–90.

18. D. Sage, *Memorabilia Domestica*, Wick, 1899, p. 131.

19. A. Cunningham (ed.), *The Works of Robert Burns*, London, 1840, p. 665: R. Burns to J. Tennant, 22 December 1788.

20. J. MacCulloch, *The Highlands and Western Isles of Scotland*, 4 vols, London, 1824, IV, p. 372. See also, *Report to the Lords Commissioner of the Treasury by the Chairman of the Board of Excise in Scotland respecting Distillery Laws*, London, 1822, p. 2.

21. NRS JP32/2/1: Sutherland Justices of the Peace, Minutes, 6 March 1816; SCRO D593/K/1/5/6: J. Loch to F. Suther, 30 December 1817; SCRO D593/K/1/3/7: F. Suther to J. Loch, 17 July 1819.

22. J. Mitchell, *Reminiscences of My Life in the Highlands*, 2 vols, London, 1883, II, pp. 60–61.

23. D. Stewart, 'Observations on the Origins and Cause of Smuggling in the Highlands of Scotland', *Quarterly Review of Agriculture*, I, 1828, p. 360.

24. Keir Strickland: Personal communication to the author, 20 August 2014; Mitchell, *Reminiscences*, II, p. 61.

25. SCRO D593/K/1/5/2: J. Loch to W. Young, 3 April 1813; NLS 313/1580: W. Young to Lady Stafford, 6 February 1813; NLS 313/991: P. Sellar, Note concerning Sutherland, 24, 31 May 1816.

26. Keir Strickland: Personal communication to the author, 20 August 2014.

27. H. Miller, *Sutherland As It Was and Is*, Edinburgh, 1843, p. 16; H. Miller, *My Schools and Schoolmasters*, Edinburgh, 1854, p. 91.

28. T. M. Devine, *The Scottish Nation, 1700–2007*, London, 2006, pp. 340–41.

29. Miller, *Schools and Schoolmasters*, p. 91.

30. The account of longhouse construction given here comes from a wide variety of sources. Contemporary descriptions can be found in, for example, J. Henderson's *General View of the Agriculture of the County of Sutherland*, London, 1812. A more modern analysis, based on archaeological inquiry, is available in H. Fairhurst, 'Rossal: A Deserted Township in Strathnaver', *Proceedings of the Society of Antiquaries in Scotland*, 100, 1967. The average floor area of new built homes in Britain in 2009 was 818 square feet – equivalent to that of longish longhouse.

31. There is a growing literature on the Tambora eruption and its consequences. Two recent accounts are W. K. Klingaman and N. P. Klingaman, *The Year Without A Summer: 1816 and the Volcano that Darkened the World*, New York, 2013; G. D. Wood, *Tambora: The Eruption that Changed the World*, Princeton, 2014. This and the subsequent paragraph draw heavily on those books. See also, J. D.

Post, *The Last Great Subsistence Crisis in the Western World*, Baltimore, 1977.

32. See, inter alia, P. Webb, 'Emergency relief during Europe's famine of 1817 anticipated crisis response mechanisms of today', *Journal of Nutrition*, 132, 2002.

33. Wood, *Tambora*, pp. 171–98; M. W. Flinn, 'The Poor Employment Act of 1817', *Economic History Review*, 14, 1961, pp. 82–92; J. R. Lee, *Climate Change and Armed Conflict: Hot and Cold Wars*, Oxford, 2009, pp. 49–50; A. Dawson, *So Foul and Fair a Day: A History of Scotland's Weather and Climate*, Edinburgh, 2009, p. 157; G. W. T. Omond, *The Lord Advocates of Scotland*, 2 vols, Edinburgh, 1883, II, 232; *Scots Magazine*, August 1816, pp. 633–34; *Caledonian Mercury*, 12 August, 19 September 1816; H. Cockburn, *Memorials of His Time*, Edinburgh, 1856, p. 306.

34. SCRO D593/K/1/3/4: G. M. Grant to Lady Stafford, 19 November 1816; SCRO D593/K/1/3/4: P. Sellar to Lady Stafford, 16 November 1816.

35. NLS 313/991: G. M. Grant, Observations on an excursion into the interior of the Sutherland Estate, 1816; Adam, *Sutherland Estate*, I, pp. 191–95: J. Loch, Memorandum respecting the management of the Estate of Sutherland, 18 August 1816.

36. Loch, *Account of Improvements*, p. 12; SCRO D593/K/1/5/5: J. Loch to P. Sellar, 5 November 1816; SCRO D593/K/1/5/5: J. Loch to P. Sellar, 16 December 1816; SCRO D593/K/1/5/6: J. Loch to K. MacKay, 5 April 1817.

37. Loch, *Account of Improvements*, p. 82.

38. NLS 313/1139: J. Loch to F. Suther, 17 February 1819; HA CH2/508/2: Tongue Presbytery Minutes, 19 October 1818; SCRO D593/K/1/5/6: G. M. Grant to J. Loch, 14 July 1818; SCRO D593/K/1/5/6: P. Sellar to J. Loch, 25 September 1818.

39. SCRO D593/K/1/5/5: J. Loch to Lady Stafford, 27 November 1816; Loch, *Account of Improvements*, pp. 82–85.

40. SCRO D593/L/2/1: J. Loch, Memorandum Book, 26 September 1818.

41. NLS 313/1589: G. Reed to Lady Stafford, 29 August 1816.

42. *Inverness Journal*, 16 April 1819, 9 August 1821.

43. SCRO D593/K/1/3/5: P. Sellar to J. Loch, 16 October 1817; SCRO D593/K/1/3/5: J. MacKay to J. Loch, 10 October 1817; Sage, *Memorabilia*, pp. 206–07; Loch, *Account of Improvements*, pp. 85–86.

44. SCRO D593/K/1/3/5: A. Marshall to J. Loch, 27 December 1817; SCRO D593/K/1/5/7: J. Loch to A. Marshall, 2 January 1818.

45. SCRO D593/L/21: J. Loch, Memorandum Book, 19 August 1818.

46. SCRO D593/K/1/3/5: Lady Stafford to J. Loch, 21 October 1817; NLS 313/1591: J. Loch to Lady Stafford, 3 November 1817.

47. Loch, *Account of Improvements*, p. 86; SCRO D593/K/1/5/7: J. Loch to H. Morton, 1 May 1818.

48. SCRO D593/K/1/3/6: F. Suther to J. Loch, 30 April 1818.

49. Loch, *Account of Improvements*, p. 89; SCRO D593/K/1/5/7: J. Loch to F. Suther, 17 June 1818.

50. SCRO D593/K/1/5/5: J. Loch to P. Sellar, 25 October 1816.

51. NLS 313/1578: Lady Stafford to Lord Stafford, 21 August 1815.

52. SCRO D593/K/1/5/5: Lady Stafford to D. MacKenzie, 16 May 1816.

53. SCRO D593/K/1/5/5: Lady Stafford to A. Sage, 16 May 1816.

54. D. MacLeod, *Gloomy Memories in the Highlands of Scotland*, Glasgow, 1892, pp. i, 1, 46, 49–51; HA OPR, Farr, 20 January 1818; J. Prebble, *The Highland Clearances*, Harmondsworth, 1969, p. 71. (The 'Preface' to the 1892 edition of *Gloomy Memories*, cited here, was written by *Fionn*, the pen-name of Henry Whyte, then a leading figure in pro-Gaelic and pro-land reform circles. Its accuracy as to MacLeod's family history is borne out by the Farr parish register entry recording MacLeod's marriage.)

55. MacLeod, *Gloomy Memories*, pp. xv–xvi.

56. Sage, *Memorabilia*, p. 54.

57. HA D1249/4/2/1: A. Sage to D. Sage, 1 November 1819; SCRO D593/K/1/3/7: F. Suther to J. Loch, 17 November 1819.

58. MacLeod, *Gloomy Memories*, pp. 21–22. For an extended defence of clerical attitudes to clearance, see, D. Paton, *The Clergy and the Clearances: The Church and the Highland Crisis, 1790–1850*, Edinburgh, 2006.

59. HA CH2/1290/4: Presbytery of Dornoch, Minutes, 24 August 1813; HA CH2/1290/4: Presbytery of Dornoch, Minutes, 24 August 1813; NLS 313/1578: P. Sellar to Lady Stafford, 15 October 1813.

60. MacLeod, *Gloomy Memories*, p. 54.

61. MacLeod, *Gloomy Memories*, p. 54; Sage, *Memorabilia*, p. 211. A degree of inference is involved here. MacLeod's father-in-law was certainly Charles Gordon. Sage refers to Charles Gordon, Rivigill, without making a link to MacLeod. Evicted tenants from Rivigill were sent to Skail where Jane Gordon, MacLeod's wife, lived before her marriage.

62. MacLeod, *Gloomy Memories*, p. 18.

63. SCRO D593/K/1/3/6: J. Loch to D. MacKenzie, 17 February 1818.

64. SCRO D593/K/1/3/6: D. MacKenzie to J. Loch, 19 March 1818.

65. Sage, *Memorabilia*, pp. 181, 208.

66. SCRO D593/K/1/5/7: J. Loch to J. MacKay, 30 January 1818; SCRO D593/K/1/3/6: F. Suther to J. Loch, 23 April 1818; SCRO D593/K/1/3/5: P. Sellar to Lady Stafford, 8 May 1817; SCRO D593/K/1/3/5: P. Sellar to J. Loch, 24 August 1817. Sellar, in 1816, had dealings with a Charles Gordon, a Langdale subtenant. See, Adam, *Sutherland Estate*, I, p. 189: Report concerning woods on the Sutherland Estate, 27 July 1816.

67. NLS 313/1588: P. Sellar to Lady Stafford, 14 September 1816; SCRO D593/K/1/5/5: J. Loch to Lady Stafford, 15 May 1816; SCRO D593/K/1/5/5: J. Loch to W. MacKenzie, 23 October 1816; SCRO D593/K/1/5/6: J. Loch to Lady Stafford, 13 May 1817.

68. SCRO D593/L/2/1: J. Loch, Memo Book, copy advertisement, n.d.; J. Loch, *Account of Improvements*, Appendices, p. 106.

69. SCRO D593/K/1/3/6: F. Suther to J. Loch, 6 March 1818; SCRO D593/K/1/5/7: J. Loch to P. Sellar, 5 October 1818; SCRO D593/K/1/5/7: J. Loch to F. Suther. 1 December 1818.

70. *Scots Magazine*, June 1816, pp. 427–28; SCRO D593/K/1/3/6: P. Sellar to J. Loch, 13 October 1818; SCRO D593/K/1/3/6: F. Suther to J. Loch, 22 November 1818; SCRO D593/K/1/3/7: J. Loch to F. Suther, 21 December 1818.

71. SCRO D593/K/1/3/6: P. Sellar to J. Loch 12 December 1818; SCRO

D593/K/1/3/6: G. M. Grant to J. Loch, 14 July 1818; Paton, 'Brought to a Wilderness', pp. 95–96.

72. SCRO D593/K/1/3/6: D. MacKenzie to J. Loch, 19 March 1818.

73. SCRO D593/K/1/5/7: J. Loch to D. MacKenzie, 30 March 1818.

12 'The year of the burnings'

1. SCRO D593/K/1/5/6: J. Loch to A. Marshall, 2 October 1817; D. Sage, *Memorabilia Domestica*, Wick, 1899, p. 197.

2. Sage, *Memorabilia*, p. 198.

3. Sage, *Memorabilia*, pp. 215–16.

4. Sage, *Memorabilia*, p. 216; SCRO D593/K/1/3/7: J. MacKay to J. Loch, 12 June 1819.

5. Sage, *Memorabilia*, p.216; *Inverness Journal*, 20 December 1822.

6. A. MacKay, *The Book of MacKay*, Edinburgh, 1906, pp. 242–69 (especially p. 264); Sage, *Memorabilia*, p.203.

7. Sage, *Memorabilia*, p. 203.

8. Sage, *Memorabilia*, p. 216.

9. Sage, *Memorabilia*, p. 215.

10. SCRO D593/K/1/5/7: J. Loch, Circular to Ministers, 19 November 1818.

11. J. Loch, *An Account of the Improvements on the Estates of the Marquis of Stafford*, London, 1820, p. 89; SCRO D593/K/1/3/7: F. Suther to J. Loch, 19 March, 1, 29 April 1819.

12. SCRO D593/K/1/3/7: F. Suther to J. Loch, 29 April 1819.

13. SCRO D593/K/1/3/6: J. Loch to J. MacKay, 27 March 1817.

14. NRS JP32/7/3: JP Minutes, 6 October 1820; SCRO D593/K/1/3/7: F. Suther to J. Loch, 26 May 1819; *Military Register*, 11 August 1819.

15. SCRO D593/K/1/3/7: F. Suther to J. Loch, 12 May 1819.

16. SCRO D593/K/1/3/7: F. Suther to J. Loch, 26 May 1819; SCRO D593/K/1/3/7: F. Suther to J. Loch, 3 June 1819.

17. SCRO D593/K/1/3/7: F. Suther to J. Loch, 5 June 1819.

18. SCRO D593/K/1/3/7: J. MacKay to J. Loch, 7 May 1819; SCRO D593/K/1/3/7: F. Suther to J. Loch, 12 May 1819.

19. SCRO D593/K/1/5/8: J. Loch to J. MacKay, 15 May 1819; SCRO D593/K/1/5/8: J. Loch to K. MacKay 8 June 1819.

20. NLS 313/1139: J. Loch to F. Suther, 27 May 1819.

21. Sage, *Memorabilia*, p. 218.

22. Sage, *Memorabilia*, pp. 217–18; NLS 313/1015: Note of Removals on the Estate of Sutherland in May 1819.

23. Sage, *Memorabilia*, pp. 216–17. For an account of wives and women-folk's role in the army of this era, see, R. Holmes, *Redcoat: The British Soldier in the Age of Horse and Musket*, London, 2001, pp. 292–306.

24. Sage, *Memorabilia*, p. 217.

25. *Report of the Royal Commission (Highlands and Islands)*, 2 vols, London, 1895, I, p. 583; C. I. Maclean, *The Highlands*, London, 1959, p. 32.

26. SCRO D593/K/1/3/7: F. Suther to J. Loch, 29 May 1819.

27. SCRO D593/K/1/3/8: Tenants removed at Whitsun 1819 (enclosed with F. Suther to J. Loch, 3 February 1820); *Report of Commissioners of Inquiry into the Condition of the Crofters and Cottars in the Highlands and Islands of Scotland*, 5 vols, London, 1884, Evidence, IV, p. 3221.

28. *Military Register*, 28 July, 11 August 1819; *Observer*, 2 August 1819.

29. *Observer*, 2 August 1819.

30. *Times*, 14 July 1819.

31. A. Allardyce (ed.), *Letters To and From Charles Kirkpatrick Sharpe*, 2 vols, Edinburgh, 1888, II, p. 206: Lady Stafford to Sharpe, 25 July 1819.

32. NLS 313/1139: J. Loch to F. Suther, 18 July 1819.

33. SCRO D593/K/1/3/8: J. Loch to W. Rae, 18 July 1819; SCRO D593/K/1/3/8: J. Loch to A. Brown, 15 July 1819; SCRO D593/K/1/3/7: W. MacKenzie to J. Loch 20, 29 June 1819; SCRO D593/K/1/3/9: J. Loch to F. Suther 27 January 1820; *Scotsman*, 13 August 1819.

34. *Morning Chronicle* and *Times*, 19 July 1819; *Caledonian Mercury*, 28 August 1819.

35. NLS 313/1139: J. Loch to F. Suther, 18 July 1819.

36. T. H. Ford. 'Political Coverage in *The Times*, 1811–41: The Role of Barnes and Brougham', *Historical Research*, 85, 1986, p. 95; *Morning Chronicle*, 15 March 1820. See also, D. Hudson, *Thomas Barnes of The Times*, Cambridge, 1943.

37. HA CH2/350/1: Tarbat Kirk Session Minutes, 28 June, 6, 25 July 1803.
38. HA CH2/350/1: Tarbat Kirk Session Minutes, 22 August 1803, 1, 15 May 1809; HA Fearn Old Parish Registers, 1810–19.
39. NLS 313/1575: P. Sellar, Memorandum as to Morvich, 10 September 1810; NLS 313/1574: W. Young to Lady Stafford, 5 May 1811; NLS 313/1128: W. Young to Lord Gower, 26 April 1812; SCRO D593/K/1/3/7: F. Suther to J. Loch, 11 June 1819.
40. SCRO D593/K/1/5/8: J. Loch to W. MacKenzie, 25 June 1819; *Inverness Journal*, 4 June 1819; SCRO D593/K/1/3/7: F. Suther to J. Loch, 27 December 1819; T. Dudgeon, *A Nine Years Residence in the States of New York and Pennsylvania*, Edinburgh, 1841, p. 47.
41. SCRO D593/K/1/3/7: F. Suther to J. Loch, 27 December 1819.
42. *Inverness Journal*, 18 June 1819; *Morning Chronicle*, 1 July 1819.
43. SCRO D593/K/1/3/7: F. Suther to J. Loch, 24 July 1819; *Inverness Journal*, 23 July 1819; *Military Register*, 4 August 1819.
44. Loch, *Account of Improvements*, pp. 10–11. Also, SCRO D593/K/1/3/7: F. Suther to J. Loch, 24 July 1819.
45. *Inverness Journal*, 19 November 1819; SCRO D593/K/1/3/7: K. MacKay to J. Loch, 20 December 1819; SCRO D593/K/1/3/7: F. Suther to J. Loch, 24 July 1819; NLS 313/991: A. Sutherland to W. Ross, 20 July 1815; *Military Register*, 11 August 1819; R. W. and J. Munro, *Tain Through the Centuries*, Edinburgh, 2005, p. 108.
46. SCRO D593/K/1/3/7: P. Sellar to J. Loch, 22 June 1819; SCRO D593/K/1/3/7: F. Suther to W. MacKenzie, 17 November 1819.
47. *Appeal on Behalf of the Royal Tain Academy and Report of Its Funds*, London, 1819, pp. 19–25; Dudgeon, *Nine Years Residence*, p. 4; SCRO D593/K/1/3/8: F. Suther to J. Loch, 25 November 1820; J. M. Bulloch, *The Families of Gordon of Invergordon, Newhall and Carrol*, Dingwall, 1906, p. 108. See also, B. B. King, *Partner in Empire: Dwarkanath Tagore and the Age of Enterprise in Eastern India*, Los Angeles, 1976.
48. R. M. Cowan, *The Newspaper in Scotland: A Study of its First Expansion, 1815–1860*, Glasgow, 1946, pp. 41–42; NLS 313/1139: J. Loch to F. Suther, 30 November 1819.

49. Loch, *Account of Improvements*, p. 57; SCRO D593/K/1/5/8: J. Loch to H. Brougham, 27 December 1819; NLS 313/1015: J. Loch to F. Suther, 21 January 1820. Early twentieth-century land raids are explored in J. Hunter, *The Making of the Crofting Community*, Edinburgh, 1976, pp. 184–206.

50. Loch, *Account of Improvements*, pp. 57–58; NLS 313/1015: J. Loch to F. Suther, 21 January 1820; NLS 313/1119: J. Loch to F. Suther, 25, 30 November 1819; A. MacKay, *Sketches of Sutherland Characters*, Edinburgh, 1889, p. 159.

51. E. Richards, *A History of the Highland Clearances: Emigration, Protest, Reasons*, London, 1885, p. 311; *Inverness Journal*, 19 November 1819; *Morning Chronicle*, 11 December 1819.

52. SCRO D593/K/1/5/8: J. Loch to J. MacKay, 17 November 1819; SCRO D593/K/1/5/8: J. Loch to K. MacKay, 14 December 1819.

53. SCRO D593/K/1/5/8: J. Loch to W. MacKenzie, 17 November 1819.

54. *Morning Chronicle*, 11 December 1819.

55. *Hansard*, House of Commons, 9 December 1819.

56. NLS 313/1139: J. Loch to F. Suther, 10 December 1819; NLS 313/1016: Copy of Dudgeon letter to an unidentified recipient, 18 December 1819; Dudgeon, *Nine Years Residence*, p. 4; SCRO D593/K/1/3/7: W. Wilberforce to J. Loch, 28 December 1819; SCRO D593/K/1/3/8: J. Loch to W. MacKenzie, 31 December 1819. See also, W. Hague, *William Wilberforce: The Life of the Great Anti-Slave Trade Campaigner*, London, 2007.

57. SCRO D593/K/1/3/7: H. Brougham to J. Loch, 27 December 1819; SCRO D593/K/1/3/8: J. Loch to H. Brougham, 27 December 1819.

58. SCRO D593/K/1/3/7: H. Brougham to J. Loch, 30 December 1819.

59. A. Aspinall, D. C. Charles and A. Smith (eds), *English Historical Documents, 1783–1832*, London, 1996, p. 337.

60. *Inverness Journal*, 24 December 1819.

61. SCRO D593/K/1/3/8: W. MacKenzie to F. Suther, 27 December 1819.

62. NRS JP32/7/3: F. Suther to W. Taylor, 1 January 1820; SCRO D593/K/1/3/8: F. Suther to J. Loch, 15 January 1820.

63. *Inverness Journal*, 28 January 1820.

64. SCRO D593/K/1/3/8: F. Suther to J. Loch, 2 January 1820.

65. NRS JP32/2/1: Justices of the Peace, Minutes, 4 January 1820; NRS JP32/7/3: F. Suther to W. Taylor, 1 January 1820.

66. NRS JP32/7/3: Proclamation for dispersing persons assembled in Golspie, 4 January 1820; *Military Register*, 19 January 1820; *Morning Chronicle*, 20 January 1820; SCRO D593/K/1/3/8: F. Suther to J. Loch, 9, 14 January 1820.

67. *Inverness Courier*, 27 January 1820; NLS 313/1140: J. Loch to F. Suther, 12 January 1820.

68. *Inverness Journal*, 17 March 1820.

13 'Law is one thing and humanity may be another'

1. NLS 313/1139: J. Loch to F. Suther, 30 November 1819; SCRO D593/K/1/5/8: J. Loch to F. Suther, 6 December 1819; 313/1139: J. Loch to F. Suther, 5 November 1819; SCRO D593/K/1/5/8: F. Suther to J. Loch, 29 April 1820.

2. SCRO D593/K/1/3/8: F. Suther to J. Loch, 15 January 1820.

3. HA D538/A/8/1: P. Brown to K. MacKenzie, 20 February 1820.

4. *Morning Chronicle*, 15 March 1820; HA D538/A/8/1: J. MacKenzie to K. MacKenzie, 4 February 1820; HA D538/A/8/1: Case for Munro of Novar, Culrain Removings, 1820; NRS AD14/20/263: Culrain Precognitions, (Statement of J. Stewart), 15 February 1820.

5. NRS AD14/20/263: Culrain Precognitions, (Statement of J. Stewart), 15 February 1820.

6. NRS AD14/20/263: Culrain Precognitions, (Statements of J. Stewart and A. Ross), 15 February 1820.

7. NRS AD14/20/263: Culrain Precognitions, (Statement of J. Stewart), 15 February 1820.

8. NRS AD14/20/263: Culrain Precognitions, (Statement of J. Stewart), 15 February 1820.

9. NRS AD14/20/263: Culrain Precognitions, (Statement of J. Stewart), 15 February 1820.

10. NRS AD14/20/263: Culrain Precognitions, (Statements of J. Stewart and W. Munro), 15 February 1820.

11. NRS AD14/20/263: Culrain Precognitions, (Statements of J. Stewart and A. Ross), 15 February 1820.

12. HA D538/A/1: J. MacKenzie to K. MacKenzie, 4 February 1820; NRS AD14/20/263: Culrain Precognitions, (Statements of A. Ross, J. Stewart and W. Munro), 15 February 1820.

13. SCRO D593/K/1/3/9: F. Suther to J. Loch, 11 April 1821.

14. HA D538/A/8/1: J. MacKenzie to K. MacKenzie, 4 February 1820.

15. HA D538/A/8/1: H. Munro to K. MacKenzie, 15 February 1820; SCRO D593/K/1/3/8: F. Suther to J. Loch, 5 March 1820; *Glasgow Herald*, 24 March 1820; *Inverness Courier*, 30 March 1820; HA D538/A/8/1: J. MacKenzie to K. MacKenzie, 4 February 1820; *Inverness Journal*, 7 July 1820; NRS AD14/20/263: Culrain Precognitions, (Statement of J. Stewart), 15 February 1820.

16. HA D538/A/8/1: J. MacKenzie to K. MacKenzie, 18 February 1820; HA D538/A/8/1: D. MacLeod to J. MacKenzie, 11 February 1820; SCRO D593/K/1/3/8: W. MacKenzie to J. Loch, 30 March 1820; *Inverness Courier*, 30 March 1820.

17. HA D538/A/8/1: J. MacKenzie to K. MacKenzie, 18 February 1820; *Inverness Journal*, 17 March 1820: Letter from D. MacLeod; NRS AD14/20/263: Culrain Precognitions, (Statement of J. Stewart), 15 February 1820; NRS AD14/20/263: D. MacLeod to H. Warrender, 17 February 1820.

18. HA D538/A/8/2: J. MacKenzie to W. MacKenzie, 5 April 1821.

19. HA D538/A/8/1: D. MacLeod to W. Rae, 2 March 1820; *Inverness Journal*, 17 March 1820: Letter from D. MacLeod.

20. HA D538/A/8/1: D. MacLeod to W. Rae, 2 March 1820; *Inverness Journal*, 17 March 1820: Letter from D. MacLeod

21. SCRO D593/K/1/3/8: F. Suther to J. Loch, 5 March 1820; HA D538/A/8/1: D. MacLeod to W. Rae, 2 March 1820; *Inverness Journal*, 17 March 1820: Letter from D. MacLeod; *Caledonian Mercury*, 6 March 1820.

22. HA D538/A/8/1: D. MacLeod to W. Rae, 2 March 1820; *Inverness Journal*, 17 March 1820: Letter from D. MacLeod; SCRO D593/K/1/3/8: F. Suther to J. Loch, 5 March 1820.

23. *Inverness Journal*, 17 March 1820: Letter from D. MacLeod.

24. *Inverness Journal*, 17 March 1820: Letter from D. MacLeod.

25. HA D538/A/8/1: D. MacLeod to W. Rae, 2 March 1820.

26. *Morning Chronicle*, 15 March 1820.

27. E. Richards, 'The Social and Electoral Influence of the Trentham Interest, 1800–1860', *Midland History*, 3, 1975, pp. 132, 137; *Times*, 13 March 1820; SCRO D593/K/1/5/9: J. Loch to F. Suther, 20 March 1820.

28. SCRO D593/K/1/5/10: J. Loch to H. Brougham, 25 December 1820; NLS 313/1140: J. Loch to F. Suther, 17 March 1820.

29. NRS AD14/20/263: Culrain Precognitions (Note by W. Rae on precognition sleeve), 24 March 1820; NLS 313/1140: J. Loch to F. Suther, 1 April 1820; SCRO D593/K/1/5/9: J. Loch to C. Ross, 1 April 1820.

30. *Inverness Journal*, 31 March 1820: Letter from D. MacLeod; *Inverness Journal*, 24 March 1820: Letter from A. MacBean.

31. SCRO D593/K/1/3/8: F. Suther to J. Loch, 15 June 1820.

32. SCRO D593/K/1/3/8: F. Suther to J. Loch, 19 March 1820.

33. NLS 313/1140: J. Loch to F. Suther, 17 March 1820; *Inverness Journal*, 31 March 1820: Letter from D. MacLeod; NRS AD14/20/263: Culrain Precognitions (Statement of J. Stewart), 15 February 1820.

34. SCRO D593/K/1/3/8: F. Suther to J. Loch, 19 March 1820.

35. NLS 313/1139: J. Loch to F. Suther, 30 November 1819; SCRO D593/K/1/5/9: J. Loch to F. Suther, 20, 23 March 1820.

36. NLS 313/1015: Note of Removals on the Estate of Sutherland, 1819 and 1820; SCRO D593/K/1/3/8: F. Suther to Lady Stafford, 27 May 1820; NLS 313/1140: J. Loch to F. Suther, 6 June 1820.

14 'To seek shelter in some more propitious quarter of the world'

1. SCRO D593/K/1/3/8: F. Suther to J. Loch, 19 March 1820; SCRO D593/K/1/3/7: P. Sellar to J. Loch, 22 June 1819; NLS 313/1015: Kildonan Removals, June 1819.

2. SCRO D593/K/1/3/7: F. Suther to J. Loch, 23 June 1819; SCRO D6579/9: Lady Stafford to Lord Stafford, 26 September 1820.

3. D. Sage, *Memorabilia Domestica*, Wick, 1899, pp. 221–22, 306.

4. M. MacDonell, *The Emigrant Experience: Songs of Highland Emigrants in North America*, Toronto, 1982, pp. 136–37.

5. Personal communication from Glen Matheson, 23 February 2015; J. Hunter, *Scottish Exodus: Travels Among a Worldwide Clan*, Edinburgh, 2005, pp. 138–39.

6. NSA RG 20 Series A: Petition from R. Baillie and others, 6 October 1814.

7. NSA RG 20 Series A: Petition from R. Baillie and others, 6 October 1814.

8. The Baillie–MacPherson connection with Strathbrora has been established by Glen Matheson's extensive research, drawing on Clyne's parish registers and other data in Scotland as well as on documentary sources and family traditions in Nova Scotia.

9. G. Patterson, *A History of the County of Pictou*, Montreal, 1877, pp. 277–78.

10. Patterson, *County of Pictou*, pp. 277–78; L. H. Campey, *After the Hector: The Scottish Pioneers of Nova Scotia and Cape Breton*, Toronto, 2003, pp. 134–35; Personal communication from Glen Matheson, 23 February 2015; G. R. Sutherland, *The Rise and Decline of the Community of Earltown*, Truro, 1980, pp. 4–18.

11. J. M. MacKenzie with N. R. Dalziel, *The Scots in South Africa: Ethnicity, Gender and Race*, Manchester, 2007, p. 41; L. M. Thompson, *A History of South Africa*, pp. 54–55; A. E. J. Cavendish, *An Rèisimeid Chataich: The 93rd Sutherland Highlanders*, London, 1928, p. 35.

12. SCRO D593/K/1/3/6: A. Gordon to Lady Stafford, 22 April, 1818; SCRO D593/K/1/3/6: F. Suther to J. Loch, 24 April 1818; SCRO D593/L/2/1: Memo Book of J. Loch, 26 September 1818; SCRO D593/K/1/3/6: F. Suther to J. Loch, 22 November 1818; A. S. Gordon, *A Sutherland Trail: A History of the Gordons of Dallagan, Griamachary and Drumearn*, London, 2005, pp. 84–86.

13. SCRO D593/K/1/3/7: F. Suther to J. Loch, 26 May 1819; SCRO D593/K/1/3/8: F. Suther to J. Loch, 13 June 1820.

14. SCRO D593/K/1/3/7: F. Suther to J. Loch, 26 May 1819; SCRO D593/K/1/3/8: F. Suther to Lady Stafford, 8, 20 May 1820.
15. SCRO D593/K/1/3/4: P. Sellar to J. Loch, 16, 20 October 1816.
16. SCRO D593/K/1/3/5: W. Allan to F. Suther, 7 November 1817; SCRO D593/K/1/5/6: J. Loch to W. Allan, 7 November 1817.
17. M. Harper, *Adventurers and Exiles: The Great Scottish Exodus*, London, 2003, p. 46; D. Campbell and R. A. MacLean, *Beyond the Atlantic Roar: A Study of the Nova Scotia Scots*, Toronto, 1975, p. 46.
18. C. T. Campbell, *British South Africa*, London, 1897, p. 31; MacKenzie with Dalzeil, *Scots in South Africa*, pp. 49–51; SCRO D593/K/1/5/8: J. Loch to F. Suther, 9 October 1819; SCRO D593/K/1/5/8: J. Loch to Lady Stafford, 12 October 1819.
19. *Inverness Journal*, 1 December 1820; SCRO D593/K/1/3/8: G. Gordon to J. Gordon, 25 May 1820.
20. SCRO D593/K/1/3/8: G. Gordon to J. Gordon, 25 May 1820; SCRO D593/K/1/3/8: W. MacKenzie to Lady Stafford, 18, 20 November 1820.
21. SCRO D593/K/1/3/7: Lady Stafford to J. Loch, 22 October 1819; NLS 313/1140: J. Loch to W. MacKenzie, 30 November 1820; *Inverness Journal*, 20 April 1821.
22. NRS GD268/50: Lord Stafford to J. Loch, 2 December 1820.
23. NLS 313/1015: Printed circular from Joseph Gordon, 1821; SCRO D593/K/1/3/9: F. Suther to J. Loch, 2 May 1821.
24. *Inverness Journal*, 29 June 1821, 12 July 1822.
25. NLS 313/1015: Notes of examination anent Strathbrora Removings, 13 August 1821; personal communications from Glen Matheson, 23–27 February 2015.
26. W. Glyndwr (ed.), *Hudson's Bay Miscellany, 1670–1870*, Winnipeg, 1975, p. 234; HBCA Biographical Sheets. William MacKay's career, meriting more detailed treatment than it gets here, is summarised in 'Red River Ancestry' at http://www.redriverancestry.ca/McKAY-WILLIAM-1795.php.
27. *Eastern Chronicle*, 9 July 1885. This from an obituary of Donald MacKay Junior supplied by Marsha MacKay.

28. H. H. Bruce, *History of Barney's River: Early Days in East Pictou*, Pictou, 2013, p. 12 p. 13; HBCA E/233/1: Narrative of Donald MacKay, n.d.

29. NLS 313/2149–55: List of small rents supposed irrecoverable at 1st August 1825; NLS 313/1141: J. Loch to F. Suther, 31 July 1821: NLS 313/750; Lady Stafford to Lord Stafford, 5 October 1820.

30. SCRO D593/K/1/3/7: J. Loch to W. Young, 25 December 1819; SCRO D593/K/1/3/9: F. Suther to J. Loch, 18 April 1821; SCRO D593/K/1/3/9: F. Suther to J. Loch, 27 May 1821.

31. NLS 313/1139: W. Young to J. Loch, 18 August 1819; SCRO D593/K/1/3/7: F. Suther to J. Loch, 16 December 1819; NLS 313/1139: J. Loch to F. Suther, 22 December 1819; SCRO D593/K/1/5/8: J. Loch to W. Young, 25 December 1819; NLS 313/1140: W. Young to J. Loch, 1 January 1820.

32. Bruce, *Barney's River*, p. 9.

33. SCRO D593/K/1/5/9: J. Loch to W. MacKenzie, 22 June 1820.

34. NRS AD14/21/93: Gruids Precognition, (Statement of D. Bannerman), 10 April 1821.

35. NRS AD14/21/93: Gruids Precognition, (Statements of D. Bannerman and A. Ross), 10–11 April 1821.

36. NRS AD14/21/93: Gruids Precognition, (Statements of D. Bannerman, A. Ross and A. MacKenzie), 10–11 April 1821.

37. NRS AD14/21/93: Gruids Precognition, (Statement of D. Bannerman), 10 April 1821.

38. NRS AD14/21/93: Gruids Precognition (Statement of D. Bannerman), 10 April 1821; SCRO D593/K/1/3/8: F. Suther to J. Loch, 6 April 1820; J. Loch, *An Account of the Improvements on the Estates of the Marquis of Stafford*, London, 1820, pp. 111–12.

39. NLS 313/750: Lady Stafford to Lord Stafford, 20 September 1820; D593/K/1/5/10: J. Loch to Lord Stafford, 20 April 1821.

40. SCRO D6579/9: Lady Stafford to Lord Stafford, 30 September 1820; SCRO D593/K/1/3/9: F. Suther to J. Loch 17 April 1821.

41. NRS JP32/73/3: JPs Court Minutes, 8 August 1820; NRS JP32/2/1: JPs Court Minutes, 8, 19 August, 6 October 1820.

42. SCRO D593/K/1/3/8: F. Suther to J. Loch, 20 August 1820.

43. NLS 313/1140: F. Suther to J. Loch, 12 January 1820; SCRO D593/K/1/5/9: J. Loch to F. Suther, 12 January 1820; SCRO D593/K/1/3/8: F. Suther to J. Loch, 14 February 1820; NLS 313/1153: J. Loch to Lord Stafford, 3 October 1820.

44. NLS 313/1120: J. Loch to F. Suther, 12 January 1820; SCRO D593/K/1/5/9: J. Loch to W. Young, 14 January 1820; NLS 313/1153: J. Loch to F. Suther, 3 October 1820.

45. SCRO D593/K/1/3/8: F. Suther to J. Loch, 10 April 1820; NLS 313/1147: J. Loch to Lady Stafford, 3 May 1821; SCRO D593/K/1/3/8: F. Suther to J. Loch, 14 January 1820; SCRO D593/K/1/5/10: J. Loch to W. MacKenzie, 21 March 1821.

46. NLS 313/1575: View of farms on the Estate of Sutherland, 1810; NLS 313/1015: J. Loch to F. Suther, 22 March 1821; SCRO D593/K/1/3/9: G. M. Grant to J. Loch, 25 March 1821; SCRO D593/K/1/5/10: J. Loch to W. MacKenzie, 30 March 1821; SCRO D593/K/1/5/8: J. Loch to W. Rae, 6 April 1821; SCRO D593/K/1/3/9: F. Suther to J. Loch, 27 April 1821.

47. SCRO D593/K/1/5/10: J. Loch to W. MacKenzie, 21 March 1821; SCRO D593/K/1/3/9: F. Suther to J. Loch, 6 April 1821.

48. SCRO D593/K/1/3/9: F. Suther to J. Loch, 27 March 1821.

49. NLS 313/750: Lady Stafford to Lord Stafford, 20 September 1820; SCRO D593/K/1/5/9: J. Loch to W. MacKenzie, 3 October 1820.

50. NLS 313/1153: J. Loch to Lord Stafford, 1 April 1821; NLS 313/1147: J. Loch to Lord Stafford, 17 April 1821; SCRO D593/K/1/5/10: J. Loch to W. MacKenzie, 21, 23 March 1821.

51. SCRO D593/K/1/3/9: F. Suther to J. Loch, 27 March 1821.

52. NLS 313/1147: J. Loch to Lady Stafford, 25 April 1821.

53. SCRO D593/K/1/3/9: W. MacKenzie to J. Loch, 1 April 1821; SCRO D593/K/1/3/9: C. Ross to Solicitor General, 11 April 1821; SCRO D593/K/1/3/9: F. Suther to J. Loch, 11 April 1821.

54. NLS 313/1147: J. Loch to Lady Stafford, 25 April 1821; SCRO D593/K/1/3/9: W. MacKenzie to J. Loch, 31 March 1821; SCRO D593/K/1/3/10: J. Loch to F. Suther, 4 April 1821.

55. SCRO D593/K/1/3/9: F. Suther to J. Loch, 11, 27 April 1821.

56. NLS 313/1153: J. Loch to Lord Stafford, 30 March 1821; SCRO

D593/K/1/3/9: W. MacKenzie to J. Loch, 31 March 1821; SCRO D593/K/1/3/9: F. Suther to J. Loch, 11 April 1821; *Inverness Journal*, 20 April 1821; SCRO D593/K/1/3/9: C. Ross to J. Wedderburn, 11 April 1821.

57. SCRO D593/K/1/3/9: F. Suther to J. Loch, 9 April 1821; SCRO D593/K/1/3/9: C. Ross to J. Wedderburn, 11 April 1821.

58. SCRO D593/K/1/3/9: C. Ross to J. Wedderburn, 11 April 1821; *Inverness Journal*, 20 April 1821.

59. SCRO D593/K/1/3/9: F. Suther to J. Loch, 13 April 1821; SCRO D593/K/1/3/9: C. Ross to J. Wedderburn, 15 April 1821.

60. SCRO D593/K/1/3/9: C. Ross to J. Wedderburn, 15 April 1821; SCRO D593/K/1/3/9: F. Suther to J. Loch, 15, 17 April 1821.

61. NRS JC11/63: North Circuit Minute Book, 21 April 1821; *Inverness Journal*, 20 April, 4 May 1821; SCRO D593/K/1/3/9: F. Suther to J. Loch, 28 April 1821; HA BD1/14/1: Dornoch Jail Record of Prisoners, 6 April, 3 May 1821.

62. NRS JC11/63: North Circuit Minute Book, 21 April 1821; NLS 313/1147: J. Loch to Lady Stafford, 25 April 1821; SCRO D593/K/1/3/9: F. Suther to J. Loch, 27 April 1821.

63. SCRO D593/K/1/3/9: D. MacKay to Lord Stafford, 10 July 1821; M. McLean, *The People of Glengarry: Highlanders in Transition, 1745–1820*, Montreal, 1991, pp. 9–10.

64. SCRO D593/K/1/3/9: F. Suther to J. Loch, 17, 27 April, 27 May 1821; NLS 313/1153: J. Loch to Lady Stafford, 28 July 1821.

65. SCRO D593/K/1/3/9: F. Suther to J. Loch, 4 June 1821.

66. NLS 313/1153: J. Loch to Lord Stafford, 17 June 313/1153.

15 'Indelible characters on the surface of the soil'

1. C. N. Bell, *The Selkirk Settlement and the Settlers*, Winnipeg, 1887, p. 35.

2. Bell, *Selkirk Settlement*, p. 37; HA OPR, Kildonan, 1792–1801; HBCA C.1/778: Log of *Prince of Wales*, 19 June 1813; LAC MG19-E1 1658–61: List of Passengers Landed at York Factory, 26 August 1815. In the Kildonan OPR, Donald Murray's mother's name is given as Isobel; in

the 1815 passenger list as Elizabeth. But the two sources are clearly referring to the same Suisgill family.

3. Bell, *Selkirk Settlement*, p. 38.
4. Bell, *Selkirk Settlement*, pp. 37–39. Selkirk's movements during this period are examined in, Bumsted, *Lord Selkirk*, pp. 277–358.
5. Bell, *Selkirk Settlement*, p. 37.
6. Bell, *Selkirk Settlement*, pp. 37–39; LAC Mg19-E1 8218–64: G. Simpson to A. Colvile, 31 May 1824.
7. A. Ross, *The Red River Settlement: Its Rise, Progress and Present State*, London, 1856, p. 207.
8. *Royal Commission of Inquiry into the Condition of the Crofters and Cottars in the Highlands and Islands of Scotland*, Edinburgh, 1884, pp. 1616–18.
9. *Crofters and Cottars*, p. 1615.
10. T. M. Devine, *The Great Highland Famine*, Edinburgh, 1988, pp. 46, 89, 92.
11. A. Tindley, *The Sutherland Estate, 1850–1920: Aristocratic Decline, Estate Management and Land Reform*, Edinburgh, 2010, p. 67. Angus Sutherland's career can be followed in, A. G. Newby, *Ireland, Radicalism and the Scottish Highlands*, Edinburgh, 2007.
12. *Highland News*, 22 June 1889.
13. *Crofters and Cottars*, Evidence, pp. 2431, 2440; HA OPR, Kildonan, 1790–1800.
14. *Crofters and Cottars*, Evidence, p. 1645; *Crofters and Cottars*, Report, p. 2.
15. *Crofters and Cottars*, Evidence, p. 1657; *Glasgow Herald*, 26 July 1883.
16. *Crofters and Cottars*, Report, pp. 10–11.
17. *Crofters and Cottars*, Report, p. 16.
18. SCRO D6579/9: Lady Stafford to Lord Stafford, 17, 18, 26 September, 3 October 1820.
19. SCRO D6579/9: Lady Stafford to Lord Stafford, 19 September, 4, 5 October 1820.
20. J. Loch, *An Account of the Improvements on the Estates of the Marquis of Stafford*, London, 1820, pp. vi, 6–7, 9, 12, 50–53, 73, 90, 100, 108.

21. Loch, *Account of Improvements*, p. 119.
22. SCRO D593/K/1/3/8: H. Brougham to J. Loch, 12 August 1820; J. I. Robertson, *The First Highlander: Major-General David Stewart of Garth*, East Linton, 1988, pp. 98–99.
23. J. Thomson, *The Value and Importance of the Scottish Fisheries*, London, 1849, pp. 19–20; SCRO D6579/9: Lady Stafford to Lord Stafford, 21 September 1820.
24. SCRO D6579/9: Lady Stafford to Lord Stafford, 21 September 1820.
25. SCRO D6579/9: Lady Stafford to Lord Stafford, 21 September 1820.
26. Loch, *Account of Improvements*, pp. 5–6.
27. Loch, *Account of Improvements*, p. 6.
28. Loch, *Account of Improvements*, p. xiii.
29. D. Stewart, *Sketches of the Character, Manners and Present State of the Highlands of Scotland*, 2 vols, Edinburgh, 1822, I, pp. 230–31.
30. Stewart, *Sketches*, I, pp. 161–70.
31. B. Botfield, *Journal of a Tour Through the Highlands*, Norton Hall, 1830, pp. 152–53.
32. A. MacRae, *Kinlochbervie: Being the Story of a Remote Highland Parish and its People*, Tongue, 1932, p. 51. For a wider analysis of the role of the Free Church, see, A. W. MacColl, *Land, Faith and the Crofting Community: Christianity and Social Criticism in the Highlands of Scotland, 1843–1893*, Edinburgh, 2006.
33. *Second Report from the Select Committee on Sites for Churches (Scotland)*, London, 1847, p. 117.
34. H. Miller, *Sutherland As It Was and Is*, Edinburgh, 1843, pp. 10–11.
35. Miller, *Sutherland As It Was*, p. 11.
36. Miller, *Sutherland As It Was*, p. 9; D. MacLeod, *in the Highlands of Scotland*, Glasgow, 1892, p. 71.
37. H. B. Stowe, *Sunny Memories of Foreign Lands*, 2 vols, London, 1854, pp. 301–13.
38. MacLeod, *Gloomy Memories*, 76, 91, 108.
39. K. Marx, 'The Duchess of Sutherland and Slavery', in J. Ledbetter (ed.), *Karl Marx: Dispatches for the New York Tribune*, London, 2007, pp. 113–19.

40. K. Marx, *Capital*, 3 vols, New York, 1906, I, pp. 788–805; M. Mignet (ed.), *Political Economy and the Philosophy of Government: A Series of Essays Selected from the Works of M. de Sismondi*, London, 1847, pp. 183–89.

41. A. R. Wallace, *Land Nationalisation: Its Necessity and Its Aims*, London, 1906, p. 181.

42. *Crofters and Cottars*, Evidence, pp. 1650–51.

43. I. C. Smith, *Consider the Lilies*, Oxford, 1970, p. 144.

44. A. M. Sinclair, *Comhchruinneachadh Ghlinn-a-Bhàird: The Glenbard Collection of Gaelic Poetry*, Charlottetown, 1890, pp. 200–03; D. Meek, *Tuath is Tighearna: Tenants and Landlords*, Edinburgh, 1995, pp. 54–56, 190–91.

45. I. C. Smith, *Collected Poems*, Manchester, 1992, p. 52; I. Grimble, *The Trial of Patrick Sellar*, Edinburgh, 1993, pp. 159–60; J. MacInnes, 'A Gaelic Song of the Sutherland Clearances', *Scottish Studies*, 8, 1964, pp. 158–60.

46. Meek, *Tuath is Tighearna*, p. 18.

47. *Crofters and Cottars*, Evidence, p. 3179; T. Sellar, *The Sutherland Evictions of 1814: Former and Recent Statements Respecting Them Examined*, London, 1883, p. iii. See also, D. Richardson, *The Curse on Patrick Sellar*, Stockbridge, 1999.

48. J. Hunter, 'Sheep and Deer: Highland Sheep Farming, 1850–1900', *Northern Scotland*, 2. 1975, p. 202; *Crofters and Cottars*, Report, p. 315.

49. Loch, *Account of Improvements*, p. 145; R. D. G. Clarke, *Two Hundred Years of Farming in Sutherland: The Story of My Family*, Stornoway, 2014, pp. 188–91; Hunter, 'Sheep and Deer', pp. 202–06. See also, W. Orr, *Deer Forests, Landlords and Crofters: The Western Highlands in Victorian and Edwardian Times*, Edinburgh, 1982.

50. Sellar, *Sutherland Evictions*, pp. 39–60.

51. MacLeod, *Gloomy Memories*, p. 9.

52. N. M. Gunn, *Butcher's Broom*, London, 1977, pp. 358–60.

53. N. M. Gunn, *The Silver Darlings*, London, 1969, p. 12.

54. F. H. Hart and J. B. Pick, *Neil M. Gunn: A Highland Life*, London, 1981, p. 103; N. M. Gunn, 'Caithness and Sutherland', in A. McCleery

(ed.), *Landscapes and Light: Essays by Neil M. Gunn*, Aberdeen, 1987, p. 32.

55. C. I. Maclean, *The Highlands*, London, 1959, pp. 163, 167.

56. Maclean, *Highlands*, p. 173; Dennis MacLeod in correspondence and conversation with the author.

57. Programme notes for the unveiling of Gerald Laing's sculpture by Scotland's First Minister, Alex Salmond, 23 July 2007.

58. M. Laurence, *The Diviners*, Toronto, 1993, p. 58.

59. Laurence, *Diviners*, pp. 59–61.

60. *Crofters and Cottars*, Evidence, pp. 2507–10.

61. NRS RH/1/2/827: Napier to J. MacKay, 2 November 1889. For background to this exchange, see, I. Grimble, 'The Sutherland Story: Fact and Fiction', in, M. I. Mackay (ed.), *Sar Ghaideal: Essays in Memory of Ruaraidh Mackay*, Inverness, n.d., pp. 44–45.

62. NRS RH/1/2/827: Napier to J. MacKay, 2 November 1889.

63. *Royal Commission (Highlands and Islands)*, 1895, Report, p. v.

64. Tindley, *Sutherland Estate*, pp. 120–25.

65. Congested Districts Board, *Fourth Report*, 1902, p. x; NRS AF42/750: Application for No 5 Syre from D. J. MacKay, 29 January 1901; D. MacLeod, 'Hughina Celebrates Her 100th Year', *Am Bratach*, June 2012. The late Hughina MacKellar, whose hundredth birthday this article reported, was Donald John MacKay's daughter.

66. Congested Districts Board, *Fourth Report*, 1902, p. x; Adam, *Sutherland Estate*, I, p. 22: Report on the present state of possessions in Strathnaver, 1810.

67. HA OPR, Farr. Additional family information supplied by Rosa Sutherland, one of Barbara MacKay's great-granddaughters.

68. *Hansard*, House of Commons, 1 April 1971; HIDB, *Strath of Kildonan: Proposals for Development*, Inverness, 1970, pp. 10, 29–30; J. Grassie, *Highland Experiment*, Aberdeen, 1983, pp. 69–81.

69. *Royal Commission (Highlands and Islands)*, 1895, Evidence, pp. 615, 623–34.

Appendix

1. NRS GD95/2/15: Minutes of Directors, 2 February 1826; NRS GD95/9/4: Reports of Visits to the Schools of the Society, 1827. Some further details are available in A. S. Cowper, *Gordon Ross, 1791–1868: SSPCK Schoolmaster and Disciple of Sandy Gair*, Edinburgh, 1981.

BIBLIOGRAPHY

Unpublished and archived material

Timespan Arts and Heritage Centre, Helmsdale
Copies of letters to Sutherland family, Red River, 1815–42

Highland Archive, Inverness
BD/1/1/3 Dornoch Town Council minutes, 1810–32
BD/1/14/1–3 Dornoch Jail records, 1813–40
CH2/350/1 Tarbat Kirk Session Minutes, 1800–12
CH2/508/2 Presbytery of Tongue minutes, 1810–21
CH2/1290/4–5 Presbytery of Dornoch minutes, 1810–21
D269/1 Census, Parish of Farr, 1811
D1249/4/2/1 Letter from A. Sage to D. Sage, 1819

National Library of Scotland, Edinburgh

Sutherland Papers
313/748–50 Letters of Lady Stafford to Lord Stafford, 1814–20
313/755–56 Letters of Lady Stafford to Earl Gower, 1812–22
313/825 Letters of Earl Gower to Lady Stafford, 1813–22
313/990–93 Miscellaneous estate management papers, 1810–16
313/1010 Draft report by J. Loch on Sutherland Estate, 1818
313/1015–16 Papers on removals, 1819–21
313/1124 Letters of W. Young and P. Sellar to Lady Stafford, 1809–10
313/1125 Letters of W. Young to Earl Gower, 1812–18
313/1126 Miscellaneous estate management papers, 1809–13

313/1127 Letters of C. Falconer and P. Sellar, 1808–15

313/1128 Letters of W. Young to Earl Gower, 1812–15

313/1129 Letters of W. MacKenzie to Lady Stafford, 1813

313/1130 Letters of J. Loch to Earl Gower, 1812–17

313/1131–35 Letters of J. Loch to Lord Stafford, 1813–16

313/1136–41 Letters of J. Loch to F. Suther, 1819–21

313/1145–47 Letters of J. Loch to Lady Stafford, 1817–21

313/1153 Letters of J. Loch to Lord Stafford, 1812–22

313/1573 Report by P. Sellar on estate rental, 1811

313/1574–77 Letters from W. MacKenzie, W. Young and others, 1810–12

313/1578 Letters of P. Sellar and others to Lady Stafford, 1813–14

313/1579 Letters of W. MacKenzie and others to Lady Stafford, 1813–15

313/1580–81 Letters from Lord Selkirk and others, 1813

313/1584–85 Letters of W. Young to Lady Stafford, 1815

313/1586–91 Letters of P. Sellar, J. Loch and others to Lady Stafford, 1814–19

313/2124–47 Rentals, 1811–23

313/3167–68 Register of tacks, 1819

313/3270 Plans for raising a Highland regiment, 1797–1800

313/3271 Letters concerning the military, 1793–1802

313/3485 Letters of Lady Stafford to J. Gordon, 1809

314/16 Sketch of geology of Sutherland by H. Davy, 1812–14

10853/276 Leases in Ascoilemore

National Records of Scotland, Edinburgh

Court and related records

AD14/13/9 Precognitions, Kildonan, 1813

AD14/20/263 Precognitions, Culrain, 1820

AD14/21/93 Precognitions, Gruids, 1821

CS232/S/23/2 Precognitions, Strathnaver, and related papers, 1815–17

JC11/55 High Court, North Circuit minutes, 1816

JC11/63 High Court, North Circuit minutes, 1821

JP32/2/1 Sutherland Justices of the Peace Court minutes, 1813–40

JP32/5/21–24 Sutherland Justices of the Peace Court, processes, 1811–21
JP32/7/1–4 Sutherland Justices of the Peace Court, miscellaneous, 1813–21
SC9/1/3–4 Dornoch Sheriff Court minutes, 1806–25
SC9/7/63–75 Dornoch Sheriff Court processes, 1812–21
SC9/96/5 Correspondence relating to military deployments, 1821

Home Office Correspondence
RH2/4/100–39 Letters and Papers, Scotland, 1813–21

Maps and plans
RH2/4/137 Plan of intended road, Kirk of Farr to Helmsdale, 1794

Society in Scotland for Propagating Christian Knowledge
GD95/1/7–8 Minutes of General Meetings, 1813–23
GD95/2/14–15 Minutes of Directors' Meetings, 1813–23
GD95/11/3 Society Reports, 1796–1822
GD95/11/10 Annual Reports, 1800–24

Loch Muniments
GD268/44 Diary of J. Loch, 1802–33
GD268/216–17 Letters to J. Loch from Lord and Lady Stafford, 1807–20
GD268/359 Letters from Lady Stafford and others, 1821

Maclaine of Lochbuie Papers
GD174/2313 Letter from A. Maclaine to M. Maclaine, 1813

Military records
RH2/8/99 93rd (Sutherland) Highlanders Descriptive Roll Book

Congested Districts Board
AF42/750 Syre holding application, 1901

University of Edinburgh Archives
La.II.202 Correspondence, Lord Selkirk and A. MacDonald, 1812–15

Staffordshire County Record Office, Stafford

Sutherland Collection

D593/H/2/12 Map of Sutherland, 1820
D593/K/3/1/1–3 In letters from J. Loch, 1813–16
D593/K/1/3/1–9 In letters to J. Loch, 1813–21
D593/K/1/5/2–10 Out letters from J. Loch, 1813–21
D593/L/2/1 Memo book of J. Loch, 1817–42
D593/L/3/1 Reports and memos from J. Loch, 1816–32
D593/P/18/1 Letters from J. Loch to Lord Stafford, 1816–32
D6579/6–9 Letters from Lady Stafford to Lord Stafford, 1813–22
D6579/85 Letters from Lady Stafford to Earl Gower, 1803–21

National Archives, Kew
WO/121 Military Discharge Papers, 1800–20

Nova Scotia Archives, Halifax
RG20 Series A Land Grant Petitions

Library and Archives Canada, Ottawa
MG19-E1 Selkirk Papers, 1809–50

Hudson's Bay Company Archives, Winnipeg
B42/a/139–40 Fort Churchill Post Journal, 1813–14
B42/b/59 Fort Churchill Correspondence Book, 1813–14
C.1/778 Log of *Prince of Wales*, 1813
E223/1 Narrative by Donald MacKay, n.d.

British Columbia Archives, Victoria
A/B/20/C47E Abel Edwards Papers, 1813–14

Other unpublished material

John C. Jackson, 'The Voyages of Mad Donald MacKay and his Fight for the Fur Trade of the Canadian North West'. Copy available at the UHI Centre for History, Dornoch.

Newspapers and periodicals of the clearance era

Aberdeen Journal
Annual Register
Army List
Caledonian Mercury
Gentleman's Magazine
Glasgow Herald
Highland News
Inverness Courier
Inverness Journal
Military Register
Morning Chronicle
Observer
Scots Magazine
Scotsman
Star
The Times

UK parliamentary publications

Hansard, House of Commons Debates.
Papers Relating to the Red River Settlement, 1819.
Report to the Lords Commissioner of the Treasury by the Chairman of the Board of Excise in Scotland Respecting Distillery Laws, 1822.
Reports from the Select Committee on Sites for Churches (Scotland), 1847.
Report of Commissioners of Inquiry into the Condition of the Crofters and Cottars in the Highlands and Islands of Scotland, 5 vols, 1884.
Report of the Royal Commission (Highlands and Islands), 2 vols, 1895.
Congested Districts Board for Scotland, *Annual Reports*, 1899–1905.

Published material from the clearance era

Adam, R. J. (ed.), *John Home's Survey of Assynt*, Edinburgh, 1960.

Adam, R. J., *Papers on Sutherland Estate Management*, 2 vols, Edinburgh, 1972.

Allardyce, Alexander (ed.), *Letters to and from Charles Kirkpatrick Sharpe*, 2 vols, Edinburgh, 1972.

Amos, Andrew, *Report of Trials in the Courts of Canada Relative to the Destruction of the Earl of Selkirk's Settlement on the Red River*, London, 1820.

Anon., *Appeal on Behalf of the Royal Tain Academy and Report of its Funds*, London, 1819.

Anon., *A Narrative of Occurrences in the Indian Countries of North America*, London, 1817.

Anderson, W. E. K. (ed.), *The Journal of Sir Walter Scott*, Oxford, 1972.

Aspinall, A., Charles, D. C. and Smith, A. (eds), *English Historical Documents, 1783–1832*, London, 1996.

Auld, Alexander, *Ministers and Men in the Far North*, Wick, 1868.

Barron, James (ed.), *The Northern Highlands in the Nineteenth Century*, 3 vols, Inverness, 1903–13.

Bell, Charles N., *The Selkirk Settlement and the Settlers*, Winnipeg, 1887.

Bell, Robert, *A Treatise on Leases*, Edinburgh, 1820.

Botfield, Beriah, *Journal of a Tour Through the Highlands*, Norton Hall, 1830.

Brown, Robert, *Remarks on the Earl of Selkirk's Observations on the Present State of the Highlands of Scotland*, Edinburgh, 1806.

Browne, James, *A Critical Examination of Dr MacCulloch's Work on the Highlands of Scotland*, Edinburgh, 1825.

Bruce, H. H., *History of Barney's River: Early Days in East Pictou*, Pictou, 2013.

Butler, William F., *The Great Lone Land*, London, 1873.

Calder, T. T., *Sketch of the Civil and Traditional History of Caithness*, Glasgow, 1861.

Cobbett, William, *Tour in Scotland*, London, 1833.

Cockburn, Henry, *Circuit Journeys*, Edinburgh, 1888.

Cockburn, Henry, *Journal of Henry Cockburn*, 2 vols, Edinburgh, 1874.

Cockburn, Henry, *Life of Lord Jeffrey*, 2 vols, Edinburgh, 1852.

Cockburn, Henry, *Memorials of His Time*, Edinburgh, 1856.

Coltman, W. B., *Statement and Report Relative to the Disturbances in the Indian Territories of British North America*, London, 1818.

Cunningham, Allan (ed.), *The Works of Robert Burns*, London, 1840.

De Wolfe, Barbara (ed.), *Discoveries of America: Personal Accounts of British Emigrants to North America During the Revolutionary Era*, Cambridge, 1997.

Douglas, Thomas (Earl of Selkirk), *Observations on the Present State of the Highlands of Scotland*, London, 1805.

Douglas, Thomas (Earl of Selkirk), 'Ossinoboia' [1815], in J. M. Bumsted (ed.), *The Collected Writings of Lord Selkirk, 1810–1820*, Winnipeg, 1987.

Douglas, Thomas (Earl of Selkirk), *A Sketch of the British Fur Trade in North America*, London, 1816.

Dudgeon, Thomas, *A Nine Years Residence in the States of New York and Pennsylvania*, Edinburgh, 1841.

Gleig, G. R., *The Campaigns of the British Army at Washington and New Orleans*, London, 1827.

Glyndwr, William (ed.), *Hudson's Bay Miscellany, 1670–1870*, Winnipeg, 1975.

Gordon, Robert, *A Genealogical History of the Earldom of Sutherland*, Edinburgh, 1813.

Gower, Ronald, *My Reminiscences*, London, 1883.

Gower, Ronald, *Stafford House Letters*, London, 1891.

Granville, Castalia (ed.), *Lord Granville Leveson Gower: Private Correspondence, 1781–1821*, 2 vols, London, 1916.

Grierson, H. J. C. (ed.), *The Letters of Sir Walter Scott*, 12 vols, London, 1932.

Gunn, Donald, *A History of Manitoba from the Earliest Settlements to 1835*, Ottawa, 1880.

Halkett, John, *Postscript to the Statement Respecting the Destruction of the Earl of Selkirk's Settlement on the Red River*, Montreal, 1818.

Halkett, John, *Statement Respecting the Destruction of the Earl of Selkirk's Settlement upon the Red River*, London, 1817.

Hargrave, Joseph J., *Red River*, Montreal, 1871.

Henderson, John, *General View of the Agriculture of the County of Caithness*, London, 1815.

Henderson, John, *General View of the Agriculture of the County of Sutherland*, London, 1812.

Henry, Philip, *Notes of Conversations with the Duke of Wellington*, New York, 1988.

Hill, Benson, E., *Recollections of an Artillery Office*, 2 vols, London, 1836.

James, William, *A Full and Correct Account of the Military Occurrences of the Late War Between Great Britain and the United States of America*, 2 vols, London, 1818.

Ledbetter, James (ed.), *Karl Marx: Dispatches of the New York Tribune*, London, 2007.

Leighton, Rachel (ed.), *Correspondence of Charlotte Grenville, Lady Williams Wynn*, London, 1920.

Loch, James, *An Account of the Improvements on the Estates of the Marquis of Stafford*, London, 1820.

Loch, James, *An Account of the Improvements on the Estate of Sutherland Belonging to the Marquis and Marchioness of Stafford*, London, 1815.

Loch, James, *Dates and Documents Relating to the Family and Property of Sutherland*, London, 1859.

Loch, James, *Memoir of George Granville, Late Duke of Sutherland*, London, 1834.

McAdam, Adam, *Communications in Reply to Letters of Archibald McDonald*, Montreal, 1816.

MacBeth, Roderick G., *The Selkirk Settlers in Real Life*, Toronto, 1897.

MacCulloch, John, *The Highlands and Western Isles of Scotland*, 4 vols, London, 1828.

McDonald, Archibald, *Narrative Respecting the Destruction of the Earl of Selkirk's Settlement on Red River*, London, 1816.

McDonald, Archibald, *Reply to the Letter Lately Addressed to the Earl of Selkirk by the Rev John Strachan*, Montreal, 1816.

MacDonald, James, 'On the Agriculture of the County of Sutherland', *Transactions of the Highland and Agricultural Society of Scotland*, 4th Series, 12, 1880.

MacDonell, Alexander, *A Narrative of Transactions in the Red River Country*, London, 1819.

MacDonell, Margaret (ed.), *The Emigrant Experience: Songs of Highland Emigrants in North America*, Toronto, 1982.

MacGowan, Douglas (ed.), *The Stonemason: Donald MacLeod's Chronicle of Scotland's Highland Clearances*, Westport, 2001.

MacKay, Alexander, *Sketches of Sutherland Characters*, Edinburgh, 1889.

MacKay, Angus (ed.), *Autobiographical Journal of John MacDonald, Schoolmaster and Soldier, 1770–1830*, Edinburgh, 1906.

MacKay, Angus, *The Book of MacKay*, Edinburgh, 1906.

MacKay, Robert, *History of the House and Clan of MacKay*, Edinburgh, 1829.

MacKenzie, Aeneas, *An Historical, Topographical and Descriptive View of the County of Northumberland*, 2 vols, Newcastle, 1825.

MacKenzie, Alexander, *History of the Highland Clearances*, Inverness, 1883.

MacKenzie, Alexander (ed.), *The Trial of Patrick Sellar*, Inverness, 1883.

MacKenzie, Alexander, *Voyages from Montreal Through the Continent of North America*, New York, 1902.

MacKenzie, George, *General View of the Agriculture of the Counties of Ross and Cromarty*, London, 1834.

MacLeod, Donald, *Gloomy Memories in the Highlands of Scotland*, Glasgow, 1892.

Martin, Chester (ed.), *Red River Settlement: Papers in the Canadian Archives Relating to the Pioneers*, Ottawa, 1910.

Masson, Louis R. (ed.), *Les Bourgeois de la Compagnie du Nord-Ouest*, 2 vols, Quebec, 1890.

Marx, Karl, *Capital*, 3 vols, New York, 1906.

Maxwell, H. (ed.), *The Creevey Papers*, 2 vols, London, 1903.

Mignet, François (ed.), *Political Economy and the Philosophy of Government: A Series of Essays Selected from the Works of M. de Sismondi*, London, 1847.

Miller, Hugh, *My Schools and Schoolmasters*, Edinburgh, 1854.

Miller, Hugh, *Sutherland as It Was and Is*, Edinburgh, 1843.

Mitchell, Joseph, *Reminiscences of My Life in the Highlands*, 2 vols, London, 1883.

Murdoch, Alexander (ed.), 'A Scottish Document Concerning Emigration to North Carolina in 1772', *North Carolina Historical Review*, 67, 1990.

Newsome, Albert R., 'Records of Emigrants from England and Scotland to North Carolina, 1774–75', *North Carolina Historical Review*, 11, 1934.

Paris, J. A., *The Life of Sir Humphry Davy*, London, 1831.

Parrish, Woodbine, *Two Reports on the Subject of Illicit Distillation in Scotland*, London, 1816.

Patterson, George, *A History of the County of Pictou*, Montreal, 1877.

Robertson, P., *Report of the Trial of Patrick Sellar*, Edinburgh, 1816.

Ross, Alexander, *The Red River Settlement: Its Rise, Progress and Present State*, London, 1856.

Ross, Walter, *A Discourse Upon the Removing of Tenants*, Edinburgh, 1782.

Ross, Walter, 'Parish of Clyne', *Statistical Account of Scotland*, 21 vols, Edinburgh, 1791–99 (Vol. 10).

Sage, Alexander, 'Parish of Kildonan', *Statistical Account of Scotland*, 21 vols, Edinburgh, 1791–99 (Vol. 3).

Sage, Donald, *Memorabilia Domestica: Parish Life in the North of Scotland*, Wick, 1899.

Scott, Hew (ed.), *Fasti Ecclesiae Scoticanae*, 7 vols, Edinburgh, 1915–28.

Scotus Americanus, 'Informations Concerning the Province of North Carolina', in William K. Boyd (ed.), *Some Eighteenth Century Tracts Concerning North Carolina*, Raleigh, 1927.

Sellar, E. M., *Recollections and Impressions*, Edinburgh, 1908.

Sellar, Patrick, 'Farm Reports: County of Sutherland: Strathnaver, Morvich and Culmaily Farms', in John F. Burke (ed.), *British Husbandry Exhibiting the Farm Practice in Various Parts of the United Kingdom*, London, 1834.

Sellar, Thomas, *The Sutherland Evictions of 1814: Former and Recent Statements Respecting Them Examined*, London, 1883.

Sinclair, A. MacLean, *Comhchruinneachadh Ghlinn-a-Bhàird: The Glenbard Collection of Gaelic Poetry*, Charlottetown, 1890.

Smith, Adam, *An Inquiry into the Nature and Causes of the Wealth of Nations*, 2 vols, Hartford, 1811.

Stewart, David, 'Observations on the Origins and Cause of Smuggling in the Highlands and Islands of Scotland', *Quarterly Review of Agriculture*, 1, 1828.

Stewart, David, *Sketches of the Character, Manners and Present State of the Highlands of Scotland*, 2 vols, Edinburgh, 1822.

Stowe, Harriet B., *Sunny Memories of Foreign Lands*, 2 vols, London, 1854.

Strachan, John, *A Letter to Lord Selkirk on His Settlement at the Red River*, London, 1816.

Sutherland, Alexander, *A Summer Ramble in the North Highlands*, Edinburgh, 1825.

Thomson, James, *The Value and Importance of the Scottish Fisheries*, London, 1849.

Tyrrell, James W., *Across the Sub-Arctics of Canada*, Toronto, 1897.

Wallace, Alfred, *Land Nationalisation: Its Necessity and Its Aims*, London, 1906.

Wallace, W. Stewart (ed.), *John McLean's Notes of a Twenty-Five Years Service in the Hudson's Bay Territory*, Toronto, 1932.

White, P. C. T. (ed.), *Lord Selkirk's Diary, 1803–04: A Journal of His Travels*, Toronto, 1958.

Wilcocke, Samuel H., *A Narrative of the Occurrences in the Indian Countries of North America*, London, 1817.

Other published material

Adams, Ian and Somerville, Meredith, *Cargoes of Despair and Hope: Scottish Emigration to North America, 1603–1803*, Edinburgh, 1993.

Allison, Hugh G., *Roots of Stone*, Edinburgh, 2004.

Anderson, James L., *The Story of the Commercial Bank During its Hundred Years, 1810 to 1910*, Edinburgh, 1910.

Ansdell, Douglas, *The People of the Great Faith: The Highland Church, 1690–1900*, Stornoway, 1998.

Anson, Peter F., *Fisher Boats and Fisher Folk on the East Coast of Scotland*, London, 1971.

Baldwin, John R., 'The Long Trek: Agricultural Change and the Great Northern Drove', in John R. Baldwin (ed.), *Firthlands of Ross and Sutherland*, Edinburgh, 1986.

Bangor-Jones, Malcolm, *The Assynt Clearances*, Assynt, 2001.

Bangor-Jones, Malcolm, 'From Clanship to Crofting: Landownership, Economy and the Church in the Province of Strathnaver', in John R. Baldwin (ed.), *Firthlands of Ross and Sutherland*, Edinburgh, 1986.

Bangor-Jones, Malcolm, *Historic Assynt*, Assynt, 1996.

Bangor-Jones, Malcolm, 'Land Assessments and Settlement History in Sutherland and Easter Ross', in John R. Baldwin (ed.), *Firthlands of Ross and Sutherland*, Edinburgh, 1986.

Bangor-Jones, Malcolm, 'Sheep Farming in Sutherland in the 18th Century', *Agricultural History Review*, 50, 2002.

Bangor-Jones, Malcolm, 'The Strathnaver Clearances', in Scottish Vernacular Buildings Working Group, *North Sutherland Studies*, Glasgow, 1987.

Bardgett, Frank, *North Coast Parish: Strathy and Halladale*, Thurso, 1990.

Basu, Paul, *Highland Homecomings: Genealogy and Heritage Tourism in the Scottish Diaspora*, Oxford, 2007.

Basu, Paul, 'Sites of Memory, Sources of Identity: Landscape Narratives of the Sutherland Clearances', in J. A. Atkinson, I. Banks and G. MacGregor (eds), *Townships to Farmsteads: Rural Settlement Studies in Scotland, England and Wales*, Oxford, 2000.

Beaton, Elizabeth, 'Bighouse and Strath Halladale', in John R. Baldwin (ed.), *The Province of Strathnaver*, Edinburgh, 2000.

Beaumont, Raymond M., *Norway House: A Brief History*, Winnipeg, 1993.

Beck, Roger B., *The History of South Africa*, Santa Barbara, 2014.

Begg, Alexander, *History of the North-West*, 2 vols, Toronto, 1894.

Bentinck, Charles D., *Dornoch Cathedral and Parish*, Inverness, 1926.

Berton, Pierre, *The Last Spike: The Great Railway, 1881–1885*, Markham, 1989.

Bil, Albert, *The Shieling, 1600–1840*, Edinburgh, 1990.

Black, Jeremy, *The War of 1812 in the Age of Napoleon*, Edinburgh, 1990.

Bowen, James P., 'A Landscape of Improvement: The Impact of James Loch, Chief Agent of the Marquis of Stafford, on the Lilleshall Estate, Shropshire', *Midland History*, 35, 2010.

Brandson, Lorraine E., *Churchill: Hudson Bay: A Guide to Natural and Cultural Heritage*, Churchill, 2012.

Brown, Jennifer S. H., *Strangers in Blood: Fur Trade Company Families in Indian Country*, London, 1980.

Bryce, George, *The Life of Lord Selkirk: Coloniser of Western Canada*, Toronto, 1912.

Bryce, George, *The Romantic Settlement of Lord Selkirk's Colonists: The Pioneers of Manitoba*, Toronto, 1909.

Bulloch, John M., *The Families of Gordon of Invergordon, Newhall, Ardoch and Carrol*, Dingwall, 1906.

Bulloch, John M., *The Family of Gordon of Griamachary in the Parish of Kildonan*, Dingwall, 1907.

Bulloch, John M., *The Gordons of Embo with Other Families of the Name in the County of Sutherland*, Dingwall, 1907.

Bumsted, J. M, *The Collected Writings of Lord Selkirk, 1799–1809*, Winnipeg, 1984.

Bumsted, J. M, *The Collected Writings of Lord Selkirk, 1810–1820*, Winnipeg, 1987.

Bumsted, J. M., *Lord Selkirk: A Life*, East Lansing, 2009.

Bumsted, J. M., *The People's Clearance: Highland Emigration to North America*, Edinburgh, 1982.

Burgoyne, Roderick H., *Historical Records of the 93rd Highlanders*, London, 1883.

Cameron, A. D., *Go Listen to the Crofters: The Napier Commission and Crofting a Century Ago*, Stornoway, 1986.

Cameron, Ewen A., *Land for the People: The British Government and the Scottish Highlands, 1880–1925*, Edinburgh, 1996.

Cameron, George C., *The Scots Kirk in London*, Oxford, 1979.

Campbell, Colin T., *British South Africa*, London, 1897.

Campbell, D. and MacLean, R. A., *Beyond the Atlantic Roar: A Study of the Nova Scotia Scots*, Toronto, 1975.

Campbell, J. R. D., *Some Helmsdale Memories*, Helmsdale, 1988.

Campbell, Marjorie W., *The North West Company*, Vancouver, 1983.

Campey, Lucille H., *After the Hector: The Scottish Pioneers of Nova Scotia and Cape Breton*, Toronto, 2004.

Campey, Lucille, H., *The Silver Chief: Selkirk and the Scottish Pioneers of Belfast, Baldoon and Red River*, Toronto, 2003.

Campey, Lucille H., *An Unstoppable Force: The Scottish Exodus to Canada*, Toronto, 2008.

Cavendish, A. E. J., *An Rèisimeid Chataich: The 93rd Sutherland Highlanders*, London, 1928.

Chandler, David G., and Beckett, Ian (eds), *The Oxford History of the British Army*, Oxford, 1996.

Checkland, S. G., *Scottish Banking: A History*, Glasgow, 1975.

Clarke, Reay D. G., *Two Hundred Years of Farming in Sutherland: The Story of My Family*, Stornoway, 2014.

Clyde, Robert, *From Rebel to Hero: The Image of the Highlander, 1745–1830*, East Linton, 1995.

Cole, Jean M., *Exile in the Wilderness: The Life of Chief Factor Archibald McDonald*, Seattle, 1979.

Cowan, R. M. W., *The Newspaper in Scotland: A Study of its First Expansion, 1815–1860*, Glasgow, 1946.

Cowley, D. C., *Strath of Kildonan: An Archaeological Survey*, Edinburgh, 1993.

Cowper, Alexandrina S., *Gordon Ross, 1791–1868: SSPCK Schoolmaster and Disciple of Sandy Gair*, Edinburgh, 1981.

Cowper, Alexandrina S., *SSPCK Schoolmasters, 1709–1872*, Edinburgh, 1997.

Cowper, Alexandrina S. and Ross, I., *Selected Notes on Sutherland and Reay Country Schools from SSPCK Records*, Edinburgh, 1980.

Cowper, Alexandrina S., and Ross, I., *The SSPCK and the Parish of Kildonan*, Edinburgh, 1980.

Craig, David, *On the Crofter's Trail*, London, 1990.

Darling, F. Fraser, *West Highland Survey*, Oxford, 1955.

Dawson, Alastair G., *So Foul and Fair a Day: A History of Scotland's Weather and Climate*, Edinburgh, 2009.

Devine, T. M., *Clanship to Crofters' War: The Social Transformation of the Scottish Highlands*, Manchester, 1994.

Devine, T. M., *Clearance and Improvement: Land, Power and People in Scotland*, Edinburgh, 2006.

Devine, T. M., *The Great Highland Famine*, Edinburgh, 1988.

Devine, T. M., 'The Rise and Fall of Illicit Whisky-Making in Northern Scotland', *Scottish Historical Review*, 54, 1975.

Devine, T. M., *Scotland's Empire, 1600–1815*, London, 2003.

Devine, T. M., *The Scottish Nation, 1700–2007*, London, 2006.

Devine, T. M., *To the Ends of the Earth: Scotland's Global Diaspora*, London, 2011.

Diefenbaker, John G., *One Canada: Memoirs*, Toronto, 1973.

Dodgshon, Robert, *From Chiefs to Landlords: Social and Economic Change in the Western Highlands, 1493–1820*, Edinburgh, 1988.

Duckworth, Henry W., 'The Madness of Donald MacKay: An Iron Man of the Fur Trade Made his own Claim to Immortality', *The Beaver*, June 1988.

Dunn, Charles W., *Highland Settler: A Portrait of the Scottish Gael in Cape Breton and Eastern Nova Scotia*, Toronto, 1953.

Ellis, Peter B. and Mac a' Ghobhainn, Seumas *The Scottish Insurrection of 1820*, London, 1989.

Ens, Gerhard J., *Homeland to Hinterland: The Changing World of the Red River Métis in the Nineteenth Century*, Toronto, 1996.

Evans, John, *The Gentleman Usher: The Life and Times of George Dempster*, Barnsley, 2005.

Fairhurst, Horace, 'Rossal: A Deserted Township in Strathnaver', *Proceedings of the Society of Antiquaries in Scotland*, 100, 1967.

Fairhurst, Horace, 'The Surveys for the Sutherland Clearances', *Scottish Studies*, 8, 1964.

Falk, Bernard, *The Bridgewater Millions: A Candid Family History*, London, 1942.

Fenton, Alexander and Veitch, Kenneth, *Scottish Life and Society: Farming and the Land*, Edinburgh, 2011.

Fenyó, Krisztina, *Contempt, Sympathy and Romance: Lowland Perceptions of the Highlands and the Clearances during the Famine Years, 1845–1855*, East Linton, 2000.

Flinn, M. W., 'The Poor Employment Act of 1817', *Economic History Review*, 14, 1961.

Ford, Trowbridge H., 'Political Coverage in *The Times*, 1811–41: The Role of Barnes and Brougham', *Historical Research*, 85, 1986.

Fraser, William, *The Sutherland Book*, 3 vols, Edinburgh, 1892.

Friesen, Gerald, *The Canadian Prairies: A History*, Toronto, 1990.

Fry, Michael, *The Dundas Despotism*, Edinburgh. 1992.

Fry, Michael, *Wild Scots: Four Hundred Years of Highland History*, London, 2005.

Gash, Norman, *Lord Liverpool*, London, 1984.

Gibson, Rob, *Toppling the Duke: Outrage on Ben Bhraggie*, Evanton, 1996.

Gordon, Alastair G., *A Sutherland Trail: A History of the Gordons of Dallagan, Griamachary and Drumearn*, London, 2005.

Gore, John (ed.), *Creevey's Life and Times*, London, 1934.

Gouriévidis, Laurence, *The Dynamics of Heritage: History, Memory and the Highland Clearances*, Farnham, 2010.

Gouriévidis, Laurence, 'Patrick Sellar', *Études Écossaises*, 10, 2005.

Gourlay, Robert, *Sutherland: An Archaeological Guide*, Edinburgh, 1996.

Grant, Margaret W., *Birth of a Village: Nineteenth-Century Golspie*, Golspie, 1983.

Grassie, James, *Highland Experiment*, Aberdeen, 1983.

Gray, John M., *Lord Selkirk of Red River*, London, 1963.

Gray, Malcolm, *The Fishing Industries of Scotland, 1790–1914*, Aberdeen, 1978.

Gray, Malcolm, *The Highland Economy, 1750–1850*, Edinburgh, 1957.

Greene, Jerome A., *The New Orleans Campaign of 1814–15 in Relation to the Chalmette Battlefield*, Washington, 1985.

Grimble, Ian, 'The Sutherland Story: Fact or Fiction', in M. I. Mackay (ed.), *Sar Ghaidheal: Essays in Memory of Rory Mackay*, Inverness, n.d.

Grimble, Ian, *The Trial of Patrick Sellar*, Edinburgh, 1993.

Grimble, Ian, *The World of Rob Donn*, Edinburgh, 1979.

Groves, Percy, *History of the 93rd Sutherland Highlanders*, Edinburgh, 1895.

Gunn, Adam and MacKay, John (eds), *Sutherland and the Reay Country*, Glasgow, 1897.

Gunn, Diarmid and Murray, Isobel (eds), *Neil Gunn's Country: Essays in Celebration of Neil Gunn*, Edinburgh, 1991.

Gunn, Neil M., 'Caithness and Sutherland', in Alistair McCleery (ed.), *Landscapes and Light: Essays by Neil M. Gunn*, Aberdeen, 1987.

Gwyn, Richard, *John A: The Man Who Made Us: The Life and Times of John A. Macdonald*, 1815–1867, Toronto, 2007.

Gwyn, Richard, *Nation Maker: Sir John A. Macdonald: His Life, Our Times*, Toronto, 2011.

Hague, William, *William Wilberforce: The Life of the Great Anti-Slave Trade Campaigner*, London, 2007.

Haldane, A. R. B., *New Ways Through the Glens*, Edinburgh, 1962.

Hamilton, Douglas J., *Scotland, the Caribbean and the Atlantic World, 1750–1820*, Manchester, 2005.

Harper, Marjory, *Adventurers and Exiles: The Great Scottish Exodus*, London, 2003.

Hart, F. H. and Pick, J. B., *Neil M. Gunn: A Highland Life*, London, 1981.

Healy, William J., *Women of Red River*, Winnipeg, 1923.

Highlands and Islands Development Board, *Strath of Kildonan: Proposals for Development*, Inverness, 1970.

Hilton, Boyd, *A Mad, Bad, Dangerous People: England, 1783–1846*, Oxford, 2006.

Holmes, Richard, *The Age of Wonder: How the Romantic Generation Discovered the Beauty and Terror of Science*, London, 2009.

Holmes, Richard, *Redcoat: The British Soldier in the Age of Horse and Musket*, London, 2001.

Hook, Michael, *A History of the Royal Burgh of Dornoch*, Dornoch, 2005.

Hudson, Derek, *Thomas Barnes of* The Times, *Cambridge, 1943*.

Hume, John R. and Moss, Michael S., *Scotch Whisky: A History of the*

Scotch Whisky Distilling Industry, Edinburgh, 2000.

Hunter, James, *A Dance Called America: The Scottish Highlands, the United States and Canada*, Edinburgh, 1994.

Hunter, James, *From the Low Tide of the Sea to the Highest Mountain Tops: Community Ownership of Land in the Highlands and Islands of Scotland*, Stornoway, 2012.

Hunter, James, *Glencoe and the Indians*, Edinburgh, 1996.

Hunter, James, *Last of the Free: A History of the Highlands and Islands of Scotland*, Edinburgh, 1999.

Hunter, James, *The Making of the Crofting Community*, Edinburgh, 1976 and 2000.

Hunter, James, *On the Other Side of Sorrow: Nature and People in the Scottish Highlands*, Edinburgh, 1995.

Hunter, James, *Scottish Exodus: Travels Among a Worldwide Clan*, Edinburgh, 2005.

Hunter, James, 'Sheep and Deer: Highland Sheep Farming, 1850–1900', *Northern Scotland*, 2, 1975.

Jackson, John J., 'Inland from the Bay: Mapping the Fur Trade', *Beaver*, March 1992.

Jordan, Weymouth T., *George Washington Campbell of Tennessee: Western Statesman*, Tallahassee, 1955.

Kavanagh, Martin, *The Assiniboine Basin: A Social Study of Discovery, Exploitation and Settlement*, Brandon, 1967.

Ketteringham, Lesley, *A History of Lairg*, Lairg, 1977.

King, Blair B., *Partner in Empire: Dwarkanath Tagore and the Age of Enterprise in Eastern India*, Los Angeles, 1976.

Kirk, Sylvia van, *Many Tender Ties: Women in Fur Trade Society in Western Canada*, Winnipeg, 1980.

Klingaman, W. K. and Klingaman, N. P., *The Year Without A Summer: 1816 and the Volcano that Darkened the World*, New York, 2013.

Knight, David, *Humphry Davy: Science and Power*, Oxford, 1992.

Latimer, Jon, *1812: War with America*, London, 2007.

Lee, J. R., *Climate Change and Armed Conflict: Hot and Cold Wars*, Oxford, 2009.

Lenman, Bruce P., *Integration and Enlightenment: Scotland, 1746–1832*, Edinburgh, 1981.

Lindsay, Nick, *Dalreavoch-Sciberscross, Strathbrora, Sutherland: A Report of an Archaeological Survey*, Brora, 2009.

Logue, Kenneth J., *Popular Disturbances in Scotland, 1780–1815*, Edinburgh, 1979.

MacColl, Allan W., *Land, Faith and the Crofting Community: Christianity and Social Criticism in the Highlands of Scotland, 1843–1893*, Edinburgh, 2006.

McCulloch, Margery, *The Novels of Neil Gunn: A Critical Study*, Edinburgh, 1987.

MacDonald, George, *Sketches of Some of the Men of Sutherland*, Inverness, 1937.

Macdonald, John, *Rogart: The Story of a Sutherland Parish*, Skerray, 2002.

McGilvary, George, *East India Patronage and the British State*, London, 2008.

MacInnes, Allan I., *Clanship, Commerce and the House of Stuart, 1603–1788*, East Linton, 1996.

MacInnes, John, 'A Gaelic Song of the Sutherland Clearances', *Scottish Studies*, 8, 1964.

MacInnes, John, *The Evangelical Movement in the Highlands of Scotland*, Aberdeen, 1951.

MacIver, Angus and MacIver, Bernice, *Churchill on Hudson Bay*, Churchill, 2006.

MacKay, Elizabeth R., *George Sutherland of Riarchar: The Last of the Tacksmen*, Dornoch, 1970.

MacKenzie, John M. with Dalziel, Nigel R., *The Scots in South Africa: Ethnicity, Gender and Race*, Manchester, 2007.

McKichan, Finlay, 'Lord Seaforth and Highland Estate Management in the First Phase of Clearance', *Scottish Historical Review*, 86, 2007.

MacKillop, Andrew, *More Fruitful than the Soil: Army, Empire and the Scottish Highlands, 1715–1815*, East Linton, 2000.

MacKillop, Andrew, 'The Political Culture of the Scottish Highlands from Culloden to Waterloo', *Historical Journal*, 46, 2003.

Maclean, Calum I., *The Highlands*, London, 1959.

McLean, M., *The People of Glengarry: Highlanders in Transition, 1745–1820*, Montreal, 1991.

MacLeod, Anne, *From An Antique Land: Visual Representations of the Highlands and Islands, 1700–1880*, Edinburgh, 2012.

MacLeod, Donald, 'Hughina Celebrates her Hundredth Year', *Am Bratach*, June 2012.

MacLeod, John, *The North Country Separatists*, Inverness, 1930.

MacLeod, Margaret A. and Morton, W. L., *Cuthbert Graham of Grantown: Warden of the Plains*, Toronto, 1963.

MacPhie, J. P., *Pictonians at Home and Abroad*, Boston, 1914.

MacRae, Alexander, *Kinlochbervie: Being the Story of a Remote Highland Parish and its People*, Tongue, 1932.

Martin, Chester, *Lord Selkirk's Works in Canada*, Oxford, 1916.

Martins, Susanne W., 'A Century of Farms and Farming on the Sutherland Estate, 1790–1890', *Review of Scottish Culture*, 10, 1996.

Mearns, Alexander B., 'The Minister and the Bailiff: A Study of Presbyterian Clergy in the Northern Highlands during the Clearances', *Scottish Church History Society Records*, 29, 1990.

Meek, Donald, *Tuath is Tighearna: Tenants and Landlords*, Edinburgh, 1995.

Miller, James, *The Gathering Stream: The Story of the Moray Firth*, Edinburgh, 2012.

Mitchison, Rosalind, *Agricultural Sir John: The Life of Sir John Sinclair of Ulbster*, London, 1962.

Mokyr, Joel, *The Enlightened Economy: Britain and the Industrial Revolution, 1700–1850*, London, 2009.

Morrison, S., *History of* The Times: *'The Thunderer' in the Making, 1785–1841*, London, 1935.

Moss, Michael S. and Hume, John R., *The Making of Scotch Whisky: A History of the Scotch Whisky Distilling Industry*, Edinburgh, 1981.

Mowat, Ian R. M., *Easter Ross, 1750–1850: The Double Frontier*, Edinburgh, 1981.

Munro, Donald, *Records of Grace in Sutherland*, Edinburgh, 1953.

Munro, R. W. and Munro, Jean, *Tain Through the Centuries*, Edinburgh, 2005.

Nenadic, Stana, *Lairds and Luxury: The Highland Gentry in Eighteenth-Century Scotland*, Edinburgh, 2007.

Nenadic, Stana (ed.), *Scots in London in the Eighteenth Century*, Lewisburg, 2010.

New, Chester W., *The Life of Henry Brougham*, Oxford, 1961.

Newby, Andrew G., *Ireland, Radicalism and the Scottish Highlands*, Edinburgh, 2007.

Newman, Peter C., *Caesars of the Wilderness: The Story of the Hudson's Bay Company*, New York, 1988.

Newman, Peter C., *Company of Adventurers: The Story of the Hudson's Bay Company*, New York, 1988.

Newton, Michael, *Warriors of the Word: The World of the Scottish Highlanders*, Edinburgh, 2009.

Norrie, William, *Edinburgh Newspapers Past and Present*, Edinburgh, 1891.

Omand, Donald (ed.), *The Ross and Cromarty Book*, Golspie, 1984.

Omand, Donald (ed.), *The Sutherland Book*, Golspie, 1982.

Omond, George W. T., *The Lord Advocates of Scotland*, 2 vols, Edinburgh, 1883.

Orr, Willie, *Deer Forests, Landlords and Crofters: The Western Highlands in Victorian and Edwardian Times*, Edinburgh, 1982.

Owen, John S., *Coal Mining in Brora, 1529–1974*, Inverness, 1995.

Paton, David, '"Brought to a Wilderness": The Rev David MacKenzie of Farr and the Sutherland Clearances', *Northern Scotland*, 13, 1993.

Paton, David, *The Clergy and the Clearances: The Church and the Highland Crisis, 1790–1850*, Edinburgh, 2006.

Patterson, Benton R., *The Generals: Andrew Jackson, Sir Edward Pakenham and the Battle of New Orleans*, New York, 2005.

Post, John D., *The Last Great Subsistence Crisis in the Western World*, Baltimore, 1977.

Prebble, John, *The Highland Clearances*, Harmondsworth, 1969.

Pritchett, John P., *The Red River Valley: A Regional Study*, New Haven, 1942.

Reilly, Robin, *The British at the Gates: The New Orleans Campaign in the War of 1812*, Toronto, 2002.

Remini, Robert V., *The Battle of New Orleans: Andrew Jackson and America's First Military Victory*, London, 2001.

Rich, E. E., *The History of the Hudson's Bay Company*, 2 vols, London, 1958–59.

Richards, Eric, *Britannia's Children: Emigration from England, Scotland, Wales and Ireland since 1600*, London, 2004.

Richards, Eric, *Debating the Highland Clearances*, Edinburgh, 2007.

Richards, Eric, *The Highland Clearances: People, Landlords and Rural Turmoil*, Edinburgh, 2008.

Richards, Eric, *A History of the Highland Clearances: Agrarian Transformation and the Evictions*, London, 1982.

Richards, Eric, *A History of the Highland Clearances: Emigration, Protest, Reasons*, London, 1985.

Richards, Eric, *The Leviathan of Wealth: The Sutherland Fortune in the Industrial Revolution*, London, 1973.

Richards, Eric, 'The *Military Register* and the Pursuit of Patrick Sellar', *Scottish Economic and Social History*, 16, 1996.

Richards, Eric, 'Patrick Sellar and His World', *Transactions of the Gaelic Society of Inverness*, 61, 1999.

Richards, Eric, *Patrick Sellar and the Highland Clearances: Homicide, Eviction and the Price of Progress*, Edinburgh, 1999.

Richards, Eric, 'The Social and Electoral Influence of the Trentham Interest, 1800–60', *Midland History*, 3, 1975.

Richardson, Dorothy, *The Curse on Patrick Sellar*, Stockbridge, 1999.

Robertson, Alan G., *The Lowland Highlanders*, Inverness, 1970.

Robertson, James I., *The First Highlander: Major-General David Stewart of Garth*, East Linton, 1988.

Rosie, George, *Hugh Miller: Outrage and Order: A Biography and Selected Writings*, n.d.

Ross, Alasdair, 'Improvement on the Grant Estates in Strathspey in the Later Eighteenth Century', in Richard W. Hoyle (ed.) *Custom, Improvement and the Landscape in Early Modern Britain*, Farnham, 2011.

Royle, Edward, *Revolutionary Britannia: Reflections on the Threat of Revolution in Britain, 1789–1948*, Manchester, 2000.

Scobie, Ian H. M., *An Old Highland Fencible Corps: The History of the Reay Fencibles*, Edinburgh, 1914.

Scottish Vernacular Buildings Working Group, *North Sutherland Studies*, Glasgow, 1987.

Sillett, S. W., *Illicit Scotch*, Aberdeen, 1965.

Smith, Donald C., *Passive Obedience and Prophetic Protest: Social Criticism in the Scottish Church, 1830–1945*, New York, 1987.

Smith, Gavin D., *The Secret Still: Scotland's Clandestine Whisky Makers*, Edinburgh, 2002.

Statham-Drew, Pamela, *James Stirling: Admiral and Founding Governor of Western Australia*, Crawley, 2003.

Sutherland, George. R., *The Rise and Decline of the Community of Earltown*, Truro, 1980.

Sutherland, Malcolm, *A Fighting Clan: Sutherland Officers, 1250–1850*, London, 1996.

Szasz, Margaret C., *Scottish Highlanders and Native Americans: Indigenous Education in the Eighteenth-Century Atlantic World*, Norman, 2007.

Taylor, Michael A., *Hugh Miller: Stonemason, Geologist, Writer*, Edinburgh, 2007.

Tegelberg, Laurie, 'Catherine Sutherland of Point Douglas: Woman of Head and Heart', *Manitoba Pageant*, 21, 1975.

Thomis, Malcolm I. and Holt Peter, *Threats of Revolution in Britain, 1789–1848*, London, 1977.

Thompson, F. M. L., *British Landed Society in the Nineteenth Century*, London, 1963.

Thompson, Leonard M., *A History of South Africa*, Yale, 2001.

Thomson, Duncan (ed.), *Raeburn: The Art of Sir Henry Raeburn, 1756–1823*, Edinburgh, 1997.

Tindley, Annie, *The Sutherland Estate, 1850–1920: Aristocratic Decline, Estate Management and Land Reform*, Edinburgh, 2010.

Wallace, W. Stewart, *The Pedlars from Quebec and other Papers on the Nor'Westers*, Toronto, 1954.

Watson, J. A. S., 'The Rise and Development of the Sheep Industry in the Highlands and the North of Scotland', *Transactions of the Highland and Agricultural Society of Scotland*, 5th Series, 44, 1932.

Watson, William J., *The History of the Celtic Place Names of Scotland*, Edinburgh, 1926.

Webb, Patrick, 'Emergency Relief During Europe's Famine of 1817 Anticipated Crisis Response Mechanisms of Today', *Journal of Nutrition*, 132, 2002.

Wheeler, Philip T., 'The Sutherland Crofting System', *Scottish Studies*, 8, 1964.

Whetstone, Anne E., *Scottish County Government in the Eighteenth and Nineteenth Centuries*, Edinburgh, 1981.

Willock, Ian D., *The Origins and Development of the Jury in Scotland*, Edinburgh, 1966.

Withers, Charles W. J., 'Landscape, Memory, History: *Gloomy Memories* and the Nineteenth-Century Scottish Highlands', *Scottish Geographical Journal*, 121, 2005.

Withers, Charles W. J., 'Place, Memory, Monument: Memorialising the Past in Contemporary Highland Scotland', *Ecumene*, 3, 1996.

Wood, Gillen D., *Tambora: The Eruption that Changed the World*, Princeton, 2014.

Wordie, J. R., *Estate Management in Eighteenth-Century England: The Building of the Leveson-Gower Fortune*, London, 1982.

Creative writing on the clearances

Fidler, Kathleen, *The Desperate Journey*, London, 1984.

Gunn, Kirsty, *The Big Music*, London, 2012.

Gunn, Neil M., *Butcher's Broom*, London, 1977.

Gunn, Neil M., *The Silver Darlings*, London, 1969.

Laurence, Margaret, *The Diviners*, Toronto, 1993.

MacColla, Fionn, *And the Cock Crew*, Edinburgh, 1995.

McGrath, John, *The Cheviot, the Stag and the Black, Black Oil*, London, 1981.

Smith, Iain Crichton, *Collected Poems*, Manchester, 1992.
Smith, Iain Crichton, *Consider the Lilies*, Oxford, 1970.

Selected websites

Scotland's People, http://www.scotlandspeople.gov.uk/.
Scotland's Places, http://www.scotlandsplaces.gov.uk/.
History of Parliament Online, http://www.historyofparliamentonline.org/.
Dictionary of Canadian Biography Online, http://www.biographi.ca/en/index.php.
Dictionary of National Biography, http://www.oxforddnb.com/public/index.html

INDEX